Improving Adult Literacy Instruction

Options for Practice and Research

Committee on Learning Sciences: Foundations and
Applications to Adolescent and Adult Literacy

Alan M. Lesgold and Melissa Welch-Ross, *Editors*

Division of Behavioral and Social Sciences and Education

NATIONAL RESEARCH COUNCIL
OF THE NATIONAL ACADEMIES

THE NATIONAL ACA[
Washington
www.na[

THE NATIONAL ACADEMIES PRESS   500 Fifth Street, NW   Washington, DC 20001

NOTICE: The project that is the subject of this report was approved by the Governing Board of the National Research Council, whose members are drawn from the councils of the National Academy of Sciences, the National Academy of Engineering, and the Institute of Medicine. The members of the committee responsible for the report were chosen for their special competences and with regard for appropriate balance.

This study was supported by Contract No. ED-08-CO-0142 between the National Academy of Sciences and the U.S. Department of Education. Any opinions, findings, conclusions, or recommendations expressed in this publication are those of the author(s) and do not necessarily reflect the views of the organizations or agencies that provided support for the project.

Library of Congress Cataloging-in-Publication Data

National Research Council (U.S.). Committee on Learning Sciences: Foundations and Applications to Adolescent and Adult Literacy.
  Improving adult literacy instruction : options for practice and research / Committee on Learning Sciences: Foundations and Applications to Adolescent and Adult Literacy, Alan M. Lesgold and Melissa Welch-Ross, Editors, Division of Behavioral and Social Sciences and Education, National Research Council of the National Academies.
       pages cm
  Includes bibliographical references.
  ISBN 978-0-309-21959-4 (pbk.) — ISBN (invalid) 978-0-309-21960-0 (pdf) 1. Functional literacy—United States. I. Lesgold, Alan M. II. Welch-Ross, Melissa K. III. Title.
  LC151.N385 2012
  302.2'2440973—dc23
                                        2012007109

Additional copies of this report are available from the National Academies Press, 500 Fifth Street, NW, Keck 360, Washington, DC 20001; (800) 624-6242 or (202) 334-3313; http://www.nap.edu.

Printed in the United States of America

Suggested citation: National Research Council. (2012). *Improving Adult Literacy Instruction: Options for Practice and Research.* Committee on Learning Sciences: Foundations and Applications to Adolescent and Adult Literacy, A.M. Lesgold and M. Welch-Ross, Eds. Division of Behavioral and Social Sciences and Education. Washington, DC: The National Academies Press.

THE NATIONAL ACADEMIES
Advisers to the Nation on Science, Engineering, and Medicine

The **National Academy of Sciences** is a private, nonprofit, self-perpetuating society of distinguished scholars engaged in scientific and engineering research, dedicated to the furtherance of science and technology and to their use for the general welfare. Upon the authority of the charter granted to it by the Congress in 1863, the Academy has a mandate that requires it to advise the federal government on scientific and technical matters. Dr. Ralph J. Cicerone is president of the National Academy of Sciences.

The **National Academy of Engineering** was established in 1964, under the charter of the National Academy of Sciences, as a parallel organization of outstanding engineers. It is autonomous in its administration and in the selection of its members, sharing with the National Academy of Sciences the responsibility for advising the federal government. The National Academy of Engineering also sponsors engineering programs aimed at meeting national needs, encourages education and research, and recognizes the superior achievements of engineers. Dr. Charles M. Vest is president of the National Academy of Engineering.

The **Institute of Medicine** was established in 1970 by the National Academy of Sciences to secure the services of eminent members of appropriate professions in the examination of policy matters pertaining to the health of the public. The Institute acts under the responsibility given to the National Academy of Sciences by its congressional charter to be an adviser to the federal government and, upon its own initiative, to identify issues of medical care, research, and education. Dr. Harvey V. Fineberg is president of the Institute of Medicine.

The **National Research Council** was organized by the National Academy of Sciences in 1916 to associate the broad community of science and technology with the Academy's purposes of furthering knowledge and advising the federal government. Functioning in accordance with general policies determined by the Academy, the Council has become the principal operating agency of both the National Academy of Sciences and the National Academy of Engineering in providing services to the government, the public, and the scientific and engineering communities. The Council is administered jointly by both Academies and the Institute of Medicine. Dr. Ralph J. Cicerone and Dr. Charles M. Vest are chair and vice chair, respectively, of the National Research Council.

www.national-academies.org

Acknowledgments

The Committee on Learning Sciences: Foundations and Applications to Adolescent and Adult Literacy was established to review evidence on learning and literacy to develop a roadmap for research and practice to strengthen adult literacy education in the United States. This report is the culmination of a 36-month study by the 15 experts from diverse disciplines appointed to carry out this charge. First, we would like to thank the National Institute for Literacy (NIFL) and the U.S. Department of Education for their sponsorship of the study and for turning to the National Research Council (NRC) for help in synthesizing the available research to improve literacy instruction for adults and youth in the United States.

Over the course of the study, committee members and staff benefited from discussions and presentations by individuals who brought a range of perspectives and expertise to three fact-finding meetings. The first meeting allowed us to gain a better understanding of the study charge and the work before us. We heard from experts in adult literacy education to understand adult literacy levels, the literacy needs and challenges of diverse populations, and recent large-scale adult literacy interventions. The invited experts were Judy Alamprese, Abt Associates, Inc.; Alisa Belzer, Rutgers University; Daphne Greenberg, Georgia State University; Mark Kutner, American Institutes of Research; T. Scott Murray, DataAngel Policy Research, Inc.; Dolores Perin, Teachers College, Columbia University; and John Strucker, World Education, Inc.

At the second meeting, the committee heard evidence about cognitive and neural models of reading comprehension, genetic and environmental influences on reading, the neurobiology of literacy in a second language, maturational effects on cognition and learning, the state of adult literacy assessment, and relations between oral language and literacy. Invited participants included Elena Grigorenko, Yale University; Arturo Hernandez, University of Houston; Denise Park, University of Texas, Dallas; John Sabatini, ETS; Paul van den Broek, University of Leiden and University of Minnesota; and Gloria Waters, Boston University.

The third meeting included a diverse set of presenters who provided researcher and practitioner perspectives about factors that affect persistence, motivation, and engagement for learners from late adolescence through adulthood and that are amenable to being influenced by instruction. Members also sought information about the cognitive and social factors that influence progress with literacy among English language learners. Invited experts included John Comings, World Education, Inc.; Edward L. Deci, University of Rochester; Ruth Kanfer, Georgia Tech; Judith Kroll, Pennsylvania State University; Nonie Lesaux, Harvard University; Steve Reder, Portland State University; Dan Wagner, University of Pennsylvania; and Heide Spruck Wrigley, Literacywork International.

Our work was also advanced by the contributions of able consultants who wrote papers that were invaluable to our discussions and development of report text: Eric Anderman, Ohio State University; Alisa Belzer, Rutgers University; Mary Ellen Cushman, Michigan State University; Edward L. Deci; Elena Grigorenko; W. Norton Grubb, University of California, Berkeley; Ruth Kanfer; Judith Kroll; Dolores Perin; Amy Stornaiuolo, University of California, Berkeley; Paul van den Broek; Lalitha Vasudevan, Teachers College, Columbia University; Kari L. Woods, University of Kansas; and Heide Spruck Wrigley. Francisco Rivera-Batiz of the Department of Economics and Education, Teachers College, Columbia University, was a member of the committee until other commitments required him to step down in November of 2009; we thank him for the insights and expertise he brought to the committee on issues of economics and education involving immigrant and minority populations.

We thank Peggy McCardle and Brett Miller. who facilitated access to the results of studies funded by the National Institute of Child Health and Human Development and the U.S. Department of Education while the studies were in press. We also thank those who assisted committee members with literature searches or background research, including NRC staff Julie Shuck and Matthew von Hendy, as well as Mary Ann Kasper, who ably arranged logistics for members and meetings and assisted with manuscript preparation. The committee is grateful for the guidance and support of Patricia Morison, associate executive director of the Division of Behavioral and Social Sciences and Education (DBASSE). We thank Chris McShane,

Yvonne Wise, and Eugenia Grohman of the DBASSE Office of Reports and Communication for editing the report.

This report has been reviewed in draft form by individuals chosen for their diverse perspectives and technical expertise, in accordance with procedures approved by the Report Review Committee of the NRC. The purpose of this independent review is to provide candid and critical comments that will assist the institution in making its published report as sound as possible and to ensure that the report meets institutional standards for objectivity, evidence, and responsiveness to the study charge. The review comments and draft manuscript remain confidential to protect the integrity of the deliberative process.

We thank the following individuals for their review of this report: Patricia Alexander, College of Education, University of Maryland; Roger Azevedo, Department of Educational and Counseling Psychology, McGill University; Virginia Berninger, College of Education, University of Washington; Larry Condelli, American Institutes for Research; Laurie E. Cutting, Departments of Special Education and Psychology, Radiology, and Pediatrics, Vanderbilt University Kennedy Center; Morton Ann Gernsbacher, University of Wisconsin–Madison; Susan R. Goldman, Department of Psychology and Education, University of Illinois at Chicago; Maryalice Jordan-Marsh, School of Social Work, University of Southern California; Susan Kemper, Department of Psychology, University of Kansas; Richard E. Mayer, Department of Psychology, University of California, Santa Barbara; Larry J. Mikulecky, Department of Education, Indiana University; Timothy Shanahan, Department of Curriculum and Instruction, University of Illinois at Chicago; Catherine Snow, Harvard Graduate School of Education, Harvard University; Sharon Vaughn, Department of Human Development, College of Education, University of Texas at Austin; Dan Wagner, Graduate School of Education, University of Pennsylvania; and Christina Zarcadoolas, Department of Preventive Medicine and Public Health Literacy, Mt. Sinai School of Medicine.

Although the reviewers listed above have provided many constructive comments and suggestions, they were not asked to endorse the conclusions or recommendations, nor did they see the final draft of the report before its release. The review of this report was overseen by Paul R. Sackett, Department of Psychology, University of Minnesota, and Johanna T. Dwyer, Tufts University School of Medicine and Friedman School of Nutrition Science and Policy and Frances Stern Nutrition Center, Tufts Medical Center, and Jean Mayer Human Nutrition Research Center on Aging at Tufts University. Appointed by the NRC, they were responsible for making certain that an independent examination of this report was carried out in accordance with institutional procedures and that all review comments were carefully considered. Responsibility for the final content of this report rests entirely with the authoring committee and the institution.

Alan M. Lesgold, *Chair*
Melissa Welch-Ross, *Study Director*
Committee on Learning Sciences:
Foundations and Applications to
Adolescent and Adult Literacy

Contents

Summary   1
    Recommendations, 5

1 Introduction   8
    Literacy in the United States, 8
    Study Charge, Scope, and Approach, 15
        Conceptual Framework and Approach to the Review of
            Evidence, 15
        Study Scope, 19
    Organization of the Report, 21

2 Foundations of Reading and Writing   24
    Social, Cultural, and Neurocognitive Mechanisms of Literacy
        Development, 25
        Types of Text, 26
        Literacy Tools, 27
        Literacy Activities, 28
        Teacher Knowledge, Skills, and Beliefs, 29
        Neurocognitive Mechanisms, 30
    Reading, 31
        Decoding, 34
        Vocabulary, 35
        Fluency, 37
        Reading Comprehension, 39

Writing, 45
  Components and Processes of Writing, 46
  Writing Instruction, 50
Neurobiology of Reading and Writing Development and
    Difficulties, 54
  Neurobiology of Reading, 54
  Neurobiology of Writing, 55
  Implications for Instruction, 56
Instruction for Struggling Readers and Writers, 57
  Decontextualized Interventions, 57
  Principles of Instruction for Struggling Learners, 58
Reading and Writing Across the Life Span, 64
Summary and Discussion, 67

3 **Literacy Instruction for Adults**   70
Contexts for Literacy Learning, 71
  Adult Education Programs, 71
  Literacy Instruction in Adult Education Programs, 77
  Developmental Education Courses in Colleges, 81
Instructional Practices and Outcomes: State of the Research, 84
  Assumptions and Sources of Evidence, 84
  Orientation to the Findings, 86
  Adults in Basic and Secondary Education Programs, 86
Topics for Future Study from Adult Literacy Research, 92
  Collaborative Learning, 92
  Contextualized Instruction, 93
  Instructional Materials, 94
  Writing Instruction, 95
  Funds of Knowledge and Authentic Learning Experiences, 96
  Social, Psychological, and Functional Outcomes, 96
Underprepared Postsecondary Students, 97
Summary and Directions for Research, 99

4 **Principles of Learning for Instructional Design**   106
The Development of Expertise, 107
Supporting Attention, Retention, and Transfer, 109
  Present Material in a Clear and Organized Format, 109
  Use Multiple and Varied Examples, 110
  Present Material in Multiple Modalities and Formats, 110
  Teach in the Zone of Proximal Development, 111
  Space Presentations of New Material, 113
  Test on Multiple Occasions, Preferably with Spacing, 113
  Ground Concepts in Perceptual-Motor Experiences, 113

Supporting Generation of Content and Reasoning, 115
    Encourage the Learner to Generate Content, 115
    Encourage the Generation of Explanations, Substantive
        Questions, and the Resolution of Contradictions, 116
Encourage the Learner to Construct Ideas from Multiple Points of
    View and Different Perspectives, 117
Complex Strategies, Critical Thinking, Inquiry, and Self-Regulated
    Learning, 118
    Structure Instruction to Develop Effective Use of Complex
        Strategies, 118
    Combine Complex Strategy Instruction with Learning of
        Content, 120
Feedback, 121
    Accurate and Timely Feedback Helps Learning, 121
    Qualitative Feedback Is Better for Learning Than Test Scores
        and Error Flagging, 122
Adaptive and Interactive Learning Environments, 123
    Adaptive Learning Environments Foster Understanding in
        Complex Domains, 123
    Interactive Learning Environments Facilitate Learning, 124
    Learning Is Facilitated in Genuine and Coherent Learning
        Environments, 125
Learning Is Influenced by Motivation and Emotion, 125
Summary and Directions for Research, 126

5   Motivation, Engagement, and Persistence   130
    The Psychology of Motivation and Learning, 131
        Self-Efficacy, 134
        Intrinsic Motivation, 143
    Social, Contextual, and Systemic Mediators of Persistence, 151
        Formal School Structures and Persistence, 151
        Cultural and Linguistic Differences, 152
        Social Relationships and Interactions, 153
        Potentially Negative Effects of Stereotype, 155
        Social and Systemic Supports for and Barriers to Persistence, 156
    Directions for Research, 158

6   Technology to Promote Adult Literacy   162
    Classes of Technologies for Learning, 165
    How Technologies Affect Learning, 166
    Digital Tools for Practicing Skills, 169
    Summary and Directions for Research, 177

7 **Learning, Reading, and Writing Disabilities**   **179**
   Learning Disabilities, 180
      Reading Disabilities, 182
      Writing Disabilities, 187
   Developing Brain Systems in Struggling Readers, 192
      Brain Structure and Function, 193
      Brain Plasticity, 196
   Accommodations to Support Literacy Learning, 198
      Reading Accommodations, 199
      Writing Accommodations, 201
   Summary and Directions for Research, 203

8 **Language and Literacy Development of English Language**
   Learners   **206**
   Component Literacy Skills of English Language Learners, 209
   Influences on Language and Literacy in a Second Language, 210
      First Language Knowledge and Education Level, 210
      English Language Proficiency, 214
      Age, 216
      Aptitude for a Second Language, 217
      Reading and Learning Disabilities, 218
      Cultural Knowledge and Background, 218
   Approaches to Second Language Literacy Instruction, 220
      Integration of Explicit Instruction and Implicit Learning of
         Language and Literacy, 221
      Development of Language and Knowledge for Learning and
         Reading Comprehension, 225
      Access to Language and Literacy Practice Outside
         Classrooms, 227
      Leveraging Knowledge in the First Language, When
         Available, 227
      Integrated Multimodal Instruction, 228
      Writing, 228
      Affective Aspects of Learning and Instruction, 230
      Assessment, 230
   Summary and Directions for Research, 233

9 **Conclusions and Recommendations**   **236**
   Conclusions, 238
      Adult Learners and Learning Environments, 238
      Principles of Effective Literacy Instruction, 240
      English Language Learners, 244
      Assessment, 246

Technology, 248
Adult Literacy Instruction: State of the Evidence, 250
Recommendations, 251
Research Design, 254
Priorities for Basic and Applied Research, 255
Priorities for Translational Science, 256
Large-Scale Data Collection and Information Gathering, 259
Concluding Thoughts: Leadership and Partnership, 259

References and Bibliography   263

Appendixes

A   **Biographical Sketches of Committee Members and Staff**   385
B   **Literacy in a Digital Age**   392
Adult Literacy Practices and Proficiencies, 394
Adults' Engagement with Information and Communication
    Technologies, 397
Instructional Practices and Learning Environments, 399
Future Research, 401
References, 401
C   **Interventions to Develop the Component Literacy Skills of
Low-Literate Adults**   407
A. Study Populations and Sample Characteristics, 408
B. Intervention Practices, Intensity, Duration, and Attrition
    Rates, 410
C. Study Instruments by Measurement Construct by Study, 412
References, 416
D   **Search Procedures and Reviewed Studies of Adult Literacy
Instruction***   417

---

*Appendix D is not printed in this volume but is available online. Go to http://www.nap.edu/catalog.php?record_id=13242.

Summary

A high level of literacy in both print and digital media is required for negotiating most aspects of 21st-century life—supporting a family, education, health, civic participation, and competitiveness in the global economy. Yet a recent survey estimates that more than 90 million U.S. adults lack adequate literacy.[1] Furthermore, only 38 percent of U.S. twelfth graders are at or above proficient in reading.[2]

Adults who need literacy instruction receive it in two main types of settings: (1) adult education programs, for which the largest source of federal funding is the Workforce Investment Act, Title II, Adult Education and Family Literacy Act (AEFLA), and (2) developmental education courses in colleges for academically underprepared students. Adults in adult education programs (an estimated 2.6 million in federally funded programs in 2005) show variable progress in their literacy skills, and for many, their gains are insufficient to achieve functional literacy.[3]

This report responds to a request from the U.S. Department of Education to the National Research Council (NRC) to (1) synthesize research on literacy and learning, (2) draw implications for the instructional practices used to teach reading in adult literacy programs, and (3) recommend a more systemic approach to research, practice, and policy. To inform its conclusions and recommendations, the Committee on Learning Sciences: Foundations and Applications to Adolescent and Adult Literacy reviewed

---

[1] Estimate from Kutner et al. (2007).
[2] According to the National Assessment of Educational Progress (2010).
[3] Information from Tamassia et al. (2007).

1

research from the fields of literacy, learning, cognitive science, neuroscience, behavioral and social science, and education. The committee identifies factors that affect literacy development in adolescence and adulthood in general and examines their implications for the populations in adult education programs.

In keeping with its charge, the committee defined *literacy* as the ability to read, write, and communicate using a symbol system (in this case, English) and using appropriate tools and technologies to meet the goals and demands of individuals, their families, and U.S. society. Thus, *literacy skill* includes but encompasses a broader range of proficiency than *basic skills*. The focus of the committee is on improving the literacy of individuals ages 16 years and older who are not in K-12 education; this focus is consistent with eligibility for federally funded adult education programs. The report includes research with adolescents of all ages but discusses the implications of this research (as well as research with children and adults) for instruction to be used in adult literacy education.[4]

There is a surprising lack of rigorous research on effective approaches to adult literacy instruction. This lack of evidence is especially striking given the long history of both federal funding for adult education programs and reliance on the nation's community colleges to develop and improve adults' literacy skills. Sustained and systematic research is needed to (1) identify instructional approaches that show promise of maximizing adults' literacy skill gains; (2) develop scalable instructional programs and rigorously test their effectiveness; and (3) conduct further testing to determine for whom and under what conditions those approaches work.

In the absence of research with adults whose literacy is not at high levels, the committee concluded that it is reasonable to apply findings from the large body of research on learning and literacy with other populations (mainly younger students and relatively well-educated adults) with some adaptations to account for the developmental level and unique challenges of adult learners. The available research provides guidance about principles of effective reading and writing instruction, principles of learning and motivation, and promising uses of technologies and other supports for learning.

Effective literacy instruction addresses the foundational components of reading—word recognition, fluency, vocabulary, reading comprehension, background knowledge, strategies for deeper analysis, and understanding of texts—and the component skills of writing. It combines explicit teaching

---

[4]Given the sponsor's primary interest in improving adult literacy education, we did not address the question of how to prevent low literacy in the United States. Although the report does not have an explicit focus on issues of prevention and how to improve literacy instruction in the K-12 system, many of the relevant findings were derived from research with younger populations and so they are likely to be relevant to the prevention of inadequate literacy.

and extensive practice with motivating and varied texts, tools, and tasks matched to the learner's skills, educational and cultural backgrounds, and literacy needs and goals. It explicitly addresses the automation and integration of component skills and the transfer of skills to tasks valued by society and the learner. Effective instruction includes formative (ongoing) assessments to monitor progress, provide feedback, and adjust instruction.

Students who have not mastered the foundations of reading and writing require instruction targeted to their skill levels and practice in amounts substantial enough to produce high levels of competence in the component skills. A large body of research with K-12 students provides the principles and practices of literacy instruction that are equally important to developing and struggling adult learners. Additional principles have been identified to help those with learning disabilities overcome specific areas of difficulty. The available research on accommodations for adults with learning disabilities, conducted mainly with college students, also warrant application and further study in adult education settings to remove barriers to learning.

Although findings from research specifically on effective literacy instruction for adults is lacking, research with younger populations can guide the development of instructional approaches for adults if it is modified to account for two major differences between adults and younger populations. One is that adults may experience age-related neurocognitive declines that affect reading and writing processes and speed of learning. The second is that adults bring varied life experiences, knowledge, and motivations for learning that need attention in the design of literacy instruction for them. Compared with children, adolescents and adults may have more knowledge and possess some literacy skills while still needing to fill gaps in other skills, acquire content knowledge, and develop the level of literacy needed for education, work, and practical life.

Research on learning and motivation can inform the design of supportive instructional interactions and environments. This research has not included low-literate adults: translational research is needed to design and evaluate instructional approaches consistent with these principles for this population. Although basic principles of learning and motivation apply to learners of all ages, the particular motivations to read or write are often different at different ages. Instruction for adolescents and adults may need to be designed differently to motivate these populations.

Literacy is a complex skill that requires thousands of hours of practice, but many adults do not persist in adult literacy instruction long enough or have enough time to practice outside the instructional setting to reach their goals. The problem of high attrition needs to be resolved for adults to receive sufficient practice and instruction and for rigorous research to accumulate on effective instructional methods. The available research suggests ways to design motivating instructional approaches and environments, create more time for practice, and ensure the time is efficiently used: they will need to be tested rigorously. Technologies for learning have the potential to help resolve problems of insufficient practice caused by time and space constraints. Technologies also can assist with multiple aspects of teaching, assessment, and accommodations for learning. Translational research is needed to develop and evaluate promising technologies for improving adult literacy and to demonstrate how these can be part of coherent systems of instruction.

The population of adult literacy learners is heterogeneous. Consequently, optimal literacy instruction needs to vary according to adults' goals, motivations, knowledge, assessed skills, interests, neurocognitive profiles, and language background. The population of adults who need to develop their literacy ranges from recent immigrants with only a sixth grade education in their native country, to middle-aged and older U.S.-born high school graduates who find they can no longer keep up with the reading, writing, and technology demands of their jobs, to adults who dropped out of school or whose learning disabilities were not fully accommodated in school, to highly educated immigrants who need to learn to read and write in English.

The largest subgroup of adults enrolled in adult education is adults learning English as a second language. This population is very diverse. Some are immigrants who are well educated and highly literate in their first languages. Others are recent immigrants with low levels of education and first language literacy. Another large subgroup is people who were born in the United States or came to the United States as young children but have grown up with a home language other than English. Although educated in U.S. schools, these adults often need to develop higher literacy skills for postsecondary education or work.

There has been virtually no research on effective literacy instruction for adults learning English as a second language. The available research with other populations—young second language learners and relatively well-educated students in high school or college—suggests practices that warrant further study with the larger population of adult learners. Although general principles of learning and literacy development can be applied to second language learners, literacy instruction needs to be adapted to the learner's education level, degree of literacy in the first and second language, and familiarity with U.S. culture.

Good systems of assessment to improve student learning consist of (a) *diagnostic assessment* to inform instructors about skills the learner possesses and needs to develop; (b) *formative assessment* of skills being developed that need further improvement as instruction progresses; and (c) *accountability assessment* to inform administrators, policy makers, funders, and the public of how well the program and systems that serve adult literacy learners are working. The assessments need to be aligned with common goals for learning. Assessments of literacy need to be suitable for adults, assess all the important dimensions of reading, writing, and language, and assess a range of print and digital functional literacy skills that society demands and values.

Adult literacy education is offered in a mix of programs that lack coordination and coherence with respect to literacy development objectives and instructional approaches. In addition, learning objectives for literacy lack alignment across the many places of adult education and with colleges and K-12 instruction. Literacy instructors need sufficient training and supports to assess adults' skills, plan and differentiate instruction for adults who differ in their neurobiological, psychosocial, and cultural and linguistic characteristics, as well as their levels of literacy attainment. Yet, the preparation of instructors is highly variable and training and professional development limited. These factors, as well as high attrition from adult literacy programs, present challenges to the systematic implementation and study of effective adult literacy instruction.

RECOMMENDATIONS

The committee's conclusions led to four overarching recommendations.

First, federal and state policy makers should move quickly to build on and expand the infrastructure of adult literacy education to support the use of instructional approaches, curricula, materials, tools, and assessments of learners consistent with (a) the available research on reading, writing, learning, language, and adult development; (b) the research on the effectiveness of instructional approaches; and (c) knowledge of sound assessment practices.

Second, federal and state policy makers need to ensure that professional development and technical assistance for instructors are widely accessible and consistent with the best research on reading, writing, learning, language, and adult development.

Third, policy makers, providers of literacy programs, and researchers should collaborate to systematically implement and evaluate options to achieve the persistence needed for literacy learning. These options include, among others, instructional approaches, technologies, social service support, and incentives.

Fourth, to inform local, state, and federal decisions aimed at optimizing the progress of adult learners, the committee strongly recommends strategic and sustained investments in a coordinated and systemic approach to program improvement, evaluation, and research about adult literacy learners. Translational research should be conducted in four areas: (1) instructional approaches and materials grounded in principles of learning and instruction, (2) supports for persistence, (3) technologies for learning, and (4) assessments of learners and their instructional environments. The research will need a strong instructor training component with instructor supports. To ensure investments of the appropriate scale, a sequence of research should be undertaken that includes exploration, innovation, efficacy testing, scaling up, and assessment development.

Basic and applied research is recommended in several priority areas. First, the characteristics of adult literacy learners should be studied to define instructionally meaningful subgroups to provide a strong basis for differentiating instructional approaches. Second, an empirical basis is needed to help define the literacy skills required in today's society to meet educational or career milestones and for full social and civic participation. Third, more research is need on the cognitive, linguistic, and neural influences on learning for both typical adult learners and those with learning disabilities. Fourth, the various forces that interact to affect typical and atypical literacy development across the life span—cognitive, linguistic, social, cultural, instructional, and systemic—need to be better specified.

Information about the literacy of adults in the United States rapidly becomes outdated, and adequate information is not available about the literacy instruction provided to adults or its effectiveness. The committee recommends that information about the literacy skills of the nation's adults and in the diverse systems that offer adult literacy instruction be gathered and analyzed on a continual and long-term basis to know (1) whether the population is becoming more literate and (2) whether efforts to improve literacy are effective at a macro level as well as in specific individual efficacy studies. These efforts should track progress on the components of reading and writing that have been identified in research and on proficiency in performing important functional literacy tasks. The information collected on instructional programs should include learning goals and objectives and the practices, materials, tools, and assessments in use. This information is needed to better understand current practices, plan the appropriate professional development of instructors, create effective out-of-classroom learning opportunities, and better match literacy instruction to emerging literacy demands for work, education, health, and functioning in society.

Implementation of these recommendations will require strong leadership from specific entities in the U.S. Department of Education and the U.S. Department of Labor. Given the scope of the problem, partnerships need to be developed between researchers, curriculum developers, and administrators across the systems that serve adult learners. It will also be important to enlist business leaders and faith-based and other community groups in the effort. The committee urges particular attention to three issues noted above: (1) variability of instructor preparation, (2) the existence of many different types of programs that have varied literacy development practices and that lack alignment with K-12 education and college systems that offer literacy instruction, and (3) the instructional and other supports that enable adults to persist in programs and practice skills outside the classroom. These factors affect the quality of instruction to be implemented, the feasibility of conducting the needed research, and the potential for broad dissemination and implementation of the practices that are identified as effective.

1

Introduction

The Adult Education and Family Literacy Act (Title II of the Workforce Investment Act (1998) defines literacy as "an individual's ability to read, write, and speak in English, compute, and solve problems, at levels of proficiency necessary to function on the job, in the family of the individual, and in society." The United Nations Education, Social, and Cultural Organization (UNESCO) (2004) defines literacy more broadly as "the ability to identify, understand, interpret, create, communicate, compute and use printed and written materials associated with varying contexts. Literacy involves a continuum of learning to enable an individual to achieve his or her goals, to develop his or her knowledge and potential, and to participate fully in the wider society."

LITERACY IN THE UNITED STATES

More than 90 million adults in the United States are estimated to lack the literacy skills for a fully productive and secure life, according to the National Assessment of Adult Literacy (NAAL) (Kutner et al., 2007). This report synthesizes the research on literacy and learning to improve literacy instruction for those served in adult education in the United States and to recommend a more systemic approach to research, practice, and policy.

Conducted in 2003, the NAAL is the most recent national survey of U.S. adult literacy. *Adults* were defined by the NAAL as people ages 16 years or older. The survey assessed the prose, document, and quantitative literacy of a nationally representative sample of more than 18,000 U.S.

adults living in households and 1,200 prison inmates.[1] Adults were categorized as having proficient, intermediate, basic, or below basic levels of
literacy.

According to the survey, 43 percent of U.S. adults (an estimated 56
million people) possess only basic or below basic prose literacy skills. Only
13 percent had proficient prose literacy. Results were similar for document
literacy: 34 percent of adults had basic or below basic document literacy
and only 13 percent were proficient. A comparison of the results with findings from the 1992 National Adult Literacy Survey (NALS) shows that little
progress was made between 1992 and 2003 (see Table 1-1).

Table 1-2 shows the percentage and number of adults in each race/
ethnicity category in the 2003 NAAL survey with below basic and basic
literacy. Certain groups in the 2003 NAAL survey were more likely to
perform at the below basic level: those who did not speak English before
entering school, Hispanic adults, those who reported having multiple disabilities, and black adults. The 7 million adults with the lowest levels of
skill showed difficulties with reading letters and words and comprehending
a simple text (Baer, Kutner, and Sabatini, 2009) (see Table 1-3).

Although literacy increases with educational attainment (see Table 1-4),
only 4 percent of high school graduates who do not go further in their
schooling are proficient in prose literacy, according to the NAAL; 53 percent are at the basic or below basic level. Among those with a 2-year degree,
only 19 percent have proficient prose literacy, 56 percent show intermediate
skill, and 24 percent are at basic or below basic levels. This level of literacy
might have been sufficient earlier in the nation's history, but it is likely to
be inadequate today (Organisation for Economic Co-operation and Development, 2005). For U.S. society to continue to function and sustain its
standard of living, higher literacy levels are required of the U.S. population
in the 21st century for economic security and all other aspects of daily life:
education, health, parenting, social interaction, personal growth, and civic
participation.

Civic participation requires citizens to understand the complex matters
about which they need to make decisions and on which societal well-being
depends. Although people might legitimately differ in their beliefs about
what health care policy the country should have, national surveys show
that too many people lack the literacy needed to engage in that discussion.
Parents cannot further their children's education or ensure their children's

---

[1]Prose literacy was defined as the ability to search, comprehend, and use information from
continuous texts. Prose examples include editorials, news stories, brochures, and instructional
materials. Document literacy was defined as the ability to search, comprehend, and use information from noncontinuous texts. Document examples include job applications, payroll
forms, transportation schedules, maps, tables, and drug and food labels. The survey also assessed quantitative literacy.

TABLE 1-1 Percentage of U.S. Adults in Each Literacy Proficiency Category by Literacy Task, 1992 and 2003 (in percentage)

Proficiency Category	Prose Literacy 1992	Prose Literacy 2003	Document Literacy 1992	Document Literacy 2003	Quantitative Literacy 1992	Quantitative Literacy 2003
Below basic	14	14	14	12[a]	26	22[a]
Basic	28	29	22	22	32	33
Intermediate	43	44	49	53[a]	30	33[a]
Proficient	15	13[a]	15	13[a]	13	13

NOTE: Data exclude people who could not be tested due to language differences: 3 percent in 1992 and 2 percent in 2003.
[a]Significantly different from 1992.
SOURCE: Data from the National Assessment of Adult Literacy (Kutner et al., 2007).

health when their literacy is low: adults with low literacy are much less likely to read to their children or have reading materials in the home (Kutner et al., 2007), and they have much more limited access to health-related information (Berkman et al., 2004) and have lower health literacy (U.S. Department of Health and Human Services, 2008). Many U.S. adults lack health literacy or the ability to read and follow the kinds of instructions routinely given for self-care or to family caregivers after medical procedures or hospital stays (Kutner et al., 2006; Nielsen-Bohlman, Panzer, and Kindig, 2004).

TABLE 1-2 U.S. Adults in Each Race/Ethnicity Category with Below Basic and Basic Literacy, 2003

	Percentage Below Basic	Percentage Basic	Estimated Total Number Across Both Categories (in millions)
Asian/Pacific Islander	14	32	4.1
Black	24	43	17.8
Hispanic	44	30	19.7
White	7	25	49.8
Total Number of Adults			91.4

NOTES: The NAAL included a national sample representative of the total population in 2003 (222 million people; 221 million in households and a little more than 1 million in prisons). This estimate of the number of people with low literacy (basic or below basic literacy) in each race/ethnicity category is derived from the percentage of people in each category in the NAAL survey. The table does not include the 3 percent of adults who could not participate in the survey due to language spoken or disabilities. It does not include 2 percent of respondents who identified multiple races. These findings are for prose literacy; the pattern of findings is similar for document literacy. For definitions of the literacy categories, see text.
SOURCE: Data from the National Assessment of Adult Literacy (Kutner et al., 2007).

TABLE 1-3 Correct Responses on Reading Tasks for U.S. Adults with Below Basic Literacy (by language of administration) (in percentage), 2003

	Letter Reading[a]	Word Identification[b]	Word Reading[c]	Comprehension[d]
English	80	65	56	54
Spanish	38	74	37	54

NOTES: The data cover 7 million adults, 3 percent of the population. Adults are defined in the survey as people ages 16 and older living in households or prisons. The data exclude adults who could not be interviewed because of language spoken or cognitive or mental disabilities, approximately 3 percent.

[a]Letter reading required reading a list of 35 letters in 15 seconds.

[b]Word identification required recognizing words on three word lists of increasing difficulty—from one- to four-syllable words.

[c]Word reading required decoding of nonwords using knowledge of letter-sound correspondences.

[d]Comprehension required correctly answering a question about the content of a passage written either at grades 2-6 or grades 7-8 level.

SOURCE: Data from Baer, Kutner, and Sabatini (2009).

TABLE 1-4 Percentage of U.S. Adults in Prose and Document Literacy Proficiency Categories by Educational Attainment, 2003

	Below Basic	Basic	Intermediate	Proficient
Prose				
Less than/some high school	50	33	16	1
GED/high school equivalency	10	45	43	3
High school graduate	13	39	44	4
Vocational/trade/business school	10	36	49	5
Some college	5	25	59	11
Associate/2-year degree	4	20	56	19
College graduate	3	14	53	31
Document				
Less than/some high school	45	29	25	2
GED/ high school equivalency	13	30	53	4
High school graduate	13	29	52	5
Vocational/trade/business school	9	26	59	7
Some college	5	19	65	10
Associate/2-year degree	3	15	66	16
College graduate	2	11	62	25

SOURCE: Data from the National Assessment of Adult Literacy (Kutner et al., 2007).

Adults with low literacy also have lower participation in the labor force and lower earnings (Kutner et al., 2007). Figure 1-1 shows how lifetime net tax contributions increase as education level increases. It is reasonable to assume that gains in literacy that allow increases in educational attainment would lead to a higher standard of living and the ability of more people to contribute to such costs of society as public safety and educating future generations. Adults with a high school diploma or general educational development (GED) certificate earn significantly more per year than those without such credentials (e.g., Liming and Wolf, 2008; U.S. Census Bureau, 2007). The most recent national survey of adults' literacy skills in the United States shows that the percentage of adults employed full time increases with increased facility in reading prose (Kutner et al., 2007).

If anything, data from the NAAL and other surveys and assessments are likely to underestimate the problem of literacy in the United States. Literacy demands are increasing because of the rapid growth of information and communication technologies, while the literacy assessments to date have focused on the simplest forms of literacy skill. Most traditional employment has required reading directions, keeping records, and answering business communications, but today's workers have very different roles. Employers stress that employees need higher levels of basic literacy in the workplace than they currently possess (American Manufacturing Association, 2010) and that the global economy calls for increasingly complex forms of literacy skill in this information age (Casner-Lotto and Benner, 2006). In a world in which computers do the routine, human value in the workplace rests increasingly on the ability to gather and integrate information from disparate sources to address novel situations and emergent problems, mediate among different viewpoints of the world (e.g., between an actuary's and a

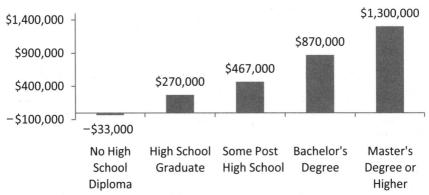

FIGURE 1-1 Lifetime net tax contributions by education level.
SOURCE: Data from Khatiwada et al. (2007).

customer's view of what should be covered under an insurance policy), and collaborate on tasks that are too complex to be within the scope of one person. To earn a living, people are likely to need forms of literacy skill and to have proficiencies in the use of literacy tools that have not been routinely defined and assessed.

A significant portion of the U.S. population is likely to continue, at least in the near term, to experience inadequate literacy and require instruction as adults: the most recent main National Assessment of Educational Progress (NAEP) (2009) shows that only 38 percent of twelfth graders performed at or above the proficient level in reading; this achievement was higher than the percentage in 2005 but not significantly different from earlier assessment years. Although 74 percent of twelfth graders were at or above basic, 26 percent were below basic near the end of high school. Table 1-5 shows the percentage of twelfth grade students at each achievement level for reading by race and ethnicity. These numbers include students identified as learning English as a second language: only 22 percent of them were at or above basic reading levels near the end of high school; 78 percent were below basic. Results were similar for twelfth graders with disabilities: 38 percent were at or above basic reading levels; 62 percent were below basic.

Similarly, according to the 2007 assessment of writing by the NAEP, only 24 percent of twelfth graders had proficient writing skills, with many fewer of the students who were learning English or with learning disabilities showing proficiency (40 and 44 percent, respectively) compared with those not identified as English learners or as having a learning disability (83 and 85 percent, respectively).

The NAEP is likely to underestimate the proportion of twelfth graders who need to develop their literacy outside the K-12 system because it does not include students who dropped out of school before the assessment, many of whom are likely to have inadequate literacy. In the 2007-2008 school year, the most recent one for which data are available, 613,379 students in the ninth to twelfth grades dropped out of school. The overall

TABLE 1-5 Percentage of Twelfth Grade Students at or Above NAEP Achievement Levels by Race/Ethnicity

	Asian/Pacific	Black	Hispanic	White
Below basic	19	43	39	19
At or above basic	81	57	61	81
At or above proficient	49	17	22	46
Advanced	10	1	2	7

SOURCE: Data from the National Assessment of Educational Progress (NAEP) 2009 Reading Assessment (U.S. Department of Education, 2011).

annual dropout rate (known as the event dropout rate—the percentage of high school students who drop out of high school over the course of a given school year) was 4.1 percent across all 49 reporting states and the District of Columbia (National Center for Education Statistics, 2010). Although students drop out of school for many reasons, it can be assumed that these students' literacy skills are below those of the rest of the U.S. population and fail to meet society's expectations for literacy. In fact, 55 percent of adults in the 2003 NAAL survey who scored below basic did not graduate from high school (compared with 15 percent of the entire adult population); adults who did not complete high school were almost four times more likely than the total adult population to demonstrate below basic skills (Baer et al., 2009).

Given these statistics, it is not surprising that, although originally designed for older adults, adult literacy education programs are increasingly attended by youths ages 16 to 20 (Hayes, 2000; Perin, Flugman, and Spiegel, 2006). In 2003, more than half of participants in federally funded adult literacy programs were 25 or younger (Tamassia et al., 2007).

The problem of inadequate literacy is also found by colleges, especially community colleges. More than half of community college students enroll in at least one developmental education course during their college tenure to remediate weak skills (Bailey, Jeong, and Cho, 2010). Data from an initiative called Achieving the Dream: Community Colleges Count provide the best information on students' difficulties in remedial instruction. The study included more than 250,000 students from 57 colleges in seven states who were enrolled for the first time from fall 2003 to fall 2004. Of the total, 59 percent were referred for remedial instruction, and 33 percent of the referrals were specifically for reading. After 3 years, fewer than 4 of 10 students had completed the entire sequence of remedial courses to which they had been referred (Bailey, Jeong, and Cho, 2010). About 30 percent of students referred to developmental education did not enroll in any remedial course, and about 60 percent of those who did enroll did not enroll in the specific course to which they had been referred (Bailey, Jeong, and Cho, 2010). Notably, according to the NAAL survey, proficiency in prose literacy was evident in only 31 percent of U.S. adults with a 4-year college degree.

For a variety of reasons, firm conclusions cannot currently be drawn about whether developmental education improves the literacy skills and rates of college completion. What is clear, however, is that remediation is costly: in 2004-2005, the costs of remediation were estimated at $1.9 to $2.3 billion at community colleges and another $500 million at 4-year colleges (Strong American Schools, 2008). States have reported tens of millions of dollars in expenditures (Bailey, 2009). The costs to students of inadequate remediation include accumulated debt, lost earnings, and frustration that can lead to dropping out.

STUDY CHARGE, SCOPE, AND APPROACH

To address the problem of how best to instruct the large and diverse population of U.S. adults who need to improve their literacy skills, the U.S. Department of Education asked the National Research Council to appoint a multidisciplinary committee to (1) synthesize research findings on literacy and learning from cognitive science, neuroscience, behavioral science, and education; (2) identify from the research the main factors that affect literacy development in adolescence and adulthood, both in general and with respect to the specific populations served in education programs for adults; (3) analyze the implications of the research for informing curricula and instruction used to develop adults' literacy; and (4) recommend a more systemic approach to subsequent research, practice, and policy. The complete charge is presented in Box 1-1.

The work of the Committee on Learning Sciences: Foundations and Applications to Adolescent and Adult Literacy is a necessary step toward improving adult literacy in the United States. Through our work, which included public meetings and reviews of documents, the committee gathered evidence about adult literacy levels both in the United States and internationally and the literacy demands placed on adults in modern life related to education, work, social and civic participation, and maintenance of health and family. We considered a wide array of research literatures that might have accumulated findings that could help answer the question of how best to design literacy instruction for adults.

Conceptual Framework and Approach to the Review of Evidence

Figure 1-2 presents the committee's conceptual model of the development of literate practice, which we used to identify research most germane to this report. We also used it to convey the range of factors that require attention in our attempt to identify the instructional practices that work for learners and the conditions that support or impede instructional effectiveness and learning. The model focuses mainly on the factors that research shows are amenable to change through particular approaches to instruction and the creation of supportive learning environments. It is derived mainly from understandings of literacy development from K-12 populations and extended to accommodate adults' motivations and circumstances, which differ from those of younger populations learning to read and write.

In view of the charge that motivates this report, we define *literacy* to be the ability to read, write, and communicate using a symbol system (in this case, English), with available and valued tools and technologies, in order to meet the goals and demands of families, individuals, and U.S. society. Literacy requires developing proficiencies in the major known components

---

BOX 1-1
Committee Charge

In response to a request from the National Institute for Literacy (NIFL), the National Research Council will convene a committee to conduct a study of the scientific foundations of adolescent and adult literacy with implications for policy and practice. In particular, the study will synthesize research-based knowledge on literacy from the multidisciplinary perspectives of education, cognitive and behavioral science, neuroscience, and other relevant disciplines; and will provide a strong empirical foundation for understanding the main factors that affect literacy learning in adolescence and adulthood generally and with respect to the specific populations served by adult education. The committee will develop a conceptual and methodological framework to guide the study and conduct a review of the existing research literature and sources of evidence. The committee's final report will provide a basis for research and practice, laying out the most promising areas for future research while informing curriculum and instruction for current adolescent literacy and adult education practitioners and service providers.

This study will (1) synthesize the behavioral and cognitive sciences, education, and neuroscience research on literacy to understand its applicability to adolescent and adult populations; (2) analyze the implications of this research for the instructional practices used to teach reading in adolescent and adult literacy programs; and (3) establish a set of recommendations or roadmap for a more systemic approach to subsequent research, practice, and policy. The committee will synthesize and integrate new knowledge from the multidisciplinary perspectives of behavioral and cognitive sciences, education, neuroscience, and other related disciplines, with emphasis on potential uses in the research and policy communities. It will provide a broad understanding of the factors that affect typical and atypical literacy learning in adolescence and adulthood

---

of reading and writing (presented in Chapter 2) and being able to integrate them to perform the activities required of adults in the United States in the 21st century. Thus, our use of the term *literacy skill* includes but encompasses a broader range of proficiency than *basic skills*.

Our synthesis covers research literature on

- cognitive, linguistic, neurobiological, social, and cultural factors that are part of reading and writing development across the life span;
- effective approaches for teaching reading and writing with students in K-12 education, out-of-school youth, and adults;
- principles of learning that apply to the design of instruction;
- motivation, engagement, and persistence;
- uses of technology to support learning and literacy for adolescents and adults;
- valid assessment of reading, writing, and learning; and

generally and with respect to the specific populations served by adult education and such related issues as motivation, retention and prevention.

The following questions will be among those the committee will consider in developing its roadmap for a more systematic approach to subsequent research, practice, and policy:

- Does the available research on learning and instruction apply to the full range of types of learners served by adult education? If not, for what specific populations is research particularly needed? What do we know, for example, about how to deliver reading instruction to students in the lowest achievement levels normally found in adult basic education?
- What are some of the specific challenges faced by adults who need to learn literacy skills in English when it is their second language? What does the cognitive and learning research suggest about the most effective instructional strategies for these learners?
- What outcome measures and methods are suggested from research addressing literacy remediation and prevention in both adolescent and adult programs?
- Where are there gaps in our understanding about what research is needed related to retention and motivation of adult literacy learners?
- What implications does the research on learning and effective instruction have for remediation and prevention of problems with literacy during middle and/or high school?
- What is known about teacher characteristics, training, and capacity of programs to implement more effective literacy instructional methods?
- Are there policy strategies that could be implemented to help ensure that the evidence base on best practices for learning gets used by programs and teachers?

- instructional approaches for English language learners and the various influences (cognitive, neurobiological, social) on the development of literacy in a second language in adulthood.

Several reviews of research relevant to the charge informed the work of this committee, among them a report of the National Reading Panel (NRP) (National Institute of Child Health and Human Development, 2000) and a recent systematic review of the literature on adult literacy instruction (Kruidener, MacArthur, and Wrigley, 2010). In such cases, we did not duplicate existing works but incorporated from previous work the core findings that we interpreted to be most relevant to our charge, augmented with targeted searches of literature as needed to draw conclusions about the state of the research base and needs for development.

We included both quantitative and qualitative research with the recognition that different types of research questions call for different methodological approaches. We concentrated mainly on the most developed

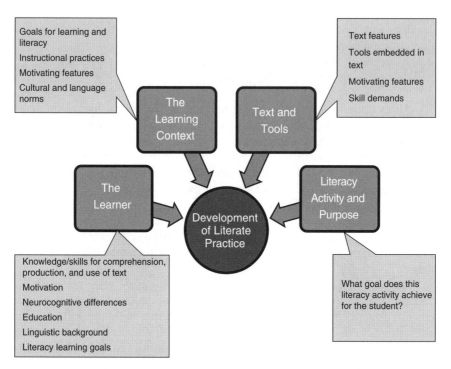

FIGURE 1-2 Conceptual model of the development of literate practice.

research findings and included promising, cutting-edge areas of inquiry that warrant further research. In reviewing the research, we asked: Are the data reliable and potentially valid for the target population? What are the limits of current knowledge? What are the most useful directions for expanding knowledge of literacy development and learning to better meet the needs of adult learners?

An assumption of our framework is that to be functionally literate one must be able to engage in literacy practices with texts and tools that are demanded by and valued in society. Thus, we include a focus on writing, which has a smaller base of research than reading. We also refer throughout the report to new literacy skills and practices enabled by a digital age and include a more complete discussion of these issues in Appendix B. Although we assume that literacy skills enabled by the use of new technologies are now fundamental to what it means to be literate, researchers are only beginning to define these skills and practices and to study the instruction and assessments that develop them in students of all ages (e.g., Goldman et al., 2011). In the final chapter, we stress the importance of including writing and emerging new literacy demands in any future efforts to define literacy development goals for adults and to identify the instructional approaches that comprehensively meet their skill development needs.

Study Scope

An examination of the relevant literatures revealed a diverse range of information and disparate literatures that seemed unknown and unconnected to each other, despite the fact that many share a focus on reading and literacy. The literatures differ in the ages of the populations studied; definitions, theories, and working understandings or models of literacy development; research topics; and research methods. Several literatures were severely underdeveloped with respect to the charge because of the nature of the topics studied or because the data are mainly descriptive or anecdotal and have not yet led to the accumulation of reliable or relevant knowledge. This information gathering led the committee to focus the charge in these ways.

We focused on a target population (to whom we refer generally as "adults") of individuals ages 16 and older not in secondary education, consistent with eligibility requirements for participation in federally funded adult literacy education programs. We considered what is known about the literacy skills and other characteristics of these adults and their learning environments in programs of four general types: (1) adult basic education, (2) adult secondary education (e.g., GED instruction), (3) programs of English as a second language, and (4) developmental (remedial) education courses in colleges for academically underprepared students. We focused mainly on research that could be applied to the development of instructional methods for these populations, and we did not focus more broadly on segments of the U.S. population, such as the elderly, who might benefit from enhanced literacy or strategies that compensate for age-related declines in literacy skills.

The lack of research on learning and the effects of literacy instruction in the target population is striking, given the long history of both federal funding, albeit stretched thin, for adult education programs and reliance on developmental education courses to remediate college students' skills. As we explain in Chapter 3, although there is a large literature on adult literacy instruction, it is mostly descriptive, and the small body of experimental research suffers from methodological limitations, such as high rates of participant attrition and inadequate controls. As a result, the research has not yielded a body of reliable and interpretable findings that could provide a reliable basis for understanding the process of literacy acquisition in low-skilled adults or the design and delivery of instruction for this population.

In contrast to the scant literature on adult literacy, a large body of research is available with younger populations, especially children. Although the majority of this work investigates the acquisition and instruction of word-reading skills, more is becoming known about how to develop vocabulary and reading comprehension. A growing body of research with adolescents in school settings focuses on such topics as academic literacy, disciplinary literacy, and discussion-based approaches that warrant further study with both adolescents and adults outside school. Although major research studies have been launched by the U.S. Department of Education, the National Institute of Child Health and Human Development, and others to increase knowledge of literacy development and effective instruction beyond the early elementary years, the efforts are too new to have produced numerous peer-reviewed publications on effective instructional practices. Similarly, research on adult cognition, learning, and motivation from other disciplines is constrained for our purposes. For the most part, such research relies on study samples of convenience (e.g., college students in introductory psychology courses) or the elderly.

Given the dearth of research on what is the target population for this report, the committee has drawn on what is available: extensive research on reading and writing processes and difficulties in younger students, a mature body of research on learning and motivation in relatively well-educated adults with normal reading capability, and comparatively limited research on struggling adolescent readers and writers and adult literacy learners. These constraints on the available literature mean the committee's analysis and synthesis focus on examining instructional practices that work for younger populations that have not been invalidated by any of the available data with adults; extrapolating with caution from other research available on learning, cognition, and motivation to make additional suggestions for improving adult reading instruction; and articulating a research agenda focused specifically on learning and reading and writing instruction for adult literacy learners. The committee decided that examining the wealth of information from the research that exists with these populations could be valuable to the development of instructional practices for adults, with research and evaluation to validate, identify the boundaries of, and expand this knowledge in order to specify the practices that develop literacy skills in adolescents and adults outside school.

Although the charge specified a focus on reading, we chose to add a focus on writing for four reasons. First, integrated reading and writing instruction contributes to the development of both reading and writing skills, as described in Chapter 2, most likely because these skills require some of the same knowledge and cognitive and linguistic processes. Second, from a practical perspective, many reading activities for academic learning or work also involve writing (and vice versa). Third, writing is a method of developing content knowledge, which adults need to develop to improve their reading, both in general and in specific content domains. Fourth, writing is a literacy skill that is important to adult literacy education, given that it is needed for GED completion and for success in college and in the workplace (Berman, 2001, 2009; Carnevale and Derochers, 2004; Kirsch et al., 2007; Milulecky, 1998; National Commission on Writing, 2004, 2005).

Because of the large variety of literatures, the report does not focus in depth on domain-specific literacies, such as quantitative literacy, financial literacy, health literacy, or science literacy. These topics are large and significant enough to deserve separate treatment (e.g., Condelli, 2006; Nielsen-Bohlman et al., 2004).

The report includes research about literacy development with adolescents of all ages as well as children. However, given the breadth of the charge and in consultation with the project sponsor about the primary interest, the committee narrowed its focus to synthesizing the implications of that research for instruction in adult literacy education (defined as instruction for individuals 16 years and older and outside K-12 education). This focus was chosen to fit with the requirement that federally funded adult literacy programs are for youth and adults older than 16 and not in the regular K-12 system. Although there is a broad universe of information on adolescent and adult literacy and the factors that affect literacy, the committee and this report covers the research findings about the factors that affect literacy and learning that are sufficiently developed and relevant for making decisions about how to improve adult literacy instruction and planning a research agenda. Consistent with the sponsor's guidance, we did not address the question of how to prevent low literacy in U.S. society, but the pressing and important problem of how to instruct adolescents and adults outside the K-12 system who have inadequate English literacy skills. Although the report does not have an explicit focus on issues of prevention and how to improve literacy instruction in the K-12 system, many of the relevant findings were derived from research with younger populations, and so they are likely to be relevant to the prevention of inadequate literacy.

ORGANIZATION OF THE REPORT

The discussion of research relevant to the population of adult learners is complicated by substantial differences in the characteristics of learners, learning goals, and the many and varied types and places of instruction. In theory, it is possible to organize this report according to any number of individual difference variables, learning goals (e.g., GED, college entrance, parental responsibilities, workplace skills), general type of instruction (adult basic education, adult secondary education, English as a second language), places of instruction, or various combinations. As Chapter 3 of the report makes clear, however, it is premature, given the limits of the research available, to disentangle the research along these dimensions. On one hand, learners across the many places of instruction share literacy development needs, learning goals, and other characteristics; on the other hand, learners at a single site vary in these characteristics. In many instances, it would not be possible to know how to categorize the research because research reports do not specify the place of instruction, describe the goals of instruction, or clearly and completely describe the study participants. Indeed, one of the critical needs for future research is to systematically define segments of the population to identify constraints on generalizing research findings and specific features of instruction that might be needed to effectively meet the needs of particular subgroups.

Thus, this report is organized according to the major topics that deserve attention in future research to develop effective instructional approaches. The topics reflect those about which most is known from research—albeit mostly with populations other than one that is the focus of our study—and that have the greatest potential to alleviate the personal, instructional, and systemic barriers that adults outside school experience with learning.

Chapter 2 provides an overview of what is known about the major components and processes of reading and writing and the qualities of instruction that develop reading and writing for both typical and struggling learners in K-12 settings. The chapter presents principles for intervening specifically with struggling learners. Although supported by strong evidence, we stress that caution must be used in generalizing the research to other populations. Translational research is needed on the development of practices that are appropriate for diverse populations of adolescents and adults.

Chapter 3 describes the adults who receive literacy instruction, including major subgroups, and the demographics of the population, what is known about their difficulties with component literacy skills, and characteristics of their instructional contexts. The chapter conveys the state of research on practices that develop adults' literacy skills and identifies priorities for research and innovation to advance knowledge of adult literacy development and effective literacy instruction.

Chapters 4 through 6 synthesize research from a variety of disciplines on topics that are vital to furthering adult literacy. Chapter 4 summarizes findings from research on the conditions that affect cognitive processing and learning. The chapter draws on and updates several recent efforts to distill principles of learning for educators and discusses considerations in applying these principles to the design of literacy instruction for adults. Chapter 5 synthesizes research on the features of environments—instructional interactions, structures, tasks, texts, systems—that encourage engagement with learning and persistence in adolescents and adults. The chapter draws on research from multiple disciplines that examine the psychological, social, and environmental factors that affect motivation, engagement in learning, and goal attainment. Chapter 6 applies what is known about literacy, learning, and motivation to examine in greater depth one aspect of the instructional environment—instructional technologies—that may motivate essential practice with literacy activities, scaffold learning, and help to assess learners' progress. Technology also may help to resolve some of the practical barriers to more extensive literacy practice related to life demands, child care, and transportation, which adult learners cannot always afford, in either dollars or time.

The next two chapters discuss the research for two subgroups of the adult learner population. Chapter 7 synthesizes what is known about the cognitive, linguistic, and other learning challenges experienced by adults with learning disabilities and the uses of accommodations that facilitate learning. Chapter 8 considers the literacy development needs and processes for the population of adults learning English as a second language, which includes both immigrants and U.S. citizens and is diverse in terms of education, language background, and familiarity with U.S. culture. This chapter points to the major challenges experienced by English language learners in developing their literacy skills and outlines the research needed to facilitate literacy development. Given that the basic principles of reading, writing, learning, and motivation have been discussed in previous chapters, this chapter focuses on issues specific to the literacy development of adults who are learning a second language.

Chapter 9 presents the committee's conclusions and recommendations in light of the research reviewed in previous chapters. Our conclusions stress that it should be possible to develop approaches that improve adults' literacy given the wealth of knowledge that exists. The challenge is to determine how to integrate the various principles we have derived from the research findings into coordinated and comprehensive programs of instruction that meet the needs of diverse populations of adults. In this final chapter, we urge attention to several issues in research and policy that impinge directly on the quality of instruction, the feasibility of completing the much-needed research, and the potential for much broader dissemination and implementation of the practices that emerge as effective.

2

Foundations of Reading and Writing

This chapter provides an overview of the components and processes of reading and writing and the practices that develop these skills. This knowledge is derived mainly from research with K-12 students because this population is the main focus of most rigorous research on reading components, difficulties in learning to read, and effective instructional practices. The findings are particularly robust for elementary school students and less developed for middle and high school students due to lack of attention in research to reading and writing development during these years. We also review a small body of research on cognitive aging that compares the reading and writing skills of younger and older adults. From all the collected findings, we distill principles to guide literacy instruction for adolescents and adults who are outside the K-12 education system but need to further develop their literacy.

Caution must be used in generalizing research conducted in K-12 settings to other populations, such as adult literacy students. Precisely what needs to be taught and how will vary depending on an individual's existing literacy skills; learning goals that require proficiency with particular types of reading and writing; and characteristics of learners that include differences in motivation, neurobiological processes, and cultural, linguistic, and educational backgrounds. Translational research will be needed to apply and adapt the findings to diverse populations of adolescents and adults, as discussed in later chapters.

This chapter is organized into five major parts. Part 1 provides an orienting discussion of the social, cultural, and neurocognitive mechanisms involved in literacy development. Part 2 describes the components and processes of reading and writing, and research on reading and writing instruction for all students (both typical and atypical learners). We summarize principles for instruction that have sufficient empirical support to warrant inclusion in a comprehensive approach to literacy instruction. Part 3 discusses the neurobiology of reading and writing development and difficulties. Part 4 conveys additional principles for intervening specifically with learners who have difficulties with learning to read and write. In Part 5, we describe what is known about reading and writing processes in older adults and highlight the lack of research on reading and writing across the life span.

Throughout the chapter, we point to promising areas for research and to questions that require further study. We conclude with a summary of the findings, directions for research, and implications for the learners who are the focus of our report: adolescents and adults who need to develop their literacy skills outside K-12 educational settings.[1]

SOCIAL, CULTURAL, AND NEUROCOGNITIVE MECHANISMS OF LITERACY DEVELOPMENT

Literacy, or cognition of any kind, cannot be understood fully apart from the contexts in which it develops (e.g., Cobb and Bowers, 1999; Greeno, Smith, and Moore, 1993; Heath, 1983; Lave and Wenger, 1991; Markus and Kitiyama, 2010; Nisbett, 2003; Rogoff and Lave, 1984; Scribner and Cole, 1981; Street, 1984). The development of skilled reading and writing (indeed, learning in general) depends heavily on the contexts and activities in which learning occurs, including the purposes for reading and writing and the activities, texts, and tools that are routinely encountered (Beach, 1995; Heath, 1983; Luria, 1987; Scribner and Cole, 1981; Street, 1984; Vygotsky, 1978, 1986). In this way, reading and writing are similar to other complex cognitive skills and brain functions that are shaped by cultural patterns and stimuli (Markus and Kitayama, 2010; Nisbett, 2003; Nisbett et al., 2001; Park and Huang, 2010; Ross and Wang, 2010). The particular knowledge and skill that develop depend on the literacy practices engaged in, the supports provided for learning, and the demand and value attached to particular forms of literacy in communities and the broader society (Heath, 1983; Scribner and Cole,

---

[1]Other documents have summarized research on the components of reading and writing and instructional practices to develop literacy skills. We refer readers to additional resources for more extensive coverage of this literature (Ehri et al., 2001; Graham, 2006a; Graham and Hebert, 2010; Graham and Perin 2007a, 2007b; Kamil et al., 2008; McCardle, Chhabra, and Kapinus, 2008; National Institute of Child Health and Human Development, 2000a).

1983; Vygotsky, 1986). Thus, how people use reading and writing differs considerably by context.

As an example, forms and uses of spoken and written language in academic settings differ from those in nonacademic settings, and they also differ among academic disciplines or subjects (Blommaert, Street, and Turner, 2007; Lemke, 1998; Moje, 2007, 2008b; Street, 2003, 2009). Recent work on school subject learning also makes it clear that content and uses of language differ significantly from one subject matter to another (Coffin and Hewings, 2004; Lee and Spratley, 2006; McConachie and Petrosky, 2010). People may develop and use forms of literacy that differ from those needed for new purposes (Alvermann and Xu, 2003; Cowan, 2004; Hicks, 2004; Hull and Schultz, 2001; Leander and Lovvorn, 2006; Mahiri and Sablo, 1996; Moje, 2000a, 2008b; Moll, 1994; Noll, 1998; Reder, 2008). Thus, as depicted in Figure 1-2, a complete understanding of reading and writing development includes in-depth knowledge of the learner (the learners' knowledge, skills, literacy practices, motivations, and neurocognitive processes) and features of the instructional context that scaffold or impede learning. The context of instruction includes texts, tools, activities, interactions with teachers and peers, and instructor knowledge, beliefs, and skills.

Types of Text

Types of text vary from books to medication instructions to Twitter tweets. Texts have numerous features that in the context of instruction can either facilitate or constrain the learning of literacy skills (Goldman, 1997; Graesser, McNamara, and Louwerse, 2004). Texts that effectively support progress with reading are appropriately challenging and well written. They focus attention on new knowledge and skills related to the particular components of reading that the learner needs to develop. They also support the learner in gaining automaticity and confidence and in applying and generalizing their new skills. To the greatest degree possible, the materials for reading should help to build useful vocabulary and content (e.g., topic, world) knowledge. Effective texts also motivate engagement with instruction and practice partly by developing valued knowledge or relating to the interests of the learner.

Adult learners will have encountered many texts during the course of formal schooling that are poorly written or highly complex (Beck, McKeown, and Gromoll, 1989; Chambliss and Calfee, 1998; Chambliss and Murphy, 2002; Lee and Spratley, 2010). Similarly, the texts of everyday life are not written to scaffold reading or writing skill (Solomon, Van der Kerkhof, and Moje, 2010). Developing readers need to confront challenging texts that engage them with meaningful content, but they also need texts that afford the practicing of the skills they need to develop and systematic support to stretch beyond existing skills. This support needs to come from a mix of instructional interactions and texts that scaffold the learner in developing and practicing new skills and becoming an independent reader (Lee and Spratley, 2010; Moje, 2009; Solomon, Van der Kerkhof, 2010).

Literacy Tools

Being literate also requires proficiency with the tools and practices used in society to accomplish valued tasks that require reading and writing (see Box 2-1). For example, digital and online media are used to communicate with diverse others and to produce, find, evaluate, and synthesize knowledge in innovative and creative ways to meet the varied demands of education and work. It is important, therefore, to offer reading and writing

---

BOX 2-1
Literacy in a Digital Age

Strong reading and writing skills underpin valued aspects of digital literacy in several areas:

- Presentations of ideas
  - Organizing a complex and compelling argument
  - Adjusting the presentation to the audience
  - Using multiple media and integrating them with text
  - Translating among multiple documents
    - Extended text
    - Summary
    - Graphics versus text
  - Responding to queries and critiques through revision and written follow-up
- Using online resources to search for information and evaluating quality of that information
  - Using affordances, such as hyperlinks and search engines
  - Making effective predictions of likely search results
  - Coordinating overlapping ideas expressed in differing language
  - Organizing bodies of information from multiple sources
  - Evaluating the quality and warrants of accessed information
- Using basic office software to generate texts and multimedia documents
  - Writing documents: writing for others
  - Taking notes: writing for oneself
  - Preparing displays to support oral presentations

SOURCES: Adapted from National Center on Education and the Economy (1997); Appendix B: Literacy in a Digital Age.

instruction that incorporates the use of print and digital tools as needed for transforming information and knowledge across the varied forms of representation used to communicate in today's world. These forms include symbols, numeric symbols, icons, static images, moving images, oral representations (available digitally and in other venues), graphs, charts, and tables (Goldman et al., 2003; Kress, 2003). Extensive research has been conducted on youths' multimodal and digital literacy learning, demonstrating that young people are experimenting with a range of tools and practices that extend beyond those taught in school (see Coiro et al., 2009a, 2009b). Continued research is needed to identify effective instructional methods that incorporate digital technologies (e.g., Coiro, 2003; see Appendix B for detailed discussion of the state of research on digital literacy).

Literacy Activities

The development of skilled literacy involves extensive participation and practice using component skills of reading and writing for particular purposes (Ford and Forman, 2006; Lave and Wenger, 1991; McConachie et al., 2006; Rogoff, 1990; Scribner and Cole, 1981; Street, 1984; Vygotsky, 1986). Because literacy demands shift over time and across contexts, some individuals may need specific interventions developed to meet these shifting literacy demands. For example, a typical late adolescent or adult must traverse, on a regular basis, workplaces; vocational and postsecondary education; societal, civic, or political contexts; home and family; and new media. Literacy demands also change over time due to global, economic, social, and cultural forces. These realities make it especially important to understand the social and cultural contexts of literacy and to offer instruction that develops literacy skills for meeting social, educational, and workplace demands as well as the learner's personal needs. The likelihood of transferring a newly learned skill to a new task depends on the similarity between the new task and tasks used for learning (National Research Council, 2005), making it important to design literacy instruction using the literacy activities, tools, and tasks that are valued by society and learners outside the context of instruction. Such instruction also would be expected to enhance learners' motivation to engage with a literacy task or persist with literacy instruction.

Instruction that connects to knowledge that students already possess and value appears to be motivating (e.g., Au and Mason, 1983; Guthrie et al., 1996; Gutiérrez et al., 1999; Lee, 1993; Moje and Speyer, 2008; Moll and Gonzalez, 1994; Wigfield, Eccles, and Rodriguez, 1998) and thus may be important for supporting the persistence of those who have successfully navigated other life arenas despite not having developed a broader range of literacy skills and practices. Successful literacy instruction for adults and adolescents should recognize the knowledge and experience brought by mature learners, even when their literacy skills are weak.

Because the motivation to engage in extensive reading and writing practice is so important for the development and integration of component skills, we discuss the topic of motivation more extensively in Chapter 5.

Teacher Knowledge, Skills, and Beliefs

Literacy development, like the learning of any complex task, requires a range of explicit teaching and implicit learning guided by an expert (Ford and Forman, 2006; Forman, Minick, and Stone, 1993; Lave and Wenger, 1991, 1998; Rogoff, 1990, 1993, 1995; Scribner and Cole, 1981; Street, 1984; Vygotsky, 1986; Wertsch, 1991). To be effective, teachers of struggling readers and writers must have significant expertise in both the components of reading and writing, which include spoken language, and how to teach them. The social and emotional tone of the instructional environment also is very important for successful reading and writing development (Hamre and Pianta, 2003). Teachers are more effective when they nurture relationships and develop a positive, dynamic, and emotionally supportive environment for learning that is sensitive to differences in values and experiences that students bring to instruction.

Effective instructors tend to have an informed mental map of where they want their students to end up that they use to guide instructional practices every day. That is, they plan activities using clear objectives with deep understanding of reading and writing processes. Descriptions of effective teachers in the K-12 system stress that they are highly reflective in their teaching, mindful of their instructional choices and how they fit into the larger picture for their students, and able to fluently use and orchestrate a repertoire of effective and adaptive instructional strategies (Block and Pressley, 2002; Butler et al., 2004; Duffy, 2005; Lovett et al., 2008b). Effective teachers use feedback from their own performance to adjust and change instruction, and they are able to transfer and apply knowledge from one domain to another (Duffy, 2005; Israel et al., 2005; Zimmerman, 2000a, 2000b). Effective teachers of reading and writing also have deep knowledge of the English language system and its oral and written structures, as well as the processes involved in acquiring various language abilities (Duke and Carlisle, 2011; Moats, 2004, 2005). Beyond the requisite knowledge and expertise, literacy teachers often need coaching, mentoring, and encouragement to question and evaluate the efficacy of their instruction.

Teacher beliefs can have a profound impact on the opportunities provided during instruction to develop literacy skills. For example, both Green (1983) and Golden (1988) demonstrated how teachers' instruction changed depending on what the teachers assumed about the literacy abilities of the students in each group. Students who were identified as reading at lower levels were not asked to think about the texts and interpret them in the same way as those at higher reading levels (see also Cazden, 1985). Being thought of as "successful" or "achieving" or, at the other extreme, "unsuccessful" and "failing" can produce low-literacy learning and even, in some cases, what is identified as disability (McDermott and Varenne, 1995).

As discussed further in Chapter 3, it is well known that the knowledge and expertise of adult literacy instructors are highly variable (Smith and Gillespie, 2007; Tamassia et al., 2007). A large body of research on the efficacy of teacher education and professional development practices for literacy instruction does not exist that could be used as a resource for instructors of adults (McCardle, Chhabra, and Kapinus, 2008; National Institute of Child Health and Human Development, 2000a; Snow, Griffin, and Burns, 2005). Neither preparation nor selection of instructors in adult literacy education or developmental college courses has been studied much at all and certainly not in terms of ability to apply the practices presented in this chapter. Thus, the issue of instructor preparation for the delivery of effective instructional practices is vital to address in future research.

Neurocognitive Mechanisms

The field of cognitive neuroscience is opening windows on the brain mechanisms that underlie skilled reading and writing and related difficulties. Much of the research has focused on identifying the neurocircuits (brain pathways) associated with component processes in reading and writing at different stages of typical reading development, and differences in the progression of brain organization for these processes in atypically developing readers. It also has focused mainly on word- and sentence-level reading. More needs to be understood from neurocognitive research about the development of complex comprehension processes. In addition, because different disciplines study different aspects of literacy, much remains to be discovered about how various social, cultural, and instructional factors interact with neurocognitive processes to facilitate or constrain the development of literacy skills.

Brain imaging studies (both structural and functional imaging) have revealed, however, robust differences in brain organization between typically and atypically developing readers (see Chapter 7). It is yet to be determined whether these observed brain differences are the cause or consequence of reading-related problems. It is possible, however, to confirm certain levels of literacy development by observing the brain activity associated with literacy function. More needs to be understood about (1) the genetic, neuroanatomical, neurochemical, and epigenetic factors that control the development of these neurocircuits and (2) the ways in which experiential factors, such as enriched learning environments, might modulate brain pathways in struggling readers at different ages and in different environments. Research on gene-brain-environment relations has the potential to inform instruction in at least three ways: (1) the development and testing of theories and models of typical and atypical development of reading and writing needed to guide effective teaching and remedial interventions; (2) development of measures that provide more sensitive assessments in specific areas of difficulty to use for instruction and research; and, though less germane to this report, (3) knowledge of neurobiological processes needed for early identification of risk with an eye toward prevention of reading and writing difficulties. The same possibilities apply for writing instruction, although neurobiological research on writing is in the early stages. In subsequent sections, we further describe what is known about the neurobiological mechanisms specific to reading and writing. A key point to keep in mind, however, is that neither the available behavioral data nor neurocognitive data suggest that learners who struggle with reading and writing require a categorically different type of instruction from more typically developing learners. Rather, the instruction may need to be adapted in particular ways to help learners overcome specific reading, writing, and learning difficulties, as discussed later in the chapter.

READING

Reading is the comprehension of language from a written code that represents concepts and communicates information and ideas. It is a complex skill that involves many human capacities that evolved for other purposes and it depends on their development and coordinated use: spoken language, perception (vision, hearing), motor systems, memory, learning, reasoning, problem solving, motivation, interest, and others (Rayner et al., 2001). Reading is closely related to spoken language (National Research Council, 1998) and requires applying what is known about spoken language to deciphering an unfamiliar written code. In fact, the correlation between comprehension of spoken and written language in adults is high, approximately .90 (Braze et al., 2007; Gernsbacher, Varner, and Faust, 1990). Conversely, being less skilled in a spoken language—having limited vocabulary, less familiarity with standard grammar, speaking a different dialect—makes it more difficult to become skilled at reading that language (Craig et al., 2009; Scarborough, 2002). Reading also depends on knowledge of the context and purpose for which the act of reading occurs (Scribner and Cole, 1981; Street, 1984; Vygotsky, 1978).

Although reading and speech are similar, they differ in important ways that have implications for instruction (Biber, 1988; Clark, 1996; Kucer, 2001). Speech fades from memory whereas most types of text are more permanent, allowing for reanalysis and use of strategies to comprehend complex written structures (Biber and Conrad, 2006). Skilled readers are attuned to the differences between texts and spoken language (e.g., differences in types and frequencies of words, expressions, and grammatical structures) (Biber, 1988; Chafe and Tannen, 1987), and they know the strategies that help them comprehend various kinds of text. Perhaps the most important difference is that people learn to speak (or sign) even when direct instruction is limited or perhaps absent, whereas learning to read almost always requires explicit instruction as well as immersion in written language.

The major components of reading are well documented and include decoding, fluency, vocabulary, and comprehension. Box 2-2 summarizes

---

BOX 2-2
Principles of Reading Instruction

Becoming an able reader takes a substantial amount of time. Reading is a complex skill, and, like other complex skills, it takes well over 1,000 hours, perhaps several times that, to acquire fully. Instruction consistent with the principles that follow must therefore be implemented and learner engagement supported at the scale required for meaningful gains.

- **Use explicit and systematic reading instruction to develop the major components of reading (decoding, fluency vocabulary, comprehension) according to the assessed needs of individual learners.** Although each dimension is necessary to proficient reading, adolescents and adults vary in the specific reading instruction they need. For example, some will require comprehensive decoding instruction; others may need less or no decoding instruction. Further research is needed to clarify the forms of explicit instruction that effectively develop component skills for adolescents and adults.
- **Combine explicit and systematic instruction with extended reading practice to promote acquisition and transfer of component reading skills.** Learning to read involves both explicit teaching and implicit learning. Explicit teaching does not negate the vital importance of incidental and informal learning opportunities or the need for extensive practice using new skills.
- **Motivate engagement with the literacy tasks used for instruction and extensive reading practice.** Learners, especially adolescents, are more engaged when literacy instruction and practice opportunities are embedded in meaningful learning activities. Opportunities to collaborate during reading also can increase motivation to read, although more needs to be known about how to structure collaborations effectively.
- **Develop reading fluency as needed to facilitate efficiency in the reading of words and longer text.** Some methods of fluency improvement have been vali-

principles of instruction related to developing each of these components. Although the components are presented separately here for exposition, reading involves an interrelated and interdependent system with reciprocity among the various components, both within reading and between reading and writing.

A substantial body of evidence on children shows that *effective reading instruction explicitly and systematically targets each component of reading skill that remains to be developed* (National Institute of Child Health and Human Development, 2000a; Rayner et al., 2001). More extensive evidence for this statement is available for younger than older learners and for word identification and decoding processes than for reading comprehension and

dated in children (e.g., guided repeated reading); these require further research with adolescents and adults.

- **Explicitly teach the structure of written language to facilitate decoding and comprehension.** Develop awareness of the features of written language at multiple levels (word, sentence, passage). Teach regularity and irregularity of spelling-to-sound mappings, the patterns of English morphology, rules of grammar and syntax, and the structures of various text genres. Again, the specifics of how best to provide this instruction to adolescents and adults requires further research, but the dependence of literacy on knowledge of the structure of written language is clear.

- **To develop vocabulary, use a mixture of instructional approaches combined with extensive reading of texts to create "an enriched verbal environment."** High-quality mental representations of words develop through varied and multiple exposures to words in discourse and reading of varied text. Instruction that integrates the teaching of vocabulary with reading comprehension instruction, development of topic and background knowledge, and learning of disciplinary or other valued content are promising approaches to study with adolescents and adults.

- **To develop comprehension, teach varied goals and purposes for reading; encourage learners to state their own reading goals, predictions, questions, and reactions to material; encourage extensive reading practice with varied forms of text; teach and model the use of multiple comprehension strategies; teach self-regulation in the monitoring of strategy use.** Reading comprehension involves a high level of metacognitive engagement with text. Developing readers often need help to develop the metacognitive components of reading comprehension, such as learning how to identify reading goals, select, implement, and coordinate multiple strategies; monitor and evaluate success of the strategies; and adjust strategies to achieve reading goals. Extensive practice also is needed to develop knowledge of words, text structures, and written syntax that are not identical to spoken language and that are gleaned from extensive experience with various texts.

reading fluency, given that research has focused mainly in these areas. Despite this caveat, this principle of reading instruction is considered to have strong research support (National Institute of Child Health and Human Development, 2000a). The emphasis of instruction within and across reading components will vary depending on each person's need for skill development, but skill needs to be attained in all the components. It is possible to design many ways to provide explicit and systematic reading instruction focused on the learner's needs using methods and formats that will appeal to learners (McCardle, Chhabra, and Kapinus, 2008).

Learning to read involves both explicit teaching and implicit learning. Explicit teaching does not negate the importance of incidental and informal learning opportunities, or the need for extensive practice using new skills. Explicit and systematic reading instruction must be combined with extended experience with reading for varied purposes in order to promote learning and the transfer of reading skills. Thus, it is important to provide forms of reading practice that develop the particular skills that need to be acquired. Learners, especially adolescents, are more engaged when literacy instruction and practice are embedded in meaningful learning activities (e.g., Guthrie and Wigfield, 2000; Guthrie et al., 1999; Schiefele, 1996a, 1996b; Schraw and Lehman, 2001).

Decoding

Decoding involves the ability to apply knowledge of letter-sound relationships to correctly pronounce printed words. It requires developing phonological awareness, which consists of phonemic awareness (an oral language skill that involves awareness of and ability to manipulate the units of sound, phonemes, in a spoken word) and alphabetic knowledge (knowing that the letters in written words represent the phonemes in spoken words) (National Institute of Child Health and Human Development, 2000b; Rayner et al., 2001).

Even highly skilled adult readers must rely on alphabetic knowledge and decoding skills to read unfamiliar words (e.g., "otolaryngology") (Frost, 1998; Rayner et al., 2001). Word reading also requires being able to recognize sight words that do not follow regular patterns of letter-sound correspondence (e.g., "yacht"). Explicit and systematic phonics instruction to teach correspondences between letters and phonemes has been found to facilitate reading development for children of different ages, abilities, and socioeconomic circumstances (Foorman et al., 1998; McCardle, Chhabra, and Kapinus, 2008; Morris et al., 2010; National Institute of Child Health and Human Development, 2000a; Torgesen et al., 1999). The evidence is clear that explicit instruction is necessary for most individuals to develop understanding of written code and its relation to speech (National Institute of Child Health and Human Development, 2000a; Snow, 2002).

The National Reading Panel, convened at the request of Congress, identified several types of effective systematic phonics programs, among them *synthetic phonics* (teaching children to convert letters into sounds or phonemes and then blend the sounds to form recognizable words) (National Institute of Child Health and Human Development, 2000a). The research shows that, although phonological awareness is the oral language building block of reading, teaching phonological awareness for those who need such instruction is most effective when coupled with the use of letters and the learning of letter-sound correspondences as part of phonics instruction.

Many adults with low literacy may experience difficulty with decoding (Baer, Kutner, and Sabatini, 2009; Greenberg, Ehri, and Perin, 1997, 2002; Mellard, Fall, and Woods, 2010; Nanda, Greenberg, and Morris, 2010; Read and Ruyter, 1985; Sabatini et al., 2010). Research on younger populations suggests that instructors may need to be prepared to explicitly and systematically teach all aspects of the word-reading system: letter-sound patterns, high-frequency spelling patterns (oat, at, end, ar), consonant blends (st-, bl-, cr-), vowel combinations (ai, oa, ea), affixes (pre-, sub-, -ing, -ly), and irregular high-frequency word instruction (sight words that do not follow regular spelling patterns). For those adults who need to develop their word-reading skills, it may be important to teach "word attack" strategies with particular attention to challenges posed by multisyllabic words and variable vowel pronunciations. Effective word attack strategies for all readers include phonological decoding and blending, word identification by analogy, peeling off prefixes and suffixes, and facility with variable vowel pronunciations (for information about these word-reading strategies and how to use them, see Lovett et al., 1994, 2000; Lovett, Lacerenza, and Borden, 2000). Even after adult learners have mastered decoding, they may need substantial practice to become able to decode words easily, freeing up limited attentional capacity for other reading processes, like comprehension (see discussion of fluency below).

Vocabulary

Vocabulary knowledge is a primary predictor of reading success (Baumann, Kame'enui, and Ash, 2003). It is associated with word identification skills at the end of first grade (Sénéchal and Cornell, 1993) and reading comprehension in eleventh grade (Cunningham and Stanovich, 1998; Nagy, 2007). In fact, for those who have acquired basic decoding skills, the aspect of lexical (word) processing that has the greatest impact on reading is vocabulary knowledge and, more specifically, the depth, breadth, and flexibility of knowledge about words (Beck and McKeown, 1986; Perfetti, 2007). Vocabulary also tends to grow with reading experience. As readers progress, lexical analysis (i.e., morphological awareness allowing the recognition of derived words, e.g., *decide→decision, decisive, deciding*) becomes increasingly important for comprehending complex and unfamiliar words and concepts (Adams, 1990; Nagy and Anderson, 1984; Nagy and Scott, 2000). Specialized vocabulary is important to develop for comprehending texts in different subject-matter areas (Koedinger and Nathan, 2004).

The National Reading Panel (National Institute of Child Health and Human Development, 2000a) concluded that explicit vocabulary instruction is associated with gains in reading comprehension. Other research reviews have been less definitive, and thus some researchers consider the evidence to be mixed (Kamil et al., 2008; Pressley, Disney, and Anderson, 2007). Differences in findings across studies may be due partly to variations in the approaches and how they were implemented, the lack of direct measures of vocabulary growth in some studies, and the use of measures that fail to assess all dimensions of word knowledge or reading comprehension. These issues should be addressed in future research with adult and adolescent populations.

Research on literacy instruction for children suggests that selecting words from the curriculum and teaching their meanings prior to reading a text help to ensure that vocabulary items are in the spoken language of the reader prior to encountering the words in print (Beck, McKeown, and Kucan, 2002; McKeown and Beck, 1988; National Institute of Child Health and Human Development, 2000a). For less skilled readers, explicit instruction, combined with discussion and elaboration activities that encourage using the words to be learned, can improve vocabulary and facilitate better reading comprehension (Curtis and Longo, 2001; Foorman et al., 2003; Klinger and Vaughn, 1999; Stahl and Fairbanks, 1986). Beck and colleagues (Beck and McKeown 2007; McKeown and Beck, 1988) articulated principles for developing a teacher's ability to deliver effective vocabulary instruction: (a) introduce vocabulary through connected language (discussion, elaboration activities) instead of only dictionary definitions, (b) provide multiple opportunities to interact with new words and word meanings in a variety of engaging contexts, and (c) use activities that engage learners in deep and reflective processing of word meanings. In addition, repeated exposure to words in multiple contexts and domains enhances vocabulary learning (Kamil et al., 2008; Nagy and Scott, 2000) and provides "an enriched verbal environment" (Beck, McKeown, and Kucan, 2002) for vocabulary growth. Findings that show no effect for vocabulary instruction have tended to look at more impoverished forms of instruction.

Having rich knowledge of words (i.e., high-quality lexical representations) allows for rapid and reliable retrieval of word meanings with profound consequences for both word- and text-reading proficiency (Perfetti, 1992, 2007). Reading is supported by knowing not only the definition of the words being read but also how the words are used, their different forms (e.g., *anxious→anxiety*), and what they connote in different situations. Findings from research on children indicate that effective approaches to vocabulary instruction will consist of strategies that build high-quality lexical representations and develop metalinguistic awareness (Nagy, 2007). These strategies include teaching not only word meanings but also multiple meanings of words and varied word forms and origins, as well as providing ample opportunities to encounter and use the words in varied contexts. As more text becomes available in electronic form, it also may be possible to develop more tools that provide text-embedded "just-in-time" vocabulary support that developing readers can call on when their reading is impeded by lack of word or lexical knowledge.

Embedding vocabulary instruction in reading comprehension activities is another method of developing high-quality lexical representations (Perfetti, 1992, 2007). This approach involves reading new texts that develop vocabulary, topic, and domain knowledge. Readers acquire new words, phrases, and concepts that appear more often in text than in speech and that would therefore lie outside most learners' experience with spoken language (Kamil et al., 2008). For example, because academic texts (e.g., those in science or history) include specialized vocabulary that is not part of everyday spoken language (Beck, McKeown, and Kucan, 2002; Kamil et al., 2008), the teaching of content needs to be integrated with explicit teaching of words and phrases used in a discipline (Moje and Speyer, 2008). Such approaches warrant study with those outside K-12 because adolescents and adults may need to develop academic or other specialized vocabulary and content knowledge for education, work, or other purposes.

Overall, findings suggest a range of vocabulary activities that may be useful in adult literacy instruction, but, at present, research on adults is extremely limited.

Fluency

Reading fluency is the ability to read with speed and accuracy (Klauda and Guthrie, 2008; Kuhn and Stahl, 2003; Miller and Schwanenflugel, 2006). Developing fluency is important because the human mind is limited in its capacity to carry out many cognitive processes at once (Logan, 2004). When word and sentence reading becomes automatic, readers can concentrate more fully on creating meaning from the text (Graesser, 2007; Perfetti, 2007; Rapp et al., 2007; van den Broek et al., 2009). Experiments with young children show that fluency instruction can lead to significant gains in both fluency and comprehension (Chard, Vaughn, and Tyler, 2002; Klauda and Guthrie, 2008; Kuhn and Stahl, 2003; Therrien, 2004; Therrien and Hughes, 2008).

The relation between fluency and comprehension is not fully understood, however, and it is more complex and bidirectional than previously thought (Meyer and Felton, 1999; Wolf and Katzir-Cohen, 2001). Comprehension appears to affect fluency as well as the reverse (Collins and Levy, 2008; Johnston, Barnes, and Desrochers, 2008; Klauda and Guthrie, 2008). Moreover, although some studies show that fluency instruction improves comprehension, other studies do not (Fleisher, Jenkins, and Pany, 1979; Grant and Standing, 1989; Oakhill, Cain, and Bryant, 2003). There are at least two possible reasons for the mixed findings to address in future research. Studies have demonstrated that there are different dimensions of reading fluency (at the level of words, phrases, sentences, and passages), and all should be considered in measuring or facilitating reading fluency. In addition, the best ways to conceptualize and measure text comprehension have yet to be identified and used consistently across research studies.

Guided repeated reading has generally led to moderate increases in fluency, accuracy, and sometimes comprehension for both good and poor readers (Kuhn and Stahl, 2003; Kuhn et al., 2006; Vadasy and Sanders, 2008). In guided repeated reading, the learner receives feedback and is supported in identifying and correcting mistakes. A critical unanswered question is whether certain types of text are more effective than others for guided repeated reading interventions (Kuhn and Stahl, 2003; Vadasy and Sanders, 2008).

Repeated reading of a text without guidance, though a popular instructional method believed to improve fluency, has not been reliably demonstrated to be effective, even with young children in K-3 classrooms (Carlisle and Rice, 2002; National Institute of Child Health and Human Development, 2000a; Stahl, 2004). At least one recent review suggests that there is not enough rigorous evidence to warrant unguided repeated reading for students with or at risk for learning disabilities (Chard et al., 2009). A well-designed controlled evaluation with high school students with reading disabilities also failed to find support for repeated reading effects on reading comprehension (Wexler et al., 2010).

Fluency has been difficult to change for adolescent and adult readers (Fletcher et al., 2007; Wexler et al., 2010). One possible reason is that older struggling readers lack sufficient reading practice and experience. Another possible reason is that instruction must focus on developing not only the reader's ability to decode or recognize individual words but to quickly process larger units of texts (e.g., sentences and paragraphs). In the future, fluent reading needs to be studied at the word level, syntactic level, and passage level. Fluency at each of these levels has been found to contribute to growth in reading comprehension for fifth graders (Klauda and Guthrie, 2008; see also Kuhn and Stahl, 2003; Young and Bowers, 1995). To encourage the practice needed for fluency, it is important to develop procedures and text types that will engage older developing readers.

Reading Comprehension

Components and Processes

Although they differ in detail, theories of reading comprehension share many assumptions about the cognitive processes involved (Cromley and Azevedo, 2007; Gernsbacher, Varner, and Faust, 1990; Graesser, Singer, and Trabasso, 1994; Kintsch, 1998; Trabasso, Secco, and van den Broek, 1984; van den Broek, Rapp, and Kendeou, 2005; Zwaan and Singer, 2003). First, comprehension requires adequate and sustained attention. In complex cognitive acts, such as reading comprehension, attention cannot simultaneously be focused in an unlimited number of ways. As mentioned earlier, facile readers develop fluent and relatively automatic decoding that allows allocating more attention to the information gleaned from words and phrases and creating coherent meaning from text (Ericsson and Kintsch, 1994; Kintsch and van Dijk, 1978; O'Brien et al., 1998). Concentration also must be sustained so that memories of previous sentences and pages do not fade before the next text is read, and this is less possible when a decoding problem diverts attention from prior content.

Second, comprehension requires the reader to interpret and integrate information from various sources (the sentence being read, the prior sentence, prior text, background knowledge, and extraneous information) (Goldman, Graesser, and van den Broek, 1999; Graesser, Gernsbacher, and Goldman, 2003; Graesser, Singer, and Trabasso, 1994; Kintsch, 1998; Kintsch and van Dijk, 1978; McCardle, Chhabra, and Kapinus, 2008; Rapp et al., 2007; Rumelhart, 1994; Snow, 2002; Trabasso and van den Broek, 1985; van den Broek, Rapp, and Kendeou, 2005). Comprehension depends heavily on background knowledge for understanding how elements in a text relate to one another to create a broader meaning (McNamara et al., 1996; O'Reilly and McNamara, 2007). Nontextual information that accompanies the text (figures or multimedia) must also be integrated to support deeper comprehension (Hegarty and Just, 1993; Lowe and Schnotz, 2007; Mayer, 2009; Rouet, 2006). Such information distracts the unskilled reader. With practice, however, strategic processes for remembering, interpreting, and integrating information become less effortful.

Third, each reader has at least an implicit standard of coherence used while reading to determine whether the type and level of comprehension aimed for is being achieved (Kintsch and Vipond, 1979; van den Broek, Risden, and Husebye-Hartman, 1995). That is, readers must decide how hard to try and how long to persist in reading a text. Effective readers keep working to better understand text until certain requirements are met. The standard varies depending on such factors as the person's reading goal, interest, and fatigue. A facile reader strives for an overall understanding of text that is rich with meaning and complete and is highly effective in adjusting the allocation of effort for particular purposes (Duggan and Payne, 2009; Kaakinen and Hyönä, 2007, 2008, 2010; Kaakinen, Hyönä, and Keenan, 2003; Kintsch, 1994; Linderholm and van den Broek, 2002; Reader and Payne, 2007; Stine-Morrow et al., 2004, 2006; Stine-Morrow, Miller, and Hertzog, 2006; Therriault, Rinck, and Zwaan, 2006; Zwaan, Magliano, and Graesser, 1995). A rich and complete understanding involves making inferences, retrieving prior knowledge, and connecting components of text that may not be contiguous on the page. It also requires attending to semantic connections given in the text. Two types of coherence relations—referential and causal—are central to many types of texts (Britton and Gulgoz, 1991; McNamara et al., 1996; van den Broek et al., 2001), but readers also use other relations in text (spatial, temporal, logical, intentional) to create meaning (Graesser and Forsyth, in press; van den Broek et al., 2001; Zwaan and Radvansky, 1998).

Although theories of reading comprehension overlap in many respects, they vary in the number and types of components emphasized and how these components interact (Graesser and McNamara, 2010). The Direct and Inferential Mediation Model (DIME; Cromley and Azevedo, 2007), for example, focuses on five general factors that affect comprehension and that every comprehension theory includes in some form: (1) background knowledge, (2) word-reading, (3) vocabulary, (4) strategies, and (5) inference procedures. These factors accounted for a substantial 66 percent of the variation in reading comprehension in a study of 175 ninth graders.

Different types of text place different demands on the reader, and skilled readers adjust their reading according to what is being read and why (McCrudden and Schraw, 2007; Pressley, 2000; Rouet, 2006). Thus, other approaches to comprehension research focus on how variations in text (genre, style, structure, purpose, content, complexity) influence how people read text and develop knowledge of text structures. Box 2-3 presents an example of one text-based model of reading comprehension.

Reading Comprehension Instruction

Although current theories and models of comprehension are useful for guiding instruction, they require further development. A more systematic and integrated approach to reading comprehension research is needed to

---

BOX 2-3
A Text-Based Model of Reading Comprehension

Proposed by Graesser and McNamara (2010), the multilevel text model, which extends earlier research by Garrod and Pickering (2004), Kintsch (1998), and Zwaan and Radvansky (1998), identifies seven main components of text processing that affect comprehension: lexical decoding, word knowledge, syntax, genre and rhetorical structure, textbase, situation model, and pragmatic communication (see also Graesser and McNamara, 2011; Kintsch, 1998; Perfetti, 1999).

- *Lexical decoding, word knowledge*, and *syntax components* refer to word- and sentence-reading skills.
- Knowledge of *genres* (narration, exposition, persuasion, description) and global text structures also aids comprehension. A proficient reader processes the *rhetorical composition* used in various genre and discourse functions of text segments (sections, paragraphs, sentences) and their relation to the overall organization of the text (citation). (Examples of rhetorical structures used to compose expository texts are cause + effect, claim + evidence, problem + solution, and compare + contrast.)
- Full processing of the *textbase* (propositions explicitly stated in the text) is needed for accurate comprehension. For example, a ubiquitous problem among unskilled readers is the tendency to minimally process propositions, rely too much on what they "know" about the topic from their own experience, and miss parts of the text that do not match their experience.
- *Situation model* refers to creating larger representations of meaning, derived both from propositions stated explicitly (the textbase) and a large number of inferences that must be filled in using world knowledge.
- *Pragmatics* refers to the communication goals of spoken and written language. Proficient, goal-directed readers search, select, and extract relevant information from text, further evaluate what they read for relevance to their goals, and use relevance to monitor their attention while reading. People best comprehend and learn from text when the pragmatic function of the text matches the readers' goals.

---

develop instruction that can be evaluated using rigorous experimental research designs.

The report of the National Reading Panel (National Institute of Child Health and Human Development, 2000a) is a main source of experimental evidence on instruction that contributes to developing comprehension. More recent research also has sought a better understanding of the components of instruction that improve comprehension among students at different ages and with different levels of reading skills (e.g., Berkeley, Mastropieri, and Scruggs, 2011; Edmonds et al., 2009). We draw on all of these sources of information in discussing what is known about effective comprehension instruction.

The National Reading Panel analyzed the results of 203 different studies of reading comprehension instruction with students in grades 4 and above and identified eight instructional procedures that had a positive effect on reading comprehension. In this analysis and in more recent research, comprehension strategy instruction emerges as one of the most effective interventions (Forness et al., 1997; Gersten et al., 2001; Kamil, 2004; Kamil et al., 2008; National Institute of Child Health and Human Development, 2000a). Similarly, an influential meta-analysis of comprehension interventions, including for students with learning disabilities (Swanson, 1999), supports the efficacy of strategy instruction models.

Several core findings have emerged from the research on comprehension strategy instruction. First, different texts and challenges to comprehension require the use of different strategies. Effective comprehension requires understanding all of the strategies, when and why to select particular strategies, how to monitor their success, and how to adjust strategies as needed to achieve the reading goal (Mason, 2004; Sinatra, Brown, and Reynolds, 2002; Vaughn, Klinger, and Hughes, 2000). The greatest benefits occur when students learn to flexibly use and coordinate multiple comprehension strategies (Kamil et al., 2008; Lave, 1988; Vaughn, Klinger, and Hughes, 2000).

Comprehensive strategy instruction is more effective if students are taught all of the preskills and knowledge they will need to use the strategies effectively. The 2008 practice guide on adolescent literacy published by the U.S. Department of Education's Institute of Education Sciences cautions that, to be effective, explicit strategy instruction must provide sufficient supports (Kamil et al., 2008). Among those supports are explicit instruction on different aspects of text structure (Williams et al., 2005, 2007), familiarity with different text genres, and recognition of the different conventions authors use to convey meaning. For example, less skilled readers often have limited knowledge of narrative or expository text structures and do not rely on structural differences in text to assist their reading (Meyer, Brandt, and Bluth, 1980; Rapp et al., 2007; Williams, 2006). As more text is available in electronic forms and as display devices become more ubiquitous, it will be possible to embed prompts and other "pop-up" preskill supports in texts to help scaffold the comprehension process.

Strategy instruction depends heavily on opportunities to draw from existing knowledge and build new knowledge (Alexander and Judy, 1989; McKeown, Beck, and Blake, 2009; Moje and Speyer, 2008; Moje et al., 2010). World, topic, and domain knowledge are important to the effective use of strategies (Alexander and Judy, 1989; Moje and Speyer, 2008). Learners with limited or fragmented knowledge of a subject typically apply general and relatively inefficient strategies in an inflexible manner (Alexander, 1997; Alexander, Graham, and Harris, 1998). As their knowledge expands and becomes better integrated, learners begin to use strategies more efficiently and flexibly. The value of some strategies declines with more knowledge about the content (rereading specific sections of text), whereas the value of others increases (e.g., mentally summarizing or elaborating main ideas that involve deeper processing of text).

Strategy instruction seems most effective when it incorporates ample opportunities for practice (Kamil et al., 2008; Pressley and Wharton-McDonald, 1997; Pressley et al., 1989a, 1989b). Incorporation of attributional retraining (Berkeley et al., 2011; Borkowski, Weyhing, and Carr, 1988; Schunk and Rice, 1992) and training to improve metacognitive processes (Malone and Mastropieri, 1992) also appear to enhance the effectiveness of strategy instruction. Understanding of text improves if readers are asked to state reading goals, predictions, questions, and reactions to the material that is read (Kamil et al., 2008; National Institute of Child Health and Human Development, 2000a; Palincsar and Brown, 1984). These practices may be effective because they engage readers in more active processing of the content or develop the metacognitive and self-regulatory skills needed for reading comprehension, which requires substantial metacognitive capability.

Knowledge of the various ways to support comprehension remains to be developed in several ways. It is known that the development of comprehension requires having extensive opportunities to practice skills with materials and engagement with varied forms of text (Rayner et al., 2001; Snow, 2002). A question for research is the degree to which explicit instruction to develop knowledge of text components facilitates comprehension. Often the components of text described in text-based models of reading (e.g., see Box 2-3) are learned mainly from practice with reading varied texts instead of from explicit teaching (Hacker, Dunlosky, and Graesser, 2009). Adults who lack reading comprehension skills developed through years of accumulated experience with reading especially might benefit from explicit instruction to develop awareness of text components that often happens implicitly.

Research on the development of literacy and language in the context of learning domain content for broader learning goals (e.g., Lee, 1993; McKeown and Beck, 1994; Moje, 1995, 1996, 1997) is promising to pursue with adolescents and adults needing both to improve their literacy skills and to develop background and specialized knowledge. One of these approaches, disciplinary literacy, seeks to make explicit the different reading and writing demands and conventions of the disciplinary domains, given that the disciplines use particular ways of reading and writing to solve real-world problems (Bain, 2000; Coffin, 2000; Hynd-Shanahan, Holschuh, and Hubbard, 2004; McConachie and Petrosky, 2010; Moje, 2007, 2008a;

Shanahan and Shanahan, 2008; Wineburg, 1991, 1998). This emerging body of research points to several important findings.

First, rich discussion about text may increase both literacy outcomes and understanding of content (Applebee et al., 2003). Similarly, instruction specific to the writing valued in the disciplines can increase both the quality of written text and the disciplinary content learned (e.g., Akkus et al., 2007; Coffin, 2006; Hohenshell and Hand, 2006; Moje et al., 2004b). Second, readers of a range of ages taught to read using texts and language practices valued in the disciplines show enhanced understanding of the content and ability to engage critically with the content (Bain, 2005, 2006; Palincsar and Magnusson, 2001). Third, close study of the linguistic structures of textbooks and related texts appears to enhance students' understanding of the content (e.g., Schleppegrell and Achugar, 2003; Schleppegrell, Achugar, and Oteíza, 2004). Research is needed to evaluate the approaches more fully with samples that include diverse populations of adolescents and adults who need to develop their reading skills.

Although experimental research has focused mainly on the use of effective reading strategies, research is needed to determine how best to combine strategy instruction with other practices that may further facilitate the development of comprehension. McKeown, Beck, and Blake (2009) demonstrated, for example, that focusing students' attention on the content of the text through the use of open-ended questions was more effective in developing comprehension than the same amount of time invested in strategy instruction. An important direction for research with adolescents and adults is to identify the best methods of integrating strategy instruction with the development of content knowledge, vocabulary, and other aspects of language competence for reading comprehension to meet the assessed needs of the learner.

Findings also suggest that the critical analysis of text, such as asking readers to consider the author's purposes in writing the text; the historical, social, or other context in which the text was produced; and multiple ways of reading or making sense of the text may encourage deeper understanding of text (Bain, 2005; Greenleaf et al., 2001; Guthrie et al., 1999; Hand, Wallace, and Yang, 2004; McKeown and Beck, 1994; Palincsar and Magnusson, 2001; Paxton, 1997, Romance and Vitale, 1992). Introducing and explicitly comparing features of texts and literacy practices across languages and cultures also may be helpful to some readers (Au and Mason, 1983; Heath, 1983; Lee, 1993). A recent meta-analysis (Murphy et al., 2009) indicates that critical thinking, reasoning, and argumentation about text all warrant more systematic attention to determine the instructional practices that are effective for developing comprehension skills.

In general, more needs to be known about individual differences in comprehension, which is a major objective of the Reading for Understanding initiative of the Institute of Education Sciences launched in 2010. Individuals may possess certain combinations of proficiencies and weaknesses in comprehension that are important to understand and to measure to guide instructional practice.

The range of skill components to be practiced and the amount of practice required are substantial for the developing reader. At the same time, available evidence suggests that adult learners do not persist in formal programs for anywhere near the amount of time needed to accomplish all of the needed preskill training and reading practice (Miller, Esposito, and McCardle, 2011; Tamassia et al., 2007). Consequently, it is important to better understand how to motivate longer and deeper engagement with reading practice by adult learners.

It is likely that selecting texts that are compatible with learning goals will result in more persistence at deep understanding. Self-reported motivation to perform certain reading tasks in the classroom predicts moderately well students' performance on the reading tasks and reading achievement scores (Guthrie and Wigfield, 2005; Guthrie, Taboada, and Coddington, 2007; Schiefele, Krapp, and Winteler, 1992). In general, it is well established that academic performance improves when motivation and engagement are nurtured and constructive attributions and beliefs about effort and achievement are reinforced. Opportunities to collaborate during reading also can increase motivation to read (Guthrie, 2004; Guthrie and Wigfield, 2000; Slavin, 1995, 1999; Wigfield et al., 2008) although more needs to be known about how to structure collaborations effectively. We highlight key findings of that research in Chapter 5.

WRITING

Writing is the creation of texts for others (and sometimes for the writer) to read. People use many types of writing for a variety of purposes that include recording and tabulating, persuading, learning, communicating, entertaining, self-expression, and reflection. Proficiency in writing for one purpose does not necessarily generalize to writing for other purposes (Osborn Popp et al., 2003; Purves, 1992; Schultz and Fecho, 2000). In today's world, proficiency requires developing skills in both traditional forms of writing and newer electronic and digital modes (see Appendix B). In the last three decades, much more has become known about the components and processes of writing and effective writing instruction. As with reading, most of this research comes from K-12 settings.

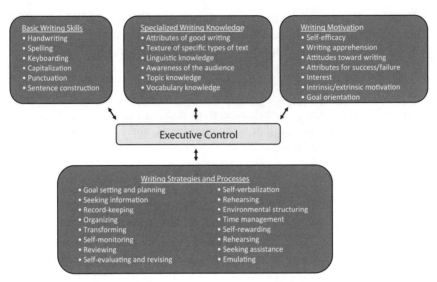

FIGURE 2-1 Model of the components and processes of writing.

Components and Processes of Writing

Figure 2-1 shows the component skills and processes of writing. As the figure shows, the writer manages and orchestrates the application of a variety of basic writing skills, specialized writing knowledge, writing strategies, and motivational processes when writing. The application of these skills and processes is interrelated and varies depending on the task and purpose of the writer.

Basic Writing Skills

Basic writing skills include planning, evaluating, and revising of discourses; sentence construction (including selecting the right words and syntactic structure to convey the intended meaning); and text transcription skills (spelling, handwriting, keyboarding, capitalization, and punctuation; Graham, 2006b).

Sentence construction involves selecting the right words and syntactic structures for transforming ideas into text that conveys the intended meaning. Skilled writers can deftly produce a variety of different types of sentences for effective communication. Facility with writing does not always mean constructing more complex sentences (Houck and Billingsley, 1989). Sentence complexity varies as a function of several factors, such as genre (Hunt, 1965; Scott, 1999; Scott and Windsor, 2000). Yet better writers produce more complex sentences than less skilled writers (Hunt, 1965; Raiser, 1981), and teaching developing and struggling writers how to craft more complex sentences improves not only their sentence writing skills, but also the quality of their texts (Graham and Perin, 2007b; Hillocks, 1986).

For those developing or struggling writers who need to develop spelling, handwriting, or keyboarding skills, instruction in these areas improves these skills and enhances other aspects of writing performance (Berninger et al., 1998; Christensen, 2005; Graham, Harris, and Fink, 2000; Graham, Harris, and Fink-Chorzempa, 2002).

Specialized Writing Knowledge

Writing also depends on specialized knowledge beyond the level of specific sentences: knowledge of the audience (Wong, Wong, and Blenkinsop, 1989), attributes of good writing, characteristics of specific genres and how to use these elements to construct text (Englert and Thomas, 1987; Graham and Harris, 2003), linguistic knowledge (e.g., of words and of text structures that differ from those of speech) (Donovan and Smolkin, 2006; Groff, 1978), topic knowledge (Mosenthal, 1996; Mosenthal et al., 1985; Voss, Vesonder, and Spilich, 1980), and the purposes of writing (Saddler and Graham, 2007). In general, skilled writers possess a more sophisticated conceptualization of writing than less skilled writers (Graham, Schwartz, and MacArthur, 1993). The developing writer's knowledge about writing also predicts individual differences in writing performance (Bonk et al., 1990; Olinghouse and Graham, 2009). A small body of evidence shows that efforts to increase developing and struggling writers' knowledge about writing, especially knowledge of text structure, improve the writing performance of school-age students (Fitzgerald and Markham, 1987; Fitzgerald and Teasley, 1986; Holliway and McCutchen, 2004) and college students (Traxler and Gernsbacher, 1993; Wallace et al., 1996).

Writing Strategies and Self-Regulation

Writing depends on the use of strategies and knowledge that must be coordinated and regulated to accomplish the writer's goal (Graham, 2006a; Hayes and Flower, 1980; Kellogg, 1993b; Zimmerman and Reisemberg, 1997). These include goal setting and planning (e.g., establishing rhetorical goals and tactics to achieve them), seeking information (e.g., gathering information pertinent to the writing topic), record-keeping (e.g., making notes), organizing (e.g., ordering notes or text), transforming (e.g., visualizing a character to facilitate written description), self-monitoring (e.g., checking to see if writing goals are met), reviewing records (e.g., reviewing notes or the text produced so far), self-evaluating (e.g., assessing the quality of text or proposed plans), revising (e.g., modifying text or plans for writing), self-verbalizing (e.g., saying dialogue aloud while writing or personal articulations about what needs to be done), rehearsing (e.g., trying out a scene before writing it), environmental structuring (e.g., finding a quiet place to write), time planning (e.g., estimating and budgeting time for writing), self-rewarding (e.g., going to a movie as a reward for completing a writing task), seeking social assistance (e.g., asking another person to edit the paper), and emulating the writing style of a more gifted author (Scardamalia and Bereiter, 1985; Zimmerman and Riesemberg, 1997).

As in reading, the strategies must be applied intelligently with an understanding of when and why to use a particular approach (Breetvelt, Van den Bergh, and Rijlaarsdam, 1994, 1996; Van den Bergh and Rijlaarsdam, 1996). For example, in a study of high school students' use of 11 writing strategies, use of strategy at the most opportune time was a strong predictor of the quality of writing. Skilled writing especially requires planning and revising (Graham and Harris, 2000a; Hayes and Flower, 1980; Zimmerman and Reisemberg, 1997). For example, children and adolescents spend very little time planning and revising, whereas more accomplished writers, such as college students, spend about 50 percent of writing time planning and revising text (Graham, 2006b; Kellogg, 1987, 1993a). Explicit teaching of strategies for planning and revising has a strong and positive effect on the writing of both developing and struggling writers (Graham and Perin, 2007b; Rogers and Graham, 2008). Similar results have been found for adults needing to develop their writing skills (MacArthur and Lembo, 2009).

Writing Motivation

Despite its importance, motivation is one of the least frequently studied aspects of writing. In this small literature, the most commonly studied topics are attitudes about writing, including self-efficacy, interest, and writing apprehension, and goals for writing (Brunning and Horn, 2000; Graham, Berninger, and Fan, 2007; Hidi and Boscolo, 2006; Madigan, Linton, and Johnston, 1996; Pajares, 2003).

Attitudes toward writing predict writing achievement (Knudson, 1995; see also Graham, Berninger, and Fan, 2007), and poor writers have less positive attitudes about writing than good writers (Graham, Schwartz, and MacArthur, 1993). Thus, it is important to establish positive attitudes about writing. Attitudes may be influenced by self-efficacy or belief in one's ability to write well. Self-efficacy predicts writing performance (Albin, Benton, and Khramtsova, 1996; Knudson, 1995; Madigan, Linton, and Johnston, 1996; Pajares, 2003), and, with only some exceptions (Graham, Schwartz, and MacArthur, 1993), weaker writers have a lower sense of self-efficacy than stronger writers (Shell et al., 1995; Vrugt, Oort, and Zeeberg, 2002).

Self-efficacy is especially important to the social-cognitive model of writing proposed by Zimmerman and Reisemberg (1997; Zimmerman, 1989), which specifies that writing is a goal-driven, self-initiated, and self-sustained activity that involves both cognition and affect. The model, which is derived from empirical research and professional writers' descriptions of how they compose, specifies the self-initiated thoughts, feelings, and actions that writers use to attain various writing goals. Related findings show that the perceived level of success (or failure) in the self-regulated use of writing strategies enhances (or diminishes) self-efficacy and affects intrinsic motivation for writing, further use of self-regulatory processes during writing, and attainment of writing skills and goals. Goals are important because they prompt marshaling the resources, effort, and persistence needed for proficient writing (Locke et al., 1981). Setting goals is especially important when engaging in a complex and demanding task such as writing, which requires a high level of cognitive effort (Kellogg, 1986, 1987, 1993a). As noted earlier in this chapter, arranging writing tasks so that they are consistent with learners' goals is especially helpful.

Linguistic and Cognitive Foundations of Writing

Writing systems developed as a way to record speech in more permanent form for such purposes as extending memory or creating legal records (Nissen, Damerow, and Englund, 1993). Thus, it is not surprising that facility with reading and writing draws on many of the same skills and that these overlap with those of spoken language (Nelson and Calfee, 1998; Tierney and Shanahan, 1991). These include knowledge of alphabetics (phonemic and phonological awareness), English spelling patterns, vocabulary and etymology (word origins), morphological structures, syntax and sentence structures, and text and discourse structures.

Skilled writing also involves cognitive capacities that evolved earlier and separate from literacy (Graham and Weintraub, 1996; McCutchen, 2006; Shanahan, 2006). Key among these is working memory (Hayes, 1996; Swanson and Berninger, 1996), which is needed, for example, to create interconnections that increase the coherence of text. Writing also requires use of executive functions to coordinate and flexibly use a variety of writing strategies (Graham, 2006b) and more generally purposefully activate, orchestrate, monitor, evaluate, and adapt writing to achieve communication goals (Graham, Harris, and Olinghouse, 2007).

Writing Instruction

A number of principles for writing instruction are supported by re-search (see Box 2-4), although the body of research is smaller than for reading. This research includes a focus on both narrative and expository writing (Graham and Perin, 2007a).

A key principle from this research is that *explicit and systematic in-struction is effective in teaching the strategies, skills, and knowledge needed to be a proficient writer.* Almost all the effective writing practices identified in three meta-analyses of experiments and quasi-experiments (grades 4-12, Graham and Perin, 2007a; grades 3 through college, Hillocks, 1986; and grades 1-12, Rogers and Graham, 2008) involved explicit instruction. These practices proved effective with a range of writers, from beginners to college students, as well as with those who experienced difficulty in learning to write. What should be taught, however, depends on the writer's develop-mental level, the skills the writer needs to develop for particular purposes, and the writing task.

A comprehensive meta-analysis of experiments and quasi-experiments by Graham and Perin (2007a) conducted with students in grades 4-12 supports use of the practices in Box 2-5. This meta-analysis also shows that learners can benefit from the process approach to writing instruc-tion (Graves, 1983), although the approach produces smaller average ef-fects than methods that involve systematic instruction of writing strategies (Graham and Perin, 2007a). In another recent meta-analysis, the process approach was not effective for students who were weaker writers (Sandmel and Graham, in press). The process approach is a "workshop" method of teaching that stresses extended writing opportunities, writing for authentic

---

BOX 2-4
Principles of Writing Instruction

- Explicitly and systematically teach the strategies, skills, and knowledge needed to be a proficient writer.
- Combine explicit and systematic instruction with extended experience with writing for a purpose, with consideration of message, audience, and genre.
- Explicitly teach foundational writing skills to the point of automaticity.
- Model writing strategies and teach how to regulate strategy use (e.g., how to select, implement, and coordinate writing strategies; how to monitor, evaluate, and adjust strategies to achieve writing goals).
- Develop an integrated system of skills by using instructional approaches that capitalize on and make explicit the relations between reading and writing.
- Structure instructional environments and interactions to motivate writing prac-tice and persistence in learning new forms of writing.

BOX 2-5
Effective Practices in Writing Instruction

- Strategy instruction for planning, revising, and/or editing compositions.
- Summarizing reading passages in writing.
- Peer assistance in planning, drafting, and revising compositions.
- Setting clear, specific goals for purposes or characteristics of the writing.
- Using word processing regularly.
- Sentence-combining instruction (instruction in combining short sentences into more complex sentences, usually including exercises and application to real writing).
- Process approach to writing with professional development.
- Inquiry approach (including clear goals, analysis of data, using specified strategies, and applying the analysis to writing).
- Prewriting activities (teaching students activities to generate content prior to writing).
- Analyzing models of good writing (discussing the features of good essays and learning to imitate those features).

NOTE: The practices are listed in descending order by effect size.
SOURCE: Adapted from Graham and Perin (2007a).

---

audiences, personalized instruction, and cycles of writing. It relies mainly on incidental and informal methods of instruction. The approach is most effective when teachers are taught how to implement it (Graham and Perin, 2007a). It is possible that process approaches would be more effective if they incorporated explicit and systematic instruction to develop essential knowledge, strategies, and skills, especially for developing writers. This is a question for future research.

As with reading, *it is important to combine explicit and systematic instruction with extended experience with writing for a purpose* (Andrews et al., 2006; Graham, 2000; Graham and Perin, 2007a; Hillocks, 1986). It is important to note that most of the evidence-based writing practices suggest the importance of considerable time devoted to writing and the need to practice writing for different purposes. These findings are consistent with qualitative research showing that two practices common among exceptional literacy teachers are (1) dedicating time to writing and writing instruction across the curriculum and (2) involving students in varying forms of writing over time (Graham and Perin, 2007b).

Some foundational writing skills need to be explicitly taught to the point of automaticity. Spelling, handwriting, and keyboarding become mostly automatic for skilled writers (Graham, 2006b), and individual differences in handwriting and spelling predict writing achievement (Graham et al., 1997), even for college students (Connelly, Dockrell, and Barnett, 2005). Thus, it is important that writers learn to execute these skills fluently and automatically with little or no thought (Alexander, Graham, and Harris, 1998). When these skills are not automatized, as is the case for many developing and struggling writers, cognitive resources are not available for other important aspects of writing, such as planning, evaluating, and revising (McCutchen, 2006). Use of dictation to eliminate handwriting and spelling also has a positive impact on writing performance for children and adults, especially on the amount of text produced (De La Paz and Graham, 1995), although functional writing capability in everyday life probably needs to include the ability to write via other means than dictation. Overall, it is clear that automating what can be automated helps improve writing competence. Some aspects of writing, such as planning or sentence construction, require decisions and cannot be fully automated (Graham and Harris, 2000a). Other, more strategic processes need to be taught and practiced to a point of fluent, flexible, and effective use (Berninger and Amtmann, 2003; Berninger et al., 2006; Graham and Harris, 2003; Graham and Perrin, 2007b).

Instructional environments must be structured to support motivation to write. Although some studies have focused specifically on enhancing motivation to write with positive results (Hidi, Berndorff, and Ainley, 2002; Miller and Meece, 1997; Schunk and Swartz, 1993a, 1993b), the evidence base related to motivation and instruction stems mainly from a few ethnographic, qualitative, and quasi-experimental studies. A small number of experiments show practices that improve the quality of writing and that reasonably could affect motivation to write or engage with writing instruction, although motivation itself was not measured. These practices include setting clear goals for writing; encouraging students to help each other plan, draft, or revise (Graham and Perin, 2007a); use of self-assessment (Collopy and Bowman, 2005; Guastello, 2001); and providing feedback on progress (Schunk and Swartz, 1993a, 1993b). Several single-subject design studies with adolescent learners have demonstrated that social praise, tangible rewards, or both can improve students' writing behaviors (Graham and Perin, 2007b).

Experiments are needed to identify how to deliver motivating instruction that encourages engagement with and persistence in writing and to explain how the practices work (via improved self-efficacy, improved self-regulation, etc.) to improve writing. This research might also draw on observational studies that describe instructional routines used by teachers to support engagement with writing and that enable developing writers to become a source of writing improvement for their peers (Dyson, 1995; Lensmire, 1994; Prior, 2006; Russell, 1997; Schultz, 1997; Schultz and

Fecho, 2000). Other qualitative research with exceptional literacy teachers of elementary school students suggests additional instructional approaches for engaging learners that warrant further study with older populations (see Graham and Perin, 2007b).

When the connections between reading and writing are made explicit during instruction, a more integrated system of literacy skills develops and learning is facilitated. Historically, reading and writing have been taught as separate language skills (Nelson and Calfee, 1998). As Fitzgerald and Shanahan (2000) note, this may be due to a variety of factors, such as greater value placed on reading than writing, professional division between those who teach and study these two skills, and gaps in teachers' skills and knowledge. Yet reading and writing depend on similar knowledge and cognitive processes, so insights in one area can lead to insights in the other. Making reciprocities explicit between reading and writing systems will facilitate skill development, contribute to metalinguistic awareness, and enhance retrieval of and access to text forms and meanings (see Graham, 2000; Graham and Hebert, 2010; Wolf, 2007).

Spelling instruction, for example, deepens awareness of correspondences between letters or letter patterns and speech sounds and thus enables forming a more specific mental representation of words for faster word reading (Ehri, 1987; McCardle, Chhabra, and Kapinus, 2008; Snow, Griffin, and Burns, 2005). A meta-analysis involving students in grades 1 to 7 shows that reading fluency is enhanced through teaching spelling or sentence construction skills (Graham and Hebert, 2010). Similarly, alphabetics instruction for reading improves spelling (Graham, 2000).

Reading comprehension improves with frequent writing, according to a recent meta-analysis of 60 experiments involving elementary school students (Graham and Hebert, 2010). Process approaches to writing, teaching sentence construction skills, and teaching text structure as part of a writing activity had a small-to-moderate impact on reading comprehension. Activities included writing questions and answers about the material read, taking notes about text, summarizing text, and analyzing and interpreting text through writing.

Teachers need to understand the components of skilled reading and writing and how they reinforce each other so that a coherent system of skills can be taught, but the differences between reading and writing should not be overlooked. Both reading and writing involve the mastery of specialized skills, knowledge, and processes and thus require dedicated instruction. Instructional programming can be designed and delivered so that all reading and writing components are developed as needed and support each other (Englert et al., 1995, 1998; Roberts and Meiring, 2006).

NEUROBIOLOGY OF READING AND WRITING DEVELOPMENT AND DIFFICULTIES

Neurobiology of Reading

Early findings on the brain pathways (neurocircuits) for reading and reading disorders came primarily from studies of acquired dyslexia associated with brain injury (Damasio and Damasio, 1983; Dejerine, 1891; Geschwind, 1965; Warrington and Shallice, 1980) or postmortem histological studies of individuals with a history of reading disability (Galaburda, 2005; Galaburda et al., 2006). Early studies implicated several posterior regions of the left hemisphere (LH) as critical to reading behavior, including the angular gyrus in the parietal lobe and the fusiform gyrus in the occipitotemporal region. In recent years, structural (MRI) and functional (EEG, MEG, PET, fMRI) neuroimaging technologies have provided a new window on neurocircuits involved in reading and its disorders (Pugh et al., 2010). The new technologies, some of which are relatively unobtrusive, allow observing levels of brain activity associated with reading and writing components. A more extensive reading circuitry has been documented with these new technologies, and the findings are broadly consistent with earlier neuropsychological research.

Specifically, across a large number of studies with skilled readers, it is seen that visual word reading (fluent decoding) involves a largely LH circuitry with temporoparietal (TP), occipitotemporal (OT), frontal, and subcortical components (for reviews, see Pugh et al., 2010; Schlaggar and McCandliss, 2007). In typically developing readers, all three of these components (with subcortical mediating influences from the basal ganglia and thalamus) come to function in a highly integrated manner (Bitan et al., 2005; Hampson et al., 2006; Seghier and Price, 2010). Indeed, at the level of neurocircuits, a foundation of skilled reading appears to be the establishment of adequate connections among distributed LH regions (operationally defined with measures of functional connectivity). This LH circuitry, when established through reading experience, supports efficient mapping of visual percepts of print onto knowledge of the phonological and semantic structures of language for fast and automatic word recognition during reading (Booth et al., 2001; Church et al., 2008; Cohen et al., 2000, 2002; Shaywitz et al., 2002).

By contrast, for both children and adults with reading disabilities (RD), there are marked functional differences, relative to typically developing readers, in language processing (see Pugh et al., 2010, for reviews) with reduced activation and connectivity at both TP and OT sites. Moreover, these differences in brain function appear to be associated with anomalies in brain structure. Structural MRI studies have identified differences, such as reduced gray matter volumes in RD, at those regions showing functional anomalies (e.g., Brambati et al., 2004). Several studies using diffusion tensor imaging (DTI) also reveal reduced white matter connectivity for several pathways that support interregional communication among these LH foci (e.g., Niogi and McCandliss, 2006).

While establishment of this LH circuitry for fluent decoding is necessary, the goal of reading is comprehension. Research on neurocircuits that support reading beyond the word level is beginning to focus on how neurocircuits organize as readers cope with syntactic, pragmatic, and cognitive processing demands associated with sentence and text reading and comprehension (Caplan, 2004; Cooke et al., 2006; Cutting and Scarborough, 2006; Ferstl et al., 2008; Kuperberg et al., 2008; Shankweiler et al., 2008). In general, the same broad LH circuitry evident for word-level reading is observed, with additional increased activation in regions beyond those activated by simple word reading tasks (Cutting and Scarborough, 2006). A recent meta-analysis of neuroimaging studies (Ferstl et al., 2008) confirms that these higher order language processes involve an extended neural network that includes dorso-medial prefrontal cortex, posterior cingulate cortex, and heightened right hemisphere (RH) involvement. As with research on word reading, recent studies contrasting skilled and less skilled "comprehenders" reveal anomalies across these extended LH networks (Keller, Carpenter, and Just, 2001; Rimrodt et al., 2010).

Neurobiology of Writing

Reading and writing make common demands on orthographic, phonological, and semantic processing and so must involve at least partially overlapping neurocircuits (Berninger and Richards, 2002; Berninger and Winn, 2006). Available studies indicate substantial overlap (Philipose et al., 2007; Purcell et al., 2010). Research on the component systems associated with writing-related behaviors, such as handwriting (James and Gauthier, 2006; Katanoda, Yoshikawa, and Sugishita, 2001; Menon and Desmond, 2001) and spelling (Bitan et al., 2005; Booth et al., 2001; Richards, Berninger, and Fayol, 2009) is rapidly increasing. Together, these studies implicate a highly integrated perception-action neurocircuitry for writing that overlaps substantially, but not entirely, with the neurocircuitry involved in reading words and sentences. Connections between writing and reading also have been identified in the higher order aspects of writing, such as planning of written and spoken messages (see Indefrey and Levelt, 2004, for a meta-analysis), which in turn overlap with the broad circuitry for comprehension (Ferstl et al., 2008) and lexical finding (i.e., finding the right word to convey the writer's intended meaning). It is known that reading and writing difficulties often co-occur in learners at different ages and that some of these learners struggle more at the word level (Wagner et al., 2011) while others struggle at more abstract levels of processing (Berninger, Nagy, and Beers, 2011). More needs to be understood about shared and unshared neurocircuits at each level to better understand individual differences in the difficulties learners experience with writing.

Implications for Instruction

It is possible in future research to track populations with different literacy challenges that receive different instructional approaches to see which produce the most efficient change in neural circuitry. Although this information does not directly or completely test the effectiveness of instructional approaches, such knowledge of brain processes will be important for validating theories of reading and writing and skill acquisition. With a better understanding of how brain processing changes with age, one can also better determine whether and why certain instructional approaches are likely to generalize across populations of different ages. It will be important to extend the research to reading beyond the word level and to writing.

It will be especially valuable to understand how neurocircuits involved in reading and writing become organized, why they fail to organize properly in individuals with reading problems, how they are modified by experiential factors that include instruction and intervention, and why they do not develop as expeditiously with learning and practice in some subpopulations. More knowledge about how shared and unshared neurocircuits organize for reading and writing could help in the design of instruction that maximizes the carryover of skills from one domain to the other (e.g., identifying when and why focusing on spelling might impact silent reading or vice versa).

Ongoing developmental research is examining both structural (Giedd et al., 1997; Hua, Tembe, and Dougherty, 2009) and functional (Booth et al., 2001; Shaywitz et al., 2002) brain changes as individuals mature from early childhood into adulthood. Such research will be invaluable for understanding how learning to read and write differs at different ages. This information can be used to design optimal learning environments that take advantage of neurocognitive strengths and compensate for declines at different points in the life span. It is also important to learn how structural or functional factors constrain the basic computational skills on which learning to read depends (memory capacity, consolidation, speed of processing) (Just and Varma, 2007).

More knowledge about gene-brain-behavior relationships will be critical for understanding changes in plasticity that may affect learning to read and write in adulthood. In particular, more needs to be known about individual and developmental differences in the sensitivity of reading and writing neurocircuits. Ongoing treatment studies, which suggest that gains in reading skill after intense reading intervention produce more "normalized" brain organization for reading (Shaywitz et al., 2004; Simos et al., 2001; Temple et al., 2003), have focused mainly on younger learners. Generalization to adult learners may not be straightforward. One recent study does suggest a good deal of plasticity following reading remediation even for those disabled readers who had adequate opportunities to learn to read at a young age but did not develop adequate skills (Eden et al., 2004). Thus, it is reasonable to hypothesize that those learning to read later in life, whether because of inadequate access to instruction or learning disability, are able to achieve at least some degree of brain reorganization that is common among more typically developing readers as a result of effective instruction. An understanding of why reorganization does or does not occur and for whom it occurs requires further study.

INSTRUCTION FOR STRUGGLING READERS AND WRITERS

The principles of reading and writing instruction presented thus far are equally important for both typically developing and struggling learners. A separate, sizeable literature on interventions for struggling K-12 learners points to additional principles of instruction to help overcome specific areas of difficulty through targeted remediation. Both children and adults experience difficulties with cognitive and linguistic processes of reading and writing that require attention during instruction to develop literacy proficiency. In Chapter 7, we describe in more detail the difficulties with component reading and writing processes that adults with learning difficulties may experience and review the literature on accommodations, used mainly in college settings, which enable students to benefit from academic instruction and demonstrate their knowledge and skills. Because research on interventions to develop the reading and writing skills of adults with learning disabilities is limited, we describe here what is known from research with children and to some degree adolescent students about how to intervene with struggling readers and writers.

Decontextualized Interventions

Before discussing additional principles of instruction for learners with disabilities, we first note that there has been a tradition in the field of learning disabilities to offer students with reading and writing difficulties training targeted to general cognitive or sensory processing deficits believed to cause the person's problem with academic learning. This has led to interventions involving balance beams, colored lenses, and brain retraining exercises; such programs are often designed to remediate what some researchers have identified as core deficits in specific lower level sensory or motor processes (visual, auditory, cerebellar) believed to underlie the academic learning problems (see, e.g., Lovegrove, Martin, and Slaghuis, 1986; Nicolson, Fawcett, and Dean, 2001; Stein, 2001; Tallal, 1980, 2004). Training in motor, visual, neural, or cognitive processes without academic content, however, does not lead to better academic outcomes for children with learning disabilities (Fletcher et al., 2007). There is no evidence that nonreading interventions of this sort will improve the reading outcomes of those with reading disabilities. This is not to say that interventions targeting cognitive processes used in reading would never be helpful, but that it is only useful to develop and practice these processes as they are needed in the context of literacy instruction and literacy practice.

Thus, the first principle below is supported by findings that argue against this type of decontextualized intervention for reading and writing difficulties. The principles that follow specify further that, rather than needing instruction that is qualitatively different from the instruction that is effective with typically developing learners, learners who struggle benefit from certain adaptations—even more explicit and systemic reading and writing instruction; enhanced supports for the transfer and generalization of skills and opportunities for practice; attention to maladaptive attributions, which can be particularly important to address for struggling learners; and scaffolded and differentiated instruction that targets specific difficulties while continuing to develop all the skills needed for reading and writing development.

Principles of Instruction for Struggling Learners

- **Interventions that directly target specific literacy difficulties in the context of explicit reading and writing instruction result in better literacy outcomes for struggling readers and writers.**

This principle is based on solid evidence (but often from studies of young students) that effective intervention for literacy learning problems directly targets specific difficulties in literacy skills (Fletcher et al., 2007; Foorman et al., 1998; Lovett, Barron, and Benson, 2003; Morris et al., 2010; Swanson, Harris, and Graham, 2003; Torgesen et al., 1999). As mentioned earlier in this chapter, good remedial interventions that address core areas of processing deficit in the context of literacy instruction appear to partially normalize patterns of brain activation for those with learning disabilities: their brain activation profiles after effective intervention come to resemble those of more able readers as they perform reading-related tasks— for example, judging whether two nonwords (e.g., lete and jeat) rhyme, a task with both phonological and orthographic processing demands (Meyler et al., 2008; Shaywitz et al., 2004; Simos et al., 2002a; Temple et al., 2003).

Most who struggle with reading and writing, particularly those with severe literacy learning disorders, have specific difficulties in aspects of speech or language that impact their ability to learn to read and write, such as poor phonological awareness and phonological processing skills, lags in oral language development (e.g., vocabulary, syntax), and slow naming speed (that may or may not be independent of phonological deficits) (Catts and Hogan, 2003; Liberman, 1971; Liberman and Shankweiler, 1991; Pennington and Bishop, 2009; Schatschneider et al., 2004; Shankweiler and Crain, 1986; Share and Stanovich, 1995; Vellutino et al., 2004; Wagner et al., 1997; Wagner, Torgesen, and Rashotte, 1994; Wolf and Bowers, 1999). Based on studies mostly with younger participants, it is reasonable to assume (subject to needed empirical verification with adults) that these difficulties can be remediated by increasing the time and intensity of instruction that is focused on building the language skills on which fluent reading and writing skills depend.

Targeted interventions also improve the performance of struggling writers. Although some who experience difficulties with writing have other difficulties with learning (Graham and Harris, 2005) or language processing (Dockrell, Lindsay, and Connelly, 2009; Smith-Lock, Nickels, and Mortensen, 2008), not all aspects of writing are necessarily affected (see, e.g., Mortensen, Smith-Lock, and Nickels, 2008). In these cases, interventions that target a specific component skill on which writing depends have had some success. Teaching the language skill of phonological awareness, for example, results in better spelling performance for those who are weak spellers (Bradley and Bryant, 1985; O'Connor, Notari-Syverson, and Vadasky, 1996). A few studies have shown that teaching vocabulary to developing writers enhances their writing performance (Duin and Graves, 1987; Popadopoulou, 2007; Thibodeau, 1964). Sentence combining, an oral language practice that often relies heavily on combining smaller sentences into larger ones when speaking, has improved the quality of writing in adolescents (Graham and Perin, 2007b). In addition, some limited evidence with elementary school students experiencing difficulties with regulating attention shows that teaching ways to monitor attention while writing improves writing skills and increases the amount of text written (Harris et al., 1994; Rumsey and Ballard, 1985). Again, these findings must be verified with adult learners. Common to almost all effective interventions is that they targeted specific areas of processing as part of teaching and practicing the act of writing, instead of trying to remediate processing problems in isolation.

Notably, the process-writing approach, which does not systematically target specific difficulties (Graves, 1983), has not been effective with struggling writers in a recent meta-analysis of five studies (Sandmel and Graham, in press). Varied forms of the approach are often used, however, and research is needed to determine whether some form is effective with some struggling learners.

- **Struggling learners benefit from more intense instruction, more explicit instruction, and even more opportunities to practice.**

The most significant gains obtained in reading interventions are associated with more intense, explicit, and systematic delivery of instruction (Fletcher et al., 2007; Torgesen et al., 2001). Reading interventions are especially effective if they teach to mastery, include academic content, monitor progress, and offer sufficient scaffolding of skills and emotional support (Fletcher et al., 2007). Greater time devoted to literacy activities allows for the additional explicit instruction required to remediate skills; opportunities to address gaps in vocabulary and language knowledge; and the additional exposures needed to consolidate, review, and explicitly teach for the generalization of newly acquired skills (Berninger et al., 2002; Blachman et al., 2004; Lovett et al., 2000; Torgesen et al., 2001; Wise, Ring, and Olson, 2000).

Similarly, almost all of the strategies that have proven to be effective in teaching struggling writers have involved intense and explicit instruction with ample opportunities to practice taught skills (see the meta-analysis by Graham and Perin, 2007a; Rogers and Graham, 2008). This research included teaching planning strategies together with genre knowledge (see the meta-analysis by Graham and Harris, 2003), revision (Graham, 2006a; Schumaker et al., 1982), handwriting and spelling (Berninger et al., 1997, 1998; Graham, 1999), as well as sentence construction (Saddler and Graham, 2005) and paragraph construction skills (Sonntag and McLaughlin, 1984; Wallace and Bott, 1989). In addition, the self-regulated strategy development model for teaching writing strategies has been more effective than other approaches for teaching writing strategies to struggling writers (Graham, 2006a). It involves explicitly teaching how to regulate the use of strategies and requires developing skills to a criterion, unlike other approaches that are time-limited.

- **Struggling learners need enhanced support for the generalization and transfer of new literacy skills.**

A majority of struggling learners do not apply and transfer newly learned literacy skills spontaneously. To be effective, instruction for all learners must attend to the generalization of new skills and knowledge and include opportunities to practice these in varied tasks outside the intervention context. This observation is particularly true, however, for those with reading disabilities. For example, children with reading disabilities demonstrate problems with transfer that are specific to printed language; these difficulties are not evident on learning tasks with parallel cognitive demands but no phonological processing requirements (Benson, 2000; Benson, Lovett, and Kroeber, 1997; Lovett, Barron, and Benson, 2003). Children with severe reading disabilities also demonstrated marked transfer-of-learning failures even when instructed target words were well learned and remembered (Lovett et al., 1989, 1990). For example, in one study, those who learned to read the word *bake* and practiced on words with the same spelling pattern (e.g., *rake, fake, lake*) could not later reliably identify *make* (Lovett et al., 1990).

A recent synthesis of intervention research with adolescent struggling readers (Edmonds et al., 2009) confirmed that older struggling readers do benefit from explicit reading comprehension strategy instruction, but these skills did not generalize well. It is possible that more explicit training and scaffolding would support generalization, as might more practice opportunities.

Struggling readers experience particular difficulties in acquiring self-regulatory strategies across a variety of literacy tasks (Levin, 1990; Pressley, 1991; Swanson, 1999; Swanson and Alexander, 1997; Swanson and Saez, 2003; Swanson and Siegel, 2001; Wong, 1991), and these difficulties are likely to affect the transfer and generalization failures observed among struggling learners (Harris, Graham, and Pressley, 1992; Meltzer, 1994). For example, when children with reading disabilities have received strategy instruction, some appear to remain novices relative to their more able peers because they fail to transform simple strategies into more efficient forms (Swanson, Hoskyn, and Lee, 1999; Zimmerman, 2000a, 2000b). Multidimensional interventions that combine explicit skills instruction with the teaching of specific strategies for reading can help those with reading disabilities to generalize strategies and skills (Lovett et al., 2003, 2005; Lovett, Lacerenza, and Borden, 2000; Morris et al., 2010; Swanson, 1999). Faster growth and better outcomes in word identification, for example, are attained when a multidimensional intervention is adopted, particularly one that combines direct and dialogue-based instruction, explicit teaching of different levels of syllabic segmentation, and teaching of multiple decoding strategies. Although most of this research has focused on word reading, the critical importance of explicit instruction for developing the flexible use of strategies to identify words and read extended text cannot be over-emphasized when it comes to achieving generalization and maintenance of remedial gains.

Although the evidence base for struggling writers is smaller than for reading, it suggests that struggling writers also have difficulty maintaining and generalizing gains from instruction (Wong, 1994). The findings need to be interpreted cautiously, however, because maintenance decrements do not appear to be severe (Graham, 2006a; Graham and Harris, 2003), and in most research maintenance of gains was assessed for no more than a month from the end of the intervention. Generalizing specific writing skills to tasks and contexts beyond those in which they were taught is not an all-or-none phenomenon, and transfer often appears to generalize to some degree (Graham, 2006a; Graham and Harris, 2003).

A very small body of research with elementary and middle school students who are struggling writers shows that maintenance and generalization of taught writing skills and strategies can be facilitated by teaching target material to mastery, having students set goals for using the skills and strategies and monitoring their progress in doing so, analyzing when and how to use the skills and strategies, and enlisting peers as a resource for reminding and helping struggling writers to apply new skills (Harris, Graham, and Mason, 2006; Sawyer, Graham, and Harris, 1992; Stoddard and MacArthur, 1993).

- **Maladaptive attributions, beliefs, and motivational profiles of struggling learners need to be understood and targeted during instruction.**

The motivational profiles of struggling and typical readers and writers can be very different. Struggling learners are usually lower in intrinsic motivation and a sense of self-efficacy for reading and writing, more likely to be extrinsically motivated or unmotivated, and more likely to attribute failure to internal factors (e.g., ability) and success to external factors (e.g., luck)—all of which lead to disengagement from reading and writing activities, less reading and writing experience, and markedly lower literacy achievement (Deci and Ryan, 2002b; Graham, 1990a; Graham, Schwartz, and MacArthur, 1993; Guthrie and Davis, 2003; Harter, Whitesell, and Kowalski, 1992; Moje et al., 2000; Morgan et al., 2008; Ryan, Stiller, and Lynch, 1994; Sawyer, Graham, and Harris, 1992; Taboada et al., 2009; Wigfield et al., 2008). Specific difficulties in these domains include maladaptive attributions about effort and achievement, learned helplessness rather than mastery-oriented motivational profiles, immature and poorly developed epistemic beliefs, and disengagement from reading and writing activities.

There is a dearth of experimental evidence on how to build adaptive attributions and motivations for struggling adult readers and writers during the course of intervention, although research with children and adolescents with reading disabilities is emerging (Guthrie et al., 2009; Lovett, Lacerenza, and Borden, 2000; Morris et al., 2010; Wigfield et al., 2008; Wolf, Miller, and Donnelly, 2000). In other research, positive attributional change has been observed for children in middle school with the effective remediation of reading disabilities. Emerging research with struggling adolescent readers suggests the importance of intervening directly to address the attributional and motivational correlates of literacy learning difficulties (see Guthrie, Wigfield, and You, in press). In this research, adding attributional retraining to comprehension strategy instruction was associated with better maintenance of gains (Berkeley, Mastropieri, and Scruggs, 2011).

Similarly, few writing studies have examined how to address the maladaptive attributions and beliefs that affect struggling writers (Wong et al., 2003). Adding attribution retraining to strategy instruction in writing is a promising approach that has enhanced the compositions of struggling writers (Garcia-Sánchez and Fidalgo-Redondo, 2006; Sexton, Harris, and Graham, 1998). For example, one writing program improved struggling writers' motivation to write by including components for enhancing multiple affective factors, including self-efficacy, self-esteem, expectations, and beliefs about writing (García and de Caso, 2004).

- **Intervention should be differentiated to scaffold learning and meet the individual needs of those who struggle with literacy.**

Scaffolding is the term used to describe teaching approaches in which the instructor or presentation of tools supports execution of a skill until the student gradually develops full mastery. *Differentiated instruction* is the term used for teaching that meets individual and small group needs by providing learning activities and supports for the development of skills that have not yet been acquired but that are necessary to move through an instructional sequence. With this type of scaffolded and integrated instruction and intervention model, learning deficits are addressed and remediated while teaching all of the necessary skills for reading and writing development that enable struggling students to participate and move through the broader program of instruction (National Institute of Child Health and Human Development, 2000a). Differentiation avoids provision of extra or specialized instruction to those who do not need it, which is counterproductive and could lead learners to view literacy activity as uninteresting.

One of the premises of special education, the arm of educational practice that specializes in learning difficulties, is that instruction should be further tailored to meet the processing needs of individual students (Edmonds et al., 2009; Scammacca et al., 2007). As discussed earlier, to date, little evidence from controlled intervention studies supports the tailoring of literacy instruction to difficulties with more general processing; what seems most important is that the intervention offer explicit, systematic, and intense reading remediation targeted to develop component literacy skills in the context of reading instruction and reading practice (Fletcher et al., 2007; Morris et al., 2010; Torgesen et al., 2001).

Differentiation of instruction also appears to be effective for writing. Most of this research has focused on teaching planning strategies to struggling writers who spend little time systematically planning their papers (e.g., Englert et al., 1991). The instruction has a positive impact on the quality and structure of text produced by struggling writers (see meta-analyses by Graham, 2006a; Graham and Harris, 2003; Graham and Perin, 2007a; Rogers and Graham, 2008). MacArthur and Lembo (2009) also found this to be a productive strategy with adult literacy learners. Similarly, a few studies show that instruction that targets the handwriting or spelling of elementary school students experiencing difficulties with these skills improves these skills as well as how much the students write and their facility with constructing sentences (Berninger et al., 1997, 1998; Graham, Harris, and Fink, 2000; Graham, Harris, and Fink-Chorzempa, 2002). In addition, the writing performance of middle and high school struggling writers was enhanced when they were taught sentence construction skills (e.g., Saddler and Graham, 2005; Schmidt et al., 1988).

READING AND WRITING ACROSS THE LIFE SPAN

Although much is known from research about the processes involved in the development of reading and writing and effective instruction for typically developing readers and writers and those who struggle, almost no research has focused on changes in reading and writing processes from early childhood through adulthood. This research will be needed to establish whether adults with low literacy have not yet achieved an asymptotic level of skill along a common learning trajectory or, perhaps less likely, whether they need truly alternative pathways to competence. A small body of research on cognitive aging has, however, examined differences in reading and writing processes between younger and older adults, although some studies examine change in cognitive functions from the late 30s or 40s. Most of those who receive adult literacy instruction are older adolescents and young adults (e.g., according to Tamassia et al., 2007); in the program year 2001-2002, 34 percent were 16- to 24-years old and 46 percent were 25- to 44-years old. Yet a significant portion of adult learners (18 percent) are older than 44. Thus, we review this research with older populations to identify whether adults may experience unique challenges in developing and using their literacy skills in midlife and beyond. There is a lack of research on changes in literacy (and learning processes) from young adulthood to middle adulthood because most research has focused on young populations or older adults.

An important caveat to the findings reported here is that the research has focused not on older adults who need to develop their literacy but on relatively well-educated and literate populations. The research typically compares the performance of older adults to that of college students who serve as samples of convenience. Thus caution must be applied in generalizing the findings to populations of adults who need to develop literacy skills later in life.

In general, the processes involved in the component skills of reading and writing studied thus far appear mostly preserved into later adulthood, although older adults do experience declines in areas affected by perception and speed of processing (Durgunoğlu and Öney, 2002; Stine-Morrow, Loveless, and Soederberg, 1996). Word recognition reappears to be fundamentally preserved throughout the adult life span. With age, readers tend to rely more on recognizing a whole word as a unit instead of decoding it using phonics skills (Spieler and Balota, 2000), although phonics facility remains essential for reading new words. As in younger readers, eventual automatic recognition of newly learned words occurs through adulthood (Lien et al., 2006). In both spoken and written communication, aging may bring reliance on the broader discourse context to decode individual words (Madden, 1988; Stine and Wingfield, 1990; Stine-Morrow et al., 2008; Wingfield et al., 1985).

Vocabulary knowledge is maintained and has the potential to grow throughout adulthood (Birren and Morrison, 1961; Schaie, 2005). For example, the ability to recognize the meanings of words in a text appears to be intact (Burke and Peters, 1986; Burke, White, and Diaz, 1987; Light, Valencia-Laver, and Zavis, 1991). It is possible, however, for vocabulary growth to decelerate later in life, perhaps because declines in working memory hinder inferring the meanings of novel words in the course of ordinary reading (McGinnis and Zelinski, 2000, 2003).

Reading comprehension can become compromised in several respects with age. Sensory impairment, which becomes more prevalent in later adulthood, may require adult readers (and listeners) to allocate more attention to decoding the surface form, which reduces cognitive resources available for understanding the meaning of text (Dickinson and Rabbitt, 1991; Stine-Morrow and Miller, 2009; Wingfield, Tun, and McCoy, 2005). Phonological skills also may be affected by sensory acuity deficits (Hartley and Harris, 2001), presenting a barrier to comprehension.

Skills in basic parsing of syntax may remain intact throughout the life span (Caplan and Waters, 1999), although age-related declines in processing capacity may reduce comprehension of syntactically complex text (Kemper, 1987; Norman, Kemper, and Kynette, 1992). The production of utterances in both speech and writing shows reliable trends toward syntactic simplification and reduced informational density with age (Kemper, 1987; Kemper et al., 2001; Norman, Kemper, and Kynette, 1992), so one would assume reasonably that the ability to read more complex and dense texts might be slowed or otherwise compromised. Comprehension of complex constructions may require more controlled/executive processing with age (Wingfield and Grossman, 2006). For example, older adults may find it more necessary to use such strategies as making notes and rereading text elements.

Decreased ability to rapidly construct meaning from language may result from age-related declines in mental processing capacity (Federmeier et al., 2003; Hartley, 1988; Hartley et al., 1994; Stine and Hindman, 1994). Aging readers also may allocate relatively less attention to the semantic analysis of sentences (Radvansky et al., 2001). With age, people usually experience decreases in memory for text (Johnson, 2003; Radvansky et al., 2001; Stine-Morrow and Shake, 2009; Zelinski and Gilewski, 1988), perhaps beginning as early as midlife (ages 40-45) (Ferstl, 2006; Van der Linden et al., 1999). These declines are mitigated by routinely engaging in activities that require text memory, by having high verbal ability, and by having knowledge related to the topic of the text (Hultsch and Dixon, 1983; Meyer and Rice, 1989; Stine-Morrow et al., 2008).

Older readers tend to remember information from elaborated texts that provide redundant support for key information better rather than isolated facts (Daneman and Merikle, 1996; Stine and Wingfield, 1990; Stine-Morrow et al., 2008). The ability to generate inferences about the larger situation described by a text is mostly intact (Radvansky and Dijkstra, 2007). Yet comprehension skills can be affected by decreased capacity for making inferences as a result of memory decline. For example, older adults can have difficulty with important inferences that require remembering text from one sentence to later ones. As a consequence, they may create a fuzzier or less complete representation of the text (Cohen, 1981; Hess, 1994; Light and Capps, 1986; Light et al., 1994; McGinnis, 2009; McGinnis et al., 2008; Noh et al., 2007).

An important strength of adulthood is accumulated knowledge that often occurs as a consequence of literacy. The dependence on knowledge in reading may increase throughout adulthood (Meyer, Talbot, and Ranalli, 2007; Miller, 2003, 2009; Miller and Stine-Morrow, 1998; Miller, Cohen, and Wingfield, 2006). Knowledge has a variety of forms, including the ability to articulate ideas (declarative knowledge), skilled performance (procedural knowledge), and implicit processes in work and social contexts (tacit knowledge), and encompasses the range of human experiences (e.g., cultural conventions, facts, conceptual systems, schemas that abstract essential elements of a system and their organization). Such knowledge can enhance text comprehension through a number of routes (Ackerman, 2008; Ackerman and Beier, 2006; Ackerman et al., 2001; Barnett and Ceci, 2002; Beier and Ackerman, 2001, 2005; Charness, 2006; Ericsson,

2006; Graesser, Haberlandt, and Koizumi, 1987; Griffin, Jee, and Wiley, 2009; Miller, 2009; Miller and Stine-Morrow, 1998; Miller, Cohen, and Wingfield, 2006; Miller et al., 2004; Noordman and Vonk, 1992). Knowledge enables, for example, understanding relations among concepts not obvious to the novice, understanding vocabulary and jargon, abstract reasoning (e.g., analogy), making inferences and connections in the text, and monitoring the success of efforts made to comprehend.

Less research has focused on changes in writing processes with age. Although vocabulary knowledge either stabilizes or grows through adulthood, especially if the adult continues to engage with text (Stanovich, West, and Harrison, 1995), adults may have difficulty with recalling a word, may substitute or transpose speech sounds in a word, and may make spelling errors more frequently beginning in midlife (Burke and Shafto, 2004; Burke et al., 1991; MacKay and Abrams, 1998).

As people age, the speech and writing they produce has simpler syntax and is less dense with information (Kemper, 1987; Kemper et al., 2001; Norman, Kemper, and Kynette, 1992). The tendency to produce less complex syntax is due partly to declines in working memory (Norman, Kemper, and Kynette, 1992), but also to some extent may reflect greater awareness that simpler syntax is easier for the listener or reader to understand. There is not a universal trend, however, toward simplified writing with age. For example, although syntax becomes simpler over time, narrative storytelling becomes more complex (Kemper et al., 1990).

In sum, not enough is known about the ways in which reading and writing processes change across the life span to determine whether or how instructional approaches would need to be modified to make them more effective for learners of different ages. Most research has concentrated on young children at the beginning of reading development and on older adults at the opposite end of the life span who are proficient readers benefiting from the fruition of knowledge growth but beginning to experience some declines in processing capacity. The findings available hint, however, at some of the underlying cognitive processes that are likely to remain intact in older adults. They also suggest some challenges in developing and using literacy skills later in life that may require enhanced supports.

SUMMARY AND DISCUSSION

A complete understanding of reading and writing development requires knowledge of the learner (the learners' knowledge, skills, literacy practices, motivations, and neurocognitive processes) and features of the instructional context (types of text, literacy tools, literacy activities, instructor knowledge, beliefs, and skills) that scaffold or impede learning. Because different disciplines study different aspects of literacy, research has yet to systematically examine how various social, cultural, and contextual forces interact with neurocognitive processes to facilitate or constrain the development of literacy.

The major components of reading and writing are well documented. Depending on the assessed needs of the learner, instruction needs to target decoding and strategies for identifying unfamiliar words. Instruction should focus on depth, breadth, and flexibility of vocabulary knowledge and use. Learners also need strategies for comprehending and learning from text. Instruction should support the development of knowledge, including background, topic, and world knowledge. Learners also need metalinguistic knowledge (phonology, morphology) and discourse knowledge (genre and rhetorical structure). Metacognitive skills may need to be developed to facilitate comprehension and meet goals for reading.

Figure 2-1 shows the writing skills that may need to be targeted with instruction, among them sentence construction skills, planning and revising, spelling, and usage (capitalization and punctuation skills). As for reading, knowledge to develop for writing includes background, topic, and world knowledge as well as knowledge of the potential audiences for written products. Writing instruction, like reading instruction, needs to develop facility with writing for particular purposes, contexts, and content domains. Writing also requires mastery of tools required for writing (typing, word processing, and handwriting).

Literacy development, like the learning of any complex task, requires a range of explicit teaching and implicit learning guided by an expert. Explicit and systematic instruction is effective in developing the components of reading and writing and facilitating the integration and transfer of skills to new tasks and context. Full competence requires extensive practice with varied forms of text and tasks that demand different combinations of literate skill. It also requires learning how to use tools required in a society for producing and using text for communication, self-expression, and collaboration. Principles of effective reading and writing instruction are summarized in Boxes 2-2 and 2-4. Box 2-5 lists practices shown to be effective in the development of writing. Reading and writing involve many shared components and processes. Instruction that includes activities that capitalize on and make explicit the relations between reading and writing facilitates development of a better integrated and mutually reinforcing literacy system.

A sizeable literature on efficacious interventions for struggling learners points to additional principles for teaching reading and writing to this population that include (1) direct targeting of specific areas of difficulty in the context of explicit reading and writing instruction; (2) more intense instruction, more explicit instruction, and even more opportunities to practice; (3) direct targeting of the generalization and transfer of learning; (4)

targeting of maladaptive attributions and beliefs; and (5) differentiation of instruction to meet the particular needs of those who struggle or have diagnosed disabilities in the course of broader instruction to develop reading and writing skills.

Several limitations in current knowledge of component processes indicate that research is needed to (1) develop more integrated and comprehensive models of reading comprehension processes, including metacognitive components, to develop more complete approaches to instruction and assessment; (2) understand the relation of fluency to comprehension and how best to develop fluency; (3) identify efficacious methods for developing vocabulary and other aspects of linguistic knowledge for reading and writing proficiency; (4) develop more integrated models of writing processes and writing instruction; (5) develop methods of teaching reading and writing in tandem with world and topic knowledge in academic, disciplinary, or content areas; (6) understand the neurobiology of reading and writing to test theories and models of typical and atypical developmental processes, develop more sensitive assessments, guide teaching and treatment of disability, and prevent reading and writing difficulties; and (7) understand the social and contextual forces on reading and writing and the implications both for the design of instruction to develop valued functional literacy skills and the assessment of these skills as part of evaluating the effectiveness of instructional outcomes.

Cognitive aging research suggests that adults may experience some age-related neurocognitive declines affecting reading and writing processes and speed of learning that might need consideration during instruction. Most research has concentrated on young children at the beginning of reading development and on older adults at the opposite end of the life span who are proficient readers beginning to experience some declines. As a result, more needs to be known about how reading and writing processes change across the life span to determine how to make instruction effective for learners of different ages.

As Chapter 3 makes clear, except for a few intervention studies, the study of component literacy skills and processes has not been a priority in research with adults, nor has the research fully incorporated knowledge of the practices that develop reading and writing skills in K-12 students. The population of adult learners is highly diverse. Adults bring varied life experiences, knowledge, education levels, skills, and motivations to learning that need attention in instructional design. Research with adolescents and adults will be required to validate, identify the boundaries of, and extend current knowledge of literacy to identify how best to meet the particular literacy development needs of well-defined subgroups of learners.

3

Literacy Instruction for Adults

This chapter describes research on effective instructional practices to develop the literacy of adolescents and adults and identifies needed research. Individuals needing to improve their literacy have diverse characteristics, literacy development needs, learning goals, and challenges to learning. Settings of instruction are wide-ranging and include local education agencies, community organizations, community colleges, prisons, and workplaces. Across these programs and often within a single program, the instruction has diverse aims to help adults attain employment or work skills, career advancement, a general educational development (GED) credential, a college degree, the ability to assist children with school, or other practical life goals. Thus, the first part of the chapter describes the population and the contexts of literacy instruction. Because formal literacy instruction in the United States occurs mainly in adult education programs and developmental education courses in college, we organize the discussion around these two learning contexts.

The second part of the chapter characterizes the state of research on instructional practices for adults. As explained in Chapter 1, *adult* is defined in this volume as individuals ages 16 and older not enrolled in K-12 school, consistent with the eligibility for participation in federally funded adult literacy education. A recent systematic review of research on instructional approaches for adult literacy populations has been funded by the National Institute for Literacy in partnership with the U.S. Department of Education and the National Institute for Child Health and Human Development (Kruidenier, MacArthur, and Wrigley, 2010). In synthesizing the evidence on instruction, we draw on this review, which we then augmented with additional searches of quantitative and qualitative research. We include English language learners and adults with disabilities in describing the population of adults with literacy development needs but discuss the research on instruction with these populations in subsequent chapters. The chapter concludes with a summary of the extent of current knowledge of effective practices in adult literacy instruction and directions for future research.

CONTEXTS FOR LITERACY LEARNING

There are many reasons why individuals seek to develop their literacy skills as adults. Some study to obtain a high school equivalency diploma; others seek to help their children and families with education, health, and other practical life matters; and others seek to learn English or enhance skills for new job responsibilities. Others may have a higher level of literacy but have not yet developed the reading and writing skills needed in college. Adults who wish to develop their literacy receive instruction in two main types of settings: adult education programs and developmental courses in college, especially in community colleges. Two types of adult education are found in college settings: (1) adult literacy programs for individuals who wish to complete their secondary education and (2) developmental education[1] for students formally enrolled in college programs.

Adult Education Programs

The U.S. Department of Education reports that nearly 2.6 million adults enrolled in federally supported adult education programs during the 2006-2007 fiscal year, the most recent year for which complete data are available. Adult education programs are largely supported by federal and state funding, which together provides about two-thirds of the funding for adult literacy programs, according to a national survey of adult education programs (Tamassia et al., 2007). Other sources of funding are local governments, private donations, and, to a small degree, fees and tuition paid by the participants. The U.S. Department of Education's Office of Vocational and Adult Education administers the federal funds, which are appropriated to designated state agencies in a competitive granting process, consistent with the Workforce Investment Act, Title II, Adult Education and Family Literacy Act (AEFLA). Each state must provide matching funds to qualify for this allocation.

The Adult Education Program Survey (AEPS; Tamassia et al., 2007) provides information on a nationally representative sample of adult edu-

---

[1] We use the term *developmental education* (also called *remedial instruction*) to refer to the broad array of services and specific courses provided to college students with weak skills.

cation programs and enrolled learners during the 12-month period 2001-2002.[2] At the time of the survey, 3,108 adult education programs were offered in 29,424 learning sites. More than 1,200 adult education programs funded under the Adult Education and Family Literacy Act participated in the survey. During this period, the median budget for a program was $199,000; with a median enrollment of 318 learners per program, the median expenditure per learner was $626.

According to the survey, adult education programs offer three main types of literacy instruction:

1. Adult basic education (ABE) provides instruction to adults who lack "competence in reading, writing, speaking, problem solving or computation at a level necessary to function in society, on a job or in the family" (National Reporting System for Adult Education, 2001, p. 25).
2. Adult secondary education (ASE) is "designed to help adults who have some literacy skills and can function in everyday life,[3] but are not proficient or do not have a certificate of graduation or its equivalent from a secondary school" (National Reporting System for Adult Education, 2001, p. 25). Adults usually attend ASE classes to obtain a GED or adult high school credential.
3. English as a second language (ESL) instruction is "designed to help adults who are limited English proficient achieve competence in the English language" (National Reporting System for Adult Education, 2001, p. 25).

English as a second language serves the largest number of students, followed closely by adult basic education: 43 percent of adult learners receive ESL instruction, 40 percent receive ABE instruction, and 19 percent participate in ASE instruction. Most English language learners (85 percent) who attend a program attend ESL programs. Of native language learners, two-thirds attend ABE and one-third attend ASE programs.

Instruction is offered in many different places and programs that vary widely in size and number of learning sites. According to the AEPS, local education agencies are the major providers of adult education, offering 54 percent of the programs surveyed, followed by community-based organizations (25 percent), community colleges (17 percent), and correctional

---

[2]The AEPS, funded by the U.S. Department of Education, was designed and conducted by the Educational Testing Service and Westat, Inc., with the involvement of staff of the Office of Vocational and Adult Education and the National Center for Education Statistics.

[3]Since these definitions for adult basic education and adult secondary education were produced, there has been a trend for jobs that pay above a poverty wage to require higher levels of literacy.

institutions (2 percent). And 3 percent of programs were offered by "other" entities, such as libraries, departments of human services, institutions for people with disabilities, and coalitions made up of the various provider types. Community colleges offer the largest programs in terms of the median number of students enrolled.[4] Table 3-1 shows the percentage of program types (ABE, ASE, ESL) offered by each type of provider.

There is not a simple alignment of learning goals with program type or location. For example, English language learners may be taught reading and writing skills in ESL classes in a workplace education setting or in a community college ABE program. Although the major goal of students in both settings may be to increase English language proficiency, the instructional aims will differ, with one focused on meeting specific job requirements and the other on developing more general literacy practices. Similarly, the goal of earning a GED certificate may be addressed in settings as diverse as prisons and volunteer library literacy programs.

Most participants (80 percent) in adult education programs surveyed in 2001-2002 were adolescents and young adults ages 44 and younger pursuing goals related to education, family, and work: 34 percent were ages 16 to 24; 46 percent were ages 25 to 44; 16 percent were ages 45 to 59; and 2 percent were ages 60 and older. Although originally designed for adults, the programs are increasingly attended by youth ages 16 to 20 (Hayes, 2000; Perin, Flugman, and Spiegel, 2006). Nonnative adults participating in ESL programs (those not born in the United States) were somewhat older than native adult learners in ABE and ASE programs, with 60 percent between the ages of 25 and 44 (versus 46 percent for native adults).

The diversity of languages spoken by English language learners points to a need to understand the factors that influence the development of literacy in English for speakers of different languages and respond to the practical challenge of delivering instruction effectively to linguistically diverse learners. According to the AEPS, 57 percent of adults in adult education programs were native to (born in) the United States. English was the home language for 94.7 percent of these adults; Spanish was the home language

---

[4]Community colleges are defined in the AEPS as institutions of higher education (e.g., junior colleges without residential facilities) that offer degrees below a bachelor's degree or technical degrees or certificates, such as in mechanical or industrial arts and applied sciences (e.g., technical colleges). Community colleges also provide continuing education, apart from the college programs, which are the site of ABE programs; college degrees or certificates are not awarded as part of these programs.

Community-based organizations are religious and social service groups, libraries, volunteer literacy organizations, literacy coalitions, community action groups, and other kinds of public or private nonprofit groups. Local education agencies are typically public schools or school districts, which in addition to providing K-12 education offer adult education classes open to all members of the community. Correctional institutions are prisons and jails funded by the state to provide adult basic education services to incarcerated adults.

TABLE 3-1 Instructional Program Types Offered by Each Type of Provider (in percentage)

Program Type	Local Education Agency (54% of programs surveyed)	Community-Based (25% of programs surveyed)	Community College (17% of programs surveyed)	Correctional (25% of programs surveyed)
Adult basic education	36	35	42	52
Adult secondary education	20	11	17	18
English as a second language	44	55	42	31

SOURCE: Data from the Adult Education Program Survey (Tamassia et al., 2007). Data are from a nationally representative sample of 3,108 programs during 2001-2002.

for 4.5 percent.[5] Almost 43 percent of adults were nonnative to the United States (versus 14 percent in the general population in 2002, the year of the survey). Of these adults, 3 percent spoke English as the home language, 62 percent spoke Spanish, 15.8 percent spoke an Asian language, 3.8 percent spoke a European language, and 14.7 percent spoke a language categorized in the survey as "other."

Education

Most native-born adults in adult education have completed ninth to eleventh grade (68 percent); about 14 percent had less education than that, and 20 percent had more (16 percent completed high school or received a GED credential, and 4 percent reported having "some college"). Nonnative learners show a broader range of educational attainment compared with native-born adults; that is, they appear in larger numbers at both the highest and lowest levels of education. More nonnative learners had completed some college (28 percent) and more had completed high school (22 percent), but more also reported having an education lower than ninth grade (28 percent); 17 percent completed ninth to eleventh grade. This variation within and across populations presents an additional challenge to programs that must design instruction for adults with such diverse educational backgrounds and degrees of proficiency in a first and second language.

---

[5]Home language was defined as the first language learned at home in childhood and still understood as an adult.

Learning Disabilities

A portion of adults participating in adult basic literacy studies can be expected to have some form of learning disability that would require differentiated instruction and the provision of appropriate accommodations. There is no consensus, however, on the estimated numbers of adult learners who may have such a disability. The estimates range from one-tenth to more than half (Patterson, 2008). There are no program reporting requirements regarding the prevalence of learning disabilities among participants in federally supported literacy programs. According to the AEPS, only 34 percent of programs reported screening for learning disabilities, and of these, only 4 percent reported using cognitive or clinical instruments. Most—62 percent—relied on self-reports. Thus, it is likely that many adults may have gone unrecognized as having a learning disability, especially older students. Others may have been mislabeled, may not remember or have known that they were identified as having a learning disability, or may be uncomfortable disclosing their learning disability. With this caveat, 89 percent of programs reported providing services to at least one adult with learning disabilities. There is a need for more reliable information about students with learning disabilities in programs and for research on instructional effectiveness to clearly define these samples and identify the practices that promote their progress.

Component Skills

As described in Chapter 2, reading is generally understood to be comprised of the fluent reading of words and sentences and the comprehension of text. One source of information about the component skills of low-literate adults (third to eighth grade reading-level equivalent) comes from a research initiative funded by the U.S. Department of Education, the National Institute of Child Health and Human Development, and the National Institute for Literacy to develop instructional interventions for low-literate adults in adult education programs and to evaluate their effectiveness (see Appendix D for details about these studies). Findings from these studies and other research (see Kruidenier, MacArthur, and Wrigley, 2010) show that adults can have difficulties with any or all of the crucial aspects of reading: alphabetics (phonemic awareness and word analysis), fluency, vocabulary, or comprehension. Thus, it is important to comprehensively assess adults' profile of starting skills to plan the appropriate instruction.

According to these studies, lack of fluent decoding is a source of reading difficulty for a significant number of low-literate adults, especially below the eighth grade reading-level equivalent (Alamprese et al., 2011; Greenberg et al., 2011; Hock and Mellard, 2011; Sabatini et al., 2011). Decoding difficulties are observed among adults performing at each of the six levels of the National Reporting System, the system used to assess the literacy performance of adults in federally funded adult education programs (Mellard, Fall, and Mark, 2008; Mellard, Woods, and Fall, 2011). Thus, even at higher levels in the National Reporting System (NRS), adults can differ greatly in their word-level reading skills.

Three studies have tested whether the reading component patterns of adults match similar models of reading developed with children (MacArthur et al., 2010a; Mellard, Fall, and Woods, 2010; Nanda, Greenberg, and Morris, 2010). These studies suggest that for adults with low literacy, the reading models were not similar. Specifically, low-literate adults appear to lack the fluent integration of word reading, language, and comprehension skills shown by young children who learned to read on a normative timetable. The comprehension skills of the low-literate adults were more similar to those of children with low reading skills than to typically developing child readers, in that they did not generate an integrated representation of the meaning of a passage by connecting words, phrases, sentences, and paragraphs and making inferences using information provided in the text and background knowledge (see the discussion of comprehension in Chapter 2).

The measurement of reading comprehension for either research or practice remains a challenge. As mentioned in Chapter 2, a more integrated approach needs to be taken to the study and assessment of reading comprehension. Depending on the assessment chosen, different subskills of reading comprehension are tapped or assessed to a greater or lesser degree (Cutting and Scarborough, 2006; Hock and Mellard, 2005). Some reading comprehension tests relate more strongly to word recognition skills, others relate more strongly to oral language ability, and the tests have only low-to-moderate correlations with one another (Keenan, Betjemann, and Olson, 2008). Furthermore, the format of the reading comprehension assessment appears to affect test performance (Eason and Cutting, 2009; Francis et al., 2005; Spear-Swerling, 2004). Reading comprehension measures for research and practice are needed with adult norms and that comprehensively assess components of reading comprehension in the context of valued everyday literacy activities.

Despite the capacity of writing to facilitate reading development and the need for adults to be able to write for work, education, and other purposes, writing has not been included in major surveys of adult learners, nor have writing skills been a focus of adult literacy research (Gillespie, 2001). It is known, however, that low-literate adults spell less accurately, their spellings are inconsistent (Dietrich and Brady, 2001), and their errors show more nonphonetic and morphological errors in comparison to the spelling of reading-matched adults (Greenberg, Ehri, and Perin, 1997, 2002; Worthy and Viise, 1996). Adult literacy students also have been reported to have great difficulty with descriptive and argumentative writing (Berry and Mason, in press; MacArthur and Lembo, 2009). Few standard tests of writing achievement are available to assess progress over time with norms for adults, much less adults with basic literacy development needs. The time required to score written compositions can present a challenge to the valid assessment of writing in research and for instruction.

Literacy Instruction in Adult Education Programs

Instructional Time

Information about the instructional practices used in adult education programs is not available from the Adult Education Program Survey, although general characteristics are provided, such as whether the instruction was classroom-based or one-on-one instruction. On average, learners participated in adult education programs for less than 100 hours over the course of a program year, according to the Adult Education Program Survey. Only about one-third of adults made reading gains equivalent to a grade level during the program year. These findings are consistent with the levels of participation and progress reported in the few published studies of interventions designed to develop the literacy of adults with low-to-intermediate skills (see Appendix C) and other information gathered from individual researchers and practitioners working in the field. Reading is a complex skill, and research on the development of complex skills and expertise suggests that about 3,000 hours are required for mastery (Chi, Glaser, and Farr, 1988); 100 hours represent 3 percent of that amount, and so it is likely to be insufficient for learning for many adults, even if the goal is not expert mastery. Thus, one primary reason for limited progress may be that adults lack sufficient amounts of instruction and practice for improving skills.

It is not clear why some adults persist with literacy instruction and others do not. Sabatini et al. (2011) reported that those who persisted with a literacy intervention tended to be older, on average, with poorer basic reading skills. This finding is consistent with the higher dropout rates reported for younger adult education students (Flugman, Perin, and Spiegal, 2003). Younger students who have lower reading scores when entering ABE and GED programs are more likely to drop out of the programs than older, higher skilled students (Dirkx and Jha, 1994). Adults report a wide range of factors that positively or negatively affect persistence in adult education, which include transportation, competing life demands, supportive relationships, and self-determination (Comings, 2009). Reasons reported for dropping out of adult education include family problems, the pace of instruction (either too fast or two slow), health issues, dislike of classwork, and inconvenient class location or schedule (Perin and Greenberg, 1994). About one-third of adult education programs report that they provide noninstructional support services (transportation, child care, psychological counseling) in an attempt to ease some of the barriers that adults experience, paid for with in-kind services contributed by the community (Tamassia et al., 2007).

Literacy Instructors

For all providers, instruction was delivered mainly by part-time staff members and volunteers, with larger percentages of individuals in these categories (versus full-time staff) filling an instructional role (see Table 3-2). The expertise of instructors in adult education programs is highly variable (see Table 3-3 and Box 3-1). According to the Adult Education Program Survey, across provider types, instructional staff is the largest program expenditure; professional development is the smallest. Volunteers deliver a significant portion of the instruction in adult basic literacy programs, and the most commonly reported educational requirement for volunteers was a high school diploma or equivalent. The most commonly reported education requirement for full-time and part-time instructors was a bachelor's degree, followed by K-12 certification. Table 3-3 shows instructor credentials as reported by ABE, ASE, and ESL programs in 2001-2002. It appears that the bulk of instructors have inadequate or no specific training in best methods for teaching in adult literacy programs (see also Box 3-1).

When special needs are considered, the situation is even more extreme (Tamassia et al., 2007). It is vital to use reliable methods to diagnose learning and reading disabilities and to adjust instruction accordingly. Across ABE, ASE, and ESL instruction, about 2 percent or fewer of programs required their full-time, part-time, or volunteer instructors to have special education certification. This problem is compounded by the fact that special education degree programs rarely focus on the needs of adult literacy students.

ESL instructors and the learners they serve face the dual challenge of

TABLE 3-2 Percentage of Staff in an Instructional Role by Role and Staff Type

Instructional Role	Fulltime	Parttime	Volunteer
Instructor	52.1	75.4	60.2
Instructional aid	6.5	8.6	27.2
Instructional support	6.4	5.2	7.8

SOURCE: Data from the Adult Education Program Survey (Tamassia et al., 2007).

TABLE 3-3 Credentials of Instructors in Adult Education Programs by Staff Type and Type of Instruction (percentage of each staff type with the credential)

Staff Type	Type of Instruction		
	ABE	ASE	ESL
Fulltime			
K-12 teaching certificate	28	23	13
Adult education certificate	13	10	6
TESOL	—	—	5
Parttime			
K-12 teaching certificate	49	42	36
Adult education certificate	18	15	12
TESOL	—	—	12

NOTE: The table includes the three most common instructor credentials reported by programs in a nationally representative survey of adult education programs.

ABE = adult basic education; ASE = adult secondary education; ESL = English as a second language; TESOL = teachers of English to speakers of other languages.

SOURCE: Data from the Adult Education Program Survey (Tamassia et al., 2007).

BOX 3-1
Characteristics of Adult Literacy Instructors

Adult basic education teachers

- work mostly part time.
- may leave the field more often than K-12 teachers.
- are often required to teach in multiple subject areas.
- have scant formal education related to teaching adults, although many are qualified and have taught in K-12.
- have in-service preparation as their primary form of professional development.
- are not consistently funded to participate in in-service professional development.
- have access mostly to short-term training and conferences.
- are hindered by systemic constraints from participating in professional development.

SOURCE: Adapted from Smith and Gillespie (2007).

improving both spoken language and literacy skills in English, and, as mentioned earlier, their students speak a variety of languages. This challenge to instructors is expected to grow: U.S. Census Bureau projections show net international migration is likely to account for more than half of the nation's population growth between 2000 and 2015 (Kirsch et al., 2007).

Although some part-time and full-time adult literacy instructors have K-12 teaching certifications and have taught in K-12 schools, evidence suggests that many teachers of grades 1 through 12 do not feel confident in teaching reading and writing and are likely to lack the requisite knowledge and skills. To illustrate, results from a survey published in 1994 on the phonics knowledge of experienced reading teachers showed that only 10-20 percent of the teachers could accurately identify consonant blends in written words, only 21 percent knew what an inflected verb was, and only 27 percent could identify morphemes in a word (Moats, 1994, 2004). Teachers with limited knowledge of language structure will be less able to teach effectively to learners at any age. Furthermore, in one survey, only 32 percent of K-12 teachers whose classes included students with disabilities felt well prepared to address their academic needs (National Center for Education Statistics, 2010a).

With respect to writing, one-third of primary grade teachers have reported that they were poorly prepared to teach writing by their college teacher preparation program (Cutler and Graham, 2008). The number increased to 66 percent in grades 4 to 6 (Gilbert and Graham, 2010), dropped to 47 percent in middle school (Graham et al., 2010) but appears most problematic among high school teachers (Cutler and Graham, 2008; Graham and Gilbert, 2010), with 71 percent reporting that they were inadequately prepared (Kiuhara, Graham, and Hawken, 2009).

Although no data were identified on the preparation of instructors of adults specific to reading and writing, it is reasonable to assume from the information available that the knowledge and skills of the instructors are highly uneven. Many instructors also are likely to have a view of the trajectory for adult literacy instruction that fits better with the world of formal K-12 schooling developed prior to the information age than to adult learners and the levels and forms of literacy needed today.

Technology

Most programs in the AEPS reported having access to educational technologies, although it is not clear how appropriate the technologies were for literacy practice and instruction. Most programs reported having computers, audiovisual equipment, and Internet connectivity; however, it is not evident what access learners have to computers during each classroom session, the supports that would be needed to secure access outside class, and the supports needed by learners and instructors to use technology tools effectively.

Assessment

In the AEPS, programs reported that adult learners were assessed on a regular basis, although the assessments that programs reported using most often were measures to meet federal accountability requirements. The NRS is the system through which all federally supported adult education programs report their annual program data, which must include assessments of learners' progress. Currently, although not at the time of the survey, states must use one or more assessments that have been determined to be valid and reliable measures and programs must administer pre- and posttests in accordance with the test publishers' guidelines. The U.S. Department of Education uses a panel of experts to review the standardized tests annually as part of its process for approving assessments submitted by the states.[6] These measures are for accountability purposes, however, and reliable information is not available about the range of assessments and assessment practices that instructors and programs use to plan the appropriate instruction. A sound approach to assessment to support and monitor learning at the individual, program, and systems levels is systematic, with linkages among the various purposes of assessment and extensive professional training and supports needed to implement the assessments reliably. More information is needed about the methods used for diagnostic, placement, and formative assessment to ascertain adults' skill development needs in order to plan instruction and track progress in component reading and writing skills and functional literacy related to broader learning goals.

Developmental Education Courses in Colleges

The precise number of academically underprepared college students is not known: estimates for community college entrants range widely, from 40 to 90 percent (Perin and Charron, 2006). National data have not been reported on the specific limitations in college students' reading and writing skills. Wang (2009) reported in a study of first-year college students enrolled in a developmental reading course that only 55 percent could identify explicitly stated main ideas in text, only 42 percent could comprehend implicit main ideas, and only 11 percent were aware of a global main idea in text. Similarly, Perin, Keselman, and Monopoli (2003) found in a study of community college students that many students attending the highest level

---

[6]A current list of approved assessments may be found at http://www.nrsweb.org/foundations/implementation_guidelines.aspx [Jan. 2012].

of developmental education had great difficulty identifying the main ideas in text in order to write summaries.

At present there is not a universally accepted definition of college readiness. The policies and regulations that govern eligibility for enrollment in credit-bearing courses, as well as student assessment and placement, pedagogy, staffing, and completion, vary from state to state, college to college, and program to program. There is also considerable variability across types of higher education institutions about the level of writing and reading proficiency that necessitates remediation.

Conventionally, community colleges and other open-enrollment colleges give placement tests to all incoming students and consider anyone above a cut point to be prepared for postsecondary learning. Other colleges may use placement measures for students admitted with lower grades or SAT scores. Placement measures vary across colleges and, among colleges using the same measures, cut scores vary and are adjusted from time to time within colleges for reasons that are not easy to determine (Perin, 2006). Furthermore, it is not clear from research that the placement scores in use or the literacy skills they assess are valid predictors of college academic performance (Hughes and Scott-Clayton, 2011). In research, readiness for postsecondary learning has not been assessed using measures derived from research on reading and writing. In practice, states and test services companies write descriptions of reading and writing capabilities for twelfth graders that currently serve as default standards but have no empirical grounding or predictive validity (e.g., ACT, undated; Grigg, Donahue, and Dion, 2007; Salahu-Din, Perskey, and Miller, 2008; University of the State of New York, 2005). A recent national effort to develop K-12 Common Core Standards includes literacy standards for twelfth grade and may inform future definitions (National Governors Association and Council of Chief State School Officers, 2009).

Developmental education courses are the primary mechanism used to increase students' skills in colleges (Kozeracki and Brooks, 2006).[7] More than half of community college students enroll in at least one developmental education course during their college tenure (Bailey, Jeong, and Cho, 2010). One study of 250,000 students from 57 colleges in 7 states found that, among students enrolled for the first time in fall 2003 to fall 2004, 59 percent were referred for remedial instruction and 33 percent of the referrals were specifically for reading (Bailey, Jeong, and Cho, 2010). Remedial reading and writing instruction in college is widely reputed among education researchers to focus on drill and practice on small subskills

---

[7]Funding for developmental education varies by state. Sources of funding may include state and local appropriations, tuition, and federal funds to the extent that students use federal financial aid to pay tuition (Education Commission of the States, 2000).

without strong linkages to the literacy activities that are part of the college curriculum (Grubb, 2010). Although there are many descriptive reports on instructional practices used in single classrooms and colleges, few quantitative data are available on the outcomes for students.

Alternate or complementary approaches to addressing the skill needs of underprepared college students include "college success" courses, college learning centers, and the incorporation of literacy skill development into disciplinary coursework. College success courses, which are increasingly required for incoming students, do not explicitly teach reading and writing skills but rather college study and research strategies that require the use of reading and writing (Derby, 2007; Pan et al., 2008; Zeidenberg, Jenkins, and Calcagno, 2007). College learning centers provide assistance from peer or professional tutors in a variety of areas that include reading and writing (Brittenham et al., 2003; Gordon, 2008; Hock, Deshler, and Schumaker, 1999; Hodges and White, 2001; Perin, 2004). They also offer legally mandated supports for students with disabilities, which can involve classroom accommodations (Gordon, 2004) or specialized tutoring (Hock, Deshler, and Schumaker, 1999; Mull, Sitlington, and Alper, 2001).

Some college instructors choose to teach basic skills to underprepared students who do not attend developmental education courses to enable them to comprehend and write about what is being taught in a discipline. These instructors intentionally incorporate literacy skills into disciplinary coursework (Juchniewicz, 2007) similar to content area literacy in secondary education (Moje and Speyer, 2008). This type of basic skills instruction is not formally recognized, and it has been referred to as "remediation in disguise," "hidden remediation," and "submerged remediation" (Grubb, 1999, pp. 194-195).

ESL courses are offered in colleges to teach language skills to students with low English language proficiency. These courses tend to be administered separately from developmental education, although they may integrate written and oral language instruction (Kaspar, 1996; Scordaras, 2009; Song, 2006). Between 1979 and 2008, the number of school-age children ages 5 to 17 who spoke a language other than English at home increased from 3.8 to 10.9 million, or from 9 to 21 percent of the population in this age range (National Center for Education Statistics, 2010b). Thus, the proportion of English language learners in higher education is increasing, especially in community colleges (Cohen and Brawer, 2003; Smith, 2010a). College students who are not fully proficient in English include "Generation 1.5" students: these students have a primary language other than English, have attended school in the United States for some period of time, and are fluent in informal but not academic English. They tend not to self-identify, however, as needing to take ESL courses (Blumenthal, 2002; DiGennaro, 2008; Goldschmidt, Notzold, and Miller, 2003; Matsuda, 2003). Those who do complete ESL courses can still require additional reading or writing instruction in college.

We identified no source of information about the qualifications (training, credentials, skills) of the nation's developmental education instructors to teach reading and writing, despite increasing concerns about the quality of developmental education (e.g., Grubb, 2010) and the need to better support the academic progress of community college students (Sperling, 2009; Zachry and Schneider, 2010). In one qualitative study (Kozeracki, 2005), 36 developmental English instructors who responded to structured interviews pointed to challenges that include a lack of maturity and motivation of students to do college work, language differences that may be best addressed in ESL classes, possible learning disabilities that may never have been diagnosed, socioeconomic conditions that make it very difficult for students to progress academically, and expressed student anger over being placed in developmental classes. The faculty from colleges in two states with an enrollment greater than 15,000 students and varied organizational structures for their developmental education programs report that they do not feel competent to address the needs of their developmental education students. The knowledge faculty gain from their own graduate training is significantly different from the knowledge they need to teach developmental classes. Although they hold advanced degrees in their discipline (e.g., English), the instructors may not be familiar with evidence-based techniques for teaching low-skilled readers and writers.

INSTRUCTIONAL PRACTICES AND OUTCOMES: STATE OF THE RESEARCH

Assumptions and Sources of Evidence

As the committee examined the research literature on instructional practices, we made certain assumptions. First, our central concern is to understand the state of the research on effective practices to develop reading and writing skills among low-literate adults and college students, including students who are proficient speakers of English and those who are learning English. Although other populations may need assistance to develop literacy or compensate for declines in their literacy, we focus on research with these populations because they represent the overwhelming majority of participants in adult education programs and developmental education courses who experience particular difficulty in achieving the literacy levels needed for economic, educational, social, and personal success in U.S. society. We do include, however, studies on the out-of-school literacy practices of disaffected youth who are still in K-12 education because these students are at risk for dropout and may eventually attend adult literacy programs.

Second, we recognize that different types of research questions call for different methodological approaches. Questions about effectiveness are best answered with well-designed randomized controlled trials and other controlled experiments, which yield the most interpretable findings. We also reviewed correlational data that controlled for extraneous factors and that were analyzed with such methods as hierarchical linear regression to yield insights about hypotheses to pursue with experimental methods. We included studies that had at least one quantitative outcome pointing to an association between an instructional practice and the learning of reading and/or writing skills. Appendix D describes more fully the procedures used to conduct the research reviews and describes the studies retained for further consideration by the committee. Quantitative studies were excluded if they did not describe specific instructional practices or curricula (e.g., they assessed program attendance on a literacy outcome) or if the outcome was derived from self-report and not a direct measure of skills.

Many quantitative studies of the effectiveness of adult literacy instruction have serious methodological flaws that limit the ability to determine best practice. However, we adopted a pragmatic approach and assumed that, although the research was not of optimal quality for this purpose, it would be useful to examine for themes that suggest directions and hypotheses for future research.

We examined descriptive and qualitative research to reveal the variety of goals, techniques, and materials that are being used and studied in relation to reading and writing instruction. We assume that qualitative research makes the strongest contribution to knowledge when it follows established procedures for qualitative research (e.g., Denzin and Lincoln, 2005) and also systematically (1) states explicit goals for literacy instruction, (2) describes the practices used to achieve stated goals, and (3) analyzes links between observed practices and well-described literacy outcomes. Such findings can provide information for generating hypotheses to test in effectiveness research. We focused our search on identifying qualitative research studies with these features. When used in conjunction with quantitative experiments, qualitative research can provide rich descriptive information about learners and the instructional context, such as how the instructional practices were implemented and the provision of other supports for learning. This information helps to interpret experimental research findings and identify the conditions that may facilitate or hinder instructional effectiveness.

Sources of information gathered include a recent comprehensive review of literature on adult literacy instruction (Kruidenier, MacArthur, and Wrigley, 2010), augmented with targeted literature searches as needed to draw conclusions about the state of the research base and needs for development. These reviews focused on studies of practices to develop the reading and writing skills of adults in basic and secondary education and academically underprepared students in college (see Appendix D; findings in the appendix for adults learning English are discussed in Chapter 8). An additional search was conducted of practices used in programs for adults with low literacy in other countries to identify practices to study with adults in basic and secondary education in the United States. We also explored the literature available on the effectiveness of practices used in programs for disengaged youth.

Orientation to the Findings

Although there is a large literature on adult literacy, the committee found a striking lack of useful, high-quality research for identifying the features of effective instructional practice. There are at least four reasons for this state of affairs:

1. Progress in adult literacy research has been hampered by the high attrition of research participants.
2. The research has lacked systematic focus on the development of reading and writing skills.
3. The research, whether quantitative or qualitative, does not include methods for systematically identifying associations or cause-effect relations between an instructional practice and outcomes.
4. Research funders and thus researchers of literacy have chosen to focus mainly on preschool and K-12 populations, a situation that has constrained the amount of research on how to further develop the literacy of adults outside school.

Despite such shortcomings in the research base, it is important to examine the existing corpus of research to try to understand the variety of instructional practices in use and to identify specific needs for future research on instructional effectiveness.

Our search terms and the other resources from which we draw directly targeted the many disparate types and locations of literacy instruction. We organize our discussion here into the two general categories of instruction for adults in education programs and instruction for academically underprepared college students. We discuss findings on literacy instruction for English language learners and those with learning disabilities in later chapters.

Adults in Basic and Secondary Education Programs

The National Institute of Child Health and Human Development, the Office of Vocational and Adult Education, and the National Institute for Literacy invested $18.5 million from 2002 to 2006 in large-scale research to develop and evaluate effective approaches to literacy instruction for adults with low literacy (i.e., third to eighth grade reading-level equivalent). The research applied knowledge of the components of reading and writing and effective practices validated with children and adolescents in K-12 settings. Appendix D reports details of these studies.

A main finding from this body of work is that the interventions tested with low-literate adults did not differ from "business as usual" in adult education programs, despite being more systematic and structured in their approach. A second finding is that both the interventions and business as usual had small effects or no effects on various component skills. Notably, although the adults in these interventions did show decoding problems, as described earlier, the interventions with a strong decoding component were no more effective in remediating componential or functional skills than interventions without a strong decoding component or business as usual in programs. One exception was a structured decoding curriculum that included an emphasis on spelling and showed gains on some decoding and word recognition measures (Alamprese et al., 2011). Instruction that targeted fluency and comprehension also either produced no effect or gains that did not differ from the gains experienced with the less systematic and structured approaches used in programs.

Thus, it is not clear from this set of studies what range of approaches might be effective in developing skills sufficiently for fluent reading with comprehension. The instruction may need to be more explicit than what was offered in these interventions, with more opportunities for extensive practice. The instruction also may need to target particular areas of decoding difficulty and develop vocabulary to a greater extent, while providing more opportunities to practice and integrate skills in the context of reading actual text with scaffolding and feedback. Low-literate adults show difficulty understanding the meaning of text beyond the word or sentence level (e.g., Mellard, Fall, and Woods, 2010). Thus, they may need to develop the knowledge and skills for making connections across text elements, drawing inferences, and generating an overall representation of the meaning of a text. These adults may benefit from explicit instruction in comprehension strategies and development of vocabulary and background knowledge relevant to the text. All of these hypotheses, which remain to be tested, are consistent with principles of effective instruction for struggling readers from K-12 research (see Chapter 2).

The intervention studies displayed several limitations and constraints that may have affected the results. The researchers reported that instructional procedures were difficult to implement as intended in the context of adult education, given that many participants did not persist to the end of the studies. To combat the high attrition rates throughout adult education programs, some studies tested shortened versions of interventions that are effective in K-12 settings. Furthermore, a sizeable percentage of the participants reported having learning disabilities, consistent with what would be expected from other studies with the population (Mellard and Patterson, 2008). Although several of the interventions were adapted from those that have been effective with children and adolescents with learning disabilities, the interventions or the placement procedures that were used may not have addressed underlying skill deficits. In addition, most of the outcome measures used in this research were developed and normed for children, and patterns of observed adult skills do not fit into the literacy levels available (Greenberg et al., 2009).

Beyond these intervention studies, a coherent and sustained base of research does not exist on the effectiveness of adult literacy instruction. There are only a handful of quantitative research experiments that include outcomes measured with standardized tests or researcher-developed measures of the components of reading (alphabetics, decoding and word recognition, fluency, vocabulary, and reading comprehension) spelling, and writing. One large study compared gains from a variety of instructional approaches in 130 ABE classrooms and found that the greatest gain was found for structured instruction in alphabetics with effect sizes of .37 to .42 (Alamprese, 2009). Most studies use designs, however, that are not adequate for concluding that the instructional approach caused the observed results.

Some studies have reported pre-post gains in terms of grade levels, but the reasons for the gains are not clear, and the amount of gain varies substantially (Gold and Horn, 1992; Gold and Johnson, 1982; Maclay and Askov, 1988; Messemer and Valentine, 2004; Shippen, 2008). There are major problems in using grade equivalents to denote adult literacy levels or progress in the literacy learning of children or adults. Grade equivalent scores do not represent an absolute standard, nor do they represent equal units at different levels of development.[8] For adult learners, some assessment instruments are calibrated to important everyday literacy demands, and the scales from such instruments may be a far better indicator of adult literacy progress than grade equivalents.

---

[8]The misconceptions about what grade equivalent scores mean have been widely noted (e.g., Airasian, 1994; American Educational Research Association, American Psychological Association, and National Council on Measurement in Education, 1985; Miller, Linn, and Gronlund, 2009; Stiggins, 1997). The grade equivalent scale is not an equal-interval scale, although grade equivalent scores are often treated as if they represent equal units. This leads to the common misperception that someone who moves from 2.5 to 2.9, for example, has "grown" the same amount as someone who moves the same number of grade equivalents at a different level on the scale (e.g., from 8.5 to 8.9). Yet the amount of growth in ability needed to move from 2.5 to 2.9 is much greater than the amount required to move from 8.5 to 8.9. Furthermore, because grade equivalent units are not an equal-interval scale, they should not be used in mathematical calculations, such as determining the mean.

All of the gains in research to date are small relative to the amount of gain that would be needed for someone to achieve levels of literacy required for functional literacy (e.g., obtaining a high school diploma or postsecondary certificate or degree). The degree to which literacy gains may be accelerated is not clear nor the rate of gain to expect with engagement in instruction that has been demonstrated to be effective. A priority for research is to experiment with a variety of ways to more fully engage learners for longer periods of time to determine how to maximize literacy gains depending on the particular skills to be developed, the characteristics of the learner, and the features and intensity of the instruction. An additional priority is to develop more valid ways of measuring adults' literacy gains than grade level equivalents with assessments normed for the population and designed to show progress in the specific component skills targeted and related improvements in valued literacy capabilities. One example of this approach is the Degrees of Reading Power (DRP) measure, which is a criterion-referenced assessment for use in grades 1 through 12 designed to measure reading facility needed for valued everyday activities (a specific level on the DRP implies the ability to read a job application, another level implies the ability to read a driving license test, etc.).

A large literature is available on practices used in literacy programs for adults in other countries. Few studies have tested whether particular curricula or pedagogies used in the programs result in better literacy skills or include quantitative assessments of the cognitive and literacy skills of learners. There are notable exceptions, however, that provide insight into practices that may be effective with low-literate adults in the United States (Abadzi, 2003; Baynham et al., 2007; Brooks et al., 2001, 2007). These include an evaluation of a research-based, functional adult literacy program developed and implemented for women in Turkey and evaluations of a program implemented in England (Skills for Life) and Northern Ireland (Essential Skills) as part of a national effort to increase adult literacy and numeracy skills. Many of the findings from these studies are consistent with K-12 research on effective practices for teaching reading and writing. An important feature of the research studies is that they include descriptive information about learners, learning contexts, and available supports to help interpret experimental research findings and understand the conditions that influence instructional effectiveness.

The functional literacy program developed in Turkey aims to develop dimensions of literacy (e.g., word recognition, listening and reading comprehension, writing), cognitive skills (e.g., critical thinking), and functional skills (e.g., performing everyday tasks) (Durgunoğlu, 2000; Durgunoğlu, Oney, and Kuscul, 2003; Kagitcibasi et al., 2005). It also includes components to promote the confidence and empowerment of women in society (e.g., discussion of legal rights). Volunteer tutors who implement the curriculum receive intensive training in literacy and numeracy and how to teach adults and communicate with them effectively. Compared with existing courses, the new curriculum was more effective in meeting literacy skill goals (e.g., word recognition, spelling, reading comprehension), affective goals (e.g., increased self-confidence), functional goals (e.g., being able to find the right bus) and sociocultural goals (e.g., knowing about rights and voting). Affective and societal outcomes were evident 1 year later. Sustaining cognitive and literacy skills depended on the starting levels of skill, with students at higher levels of skill and continued self-study showing more sustained benefits.

In other research, between 2003 and 2006 the National Research and Development Centre (see http://www.nrdc.org.uk [Jan. 2012]) conducted a large-scale pre-post examination of a total of 1,649 adults who participated in programs in England to identify the effectiveness of the literacy, numeracy, and ESL practices that were implemented (Rhys-Warner and Vorhaus, 2007). A study of 298 participants at varied reading levels showed that gains in reading comprehension were modest and highly variable (Brooks et al., 2007). Predictors of progress included starting levels of literacy, self-study outside class, and having time to engage in pair and group work in class.

With respect to writing, for 199 learners studied who received between 40 and 79 hours of instruction (average 51 hours), progress in writing was slow, but several factors distinguished the classes with the greatest increases in writing scores: (1) learners spent time on the composition of texts of different kinds; (2) writing skills, such as spelling, grammatical correctness, and punctuation, were developed in the context of meaningful writing tasks; (3) there was time to discuss the writing process and the writing task; and (4) individual feedback and support were provided as learners drafted, revised, and proofed their work (Grief, Meyer, and Burgess, 2007).

Embedded case studies allowed for a deeper examination of effective instructional practices and point to several predictors of progress that warrant future attention in research with low-literate adults. These include (1) clear planning by the teachers, both strategic and on the spot (i.e., using the opportunities of the moment to teach); (2) explicit framing for the learner to provide a rationale for what is to be learned, the activities to be completed, and how these will help the learner; (3) focusing attention on how language is structured while encouraging and supporting talk in the language to be developed; (4) repeated reviewing and reworking of linguistic items (e.g., new words or structures) in different contexts; (5) professional vision and an understanding of objectives about language teaching and the ability to use and combine materials and activities creatively to work toward these objectives; (6) learning spoken and written language for practical purposes; (7) collaborative group work; (8) safe and fun learning to create a motivating environment that avoids labels and feelings of failure if one's written and spoken language is not consistent with certain standards; (9) avoidance of practices associated with decreased sustained engagement with literacy (irrelevant content, inappropriate teaching methods, inadequate teacher training, failure to take account of students' expectations and needs, poor initial learning, top-down, didactic programs, and discrete skill instruction removed from content); and (10) skilled teachers who have time for professional development.

For some adults in these studies, shorter term deliberate instruction on fluency and phonological processing helped reading comprehension (Abadzi, 2003; Burton et al., 2010; Durgunoğlu, Oney, and Kuscul, 2003). Other adults showed little or no improvement, however, consistent with findings from the large-scale interventions for low-literate adults discussed earlier. These results point to the need to study in detail why progress in developing these skills is slow for many adults and why certain interventions are effective for some adults but not others. Learners reported several factors they perceived to help their progress: peer support, trusting the teacher, and explicit feedback, especially validation of their efforts and progress (Hannon et al., 2006; Ward and Edwards, 2002). Such findings indicate a need to develop various methods of assessment so that learners can continually assess themselves and each other to monitor progress toward learning goals (Dymock and Billett, 2008; Prins, 2010; Ward and Edwards, 2002).

The provision of professional development and support for educators affected program effectiveness (Balatti, Black, and Falk, 2007; Durgunoğlu, Oney, and Kuscul, 2003; McNeil and Smith, 2004). Fostering persistence with learning was a challenge in these studies that was met with efforts to provide programs in communities that are easily accessible by learners (Brooks et al., 2001; Guenther, 2002; McNeil and Smith, 2004). Practices associated with sustained effects on persistence over time include developing learners' confidence and integrating literacy into their everyday lives, so that skills are used in meaningful and relevant ways and continue to be practiced (Aoki, 2005; Brooks et al., 2007; Dardour, 2000; Durgunoğlu, Oney, and Kuscul, 2003; McNeil and Smith, 2004; Prins, 2010; Puchner, 2003; see also Hurry et al., 2010; Thompson, 2002).

Beyond the intervention research we have described, most research in adult literacy education has been descriptive and qualitative (e.g., Kruidenier, 2002; see Appendix D). As mentioned earlier, the research is limited in its ability to identify practices and other influences on reading, writing, and literacy and, in fact, often did not set out to meet such goals. Yet an examination of this research as well as research on practices used with disengaged youth reveals topics that are important to pursue in future research to identify effective approaches to adult literacy instruction. The research often converges with findings from K-12 research on reading and writing and with research on learning.

TOPICS FOR FUTURE STUDY FROM
ADULT LITERACY RESEARCH

Several themes from the available research about adult literacy warrant particular attention as topics for future research on adult literacy instruction: collaborative learning; contextualized instruction; instructional materials; writing instruction; funds of knowledge and authentic learning experiences; and social, psychological, and functional outcomes of literacy instruction. Before describing these topics, we note our examination of the literature reveals a number of popular theoretical frameworks used to guide the development of instructional programs for adults. The primary approaches include andragogy (Knowles, Holton, and Swanson, 2005), transformational learning (Mezirow, 1981, 1998), theories of self-directed learning or autonomy (Garrison, 1997; Tough, 1978), learning styles (see http://www.c-pal.net/course/module4/m4_learning_styles.html [Jan. 2012]), and multiple intelligences theory (Gardner, 1999, 2004). All of these approaches make assumptions about the learning preferences and needs of adults that have not been adequately tested.

Many of these approaches have not been informed by theory substantiated with empirical findings in cognitive science, motivation, developmental science, or neuroscience. For example, there is scant evidence that instruction matched to self-reported learning styles (visual, verbal, auditory) or distinct intelligences (linguistic, logical mathematical, musical, intrapersonal) improves instructional outcomes. In some of the approaches, the concepts are not defined well enough to measure, and findings (and the theories themselves) are underdeveloped even when measurement is plausible. Tailoring instruction to build on a student's strongest skills, as a by-product, also decreases opportunity to build up weaker areas of skill. In general, there has been a rush to apply these approaches in adult education and literacy instruction without empirical examination of their core principles. This is not to say that all of the claims embedded in these approaches are inaccurate. Some claims (e.g., that autonomy and self-direction are important for learning and that collaborative learning and group work are beneficial) are supported by research in various disciplines and thus need further specification and evaluation in the context of adult literacy instruction.

Collaborative Learning

Collaborative learning has been assumed to facilitate learning for several possible reasons. It has the potential to create a sense of community and connection that supports engagement with learning (Sissel, 1996; Soifer, Young, and Irwin, 1989), and it presents authentic opportunities to engage adults in literacy tasks in communities of practice (Street, 2005; Taylor et al., 2007). Collaboration is also hypothesized to develop independence and familiarity with each learner's strengths and challenges that can shape modeling and coaching (Taylor et al., 2007) and provide social support (Tett and Maclachlan, 2008).

It is uncertain, however, whether collaboration works in the ways hypothesized to develop valued literacy outcomes. Findings from K-12 research on reading and writing suggest that collaborative learning activities may facilitate learning under some conditions (see Chapter 2). The conditions that enable adults to benefit from collaboration need to be determined in future research. As others have noted (e.g., Bryan, 1996; Fingeret and Drennon, 1997; Hofer and Larson, 1997; Street, 2005; Taylor et al., 2007), such research must pay attention to setting explicit goals, the structure of the instruction and how groups are established, the literacy tasks used, and the quality of interpersonal interactions in groups.

Contextualized Instruction

Contextualized instruction is of particular interest to adult literacy practitioners both in the United States and internationally (Aoki, 2005; Casey et al., 2008; Guenther, 2002; McNeil and Smith, 2004; Thompson, 2002). The contextualization of skills is defined here as an instructional approach that creates explicit connections between the teaching of reading and writing and instruction in an academic discipline or content area (e.g., science, history, financial management, health, parenting, civics and government, engineering, mechanics). Many terms have been used to refer to contextualization, including contextual teaching and learning (Baker, Hope, and Karandjeff, 2009; Johnson, 2002), contextualized instruction (Parr, Edwards, and Leising, 2008; Wisely, 2009), content-area literacy (McKenna and Robinson, 2009), embedded instruction (Simpson et al., 1997), writing-to-learn (Klein, 1999), integrative curriculum (Dowden, 2007), situated cognition (Stone et al., 2006), theme-based instruction (Dirkx and Prenger, 1997), anchored instruction (Bottge et al., 2007), curriculum integration (Badway and Grubb, 1997), academic-occupation integration (Grubb and Kraskouskas, 1992; Perin, 2001), infused instruction (Badway and Grubb, 1997; Perin, 2001), developmental education learning communities (Weiss, Visher, and Wathington, 2010), workplace literacy (Mikulecky and Lloyd, 1997), and functional context education (Sticht, 2005).

Whatever term is used, the work tends to converge on the themes of (1) teaching skills with direct reference to real-world events and practices (Berns and Erickson, 2001; Carrigan, n.d.; Dirkx and Prenger, 1997; Fuchs and Fuchs, 2001; Goldman and Hasselbring, 1997; Johnson, 2002;

Jurmo, 2004; Karweit, 1998; Orpwood et al., 2010; Sticht, 2005; Stone et al., 2006; Weinbaum and Rogers, 1995) and (2) instruction in the basic skills needed in content courses (Boroch et al., 2007; Martino, Norris, and Hoffman, 2001; Perin et al., 2010; Snyder, 2002; Wisely, 2009). In some cases, contextualization occurs through the merging of basic skills and subject-matter instruction (Grubb, 1996; Guthrie et al., 1999; Paquette and Kaufman, 2008). Furthermore, the connection between basic skills and disciplinary learning is also seen in the newly developed national literacy standards for career and college readiness, which specify competencies for reading and writing in history, social studies, and science (National Governors Association and Council of Chief State School Officers, 2009).

The effectiveness of contextualized instruction has not been sufficiently evaluated for any population, including adult literacy students. Research is needed to identify the features of various contextual approaches that lead to both development of literacy skills and achievement of broader learning goals. A recent review yielded a small body of descriptive and experimental research with adolescents and adults that linked specific instructional practices to reading, writing, and mathematics outcomes, suggesting the value of pursuing this approach (Perin, 2011).

Instructional Materials

Much of the available research on adult literacy describes the use of authentic texts gathered from actual contexts in which adults used these materials (e.g., a workplace, a restaurant) or ways of reading fiction and nonfiction (Beaverstock, Bhaskaran, and Brinkley, 2009; Castleton, 2002; Fallon, 1995; Fingeret and Drennon, 1997; Forell, 2006; Pinsent-Johnson, 2007; Rhoder and French, 1994) and descriptions of how to match a learner with text and "debugging" it to bring it into the "learners' instructional zone" (Rogers and Kramer, 2008). Notably absent from the literature are uses of instructional texts and materials systematically developed to match adults' skill development needs, that connect with the interests of adult learners, and that draw from knowledge of other populations about the importance of reading varied forms of text for development of reading comprehension. The only quantitative study (nonexperimental) of the effects of authentic literature on the development of adults' component skills was designed to study the effects of extensive reading and combined extensive silent reading of authentic literature chosen by students with teacher read-alouds and group discussion to teach beginning readers (reading at grade equivalent 1-3). This approach showed mixed findings. It was associated with increases in expressive vocabulary and fluency but not word analysis, receptive vocabulary, or reading comprehension (Greenberg et al.,

2009). A priority for research is the development of instructional materials and texts and effective practices for their use in developing both adults' componential literacy skills and functional literacy outcomes.

Writing Instruction

A very small body of research focuses on writing in basic education students. Descriptions of instructional practices across studies are consistent with many classrooms adopting versions of the writing process approach first made popular by researchers of children's learning to write, such as Graves (1983) and Calkins (1994) and, at the middle school level, Atwell (1987) (see Chapter 2). The process taught is meant to model what good writers do—brainstorm, draft, get feedback, revise, and edit (not necessarily in a rigid order)—(Beaverstock and McIntyre, 2008; Fiore and Elsasser, 1987; Padak and Baradine, 2004; Weibel, 1994). In most cases, students have the choice of what to write about in process approaches but are encouraged to draw on life experiences for topics and to write in the narrative form (Carter, 2006; Gaber-Katz and Watson, 1991; Moni, Jobling, and van Kraayenoord, 2007; Pharness, 2001; Shor, 1987; Siegel, 2007; Street, 2005; Woodin, 2008). This approach is believed to create feelings of ownership and help students be less reluctant to write (Street, 2005). The approaches sometimes include mini-lessons to teach specific technical aspects of writing (Fuller, 2009) and various forms of feedback (student to student or teacher to student).

The research we identified does not tend to focus, however, on practices to develop adults' writing skill. The emphasis is more on documenting how teachers might help adults feel comfortable with writing, find their voice, develop an identity as a writer, understand how writers write, and use writing to bring about social change than on documenting how teachers engaged students in improving the technical aspects of writing for practical purposes. The instruction stresses writing for self-expression and communication; the process is assumed to be as important as the product. Thus, whether these various forms of writing instruction develop the component skills needed to perform literacy tasks for practical purposes, such as GED attainment, career success, financial management, health maintenance, and fulfillment of parental responsibilities, is not systematically studied and requires further research. Such research needs to consider findings from K-12 (see Chapter 2), which indicate that the process approach to teaching writing works best with professional development, that it may be more effective when combined with explicit instruction to develop specific skills, and that it may not be as effective in developing writing skill for those adults who struggle with writing.

Funds of Knowledge and Authentic Learning Experiences

Research on youth literacy practices suggests several approaches used with youth out of school that might inform the development of instructional practices for adolescents and adults in basic and secondary education programs. The approaches include a "funds of knowledge" framework, disciplinary literacy, cultural modeling, inquiry-based instruction, and anchored instruction. All of these approaches assume that people bring knowledge and experiences as well as literacy practices to learning that educators should understand and use to build new knowledge, support engagement, and establish shared expectations for learning. Curricular interventions that draw from community, family, and peer group funds of knowledge have been developed for elementary school children (e.g., Au and Mason, 1983; Heath, 1983; Moll, 1992; Moll and Greenberg, 1990; Moll and Whitmore, 1993), as well as adolescents (Gutiérrez, Rymes, and Larson, 1995). For example, teachers have used language and concepts drawn from students' lives as a bridge to support their development of deep understandings of academic language (see Gutiérrez et al., 1999) and to build disciplinary knowledge and language (e.g., Lee, 1993, 1995, 2001; Moje et al., 2001a, 2001b, 2004a, 2004b; Morrell, 2002, 2004).

There has been a long tradition of community-based and after-school programs of media-intensive and arts-based instruction, especially for marginalized youth (e.g., Buckingham, 2003; Eccles and Gootman, 2002; Kafai, Peppler and Chiu, 2007; Peppler and Kafai, 2007; Soep and Chavez, 2005). Often drawing on popular cultural forms, including music and film and digital media, such programs include literacy-related skills and practices by immersing participants in language-rich and multimodal activities to reengage youth with learning. Although such programs do not typically measure success via academic literacy gains, research that has compared students who participate in these programs with nonaffiliated youth has suggested superior academic and social performance (Heath, Soep, and Roach, 1998; see Hull et al., 2006).

Social, Psychological, and Functional Outcomes

The qualitative research on adult literacy (see Appendix D) suggests an array of psychological, social, and functional factors that may result from or influence effective instruction to develop literacy skills. Similarly, the ultimate purposes of adult literacy programs in other countries are broad and studies of their effectiveness have included psychological outcomes (e.g., self-confidence, achievement of personal goals), functional outcomes (e.g., better performance at work), economic outcomes (e.g., employment), and social outcomes (e.g., positive engagement with family or society) (Andersen and Kooij, 2007; Aoki, 2005; Balatti, Black and Falk, 2007; Casey et al., 2008; Durgunoğlu, Oney, and Kuscul, 2003; Dymock, 2007; Guenther, 2002; Hannon et al., 2006; Hua and Burchfield, 2003; Hurry et al., 2010; Kagitcibasi, Goksen, and Gulgoz, 2005; Prins, 2010; Prins, Toso, and Schafft, 2009; Puchner, 2003; Thompson, 2002). Far from being tangential, assessments of such broader social, economic, and functional outcomes can help to reveal both the conditions that support effective learning and instruction and the full impact of a literacy program that is measured not only in terms of literacy skill outcomes but greater and more effective involvement in family, work, and society. There is a need, however, to develop more reliable assessments of the full range of social, psychological, instrumental, and functional outcomes associated with effective adult literacy instruction (Dymock and Billett, 2008; Prins, 2010).

UNDERPREPARED POSTSECONDARY STUDENTS

As in adult education, research has not focused on evaluating instructional approaches to improve the literacy skills of underprepared college students; for example, the committee identified only seven small studies from 1990 to 2009 (see Appendix D; Caverly, Nicholson, and Radcliffe, 2004; Friend, 2001; Hart and Speece, 1998; Martino, Norris, and Hoffman, 2001; Rochford, 2003; Scrivener et al., 2008; Snyder, 2002). Most reported small gains in various aspects of literacy, but problems with the study designs prevent drawing conclusions about effectiveness. Only one study included a randomized design; it tested the effects of a learning community approach that produced small gains (e.g., higher pass rates for college placement reading and writing test) (Scrivener et al., 2008). None of the studies compared teaching methods. The number of teaching methods researched was approximately equal to the number of studies; thus, a sustained program of research is not available for understanding which approaches are likely to work well for which students if implemented on a large scale, how to implement the approaches, and the conditions that support effectiveness. Progress in the reading and writing skills that were taught in these studies was not commonly or directly measured.

Similarly, descriptive studies with the population lack sustained and programmatic research on instructional approaches (see Appendix D). As for adult education, descriptive studies of practices used to develop reading and writing skills did not usually describe outcomes or analyze links between the practices and change in the outcomes of students.

A body of work on writing with low-skilled postsecondary students, especially studies focused on text-based analyses and cognitive process approaches, converge with findings from the K-12 literature and warrant further mention. This research has consisted of quantitative experiments, quasi-experiments, and longitudinal correlational studies, as well as content analysis, discourse analysis, and case studies.

Text-based analyses of the writing of college students and English language learners in college have focused on error correction, sentence length and variation, audience awareness, and proficiency with specific genres. These studies report the nature, timing, and modality of feedback on elements of writing (Duijnhouwer, Prins, and Stokking, 2010; Hassel and Giordano, 2009; Morra and Assis, 2009; Sheen, Wright, and Moldawa, 2009; Yeh, Gregory, and Ritter, 2010). For example, the modality of instructors' comments (i.e., written or audio-recorded) (Morra and Assis, 2009) and the type of feedback instructors provide (Duijnhouwer, Prins, and Stokking, 2010) can affect students' abilities to cope with increasing difficulty in assignments (Hassel and Giordano, 2009) and increase their self-efficacy and motivation to continue tasks with difficult writing prompts, although the feedback on progress did not affect students' actual writing performance (Duijnhouwer, Prins, and Stokking, 2010). Several approaches are associated with students' ability to self-correct errors in sentences. Explicitly correcting their errors for them appears to be less effective than explicitly teaching types of error patterns (Shaughnessy, 1979) or teaching students to identify errors in their own writing, using such strategies as reading aloud (Bartholomae, 1980), proofing their own papers with explicit instruction in error labeling (Morra and Assis, 2009), or using online error correction and analysis feedback systems (Yeh, Gregory, and Ritter, 2010).

In the early 1980s, research proliferated on the cognitive processes of students' writing and the problems experienced by students referred to as at-risk, underprepared, basic, or remedial college writers (Hull and Bartholomae, 1984). Often single-subject designs and case studies document writers' cognitive processes using think-aloud protocol analysis and qualitative observations of students' writing. Cognitive process approaches for basic writers have focused on helping students to be attentive to the needs of audiences (Flower, 1979) and become aware of times when they might be prone to writer's block (Rose, 1984) or to overedit their writing (McCutchen, Hull, and Smith, 1987). Students also become aware of "rigid rules and inflexible plans" (Rose, 1984) that limit their abilities to produce the drafts needed to successfully complete assignments. With explicit instruction that targets these barriers to writing, students have produced longer and more detailed first drafts (Eves-Bowden, 2001). With explicit instruction to develop self-regulated learning, students demonstrate a wider range of metacognitive abilities to guide their writing processes (Nuckles, Hubner, and Renkl, 2009). Specific types of mini-lessons also have emerged from this research and warrant further study of their effectiveness with adults. These lessons include drafting to move students from writer-based prose to audience awareness, error identification, and the use of software and approaches to help them develop text and manage their writing process. Consistent with K-12 studies showing the benefit of peer assistance with writing and the positive effect of writing on comprehension and the learning of content, college students who have opportunities to receive feedback from peers about their writing show increased learning of subject matter (Cho and Schunn, 2007, 2010; Cho, Schunn, and Kwon, 2007). These were not students in developmental education courses, however, and thus the approaches need to be evaluated with college students who need to develop their literacy skills.

SUMMARY AND DIRECTIONS FOR RESEARCH

There is a severe shortage of research on effective reading and writing instruction for adults, despite the large population of U.S. adults needing to develop their literacy skills (Baer, Kutner, and Sabatini, 2009; Kutner et al., 2007) and the fact that adult literacy instruction has been offered for many years (Sticht, 1988). The shortage exists for several reasons, including the high attrition rate of research participants, a lack of attention to reading and writing skills as an outcome of literacy instruction, and the use of methods that do not allow for identification of cause-effect relations between an instructional practice and outcomes. More broadly, the field has lacked a comprehensive, sustained, and systematic agenda to produce curricula, practices, texts, and other tools that meet the skill development needs of adult learners. Research funders and thus researchers of literacy have chosen to focus mainly on preschool and K-12 populations, a situation that has constrained the amount of research with adults outside school.

The research that does exist has several limitations, consistent with Beder's (1999) observations more than a decade ago. The high rates of attrition and lack of well-controlled experiments have led to a body of research with small sample sizes and results that are difficult to interpret. The research also suffers from assessments that lack validity for the population; inadequate descriptions of the subgroups of adults being studied; overreliance on self-report; vague or incomplete descriptions of instructional practices, outcomes, and study procedures; and a lack of standards against which to judge the utility and significance of findings (e.g., few agreed-on curricula or standard practices that can be tested, varying learning objectives not linked to standard measures, or expected effect sizes).

Box 3-2 summarizes priorities for research given the limited knowledge of the effectiveness of instructional approaches and adults' learning contexts. The chapter has highlighted additional specific topics that warrant

---

BOX 3-2
Needs for Research on Adult Literacy
Development and Instruction

- Development and testing of motivating instructional practices and materials and noninstructional supports for effective instruction and sustained engagement and persistence with learning.
- Controlled experiments to evaluate curricula and instructional practices with a focus on explicit and systematic instruction, opportunities for extensive practice, and well-designed texts to build language and literacy skills related to functional learning goals.
- Valid methods of measuring component skill and functional literacy gains based on adult norms.
- Qualitative research using rigorous methods to obtain rich description and analysis to point to possible links between instructional practices and learning outcomes, help to interpret findings from effectiveness research and establish the boundary conditions of an instructional effect, and assess implementation fidelity (how practices were actually implemented).
- Establishment of standard research protocols for defining subgroups of learners and generating more complete and comparable information across studies related to the characteristics of learners, instructional practices, the quality of implementation, and instructional outcomes.
- Alignment of standards for literacy instruction, with empirical linkages among literacy activities, goals, and standards, across the programs and systems that provide literacy instruction (K-12, adult education programs, postsecondary education).
- Ongoing collection of educationally meaningful data across the systems that provide literacy instruction on learners' skills, learners' characteristics, the quality of instruction, and learning environments to enable effective instructional planning and delivery.
- Studies to identify (1) learning progressions for diverse subgroups of adults in the context of instruction and (2) how instructional approaches might need to differ at various points in the lifespan and according to the needs of particular subgroups of adults.
- Development and testing of professional development systems to ensure that teachers have the knowledge and skills required to implement instruction effectively and differentiate instruction to meet learners' needs.

---

future study, such as collaborative learning and contextualized approaches to teaching reading and writing.

To elaborate on these priorities, only a handful of interventions have been tested to develop the skills of low-literate adults in adult basic education, adult secondary education, or colleges. Although gains have been reported, they are not substantial for this population either in terms of the size of intervention effects or gains observed against the amount of gain needed to be functionally literate. More needs to be known about the features of instruction and the intensity and duration required to maximize gains for adults who vary widely in their literacy skills.

Except for a few studies, research on component literacy skills has not been a priority and has not drawn on findings about effective literacy instruction with K-12 students. Although research with young children yields information about the targets of instruction and effective practices, the instruction may not always work as well for adults. Research is required to validate, identify the boundaries of, and extend this knowledge for the adult population. For example, it is clear that the adults who read at the eighth grade equivalent level and lower lack sufficient reading fluency to support optimal comprehension. That is, their word recognition processes are slow and divert cognitive capacity from making sense of the text. A substantial number of adult learners lack some word recognition (decoding) skills. Although research shows that direct decoding instruction is effective in developing word reading for most young students, the conflicting findings obtained thus far for adult learners suggest that the approaches used with children may not be as effective. They may not be sufficiently motivating or may not be implemented with the intensity or duration needed to be effective for some learners. Differences in cognitive function at different ages (e.g., size of any short-term phonological store, attentional capacity that might allow the use of strategies that are not possible with children) also may call for different phonemic awareness and word analysis strategies to accelerate progress. Longitudinal studies will be valuable for discovering how the processes of reading and writing might change with age and how instruction to develop reading and writing skills might need to differ at various points in the life span.

Consistent with K-12 research, it is likely that multiple approaches, if designed following principles of learning and instruction reviewed in this volume, may prove to be effective. Regardless of the approach, it can be assumed that the instruction should create a positive climate for adults that draws on their knowledge and life experiences, uses materials and learning activities that develop valued knowledge and skills, and supports adults as much as possible in regulating their own learning. It is also important to ensure that instructional activities to develop such skills as word recognition and decoding are provided when specific diagnostic evidence suggests that they are needed.

Research needs to identify the approaches that are effective for identified subgroups of adults, unless there is evidence that a particular approach works for all. At some level, it is obvious that instruction needs to be differentiated, just as in K-12 research, depending on the particular skills and other characteristics of learners and larger learning goals. Research is required to understand the constraints on generalizing findings across subgroups and how to effectively differentiate instruction. A significant portion of adult learners will have multiple disabilities, including learning disabilities. This fact is inevitable, since K-12 students with diagnosed disabilities have lower literacy levels than students without disabilities (National Assessment of Educational Progress, 2010). This fact suggests both the need for careful assessment to drive choices in reading and writing instruction for adults and the likely need for instruction to overcoming specific reading and writing disabilities. As described in Chapter 2, research with K-12 students does not suggest that reading and writing instruction for students with and without learning disabilities is qualitatively different; rather younger populations with disabilities have benefitted from more intensive, explicit, and systematic instruction that targets specific reading and writing difficulties and the transfer of learned skills, and they require more opportunities to practice.

An important area for research is the development and evaluation of texts and other tools for learning experiences that are linked to well-defined instructional objectives and to adults' skill development needs. Instructors now select and adapt texts and materials with little guidance from research and in an ad hoc fashion. An interdisciplinary effort involving researchers, practitioners, and curriculum developers would help to address the lack of supportive reading materials for instruction and practice. These materials need to (a) be appropriately matched to assessed proficiencies and scaffold the practice needed to become facile in applying component reading skills, (b) present topics of interest to the reader and valued content related to broader learning goals, and (c) draw from research on what is known about practice with varied forms of texts to facilitate reading comprehension.

Any effort to apply what is known from K-12 research should be informed by research on learning with adults (see Chapter 4). For the extrapolations to work, however, and to engender confidence in the proposed approaches, they must be grounded in a theory of learning that is supported and understood well enough to provide a basis for the extrapolation. To date, popular frameworks in the adult education field about how adults learn lack sufficient empirical support, and the theories of adult cognition and learning from psychology and cognitive science have been developed with homogeneous populations and, most often, samples of convenience. Substantial conceptual and empirical work is needed to validate and further develop theories of learning in research studies that include broader populations of adults, such as those needing to develop their literacy skills. Some of this work could be accomplished in the context of research designed to identify effective approaches to reading and writing instruction.

It is difficult to interpret the available literature because the research does not include standard descriptions of subgroups of the population or account for possible group differences in the findings. The adult literacy learner population is diverse in terms of age, culture, languages spoken, learning disabilities, literacy attained to date, educational background, and other life experiences that require systematic attention. In addition, reading ability is confounded with many psychological and social variables that may influence the effectiveness of instruction. For example, reading ability, major depression, and conduct disorders, all significantly predict dropping out of high school, and reading ability in high school is related to minority status and lower socioeconomic status (Daniel et al., 2006). Poor adolescent readers self-report higher levels of depression, trait anxiety, and somatic complaints than typical readers (Arnold et al., 2005). Enhanced descriptions of learners would help to identify constraints on learning that need attention and help to interpret the results of effectiveness research. Similarly, research reports lack critical information about the components of the interventions or how they were implemented. As a result, it is difficult to ascertain the precise nature of the instructional practices that have led to (or failed to produce) gains. A more coordinated approach with established research protocols is needed to accumulate useful information about well-defined subgroups of learners and to produce a more coherent and interpretable body of information about effective instruction.

Qualitative research in adult literacy has suffered from thin descriptions and inadequate analysis of linkages among instructional goals, practices and outcomes. It also lacks attention to component literacy skills. There is an unfortunate alignment of research methods with the instructional goals and practices studied. Qualitative methods are used in studies grounded in sociocultural theories of learning and literacy. These studies focus mainly on social and psychological goals for literacy instruction and not on the teaching of reading and writing skills. Quantitative methods are used in research on reading and writing skills grounded in cognitive theories of learning. These studies focus on explicit and systematic instruction to facilitate acquisition of component skills (e.g., decoding, vocabulary, and comprehension).

If established standards for analytic methods are followed, qualitative research, which ranges from ethnography to basic observation checklists, has the potential to contribute in at least three ways to the identification of effective literacy instruction for adult learners: (1) it points to possible links between instructional practices and learning outcomes; (2) it yields rich descriptions of individuals and environments that help to establish the boundary conditions of an instructional effect; and (3) it helps to assess implementation fidelity (how practices were actually implemented). The research, whether quantitative or qualitative, needs to be designed to establish a clear relationship between an instructional practice and literacy outcomes that incorporate both component literacy skills and functional literacy tasks related to learning goals.

For many adults, the enhancement of component reading and writing skills itself is not the ultimate objective, but the attainment of larger life goals related to career and educational advancement and improvement in the lives of their families. The instructional practices studied in research must have clearly stated learning goals and objectives. These should take into account both the need to develop component skills of reading and writing and the literacy facility needed for education, work, parenting, and other purposes. It is also important to empirically document the particular constellations of component literacy skills needed to perform important literacy tasks associated with larger learning goals (e.g., GED preparation, college entry and completion, fulfillment of parental responsibilities, performance of workplace skills, participation in civic responsibilities).

Although learners across programs share literacy development needs and learning goals, the current system of instruction is a loose mix of programs in many places that lack coordination and coherence with respect to what is taught and how. There also is a lack of alignment to be addressed in the learning objectives for literacy development across adult education, colleges, and K-12 instruction. Adult literacy research is hampered by the lack of a coherent system and established curricula with materials and standard practices that can be tested. An empirical mapping of component skills to literacy tasks and learning goals would offer a basis for aligning literacy instruction across places and systems of instruction and for developing standard instructional curricula and practices to meet the needs of diverse learners across learning contexts.

At present, information is limited from adult education programs and colleges about the specific reading and writing development needs of the adults they serve; the instruction that is used and whether it is implemented effectively; and whether the instruction facilitates development of reading and writing skills needed to achieve broader learning goals. There is a need for ongoing collection across the systems that provide literacy instruction of data on learners' skills, the quality of instruction they experience, and other characteristics of learners and learning environments to enable planning and implementing instruction effectively and the tracking of progress. A sound assessment system is needed to support and monitor learning at the individual, program, and systems levels to plan instruction and track progress in the component reading and writing skills and functional literacy skills related to broader learning goals.

A primary problem to resolve is how to engage adults in the amount and intensity of instruction and practice that is required to develop literacy skills and conduct the needed research. High attrition rates, which are typical of both adult literacy and college developmental education programs (Alamprese, 2009; Comings, 2009; Goldrick-Rab, 2007), compromise the integrity of research findings and can be a disincentive to research. Several factors that are known to affect the amount and intensity of instruction and sustained engagement with learning need attention in future research. As discussed in more detail in Chapter 5, there are several ways in which an instructional approach or environment can affect motivation to persist, among them inappropriate focus or inadequate quality of the instruction, lack of clear learning objectives, failure to be explicit about or to set appropriate expectations about progress, lack of awareness of the progress that has been made, and unwanted identity as a remedial student or low-literate adult. As discussed in this chapter, studies of low-literate adults in other countries also show possible reasons for the lack of sustained engagement with literacy.

Time for learning is usually constrained for adults because of limited program funds and locations (a few hours of instruction are offered a few days per week), participants' work schedules, transportation difficulties, child care responsibilities, and other life demands. Even when personal motivation is high and instruction is appropriately motivating, some subgroups are unlikely to persist, such as those with jobs who need several hours to get to and from a learning site. Some low-literate adults have social service needs associated with poverty (Alamprese, 2009; Tamassia et al., 2007)—teenage pregnancy, physical disability, illness, alcoholism, drug addiction, or domestic violence—(Sandlin and Clark, 2009) that need to be addressed. These various barriers and problems may lead teachers and programs to offer services and advocacy in conjunction with literacy instruction, which, as covariates in impact studies, can be hard to control or measure. Although some amount of attrition may be handled with more effective instruction, expanding the scope of instructional research to systematically account for these other factors and reduce barriers to learning appears necessary if reading and writing instruction is to be effective—and effectively studied—with this population.

Another clear impediment to instructional effectiveness and to conducting the needed research is the highly variable knowledge and expertise of adult literacy instructors (Smith and Gillespie, 2007). Instructors vary in their knowledge of reading and writing development, assessment, curriculum development, and pedagogy. The training instructors receive is generally limited and professional development is constrained by lack of funding, inflexible locations, work, and other life demands. Nonetheless, the instructors must reliably assess learners' skills, plan and differentiate instruction, and select and adapt materials and learning activities to meet the skill development needs of learners who differ greatly in their neurobiological, psychosocial, cultural, and linguistic characteristics. To be effective, teachers will need to have the requisite tools for instruction, the technical knowledge and expertise, professional development, and ongoing supports.

4

Principles of Learning for Instructional Design

Much is known from decades of research with children, college students, and older adults about the conditions that affect cognition and learning and how cognition and learning change across the life span. In this chapter, we describe principles of learning that have sufficiently strong and broad support to warrant their application to the design of instruction for adolescents and adults. We draw on and update several recent efforts to distill principles of learning from research for educators that include

- *Organizing Instruction and Study to Improve Student Learning* (Pashler et al., 2007), an initiative of the Institute of Education Sciences (IES) in the U.S. Department of Education.
- *Lifelong Learning at Work and at Home* (Graesser, Halpern, and Hakel, 2007), an initiative of the Association of Psychological Sciences (APS) and the American Psychological Association.
- *How People Learn* (National Research Council, 2000).
- *What Works in Distance Learning Guidelines* (O'Neil, 2005).
- *e-Learning and the Science of Instruction* and *Multimedia Learning* (Clark and Mayer, 2003; Mayer, 2009).

These reports and hundreds of published studies inform the committee's conclusions about the elements of instruction with potential to support adult learning and the research that is needed to discover how to apply these principles most effectively to improve the literacy skills of diverse populations of adult learners.

There is substantial convergence between the conditions that facilitate learning in general and the principles of effective literacy instruction for typical and struggling learners presented in Chapter 2. This convergence leads to having greater confidence in the findings and further indicates the value of incorporating them into the design of instruction for other populations, such as adult learners. How to use the principles of learning and effective literacy instruction presented in this report to substantially enhance the literacy of diverse populations outside school is an important question for future research.

THE DEVELOPMENT OF EXPERTISE

The ideal culmination of successful learning is the development of expertise. Learners who achieve expertise tend to be self-regulated (Azevedo and Cromley, 2004; Pintrich, 2000b; Schunk and Zimmerman, 2008; Winne, 2001). They formulate learning goals, track progress on these goals, identify their own knowledge deficits, detect contradictions, ask good questions, search relevant information sources for answers, make inferences when answers are not directly available, and initiate steps to build knowledge at deep levels of mastery. The "meta" knowledge of language, cognition, emotions, motivation, communication, and social interactions that is part of self-regulated learning is well developed. The expert learner forms conceptually rich and organized representations of knowledge that resist forgetting, can be retrieved automatically, and can be applied flexibly across tasks and situations. The development of expertise has specific features:

1. Experts acquire and maintain skill through consistent and long-term engagement with domain-relevant activities, deliberate practice, and corrective feedback (Ericsson, 2006).
2. Experts notice features and meaningful patterns in situations and tasks that are not noticed by novices (Chase and Simon, 1973; Chi, Glaser, and Rees, 1982; Rawson and van Overschelde, 2008).
3. Experts have content knowledge that is organized around core mental models and concepts that reflect deep understanding (Mosenthal, 1996; Vitale, Romance, and Dolan, 2006).
4. Experts have the metacognitive skills to think about and apply strategies (Hacker, Dunlosky, and Graesser, 2009).
5. Expert knowledge is tuned and conditionalized, so it includes representing the contexts in which particular knowledge, skills, and strategies apply (Anderson et al., 1995).
6. Experts retrieve and execute relevant knowledge and skills automatically, which enables them to perform well on complex tasks and to free cognitive resources for more attention-demanding activities (Ackerman, 1988).

7. Experts approach tasks flexibly, so they recognize when more knowledge is needed and take steps to acquire it while monitoring progress (Bilalić, McLeod, and Gobet, 2008; Metcalfe and Kornell, 2005; Spiro et al., 1991).
8. Within certain physical limits of speed and endurance associated with aging and health status, experts retain domain-related skills through adulthood as long as they are practiced (Krampe and Charness, 2006).

Expertise is usually difficult to achieve—and for a complex skill such as literacy requires many hours of practice over many years—experts tend to have 1,000-10,000 hours of experience in their field of expertise (Chi, Glaser, and Farr, 1988). With respect to literacy expertise taught in schools, an hour per day from kindergarten through twelfth grade amounts to about 2,000 hours in total, after taking out the inevitable days when no real instruction occurs, which is at the low end of the range needed to gain expertise. Adult literacy learners can be assumed to have missed out on many of these hours or to need substantially more practice. Adults bring varied goals to adult literacy education, but it is clear that given the hours of practice needed to develop literacy skills for functioning well in the realms of work, family, education, civic engagement, and so on, instruction needs to be designed to ensure that learning proceeds as efficiently as possible. Efficiency is especially important considering that adolescents and adults live in complex worlds with many competing demands (Riediger, Li, and Lindenberger, 2006).

Learning involves being proficient with the tools needed to complete the tasks to be mastered and so requires practice with using tools. Tools can be anything from a physical tool (pen, computer, textbook, or graphic organizer) to more abstract tools—such as the appropriate lexicon of a particular domain or knowledge of how people in a domain construct written arguments or literature. Tools can contribute to the development of deeper understandings of a concept or idea by presenting learners with varied ways of representing the idea (Eisner, 1994; Paivio, 1986; Siegel, 1995).

The learning principles described in this chapter vary in their attention to explicit and implicit teaching and learning. Both explicit and implicit learning contribute to the development of expertise in complex skills, such as reading and writing, as illustrated in previous chapters. The principles also vary in their emphasis on promoting initial acquisition of knowledge and skills over transfer and generalization of acquired knowledge and skills to new situations. Initial acquisition involves attention to and encoding of relevant material, so that it can be retrieved from memory or applied to problems within short retention intervals. Transfer and generalization are maximized when acquired knowledge and skills are successfully applied to relevant new situations that differ from the initial context of acquisition (Banich and Caccamise, 2010). It has been widely acknowledged in the cognitive sciences for decades that transfer and generalization can be very difficult or nearly impossible when the surface characteristics of the material and context differ between training and transfer problems and when the correspondences are not highlighted or recognized (Forbus, Gentner, and Law, 1995; Gick and Holyoak, 1980; Hayes and Simon, 1977). For example, Hayes and Simon's classic study shows that college students experienced zero transfer between successive problems that were solved when the problems were structurally identical at a deep level but had different surface features (e.g., missionaries and cannibals versus monsters and globes). Each of the learning principles can be analyzed from the standpoint of ease of initial acquisition versus successful transfer and generalization. However, the principles that favor the latter are far from settled (Banich and Caccamise, 2010).

SUPPORTING ATTENTION, RETENTION, AND TRANSFER

Researchers have identified a number of factors that improve retention of information and transfer of acquired knowledge to new situations. These factors are important for educators and product developers to consider when designing curricula, texts, materials, and technologies and selecting or creating lesson plans for use in adult education programs. For adult learners who have underdeveloped literacy skills, following these guidelines is especially important for ensuring that new concepts are absorbed, even though literacy skill is, to some extent, the ability to overcome the less-than-optimal designs of information sources.

Present Material in a Clear and Organized Format

Novices or those working to further develop their knowledge and skills often need help in attending to the parts of a task that are most relevant to their learning goal. Adults of all ages benefit from a clear (Dickinson and Rabbitt, 1991; Gao et al., 2011; Wingfield, Tun, and McCoy, 2005) and organized presentation that helps them to learn and remember new information (Craik and Jennings, 1992; Hess and Slaughter, 1990; Morrow et al., 1996; Smith et al., 1983). It is important to remove any irrelevant information, even if interesting, that could detract from learning to minimize cognitive load and competing demands on attention (Kalyuga, Chandler, and Sweller, 1999; Moreno, 2007; Van Merrienboer et al., 2006). Seductive details that do not address the main points to be conveyed also risk consuming the learner's attention and effort so that they miss the main points. Visual displays that are hard to read or spoken presentations that are presented in noisy environments can compromise learning because they distract attention away from deeper semantic processing (Dickinson and Rabbitt, 1991; Heinrich, Schneider, and Craik, 2008).

According to the coherence principle, learners need to get a coherent, well-connected representation of the main ideas to be learned. Providing structure and organization is important to help them understand concepts and how they relate to one another. The particular method used to organize ideas depends on the relations to be depicted. Outlines can be used to show structural hierarchies (Ausubel, 1968). Graphic organizers show the structure of interrelated ideas pictorially, with ideas represented as concepts in circles and relationships as lines that connect the circles (Vitale and Romance, 2007). Tables can be used to organize ideas in two or three dimensions, and diagrams can help to convey more complex relationships.

According to the contiguity principle, materials and lesson plans should be organized so that the elements and ideas to be related are presented near each other in space and time (Clark and Mayer, 2003; Mayer, 2005; Mayer and Moreno, 2003). For example, the verbal label for a picture needs to be placed spatially near the picture on the display, not on the other side of the screen. An explanation should be given at the time a concept is depicted rather than many minutes, hours, or days later. According to the segmentation principle, new material should be presented in discrete units so that new learners are not overwhelmed with too much new information at once.

Use Multiple and Varied Examples

There is substantial evidence that knowledge, skills, and strategies acquired across multiple and varied contexts are better generalized and applied flexibly across a range of tasks and situations (Atkinson, 2002; Catrambone, 1996; Paas and van Merrienboer, 1994; Schmidt and Bjork, 1992; Spiro et al., 1991). Memories are triggered by multiple cues so knowledge is available when needed. Acquisition can be slower, but learners retain and transfer their knowledge and skills better than if learned only in one context (Swezy and Llaneras, 1997).

Present Material in Multiple Modalities and Formats

Information is encoded and remembered better when it is delivered in multiple modes (verbal and pictorial), sensory modalities (auditory and visual), or media (computers and lectures) than when delivered in only a single mode, modality, or medium (Clark and Mayer, 2003; Kalchman and Koedinger, 2005; Kozma, 2000; Mayer, 2009; Mayer and Moreno, 2003; Moreno and Mayer, 2007; Paivio, 1986). For example, it is effective to combine graphics with text, graphics with spoken descriptions, speech sounds with printed words, and other combinations of modalities. Graphic depictions with spoken descriptions are particularly effective for subject matter in science and technology (Mayer, 2009). Multiple codes provide richer and more varied representations that allow more memory retrieval routes.

However, implementation of this principle must be balanced against Principle 1: the amount of information should not overwhelm the learner to the point of attention being split or cognitive capacities being overloaded (Kalyuga, Chandler, and Sweller, 1999; Mayer and Moreno, 2003; Moreno, 2007; Sweller and Chandler, 1991). There needs to be a careful selection of the pictures, graphs, or other visual representations in order to be relevant to the material being taught. Graphics do not have to be completely realistic to be useful; sometimes a more abstract or schematic picture will best illustrate a key idea, whereas a more photorealistic graphic may actually distract the learner with details that are irrelevant to the main point. There is also substantial evidence that memory retention increases when a person studies the material at deeper, semantic levels of processing than exclusively at the surface levels of processing (Craik and Lockhart, 1972; Kintsch et al., 1990).

There is some evidence that, with aging, learners can increasingly benefit from the environmental support provided by augmenting the material to be learned with multimodal presentations (Craik and Jennings, 1992; Luo et al., 2007). However, multimodal presentations can be relatively less effective for older adults if the information across modalities is difficult to integrate (Luo et al., 2007; Stine, Wingfield, and Myers, 1990).

Teach in the Zone of Proximal Development

According to Vygotsky's (1986) concept of the zone of proximal development (ZPD), the effectiveness of a text, technology, tutor, or instructional approach in promoting learning can be assessed by comparing performance with and without the supports provided in the intervention. Does the intervention allow the person to perform better than they would have been able to without the particular material, tool, or approach to instruction? There is moderate evidence that the answer depends partly on the selection of learning goals, materials, and tasks, which should be sensitive to what the student has mastered and be appropriately challenging—not too easy or too difficult, but just right (Metcalfe and Kornell, 2005; VanLehn et al., 2007; Wolfe et al., 1998).

Consider a text used to help an adult learn about a medical procedure: if the text is extremely easy and overlaps perfectly with what readers already know, then the text will not stretch their knowledge beyond what they already knew without the text. Similarly, the adult will not gain much medical knowledge by reading a text that is too complex and riddled with technical jargon far beyond what he or she can handle. People will learn most from a text that appeals to some of what they already know and expands knowledge in a way that is neither too challenging nor redundant.

Individualized student instruction is expected to be more effective when it takes into account the ZPD of individual learners. The U.S Common Core Standards for reading and writing have adopted the ZPD principle by proposing that text assignments push the envelope on text difficulty, as reflected in Lexile scores and other text characteristics, but not too much beyond what the student can handle. Evidence is accumulating that reading skills are acquired better when interventions consider the characteristics of individual learners. This has been demonstrated for beginning reading in children, in that some types of readers benefit from one instructional method and other types of readers benefit from another (Connor et al., 2007). In that research, Assessment to Instruction (A2i) web-based software was used to compare students' lexical decoding skills (i.e., letter and word reading skills) and vocabulary. Instruction methods were differentially effective depending on the readers' starting skill levels on these dimensions. Readers with low lexical decoding benefited most from explicit teacher-managed code-focused instruction; this instruction was not helpful to readers with higher lexical decoding skills but low vocabulary. Readers with low vocabulary needed a combination of explicit teacher-managed code-focused instruction and explicit meaning-focused instruction. Those with high vocabulary benefited from explicit meaning-focused instruction or independent reading. Indeed, students with high lexical decoding skills and vocabulary would best be left alone to conduct independent reading on topics they are interested in.

Several factors affect growth experienced in the ZPD. First, having more knowledge about the domain to be learned can increase the efficiency of learning (Beier and Ackerman, 2005; Miller, 2009; Miller, Cohen, and Wingfield, 2006; O'Reilly and McNamara, 2007). During adulthood (in contrast to childhood) knowledge is highly individualized (Ackerman, 2008), so instruction should first assess and then build on the knowledge the learner already has. Finally, gradual age-related declines in speed of processing, attentional control, associative binding, and working memory may decrease learning efficiency (Hertzog et al., 2008; Myerson et al., 2003; Park et al., 2002; Waszak, Li, and Hommel, 2010), so slower pacing or more practice or both may be required to reach a given level of performance.

Space Presentations of New Material

It is better to distribute the presentation of materials and tests over time than to concentrate the learning experiences within a short time span (Bahrick et al., 1993; Bloom and Shuell, 1981; Cepeda et al., 2006; Cull, 2000; Rohrer and Taylor, 2006). When studying for an exam, it is better to space the same amount of study over days and weeks than to cram it into a single study session the night before the test. Spaced practice has been shown to be advantageous for adults of a variety of ages (Kausler, Wiley, and Philips, 1990; Kornell et al., 2010; Logan and Balota, 2009).

Reexposure to course material after a delay often markedly increases the amount of information that students remember. Delayed reexposure can be promoted through homework assignments, in-class reviews, quizzes, and other instructional exercises (Pashler et al., 2007). Evidence for this principle is primarily based on memory for isolated information units (such as facts or vocabulary definitions). However, there is evidence that rereading can enhance metacomprehension skills and long-term retention of text material, especially if it is spaced and especially for low-ability students (Griffin, Wiley, and Thiede, 2008; Rawson and Kintsch, 2005; Rawson, Dunlosky, and Thiede, 2000).

Test on Multiple Occasions, Preferably with Spacing

There is substantial evidence that periodic testing helps learning and slows down forgetting (Bangert-Drowns et al., 1991; Bjork, 1988; Butler and Roediger, 2007; Dempster, 1997; Karpicke and Roediger, 2007; McDaniel, Roediger, and McDermott, 2007; McDaniel et al., 2007; Roediger and Karpicke, 2006). One indirect benefit is that regular testing, which can be quite brief and embedded in instructional materials, keeps students constantly engaged in the material and guides instructors or computers in making decisions about what to teach (Shute, 2008). The precise frequency of testing presumably depends on the nature of materials to be learned. Students benefit more from repeated testing when they expect a final exam than when they do not expect one (Szupnar, McDermott, and Roediger, 2007). Spacing retrieval has been shown to improve performance for adults from a wide age range (Bishara and Jacoby, 2008).

Ground Concepts in Perceptual-Motor Experiences

There is substantial evidence that it is important to link concepts to be read or learned to concrete perceptions and actions (Glenberg and Kaschak, 2002; Glenberg and Robertson, 1999; Glenberg et al., 2004; Piaget, 1952). For example, when reading instructions on assembling a piece of furniture, it helps to be able to view and hold the parts while reading the instructions. Perceptual-motor experience is particularly important when there is a need for precision of ideas and communication and when a concept is first introduced. Some cognitive frameworks have emphasized the importance of grounding comprehension and learning in perceptual-motor experience (called embodied cognition), but there is a debate on the role of abstract representations and symbols in comprehension in addition to the embodied perceptual-motor representations (de Vega, Glenberg, and Graesser, 2008; Glenberg, 1997). As noted below, there is some evidence that it is effective to integrate abstract with concrete representations of concepts. It is critical to keep in mind that new knowledge is built on and interpreted in light of existing knowledge, and much knowledge comes from everyday activities. Building atop barely learned and abstract ideas is much more difficult and error-prone than building atop well-learned concepts that are experienced daily.

Stories and other types of narrative are usually about everyday experiences and create perceptual-motor memories similar to daily experience. There is substantial evidence that stories are easier to read, comprehend, and remember than other types of learning materials (Bower and Clark, 1969; Casey et al., 2008; Graesser and Ottati, 1996; Rubin, 1995). For many millennia, the primary way of passing wisdom down from generation to generation was through stories. Stories have concrete characters, objects, locations, plots, themes, emotions, and actions that bear some similarity to everyday experiences and are natural packages of knowledge (Bower, Black, and Turner, 1979; Graesser, Olde, and Klettke, 2002).

It is interesting to note that active experiencing, a theatrical technique in which dialogue is learned by acting out scenes with physical and emotional expression, facilitates learning large passages of dialogue without explicit memorization (Noice and Noice, 2006, 2008; Noice et al., 1999; Noice, Noice, and Kennedy, 2000). This finding is consistent with the notion that stories are easier to understand and remember partly because of the generation of perceptual-motor memories similar to the memories of everyday experience. Perceptual-motor memory is well preserved, if not enhanced, in adulthood (Dijkstra et al., 2004; Radvansky and Djikstra, 2007; Radvansky et al., 2001) and performing actions related to material to be remembered enhances memory for adults in a wide age range (Bäckman and Nilsson, 1985; Feyereisen, 2009). Thus, stories may be powerful tools for practicing and building comprehension skills and developing and reinforcing background knowledge across the life span.

At the same time, there also is a tendency for other genres than narratives to be underused in literacy instruction, and literacy does require the ability to handle a number of forms other than stories. In order to acquire the ability to read and write in other forms, practice on those forms will be required.

SUPPORTING GENERATION OF CONTENT AND REASONING

Interventions are needed that encourage the learner to actively generate language, content, and patterns of reasoning rather than passively processing the material delivered by the learning environment. Learning is enhanced when learners have to organize the information themselves and exert cognitive effort during acquisition or retrieval. Simply put, it is the student who should be doing the acting, thinking, talking, reading, and writing for learning. Encouraging learners to engage in deeper levels of thinking and reasoning is especially helpful to adults needing to develop these skills for education, work, and other purposes involving complex materials and tasks.

Encourage the Learner to Generate Content

Learning is enhanced when learners produce answers themselves instead of reading or recognizing them (Chi, Roy, and Hausmann, 2008; National Research Council, 2000; Tulving, 1967). This fact explains why free recall or essay tests that require the test-taker to generate answers with minimal cues often produce better retention than recognition tests and multiple-choice tests in which the learner only needs to be able to recognize correct answers. It also explains why tutors learn more than tutees in peer tutoring when students start out on an even playing field (Fuchs et al., 1994; Mathes and Fuchs, 1994; Topping, 1996). Learner-generated content can lack detail and contain misconceptions, however, that need to be monitored to ensure adequate learning and to prevent learning incorrect information.

Strategies that require learners to be actively engaged with reading material also produce better retention over the long term (McNamara, 2007a, 2007b; Pressley et al., 1998). Learners can, for example, develop their own mini-testing situations as they review material, such as stating the information in their own words (without viewing the text) and synthesizing information from multiple sources, such as from class and textbooks (Bjork, 1994). Programs exist to help students learn to do this (Beck and McKeown, 2006). Although the strategies require cognitive effort, their use is important to encourage since they improve learning and are underdeveloped in many children and adults (Pearson and Duke, 2002; Pressley, 2002; Snow, 2002). For complex and coherent bodies of material, outlining, integrating, and synthesizing information produce better learning than rereading materials or other more passive strategies.

There is evidence that adults from a wide age range benefit from content generation to improve learning (Johnson, Schmitt, and Pietrukowicz, 1989; Mitchell et al., 1986; Taconnat et al., 2008). Past their 20s, learners slowly may become less likely to spontaneously generate content that is rich, elaborative, and distinctive if they are learning in a domain outside their previous knowledge and experience; consequently, more contextual support may be needed as the learner generates content to optimize the benefits of generation (Dunlosky, Hertzog, and Powell-Moman, 2005; Luo, Hendricks, and Craik, 2007).

Encourage the Generation of Explanations, Substantive Questions, and the Resolution of Contradictions

There is substantial evidence that learning is facilitated by constructing explanations and arguments (Ainsworth and Loizou, 2003; Anderson et al., 2001; Chi et al., 1994; Magliano, Trabasso, and Graesser, 1999; McNamara, 2004; McNamara and Magliano, 2008; Reznitskaya et al., 2008; VanLehn et al., 2007). Explanations consist of causal analyses of events, logical justifications of claims, and functional rationales for actions. Explanations provide coherence to the material and justify why information is relevant and important. Students may be prompted to give self-explanations of material by thinking aloud or answering questions that elicit explanations connecting the material to what they already know. The self-explanations of students can be improved by explicit instruction on self-explanations and by setting up collaborations with a student or tutor to help with the process of constructing useful explanation. Studying good explanations facilitates deeper comprehension, learning, memory, and transfer.

Explanations of material and reasoning are elicited by deep questions, such as why, how, what-if, and what-if not, as opposed to shallow questions that require the learner to simply fill in missing words, such as who, what, where, and when (Graesser and Person, 1994). There is substantial evidence that training students to ask deep questions facilitates comprehension of material from text, classroom lectures, and electronic media (Beck et al., 1997; Craig et al., 2006; Dillon, 1988; King, 1994; Pressley et al., 1992; Rosenshine, Meister, and Chapman, 1996). The learner gets into the mindset of having deeper standards of comprehension (Baker, 1985), and the resulting representations are more elaborate.

One method of stimulating thought, content generation, and reasoning is to present some challenges, obstacles, or contradictions that place the learner in "cognitive disequilibrium." The occurrence of cognitive disequilibrium is anticipated by instructors who purposefully select topics, texts, and questions that clash with the students' knowledge, beliefs, or attitudes. Cognitive disequilibrium is confirmed when students ask relevant questions

(Graesser and McMahen, 1993; Rosenshine, Meister, and Chapman, 1996), when a classroom launches into a spirited discussion addressing the challenge (Nystrand, 2006), and when students exhibit facial expressions of confusion (D'Mello and Graesser, 2010). Such "desirable difficulties" slow down initial learning but promote long-term retention and transfer (Bereiter and Scardamalia, 1985; Bjork, 1988, 1999; Bjork and Linn, 2006). Presenting a challenging problem before students read a text can stimulate inquiry, curiosity, thinking, deep questions, and deeper learning during text comprehension (Schwartz and Bransford, 1998). Cognitive disequilibrium and questions occur when there are obstacles to goals, contradictions, conflicts, anomalous events, failures of the text to satisfy a task need, salient gaps in knowledge, uncertainty, equally attractive alternatives, and other types of impasses (Chinn and Brewer, 1993; Graesser and McMahen, 1993; Graesser and Olde, 2003). When these impasses occur, adaptive learners engage in reasoning, thought, problem solving, and planning en route to restoring cognitive equilibrium. Adaptive readers slow down and construct elaborations or explanations while reading misconceptions, contradictions, and false information (Kendeou and Van den Broek, 2007; O'Brien et al., 1998; Rapp, 2008).

However, it is noteworthy that readers often do not notice blatant contradictions (e.g., burying survivors, tranquilizing stimulants) that on second glance appear to be quite obvious (Daneman, Lennertz, and Hannon, 2006; Hannon and Daneman, 2004). Less skilled readers are more vulnerable to such shallow processing, so that explicit instruction and practice in monitoring coherence and self-explanation (McNamara and Magliano, 2009) may be useful.

Encourage the Learner to Construct Ideas from Multiple Points of View and Different Perspectives

There is moderate evidence that opportunities to consider multiple viewpoints and perspectives about a phenomenon contribute to understanding a concept and to greater cognitive flexibility in accessing and using the concept in a range of contexts. If a concept is understood in only a specific and rigid manner, it will be encoded, accessed, and used in a more restricted way. Cognitive flexibility increases when interventions support multiple layers of knowledge that interconnect facts, rules, skills, procedures, plans, and deep conceptual principles (Spiro et al., 1991). The cognitive complexity and multiple viewpoints are believed to be helpful when learners need to transfer knowledge and skills to tasks that have unique complexities that cannot be anticipated.

Two examples illustrate attempts to promote multiple points of view and perspectives. Kozma (2000) developed a computerized learning environment for chemistry that shows four different viewpoints simultaneously during the course of a chemical reaction, such as the action of a person mixing chemicals in beakers, the action of molecules, mathematical formulae, and graphs that plot measures over time. The extent to which a student views the different perspectives depends on their preferences and prior training, so their mental models do not necessarily converge on a single correct understanding. As another example, readers who comprehend stories can be instructed to adopt the perspectives of different characters and their resulting recall protocols and story representations end up being quite different (Anderson and Pichert, 1978). Readers eventually can be trained to adopt multiple character viewpoints while reading stories and thereby achieve greater cognitive flexibility.

Laboratory experiments and classroom studies have shown the benefits of connecting and interleaving both abstract and concrete representations of problems at the K-12 and college levels, particularly in the domains of mathematics, science, and technology (Bottge et al., 2007; Goldstone and Sakamoto, 2003; Goldstone and Son, 2005; Sloutsky, Kaminisky, and Heckler, 2005). Students have an easier time acquiring an initial understanding of a concept presented in a concrete form, but they also need a more abstract symbolic representation to apply that knowledge in a different context. So, for example, when most college students read texts on physics and technology, they do not acquire a deep enough representation or understanding to support inferences and the building of situation models without some pedagogical activities that encourage multiple representations and cognitive flexibility (VanLehn et al., 2007; Wiley et al., 2009).

COMPLEX STRATEGIES, CRITICAL THINKING, INQUIRY, AND SELF-REGULATED LEARNING

Students often lack the knowledge, skills, and meta-awareness needed to focus attention on content relevant to a task or goal, to comprehend text, to study material sufficiently, or to perform effectively on complex cognitive tasks. In particular, reading strategies at deeper levels are underdeveloped in many children and adults, especially for expository text, so they would benefit from comprehension strategy training (McNamara, 2007a; Pearson and Duke, 2007; Pressley, 1998; Snow, 2002).

Structure Instruction to Develop Effective Use of Complex Strategies

There is moderate evidence that complex strategies can be acquired by well-engineered instruction that is structured, explicit, scaffolded, and intensive. Scaffolded instruction is the systematic selection and sequencing of content, materials, and tasks that both prompt the student to provide information and deliver relevant information to achieve learning. This is well documented for comprehension strategy instruction (McNamara, 2007b; Pressley, 2000; Williams et al., 2009; Williams, Hall, and Lauer, 2004). The instruction typically goes from simple to complex, with substantial practice at each step. It incorporates meaningful and interactive tasks, as well as clear templates that exhibit instruction points.

Strategies of solving mathematical problems can also be acquired by observing experts solving example problems step by step or by interleaving worked example solutions with problem-solving exercises. That is, students learn more by alternating between studying examples of worked-out problem solutions and solving similar problems on their own than they do when just given problems to solve on their own (Catrambone, 1996; Cooper and Sweller, 1987; Kalyuga et al., 2001; Pashler et al., 2007). Procedural skills can be modeled effectively through modeling-scaffolding-fading (McNamara, 2007a; Renkl, Atkinson, and Grosse, 2004; Renkl et al., 2002; Rogoff, 1990; Rogoff and Gardner, 1984): the expert first models the solution, then the student tries with periodic feedback and scaffolding from the expert, and then the expert assistance eventually fades. Strategies of argumentation can be developed from structured practice with argument stratagems in collaborative reasoning that transfer to writing (Anderson et al., 2001; Reznitskaya et al., 2008). One central question is how much learning of knowledge, strategies, and skills can be acquired through information delivery and scripted exercises without the more flexible and interactive scaffolding (Connor et al., 2007; McNamara, 2007b).

There is some evidence that adults from a wide age range can benefit from instruction in memory monitoring strategies to improve memory performance (Dunlosky, Kubat-Silman, and Hertzog, 2003). Mnemonic training, especially if embedded in otherwise valued classroom literacy activities, may be more effective in augmenting the repertoire of memory skills of adolescents and young adults than of children (Brehmer et al., 2007, 2008). Although even older adults benefit, it is possible that age-related decreases in fluid abilities may slow the acquisition of new strategies in later life (Brehmer et al., 2007, 2008; Hertzog et al., 2008).

It is well documented that both children and adults can experience serious limitations in metacognition (Hacker, Dunlosky, and Graesser, 2009)—their ability to understand, assess, and act on the adequacy of their memory, comprehension, learning, planning, problem-solving, and decision processes. One would expect children to have limited metacognitive knowledge, but it is somewhat remarkable that adults also have limited metacognitive proficiency after their years of experience. More specifically, the vast majority of adults are not good at judging their own comprehension of text (Dunlosky and Lipko, 2007; Maki, 1998). They also are not good at planning, selecting, monitoring, or evaluating their strategies for self-regulated learning (Azevedo and Cromley, 2004; Azevedo and Witherspoon, 2009; Winne, 2001), inquiry learning (Graesser, McNamara, and VanLehn, 2005; White and Frederiksen, 2005), or discovery learning (Kirschner, Sweller, and Clark, 2006; Klahr, 2002). Therefore, explicit training, modeling, and guided practice are needed before students acquire adequate strategies of comprehension, critical thinking, metacomprehension, self-regulated learning, and discovery learning (Dunlosky and Hertzog, 1998). Domain knowledge can also enhance self-regulated learning (Griffin, Jee, and Wiley, 2009).

Combine Complex Strategy Instruction with Learning of Content

There is moderate evidence that strategy instruction should be deeply integrated with subject-matter content rather than being lists of abstract rules or scripted procedures that ignore the content (National Research Council, 2000). For example, it is a good strategy for readers to be asking the question "why" when reading texts because it encourages the student to build explanations of the content. This strategy is ideally implemented across the curriculum, so students ask such questions as why catalysts are important when reading a chemistry text, why the Spanish-American War was important in U.S. history, why an action of a character in a novel has a particular motive, and why an author bothers to describe the layout of a city. Substantial subject-matter knowledge is needed to effectively apply many reading strategies because comprehension involves the integration of prior knowledge and text.

Many reading researchers claim that comprehension skills and strategies are facilitated when they are embedded in content areas (e.g., science, history, social studies) (Duke and Pearson, 2002; Guthrie et al., 2004; Moje, 2008b; Neufeld, 2005; Pearson and Duke, 2002; Pressley, 2002; Williams et al., 2009), although some claim that more evidence should be amassed to have greater certainty (Lee et al., 2006). Comprehension can improve after instruction on the structure of expository text, such as compare-contrast, problem-solution, cause-effect, description, sequence, and other rhetorical frames (Chambliss, 1995; Meyer and Poon, 2001; Williams, Hall, and Lauer, 2004; Williams et al., 2005, 2009). Such structure training, which is often contextualized in subject matter, can improve comprehension for adults from a wide age range (Meyer and Poon, 2001; Meyer, Young, and Bartlett, 1989).

FEEDBACK

Feedback affects learning in a number of ways that are well documented (Azevedo and Bernard, 1995; Kluger and DiNisi, 1996; Shute, 2008). Adults from young to old can take advantage of feedback to acquire new skills (Hertzog et al., 2007; Stine-Morrow, Miller, and Nevin, 1999; West, Bagwell, and Dark-Freudeman, 2005). Feedback helps learners fine-tune their knowledge, skills, and strategies. It can be explicitly delivered by people or computers (supervised learning), or it can be implicitly provided in situations that are engineered to make knowledge and skill gaps evident to the learner (unsupervised learning). The feedback may identify and possibly correct inaccurate skills (bugs) and misconceptions (errors of commission) or may identify missing information (errors of omission).

Accurate and Timely Feedback Helps Learning

There is substantial evidence that students benefit from feedback on their performance in a learning task, but the optimal timing of the feedback depends on the task (Pashler et al., 2005; Shute, 2008). Immediate feedback has the advantage of maximizing contiguity of correct information and of preventing elaboration of incorrect information. Just as people learn correct information from accurate feedback, they also can learn incorrect information. For example, when incorrect alternatives on multiple-choice tests are presented, the wrong answers can be learned instead of the correct answers (Butler and Roediger, 2007; Roediger and Marsh, 2005; Toppino and Luipersbeck, 1993), and accuracy may be compromised as a function of the number of distracters (Roediger and Marsh, 2005). This may also occur for true-false tests (Toppino and Brochin, 1989) and when misconceptions are planted in texts (Kendeou and van den Broek, 2005). These effects can be reduced when learners receive feedback immediately after a test (Butler, Karpicke, and Roediger, 2008; Kang, McDermott, and Roediger, 2007; Metcalfe and Kornell, 2007; Roediger and Marsh, 2005) or while performing an action in a procedure (Anderson et al., 1995; Ritter et al., 2007) or completing a task. They can also be reduced by a rhetorical structure (Kendeou and van den Broek, 2007) or critical stance (Wiley et al., 2009) that encourages the learner to be skeptical or to refute the presented information.

Immediate feedback can be useful under many conditions, but it does have potential liabilities. A learner's motivation can be threatened when there is a barrage of corrections and negative feedback. Frequent interruptions of organized action sequences (such as reading a text aloud) can be not only irritating but also counterproductive in the acquisition of complex motor skills. Immediate feedback blocks the possibility of the students' correcting their own reading errors and regulating their own learning more generally. The impact and timing of feedback differ for tasks that involve memory, simple procedural skills, reasoning, problem solving, and complex domains of knowledge that have entrenched misconceptions.

The optimal administration of feedback is a complex mechanism that depends on timing, the nature of the knowledge or skill to be developed, and characteristics of the student. It is unlikely that an instructor can track all of these levels for 30 students in a class—or even a single student for a tutor. As discussed further in Chapter 6, technologies can keep track of the details that are beyond the horizon of human capacities. Computerized learning environments are poised to provide adaptive feedback that is sensitive to all of these constraints.

Qualitative Feedback Is Better for Learning Than Test Scores and Error Flagging

There is moderate evidence that feedback should both point out errors to the learner and explain why the information is incorrect instead of merely flagging that an answer is incorrect or giving a student an overall score that does not provide information about the nature of the needed improvements (Aleven et al., 2003; Ritter et al., 2007; Roscoe and Chi, 2007; Shute, 2008). Much of this research is on subject-matter content rather than literacy per se, but the principles are expected to apply universally. That said, more research is needed on the type of qualitative feedback that is optimal for different types of material and different types of learners (Shute, 2008). How specific should the feedback be (Ritter et al., 2007)? At what point will a negative feedback frustrate or dispirit students, especially those with low self-efficacy (Graesser, D'Mello, and Person, 2009; Lepper and Woolverton, 2002)? How can task-specific feedback productively guide subsequent learning (Hunt and Pellegrino, 2005; Shute, 2008)? When should students have control over the nature and extent of feedback they receive (Aleven et al., 2003)? Under what conditions is it appropriate to have an open learning environment, in which the students have full knowledge of their extent of mastering knowledge, skills, and strategies at a fine-grained level (Bull and Kay, 2007)? As in much of instructional design, there are a number of trade-offs and sensitivities to the nature of the knowledge and skills being trained. Instructionally perfect feedback may be expensive to provide, but to the extent that technology can be recruited, costs can decrease. Fine-grained feedback is best for specific well-defined skills, but some modicum of feedback is also appropriate for general, ill-defined skills. Excessive feedback also runs the risk of preventing the development of self-regulated learning, and so a fading process is needed to gradually shift control to the student.

There is some evidence among older learners that quantitative feedback on skill acquisition is more effective if it is framed in terms of positive feedback (what is good about one's performance) relative to goal attainment, compared with a raw score (West et al., 2005). Also, adult learners with initially high levels of perceived control may benefit more from feedback than those with lower levels of perceived control (Miller and West, 2010). (This may be true for younger populations, although further data are needed.)

ADAPTIVE AND INTERACTIVE LEARNING ENVIRONMENTS

As previously discussed, training in complex strategies, metacognition, and self-regulated learning may to some extent be accomplished by well-engineered training materials that guide all learners through the same regimen in a scripted fashion. However, some researchers think that students need to be guided by knowledgeable tutors, mentors, and computer learning environments that adaptively interact in a fashion that is sensitive to the characteristics of the learner, called the learner profile (Conley, Kerner, and Reynolds, 2005; Connor et al., 2007; Graesser, D'Mello, and Person, 2009; McNamara, 2007b; Woolf, 2009). In essence, human or machine intelligence facilitates learning when it fits the needs of the particular student in a context-sensitive fashion, particularly in the case of complex skills and knowledge (see Chapter 6 for more on technology). This research is consistent with sociocultural theories of learning positing that learning depends on interaction with a more knowledgeable other (Lave and Wenger, 1991, 1998; Rogoff, 1990, 1993, 1995; Rogoff and Lave, 1984; Rogoff and Wertsch, 1984; Scribner and Cole, 1981; Vygotsky, 1986; Wertsch, 1991).

Adaptive Learning Environments Foster Understanding in Complex Domains

There is moderate evidence that learning of complex material requires adaptive learning environments that are sensitive to the learner's general profile and to the level of his or her mastery at any given point in time. Indeed, this assumption underlies research showing learning gains through intelligent tutoring systems and learning environments (Anderson et al., 1995; Dodds and Fletcher, 2004; Doignon and Falmagne, 1999; Koedinger et al., 1997; Lesgold et al., 1992; Ritter et al., 2007; VanLehn, 2006; Woolf, 2009) and other reading systems that adapt to the learner, either computer systems (Connor et al., 2007; McNamara, 2007a; Meyer and Wijekumar, 2007) or human tutors (Palincsar and Brown, 1984; Rosenshine and Meister, 1994). When the knowledge conveyed by a text is complex, fine-tuned diagnosis and remediation may need to be sensitive to a large spectrum of learners' states of knowledge, skills, and strategies, as well as how the presence or absence of various supporting knowledge and skills impacts other components of effective performance (Connor et al., 2009).

At this point, researchers have not differentiated the contributions of context-sensitive adaptive strategies from the content in the learning experience. Simply put, is it adaptive instruction or the content of the instruction that matters? Individualized adaptive training has been used successfully to build cognitive skills among older learners (Erickson et al., 2007; Jaeggi et al., 2008; Kramer et al., 1999; Kramer, Larish, and Strayer, 1995). However, as for younger populations, there is a lack of experimentation that isolates the adaptive nature of the instruction as a cause of learning gains. Differentiating the two requires a precise mathematical treatment of the information delivered by the interventions. Such control over content is rarely imposed in research investigations (although see VanLehn et al., 2007).

Computer environments, rather than human instructors, may have the most promise in manipulating and controlling these complex interventions because of the complexity of diagnoses and remediation mechanisms. For example, accomplished human tutors have a difficult time being adaptive to many aspects of the learner (Chi, Roy, and Hausmann, 2008; Chi, Siler, and Jeong, 2004; Graesser, D'Mello, and Person, 2009). Examples of the kinds of computer interventions that can be achieved include analysis of reading times for segments of a text against models of the strategies that would distribute time in a given way, followed by coaching of specific ways to read more effectively. Even without any machine intelligence, it is possible to mark text segments according to the amount of time past readers have spent on them and thus guide students to consider their efforts more carefully.

Interactive Learning Environments Facilitate Learning

There is moderate evidence that learners benefit from instructional interactions in which they receive fine-grained feedback (i.e., feedback specific to the immediate momentary task at hand) with hints that prompt them to generate knowledge (Ainsworth, 2008; Chi, Roy, and Hausmann, 2008; Graesser, D'Mello, and Person, 2009; Graesser, Person, and Magliano, 1995; VanLehn et al., 2007). Various teaching methods include such interactions: reciprocal teaching method, modeling-scaffolding-fading, the Socratic method, refutation, and others. Efficacy studies are needed, however, to determine the effects on learning and if the effects vary for different learners (see McNamara, 2007b).

Learning Is Facilitated in Genuine and Coherent Learning Environments

Learning is enhanced by opportunities to practice and use skills for a purpose (Ford and Forman, 2006; Forman, Minick, and Stone, 1993; Lave and Wenger, 1991; Rogoff, 1990; Street, 1984). There is some evidence that anchored learning practices help learning (Bottge et al., 2007; Collins, Brown, and Newman, 1989; Dede and Grotzer, 2009; National Research Council, 2000). Anchored learning refers to developing knowledge and skill while working on problems encountered in the real world. Students often work in teams for several hours or days trying to solve a practical problem that matters to them and that connects to their knowledge. The problem is also challenging, so learners need to engage in problem solving and recruit multiple levels of knowledge and skills. With coaching, these activities can be organized coherently around solving the practical problem.

Examples of anchored learning are problem-based curricula in medical schools, in which students work on genuine medical cases, and communities of practice, in which students try to solve problems of pollution in their city. The students may spend 2 weeks learning about ecology to explain why fish are dying in a pond or how to save an eagle in a forest. Medical students may spend days analyzing the cases of patients in a hospital for diagnosis and treatment (Vernon and Blake, 1993).

Anchored learning has features that are likely to motivate struggling adult learners who are sensitive to the value of their learning experience. Yet much needs to be understood about how to design effective anchored learning experiences to achieve goals related to literacy and learning. For instance, for any particular topic, what learning goals do students pursue and what material should be read to achieve the learning goals? When an article is accessed, what do they read, how much do they read, and when do they give up? How much of the information in an article gets incorporated in messages to peers, documents they write, and behavior? What deficits in reading components present barriers to effective participation in a community of learners? There is little or no empirical evidence on answers to these fundamental questions about goal-based reading (McCrudden and Schraw, 2007). More research is needed on the principles and dynamics of how adults sift through and select material for focused study (Pirolli, 2005, 2007; Pirolli and Card, 1999).

LEARNING IS INFLUENCED BY MOTIVATION AND EMOTION

Motivation is inextricably bound to learning, and decades of research have attempted to explain the relationship (Deci and Ryan, 2002a; Dweck, 2002; Lepper and Henderlong, 2000; Linnenbrink and Pintrich, 2002;

Meyer and Turner, 2006). Chapter 5, on supporting persistence, reviews in detail research findings related to motivation and distills principles for creating learning environments to inspire and support persistence and engagement. We note two important points here. First, the affective response that learners have to the learning experience influences not only engagement and persistence in a task, but also their capacity for cognitive processing. It is well known that adults are more motivated when the learning experience and materials are consonant with existing interests and dispositions (Ackerman and Rolfhus, 1999; Beier and Ackerman, 2001, 2003, 2005), and when engaged in reading or writing for a real purpose. Engaging narrative, expository, or procedural texts on topics that interest the learner and deliver knowledge the learner values are more likely to sustain the attention needed for learning (Hultsch and Dixon, 1983; Morrow et al., 2009; Stine-Morrow et al., 2004).

Second, motivation among adults is also more likely to be enhanced when instruction helps to build self-confidence and self-efficacy and develops the student's identity as a person who reads. Adults with literacy problems often have experienced being stigmatized or marginalized, which makes enhancing self-confidence especially important. Because past experiences may have been very painful, interventions need to accommodate the occurrence of negative emotions, such as frustration, anger, boredom, and disengagement. Social support from peers, family members, tutors, and mentors facilitate motivation and mitigate their dropping out of adult literacy programs.

SUMMARY AND DIRECTIONS FOR RESEARCH

Research on cognition and learning shows elements to include in the design of instruction (see Box 4-1). Some of these findings have emerged from research on literacy. The principles are expected to generalize across populations, but how to apply them to the development of effective literacy instruction for diverse adult learners in various forms of adult education and developmental instruction in college must be determined in future research. Given the findings from research on learning, three questions should guide this research.

1. There is a high level of complexity involved in the design of learning environments consistent with principles of learning (e.g., ideal levels of information delivery, task difficulty, and feedback tailored to the individual learner). This complexity must be considered in the development of hypotheses and research designs. The research must also determine the expertise required to flexibly deliver instruction consistent with the principles once developed. To what

extent can technology leverage and augment the literacy instructor's expertise to provide the adaptive learning environments that are optimal for the learner?

2. For adolescents and adults to invest the time required to develop their literacy, the instruction they receive must provide valued content knowledge and literacy skills (see Chapter 5 on motivation, engagement, and persistence). Thus, a promising direction for practice and research that is consistent with principles of learning and motivation is to discover how to build effective literacy instruction (curricula, practices, texts, and tools) that connects with the personal interests of learners and delivers the knowledge they need in content domains (e.g., electronics). To what degree is it possible for reading and writing instruction to piggyback onto instruction to develop content knowledge, instead of content knowledge being secondary to the acquisition of reading and writing skills? In other words, to what extent can content drive the development of adults' literacy?

3. Similarly, certain skills are in demand in the 21st century for social interaction and for success in college and in the workplace. To what extent can reading and writing skills be developed as part of developing these forms of literate practice? Given that most literate practice in today's world involves technologies, a goal for research is to determine how to effectively integrate important technologies into literacy instruction and practice to enable adults to function effectively in their educational, work, and social environments.

BOX 4-1
Summary of Principles of Learning for Instructional Design

Attention, Retention, and Transfer

- **Present material in a clear and organized format.** To facilitate learning, remove irrelevant information, even if interesting, to minimize distraction, provide structure and organization (coherence principle), present related elements to be learned near each other in space and time (continuity principle), and present new material in units that do not overwhelm with information (segmentation principle).
- **Use multiple and varied examples.** Knowledge, skills, and strategies acquired across multiple and varied contexts are better generalized and applied flexibly across a range of tasks and situations,
- **Present material in multiple modalities and formats.** Information is encoded and remembered better when it is delivered in multiple modes (verbal and pictorial), sensory modalities (auditory and visual), or media (computers and lectures) than when delivered in only a single mode, modality, or medium.
- **Teach in the zone of proximal development.** Select learning goals, materials, and tasks that are sensitive to what the student has mastered and that are appropriately challenging. Scaffold learning with instructional interactions and systematic selection and sequencing of content, materials, and tasks that are both at the appropriate level of difficulty and provide prompts and information needed to learn.
- **Space presentations of new material.** Learning is facilitated by the temporally distributed presentation of materials and tests instead of concentrated learning experiences within a short time span. Reexposure to course material after an optimal amount of delay often markedly increases the amount of information that students remember.
- **Test on multiple occasions, preferably with spacing.** Periodic testing helps learning and slows down forgetting. Regular testing, which can be quite brief and embedded in instructional materials, keeps students constantly engaged in the material and guides instructors or computers in making decisions about what to teach.
- **Ground concepts in perceptual-motor experiences.** Learning of concepts is facilitated with instruction that employs or evokes concrete perceptions and actions. Stories, for example, which generate perceptual-motor memories similar to the memories of everyday experience, may be powerful tools for practicing and building comprehension skills and developing and reinforcing background knowledge. Consider using content presented in stories to scaffold learning from other genres.

Generation of Content and Reasoning

- **Encourage the generation of explanations, substantive questions, and the resolution of contradictions.** These active learning processes impart coherence and meaning to the material to be learned, facilitates habitual generation of complex representations of information, and result in deeper understanding. Learner-generated content can lack detail and contain misconceptions that must be monitored and corrected.

- **Construct ideas from multiple points of view and different perspectives.** Considering multiple viewpoints and perspectives contributes to understanding a concept and to greater cognitive flexibility in accessing and using the concept in a range of contexts.

Complex Strategies, Critical Thinking, Inquiry, and Self-Regulated Learning

- **Structure instruction to develop the effective use of complex strategies.** Explicit training, modeling, and guided practice in the use of complex strategies is especially important for those with serious limitations in metacognition (the ability to understand, assess, and act on the adequacy of one's memory, comprehension, learning, planning, problem-solving, and decision processes) and difficulties with regulating their own strategy use.
- **Combine complex strategy instruction with the learning of content.** To facilitate learning and application of new knowledge in a subject domain, strategy instruction should be integrated with subject-matter content.

Feedback

- **Effective feedback is immediate, accurate, and timely.** Feedback should not contain too many corrections, too much negative feedback, or frequent interruptions of organized action sequences (such as reading a text aloud) because these can be demotivating and counterproductive in the acquisition of complex skills.
- **Qualitative feedback is better for learning than test scores and error flagging.** Feedback is more effective if it points out errors and explains why the response is incorrect. The type of qualitative feedback that is optimal for different types of material and different types of learners requires further study.

Adaptive and Interactive Learning Environments

- **Adaptive learning environments foster understanding in complex domains.** Adaptive learning environments are sensitive to the learner's general profile, and level of mastery at any given point in time can facilitate the learning of complex material. The degree to which adaptive instruction from human instructors and computerized learning environments can facilitate and accelerate learning requires further study.
- **Interactive learning environments facilitate learning.** Fine-grained feedback provided while learners engage in a task with hints that prompt generation of knowledge facilitates learning. Research is needed to evaluate the effectiveness of specific interactive instructional approaches (e.g., reciprocal teaching method, modeling-scaffolding-fading, the Socratic method, refutation).
- **Learning is facilitated in genuine and coherent learning environments.** Learning is enhanced by opportunities to practice and use skills for a purpose, although the effectiveness of specific approaches consistent with this principle remains to be tested.

Motivation and Emotion

- **Motivation is essential for learning.** A learner's affective response to the learning experience influences not only engagement and persistence in a task but also the capacity for cognitive processing.

5

Motivation, Engagement, and Persistence

Adults lead complex lives with many responsibilities and constraints on their availability to engage in formal learning. This reality, combined with the amount of effort and practice needed to develop one's literacy skills, makes supporting persistence one of the most challenging aspects of designing effective adult literacy programs. Adults and adolescents who lack adequate literacy need substantial amounts of literacy practice, on the order of many hundreds of hours, but the average duration of participation in literacy programs is nowhere close to what is needed. This chapter addresses the practical question of what can be done to motivate adolescents and adults from a range of backgrounds to persist in their efforts to learn. Specifically, what features of learning environments, which include instructional interactions, structures, systems, tasks, and texts, encourage persistence?

Different terms are used in the research literature to refer to learners' motivation and engagement with learning. We use the word "persistence" because it aptly describes the situation of adult learning. Many adults want to improve their literacy skills, but they do not persist, perhaps because of competing demands on their time, unpleasant past experiences with learning, or instruction that does not support sustained engagement or that is otherwise ineffective. It is also easy to underestimate the amount of effort and practice needed to develop literacy. Certainly the conditions that motivate or demotivate learners to persist with complicated tasks such as reading and writing are complex. Although lack of persistence is often discussed solely in psychological or dispositional terms, such as being intrinsically motivated or self-regulated, most contemporary researchers of motivation recognize the power of the learner's environment—instructional interactions and structures, relationships, and broader social and cultural experience—to affect motivation, engagement, and goal attainment (e.g., Anderman and Anderman, 2010). This chapter integrates findings from disciplines that offer complementary perspectives on these issues (psychology, anthropology, and sociology) to obtain a more complete understanding of where to focus efforts to increase adults' persistence with learning.[1] The framework for the chapter, shown in Figure 5-1, specifies the multiple dimensions of persistence and puts at the center the question of how to support it through the design of effective learning environments.

Box 5-1 identifies principles that are reasonable to use and further study to determine how best to support adults' persistence in developing literacy given current research. The principles are derived mainly from decades of research with students in school settings, adolescents in programs outside school, adults in workplace training, and adult behavior change more generally. Studies of high school dropouts, community college and university students, and adults in literacy education were included when available. The principles must be studied further, however, with adults needing to improve their literacy since they have for the most part not been included in the research studies. The chapter concludes with needs for future research, which are summarized in Box 5-2.

THE PSYCHOLOGY OF MOTIVATION AND LEARNING

An impressive array of contributors to individual motivation has been identified in psychological studies, among them self-efficacy (e.g., Bandura, 1977; Eccles et al., 1983), self-control (e.g., Findley and Cooper, 1983), goal orientations and task choice (e.g., Ames, 1992; Nicholls, 1984; Pintrich and Garcia, 1991; Urdan and Maehr, 1992), interest (e.g., Alexander, Kulikowich, and Jetton, 1994; Renninger, Hidi, and Krapp, 1992; Schiefele, 1996a; Wade, 1992; Wade et al., 1993), self-regulation (e.g., Butler and Winne, 1995; Pintrich and DeGroot, 1991; Pintrich, Marx, and Boyle, 1993; Schunk and Zimmerman, 1994; Zimmerman, 1989), self-concept of ability (Eccles et al., 1983), and others. Before examining these constructs in greater depth, there are several general points to note. First, each factor, although distinguishable and discussed separately, interacts with the others in complex ways to influence motivation to persist. For instance,

---

[1]The most profound area of difference among these three disciplines lies in how the relationship between individuals and social systems is conceptualized. The different fields use different terms to discuss motivation, resilience, and persistence. These different terms connote unique meanings specific to the theoretical underpinnings of each field, and so the distinctions are retained in this chapter to signify important differences among the various perspectives that are likely to be useful for conceptualizing effective practices.

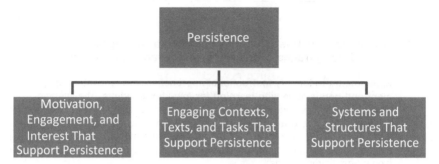

FIGURE 5-1 Factors that support or constrain persistence in learning.

the goals people set are related to their sense of self-efficacy, or perceived ability to perform well on a task, and the value they assign to the task. Second, although often discussed as stable attributes of an individual, a person's self-efficacy, self-regulation, goal orientation, and so on can differ depending on the context and the activity. Third, each of these contributors

---

BOX 5-1
Design Principles from Research on
Motivation, Engagement, and Learning

- Develop self-efficacy and perceptions of competency.
- Help learners set appropriate and valuable learning goals.
- Set expectations about the amount of effort and practice required to develop literacy skills.
- Help learners develop feelings of control and autonomy.
- Foster interest and develop beliefs about the value of literacy tasks.
- Help learners monitor progress and regulate their behavior toward goal attainment.
- Teach students to make adaptive attributions for successes and failures.
- Provide learners' with opportunities for success while providing optimal challenges to develop proficiencies.
- Foster social relationships and interactions known to affect learning.
- Use classroom structures and select texts and materials to help learners identify with learning and literacy tasks that counter past negative experiences with schooling.
- Assist with removing barriers to participation and practice to ensure that learners have the motivating experience of making progress.
- Give learners access to knowledgeable and skilled teachers and appropriately designed materials.

BOX 5-2
Directions for Research on the Motivation, Engagement, and Persistence of Learners in Literacy Instruction

- **Experiments to identify instructional approaches that motivate engagement and persistence with learning for low-literate adults.** The interventions should aim to understand how individual, social, cultural and systemic influences interact to affect persistence. The research should focus at the task and instructional program levels. It should also evaluate ways to support students in meeting immediate literacy goals and sustained learning to meet longer term literacy needs.

- **Development of measures to assess student motivation and test hypotheses about how to motivate adult learners' persistence.** Reliable and valid measures are needed to assess motivation and related constructs, such as engagement and interest, which are geared toward the adult literacy education context. These measures need to be developed for use in intervention research at the task, program, and sustained learning levels.

- **More thorough understanding of adult learners.** Rich descriptive information is needed of learners' circumstances and contexts (e.g., educational experiences, job, family, health), and how these relate to the effectiveness of various strategies to support engagement and persistence in adult literacy instruction.

- **How the various components of motivation relate to one another to affect persistence in the adult instruction context.** Constructs and models of motivation need to be clarified, applied, and tested in the context of helping people to persist in adult literacy education.

- **Texts and tasks for adult literacy instruction.** It is important to understand how the texts and tasks made available to learners, and how their perceptions of these texts and tasks affect motivation to persist, even in the face of linguistic and cognitive challenges.

- **Group differences and similarities in the factors that influence motivation to persist with learning, reading, and writing.** Although principles of motivation apply across populations, group differences in persistence can be expected according to age and other characteristics of the learner.

- **Technology.** Key areas for study are the features and formats of technologies that motivate persistence and the best ways to introduce technologies and support their use. Outcomes that may be measured include attitudes toward literacy, task enjoyment, perceived task difficulty, expectations for success, and literacy skills.

- **Conditions that motivate enrollment in literacy courses.** The circumstances (e.g., mandatory enrollment) and incentives that affect decisions to enroll in literacy courses must be determined both to influence enrollment and identify moderators of instructional effectiveness.

- **Development and implementation of support systems for motivating persistence.** The contexts, texts, tasks, systems, and structures of adult literacy instruction require as much research-based attention as do the individuals who must persist in learning.

is amenable to change and is developed and affected by various aspects of the learner's environment.

Self-Efficacy

When learners expect to succeed, they are more likely to put forth the effort and persistence needed to perform well. More confident students are likely to be more cognitively engaged in learning and thinking than students who doubt their capabilities (e.g., Pintrich, 1999; Pintrich and Schrauben, 1992; Schunk, 1991). Indeed, self-efficacy is a strong predictor of many educational, physical, and mental health outcomes (Bandura, 1997) and has been associated with better literacy skills (Pajares, 2003). Self-efficacy beliefs relating to the ability to write, for instance, have been associated with better writing performance (see Pajares, 2003), whereas apprehension about writing usually predicts weak performance in writing (e.g., Madigan, Linton, and Johnston, 1996).

Self-efficacy is often confused with global self-esteem. Whereas self-efficacy refers to learners' beliefs about their abilities in a certain area, such as literacy, or their ability to complete a specific type of literacy task (e.g., writing short stories, reading the newspaper, reading a mystery novel, reading and comprehending an instruction manual), global self-esteem refers to how one feels about oneself generally (Crocker, Lee, and Park, 2004; Wigfield and Karpathian, 1991; Wylie, 1979). It is possible to have high self-esteem generally while having low self-efficacy in one domain. Whether or not low self-efficacy in one area affects global self-esteem depends partly on how important that particular skill or behavior is to the person's identity and goals and whether it is valued by the people that matter to the learner (Harter, 1999; Roeser, Peck, and Nasir, 2006).

Self-efficacy and self-esteem also relate differently to learning and other outcomes. Whereas self-efficacy in a particular domain, such as education or health, relates positively to outcomes in that domain, the relation between general self-esteem and any given outcome is weak. Indeed, there is little evidence that enhancing students' general self-esteem leads to increases in achievement (Baumeister et al., 2003; Wylie, 1979). Thus, although raising general self-esteem often is promoted as a panacea, the actual relations between self-esteem and beneficial outcomes are minimal (Baumeister, Smart, and Boden, 1996; Kohn, 1994).

Many adults are likely to have experienced difficulty with literacy starting in childhood (Corcoran, 2009). It can be expected that some adults enter literacy education questioning their ability to learn to read and write. Many may not have the confidence to enter literacy education programs, and, if they do enter, lack the self-efficacy needed to persist. How, then, might teachers increase self-efficacy? Research points to three areas that require attention: (1) setting appropriate goals, (2) provision of feedback to achieve appropriate attributions for success and failure, and (3) progress monitoring.

Appropriate Goals

Goals are extremely important in motivating and directing behavior (Austin and Vancouver, 1996). Adults often have very general ideas about why they need or want to learn to read or write. Instructors need to assist learners with breaking down their learning goals into short-term literacy goals (i.e., proximal goals) and long-term literacy goals (i.e., distal goals) to motivate persistence and progress. Setting proximal goals, not just distal ones, is much more likely to result in experiencing success, which enhances self-efficacy (Schunk, 1991). Opportunities to achieve short-term goals are especially motivating in complex domains such as reading and writing, in which substantial time and effort are required and reaching distal goals can take months or even years (Schunk, 2003).

Supporting students' awareness of progress week by week can motivate persistence. As students reach proximal goals and recognize that short-term achievements are the path toward reaching long-term goals, they will be motivated to set and work toward new goals and thus continue to learn. In contrast, if focused only on distal goals, students can become frustrated with what appears to be minimal progress, and so self-efficacy and then persistence may suffer.

Learning proceeds best if students engage in activities that afford opportunities to be and feel successful but that also develop new proficiencies. People persist at a task when the activity is optimally challenging, meaning that the activity is well matched with the person's skill level (e.g., Csikszentmihalyi, 1975; Csikszentmihalyi, Abuhamdeh, and Nakamura, 2005; Deci, 1975; Payne et al., under review). People also attempt to regulate learning so as to allocate effort to material and activities that are neither too easy nor too hard (Kornell and Metcalfe, 2006; Metcalfe, 2002; Metcalfe and Kornell, 2003, 2005; Son and Metcalfe, 2000). Allocating attention in this way to optimize learning may be especially important for older adults (Miles and Stine-Morrow, 2004). One strategy to encourage persistence is to help learners set short-term, or proximal, literacy goals that are optimally challenging and reachable within a short period of time (Manderlink and Haraciewicz, 1984; Schunk, 1991, 1996). Appropriate scaffolding can support learners in moving toward those goals (Bruner, 1960; National Research Council, 2000; Vygotsky, 1978) and experiencing the motivating positive affect that comes from success.

Research on goal orientation theory (also referred to simply as "goal theory") has identified the personal goals that motivate learners to achieve and that are shaped by aspects of their environment (e.g., classroom learning environments) (Ames, 1992; Ames and Ames, 1984; Midgley, 2002). Personal goal orientation refers to learners' individual beliefs about their reasons for engaging with academic tasks; goal structures refer to students' perceptions of the goals that are emphasized in such environments as classrooms (Anderman and Wolters, 2006; Midgley, 2002). In research on achievement motivation, personal goal orientations are often broken down into three types of goals: mastery goals, performance-approach goals, and performance-avoidance goals. An additional type of goal, discussed further in the next section, is extrinsic goals in which individuals engage with a task to achieve or earn some type of reward (Anderman, Maehr, and Midgley, 1999; Pintrich et al., 1993).

When a student holds a mastery goal, he or she engages with a task (e.g., reading a book) in order to improve ability; the goal is to truly master the task. When students hold mastery goals, they use themselves as points of comparison (i.e., the student compares her or his present performance to past performance and gauges improvement in terms of self-growth) (Ames and Archer, 1988). The second type of goal is actually a class of goals referred to as performance goals. Conceptualizations of performance goals since the mid-1990s distinguish between performance-approach and performance-avoidance goals (Elliot and Harackiewicz, 1996; Middleton and Midgley, 1997). When a student holds a performance-approach goal, the goal is to demonstrate his or her ability relative to others. With performance-approach goals, students compare their own performance to the performance of other individuals, with the ultimate goal of demonstrating that the student is more competent (e.g., a better reader) than others. In contrast, when a student holds a performance-avoidance goal, the student's goal is to avoid appearing incompetent or "dumb"; such students would want to avoid appearing to others as if they have poor literacy skills.

It is possible to structure learning environments to facilitate different types of goals in learners (Maehr and Anderman, 1993; Maehr and Midgley, 1996). Goal orientation theorists argue, and research has demonstrated, the goal structures that are emphasized in classrooms and schools predict the types of personal goals that students adopt (Anderman, Maehr, and Midgley, 1999; Maehr and Midgley, 1996; Meece, Anderman, and Anderman, 2006; Roeser, Midgley, and Urdan, 1996). Specifically, when students perceive a mastery goal structure, they perceive that mastery, effort, and learning for the sake of learning are stressed in the classroom by the instructor; when students perceive a performance goal structure, they perceive that learning is defined in terms of demonstrating one's ability and other external consequences (Kaplan et al., 2002). If a teacher emphasizes the importance of mastering literacy skills, students are likely to adopt mastery goals; if a teacher emphasizes relative ability (i.e., the teacher inadvertently makes comments that position adult learners as "good" or "bad" readers), students are likely to adopt performance goals. Mastery is also easier to link to successful behavior in life: people do well if they can comprehend instructions on the job and write reports that colleagues value, not because they got an A in a course.

In one literacy intervention based on goal achievement theory (e.g., Ames, 1992; Ames and Archer, 1988), Meece and Miller (1999) worked with elementary school teachers to develop literacy activities that involved reading extended passages of prose and writing detailed responses. When implemented well, students' endorsement of performance goals decreased (i.e., students became less focused on comparing their own literacy skills to those of others), and work-avoidance goals decreased for low-achieving students.

Much research indicates that both students' personal goals and their perceptions of classroom goal structures predict valued educational outcomes. Personal mastery goals have predicted adaptive outcomes that include persistence at tasks, choosing to engage in similar activities in the future (Harackiewicz et al., 2000), and the use of adaptive cognitive strategies and more effective self-regulatory strategies (Elliot, McGregor, and Gable, 1999; Meece, Herman, and McCombs, 2003; Wolters, 2004). Performance-avoidance goals consistently predict maladaptive outcomes that include increased use of self-handicapping strategies (Midgley and Urdan, 2001) and poor achievement (Skaalvik, 1997). Results for performance-approach goals are mixed, with some studies finding that their adoption is related to adaptive outcomes (Elliot, McGregor, and Gable, 1999), and others indicating that they are related to maladaptive outcomes (Middleton and Midgley, 1997; Wolters, 2004).

Personal goals tend to correspond with certain beliefs about intelligence that can affect self-efficacy. Carol Dweck and her colleagues have demonstrated that students hold incremental and entity views of intelligence. Students who hold an incremental view of intelligence believe that intelligence is malleable and that it is possible to learn just about anything; in contrast, students who hold an entity view of intelligence believe that intelligence is fixed, so a person cannot effectively learn more than they are naturally capable of learning.

Students who hold an incremental view of intelligence are likely to adopt mastery goals, and students who hold entity views of intelligence are likely to adopt performance goals (Dweck and Leggett, 1988). It appears possible, however, to alter beliefs about intelligence via interventions or manipulations (Dweck, 2008). For instance, feedback that focuses learners' attention on the processes of learning, including the use of strategies, effort, practice, and the general changeable and controllable nature of learning, can foster more incremental views of ability with positive outcomes. One challenge to implementing these practices, however, is that teachers may hold similar views about the malleability of intelligence, as in one study of two university teacher preparation courses (Moje and Wade, 1997). Although documented in only one study, adult educators may benefit from professional development to develop teaching practices that support students in developing personal mastery rather than personal performance goals.

The broader environments of learners also can affect how they think about themselves in relation to other groups and social systems, thereby influencing their goals. Markus and Nurius suggest that young people make decisions and set goals on the basis of who they think they might become or, alternatively, who they do not wish to become, thereby shaping their successes. Thus, this concept of "possible selves" (see Markus and Nurius, 1986) represents an important idea to pursue in research on self-efficacy and persistence with literacy education, especially among adolescents and emerging adults. A question is how to foster resilience—the capacity of those exposed to risk to overcome those risks and to avoid negative outcomes—which is known to help people cope and avoid negative outcomes in other areas that have included delinquency and behavioral problems, psychological maladjustment, academic difficulties, and physical complications (see Rak and Patterson, 1996).

By contrast, Ogbu (1987, 1993) argued that a "cultural frame of reference" shapes the school successes of different groups by positioning some groups in opposition to conventional notions of academic success, although his findings have been challenged by social and cultural perspectives on achievement (see Foley, 1999; Moje and Martinez, 2007; O'Connor, 1997), as discussed in later sections. Similarly, other psychological studies offer a challenge to Ogbu's theories. Eccles and colleagues (e.g., Eccles and Midgley, 1989; Eccles et al., 1993a, 1993b), for example, suggest that a mismatch between formal school structures and adolescents' development needs produces negative behaviors among adolescents, because, even as youth are exhorted to act as responsible, decision-making beings, the capacity to make decisions and plot a possible future is taken from them by overly controlled school environments. Thus, many adults who seek adult literacy instruction may not have had opportunities to envision and enact a wide range of possible selves and self-regulated practices in past schooling.

Research on possible selves (Kemmelmeier and Oyserman, 2001; Oyserman, 1987; Oyserman, Bybee, and Terry, 2003) reveals both the power of limiting social identities (negative gender, race, or class-based perceptions) and the potential for interventions (Oyserman, Brickman, and Rhodes, 2007; Oyserman, Bybee, and Terry, 2006) to help adolescent learners set goals and identify and monitor necessary life practices for persisting toward and attaining those goals. In general, a lack of understanding for how to achieve desired goals ultimately chips away at motivation to persist because individuals often think they are taking appropriate steps toward goals, when, in reality, their daily practices interfere with taking appropriate and realistic steps toward achievement. Possible selves interventions have been documented to assist youth in clarifying their goals, evaluating their current practices, and developing plans for meeting goals (Oyserman, Brickman, and Rhodes, 2007; Oyserman, Bybee, and Terry, 2006). Similar interventions could be designed for adult literacy instruction in ways that would support both adult literacy educators and adult learners.

Beliefs about personal efficacy (and control) can decrease in older adulthood (Lachman, 2006; Miller and Gagne, 2005; Miller and Lachman, 1999), although individual differences are observed (e.g., adults with active lifestyles also have more positive self-efficacy beliefs; Jopp and Hertzog, 2007). Such beliefs can be modified, however, with cognitive restructuring (Lachman et al., 1992) and experience with cognitive tasks in which realistic goals are set and progress is monitored relative to those goals (West, Thorn, and Bagwell, 2003). Research shows it is important to attend to changing self-efficacy beliefs in adulthood: positive beliefs about one's cognitive capacity in adulthood can affect performance by enhancing perseverance in the face of cognitive challenge (Bandura, 1989b) and by engendering the use of effective strategies for learning (Lachman and Andreoletti, 2006; Stine-Morrow et al., 2006a). Self-efficacy beliefs at midlife predict changes over time in cognitive ability (Albert et al., 1995; Seeman et al., 1996). Similarly, beliefs in one's own capacity to be effective with cognitive activities (e.g., self-efficacy, control beliefs) predict cognitive and intellectual performance across the life span (Bandura, 1989b; Jopp and Hertzog, 2007; Lachman, 1983).

Altogether, research on goals and goal setting indicates that the instructional practices used in classrooms are likely to affect learners' adoption of goals that affect self-efficacy. Goals should be optimally challenging to increase engagement and persistence with learning as well as progress. If instructors emphasize mastery, effort, and improvement, then students will be more likely to adopt personal mastery goals; the adoption of mastery goals subsequently predicts valued learning outcomes, including persistence at reading, choosing to engage in additional literacy activities in the future, and the use of more effective reading strategies. If, however, instructors emphasize grades, relative ability, and differences in progress and achievement, students will be more likely to adopt performance goals (either approach or avoid) and experience maladaptive outcomes (e.g., use of less effective reading and writing strategies) (Ames and Archer, 1988; Anderman and Wolters, 2006; Nolen, 1988; Nolen and Haladyna, 1990). Thus, it is particularly important for adult educators to have training and professional development that helps them to recognize the importance of goal orientations and structures and to become skilled in the use of instructional practices that will foster the adoption of appropriate goals and adaptive goal orientations and structures in their students.

Feedback and Framing: Adaptive Explanations for Success and Failure

Adaptive self-efficacy requires having fairly accurate perceptions of one's current competencies, which in turn requires the opportunity to receive feedback and monitoring of progress. Overestimating one's ability to read and understand a text, for instance, will not lead to engaging in the behaviors needed to develop new skills (e.g., Pintrich, 2000b; Pintrich and Zusho, 2002); similarly, underestimating one's abilities may lead to coping or hiding behaviors that prevent the learner from making use of their existing skills and resources for learning (Brozo, 1990; Hall, 2007). Clear, specific, and accurate feedback that focuses on competence, expertise, and skill is needed to promote self-efficacy. The feedback should be appropriate to the learners' level of progress and relate directly to the specific area that needs improvement, which requires sound assessment. Dynamic assessments, although they need further development, are promising in this regard because they can provide the feedback needed to target supports and instruction within the learners' zone of proximal development (Vygtosky, 1978, 1986).

Experiences with learning can trigger questions such as: Why did I do badly? (after receiving a low score on an evaluation).Why can't I understand this? (after failing to comprehend a paragraph). Why can't I write sentences that make sense? (after being unable to write a coherent short story). The attributions students form in response to such questions will either motivate or demotivate their persistence. Those who have struggled with reading and writing and perhaps with continuing their literacy education in the past are likely to have formed attributions that lead to lack of persistence.

To persist, learners need feedback and models that help frame their experiences with learning and develop adaptive explanations for successes and failures. Consistent with attribution theory (Weiner, 1985, 1986, 1992), a learner who is experiencing failure or difficulty comprehending a text, for example, will be more likely to persist if he or she attributes the difficulty to something external (e.g., a boring text), something uncontrollable (e.g., being ill), or something unstable (e.g., feeling depressed that day). A learner who experiences success at a task will be more likely to persist if progress is attributed to something internal (e.g., personal enjoyment of reading), controllable (e.g., practice, spending a lot of time working on the text), and stable (e.g., a belief in one's ability as a reader) (Schunk and Zimmerman, 2006).

Many adults in need of literacy development are likely to have experienced years of combined low interest, low perceptions of literacy ability, and poor achievement in literacy (Denissen, Zarrett, and Eccles, 2007). After experiencing years of difficulty with reading and writing, some adults can enter into each literacy task with the assumption that their capacities are limited, an assumption that threatens motivation to persist at the task and perhaps with literacy education in general (Brozo, 1990; Hall, 2007). Instructors can help adults to overcome the potentially demotivating effects of past experiences if they attempt to understand the learning histories of adults and actively seek to shape the attributions they could be making to explain their experiences during the course of instruction.

Students of all ages can find errors demotivating. Research from organizational psychology and adult training studies suggests the benefits of error management—that is, leading adults to expect errors as a part of the learning process and then providing strategies for coping with and learning from errors (Keith and Frese, 2008; Van der Linden et al., 2001). Likewise, in education, instructors need to know how to recognize and correct ingrained negative attributions by providing feedback that stresses the processes of learning, such as the importance of using strategies, monitoring one's understanding, and engaging in sustained effort, even in the face of challenge. When a student does not experience success (e.g., is unable to make sense of the overarching point of a short story), instructors can help the learner employ reading strategies that can elucidate the meaning and provide a different frame for thinking about successful reading. With repeated reframing, instructors can help learners develop attributional styles that motivate persistence and move beyond dichotomous attributional frames (i.e., "the problem is entirely inside my head or the problem is entirely in the text, task, or setting") and toward frames that allow learners to employ strategies and skills for constructing meaning in a wide range of literacy tasks.

If learners attribute poor performance on an assignment or assessment to uncontrollable circumstances, they may feel helpless and become less motivated to engage with literacy activities in the future (Anderman and Anderman, 2010). However, if the learners attribute poor performance to something controllable (e.g., a lack of appropriate effort or the use of inappropriate reading strategies), then motivation may not suffer, since the student should realize that exerting greater effort or using different strategies should lead to better results.

Vicarious experience (i.e., observing others successfully perform specific tasks or use specific strategies) (Bandura, 1997) is another way to frame learner's attitudes toward learning and increase self-efficacy. For instance, instructors or students might model literacy strategies or other learning behaviors. This approach has been effective with struggling early adolescent readers using such methods as reciprocal teaching (Brown and Palincsar,

1982; Palincsar and Brown, 1984) or questioning the author (Beck and McKeown, 2002; McKeown, Beck, and Blake, 2009). It is always important, however, to adhere to good practice for modeling literacy strategies (Palincsar and Brown, 1984).

Attribution theory and research suggest that teachers can contribute to the development of negative attributions in a variety of ways. One obvious way is to communicate, intentionally or unintentionally, to learners that a reading problem is internal to them. Teaching practices that could build negative internal attributions include labeling readers and writers as strong or struggling; making obvious assignments of readers and writers to working groups by skill level; and encouraging some learners to excel, while exhibiting clearly low expectations for others. In addition, providing inadequate or no feedback can also signal the idea that skills are inherent and immutable. For example, if a teacher responds to an answer with, "No, that is wrong" and does not provide feedback or suggestions for development, then the student may develop or apply a maladaptive attribution (e.g., "I must be stupid"); an internal, stable, and uncontrollable attribution for failure that is unlikely to enhance motivation to read.

Progress Monitoring and Self-Regulation

Students who are self-regulating—who set goals, make plans for reaching their goals, and then monitor and regulate their cognitions and behavior—are more likely to do well on academic tasks. Although much research focuses on the cognitive aspects of self-regulation (e.g., use of cognitive and metacognitive strategies during reading and writing tasks), less attention has been paid to how students monitor and control their learning-related motivations and affect (Pintrich, 2003). They may need help, however, with recognizing and appreciating their progress so that they feel efficacious and persist.

Assessments of progress are important and are hallmarks of American education. However, the ways in which assessments are administered and the ways in which feedback is presented can have important effects on motivation. Discourse in the adult education classroom that stresses the importance of assessments and tests can lead students to adopt performance goals (Anderman and Maehr, 1994). As discussed previously, the adoption of performance goals is related to some problematic academic outcomes, particularly when students adopt performance-avoid goals (i.e., to avoid appearing incompetent) (Middleton and Midgley, 1997). When students are focused on how they compare to others academically, they may use less efficient cognitive strategies (Anderman and Young, 1994; Nolen, 1988; Nolen and Haladyna, 1990), and they may engage in various self-handicapping behaviors (Urdan, 2004; Urdan and Midgley, 2001; Urdan, Midgley, and Anderman, 1998).

A number of research-based instructional strategies for administering assessments can help to avoid demotivating students. First, results of assessments should be presented privately. The presentation of assessment results in a public manner is highly conducive to the adoption of performance rather than mastery goals (Anderman and Anderman, 2010; Maehr and Anderman, 1993). Second, whenever possible, adult educators should encourage students to focus on effort and improvement. Motivation is enhanced if students feel they can improve if they work hard at a task. If a student does not receive an acceptable score on an assessment, motivation research suggests that an effective strategy is to allow him or her to take the assessment again. As discussed further in the next section, intrinsic motivation is enhanced when students are rewarded on the basis of their improvement rather than absolute scores (MacIver, 1993) or other external rewards that can decrease effort and academic performance.

Intrinsic Motivation

Intrinsic motivation refers to undertaking a behavior for its own sake, enjoyment, and interest and with a high degree of perceived autonomy—or willingness, volition, and control (Deci and Ryan, 1985). Students who are more intrinsically motivated or perceive their behaviors as autonomous show better outcomes for text recall (Ryan, Connell, and Plant, 1990), physical education high school coursework (Boiché et al., 2008), college student well-being (Levesque et al., 2004), and college course grades (Burton et al., 2006). Intrinsic motivation is affected by rewards for performance, the degree to which the learner values the learning activity and task, the learner's interest in the activity or task, and opportunities for choice or other ways of participating in learning to develop autonomy.

Extrinsic Rewards

The effects of extrinsic rewards on perceptions of control and autonomy, and thus on the development of intrinsic motivation, are debated (Cameron and Pierce, 1994, 1996; Cameron, Banko, and Pierce, 2001; Deci, Koestner, and Ryan, 1999, 2001; Eisenberger, Pierce, and Cameron, 1999; Henderlong and Lepper, 2002; Kohn, 1996; Lepper, Greene, and Nisbett, 1973; Lepper and Henderlong, 2000; Lepper, Keavney, and Drake, 1996; Ryan and Deci, 1996). Some argue that extrinsic incentives are not harmful to intrinsic motivation (e.g., Cameron, Banko, and Pierce, 2001; Eisenberger, Pierce, and Cameron, 1999), and others argue that they ultimately lower intrinsic motivation. The case against extrinsic rewards has been confirmed in a meta-analysis of 128 experiments (Deci, Koestner, and Ryan, 1999; see also Deci, Koestner, and Ryan, 2001). For instance, extrinsic rewards can lead to more rigid, less flexible, and slower problem solving (e.g., Glucksberg, 1962; McGraw and McCullers, 1979). Performance decrements can result from large financial incentives (Ariely, Gneezy, and Lowenstein, 2009). Undermining effects have been especially prominent under certain conditions: when the rewards were salient (Ross, 1975), expected (Lepper, Greene, and Nisbett, 1973), or contingent on doing a task (Deci, 1972). One possibility is that extrinsic rewards thwart the person's sense of autonomy and control (intrinsic motivation), as has long been hypothesized (see de Charms, 1968; Heider, 1958).

The conditions under which extrinsic rewards or incentives for adults affect their participation and persistence in adult literacy programs are not known. State and federally funded adult literacy programs at times offer incentives for enrollment. For example, many adult education courses, which include various courses in literacy, are provided free of charge in the city of Philadelphia. In this type of program, the concept of incentive was reframed as an opportunity that made it possible for adults to enroll in the courses (i.e., the payment was provided prior to enrollment, thus affording opportunity). When opportunities, such as support for child care, coverage of costs of enrollment, or replacement of lost wages are used up front to minimize barriers to participation, such opportunity enhancers may not have the negative impact documented for simple extrinsic rewards. By contrast, other programs provide incentives upon completion of programs or during program participation.

Research suggests that some type of opportunity or incentive system will continue to be used, and in some instances they may have positive effects. For example, the state of Tennessee recently implemented a cash-incentive program (i.e., students received cash incentives for participating in adult education classes); the results of a nonexperimental study suggested that the introduction of rewards was related to achievement and to passing the general educational development examination among welfare recipients (Ziegler, Ebert, and Cope, 2004). The issue of the effects of various types of incentives is complex in the context of understanding persistence in adult literacy programs and is worthy of further research to determine the conditions under which some types of incentives might motivate certain learners under particular circumstances.

Research suggests, however, that if students enroll in adult literacy courses simply to be able to obtain an extrinsic reward, such as job referrals, their motivation to subsequently use and engage with subsequent literacy activities may diminish or be undermined once the reward (i.e., a job or a job placement referral) is received. Although the aim of adult literacy programs may be to enhance the literacy skills of adult learners, it is possible that some types of rewards might undermine their motivation to continue to read or write for other purposes, but this is an open research question. If extrinsic incentive programs are offered, then research clearly indicates that it is important to implement such programs in a way that enhances engagement so that any intrinsic motivation toward literacy is not diminished. Specifically, extrinsic rewards should be presented so that students perceive them as providing information about their progress rather than as controlling their behavior (Deci and Ryan, 1987; Pittman et al., 1980). The reward should be contingent on the student's having learned specific literacy skills or reached specific goals, rather than for simply engaging with or completing a literacy task or course, which is more likely to be experienced as controlling (Deci, 1975; Deci and Ryan, 1987). For instance, if the reward provided by an adult education course is a job referral, then the job referral should be offered for having learned specific skills (e.g., being able to write a coherent essay), not for merely having completed a set of tasks (e.g., completing all exercises in a course). In this case, the learner's intrinsic motivation is less likely to be undermined because he or she is likely to perceive the reward to be a natural consequence of having learned specific skills.

In sum, it is not completely clear, especially in the context of adult literacy education, how extrinsic rewards contribute to persistence when used in conjunction with other practices known to develop a person's autonomy, interest, and beliefs about the value of the behavior to be performed. Research is needed with adults to determine more fully how various types of rewards combine with other factors to support and maintain student motivation and persistence. The effects of rewards and incentives are likely to differ depending on characteristics of learners and their circumstances.

Interest

Adult learners are likely to put forth more effort and stay engaged in tasks they find interesting (Wigfield and Eccles, 1992). Researchers have made a useful distinction between personal and situational interest (Hidi and Harackiewicz, 2000; Krapp, Hidi, and Renninger, 1992; Renninger, 2000), which has implications for motivating adult learners. Personal interest is the interest that learners bring into classrooms; it represents long-standing preferences of learners. When students are personally interested in topics covered in reading passages, recall of the main ideas of the passages is enhanced (Schiefele, 1996a) and subsequent motivation in related texts is maintained (Ainley, Hidi, and Berndorff, 2002). In contrast, situational interest is transitive; it is the type of interest that is inspired by a particular event or characteristic of an experience, which might include features of a text or task. Situational interest is related to engagement with literacy activities in adult college students (Flowerday, Schraw, and Stevens, 2004) and in young children (Guthrie et al., 2006b). A student who has not previously expressed any interest in a skill, such as writing persuasive essays, might become interested in the topic if presented in a manner that inspires interest (e.g., the opportunity to experience the value of the persuasive essay for college or job applications, changing public opinion, or simply self-expression).

The real challenge, however, is moving learners from situational to personal, or sustained, interest in a way that inspires persistence even when faced with challenging reading tasks or lack of background knowledge.

Guthrie and colleagues (2006a) have demonstrated how situational interest can be used to motivate initial reading and, with scaffolded knowledge development and the teaching of reading strategies, children can develop sustained interest and proficient skills necessary to read and learn in the domain of science. The value of giving readers opportunities to choose texts that connect with or expand their interests is a major finding of reading motivation research (Baker, 1999; Guthrie and Wigfield, 2000; Moje et al., 2010). When young readers are more engaged by the topic of a text, for whatever reason (i.e., to solve a problem or simply to read for amusement), they are more motivated to continue reading (Guthrie and Wigfield, 2000). Similarly, interest in the topic or purpose of a writing task predicts the writing performance of students in secondary schools (Albin, Benton, and Khramtsova, 1996).

Studies, mostly qualitative, on writing in adult education settings (Branch, 2007), on college freshman's attitudes about their writing (Jones, 2008), and on basic writers' sense of appreciation and motivation (McAlexander, 2000; Minnot and Gamble, 1991) suggest that instruction that facilitates motivation and investment in learning and increases a learner's sense of ownership, involvement, and sense of self-efficacy contributes to successful ongoing learning.

To support persistence, adult literacy instructors can use easy and cost-effective ways to learn about students' personal interests (e.g., asking them to share with the instructor only on a sheet of paper five topics they find personally interesting and five they view as boring). Instructors can use this information to select meaningful texts, tasks, and writing prompts and assignments to engage learners, support feelings of autonomy and control, and facilitate continued intrinsic motivation and engagement (Padak and Bardine, 2004). Situational interest can be generated and personal or sustained interest can be developed if instructors use well-written texts, videos, and graphics that incorporate vivid imagery and facilitate connectivity among ideas (Wade, Buxton, and Kelly, 1999).

A recent review identified six research-based strategies that literacy instructors can employ to enhance situational interest among students (Schraw and Lehman, 2001). These include (1) offering meaningful choices to students (e.g., allowing them to occasionally choose from among several texts), (2) using well-organized texts, (3) using texts that include vivid imagery, (4) using texts about which students have some prior knowledge, (5) encouraging students to actively and creatively think about the material they are reading, and (6) providing relevant cues for students (e.g., prompting them while reading or providing advance organizers to help make sense of the material).

Guthrie and colleagues' work further demonstrates that when situated in interesting material, reading strategy instruction improved children's motivation and reading skill. Specifically, Guthrie's Concept-Oriented Reading Instruction (CORI)—tested with elementary school children—embeds the teaching of reading in cycles of activity that occur around particular science concepts. CORI involves firsthand experiences, reading, strategy instruction, peer collaboration, and public forms of communication. Key to the success of the CORI model is that instruction focuses on integrating instruction designed to motivate readers, develop conceptual knowledge in the domain, and foster the use of reading strategies. A year-long CORI intervention resulted in increased elementary school students' strategy use, conceptual learning, and text comprehension compared with control classrooms (Guthrie et al., 1999).

Digital media are a promising way to give access to a broad range of text genres and topics to stimulate interest in reading and writing for all students, including adults. The use of digital technologies for exposure to genres and topics, for scaffolding, and for practice are likely to motivate interest in at least three ways: they are novel; they can ease the unpleasant parts of practice, and they can empower the learner through development of valued, relevant digital literacy skills.

Values

It is possible to distinguish between the motivating forces of value and interest. A person may persist with a task that is not initially intrinsically interesting if it is valued. Value refers to learners' beliefs about whether a domain or task is (1) enjoyable (intrinsically interesting), (2) useful, (3) important to identity or sense of self, and (4) worth investing time in (Eccles and Wigfield, 2002; Eccles et al., 1983; Wigfield and Eccles, 1992, 2000, 2002). In fact, motivation research from an expectancy-value framework (Wigfield and Eccles, 1992) points to several potential paths for motivating adults to learn and maintain literacy skills. In this framework, expectancy beliefs, like self-efficacy, refer to learners' beliefs about their abilities to succeed in an academic domain (e.g., writing) (Eccles et al., 1983).

Key to the theory is the idea that these dimensions work together; a less-than-skilled reader may nevertheless approach a difficult reading task with strong motivation to persist in the task if it is interesting, useful, or important to the reader's identity. Moje and colleagues (2008), for example, illustrated the value that adolescent readers attached to various texts because those texts taught them important life lessons or provided them information necessary for fitting in with a group or social network. Similarly, Dinsmore and colleagues (2010) demonstrated the multiple dimensions that motivate late adolescent readers (undergraduate students) who might lack reading skill to persist as "effortful processors" (Alexander, 2003) in the face of difficult text. Longitudinal studies have shown that value beliefs predict such choices as intentions to enroll in future mathematics courses and actual course enrollment, whereas expectancy beliefs relating to self-concept of ability predict achievement in English classes once enrolled (e.g., Durik, Vida, and Eccles, 2006). However, as previously discussed, recent evidence suggests that self-concept of ability, in particular, predicts both time spent in voluntary reading and achievement in both general and some domain-specific reading tasks (e.g., on science and social studies text passages), even more than time spent in voluntary reading (Moje et al., 2010).

Although valuing an activity is important for learning in the context of compulsory education, it is vital to persisting in adult literacy education (see Anderman and Anderman, 2010, for a review). When individuals value a particular literacy activity, such as reading about current events, they are more likely to choose to engage in it in the future (Meece, Wigfield, and Eccles, 1990; Wigfield and Eccles, 1992). Adults are likely to enter literacy instruction holding beliefs about the degree to which they value or like reading and writing and the types of literacy activities they value given that such beliefs form early in childhood and predict engagement with literacy activities in later grades (Durik, Vida, and Eccles, 2006).

To summarize, research suggests that if adults are enrolled in adult education courses and develop and maintain positive values about the literacy activities they engage in (i.e., they come to believe that the courses are useful, important, interesting, and worth their time), then they will be more likely to persist with learning. Although it is clear that instructors need to help their students develop these values and that the development (or internalization) of values relating to learning and literacy is possible, most of the relevant findings are drawn from populations other than adults needing literacy improvement, and more research is needed on how to affect adults' values related to literacy and literacy tasks over time.

Control and Autonomy

When students (children and adolescents) believe that they have some control over their own learning, they are more likely to take on challenges and to persist with difficult tasks, compared with students who perceive that they have little control over their learning outcomes (Schmitz and Skinner, 1993; Skinner, 1995; Skinner, Zimmer-Gembeck, and Connell, 1998). A controlling or pressured climate in a classroom (Ryan and Grolnick, 1986), home (Grolnick and Ryan, 1989), or work group (Deci, Connell, and Ryan, 1989) is known to decrease motivation to perform a variety of behaviors. The factors that promote versus diminish control and the motivating effects of autonomy have been studied in areas as varied as the following:

- parenting (Grolnick and Ryan, 1989),
- management (Baard, Deci, and Ryan, 2004),
- dentistry (Halvari and Halvari, 2006),
- environmental sustainability (Pelletier et al., 1999),
- sport (Chatzisarantis and Hagger, 2007),
- virtual worlds (Ryan, Rigby, and Przybylski, 2006),
- psychotherapy (Ryan and Deci, 2008),
- religion (Ryan, Rigby, and King, 1995),
- politics (Koestner et al., 1996), and
- friendship (Deci et al., 2006).

Experiencing higher levels of perceived self-control predicts numerous positive outcomes, among them engagement in school and academic achievement (e.g., Skinner, Zimmer-Gembeck, and Connell, 1998). Research in education settings with elementary students, high school students, college students, and medical or law school students has relied mainly on students' reports about whether they perceive their learning behaviors to be autonomously driven or controlled. Students' intrinsic motivation is higher when they are taught in classrooms in which instructors are perceived as being supportive of student autonomy (Deci et al., 1981). Teachers and parents of young adults and adolescents who provide more autonomy support, either on their own or after training, have students or children with a greater sense of autonomy, which in turn predicted better learning and performance in school, greater retention, higher well-being, persistence with finding employment, and pursuit of additional learning opportunities (Black and Deci, 2000; Hardre and Reeve, 2003; Niemiec et al., 2006; Soenens and Vansteenkiste, 2005; Vallerand and Bissonnette, 1992; Vallerand, Fortier, and Guay, 1997; Vansteenkiste et al., 2004). Similarly, children of teachers who were more supportive of autonomy were judged to be more competent and better adjusted (Grolnick and Ryan, 1987). Similar findings have emerged for students in professional schools (Sheldon and Krieger, 2007; Williams and Deci, 1996; Williams et al., 1997). The amount of autonomy any learner desires, however, appears to depend on how competent and self-efficacious he or she feels. If the task is new or especially challenging, an individual may appreciate having little autonomy.

Providing people with choice about what activities to do and how to do them can increase intrinsic motivation (Zuckerman et al., 1978). Intrinsic motivation appears to be enhanced through choice when a moderate (and so not overwhelming) number of options are provided (Iyengar and Lepper, 2000). Motivation to learn in particular is enhanced when students are able to make meaningful choices during instruction (Moller, Deci, and Ryan, 2006; Ryan and Grolnick, 1986). This is clear from studies of engaged reading and writing among children and adolescents (Baker, 1999; Moje, Dillon, and O'Brien, 2000; Moje et al., 2008; Moje, Willes, and Fassio, 2001). Thus, to develop motivation, learners should be allowed to make some decisions about their instruction and control their outcomes (see Eccles and Midgley, 1989; Eccles et al., 1993a, 1993b; Urdan, Midgley, and Anderman, 1998).

It is important to note that building a sense of learner autonomy and control does not mean abandoning adults to learn on their own. There are a number of ways that adult education instructors can provide their students with opportunities to experience autonomy that do not require sacrificing such best practices as giving specific feedback, explicit and clear modeling of strategies, presenting challenging literacy tasks, and helping to monitor progress, all of which develop proficiencies and so support greater autonomy. The choices allowed can be quite small and still have important effects on motivation. Teachers can guide readers in making choices that expand exposure to different topics and genres and develop background knowledge and literacy skill. Other options can be provided to enable practicing skills within a known and comfortable genre or topic domain. Instructors can offer students guidance on how to make their own choices depending on what they need to practice, their skill levels, and their learning goals. It is possible for students to be involved with other small-scale decisions about instruction. For example, instructors can encourage adult learners to choose whether they want to work on a reading passage individually or in small groups, choose the order of activities during a class session, or choose the genre of the next text that they will read.

Providing a rationale for a task or behavior also can support perceived autonomy. For instance, Deci and colleagues (1994) found that providing a meaningful rationale for doing an uninteresting activity, acknowledging that participants might not want to do the activity, and minimizing the use of controlling language while highlighting choice led to increased reports of autonomy. There is a need for more research on promoting autonomous motivation, especially in the context of adult learning and literacy and its effects on learning outcomes. Overall, however, the existing evidence is consistent with the principle of creating learning environments that support learner autonomy.

Adult literacy educators should also assess the learning activities they have designed when students struggle to complete them; instead of the learner's skill being compromised, it may be that the learning task is inappropriate for his or her development. The task of matching tasks to a learner's developing skill is extremely challenging and depends heavily on access to data on reading and writing skills, interests, knowledge, and needs. Adult literacy educators should also consider the role of the texts being used for instruction. Many school-based texts are poorly structured, dense, and devoid of the author's voice (Anderson and Armbruster, 1984; Armbruster and Anderson, 1985; Chamblis, 1998; Chambliss and Calfee, 1998; Paxton, 1997; Schleppegrell, 2004), often creating confusion, misconception, or boredom for adolescent readers. The texts used for instruction in adult literacy courses are even more broad-ranging and complex than those of secondary education, thus potentially contributing to more challenges for learners. Adult literacy educators need to carefully analyze texts intended for instruction. Educators need to choose texts at a reader's instructional level and encourage writing tasks appropriate to instructional levels. Texts and tasks also need to engage and interest the reader or writer.

SOCIAL, CONTEXTUAL, AND SYSTEMIC MEDIATORS OF PERSISTENCE

While good instruction attempts to change individual beliefs and attitudes that can hinder persistence, it is also essential to attend to the broader environmental mediators of learning to support adults in attaining their learning goals (see McDermott, 1978; Moll and Diaz, 1993; Smith et al., 1993). Issues about systems and structures are highly relevant to persistence, especially because adults have many demands on their time (i.e., work, family responsibilities), but limited systematic intervention research is available to help address these issues. In this section we draw mainly from the literature in social psychology, anthropology, sociology, the learning sciences, and reading to identify features of the learning context, including social structures and systems, texts, and tasks with potential to motivate or demotivate adult learning and persistence.

Research conducted from anthropological and sociological perspectives seeks to describe conditions that may explain lack of persistence. The research has focused mainly on K-12 populations. What follows are findings from research about aspects of the learners' contexts that can make attaining learning goals challenging for some populations and why youth (and by extension, perhaps, adults) may fail to persist and thus fail to attain their aspirations. They offer insights into ways to create more motivating learning conditions for adults and adolescents.

Formal School Structures and Persistence

Motivation, especially in adolescence, comes in part from personal perceptions of having a choice in one's activities. Researchers have argued that the structures of rules, assignment of classes, and grading in secondary schools match poorly with adolescent needs for more space in which to make and take responsibility for decisions about actions and self-regulation (Eccles and Midgley, 1989; Eccles, Lord, and Midgley, 1991; Eccles et al., 1993a, 1993b; MacIver and Epstein, 1993). Supporting this view, Connell and Wellborn (1991) found that young people's beliefs—particularly those who are at risk (see Connell, Spencer, and Aber, 1994)—about their ability to control, and thus self-regulate, academic and social outcomes depended on the availability of contexts and experiences that allowed them some autonomy while also guiding and facilitating their decision making. Similarly, Werner's (1984) research on resilience suggests that youth who are required to engage in activities that help others (e.g., working to support family members, etc.) are more resilient, or persistent, in the face of challenges. Research also suggests that ability grouping and other related practices may have negative side effects on resilience and self-regulation (Blumenfeld, Mergendoller, and Swarthout, 1987; Guthrie et al., 1996; Urdan, Midgley, and Anderman, 1998; Wilkinson and Fung, 2002). This research is worth pursuing further in order to clarify the ways in which the design of school environments and processes can support or inhibit the development of self-regulatory capabilities that are needed in order to engage in literacy practice.

Students who see themselves as marginalized resist mainstream school structures and practices in ways that often reproduce their own marginalization and lack of attainment. These moves may appear to represent a lack of motivation. Willis (1977), for example, studied how two groups of boys in a British school appeared to be unmotivated to learn when in fact they were unmotivated to participate in social structures that they felt were inequitable. Similarly, MacLeod's (1987, 1995) analysis of two groups of young men of the same social class but of different races documented the low attainment and lack of resilience or persistence in the two groups (MacLeod, 1995). Although all the youth in his study struggled in school, those who lacked awareness of how their racial and class status shaped their treatment were more likely to fail in the long term.

These studies of how both social structures and the corresponding structures of formal schooling shape aspirations, persistence, and attainment shed light on why some adolescents and adults in literacy programs may have left school and how their motivation to learn may have been, and may continue to be, compromised. As a result, these studies offer important implications for different ways of structuring adult literacy programs, especially when considered in concert with psychological perspectives on autonomy and intrinsic motivation, already reviewed.

Cultural and Linguistic Differences

Some of the most compelling anthropological studies of education include micro-ethnographies that have focused on how linguistic and cultural difference played a part in young people's school successes and failures (see Erickson and Mohatt, 1982; Gumperz, 1981; Philips, 1972, 1983). These studies illustrated ways in which students from other than white middle-class groups struggled in the classroom because they did not possess "communicative competence" (Cazden, Hymes, and John, 1972). In other words, they did not use the language, gestures, or even body cues (e.g., making eye contact) that their teachers and other students understood as part of the proper classroom norms.

Heath's (1983, 1994) study of the language, literacy, and cultural practices of three communities augmented this research by asserting that the young people in the working-class communities were marginalized because schools valued the linguistic and symbolic capital of the children from the middle-class community. Mehan, Hertweck, and Meihls (1986) illustrated the "mediating mechanisms" of school practices, such as tracking, ability grouping, and evaluation, which affect the different kinds of cultural capital that students bring or do not bring to their school practices. They argued that the ways children use their cultural capital have less to do with their social background or ability than with what teachers and other school personnel do to work with and build cultural capital among students.

Social Relationships and Interactions

According to sociocultural theories of literacy, reading and writing are activities that participants perceive to have meaning in specific social and cultural contexts, which impart their own motivations (see Heath, 1983; Scribner and Cole, 1981). Classroom collaboration is one such activity because it fosters discourse practices in the community, from which the participants derive motivation. Research from varied disciplines points to several ways in which interpersonal or group activity—variously termed "cooperation," "collaboration," and "collective struggle"—is likely to motivate persistence and goal attainment.

First, it is important for students to interact in a learning community as they use literacy to research and solve problems (see Garner and Gillingham, 1996; Mercado, 1992; Moll and Gonzales, 1994; Moll and Greenberg, 1990). Learning environments and experiences that help establish positive relations with others while developing competence in particular skills also shape engagement, motivation, and persistence (see Guthrie et al., 2004; National Research Council, 2000; Palincsar and Magnusson, 2005). In fact, McCaslin and Good (1996) argue for reconceptualizing the idea of self-regulation by positing the notion of coregulation. Specifically, classroom teachers and researchers should examine how regulating one's learning activity is dependent on the social interactions and relationships developed in classroom settings. Engaging learners in working together may have positive social and literacy learning benefits.

A common means for enhancing engagement and persistence is to have learners work together. In learning to write, collaborative arrangements in which students work together to plan, draft, revise, or edit their texts have a positive impact on the quality of their writing, as illustrated in a meta-analysis by Graham and Perin (2007a). A distinguishing feature in these studies was that collaborative activities that students engaged in were structured so that they clearly knew what they were expected to do as they worked with others.

One challenge to the motivating effects of social interaction and group work, however, is the possibility for actual or perceived negative perceptions and actions on the basis of differences, particularly race, gender, sexual orientation, and social class. Among adults, these effects have been observed in many settings, as theories of status and related performance expectations have demonstrated (e.g., Ridgeway, 2001; Ridgeway et al., 1998). In classrooms, Cohen and colleagues (Cohen, 1994; Cohen and Lotan, 1997) provide evidence that the structure of the task and the nature of the group composition can exacerbate or mitigate perceived status differences and their negative effects (see also Wilkinson and Fung, 2002).

Models of group engagement around a task, or what is sometimes referred to as collective struggle, appear to be important to supporting youths' aspirations and attainment. In contrast to Ogbu's (1978, 1987, 1991, 1993) research suggesting that an awareness of oppression contributes negatively to students' lack of resilience and achievement in school, O'Connor (1997) found that a sense of the importance of collective struggle, combined with role models who demonstrated how to challenge oppressive practices in positive ways, contributed to the high resilience and achievement among the 47 black students she studied. Specifically, what distinguished high-achieving adolescents from the larger group was their access to family members and community structures that modeled positive struggle and resistance in the face of oppression (see Ward, 1990).

Similarly, in their analysis of various community-based education and activity programs, Heath and McLaughlin (1993) and Lakes (1996) illustrated that when provided opportunities for engaging in participatory, action-oriented learning and acts of required helpfulness (Werner, 1984), young people were able to engage in identity construction that supported persistence, motivation, resilience, and attainment in school and social settings.

These studies suggest that adult literacy programs might benefit from engaging learners in opportunities to use reading and writing to examine social and political issues of interest to them (see Freire, 1970, for an example of success in teaching basic reading skills to illiterate adult peasants in Brazil). A report of the National Research Council (2005) draws from a host of studies of how students learn in classrooms to offer a basic design principle of learning environments and instruction as "community-centered," thus supporting a "culture of questioning, respect, and risk-taking" (p. 13). Adults may become more engaged in reading and writing tasks that provide opportunities to work with other adults to solve real-world problems or allow them to make positive change in their living or work conditions. In addition to increasing the utility of literacy-based tasks and the sense of autonomy and control people have over their lives, collective literacy activities may provide them with the community support needed to persist in literacy learning even in the face of challenge.

Potentially Negative Effects of Stereotype

A robust literature on what Claude Steele and Joshua Aronson (1995) termed *stereotype threat* also offers important cautions in how teachers use group work of any size—from pairs to small groups to whole-class interactions. Stereotype threat is an individual's concern that others in a group will judge her or him by a dominant stereotype (Steele, 1997). Stereotype threat has been documented as strong enough to disrupt performance and is typically heightened in situations in which individuals who might be connected with such a stereotype (e.g., "women are not good at mathematics") represent only a small number in the overall group. For example, Steele and Aronson (1995) demonstrated that black college students who had demonstrated high capability in other testing situations performed poorly when told that their intelligence was being measured; these racial stereotype threats were documented among members of other racial and ethnic groups as well (see Aronson et al., 1999). Moreover, stereotype threat is not limited to racial stereotypes: gender and other aspects of difference have also been studied (e.g., Maas, D'Etole, and Cadinu, 2008). In other studies, researchers have situated members of racial, gender, and cultural groups in testing settings in which they are the numerical minority (e.g., small numbers of one group for whom a stereotype might be salient in large groups of students who might hold that stereotype; see Sekaquaptewa and Thompson, 2003) or have actively positioned groups against each other (e.g., women playing chess against men; see Maas, D'Etole, and Cadinu, 2008). In each testing setting, the group for whom a negative stereotype was activated, even in only implicit ways, performed worse than the other group and worse than they had in past testing situations.

Although most of the research on stereotype threat has been conducted in testing, game, or other high-pressure/high-stakes conditions, the consistent finding that stereotype threat can be activated by implicit statements and by group configurations has important implications for any adult literacy program in which groups come together from a variety of racial, cultural, and linguistic backgrounds. This work also has important implications for mixed gender groups.

Importantly, stereotype threat studies have been conducted largely among college students at elite universities. Thus, the history of struggle that many who attend adult literacy programs bring into the classroom has the potential to further divide groups on the basis of race, class, gender, and skill differences. These studies suggest that what is known about how society typically values various social identities needs to be considered and planned for in enacting opportunities for group work.

Indeed, available research suggests that stereotype threat can compromise learning in adult populations precisely because it can be triggered by age. In Western culture, education is often highly age-segregated (Riley and Riley, 1994, 2000) in being most strongly associated with childhood and early adulthood, and adult participation in formal instruction may be perceived to be "off-time." Stereotypes associated with adult learners, aging learners, and/or minority learners may constrain the effective allocation of attention needed to perform well on a task and impact self-regulation (Hess et al., 2003; Rahhal, Hasher, and Colcombe, 2001; Steele, 1997).

There is evidence that when stereotypes are activated (i.e., features of the stereotype that are relevant to the learner are made salient), working memory resources that are needed for effective performance may be consumed with distracting thoughts (Beilock, 2008; Beilock, Rydell, and McConnell, 2007; DeCaro et al., 2010). Stereotype threat may also make it more difficult for learners to use automatic attentional mechanisms (Rydell et al., 2010). It can be activated by seemingly innocuous features of the learning situation, like reporting one's gender on a mathematics test, but also by teachers' own anxieties about stereotypes (Beilock et al., 2010). Because such worries about whether one will confirm a stereotype to some extent involve inner speech, interventions that promote task-focused verbalizations have been found to mitigate against stereotype threat (DeCaro et al., 2010).

Social and Systemic Supports for and Barriers to Persistence

When designing adult education programs, it is important to consider the contexts of adults' lives and how to remove demotivating barriers to access and practice (Hidi, 1990; Krapp, Hidi, and Renninger, 1992). For adults to consider enrolling and continue participating in adult literacy courses, they must perceive the courses as being important, useful, interesting, and worth the investment of time (Wigfield and Eccles, 1992). They must also believe they can handle the short-term consequences of spending time on literacy improvement.

In fact, people selectively allocate resources to prioritize important goals, balancing responsibilities across work, family, parenting, community, and so on. Resources are also adaptively allocated across different functional domains: cognitive, physical, and emotional (Li et al., 2001; Riediger, Li, and Linderberger, 2006; Schaefer et al., 2008). So, for example, in the face of physical threat (health, safety, security) cognitive resources may be directed away from cognitive activities and toward changing conditions to protect physical well-being. Effective functioning in adulthood requires selectively allocating effort toward the most important and pressing goals in accord with the opportunities available (Heckhausen, Wrosch, and Schulz, 2010), and well-being appears to be enhanced in adulthood among those who engage in such "selective optimization" (Baltes and Baltes, 1990; Freund and Baltes, 1998, 2002; Riediger, Li, and Lindenberger, 2006; Wrosch, Heckhausen, and Lachman, 2000). In this light, lack of persistence in adult literacy instruction, while appearing to be a poor choice, actually may be a self-regulated, adaptive response to the constraints of competing pressures, demands, and trade-offs.

Descriptive data from intensive interviews collected from 88 adults in rural Kentucky reveal several factors that can affect decisions about whether or not to enroll in adult literacy classes despite being eligible for reduced fees (Anderman et al., 2002). Because local economies had been devastated, adults perceived that jobs would not be available at that time even if they earned a GED. Older interviewees reported that there was less stigma related to not completing high school in the past, and consequently they felt less reason to enroll in adult education courses in the present; they did not believe that adult literacy courses would be useful to them. Women, but not men, said they would attend to help their children with school. These and other findings from this research illustrate the value of conducting research to better understand the factors that motivate or demotivate the potential market for adult literacy programs. These interview responses are consistent with other research on how adults analyze such trade-offs: there is evidence that investment in goals perceived to be attainable is beneficial, but that perseveration in striving for goals incongruent with available opportunities can negatively impact well-being and mental health (Heckhausen, Wrosch, and Schulz, 2010). If the individual comes to believe that the opportunities to achieve the goal are unavailable, goal disengagement is likely, in which the goal itself is devalued.

Significantly, child care emerged in this and other descriptive studies as a serious practical issue that affects participation and persistence. It is likely that programs to increase the availability of child care, particularly at no cost or at reduced rates, would greatly facilitate the participation of many adults.

Longitudinal studies have examined people's motivation to persist in adult literacy programs (Comings, 2009). In the most recent report, persistence was related to variables that included (1) having previously engaged in learning experiences after formal schooling, (2) having a strong social support network, and (3) having a personal goal (e.g., helping one's children or obtaining a more lucrative job). In contrast, persistence was undermined by the demands of everyday life, low levels of social support, and lack of motivation.

DIRECTIONS FOR RESEARCH

Studies on motivation and adult literacy are scarce (Comings and Soricone, 2007). The principles outlined in this chapter are offered with the caveat that, although they are well researched with other populations, on other targeted skills, and in other settings, they must be studied further with many different groups of adult literacy learners in their varied learning environments. It is likely that significant advances can be made in understanding how to motivate adult learners to persist if interventions aim to understand how individual, social, cultural, and systemic influences interact to affect persistence (for a similar view, see Pintrich, 2003). Research in the following areas is especially needed.

Experiments to identify instructional approaches that motivate engagement and persistence with learning for low-literate adults. Experiments, including randomized controlled trials, are needed to learn how to implement and structure instruction to motivate engagement, persistence, and progress. The committee found only a handful of randomized controlled trials focused on motivation and self-regulated learning for adolescents or adults (e.g., Oyserman, Brickman, and Rhodes, 2007; Oyserman, Bybee, and Terry, 2006) and none focused on motivation or persistence in the context of reading and writing performance of adolescents and adults, other than studies of adolescents in middle and high school education settings. Randomized studies of literacy have been conducted with younger populations (e.g., Justice et al., 2008; Kemple et al., 2008), but research with adult populations is mainly descriptive or quasi-experimental. Although true randomization conditions are difficult to establish, studies that incorporate wait-list control designs (in which control groups receive the experimental approach at a later time) could be an alternate approach that would benefit both researchers and future adult learners.

As noted by Maehr (1976), continuing motivation to learn is an often neglected but extremely important educational outcome, since adults often hope to continue learning independently between bouts of program attendance. Thus, experimental research is needed that not only evaluates ways to help students develop proficiencies for meeting an immediate literacy goal, but that also encourages continued learning to meet longer term literacy needs.

Development of measures to assess student motivation and test hypotheses about how to motivate adult learners' persistence. One reason for the limited experimental research could be the lack of reliable and valid measures for assessing motivation and related constructs, such as engagement and interest. Providers of adult education need standard ways to assess the specific motivational needs of their students to inform the use of practices that meet such needs. Although many general motivation measures have been developed in research on goal orientation theory (Midgley and Urdan, 2001), expectancy-value theory (Jacobs et al., 2002), and self-efficacy (Bandura, 1997), with few exceptions (e.g., Moje et al., 2008) most are not geared toward assessing adult motivation toward literacy. The few promising instruments that exist could be developed further and specifically for adults seeking literacy instruction. For instance, one reliable and valid measure of adult reading motivation contains subscales that assess reading efficacy, reading as part of one's identity, reading for recognition, and reading in order to excel in other life domains (Schutte and Malouff, 2007). It would be especially helpful to have ways to measure actual persistence in literacy tasks in addition to survey or other self-report data. There is reason to think that perception of effort does not always relate directly to extent of effort (Steinberg, Brown, and Dornbush, 1996).

Qualitative and mixed methods for more thorough understanding of adult learners. Qualitative studies of adult literacy and mixed-methods approaches are needed to ascertain more about learners' motives and circumstances and how these relate to the effectiveness of various strategies for influencing motivation, engagement, and persistence (e.g., Anderman et al., 2002). For instance, the mixed quantitative-qualitative approach to examining motivation to enroll in adult literacy courses among eligible adults in Kentucky was particularly useful, since many of the participants did not have basic literacy skills and thus could not complete survey instruments, despite being eager to participate. Use of qualitative methods allows researchers to more thoroughly examine the effects of people's life contexts (e.g., jobs, families, health issues) on their decisions to enroll in and persist in adult literacy courses than relying only on quantitative methods, such as surveys.

Research on how the various components of motivation relate to one another to affect persistence. Different theories of motivation invoke an array of similar constructs that partially overlap and that make different hypotheses about how the components of motivation relate to one another to affect behavior. Models of motivation need to be applied and tested in the context of helping people to persist in adult literacy education.

Research on texts and tasks for adult literacy instruction. Many features of a text or task can motivate or demotivate a reader to persist in the face of reading challenges (Moje, 2006b). And these features change dramatically as children become adolescents and move through the grades from primary to secondary school. In adolescence and adulthood, reading demands are shaped by knowledge domains, each with specific types of texts and with expectations—often unspoken—for the kinds of texts to be read and written. It is important to understand how the texts and tasks made available to learners and how their perceptions of these texts and tasks affect motivation to persist, even in the face of linguistic and cognitive challenges. What tasks will engage learners in questions of interest to them (see Goldman, 1997; Guthrie and McCann, 1997; Guthrie et al., 1996)? What texts are available to learners in formal adult literacy programs? What texts typically are used and how? What texts should be used and how? A range of research methods should be used to investigate these questions, including large-scale surveys and inventories of the texts available and used for instruction in adult literacy settings; in-depth qualitative and ethnographic studies of how texts are used and perceived by adolescent and adult learners; and small-scale experimental studies that manipulate tasks and text types with different types of readers to ascertain more and less engaging text styles, types, and content.

Studies of group differences and similarities in the factors that influence motivation to persist with learning, reading, and writing. Although principles of motivation apply across populations, group differences in persistence can be expected according to age and other characteristics of the learner. Research is needed to understand how to address the particular challenges some learners have with motivation and persistence. This need is illustrated in research on writing: self-efficacy for writing declines with age in some studies and increases in others (see Pajares, 2003, for a review); similar mixed findings have been found for attitudes toward writing, with declines evident in some studies (e.g., Knudson, 1991, 1992) but not others (e.g., Graham et al., 2003; Graham, Berninger, and Fan, 2007; Graham, Harris, and Olinghouse, 2007). Several studies show that interest in writing develops over time (Lipstein and Renninger, 2007; Nolen, 2003). One's attributions for success with writing may also vary with age: younger students in one study were more likely than older ones to give higher ratings to effort and luck as a cause of success (Shell, Colvin, and Brunning, 1995). Research on adult training in the workplace also suggests that the age diversity of classrooms could have negative effects on learning and that the learning environment may be more favorable for older students if structured to avoid unfavorable social comparisons, such as those related to speed of learning that might lower self-efficacy.

Technology. Technology use for older learners needs to be studied with attention to the features that motivate persistence and how technologies are best introduced and their use supported. Research is needed on how different technology formats influence conceptions and attitudes toward literacy, such as task enjoyment, perceived task difficulty, and expectations for success, and how these attitudes in turn relate to literacy outcomes.

Research to identify the conditions that affect motivation to enroll in adult literacy courses. The effects of compulsory enrollment on motivation and learning should also be studied. The circumstances and incentives that affect decisions to enroll in literacy courses needs to be determined both to influence enrollment and to identify moderators of instructional effectiveness. In the job context, for instance, organizations often require their employees to attend job-related training programs, but the mandatory enrollment can promote feelings of external control and reduce motivation during training. Findings by Baldwin, Magjuka, and Loher (1991), Guerrero and Sire (2001), and others (see Mathieu and Martineau, 1997), for example, show that employees who are not allowed to decide whether to attend an organizationally sponsored or supported training program reported lower levels of motivation for training than employees who were allowed to participate in the enrollment decision. Consistent with motivational theories that emphasize self-determination and findings on the role of participation in goal setting, adults who are allowed to participate or control the decision are also more likely to report higher levels of training commitment, to allocate more time and effort to attending classes, and to spend more time engaged in on-task learning activities than adults who are not allowed choice over enrollment.

Development and implementation of support systems for motivating persistence. In educational settings, a student's family and peers are often identified as key influences on learning motivation. In the working adult's environment, family members, supervisors, and coworkers also exert important influences on motivation related to training and development. Research is needed to determine if sustained engagement with learning is helped by establishing appropriate expectations about the amount of time and effort that will be required to meet the learners' literacy goals and by providing support for overcoming logistical difficulties. Encouraging significant others to participate in pretraining could also help to clarify the demands and the role of social support for learning and practice.

A final point about needed research on the barriers to persistence is critical: although research on individual motivation, engagement, and interest is useful, it is unlikely that adolescents and adults with pressing social, familial, and economic demands on their lives will make the time and effort necessary to persist unless strategies are in place to help them cope in significant and sustained ways with these demands. Adult literacy programs can offer significant and sustained means of supporting persistence. The contexts, texts, tasks, systems, and structures of adult literacy instruction require as much research-based attention as do the individuals who must persist in learning.

6

Technology to Promote Adult Literacy

In this chapter, we examine the types of technologies that are available or could be developed for adult literacy instruction. Part one presents classes of technologies that are available and could be used to support growth in adults' literacy skills. Part two describes why these technologies would be expected to improve learning and literacy skill development. Part three describes specific digital tools and instructional approaches for practicing literacy skills. The chapter concludes with a summary and discussion of directions for research.

We argue from the findings that technologies can be designed and used to scaffold literacy growth in ways that may not occur in available forms of interaction between human teachers and students. Although it is likely that using technologies will add to the cost of literacy programs, the degree of differentiated and sustained support adults need to develop their skills is great enough that investments in technology may be the most cost-effective solution. Thus, it is worth developing and testing the most promising new approaches so that their costs and benefits are better understood.

In reviewing the research, we recognize that many studies of technology effectiveness in education show minimal and sometimes null results. This is not surprising. Technology does not of itself produce learning. It simply amplifies and extends instructional strategies. Too often, studies of technology effectiveness have paid inadequate attention to the content of the instruction and assumed that amplifying any strategy would be effective. Neither do the studies attend sufficiently to the engineering and training required to implement the technologies effectively.

In this chapter, we describe promising technologies that, if well engineered and supported, could be used to amplify effective instructional approaches. In some cases, we provide clear supporting evidence; in other cases, the evidence is indirect, and efficacy studies are needed. In virtually every case, translational research will be needed to demonstrate how the technologies can be part of coherent systems of instruction. We point to all of these technologies because of their potential to alleviate some of the barriers adults experience with learning due to restricted times and places of in-person instruction. Rising education costs also make amplification of human effort especially important in fields, such as adult education, that lack a strong funding base.

Furthermore, adults need opportunities to access tools and develop proficiencies that are part of what it means to be literate in the 21st century. As described in Chapter 2, literacy always includes a mediating technology that makes possible the inscription and transmission of words and meanings, whether a stone tablet, a quill pen, a book, a typewriter, or a word processor. What is new in the digital age—and what makes it essential to emphasize the role of new technologies in efforts to promote adolescent and adult literacy—is the unprecedented nature, speed, and scale of change in technologies for literacy that have occurred as a result of the Internet and related information technologies, commonly referred to as Web 2.0.

An assessment by the editors of the *Handbook of Research on New Literacies*, a compendium devoted to an exploration of new technologies, provides a sense of the vast shifts now occurring as a result of the Internet (Coiro et al., 2009a, pp. 2-3):

> No previous technology for literacy has been adopted by so many, in so many different places, in such a short period, and with such profound consequences. No previous technology for literacy permits the immediate dissemination of even newer technologies of literacy to every person on the Internet by connecting to a single link on a screen. Finally, no previous technology for literacy has provided access to so much information that is so useful, to so many people, in the history of the world. The sudden appearance of a new technology for literacy as powerful as the Internet has required us to look at the issue of new literacy with fresh lenses.

Many researchers in literacy and related fields are actively investigating the implications of Internet and related information and communication technologies (ICTs) for literacy, schooling, civic engagement, and work. To name a few such efforts, there is interest in the strategies that readers use for comprehending text online (e.g., Coiro and Dobler, 2007); multimodal text production and comprehension (e.g., Hull and Nelson, 2005; Jewitt and Kress, 2003); identifying and developing new online spaces that provide opportunities for language learning and literacy development (e.g.,

Hull, Stornaiuolo, and Sahni, 2010; Lam, 2000); and documenting the startling growth and new patterns of use of digital technologies, including cell phones and social networking sites, in mostly out-of-school contexts (Ito et al., 2009; Pew Internet & American Life Project, see http://www. pewinternet.org/ [Jan. 2012]).

There are several constraints on the evidence available. Currently, out-of-school uses of digital technologies for communication, self-presentation (on such sites as Facebook), work, and play far outstrip their use in schools for educational purposes. Educational institutions can lag greatly in their uptake and appropriation of new literacy tools and practices (Beach, Hull, and O'Brien, in press; Davies and Merchant, 2009; Greenhow, Robelia, and Hughes, 2009), thereby limiting the available research. With few exceptions, such as studies of the out-of-school digital literacy practices of youth (Hull et al., 2006; Ito et al., 2009; Lam, 2000; Lankshear and Knobel, 2003), which are only time-bound snapshots, the research base on ways to use new technologies outside classrooms to develop adults' literacy also is slight.

Certain factors have constrained the use and study of technologies for adult learning. Historically, adult education has been underresourced, in terms of both access to literacy-related technologies and instructional tools and teachers skilled in their instructional use. Currently, some populations still lack Internet connectivity and access to instructional uses of digital technologies, although such gaps are quickly narrowing (Pew Internet & American Life Project, see http://www.pewinternet.org/ [Jan. 2012]). The technology usage studies described earlier, for example, may not generalize to the adult literacy learner population, or they may apply to only part of that population. Technology access for learning also can be a complex matter. Although access to technologies for particular subgroups of learners needs to be verified and understood better,[1] we turn next to the large landscape of technologies for learning that are potentially available to adolescents and adults who need to enhance their literacy. Most are readily accessible on the Internet.

---

[1]An interesting example of the underlying complexity of availability arose in an urban school near one committee member. In that school, a foundation provides laptops for the students. However, only students whose parents attend weekend orientation sessions may take the computers home. So, all students have some access, but the subset with greater access has parents able and willing to attend a couple Saturday sessions. Many students have computers at home, but other family members compete for them and they may not contain support for instructional affordances.

CLASSES OF TECHNOLOGIES FOR LEARNING

A report of the National Research Council (2008) identified 10 classes of technologies for learning:

1. conventional computer-based training,
2. multimedia,
3. interactive simulation,
4. hypertext and hypermedia,
5. intelligent tutoring systems,
6. inquiry-based information retrieval,
7. animated pedagogical agents,
8. virtual environments with agents,
9. serious games, and
10. computer-supported collaborative learning.

To this list must be added the everyday tools of word processing. The ability to easily and quickly compose and edit prose is a major determiner of writing achievement, and word processing tools replace laborious writing and complete rewriting with faster (after practice) typing and editing that does not require recopying the entire written product (see Berninger et al., 1998; Christensen, 2005; Graham, Harris, and Fink, 2000; Graham, Harris, and Fink-Chorzempa, 2002).

Most of the items on the list above (3-10) were not widely available 20 years ago, and most are not mainstream technologies in schools today. Many of these technologies are unfamiliar to and unavailable to adult learners, particularly those with low literacy. This means that learning systems, like systems used for marketing and other commercial purposes, need highly intuitive interfaces and modes of learning activity. The labels, icons, graphics, layout, and semiotic foundations of symbols need to be easily understood and generally fully accessible without training or instruction manuals. This often is not the case for instructional technologies (Yeh, Gregory, and Ritter, 2010). It is likely that many such uses of technology that could be productive have proven disappointing in initial tests because of poor design or because a potential body of users was not part of the subculture that has absorbed knowledge of how to use a given technology. (For example, 10 years ago, high school students generally did not need instructions in how to use cell phones, but senior citizens sometimes did, because the high school culture had learned about cell phones but the senior culture had not yet absorbed this knowledge.)

One general problem in evaluating evidence on uses of technology is that the first efforts to use an approach are often designed by small teams that lack the full range of skills to make software usable, even when they have a powerful concept. Rigorous tests of the first efforts then yield minimal results, making it harder for subsequent design teams to get the funds needed to produce truly usable systems. Increasingly, tools to make software more usable are becoming more usable themselves, and it may be worth reconsidering some approaches that showed minimal results if it appears that part of the problem was poor design.

Still, many adolescents and adults in the United States and across the world (but possibly not all adult literacy learners) have adopted with alacrity and ease digital technologies for everyday life that have become inexpensive and readily available, such as cell phones. Furthermore, the literature on adolescent literacy has documented many cases of young people who acquire facility with digital tools that require reading and writing in their out-of-school lives and who have more digital expertise than teachers, although they may experience difficulties with academic literacy. The widespread use of digital tools associated with literacy in everyday life may provide a means to scaffold the development of competencies in print-based and academic literacy genres; research is needed to determine how. The existence and widespread use of such tools also challenge educators and educational institutions to expand definitions of literacy and opportunities to practice literacy to include a facility with online and multimodal texts and technologies. A related need is research on how to assess competencies with digital texts.

HOW TECHNOLOGIES AFFECT LEARNING

Computer technologies may improve learning for many reasons. They can be adaptive to the profiles of individual learners, give the learner control over the learning experience, better engage the learner, and be more efficient on many dimensions. A number of researchers have reported advantages of particular classes of technologies compared with classroom instruction, reading textbooks, and other judiciously selected controls.

For example, Dodds and Fletcher (2004; Fletcher, 2003) conducted a meta-analysis of studies with primarily adult learners that showed an advantage over controls for conventional computer-based training (.39 σ effect size), multimedia presentations (.50 σ), and intelligent tutoring systems (1.08 σ). The subject matters represented in these meta-analyses included mathematics, science, and procedural knowledge rather than reading or writing per se. Mayer (2005) reported advantages (~1.00 σ) of multimedia over conventional text on science/technology content; he also identified cognitive principles that explain when multimedia presentations do or do not help.

Successful intelligent tutoring systems have been developed to teach well-formed topics in mathematics, including algebra, geometry, and programming languages (The Cognitive Tutors—Anderson et al., 1995; Koedinger et al., 1997; Ritter et al., 2007); physics (Andes, Atlas, and Why/Atlas—VanLehn et al., 2002, 2007); electronics (Gott and Lesgold, 2000; Lesgold and Nahemow, 2001); and information technology (Mitrovic, Martin, and Suraweera, 2007). These systems do not target reading and literacy per se, but the scientific, mathematical, and technical content covered is presumably a close fit to the verbal materials that adults use in the real world and are likely to invoke and develop aspects of verbal skill related to reading and literacy skill. The systems show impressive learning gains (~1.00 σ), particularly for deeper levels of comprehension in subject areas.

Not every type of advanced computer technology has been demonstrated to facilitate learning in every subject area. Indeed, more needs to be understood about many of these technologies. Learning gains have either been nonsignificant or mixed in major investigations of hypertext/hypermedia (Azevedo, 2005; Azevedo and Cromley, 2004), animation and interactive simulation (Ainsworth, 2008; Dillon and Gabbard, 1998; Tversky, Morrison, and Betramcourt, 2002), and inquiry-based information retrieval (Goldman et al., 2003; Graesser and McNamara, in press; Klahr, 2002). This may be because most learners have inadequate strategies for inquiry learning; that is, they do not know how to use new information tools for the purposes that have been tested. Research is only emerging on the effectiveness of serious games (Kebritchi, Hirumi, and Bai, 2010; O'Neil, Wainess, and Baker, 2005; Ritterfeld, Cody, and Vorderer, 2008), virtual environments (Johnson and Beal, 2005; Johnson and Valente, 2008), and computer-supported collaborative learning (Bereiter and Scardamalia, 2003). Much remains to be explored about whether these environments can play a productive role in adult literacy improvement.

Computerized learning environments have been developed that directly focus on reading and writing. McNamara's edited volume (2007a) describes many of the recent systems that have been developed, such as iSTART, to promote deeper levels of comprehension, and Carla (Wise and VanVuuren, 2007), which focuses on more shallow levels. These computer environments as a group help students learn reading at multiple levels, including language decoding, vocabulary, semantic interpretation of sentences, generating inferences, and building self-explanations of the content. Learning gains in such system have been statistically significant, although effect sizes tend to be lower than those for mathematics and other science and technology areas. At the same time, we note that reading trainers that are commercially available for children did not show significant improvements in the 2007 report of What Works Clearinghouse assessments (Dynarski et al., 2007). There are questions about the quality of those evaluations, however, and whether the interventions adequately reflected the power of the new technologies. Regarding writing, a number of computer tools give feedback and improve different aspects of the writing process, such as Summary Street (Kintsch et al., 2007), e-rater (Attali and Burstein, 2006; Burstein, 2003), and the Intelligent Essay Assessor (Landauer, Laham, and Foltz, 2000). There are fewer writing trainers than reading trainers. Research is needed on how computer tools can support the writing development of adults with low literacy, including the integration into adult education programs of Web 2.0 technologies that have become prevalent in daily life, such wikis, blogs, and social networks.

Computer-based trainers have been developed to improve metacognition, self-regulation, and critical thinking while learners interact with multimedia environments. For example, SEEK Web Tutor helps adults evaluate the quality of information sources as they try to learn from Internet-based materials (Graesser et al., 2007; Wiley et al., 2009), and MetaTutor trains students on metacognitive and self-regulated learning strategies (Azevedo et al., 2009). These skills are important in the unedited Internet culture, in which the quality of many information sources is suspect and the goals of reading comprehension vary substantially (McCrudden and Schraw, 2007; Rouet, 2006). The impact of these trainers on comprehension and learning has either been modest or has not been fully evaluated, however.

An example of a tool now readily usable for instruction is onscreen agents that act as mini-tutors to help with using a technology or to provide other assistance. Modern learning environments increasingly incorporate animated conversation agents that speak, point, gesture, walk, and exhibit facial expressions. Agent-based systems have shown impressive learning gains, with moderate-to-high effect sizes (Atkinson, 2002; Gholson and Craig, 2006; Gholson et al., 2009; Graesser, Jeon, and Dufty, 2008; Hu and Graesser, 2004; McNamara et al., 2007b; Moreno and Mayer, 2004, 2007). The potential power of these agents is that they can mimic face-to-face communication with human tutors, instructors, mentors, peers, or people who serve other roles (Baylor and Kim, 2005). Ensembles of agents can model social interaction. Both single agents and ensembles of agents can be carefully choreographed to mimic and reflect on virtually any strategy connected to reading, writing, and learning. Agent-based systems are easy for low-literate adults to use because the human-computer interface naturally mimics everyday social experiences.

In addition to onscreen agents, there is the opportunity for human tutors to interact with students online via real-time chats, such as those that are increasingly available to support visitors to banking, shopping, and other websites. Although technologies have been used to provide real-time reading and writing instruction (e.g., such instruction was organized for children in the wake of the Haiti earthquake), the committee did not locate research on the use of real-time chats in the educational settings. Such technologies are worth testing for adult literacy programs because they allow flexible, immediate, and scaffolded interactions with instructors outside the classroom setting.

DIGITAL TOOLS FOR PRACTICING SKILLS

In the sections that follow, we describe some of the possible ways that technologies might enhance adult and adolescent literacy practice and acquisition. Many of these technologies have yet to be tested with adult literacy learners, so a program of empirical research to evaluate their effectiveness and how best to implement them is highly recommended. Nevertheless, there is empirical research that shows the promise of these technologies in K-12 and college populations.

Group collaborative communication software. In this category, we include the kinds of tools that are used in offices every day. Especially helpful to adult learning, perhaps, are the tools that are starting to emerge for exchanging comments on written materials. Other frequent forms of collaborative communication include electronic calendars, email, text messaging, Facebook, wikis, and collaboration portals. New technologies for group communication are appearing regularly.

Word processing software. The most basic tools that can help with literacy are standard word processing tools, which facilitate writing and especially editing. With a little practice, students can quickly get ideas on paper and then sharpen them. Having ideas in machine-processable form also makes it possible to use the latest tools for exchanging ideas and working in teams on written products. Controversies remain about features of software that make it easy to circumvent mastery of some literacy skills, notably spelling correction. However, for most adults and adolescents who have limited literacy, the ability to get ideas on paper, read those of others, edit initial writing, and exchange ideas that sharpen comprehension and composition is dramatically enhanced by word processing tools and should therefore be encouraged (Bereiter and Scardamalia, 2003; Graham and Perin, 2007a). In the end, the single best-established fact about literacy is that it is a form of skilled expertise, and such skills require thousands of hours of effective practice. Word processing tools support that practice. Related tools, such as presentation software, are standard ways by which empowered adults express their literacy in civic and work situations. Part of being functionally literate today is the ability to use such tools effectively.

Bulletin boards and discussion tools. Once students are creating compositions and exchanging them, they need ways to hold conversations with each other about the texts. All of this is easily possible via bulletin board systems. On such systems, threads of conversation can be started about particular topics or posted texts. Students engage in multiple literacy activities that involve reading additional documents and peer comments and then preparing their own comments and posting them. This approach is promising both because it provides engaging ways of practicing literacy and because the continuing exchanges provide natural experience with the need to write for others' understanding.

Commenting tools embedded in programs. Contemporary online word processing facilities provide commenting tools in online texts. Adobe Acrobat provides such tools for commenting on PDF files, but there also are software packages on wiki or Moodle sites that allow students to annotate texts individually as they read. Students can benefit from seeing which parts of a text prompt annotations and what their peers wrote in their notes. This turns reading into an enterprise in which quality effort is reified by artifacts and supported with those artifact tools. The use of commenting tools also mimics productive work, providing both motivation and practice in some of the 21st-century skills. For example, the chapters in this report accumulated over 100 comments each during their initial development and later editing, even prior to the formal review stage.

Virtual meeting tools. A variety of new systems support online meetings with components that permit word processing and other tools to be shared over a network. That is, multiple people can talk to each other, write to each other, show each other diagrams and other media, and jointly edit a single text, PowerPoint file, or other document. Back channel tools, such as chat windows, allow the meeting host to structure the interactions and ensure that anyone who wishes to make a point or enact a change in a document is given a chance to do so. While current systems are probably too expensive for general school use (largely because of communications charges), the price of in-house tools that could be used on a school building network can be expected to drop rapidly, following the cost curve of most new technologies.

Virtual meeting tools are used in the work world partly to support working from home. In the education world, especially for adult learners, such tools can help in overcoming transportation issues, increasing total engaged time beyond short class periods, and, for adolescents, better connecting home and after-school environments to school settings. Preliminary design and feasibility research are needed to provide a clear picture of what is possible and whether actual learning gains would be as large as one might predict.

Speech-to-text and text-to-speech tools. Computer-generated speech (called text-to-speech) and speech recognition facilities (called speech-to-text) occur throughout society (Jurafsky and Martin, 2008). Phone calls are answered by computers that then respond to spoken commands by consumers. High-end automobiles can respond to hundreds of voice commands, generally without training to handle a specific person's voice. It is entirely possible to develop texts that read themselves to a student and also systems that listen to students reading texts aloud and give corrective assistance if they make errors in their reading (Cole et al., 2003; Johnson and Valente, 2008; Mostow, 2008). A number of intelligent tutoring systems allow spoken student input as an alternative to typed input (D'Mello et al., 2010; Litman et al., 2006).

Speech-to-text technologies are achieving an acceptable level of accuracy because the speech processing task in shadowing oral reading is highly constrained. One knows what the reader should be saying, and hence it is straightforward to monitor actual student speech and correct it when appropriate. Other assistive possibilities exist as well. The computer jumps in and pronounces a word on which a student stumbles. The computer orally restates a sentence or two after a student gets stuck, thereby helping out when processing capacity is limited.

Technologies with text-to-speech and speech-to-text facilities are growing at a fast pace. Additional capabilities are described below in the section on Electronic Entertainment Technologies and Related Tools.

Embedding low-level coaching in electronic texts. Related to natural language processing technologies is the possibility of embedding pop-up questions in texts that are presented on screen. This is one way to prompt students who may get caught up in word recognition to also engage in meaning. Variations of this approach were developed at the Centre for Educational Technology in Israel two decades ago (observed by Alan Lesgold; no documentation known but screen images are available), and other variants were developed in the United States, such as Point and Query (Langston and Graesser, 1993). The basic idea is that the kinds of prompts introduced in such tools as Questioning the Author (Beck et al., 1996) can be embedded in machine-readable text and then made to appear automatically alongside the text to which they apply as the student encounters it. It is possible to have pop-up questions tailored to match a system's best understanding of how the reader is processing the text in question. For example, if the student is not spending enough time on difficult content that is important, then there can be pop-up generic questions (Are you sure you understand this section?) or specific questions that target particular ideas.

Automatic essay scoring. It is commonly held that a primary reason that students are given relatively few writing assignments is that it takes instructors too long to read and comment on them. There are two easy solutions to this problem. One is supported by the tools for collaborative text processing discussed above. Specifically, students can comment on each other's work. Although there are no data on how well this works with the adolescent and adult limited literacy population, there have been demonstrations (Cho and Schunn, 2007; Cho, Schunn, and Wilson, 2006) that it is an effective teaching strategy to have students comment on each other's written work in college courses. Positive results to date generally have involved use of writing to teach specific content rather than in literacy instruction.

In addition, it is possible to do considerable automated scoring of texts through recent advances in computational linguistics. Shermis and colleagues (2010) reviewed the performance of the three most successful automated essay grading: the e-rater system developed at Educational Testing Service (Attali and Burstein, 2006; Burstein, 2003), the Intelligent Essay Assessor developed at Pearson Knowledge Technologies (Landauer, Laham, and Foltz, 2000, 2003; Streeter et al., 2002), and the IntelliMetric Essay Scoring System developed by Vantage Learning (Elliott, 2003; Rudner, Garcia, and Welch, 2006). These systems have had exact agreements with humans as high as the mid-80s, adjacent agreements (i.e., scores the same or only one point apart in the rating scale) in the high mid-90s, and correlations as high as the mid-80s. Just as impressive, these human-machine agreement levels are slightly higher than agreement between pairs of trained human raters. Automated essay graders have been used in electronic portfolio systems to help students improve writing by giving them feedback on many features of their essays, as in the case of Criterion (Attali and Burstein, 2006) and MY Access (Elliott, 2003). Criterion scores essays on six areas related to word- and sentence-level analysis that are aligned with human scoring criteria: errors in grammar, errors in word usage, errors in mechanics, style, inclusion of organizational segments (e.g., a thesis statement, some evidence), and vocabulary content.

Intelligent tutoring systems. From 1985 to the present, there have been a number of intelligent tutoring systems developed (see citations above) that track student performance on various tasks, provide feedback, and intelligently guide students in ways that promote learning. The feedback is based on a model of how particular students must have reasoned to act as they did, or alternatively on some mixture of such "model tracing" (what set of mental rules could have produced the student performance details; see Anderson et al., 1995) and reasoning from Bayesian belief networks (Pearl and Russell, 2002). These are networks of the conditional probabilities of having one element of competence given evidence of having or not having others (Conati, Gertner, and VanLehn, 2002; Doignon and Falmagne, 1999).

Instant feedback tailored to the situation. Intelligent tutoring systems operate by trying to discover what pattern of present and missing knowledge best accounts for a student's performance. When considering reading skill training, such systems would model the comprehension skills that a learner exhibits and then provide feedback on text processing that is tailored to the learner's current level of knowledge and skill (Connor et al., 2007). A system might analyze the patterns of reading time allocated to screens of text (Conati and VanLehn, 2000) and diagnose from the processing time patterns that particular kinds of information are not being integrated. Such a system then might have an animated agent suggest to the learner that connections among related ideas be noticed and elaborated. In addition to using the temporal pattern of reading, such systems also could use learner answers to prompt questions to decide which aspects of literacy need further support (see McNamara, 2007b, for a review of such systems).

Detection and tailoring to emotion and engagement level. While the field generally is just beginning to develop, there certainly are examples already of intelligent systems that are sensitive to emotion and, thereby, to motivational state (Baker et al., 2010; D'Mello et al., 2008; Litman and Forbes-Riley, 2006). Such systems can be more flexible in engaging students if they understand when a text is not engaging the student or when a task is producing an emotional response that leads to avoidance rather than deep engagement. Engagement is a central issue in adolescent and adult literacy development, so having tools that can directly gauge emotional state and infer level of engagement should afford opportunities for substantially improved literacy practice tools.

Serious games. Serious games are designed with the explicit goal of helping students learn about important subject-matter content, strategies, and cognitive or social skills. Instead of learning by reading a textbook, listening to a lecture, or interacting with a conventional computer system, the learner plays a game that requires engaging curriculum content and provides learning opportunities as part of the game context. Serious games have revolutionary potential because the learning of difficult content becomes an enjoyable, engaging experience for the learner. Intellectual hard work is transformed into play.

Very few serious games have been around for very long, so some researchers and game developers speculate that game design may be inherently incompatible with pedagogy (Prensky, 2000). The more optimistic view is that there needs to be careful analysis of how the features of games are systematically aligned with the features of pedagogy and curriculum (Gee, 2004b; Gredler, 1996; O'Neil, Wainess, and Baker, 2005; Rieber, 1996; Shaffer, 2007; Van Eck, 2007). Van Eck (2007) has explored how Gagne's principles of instructional design (Gagne et al., 2005) are mapped onto particular features of games. O'Neil, Wainess, and Baker (2005) have presented a similar mapping of game features to Kirkpatrick's (1994) four levels of evaluating training (student reaction, learning, behavioral transfer, and systemic results) and to Baker and Mayer's (1999) model of learning that has five major families of cognitive demands (content understanding, problem solving, self-regulation, communication, and collaborative team-work). Ideally, serious games should increase enjoyment, topic interest, and what Csikszentmihaly (1990) calls the flow experience (such intense concentration that time and fatigue disappear). Engagement in the game should facilitate learning by increasing time on task, motivation, and self-regulated activities, as long as the focus is on the instructional curriculum rather than nongermane game components that distract from the knowledge and skills to be learned.

The design, development, and testing of serious games are not grounded in a rich empirical literature, but that is changing. Available reviews and meta-analyses show mixed support as to whether serious games enhance learning of content, strategies, or skills (Fletcher and Tobias, 2007; O'Neil, Wainess, and Baker, 2005; Randel et al., 1992). There are documented success cases that show the promise of serious games, such as Gopher, Weil, and Bareket's (1994) transfer of the Space Fortress game to piloting real aircraft, Green and Bavelier's (2003) transfer of action digital games to visual selective attention, Moreno and Mayer's (2004) use of experimenter-constructed games to train explanations of scientific mechanisms, and a demonstration that mathematics games can promote mathematics achievement and possibly motivation to study mathematics (Kebritchi, Hirumi, and Bai, 2010). Researchers have identified a long list of features that are good candidates for explaining why games enhance motivation (Loftus and Loftus, 1983; Malone and Lepper, 1987; Ritterfeld, Cody, and Vorderer, 2008): interest, fantasy, challenge, play, feedback, narrative, hypothetical worlds, entertainment, and so on. These hooks optimize time on task and so could be useful to learning of reading components. The integration of game components and literacy instruction seems destined to have a large future (Gee, 2007; McNamara, Jackson, and Graesser, 2010).

One important characteristic of rich gaming environments is that they allow for embedding assessment into the learning context. Shute has referred to this as "stealth assessment" because no performance is marked specifically as testing; rather, all action is simply part of the flow of a game (Shute et al., 2009). The basic approach, derived from Mislevy's concept of evidence-centered design (Mislevy, Steinberg, and Almond, 2003), is to build both assessment and instructional choices based on that assessment into the infrastructure behind a learning game. Although research on serious gaming is mostly at a demonstration stage (see National Research Council [2011] *Learning Science Through Computer Games and Simulations*), the approach is strongly anchored in well-proven theory and thus promising for further research, development, and efficacy testing.

Immersion environments. An interesting example of the sophisticated level of intelligent training environments is the system called Tactical Iraqi (Johnson and Beal, 2005; Johnson and Valente, 2008; Losh, 2005), which has been expanded to a more general Tactical Language and Culture System for multiple languages. This system has intelligent tutoring system components embedded in virtual reality with multiple fully embodied animated agents. This system was developed to help junior officers prepare for duty in Iraq, where they would need to interact with local tribal leaders in a new language and culture. The learners in this system are confronted with realistic situations, such as having to negotiate movement of a medical clinic to ensure that it is not damaged during needed military maneuvers. They then interact with graphically rendered actors, such as village elders, young firebrands who believe all Americans are bad, and others, attempting to achieve the desired goal of moving the clinic. The system is highly engaging, presumably in part because the responses to learners' actions are both cognitive and emotional.

It is not yet clear that this level of realism is needed to engage adult and adolescent literacy learners or which learners would benefit most, but the mere fact that it is possible sets the stage for a range of research that examines what level of intelligent technology is cost-effective for enhancing effective literacy practice. Moreover, as the techniques used in Tactical Iraqi penetrate the electronic games industry and the marketing world, costs may drop enough to make the approach feasible for low-budget adult literacy programming.

Electronic entertainment technologies and related tools. While systems like Tactical Iraqi are expensive in the economic context of adult education, it may be possible to get similar levels of effect from various kinds of entertainment tools, like role playing environments and social media. These range from simple games to rather elaborate possibilities, such as Second Life. The committee encourages both funding agencies and public-private partnerships to explore possible uses. Even if the approaches add little content to what can be done other ways, the motivational value of immersion environments is substantial, and motivation and engagement remain a critical barrier to progress in literacy for adult learners.

A variety of simple tools have been used (mainly in elementary education, some for secondary education, and very little for adult literacy) to help people practice and become more facile in basic components of literacy. The tools promote, for example, practice of basic word reading and increases in vocabulary (see Breznitz, 2006; Lyytinen et al., 2007; Scientific Learning Corporation, 2010; see also the section above on Embedding Low-Level Coaching in Electronic Texts).

Environments, such as Second Life, have quickly engaged significant portions of the adult and adolescent worlds. Their motivational value can be seen in the willingness of participants to pay real money to gain virtual resources, such as clothing, housing, etc., that exist only in the imaginary world on the screen. This level of motivational power might be extremely helpful in stimulating greater levels of literacy activity. Even in the simplest form, one could imagine students writing and revising essays in order to earn virtual clothes for an avatar or access for their avatar to a new environment.

Finally, there is a range of new social media (Second Life is partly a social medium, too), including Facebook, MySpace, and others, that generate large amounts of multimedia communication and might be useful in two ways. One is that, because they are stimuli for large amounts of verbal communication, they may provide a portion of the practice that adults need to build adequate literacy skills. It also is possible, of course, that they instead reinforce activity that never requires deeper comprehension or composition practice. This raises a second possibility, which is that social media might be shaped to require or provide incentives for more productive literacy practice. To some extent, this already may be occurring. For example, increasing numbers of adults are meeting and becoming paired through social media, which places a premium on being able to describe oneself in text and to respond to written questions. More directly, researchers have begun to design and implement social networking sites specifically to support and encourage literacy-rich educational activities for youth, such as multimodal composing, language learning, and intercultural understanding (e.g., Hull, Stornaiuolo, and Sahni, 2010). The committee thinks that this second possibility merits consideration and suggests that such approaches be included among those encouraged in funding for prototype development and validation.

Finally, the Internet, Web 2.0 technologies, and learning systems supported by technology can potentially eliminate or ameliorate constraints of space and time that have traditionally governed adults' opportunities to learn. Given web-based or agent-based tutors and the range of social and cognitive supports that can be provided online, the necessity for adults to be physically present in classrooms at designated times may be greatly lessened. We are not advocating that online tutoring, technologically mediated instruction, or distance education replace face-to-face instruction. However, we think it is important to explore what combinations of physically copresent, Internet-enabled, and computer-supported activity may be effective for adult learners. Because many of these adults must balance the need to extend their literacy learning with the considerable demands and responsibilities of work and family, highly motivating environments may be especially important in stimulating literacy practice.

It is worthwhile to consider promising technologies for adult literacy education even if current development costs are high. Initial versions of instructional software can be very expensive because of the steep learning curve, but the cost becomes much lower with subsequent versions. For example, the first version of one industrial training technology that went through five generations of development cost almost $2 million, but the cost for the fifth version was only $70,000 (Lesgold, in press). Moreover, first-generation development costs for many of the instructional approaches likely to benefit adult literacy learners may be borne by early adopters, such as the military.

SUMMARY AND DIRECTIONS FOR RESEARCH

Technologies with potential to support higher levels of adult and adolescent literacy development are appearing, changing, improving, and becoming more affordable at a very rapid pace. Technologies are vital to making the entire population literate because of their value for improving, leveraging, and making more affordable activities that require intense human effort, such as literacy instruction. Internet technologies also have the potential to alleviate barriers associated with limited times and places of instruction. Digital technologies are important to incorporate into literacy instruction as the tools required for literacy in a digital age.

Ten classes of technologies for learning are potentially available to support the literacy development of those outside K-12 schools: conventionally computer-based training, multimedia, interactive simulation, hypertext and hypermedia, intelligent tutoring systems, inquiry-based information retrieval, animated pedagogical agents, virtual environments with agents, serious games, and computer-supported collaborative learning. These computer technologies would be expected to improve learning because they enable instruction to be adapted to the needs of individual learners, give the learner control over the learning experience, better engage the learner, and have the potential to develop skills efficiently along several dimensions.

Numerous digital tools are potentially available to support adults in practicing their literacy skills and for giving the feedback that supports learning, among them group collaborative communication software, word processing, speech-to-text and text-to-speech tools, embedded low-level coaching of electronic texts, immersion environments, intelligent tutoring systems, serious games, and automatic essay scoring. Studies are needed to establish that the efficacy of effective instructional approaches can be enhanced by technology and to clarify which subpopulations of learners benefit from the technology. Some of this research is emerging with technologies for instruction, with intelligent tutoring systems among those with the strongest positive effects.

The ways in which adults will benefit from instructional technologies will depend on the subpopulation of adults. Given the technologies that are ready to be developed, studies are needed to develop and assess the effects of technologies for English language learners, adolescents and adults with less than high school levels of literacy, learners with disabilities, and college students who need to enhance their reading and writing skills. In doing the research, it will be important to understand the technology skill sets of both those who need to develop their literacy and the instructors involved in technology-facilitated instruction and to provide the needed supports.

Technology changes quickly in price, availability, and social penetration, making it extremely difficult to know which people are using which technologies at a particular point in time. For example, some may communicate largely through text messaging, and others use social networking sites or business mail systems. To help develop the capacity to use technologies for learning, it will be important to identify both the texts and tools already routinely used by various subgroups of the adult learner population and the types of texts they need to be able to produce and comprehend.

A challenge in the use of technology for adult literacy instruction may be overcoming complex institutional arrangements often involved in changing educational practice. This complexity leads to high institutional inertia in the adoption of technologies that much more rapidly penetrate the general world of consumers. A further challenge is the learning curve for any new technology, during which initial costs are high and utility is not fully developed. Understanding whether a particular technology is worth the investment will require a sophisticated research funding strategy. Such a strategy would involve deciding on the best bets for investment, sustaining the investment long enough for the technologies and their implementation to be refined sufficiently to have substantial impact, and maintaining agility in technology investment and implementation to respond to rapid evolutions in technology.

Research is needed to test new and evolving technologies and resolve inconclusive findings. Many specific uses of technology for adolescent and adult literacy instruction have been shown to be effective in small-scale, controlled studies. For these uses, the next step will be to evaluate them in studies with larger populations and diverse settings. At least as important, though, is programmatic translational research that can show the ways in which an existing instructional system or organization can benefit from the technologies that show the greatest promise.

7

Learning, Reading, and
Writing Disabilities

In this chapter, we review research on the cognitive, linguistic, and other learning challenges experienced by adults with learning disabilities and the use of accommodations that facilitate learning. We focus mainly on research with college students because the empirical research base is more comprehensive for them than for other adult learners with learning disabilities. The chapter also includes neurocognitive research that has concentrated mainly on children with learning disabilities, although adolescents and adults have been included in the research to some degree.

The chapter has four parts. Part one begins with a brief overview of learning disabilities before turning to a more specific discussion of reading disabilities, the most prevalent and best studied class of learning disabilities. Most of this research concentrates on the reading and comprehension of words and sentences. We next discuss research on writing and the component skills and processes of writing that challenge those with writing disabilities. Part two presents neurocognitive research on the development of brain structures and functions associated with some of the cognitive and linguistic processes that underlie reading disabilities. We discuss the future implications of this research for adult literacy assessment and instruction and the importance of interdisciplinary research for a better understanding of learning disabilities, specifically, the ways in which genetic, neurobiological, behavioral, and environmental forces interact to affect the typical and atypical development of reading and writing skills. Because neurocognitive research on writing disabilities is in the early stages, we focus mainly on the larger body of research on reading. Part three describes accommodations to facilitate learning for those with learning disabilities. The chapter concludes with a summary and discussion of research needed to design effective instruction and instructional supports for low-literate adolescents and adults with disabilities who need to further develop their reading and writing skills.

The findings presented here are relevant to instructors of colleges or adult basic and secondary education programs. Yet it is important to recognize that learning disabilities also are a condition defined by legal criteria in the United States, criteria to which secondary and postsecondary institutions must adhere in providing services for students with learning disabilities. The college students identified with learning disabilities who have participated in research have met this legal criterion. In addition, access for accommodating individuals with learning disabilities on standardized tests and instructional settings requires documentation that these legal criteria have been met. As a result, the findings reported in this chapter may be most relevant to adults with similar characteristics. More research of the kind described is needed to characterize a broader range of adults.

LEARNING DISABILITIES

Learning disabilities is an umbrella term that encompasses several types of developmental disorders evident as difficulties in learning specific academic or language skills, typically reading, mathematics, oral language communication, writing, and motor performance (e.g., coordination; see American Psychiatric Association, 2000, *Diagnostic and Statistical Manual of Mental Disorders*, 4th ed.). Learning disabilities have been historically difficult to define in part because they are not a unitary or homogeneous disorder and in part because they have been defined through exclusionary rather than inclusionary criteria. The rationale for an exclusionary definition remains relevant today. The diagnosis of learning disabilities is reserved for individuals with unexpected academic underachievement that cannot be attributed to known causes, such as sensory disorders, general intellectual disability, significant emotional or behavioral disorders, poverty, language differences, or inadequate instruction (Fletcher et al., 2007).

It is important to note that consensus on an evidence-based definition of learning disability has not yet been reached. There is much debate on how to improve definitions and legal criterion setting for the diagnosis and remediation of learning disability. Further research is needed to arrive at an evidence-based definition to guide research and practice.[1] Our main focus

---

[1]Traditional diagnoses of learning disabilities have depended either on (a) showing a significant discrepancy between reading, writing, or math achievement scores and the scores that would be expected based on the individual's IQ scores (IQ/achievement discrepancy definitions) or (b) substantial underachievement in an academic area in the context of average or

in this chapter, however, is on the known processing deficits experienced by those with learning, reading, and writing disabilities about which there is broader agreement.

Learning disabilities in adulthood by definition describe individuals as developmentally disordered in learning in comparison to age-expected performance and appropriate instructional opportunities. A diagnosis requires evidence that an individual is substantially limited in major life activities (e.g., reading or writing). If learning disabilities are not diagnosed before adulthood, however, it may be difficult to establish that the individual had access to sufficient high-quality instruction. Social/emotional, cognitive, oral language, and achievement abilities influence individual learning differently across the life span, and the recognition of age-specific markers may be critical to reliable and valid diagnostic decision making appropriate for the adolescent and adult population (Gregg, 2009). Adults can experience a range of learning disabilities that are important to diagnose and attend to as part of literacy instruction.

Although better information is needed about the number of adults in literacy programs with learning disabilities, over one-quarter of adults who attend adult education programs report having a learning disability (Tamassia et al., 2007). The prevalence of learning disabilities for the college-bound population is reported to be approximately 3 to 5 percent of student enrollment (National Center for Education Statistics, 2009; Wagner et al., 2005). Due to variability in eligibility criteria, the adult population with learning disabilities represents a very heterogeneous group of individuals in terms of severity, ability, and background.

Many individuals with learning disabilities do not have access to opportunities to develop and demonstrate their knowledge, with unsettling consequences for their career development and adult income (Gregg, 2009; Rojewski and Gregg, 2011). A total of 14 million undergraduates are enrolled in 2- and 4-year colleges in the United States, and the number is expected to reach 16 million by 2015. Among the U.S. population with learning disabilities, approximately 17 percent will take college entrance

---

low average intelligence, intact sensory abilities, and adequate instructional opportunities. Recent research findings, however, have a greater focus on other approaches such as response to intervention or differentiated diagnoses based on learning over time (Burns, Appleton, and Stehouwer, 2005; Fletcher, Denton, and Francis, 2005; Fuchs and Fuchs, 2005). There is growing agreement among some researchers that a hybrid model of identification is necessary to the definition of learning disabilities, which includes three criteria: (1) inadequate response to appropriate quality instruction; (2) poor achievement in reading, mathematics, or written expression; and (3) evidence that other factors are not the primary cause of poor achievement (Bradley, Danielson, and Hallahan, 2002; Fletcher et al., 2007). At present, however, there is not conclusive evidence or consensus on any one diagnostic approach to identifying learning disabilities.

exams, but only 4 percent of students who had received special education services in high school were found to be enrolled in a 4-year college or university 3 to 5 years after high school (Wagner et al., 2005, 2007). These figures are substantially lower than those for college-bound students without disabilities. The greatest growth in postsecondary attendance by students with learning disabilities is experienced at 2-year colleges (Wagner et al., 2005). Outcome data pertaining to secondary and postsecondary populations with learning disabilities raise concerns about the equity and quality of educational opportunities for these individuals (National Council on Disability, 2003; Wagner et al., 2005). Adolescents with learning disabilities are more likely to experience substandard postsecondary outcomes compared with their nondisabled peers, as evidenced by high secondary retention and dropout rates (Gregg, 2007; Newman et al., 2009; Weiss and Hechtman, 1993; Young and Browning, 2005), lower postsecondary enrollment and attainment (Stodden, Jones, and Chang, 2002; Wagner et al., 2005), restricted labor force participation (Barkley, 2006), and lower earnings (Cheeseman Day and Newburger, 2002). Several factors that contribute to the negative career outcomes of adolescents and adults with learning disabilities include lower self-esteem and greater susceptibility to the negative impact of socioeconomic background on academic achievement (Wagner et al., 2005) and career attainment (Rojewski and Kim, 2003).

Although behavioral tests are used for assessment and diagnosis, learning disabilities have come to be viewed as brain-based conditions with a pathogenesis that involves hereditary (genetic) factors. In recent years, research on assessment and treatment of learning disabilities has become a magnet for the application of new techniques and paradigms from genetics, basic neuroscience, cognitive science, and cognitive neuroscience. Research to date suggests that it is plausible to assume that the malfunctioning of the brain system that supports reading and its development may be caused by multiple deficiencies in the corresponding genetic machinery that guides early brain development (Grigorenko, 2009). Although understanding the genetic and neurobiological mechanisms that underlie learning difficulties is important to a full and adequate definition of learning disabilities, research on gene-brain-environment interactions is required to understand the complex sets of factors that make learning a challenge for many individuals.

Reading Disabilities

Some 80-90 percent of students with learning disabilities are reported to exhibit significant difficulty with reading (Kavale and Reese, 1992; Lerner, 1989; Lyon et al., 2001). The term *reading disability* is often used interchangeably with the terms *dyslexia*, *reading disorder*, and *learning disabilities in reading*. Adults with reading disabilities experience lower reading achievement than what is expected given their age, intelligence, and education. High school students with diagnosed learning disabilities have lower literacy levels than students without disabilities (National Assessment of Educational Progress, 2010). Longitudinal research has shown the persistence of a diagnosed reading disability into adulthood and behavioral and biological validation of the lack of reading fluency in adults with dyslexia across the life span (Bruck, 1990, 1992, 1993; Shaywitz, 2003; Swanson and Hsieh, 2009). As discussed in Chapter 3, there is no consensus on the estimated numbers of adult learners who may have such a reading disability. The estimates range from one-tenth to more than half (Patterson, 2008). In a national survey of adult education programs, 89 percent reported providing services to at least one adult with learning disabilities, although most (62 percent) relied on self-reports. Because only 34 percent of programs reported screening for learning disabilities, it is likely that many adults may have gone unrecognized as having a learning disability, especially older students.

A significant number of college students with learning disabilities demonstrate reading underachievement as a result of their disabilities, influencing both their school and work outcomes (Bruck, 1992; Gregg, 2009; Gregg et al., 2002; Shaywitz et al., 2003). According to data from the National Longitudinal Transitional Study-2, over 50 percent of secondary students performed below the 16th percentile on reading comprehension measures, placing them at the lower 25th percent of the general population (Wagner et al., 2005). These students experience various difficulties with the cognitive and linguistic processes involved in decoding, word identification, reading fluency, and reading comprehension.

Decoding

The importance of phonological, orthographic, and morphemic awareness to decoding and accurate word identification has been well documented.[2] The majority of research on decoding in college students with learning disabilities pertains to specific reading disabilities (dyslexia). The persistence of phonological, orthographic, and morphemic awareness deficits has been repeatedly documented (Bruck, 1993; Gregg et al., 2002; Hatcher, Snowling, and Griffiths, 2002; Holmes and Castles, 2001). However, in the absence of valid diagnostic tools normed on the adult

---

[2]Phonological awareness or knowledge refers to awareness of individual speech sounds and the ability to associate speech sounds with print (e.g., ability to identify, discriminate, and isolate phonemes for rhyming or repeating and/or manipulating spoken pseudowords). Orthographic awareness is the visual recognition of letter forms and spelling patterns within words. Morphological awareness is the recognition of morphemes (the smallest meaning units in language) and knowledge of word derivations (*create, creation, creative, creator*).

population, professionals are left to often infer how executive functioning, working memory, attention, metacognition, and oral language deficits differ across and within the broader range of the adult population with dyslexia. Professionals must retain a healthy degree of skepticism that the inferences drawn from cognitive, oral language, and achievement test batteries are equivalent across populations with and without disabilities until measures are validated for individuals with disabilities (Gregg, 2009).

Studies of college students with reading disabilities (dyslexia) have demonstrated that phonological knowledge predicts skill in decoding (Bruck, 1993; Gregg et al., 2002; Hatcher, Snowling, and Griffiths, 2002). As a group, these students over-rely on spelling-sound information, syllabic information, and context for word recognition. Bruck's research also documented that among this adult population, phonological awareness continued to be an area of deficit in comparison to their peers. The decoding errors demonstrated by individuals with phonological awareness deficits often represent "phonetically implausible" letter and word choices.

Orthographic awareness (e.g., Vellutino, Scanlon, and Chen, 1994) has not received the attention that phonemic awareness has in the literature, particularly with the college population with learning disabilities (Berninger, 1994; Foorman, 1994; Roberts and Mather, 1997). Yet researchers provide strong evidence that orthographic awareness significantly influences the ability to decode words (Cunningham and Stanovich, 1990; Kim, Taft, and Davis, 2004; Stanovich and West, 1989). Empirical verification supports that orthographic processing is a separate latent construct from phonological processing in the adult population (Carr and Posner, 1994; Eviatar, Ganayim, and Ibrahim, 2004; Gregg et al., 2008; Rumsey et al., 1997a, 1997b). However, as Foorman (1994) notes, "although orthographic and phonological processing can be dissociated statistically, they are conceptually intertwined" (p. 321).

Some college students with reading disabilities (dyslexia) demonstrate problems with both phonemic and orthographic awareness. The decoding errors of individuals demonstrating difficulty specific to orthographic processing usually are "phonetically plausible," meaning that these readers appear to overrely on their phonological abilities. Such readers may accurately represent the sounds in target words that have direct sound-symbol correspondence (e.g., cat) but may be unable to recall unusual or irregular sequences of letters that cannot be sounded out (e.g., yacht).

Proficiency with phonological, orthographic, and semantic knowledge is essential to learning morphemes (Carlisle, 2004). Much research documents the association between morphological awareness and word reading (Carlisle, 1995, 2000; Carlisle and Stone, 2003; Nagy et al., 1989). Recently, two studies investigating the Hebrew college population with learning disabilities (dyslexia) showed these individuals display specific deficits in morphological processing and a general metalinguistic deficiency that is not explained by phonological processing (Leikin and Hagit, 2006; Schiff and Raveh, 2006). Yet very little research concentrates on how morphological processing affects word knowledge and word reading in English-speaking adult populations with learning disabilities.

Reading Comprehension

Research with college students with learning disabilities points to several sources of difficulty with reading comprehension. These sources of difficulty include verbal working memory, language disorders, executive function, long-term memory, and metacognition (particularly self-regulation and comprehension monitoring). Several recent studies show the significant role of working memory in reading comprehension proficiency (Berninger et al., 2006; Swanson and Ashbaker, 2000; Swanson and Siegel, 2001; Swanson, Howard, and Saez, 2007). In a recent study of young adults, Berninger et al. (2006) investigated three executive functions of working memory (set shifting, inhibition, and monitoring/updating) and three word forms (phonological, orthographic, and morphological) to determine their relationship to reading comprehension performance. The predictive abilities of these linguistic and cognitive processes were not consistent across reading formats, suggesting the importance of assessment task to diagnostic decision making.

Some students experience difficulty with comprehension because of poor decoding, but for other adolescents and adults with learning disabilities, the core of their reading problem is a receptive language disorder (Cain and Oakhill, 2007; Catts, Adlof, and Ellis, 2006). The relationship between oral language and reading comprehension strengthens as readers mature both in age and ability level. There is strong evidence that language-based declarative knowledge and higher order language processes (e.g., inferencing and comprehension monitoring) relate to adults' reading comprehension (Floyd et al., in review). Prior knowledge helps with inference making and comprehension monitoring across the life span (Kintsch, 1998; Perfetti, Marron, and Foltz, 1996). Listening comprehension also is important for reading comprehension from ages 9 to 19, further suggesting the importance of higher order language processes, such as inferencing and comprehension monitoring, enabled by prior knowledge. Use of these language processes is common to listening comprehension and reading comprehension tasks (Perfetti, 2007). This finding is consistent with research indicating that oral comprehension places an upper limit on reading comprehension performance for children (Stothard and Hulme, 1996). Together these findings indicate the importance of investigating the influence of oral language on reading comprehension growth in the college population with learning disabilities and adult literacy learners.

Long-term memory is important to interpreting text. Readers construct a situational model during the process of listening or reading comprehension (Kintsch, 1998).[3] Long-term memory is believed to be one of the most critical underlying cognitive processes for creating a situation model because it is needed to (1) link propositions (units of meaning in the form of a statement or question) in the text to what the reader already knows and (2) integrate all of the propositions into a meaningful message or whole (Kintsch, 1998; see Chapter 2). The long-term memory measures on the majority of cognitive tests currently available do not have strong concurrent or construct validity, however, and better measurement tools are needed to assess this important construct in the context of reading instruction.

Many individuals with learning disabilities have difficulty with self-regulation and strategy use, which prevents them from using contextual information fully for comprehending text (Cain, Oakhill, and Elbro, 2002; Cain, Oakhill, and Lemmon, 2004). Difficulties with the strategic use of context cues can be manifest in such problems as using cohesive devices, flexibility with word knowledge (e.g., use of idioms, deciphering ambiguous references), and restricted working-memory processes (e.g., executive, attention).

Comprehension monitoring refers to evaluating one's ongoing understanding of text and spontaneous use of strategies to clarify inconsistencies or uncertainties and other comprehension problems while reading. Some readers with learning disabilities have significant difficulty detecting inconsistencies in what they read. Researchers suggest that difficulty with comprehension monitoring is often the result of restricted working memory and executive processes. Therefore, simply providing such an individual extra time on a reading task might not be very effective unless the reader is also taught specific cognitive strategies to enhance comprehension monitoring. Individuals with learning disabilities show particular difficulty with acquiring self-regulatory strategies and applying them efficiently (Swanson, Hoskyn, and Lee, 1999; Zimmerman, 2000a, 2000b). Thus, effective instruction in reading comprehension must target not only the acquisition of effective reading strategies but also their flexible application and monitoring.

---

[3]*Situation model* refers to creating representations of the meaning of text derived from both propositions stated explicitly (the textbase) and a large number of inferences that must be filled in using world knowledge (see Chapter 2).

Writing Disabilities

Individuals with learning disabilities often demonstrate difficulties with written expression. Findings from the fields of sociolinguistics, cognitive psychology, and neurolinguistics reveal that certain cognitive processes (e.g., working memory, executive functioning, orthographic awareness) influence specific types of written expression (Berninger and Winn, 2006; McCutchen, 2006; Shanahan, 2006; Torrance and Galbraith, 2006) and so provide information critical to the design of effective intervention and accommodation. Strategic learning relies not only on the cognitive abilities of writers, but also on their experiences, self-efficacy beliefs, and motivation (Pajares and Valiante, 2006). Sociolinguistic research verifies that written expression is influenced by affective, situation, and social variables (Englert, Mariage, and Dunsmore, 2006). Research on all of the processes known to affect writing (cognitive, linguistic, affective, and social) is necessary to effective assessment, intervention, and accommodation of adolescents and adults with learning disabilities.

Handwriting and Spelling

There is a small body of evidence that difficulties with basic writing skills, such as handwriting and spelling, constrain writing development. Poor writers often have difficulties mastering these skills (Graham, 1999). As a result, these skills demand the writers' attention, diverting resources away from other important aspects of writing, such as sentence construction and content generation. When struggling writers are explicitly taught handwriting and spelling, not only do these skills improve but so do other writing processes, such as output and sentence construction (Berninger et al., 1997, 1998; Graham, Harris, and Fink, 2000; Graham, Harris, and Fink-Chorzempa, 2002).

Handwriting. The term *graphomotor skills* refers to the cognitive, perceptual, and motor skills that enable a person to write. The three types of graphomotor deficits prevalent in the college population with learning disabilities include symbolic, motor speed, and dyspraxia disorders (Deul, 1992; Gregg, 2009). All three interfere with a writer's handwriting legibility and writing fluency. Individuals with symbolic graphomotor deficits demonstrate specific phonemic, orthographic, and morphological awareness deficits that interfere primarily with the planning and controlling functions required in handwriting (Berninger and Richards, 2002). A college student with learning disabilities and symbolic graphomotor deficits might produce excellent original drawings but not be able to produce legible handwriting. Visual-verbal production (handwriting) draws on very different neurological systems than visual-nonverbal production (pictures). Individuals with dyslexia often demonstrate symbolic graphomotor symptoms, resulting in poor handwriting performance. Since it is often difficult for these individuals to recall the letters or words they want to use in order to express their ideas, legibility and writing fluency become a problem for them. The source of this type of graphomotor disorder is symbolic (Berninger, 1994).

Individuals with motor speed deficits demonstrate problems with the timing and temporal aspects of graphomotor tasks, which also draw on the planning and execution functions of writing. These individuals usually provide legible and accurate handwriting, but the speed to produce the product is very slow (Deul, 1992). Historically, motor speed problems were called clumsiness or limb-kinetic apraxia (Liepmann, 1900).

According to Deul (1992), dyspraxia is the "inability to learn and perform age-appropriate sequences of voluntary movements in the face of preserved coordination, strength, and sensation" (Deul, 1992, p. 264). Unlike writers with more symbolic graphomotor deficits, these individuals demonstrate motor pattern difficulties regardless of whether the symbol is verbal or nonverbal. One of the most distinguishing aspects of dyspraxia is the unusual formation of letters and words. These writers will often print in distinct blocklike symbols, usually in all upper case, display inaccurate spaces between letters and words, and show difficulty with letter formation.

Spelling.   Spelling is the ability to represent words in print. Researchers have provided evidence of the regularities and opacities of English orthography itself; the role of morphology in spelling; developmental trajectories; spelling acquisition strategies; cognitive, linguistic, and environmental predictors of spelling; the role of various mental representations of words; the role of implicit memory in spelling; the relation between spelling and other academic skills (e.g., decoding); and possible reasons for spelling underachievement (Coleman et al., 2009; Gregg, 2009). There is a spectrum of spelling competency that depends on a variety of factors (e.g., exposure to print, reading style) unrelated to cognitive and language abilities. Even among college students with learning disabilities with similar levels of reading proficiency, some may be unexpectedly poor spellers (Frith, 1980; Holmes and Castles, 2001).

The persistence of spelling problems for college students with learning disabilities (dyslexia) has been supported by empirical evidence (Bruck, 1993; Gregg et al., 2002; Holmes and Malone, 2004). Some researchers suggest that difficulties with phonemic awareness may be reflected in spelling attempts that lack phonetic plausibility—that is, attempts that, if decoded according to typical grapheme-phoneme conversion rules, do not sound exactly like the target word (Coleman et al., 2009; Holmes and Castles, 2001). Recently, researchers have identified morphological awareness (sometimes called morphophonemic awareness) to be another strong predictor of spelling (e.g., Allyn and Burt, 1998; Gregg, 2009; Holmes and Castles, 2001; Leong, 1999) and an area of weakness in college students with learning disabilities (dyslexia) (Bruck, 1993; Coleman et al., 2009; Deacon, Parrila, and Kirby, 2006; Leong, 1999).

Orthographic awareness, orthographic sensitivity, and orthographic processing are all very important to spelling performance across the life span (e.g., Cunningham, Perry, and Stanovich, 2001; Foorman, 1994; Roberts and Mather, 1997; Stanovich, West, and Cunningham, 1991). As Holmes and Castles (2001) note in relation to college students with learning disabilities, "unexpectedly poor spellers are seen to misspell many words, not because of deficient phonological processing, but because their lexical entries contain inadequately specified word-specific information" (p. 321).

Interestingly, college students with attention deficit hyperactivity disorder (ADHD), while often demonstrating problems with spelling, do not demonstrate the number or types of errors characteristic of their peers with learning disabilities (dyslexia). In a recent study, Coleman and Gregg (2005) counted and categorized spelling mistakes in the impromptu essays composed by 263 young adults. The students without disabilities (n = 90) averaged 2 to 3 errors per 1,000 words, and about 80 percent of their incorrect attempts were judged to be plausible (e.g., airate for aerate). Students with ADHD (n = 44), although they made more errors (about 4 per 1,000 words), achieved a similar plausibility rate. The errors of students with learning disabilities (dyslexia, n = 77) were considerably more frequent (7 per 1,000 words) and less plausible (65 percent). This finding indicates the importance of attending to well-defined subgroups of adults in research to identify the most effective approaches for enhancing adults' writing skills.

Syntax (Sentence Level)

The term *syntax* refers to rules in a language for assembling words to form sentences. Syntactic awareness and the ability to produce sentence structures require a writer's semantic (word usage in context), grammar (e.g., agreement), and mechanical (e.g., application of punctuation and capitalization rules) abilities working in unison. Problems with any one of these features can influence fluency with written syntax. Therefore, during an evaluation, examination of word usage, word agreement, and the mechanics of writing should be conducted and taken into consideration in determining how written syntax is influenced by these features.

Research is limited on the cognitive and linguistic processes that influence the ability of college students with learning disabilities to produce written syntax (Gregg, 2009). Most researchers have relied on frequency counts, such as number of words, sentence length, or number of sentences.

Such indices treat grammatical structures as if they are isolated from words, syntactic structures, and context. Yet research from the field of linguistics, particularly sociolinguistics, shows that the context and function of language use relate to the uses of meaning and structure. The association of word meaning to grammatical structure and structure to words provides information pertinent to the understanding of language and to the ability to design instruction in reading and writing (see Biber, Conrad, and Reppen, 1998, for an in-depth discussion).

Gregg et al. (2002) examined the relationship of words and sentence features in the expository essays of four groups of young adult writers (with learning disabilities, ADHD, learning disabilities + ADHD, and normally achieving). They found that the writers with learning disabilities and ADHD had less varied and complex sentence features than the other groups. Biber identified several features of sentences most associated with sentence complexity in written text. Using these complexity indices, Coleman and Gregg (2005) found that with a group of college students with and without dyslexia, two of Biber's (1988) sentence features—integrated structures (i.e., nouns, prepositions, and attributive adjectives) and word specificity (i.e., word length and word types)—differentiated the two groups of writers. The writing of the college students with learning disabilities (dyslexia) contained significantly fewer of these features, therefore decreasing the linguistic complexity of their writing samples. Interestingly, Coleman and Gregg (2005) also found that the writers with learning disabilities (dyslexia) had more difficulty with sentence features having to do with time (as a main verb tense, prepositions, and time adverbials), a situation that could be due to the executive and attentional constraints on working memory. Another very distinct feature of the discourse of the writers with learning disabilities (dyslexia) was their overuse of hedges (e.g., at about, something like, more or less, almost, maybe, sort of, kind of, etc.). Such grammatical structures provide less specificity and more ambiguity to the meaning of the text. Underlying word knowledge and word access problems might be contributing to this overuse of hedges.

The development of age-appropriate written syntax skills depends on a number of variables. Foremost among these is oral language development (i.e., receptive and expressive syntax). An adult with an expressive (or receptive-expressive) language disorder will struggle to construct written sentences, just as he or she struggles to construct spoken ones. Of course, this is not to imply that intact oral syntax abilities automatically transfer to writing; oral skills are necessary but not sufficient for writing proficiency. Mastery of a formal writing system requires adequate functioning in other cognitive and social areas as well as extensive instruction in grammar, punctuation, word usage, and other conventions. Print exposure is also important, since familiarity and proficiency with different styles and genres (e.g., expository, narrative, technical) depend on it.

Composition (Text Level)

Text structure refers to the means by which individuals organize their ideas in written discourse. Word and sentence structures, as well as function (purpose), can be very different depending on the chosen mode of writing (e.g., narrative, expository, persuasion). The language one uses in written discourse comprises a structure just as words in a sentence determine a syntactic structure. Researchers examining the written text of adolescents with learning disabilities note that these writers often demonstrate difficulty with metacognitive strategies, such as planning, monitoring, evaluating, and revising (Englert, 1990; Graham and Harris, 1999). Little empirical evidence examining the written composition of the college population with learning disabilities is available, however.

The precise role of working memory in composing text is not clear. Some researchers find that working memory deficits influence written text underachievement (Berninger and Richards, 2002; McCutchen, 2006). Recently, Vanderberg and Swanson (2007) investigated the relationship of working memory to the macrostructure (planning, text structure, revision) and microstructure (grammar, punctuation) of writing. They validated the importance of working memory to both the microstructure and macrostructure of written text, but they also stressed that the writing process is more intricately tied to the attentional components of working memory. Other researchers suggest that long-term memory plays a greater role in the composing of text than working memory (Kintsch, 1998).

Sense of Audience

Current thinking about the writing process envisions writing as a problem-solving task that engages the writer in a dialogue with the reader. Research on composing processes reveals common writing patterns between inexperienced writers and students with a need to develop their basic writing skills. For instance, such students often differ from their higher achieving cohorts in the degree and manner in which they consider their audiences (Rubin and Looney, 1990). Studies show that basic writers have little sense of writing as a rhetorical transaction (Rubin and Looney, 1990). That is, such writers seldom view writing as a means of communication or persuasion; rather, they tend to think infrequently of potential readers and fail to use information about their readers even when it is available to them. The problems experienced with revision and audience awareness are interdependent. Rubin (1984) argues that audience awareness is fundamental to revision; to revise is to step back from the writer's own subjective understanding of a text and experience it with naïve eyes (Murray, 1978).

To investigate a writer's sense of audience requires evaluation of the writer's voice, the writer's perceptions of the audience, and the context in which the writing occurred (Gregg et al., 1996). Writer, audience, and context are all involved in the dynamic creation of text, and this leads to choices regarding concepts, vocabulary, style, and text organization. In an effort to evaluate such variables, researchers have identified a number of social cognition skills required for developing sensitivity to audience in written language. These social cognition skills affect content, execution, perspective taking, differentiation of voice, and organization of text (Gregg and McAlexander, 1989; Gregg et al., 1996).

Deficits in any one (or more) of these areas impacts a writer's ability to identify and remain sensitive to a specific audience. In a study exploring the relationship between sense of audience and learning disabilities among college writers with learning disabilities, Gregg and McAlexander (1989) emphasized that certain types of disorders are more likely to cause problems with sense of audience skills than others. Deficits in perspective-taking, which requires the writer to engage in social inference and to perceive or express various traits in others, often characterize typically developing writers as well.

Writing Fluency (Verbosity)

Fluency is a critical construct to address in the evaluation of writing. Fluency in relation to writing is often referred to as "verbosity" and measured by the length of or number of words in a composition. Gregg et al. (2002) investigated the written discourse complexity of college writers with and without learning disabilities (dyslexia). They found that verbosity (number of words), quality, and vocabulary complexity were significantly correlated. In particular, verbosity and quality could not be viewed as separate constructs but were statistically co-occurring functions. In other words, the number of words produced by writers increased their chances for higher quality scores. A critical finding from this study was that vocabulary and fluency proxies—number of words, number of different words, and number of words with more than two syllables—were the best discriminators between college writers with and without learning disabilities (dyslexia).

DEVELOPING BRAIN SYSTEMS IN STRUGGLING READERS

There is a growing body of research on neurodevelopmental changes in brain organization and how these changes relate to individual differences in language and reading competencies. The studies have examined changes in both structural organization (i.e., gray and white matter volumes) (Giedd et al., 1997; Hua, Tembe, and Dougherty, 2009) and functional organization (i.e., functional neurocircuits) of the brain for language and reading (Booth et al., 2001; Church et al., 2008; Shaywitz et al., 2003; Turkeltaub et al., 2003). The focus of the research thus far has been on phonological processing, decoding, or word reading (see Pugh et al., 2010, for a review), with more recent research beginning to examine sentence-level processing and comprehension (Cutting and Scarborough, 2006; Meyler et al., 2008; Rimrodt et al., 2010). As described in Chapter 2, these findings show how the brain organizes with reading experience from childhood to late adolescence for typically developing readers and readers with reading disabilities.

The neurotrajectory involved in reading takes years to develop for children given adequate early exposure. For children and adolescents with reading disabilities, this trajectory appears to be disrupted and is associated with structural and functional differences in brain functioning between children with and without reading disabilities. These brain differences are not necessarily fixed or immutable. Change (neuroplasticity) in neurological patterns has been observed in children and adolescents with reading disabilities as a result of effective intervention. In fact, several recent studies suggest that gains in reading skill following intense reading intervention are associated with a more "normalized" brain organization for reading for young children and that such plasticity is possible into adulthood.

We review this intervention research and studies of differences in brain structure and function between readers with and without reading disabilities because it has the future potential to inform assessment and literacy instruction for adults with disabilities as neurobiological theories of learning and reading and writing development become better explicated (Just and Varma, 2007).

Brain Structure and Function

A number of anatomical neuroimaging studies (research that uses magnetic resonance imaging, MRI, to measure gray and white matter volumes across brain regions) have identified structural differences, such as reduced gray matter volume, in the brains of people with reading disabilities. These differences have been found in several of the left hemisphere (LH) regions that functional brain imaging show to be involved in reading, including the temporoparietal and occipitotemporal areas (Brambati et al., 2004; Brown et al., 2001; Eckert et al., 2003; Kronbichler et al., 2008; Silani et al., 2005). Using a recently developed MRI technique known as diffusion tensor imaging (DTI), studies show differences in white matter tracts for those with reading disabilities. Individuals with reading disabilities have atypical white matter development in critical LH pathways linking the major reading areas. This finding suggests reduced myelin in the axonal fibers connecting distributed brain areas that form the reading circuits of the brain (Beaulieu et al., 2005; Keller and Just, 2009; Klingberg et al., 2000; Niogi and McCandliss, 2006).

These reported gray and white matter differences in brain organization of LH posterior regions between typically developing readers and those with a reading disability appear to be associated with underlying language difficulties (Niogi and McCandliss, 2006). It is not known whether these structural differences are a cause or consequence of reading disability. This question requires further study with research that includes prospective longitudinal designs with individuals before they learn to read.

Functional neuroimaging research uses such techniques as functional MRI (fMRI) to measure activation in different parts of the brain while an individual performs cognitive tasks. In studies of this type, both children and adults with reading disability show marked functional differences relative to typically developing readers in the activity generated in major components of the reading circuit (temporoparietal, occipitotemporal, and inferior frontal systems) (Brunswick et al., 1999; Meyler et al., 2008; Paulesu et al., 2001; Pugh et al., 2000; Rumsey et al., 1997b; Salmelin et al., 1996; Shaywitz et al., 1998, 2002; Temple et al., 2003). Individuals with reading disability tend to underactivate both temporoparietal and occipitotemporal regions; this disruption also is evident in reduced functional connectivity (a type of analysis that measures the degree to which brain areas show correlated activation and hence are acting as a functional circuit) (Hampson et al., 2006; Horwitz et al., 1998; Pugh et al., 2000). This atypical functional connectivity of key LH posterior regions in disabled relative to able readers suggests interregional communication difficulties in the left hemisphere. This pattern of reduced posterior activation and connectivity in the left hemisphere associated with reading disability has been observed in a large number of studies with both children and adults with reading disabilities (Pugh et al., 2010). In addition, readers with reading disabilities often show evidence of apparently compensatory responses to their LH posterior dysfunction: an increased functional role for right hemisphere (RH) temporoparietal regions (Sarkari et al., 2002; Shaywitz et al., 1998; Simos et al., 2002b) and increased frontal lobe activation in both right and left hemispheres (Brunswick et al., 1999; Shaywitz et al., 1998, 2003).

Differences in both structural and functional brain organization of LH posterior regions have been consistently observed across neuroimaging studies. It is hypothesized that these differences may reflect genetically based patterns of brain development, a subject of research for many years. Postmortem studies show cortical and subcortical cellular anomalies (ectopias, microgyria, and glial scarring) in the brains of individuals with reading disability (Galaburda et al., 1985). Genetic factors may give rise to these anomalies by way of abnormal neuronal migration during fetal brain development. Using animal models, studies that explore the ways in which these anomalies might impede both brain development and learning have been undertaken (Galaburda et al., 2006). This research holds promise for identifying critical gene-brain-behavior pathways in reading disabilities, although at present the links to core deficits in reading disability (e.g., phonological processing) are not yet fully understood.

More also needs to be understood about the brain bases of basic computational processes involved in reading. For example, reading depends on such cognitive processes as memory and attention; reading disabilities have been associated with deficits that include limited memory capacity, limited processing speed, and specific problems with learning and memory consolidation. Research to identify how structural and functional differences in reading disability may limit learning and cognitive processes will be important to developing brain-based models of reading and other learning disabilities (see Just and Varma, 2007).

The relative contributions of environmental factors (e.g., inadequate learning opportunities) and genetic factors (and their interaction) to brain differences in reading disabilities are complex and not well understood. Reading difficulties at any age or in any population are the result of a complex mix of congenital (gene-brain-behavior) and environmental factors. It is well known that genetic factors contribute to reading disabilities (Fletcher et al., 2007). The observation that reading difficulties run in families and are evident across generations was reported almost a century ago (Hinshelwood, 1917). It has been estimated that children of a parent with a reading disability face an eight times greater risk of a reading disorder themselves relative to the population as a whole (Pennington and Olson, 2005). Much less is known about the specifics, such as which genes play a role and the ways in which genetic influences occur (e.g., effects on brain development). Currently, the genetics literature contains references to about 20 potential genetic susceptibility loci, which are regions of the genome that have demonstrated a statistically significant linkage to reading disability and typically involve more than one and often hundreds of genes (Schumacher et al., 2007). The literature refers to at least six candidate genes for reading disability, which are genes located in susceptibility loci that have been statistically associated with reading disability, including *DYX1C1, KIAA0319, DCDC2, ROBO1, MRPL2,* and *C2orf3* (Grigorenko and Naples, 2009).

None of these loci or genes, however, has been either fully accepted or fully rejected by the field, and intensive research is ongoing. The information that has contributed to the identification of susceptibility loci and candidate genes for reading disability has been generated by molecular genetics studies of reading and reading-related processes. Unlike heritability and relative risk studies, these studies assume the collection of genetic material (DNA) from blood or saliva samples. More research is needed to fully understand the involvement of these genes with reading, its related processes, and their development.

A portion of the adults who need to develop their literacy skills is likely to have genetically based learning disabilities. A range of other factors, such as inadequate instruction, poverty, cultural and language barriers, and motivation, are likely to contribute substantially to the reading difficulties of low-literate adults. Interdisciplinary research aimed at building gene-brain-behavior models of typical and atypical reading development and understanding how these factors interact with environmental forces has the potential to enhance understanding of the unique challenges in developing reading and writing skills faced by adult learners.

Brain Plasticity

As noted earlier, a growing body of evidence is showing how functional neurocircuits change with reading experience from childhood to late adolescence in typically developing youth and how this development differs in populations with reading disabilities (Booth et al., 2001; Church et al., 2008; Shaywitz et al., 2002; Turkeltaub et al., 2003). In one developmental fMRI study using a cross-sectional design, Shaywitz and colleagues examined changes in functional brain organization in large typically developing and reading disabled cohorts ranging from age 7 through 17 (Shaywitz et al., 2002). A beginning reader, on a successful learning trajectory, appears to employ a widely distributed cortical system for reading-related processing, including the temporoparietal, frontal, and RH posterior areas. As typically developing readers mature, the weighting of the functional neuroanatomy for reading shifts toward a more consolidated "expert" system of activation in the LH occipitotemporal area that is known as the visual word form area (VWFA; Dehaene et al., 2002). This region appears important to the development of fluent reading (see Booth et al., 2001; Church et al., 2008; Turkeltaub et al., 2003, for similar arguments).

A full understanding of individual differences in the development of the brain for reading requires understanding not only change in functional circuits over time but also possible neuroanatomical constraints on learning. Structural imaging techniques (MRI) used to examine changes in gray and white matter volume from early childhood into late adolescence and adulthood show variable increases in white matter and decreases in gray matter volumes as brain regions develop (Giedd et al., 1997; Hua et al., 2009; Sowell et al., 2004). Some regions mature later (e.g., prefrontal cortex associated with executive function and response inhibition), whereas others mature earlier (e.g., basic sensory and motor processing systems).

A priority for research is to examine the ways in which age-related changes in gray and white matter organization affect plasticity and the impact on learning to read at later ages. The trajectory of brain development, both structural and functional, is established over a period of years for typically developing children given adequate early exposure. It is not clear whether the same patterns of neuronal reorganization would occur at later points in the life span in adults without learning difficulties but who were nevertheless deprived of early opportunities to learn; this question merits research, as it may inform how to think about the challenges to brain plasticity for those learning to read later in life. What is known, however, for both children and adolescents with reading disabilities is that, in the absence of intensive remediation, this neurotrajectory of reading-related brain changes remains disrupted (Brunswick et al., 1999; Hampson et al., 2003; Pugh et al., 2000; Shaywitz et al., 2002, 2003; Simos et al., 2002a).

It will be important to determine whether intensive and evidence-based intervention with those who experience atypical patterns of brain organization can lead to some degree of normalization in the structure or function of LH systems. New research on remediation suggests that a good deal of plasticity from childhood into adulthood may still be expected for those with reading disabilities. Several recent treatment studies indicate that, at least for younger readers, gains in reading skill with systematic and intense reading intervention are associated with a more normalized brain organization for reading. In a recent study using magnetoencephalography to measure brain changes, young children with severe reading difficulties underwent a brief but intensive phonologically based reading remediation program (Simos et al., 2002b). After intervention, significant gains in reading were observed, and the most salient change observed for every individual who received the intervention was a robust increase in the activation of the LH temporoparietal regions of the brain and a moderate decrease in the activation of the compensatory RH temporoparietal regions.

Shaywitz et al. (2004) examined three groups of young children with fMRI and performance indices (average age was 6.5 years at initial testing—Time 1) (Shaywitz et al., 2004). One group of children with reading disabilities received nine months of an intensive experimental reading intervention (treatment group). As described in Blachman et al. (2004), the intervention involved eight months of individualized tutoring in an intensive reading program that emphasized explicit instruction in phonological and orthographic patterns and oral reading of text and included some spelling and writing activities. For the fMRI study, there were two control groups: a control group of normal readers and a control group of readers with reading disabilities who received standard intervention from their community schools. Treatment participants with reading disabilities showed significant gains in reading fluency and comprehension compared with the control group with reading disabilities who received remediation in their schools. When the two reading disabled groups were compared on fMRI scans posttreatment (Time 2), significantly more activation increases in LH posterior reading areas were seen in the treatment group. Direct comparison of activation profiles showed that reading disabled children in the treatment group, but not the reading disabled controls, had reliable increases in activation in LH reading-related sites. One year after treatment, follow-up fMRI scans showed children with reading disabilities in the treatment group continued to experience patterns of brain region activation that indicated the intervention had an enduring influence on normalizing brain pathways for reading.

In research with somewhat older learners, Temple and colleagues (2003) used fMRI scans to examine the effects of an intervention on the cortical circuitry of a group of 8- to 12-year-old children with reading disabilities. After intervention, increased LH activation was observed, which in turn correlated significantly with increased reading scores. Similarly, in a study of fifth graders, Meyler et al. (2008) found that a phonologically based intervention increased LH temporoparietal activation during sentence reading tasks, indicating that successful remediation of core phonological skills can generalize to more demanding reading contexts. Observed increases in gray matter volume indicated a significant effect on both brain structure and function (Keller and Just, 2009). Structural changes that accompany successful intervention (Keller, Carpenter, and Just, 2001; Meyler et al., 2008) suggest that effective remediation normalizes structural differences observed between those with and without reading disabilities. Interventions with adults are rare, but Eden and colleagues (Eden et al., 2004) reported significant behavioral and neurobiological changes with intensive phonological remediation in adult readers with reading disabilities; they report a pattern of increase in LH posterior activation in adults similar to that observed in studies of children with dyslexia.

The fact that both structural and functional reorganization of LH brain circuitry for reading can occur after effective remediation for both children and adults with reading disabilities is potentially very important. Similar positive outcomes may occur for adult learners who have lacked the extended experiences needed to develop literacy skills, regardless of whether or not they have latent (undiagnosed) reading disabilities. Knowledge of brain-based developmental trajectories from childhood to adulthood, although still incomplete, suggests the patterns of brain activation that might be achieved with effective instruction and remediation of struggling readers. This work also has resulted in the development of neurobiological measures for research that may prove useful for evaluating interventions for adults learning to read for the first time.

ACCOMMODATIONS TO SUPPORT LITERACY LEARNING

Accommodations adjust the manner in which instructional or testing situations are presented so that individuals with documented disabilities can learn and demonstrate their learning in a fair and equitable manner (Gregg, 2009). Accommodations are not a replacement for literacy instruction. Rather, accommodations are adjuncts that remove barriers imposed by poor reading, writing, or academic learning skills (Moats and Dakin, 2007). Understanding the issues surrounding accommodation practices is critical to grasping the consequences for adolescents and adults with learning disabilities who are not provided access or equal opportunities to fully participate in instruction or demonstrate their knowledge in testing contexts. Lack of access to accommodations can have major negative effects on career development and adult income (Gregg, 2007; Gregg and Banerjee, 2005).

Reading Accommodations

As difficulties with phonological, orthographic, morphologic, and syntactic awareness slow down the process of decoding, extra time becomes a critical accommodation for adolescents or adults with learning disabilities (dyslexia). There is a significant amount of research to support the need for this accommodation for adolescents and adults with learning disabilities (Gregg, 2009; Gregg and Nelson, in press; Shaywitz, 2003).

Emerging technologies are changing the range of literacy skills needed in the worlds of school and work. For the college population with learning disabilities, these technologies offer opportunities to be better prepared for today's technology-rich schools and workplaces. A wide range of technologies are being used to accommodate learning and work environments for these individuals. In the area of reading, alternative media and the software to access these formats are essential accommodations for college students with learning disabilities. *Alt media* is a broad term that refers to a variety of formats into which printed text is converted (e.g., audiotaped text, enlarged print, electronic text, Braille).

Regardless of the alt media format, etext is not an effective accommodation for individuals with learning disabilities unless it is used in conjunction with assistive technology software. Optical character recognition (OCR) software is first used to convert scanned or bit-mapped images of text into machine-readable form. The text may then be saved on magnetic media (e.g., hard drives) or on optical media (e.g., CD-ROMs). Text converted by OCR software is then read by text-to-speech (TTS) software. TTS is a type of speech-synthesis application that is used to create a spoken version of etext on a computer or handheld device. TTS can enable the reading of computer display information for an adolescent or adult with learning disabilities, or it may simply be used to augment the reading of a text message. Anderson-Inman and Horney (2007) prefer the term *supported etext* to refer to the integration of etext with assistive software. An important feature of alt media is its portability. Digital files can be delivered to adolescents or adults via email or Internet portals and used in a variety of electronic and physical environments. Current advancements in technology now allow etext files to be downloaded easily not only to computers, but also to handheld devices, such as phones, personal digital assistants (PDAs), or MP3 players and to be read through specialized TTS software.

However, much of the TTS software cannot access or integrate with the various social media tools—from text messaging to blogging—that are becoming essential to success in school or the workplace. As colleges and universities are posting lectures on YouTube and many chief executives of major companies are communicating to their employees and customers through blogs and web pages, assistive technology software needs to integrate seamlessly with various forms of social media. The lack of empirical evidence to identify effective technologies to provide adolescents and adults with learning disabilities access to reading online and offline (traditional print-based) is of considerable concern, given the prevalence of low literacy skills among youth and young adults in society.

Reading comprehension problems are more difficult to accommodate than decoding and reading fluency problems. Current technology advancements, however, are providing professionals with more tools than ever before to help college students with functional limitations in reading comprehension. One promising technology software accommodation for reading instruction is embedded etext support: TTS and links to definitions, highlighting, and summaries of text (Gregg and Banerjee, 2005). Many of the embedded supports can significantly help readers with reading comprehension problems. Embedded supports used in combination with etext and TTS software may prove more effective than etext or TTS alone for college readers with learning disabilities. A growing body of research is providing strong validation for the effectiveness of embedded supports in enhancing reading comprehension for students with reading disorders (Anderson-Inman, 2004; Anderson-Inman and Horney, 2007; Anderson-Inman et al., 1994; Horney and Anderson-Inman, 1994, 1999).

A promising technology for enhancing the reading comprehension of at-risk readers is web-based tutors that provide online self-explanation and metacognitive reading strategies. McNamara and her colleagues (McNamara et al., 2007) developed one such program called the Interactive Strategy Training for Active Reading and Thinking (iSTART) and have provided strong research evidence to support its effectiveness. It is a web-based tutoring program designed for adolescents and adults that uses animated agents to teach reading strategies. McNamara and colleagues found iSTART to be most beneficial to at-risk readers. However, at this time, no research is available to support its effectiveness with individuals diagnosed with learning disabilities. Again, the effectiveness of software such as iSTART depends on its ease in successfully integrating with screen readers and other technologies necessary to access the online reading requirements of the program.

Extended time on assignments is a necessary accommodation for many individuals demonstrating reading comprehension underachievement. Difficulty decoding words, understanding vocabulary, or remaining sensitive to sentence or text structures often slows down the reading process for many adolescents or adults with learning disabilities. In addition, if any strategy or technology (e.g., read-aloud, embedded text) is used as an accommodation to assist the process of reading, extended time will be needed to implement such reading tools.

Writing Accommodations

Accommodation of Handwriting

Very little research is available to guide accommodations for the college population with handwriting disorders. Professionals depend on clinical experience and assessment data in choosing specific accommodations. For all three types of graphomotor disorders (i.e., symbolic, speed, dyspraxia) discussed above, extra time is an essential accommodation. Word processing and various assistive technologies also provide accommodation options appropriate for all types of graphomotor disorders. Traditional assistive technologies used with more severe motor disorders, such as adapted switches, adapted keyboards, and keyboard overlays, have not been well investigated by researchers as to their effectiveness with adult populations with learning disabilities. Although limited in number, studies are available to support the effectiveness of word processing, word prediction software, and voice input (speech to text) for enhancing the legibility and fluency of writing for adult populations (Gregg, 2009). In addition, the need is great for researchers to investigate the usefulness of touch windows and macro software for accommodating the writing of college students with learning disabilities, since these recommendations are often suggested by professionals. With the popularity and accessibility of mobile touch devices (i.e., iPad, iPhone), the application of this technology for accommodating graphomotor disorders may emerge.

Accommodation of Spelling Disorders

Spelling difficulty is a hallmark of college writers with learning disabilities (dyslexia). Although there is evidence to support the effectiveness of assistive technologies in enhancing spelling performance, research on the college population is limited. As with handwriting disorders, extra time is an appropriate accommodation for college students with significant spelling deficits, since they require more time to recall the motor and orthographic patterns necessary to spell words. Word processing also appears to enhance the fluency and spelling of young adult writers with learning disabilities

(Bangert-Downs, 1993; Goldberg, Russell, and Cook, 2003; Hetzroni and Shrieber, 2004; MacArthur, 2006). Research also supports the effectiveness of spell checkers and word prediction programs for enhancing the spelling performance of adolescent writers with learning disabilities (Handley-More et al., 2003). Speech recognition software for dictation has gained some support as a means to enhance the writing of adolescents and adults with spelling, handwriting, and fluency problems (Higgins and Raskind, 1995; MacArthur and Cavalier, 2004; Reece and Cumings, 1996).

Accommodation of Syntax Disorders

The effectiveness of accommodations for the college writer with written syntax disorders has not been well addressed. It is important to investigate the cognitive and linguistic deficits underlying difficulty in producing sentence structures as a guide in selecting specific accommodations (Gregg, 2009). For writers struggling to produce written sentences, extra time and word processing are appropriate accommodations. Students with verbal working memory deficits might be helped by word prediction and outlining/webbing software. For writers with significant attention or executive functioning deficits, outlining, webbing, and TTS software might be an effective accommodation. Research evidence is available to support TTS software for some students in helping them "hear" word choice errors so that they can make revisions (Higgins and Raskind, 1995; MacArthur, 2006). For students whose difficulty recalling words influences sentence structure production, word prediction software might be recommended. Speech-to-text software is often not as effective for writers demonstrating oral expressive syntax disorders. The technology is currently not advanced enough to deal with the oral hesitations and pronunciation errors often demonstrated by these individuals. Little research evidence exists to support the effectiveness of grammar checks as an accommodation for individuals with written syntax disorders.

Accommodation of Text Structure

A basic but important accommodation for writers experiencing difficulties producing text is the provision of extended time (Gregg et al., 2007; Gregg, 2009). Research confirms that extended time can provide these individuals a means to utilize strategies and technologies for improving their written products. If graphomotor, spelling, or syntax abilities are also areas of deficit for a writer, the accommodations previously discussed would be provided in addition.

Speech synthesis (text-to-speech) and speech recognition (speech-to-text) software have potential for enhancing the production of written text structure. Although limited research is available to provide evidence of the effectiveness of this software for the college population with learning disabilities, advances in assistive technologies appear promising (MacArthur, 2006). In the future, MP3 players (e.g., iPods) with digital voice recorders have the potential to increase the writing proficiency of college writers with learning disabilities (Banerjee and Gregg, 2009).

The effectiveness of teaching adolescent writers with learning disabilities cognitive strategies to enhance their writing competencies is well documented in the literature (Deshler, Ellis, and Lenz, 1996; Englert, 1990; Englert, Mariage, and Dusmore, 2006; Graham and Harris, 2004; Hallenbeck, 1996). For instance, the Think Sheets advocated by Englert in her Cognitive Strategy Instruction in Writing program can provide useful tools to help many of these writers manage the different aspects of writing (planning, organizing, drafting, editing, and author/reader relationship) (Hallenbeck, 1996). The research on computerized software that provides strategic planning, organization, and revising prompts to adolescent and adult writers with learning disabilities, however, has not provided conclusive evidence for the effectiveness of this software (Bonk and Reynolds, 1992; Reynolds and Bonk, 1996; Rowley, Carsons, and Miller, 1998; Rowley and Meyer, 2003; Zellermayer et al., 1991). MacArthur (2006), in a review of assistive technologies and writing, states that he identified only one study (Sturm and Rankin-Erikson, 2002) that provided evidence for the effectiveness of concept mapping software, despite its common use by professionals working with writers demonstrating writing disorders. This lack of research evidence does not diminish the potential utility of such techniques for enhancing the written text of many writers. Rather, it suggests that professionals must ensure that adequate evidence from a comprehensive evaluation provides strong support for the use of concept mapping software with a writer. With the increasing number of empirical studies in the area of hypermedia and computer-mediated communication, it is likely that new tools will be available in the near future to accommodate struggling writers that cannot be conceptualized today.

SUMMARY AND DIRECTIONS FOR RESEARCH

Adults can experience a range of learning disabilities that are important to diagnose and attend to as part of literacy instruction. The adult population with learning disabilities represents a very heterogeneous group of individuals in relation to severity of learning disabilities, reading and writing abilities, and background. Reading disabilities are the most prevalent and best studied class of learning disabilities. Most neurocognitive research has concentrated on reading. Most research on learning disabilities in adolescents and adults comes from studies of college students or other adults with relatively high levels of literacy skill. Less research is available with low-literate adults with reading and writing disabilities. The available research shows that adults experience difficulties with specific cognitive and linguistic processes involved in decoding, fluent reading of words and sentences, and reading comprehension. Students with writing disabilities experience difficulties with handwriting, spelling, syntax, composition, sense of audience, and writing fluency.

Research on the effectiveness of instruction to develop the reading and writing skills of adolescents and adults with learning disabilities is sparse, especially for those with low literacy. A priority for future research is the development of effective instructional practices for these populations. As discussed in Chapter 2, neither the available behavioral nor neurocognitive data suggest that instruction for learners who struggle with reading and writing needs to be categorically different from the instruction that is effective with more typically developing learners. Rather, the instruction that has been effective with younger populations targets specific reading and writing difficulties in the context of reading and writing instruction (instead of using decontextualized approaches directed at changing general cognitive processes, which has been shown to be ineffective). The instruction used with typically developing learners also needs to be adapted for those with disabilities to be more explicit and systematic; provide enhanced supports for the transfer and generalization of skills; provide more opportunities for practice; address maladaptive attributions, which can be particularly important to address for struggling learners; and provide scaffolded and differentiated instruction that targets specific difficulties while continuing to develop all the skills needed for reading and writing development (see principles for struggling readers and writers presented in Chapter 2). Research to test instructional approaches consistent with these principles is needed to address the cognitive and linguistic challenges described in this chapter.

Research on accommodations for college students with learning disabilities has a stronger research base. These findings warrant application and further study with all adolescent and adult learners with disabilities. It is important to identify accommodations to remove barriers imposed by poor reading, writing, or academic learning skills. Lack of access to accommodations for individuals with learning disabilities can have major negative effects on career development and adult income. Accommodations for learning need to be used in conjunction with effective instruction to support the development and assessment of literacy. Future policies and practices pertaining to accommodating learning and work environments for the populations with learning disabilities should be guided by evidence-based research.

Assessment batteries used to diagnose learning disabilities and determine who is qualified to receive accommodations in college settings measure a range of cognitive processing abilities in adolescents and adults. Although behavioral tests are used for assessment and diagnosis, learning disabilities have come to be viewed as brain-based conditions caused by hereditary (genetic) factors and complex pathways of gene-brain-behavior relationships and their interaction with environment and experience. Modern brain imaging techniques show that both children and adults with reading disabilities show marked differences in brain structure and functions relative to typically developing readers. An important next step will be to test causal relations between these structural and functional anomalies and reading using prospective longitudinal designs. In addition, research is needed to better understand the relative contributions of environment (inadequate learning opportunities) and genetic factors (and their interaction) to the different brain trajectories of those with reading disabilities. Gene-brain-behavior research is needed especially to enhance understanding of the unique challenges faced by older learners.

Neurocognitive research shows the plasticity (change) of brains in response to interventions for struggling readers extends into young adulthood, but studies are needed with older adults to determine if the same patterns of neuronal reorganization would occur later in life in response to instruction. This question is also important to ask for adults without learning difficulties but who were nevertheless deprived of early opportunities to learn. Although still incomplete, research on brain-based developmental trajectories from childhood to adulthood suggests patterns of brain activation and consequently improved literacy performance that might be achieved with effective instruction and remediation of struggling readers. This research also suggests ways of measuring neurobiological change that may be useful in evaluating the effectiveness of interventions for adult learners.

For both reading and writing, extra time, various technological supports, and the teaching of cognitive strategies are accommodations that enhance competencies, although many aspects of reading and writing remain to be addressed in research, such as syntax and reading comprehension. Likewise, most published research on brain differences between typically developing and reading disabled learners focuses on phonological processing, decoding, or word reading, and a better understanding of neurobiological processes involved in disorders of syntax, comprehension, spelling, and writing is needed.

The findings in this chapter must be generalized with caution beyond those adults who have met the legal criteria for learning disabilities to which secondary and postsecondary institutions in the United States must adhere in providing services for students with learning disabilities. More research of the kind described is needed to characterize and determine how best to intervene with a broader range of adults in literacy education.

8

Language and Literacy Development of English Language Learners

A growing number of adolescents and adults in the United States use a language other than English at home and require support to develop spoken and written English. In the United States, of the 280.8 million people ages 5 and older, 55 million (19.6 percent) speak a language other than English at home (U.S. Census Bureau, 2005-2009, American Community Survey). More than 18 percent of those who speak a language other than English at home are below the poverty level (versus 11.6 percent of those who speak only English at home), and 31.2 percent have less than a high school education (versus 11.7 percent of English only speakers). The percentage of those without a high school education is higher among those who speak Spanish or Spanish Creole at home (more than 41 percent).

According to the National Assessment of Adult Literacy (NAAL) (Kutner et al., 2007), which in 2003 assessed the literacy of native- and foreign-born adults living in the United States, approximately 11 million adults (5 percent of the U.S. population) were estimated to be nonliterate in English (though not necessarily in their first language) and so lacked sufficient English language proficiency to be assessed in English (Kutner et al., 2007). Among those with some English proficiency, the percentage of Hispanics with below average English prose and document literacy increased from 1992 to 2003.

English language learners are the largest group enrolled in adult education programs, with 43 percent of adult learners enrolled in English as a second language (ESL) programs in the 2001-2002 program year (Tamassia et al., 2007). In the 2006-2007 program year, more than 1 million adults were enrolled in ESL programs that were part of state-administered, federally funded adult education programs. This figure is likely to be an underestimate because it does not include nonnative speakers in adult basic education and adult secondary education (general educational development [GED]) classes or in ESL classes offered by private organizations.

The adults who participate in ESL classes are diverse in terms of languages spoken, education levels, literacy skill in the first language, and knowledge of English (Burt, Peyton, and Adams, 2003). Some are highly educated in their home countries and have strong academic backgrounds; others are recent immigrants with low levels of education and first language literacy. The numbers of adults in ESL classes who have limited education in their home countries continues to grow (Center for Applied Linguistics, 2010; Condelli, Wrigley and Yoon, 2009; Purcell-Gates et al., 2002; Strucker and Davidson, 2003). Other adults are born in the United States or came to the United States as young children but have grown up with a home language other than English (Tamassia et al., 2007). Though educated in U.S. schools, these adults can be unprepared for work and higher education (Burt, Peyton and Adams, 2003; Thonus 2003; Wrigley et al., 2009), and many drop out before completing high school.

Despite the need for English language and literacy instruction, adult ESL programs have had limited success. A 7-year longitudinal study of noncredit ESL classes showed that only about 8 percent of more than 38,000 learners made the transition to other academic (credit) studies (Spurling, Seymour, and Chisman, 2008). In fact, 44 percent advanced only one literacy level, as defined by the U.S. Department of Education's National Reporting System for adult literacy programs. Persistence was also an issue. Half of the learners who did not advance attended fewer than 50 hours of instruction. Most of those who advanced received 50 or more hours of instruction, taking on average 50 to 149 hours of attendance (usually referred to as "100 instruction hours") to advance one level.

This chapter has four parts. Part one presents a brief orienting discussion of the component skills of English learners. Part two summarizes research on the various factors (cognitive, linguistic, social, affective, and cultural) that influence the development of literacy in a second language. Part three identifies practices to develop language and literacy instruction that warrant application and further study with adults developing their English language and literacy skills outside school. The available research does not allow for conclusions about effective approaches to literacy instruction. Thus, the chapter concludes with a summary and discussion of priorities for research to develop effective approaches to instruction for this population.

In this chapter, we draw on several recent systematic reviews of research on effective instructional practices for English language learners, augmented with targeted searches to update or expand on previous findings. The available research is quite limited. In their study of "what works" for English language learners in adult literacy education, Condelli and Wrigley (2004) identified only one study of ESL students that measured a literacy outcome and included a design without confounds. Similarly, Torgerson and colleagues (2004) examined almost 5,000 reports on adult literacy and numeracy interventions, and only 3 randomized controlled trial designs focused on English as a second language. Adams and Burt (2002) cast a much wider net in their search for research on adult language learners between 1980 and 2001 to include experimental, descriptive, and practitioner studies from journals, books, reports, and dissertations. The 44 studies reviewed had methodological weaknesses, such as too few participants, unreliable measures, inadequately described practices and outcomes, and no comparison tasks or groups, which prevented drawing conclusions about the effectiveness of the approaches. Several of the studies focused on language learners in English preparatory classes before attending college, who are likely to differ in several ways (education level, first language literacy proficiency, socioeconomic status) from the broader population of English language learners. These results are consistent with a recent review of adult literacy instruction research available from the U.S. Department of Education (Kruidenier, MacArthur, and Wrigley, 2010). Similarly, the committee located four studies (two of adults in adult education and two of students in developmental college education courses) from 1990 to 2010 with the criterion that the research include at least one quantitative measure of literacy skill (see Appendix C). Because studies are so few and the ones available suffer from various methodological constraints, it is not possible to draw strong conclusions about effective instructional practices.

Given the limited research on the literacy development of adult English language learners in the United States, we also draw from a broader base of knowledge on second language and literacy development, which includes relatively well-educated adults and young children in K-12 education. Because a main challenge of literacy development for this population is learning a second language, we review research related to the development of both spoken and written language.

For simplicity, we use the term *English language learners* in this chapter to refer to foreign-born and native-born adults who are developing their English language skills and refer to other adults as *native English speakers*. On occasion we use more specific terms provided by study authors when referring to individual research studies. The research and sources of information reviewed in this chapter often do not include, however, precise or consistent ways of defining particular subgroups of the English learner population. In future research, more standard terms and definitions will be needed to refer to segments of this population to facilitate the accumulation of reliable, valid, and more interpretable research findings.

COMPONENT LITERACY SKILLS OF
ENGLISH LANGUAGE LEARNERS

The available research, though limited, suggests that, compared with adult native speakers with low literacy in adult education programs, adult English language learners with low literacy in these programs show weaker vocabulary, passage comprehension, and sight word reading skills but better phonological processing (decoding nonwords) and somewhat better phonological awareness (Nanda, Greenberg, and Morris, 2010; see Chapter 2 for discussion of the components of reading). Similarly, Strucker et al. (2007) find that adult native speakers and English language learners tend to have different patterns of strengths and weaknesses as beginning readers. Language learners show weaknesses in vocabulary and comprehension but relative strength in decoding, whereas native speakers with low literacy tend to show the opposite pattern (Alamprese, 2009; MacArthur et al., 2010a). Even for those highly literate in their first language, some explicit teaching of English decoding rules may be needed to fill gaps in knowledge (Davidson and Strucker, 2002).

Findings for poor readers in middle school, who are more likely than proficient readers to need literacy instruction as adults, show a range of difficulties that are comparable for both native speakers of English and students with a different home language (Lesaux and Kieffer, 2010). Some students show global difficulties with language, decoding, and comprehension of text. Others have accurate and automatic decoding but poor general and academic vocabulary that affects comprehension. Still others have accurate but slow decoding and so are not fluent readers.

With good instruction, young adolescent language learners can perform at similar levels to native speakers on word recognition, spelling, and phonological processing tasks (Lesaux, Rupp, and Siegel, 2007). Similarly, adult language learners can develop decoding skills that are equivalent to native speakers (Alamprese, 2009). For both native speakers and language learners, once decoding is efficient, English oral proficiency (usually assessed by vocabulary and listening comprehension) predicts English reading comprehension, in higher grades (Lesaux and Kieffer, 2010). However, young language learners often score considerably lower than native speakers on English reading comprehension tasks (Goldenberg, 2008; Nakamoto, Lindsey, and Manis, 2008). Although adult language learners (and native speakers) can establish basic decoding skills quickly with good instruction, they need help with developing their reading skills beyond the intermediate fourth and fifth grade levels (Sabatini et al., 2010; Strucker, Yamamoto, and Kirsch, 2007). Vocabulary and comprehension skills have been particularly difficult to change with instruction, however.

Vocabulary and background knowledge are usually underdeveloped for English learners, in part because they lack the English skills needed to learn through the texts and social and instructional interactions in schools, which are in English. Like native speakers, English language learners must gain facility with academic English, which has some features that differ from conversational English (Snow, 2010). For language learners, conversational English can develop in a few years (Collier, 1987), but becoming proficient with an academic language takes longer because it has its own jargon, linguistic structures, and formats, which can be specific to a discipline. These features of academic language need to be explicitly highlighted and supported during instruction (Achugar and Schleppegrell, 2005; de Jong, 2004; Schleppegrell, 2007). Some researchers emphasize that mastery of academic language is the single most important determinant of academic success for adolescents who have been in U.S. schools for less than 2 years (Francis et al., 2006).

INFLUENCES ON LANGUAGE AND LITERACY IN A SECOND LANGUAGE

Several factors affect the development of language and literacy in a second language and are important to consider in the design of effective instructional practices for segments of the English learner population. These factors include degree and type of first language knowledge, education level, English language proficiency, age, aptitude for language, reading and learning disabilities, and cultural and background knowledge.

First Language Knowledge and Education Level

Among adults, years of education in the primary language correlates with English literacy development (Condelli, Wrigley, and Yoon, 2009; Fitzgerald and Young, 1997; Strucker and Davidson, 2003). A detailed statistical analysis involving thousands of immigrants in Australian literacy programs shows that age and education in the home country were the two main predictors of literacy (Ross, 2000). Research with young students, including instructional intervention studies, also shows that to the degree that students have a strong literacy foundation in a first language, their first language literacy proficiency helps English literacy development (Farver, Lonigan, and Eppe, 2009; Goldenberg, 2008; for a meta-analysis, see Slavin and Cheung, 2005). For adolescents, self-reported first language and English proficiency in eighth grade predict English reading comprehension outcomes in grades 8, 10, and 12 as well as postsecondary achievement (occupational prestige, postsecondary education). Using data from the National Education Longitudinal Study (NELS), Guglielmi (2008) found that self-reported language proficiency of Hispanic learners predicted both initial levels of English reading and rates of improvement and through that, high school and post–high school achievement. (Similar results were not found, however, for Asians who spoke various first languages, such as Chinese, Filipino, or Korean.)

Effects of the first language on second language processes. Precisely how language and literacy in a first language affects second language development needs to be studied more thoroughly to understand how best to facilitate second language acquisition, especially for less educated adults. The extensive literature on bilingualism (knowledge of two spoken languages) is beginning to suggest ways in which a first language may help to support second language growth. Although more experimental research is needed, modern research methods that include behavioral, psychophysiological, and neuroimaging techniques have been used to study questions of bilingualism, such as how two languages are represented in the brain and whether parallel lexicons coexist for bilinguals or if they possess one integrated lexicon. Less is known about the development of more than two languages, and so we have restricted our focus to the bilingual case.

Psycholinguistic research has mainly looked at how knowledge of two languages affects comprehension and production of each one. Does a bilingual person using one language activate the same information in the other language while listening or speaking? Such parallel activation across languages has been observed in many experiments, in the form of cross-language ambiguity effects, for example: Whereas "hotel" has the same meanings in Dutch and English, "room" has different meanings (it means "cream" in Dutch). A Dutch-English bilingual will briefly (and unconsciously) activate both meanings of the word "room," quickly choosing the one that is appropriate to the language being used. Similarly, words that are pronounced differently in two languages (e.g., "coin" in French and English) produce interference in silent reading compared with words with very similar pronunciations (e.g., "piano"); (Kroll and Linck, 2007, 2009). Similar effects occur in comprehending sentences, as measured by word-by-word reading times, eye movements, and evoked potential measures. These effects are modulated by such factors as an individual's familiarity with each language and the relative frequencies of the word in different languages. However, they suggest that knowledge of a second language becomes closely interlinked to knowledge of a first language, making it difficult to inhibit activation of the alternative language under many conditions.

Studies using functional magnetic resonance imaging also support that the two languages share brain structures and circuits instead of having segregated ones (Abutalebi, 2008; Abutalebi, Cappa, and Perani, 2001). The degree of overlap appears to depend on such factors as the age at which the second language was learned and second language proficiency. Individuals whose knowledge of the second language is relatively weak, for example, have shown greater activation of frontal regions that reflect more cognitive effort and use of working memory. For skilled bilinguals, switching between languages involves increased attention or executive functions also associated with the frontal lobe, areas that are not as activated in monolingual language processing. These additional processes can be expected to provide cognitive benefits, specifically enhanced executive function and skill in allocating attention (see Bialystok et al., 2005).

Adults bring an already well-developed system for processing a first language that affects processing specific features of the second language. For example, language learners appear to be aware of grammatical structures that are similarly marked in both of their languages (e.g., auxiliary verbs used in progressive tense: "estar" in Spanish versus is in English) or unique to a second language (determiner gender marking "un/una" in Spanish). However, if a linguistic structure is marked differently in the second language, it may not be noticed (e.g., determiners of number agreement in "el/los" in Spanish versus "the/the" in English) (Tokowicz and MacWhinney, 2005). To summarize, recent findings from behavioral and neurobiological research imply that the role of the primary language cannot be ignored during the learning of a second language.

Literacy skills across languages and possibilities for transfer. Transfer from a native language to English depends on the overlap in characteristics between the two languages. Learning to read English involves matching distinctive visual symbols to units of sound in the spoken language (see Chapter 2; Ziegler and Goswami, 2006). Language learners may be familiar with writing systems that differ in their degree of similarity to English; for example, a native Spanish speaker will be familiar with an alphabetic system like the one for English, whereas a native Chinese speaker will know a nonalphabetic system. Moreover, some languages do not have a written form. Languages that do have a writing system represent their oral languages in different ways, both in terms of the symbols used as well as the phonological units that are represented in print. Some languages are nonalphabetic and represent morphological and phonological rather than purely phonological information (e.g., Japanese Kanji and Chinese). Some languages have alphabetic writing systems but use a non-Latin script (e.g., Korean, Russian, Hebrew). Even alphabetic languages that use the Latin script can be very different from English (e.g., Malay, Turkish, Welsh).

Languages differ in availability (which phonological units are more salient in the spoken language), consistency (the number of possible mappings in word recognition and spelling—more specifically, the number of different pronunciations for orthographic units and the number of different spellings for phonological units), and granularity (the nature of orthographic units that need to be learned to access the phonology). For example, in Chinese many different characters need to be learned, whereas in languages like Spanish a small subset of letters is enough to represent phonemes accurately. English is in between: single letters represent phonemes, but because of the inconsistencies at the phoneme level, larger units (such as onset rimes) provide more systematic information on how to pronounce a word. For example, vowel /a/ can be pronounced differently by itself in different words ("car/lake/pat"), but in a larger rime unit (such as "/-at/") it is pronounced the same way ("hat/cat/mat"). Even young beginning readers are sensitive to the characteristics of their spoken language and find it easier to perform the phonological awareness tasks that focus on the salient units in their spoken language (Durgunoğlu and Oney, 1999; Ziegler and Goswami, 2006). Depending on a language's characteristics (consistency, availability, and granularity), learning to decode can be almost trivial or take longer.

For individuals literate in their home language, the first language writing system and how it represents the oral language affects the strategies used in English decoding. For example, when college students who are highly literate in a first language are learning English, Japanese and Chinese speakers rely on visual cues more than Korean or Persian speakers because the latter two groups have a phonologically based rather than morphemically based writing system, although all four of the groups use non-Latin scripts (Akamatsu, 2003; Hamada and Koda, 2008; Koda, 1999).

If adult English learners are not literate in their first language, then literacy development in English has to include instruction to develop sensitivity to the phonological units of English, the English alphabet, and the mappings at both phonemes and larger units. For individuals who are already literate in their first language and already have a metacognitive understanding of spelling-sound mappings, word recognition and spelling skills develop rapidly (Burt, Peyton, and Adams, 2003), especially when instruction highlights the specific characteristics of English.

If certain skills and strategies are available to a learner in a first language, building on them may help to develop literacy in a second language (for reviews see Dressler and Kamil, 2006; Durgunoğlu, 2002, 2009; Genesee and Geva, 2006). For language learners, proficiency in phonological awareness is positively related across two languages, even when the first language is not similar to English (for a review, see Branum-Martin et al., 2006; Genesee and Geva, 2006; Swanson et al., 2008). Decoding skills in a first language overlap with decoding skills in English as the second language, even across a span of 10 years (Sparks et al., 2009a, 2009b), suggesting that decoding skill in a first language supports decoding in a second language. As children gain more experience in English, English decoding becomes a stronger predictor of English reading comprehension than Spanish decoding (Gottardo and Mueller, 2009; Manis, Lindsey, and Bailey, 2004; Nakamoto, Lindsey, and Manis, 2008). The results look different for spelling: spelling in a first language (mostly Spanish) is either not related or negatively related to proficiency with English spelling (Rolla San Francisco et al., 2006).

Vocabulary knowledge across the two languages of language learners is relatively independent (Cobo-Lewis et al., 2002; Nakamoto et al., 2008). However, the metacognitive aspects of vocabulary knowledge, such as knowing how to construct formal definitions, are related across the two languages (Durgunoğlu, Peynircioğlu, and Mir, 2002; Ordoñez et al., 2002). In addition, proficiency with explicit analytic processing or awareness of language (e.g., of morphology or cognates) in a first language correlates with having these skills in the second language (Deacon, Wade-Woolley, and Kirby, 2007; Nagy et al., 1993).

Good readers use similar comprehension strategies in both of their languages (Jiménez, 1997; Langer et al., 1990; van Gelderen et al., 2007). Writing proficiency is also correlated across the two languages of language learners: good writers use similar writing strategies in both of their languages (Durgunoğlu, Mir, and Arino-Marti, 2002; Schoonen et al., 2003).

These findings point to possibilities for applying knowledge and skills in a first language to the second language when the literacy tasks involve analyzing language structure (phonology, morphology) or using metacognitive strategies. When the tasks involve language-specific patterns (e.g., orthographic rules for spelling, meanings of items), the data suggest limited or no transfer. The available data are correlations, however. Experiments are still needed to determine whether specific literacy skills may be leveraged for the development of more efficient instructional approaches. In addition, it is not yet known how much these relationships are due to the learner transferring a specific skill from the first language to the second language and how much they are due to common underlying proficiencies that may be less sensitive to instruction. For example, although metacognitive strategies in a first language may be spontaneously accessed and used in the second language, or have the potential for transfer with instruction, other shared cognitive processes (e.g., working memory in phonological awareness) may be less amenable to change.

English Language Proficiency

For young language learners, proficiency with speaking English strongly predicts growth in English reading comprehension, and those with higher English proficiency reach reading comprehension levels of their native speaker peers (Kieffer, 2008). One crucial influence on reading comprehension is vocabulary. Grabe and Stoller (2002) and Laufer (1997) estimated that one needs at least 3,000 words in a second language to read independently in that language. The greater the number of unknown words in a text, the more text comprehension suffers (Hsueh-chao and Nation,

2000). Zareva, Schwanenflugel, and Nikolova (2006) found that in order to comprehend a college-level academic text, a vocabulary of about 9,000 words is needed. In addition to vocabulary breadth, the depth of one's vocabulary correlates with reading comprehension (Qian, 1999). Based on their empirical work, Perfetti and Hart (2002) proposed the lexical quality hypothesis, which states that rich, stable, and integrated word knowledge (that includes orthographic, phonological, syntactic-semantic information) facilitates word recognition, especially when decoding cues are weak (see also Stanovich, 1980).

Explicitly teaching vocabulary can lead to significant improvement in word knowledge and comprehension for both monolinguals and language learners (August et al., 2009; Carlo et al., 2004; Lesaux et al., 2010; McKeown et al., 1985; Vaughn et al., 2009). Vocabulary develops not only through explicit teaching but also through routine exposure to language, especially print, which contains words and word structures used less often in speech (Nagy, Herman, and Anderson, 1985). In native speakers, literacy and degree of print exposure both predict growth in reading comprehension. Individuals with high levels of literacy do more reading and so develop their vocabulary, comprehension, and general knowledge through text, whereas those with lower proficiencies get less and less benefit from print. Not only in childhood, but across the life span, vocabulary and knowledge are predicted by print exposure (Stanovich, 1986; Stanovich, West, and Harrison, 1995). This pattern has not been studied specifically with adult language learners, but it is reasonable to expect that increased opportunities to learn from print and other exposure to spoken English beyond explicit instruction would help all learners.

For language learners in elementary and middle school, proficiency in oral communication develops rapidly, whereas decontextualized and formal language structures, such as those in academic settings, tend to take longer to acquire through exposure to varied texts and routine social interactions that support learning and practicing those forms of spoken and written language. The development of academic language has not been systematically investigated with adults, but a similar pattern can be expected. Most adult language learners, especially if they were born in the United States, report having good speaking skills, but according to the NAAL only a third had literacy skills beyond the basic level (Wrigley et al., 2009).

An analysis of U.S. census data (Batalova and Fix, 2010) showed that adults (both nonnative and native English speakers) who self-reported poor oral English skills (ratings of not very well/not at all) also had poor document literacy, but self-reports of good oral proficiency (ratings of very well/well) did *not* predict literacy performance. For example, only 13 percent of native speakers and only 9 percent of nonnative speakers (and only 13 percent of native speakers) who reported having good spoken English skills

were proficient on document literacy tasks. Although these self-reported results need to be interpreted with caution, they suggest a difference between
everyday communication skills in English and the English language skills
needed to comprehend more sophisticated material in different domains.
(The report did not state how many of the native speakers were second-
generation immigrants or Generation 1.5 who had not completed their
education.)

Age

An important question in the teaching of adults is whether age affects
the ability to acquire spoken and written language. In childhood, a first language is learned rapidly and without explicit instruction or consistent feedback. Children exposed to two languages are able to learn both (Bialystok
and Hakuta, 1995), and hearing children of deaf parents become bilingual
in both speech and sign (Mayberry, 2009). Because the bilingual's learning
task is more difficult, there are some differences in patterns of language
development compared with the single language learner (Genesee, 2001).
Some have hypothesized that a critical period for developing language
ends with puberty (Lenneberg, 1967), and others propose that the window
closes earlier (e.g., Pinker, 1994). Regardless of the exact timing, it is well
established that the ability to learn a second language declines with age.
The declines observed do not suggest, however, that literacy in a second
language cannot be achieved in adulthood at the levels required for career
and academic success. What they do imply is that learning a second language will take more time and practice at later ages, and that even at high
levels of second language facility differences in spoken language might be
expected between a native and nonnative English speaker.

There are competing explanations for why the decline occurs, which
differ in their emphasis on biological versus environmental influences.
One theory emphasizes the role of neurobiological development (Newport,
1990; Stromswold, 1995): whereas the young brain is well suited to acquiring languages rapidly and effortlessly, this capacity decreases because of
neurodevelopmental processes, such as dendritic proliferation and prun-
ing, and synapse elimination (Buonomano and Merzenich, 1998; Hensch,
2003). These neurodevelopmental changes are seen as similar to ones that
affect other capacities (e.g., vision, Daw, 1994) and occur in other species
(Doupe and Kuhl, 1999). This theory predicts an age-related discontinuity
in second language attainment associated with the closing of the critical
period for acquiring the skills of a native speaker (Johnson and Newport,
1989). Data from a recent large-scale study using U.S. census responses
show linear age-related declines in second language attainment but not the

discontinuity that would implicate a biologically determined window of opportunity (Hakuta, Bialystok, and Wiley, 2003).

A second hypothesis is that plasticity declines because of success in learning a first language (Bever, 1981; Seidenberg and Zevin, 2006), rather than brain development. Learning a second language requires adjusting neural networks that support the first language. Adjusting existing neural networks for second language processing is very difficult, especially since in adults those networks have been stabilized and are still successfully used in first language processing (Seidenberg and Zevin, 2006). A third possibility is that critical period effects reflect changes in the conditions (social, environmental) under which the second language is learned (Flege, Yeni-Komshian, and Liu, 1999). Older learners of a second language may have more restricted exposure to the second language or less motivation to use it, limiting what is learned.

Regardless of the underlying explanation, age constraints on language learning may help to explain slower growth in older adults' reading comprehension in general or second language reading comprehension (Alamprese, 2009) and other basic reading skills (Condelli, Wrigley, and Yoon, 2009). Certain linguistic structures in a second language may be more difficult to automatize and integrate later in life, which may affect comprehension of text. For example, Jiang (2007) found that late Chinese-English bilinguals were accurate in detecting violations of English morphological structure (plural -s) in unspeeded, written tests, indicating they had explicit knowledge of this structure. However when faster, computer-based tests were used, these bilinguals showed less sensitivity to such errors. Age-related differences in working memory also may affect second language and literacy acquisition, rather than a biological window for learning a language (Birdsong, 2006). For example, working memory affects second language acquisition, since it is involved in the implicit recognition of statistical properties and patterns of language, such as memory for instances and associations (see Ellis, 2005, for a review; McDonald, 2006).

Aptitude for a Second Language

General language aptitude predicts second language proficiency (Abrahamsson and Hyltenstam, 2008). In studies with high school and college students learning a second language in school, general second language aptitude as assessed using the Modern Language Aptitude Test (MLAT) strongly predicts the potential for reading comprehension, writing, listening, and speaking in a second language (Sparks et al., 2009b). It measures aptitude using tasks, such as learning the numbers or word meanings in a made-up language, mapping nonsense syllables to their transcriptions, and identifying grammatical functions. These tasks require phonological, orthographic, semantic, and syntactic processing and inductive reasoning and so, as would be expected, the aptitude scores also relate to first language skills (Sparks et al., 2009b). It should be noted that although aptitude as measured by the MLAT can indicate how much effort and instruction will be needed to teach a second language, the measure is not designed to diagnose a learning disability.

Reading and Learning Disabilities

When language learners experience reading and writing difficulties in a second language, it is hard to determine whether the cause is a true disability or not-yet-developed second language skills (Klingner, Artiles, and Méndez Barletta, 2006; Lovett et al., 2008a; McCardle et al., 2005). First language literacy levels can be a useful indicator: if learners have not developed first language literacy skills despite having had opportunities to do so, then a disability diagnosis can be considered (Durgunoğlu, 2002). For young language learners with reading difficulties, weak word and nonword recognition skills and phonological processing problems are found in both of their languages (Manis and Lindsey, 2010). This group can be distinguished from children who have reading comprehension problems because of underdeveloped oral language skills or sociocultural barriers. Just as with struggling native speakers, struggling language learners have similar risk factors, such as low socioeconomic status and attending low-achieving schools (de Jong, 2004; Grubb, 2008).

Children who have reading difficulties not related to exposure or quality of instruction show similar precursors and profiles and benefit from similar types of interventions regardless of whether they are native speakers or second language learners (Lesaux and Geva, 2006; Lovett et al., 2008b). More research is needed to determine how best to diagnose and intervene to develop literacy of both adult English native speakers and English language learners who have disabilities.

Cultural Knowledge and Background

Research suggests that it is important in both practice and research to understand variations in learners' cultural knowledge in order to develop effective learning environments. As described in Chapter 2, the component skills of literacy develop through participating in routine literacy practices in a culture for particular purposes and with the materials and tools available in the culture, which include uses of technologies for reading and writing inside and outside the classroom. Even when basic decoding is mastered, readers can struggle depending on the particular type of text they are asked to read, their level of background knowledge or interest, and the task they are asked to do (Moje, 2009). While these contextual factors affect literacy instruction and performance for native English speakers, they are especially important to consider in practice and research with adults learning a second language, because these adults bring more diverse cultural and educational backgrounds and literacy experiences.

Decades of literacy research have shown that comprehension involves interpreting the meaning of text using preexisting knowledge, beliefs, and opinions. The more one knows about a topic, the better one comprehends the material (Anderson and Pearson, 1984a, 1984b; McNamara, de Vega, and O'Reilly, 2007). Errors in comprehension can occur if the reader has incorrect or misleading information (Kendeou and van den Broek, 2005). For language learners, lack of cultural knowledge can hamper reading and listening comprehension (Center for Applied Linguistics, 2010; Droop and Verhoeven, 1998; Lesaux et al., 2006). Even for college students learning a second language, cultural knowledge plays a role in their comprehension (Brantmeier, 2005; Carrell, 1984; Fitzgerald, 1995). Although advanced language learners have very rich semantic networks in English, these networks may differ from those of native speakers (Zareva, Schwanenflugel, and Nikolova, 2005) indicating that differences in cultural experience shape how learners create word associations (or understand and remember relations between words).

Cross-cultural studies show certain cognitive processes are not necessarily universal, even for highly educated college students. Some basic processes, such as categorization, perception of an object in relation to its background, and making causal attributes, have been shown to be affected by the cultural context in which an individual was raised and educated (Ceci, 1991; Choi, Koo, and Choi, 2007; Choi, Nisbett, and Norenzayan, 1999; Nisbett et al., 2001; Norenzayan and Nisbett, 2000). Behavioral and brain scan data also show that monolinguals who did not have the opportunity to develop literacy skills because of social or cultural obstacles (rather than a neurological problem) perform more poorly on certain cognitive tasks, such as two-dimensional naming, phonological processing, memory, verbal abstraction hypothesis testing, and decision making, but not on verbal fluency or word repetition (Dellatolas et al., 2003; Reis, Guerreiro, and Petersson, 2003; Stanovich, West, and Harrison, 1995). All of these results highlight the importance of studying how culture affects cognition related to language and literacy.

In addition to cognitive factors, affective factors associated with culture can influence language learning. In particular, language learners can feel insecure about their English skills and cultural differences and feel conflicted between a desire for cultural integration and a desire for preserving their own home culture. Anxiety and motivation also have been shown to relate to second language achievement. For instance, Sparks et al. (2009a) found that U.S. high school students' second language achievement correlated with self-reported motivation and anxiety with respect to learning English. A Canadian descriptive study showed that, especially for individuals with minimal literacy and schooling in their first language, ESL classes can be frustrating and embarrassing, leading to an unwillingness to participate in classroom settings (Klassen and Burnaby, 1993). A meta-analysis showed that identity with the second language community and effort and desire to learn the second language correlated with second language achievement among Canadian students (Masgoret and Gardner, 2003), although it should be noted that the participants were required to learn an official second language and so the particular findings may not generalize. Nonetheless, findings such as these show the importance of considering adults' affective responses to instruction and the learning environment in research and practice.

APPROACHES TO SECOND LANGUAGE LITERACY INSTRUCTION

This section describes promising approaches to consider in the development of effective second language literacy instruction for adult learners. We draw on three sources of information. First, given the importance of language development to literacy, we review research on teaching a second language to high school or college students. This research has focused mainly, however, on developing linguistic structures and vocabulary for those who are highly literate in their first language. We also review studies of children who have limited literacy in their first language and who are developing both oral and written language skills in English. These findings may provide insights into effective practices for adults with no or very limited education or literacy facility in their first language. A third source of information is practitioner descriptions of practices that appear to be effective or ineffective in ESL adult education classes and that may be studied more systematically in future research. The practices gathered from these sources of information, which we describe next, suggest the importance of (1) integrated explicit instruction and opportunities for the implicit learning of language and literacy, with a focus on both linguistic form and meaning with feedback, (2) development of vocabulary and content knowledge for learning and reading comprehension, (3) extensive practice outside the classroom, (4) leveraging knowledge of the first language, (5) multimodal instruction, (6) attention to writing, (7) attention to the affective aspects of learning and instruction, and (8) sound assessment of literacy skill and affective and psychological outcomes of instruction.

Integration of Explicit Instruction and Implicit Learning of Language and Literacy

Second language learning involves both implicit learning as well as explicit knowledge about language. Across the years, methods for teaching a second language have fluctuated between emphasizing sequenced explicit instruction of grammatical structures and using language to communicate for a purpose (Long, 2009). One promising approach is task-based language teaching (see Box 8-1) (for a thorough review, see Ellis, 2005; Vouloumanos, 2008).

Research is required to know precisely how to configure instruction with the appropriate balance and emphasis and whether it depends on characteristics of the learner and other factors (Long, 2009; Long and Crookes, 1992; Norris and Ortega, 2000; Spada and Lightbown, 2008). Most empirical evaluations of instructional approaches have been short-term studies of very specific language structures (e.g., use of Spanish clitic pronouns) in college foreign language classes. In one study of 256 adults in ESL programs in the United Kingdom, however, the main factor that predicted increased

---

BOX 8-1
Task-Based Language Teaching

The task-based language teaching method is a promising approach that integrates explicit instruction and implicit learning and emphasizes that language is learned from communications used to accomplish certain tasks and goals (Ellis, 2005; Long and Crookes, 1992; Robinson and Ellis, 2008). Language instruction occurs as tasks are performed. The tasks are selected to be relevant and meaningful to the learners, consistent with observations that relevance and connections to communicating for real-world purposes are especially important for adult language learners (Condelli, Wrigley, and Yoon, 2009). In task-based language teaching, the first step is to analyze the learner's practical literacy needs (e.g., reading technical manuals, communicating with a child's teacher, navigating bureaucratic mazes, taking lecture notes) and the learner's developmental levels. This information is used to inform the design of systematic and structured instruction. Instruction involves gradually increasing the complexity of the communicative and conceptual demands of the tasks, while directing the learner's attention to the language structures and tools (such as those used for understanding the referents of pronouns) available in the language.

Genuine materials are used which differ from "authentic" materials in actual use in that they are designed to have features that systematically scaffold learning while enabling engagement with meaningful and valued content. Task-based language teaching includes a systematic focus on the grammatical form of language and not only a focus on meaning.

oral language proficiency (grammar and vocabulary) was the observed balance and variety of instruction, which was defined as connections among lessons; integrated reading, writing, and speaking; and use of a wide range of activities and materials (Baynham et al., 2007). Longer term intervention studies are needed with a broader range of language structures and populations to determine how best to integrate explicit instruction techniques and genuine experiences with communicating, depending on the language development needs of learners in adult literacy education.

Explicit Teaching

A principle of learning is that most students have trouble discovering important principles on their own, without careful guidance, scaffolding, or well-crafted materials. English language learners are usually exposed to much more input than they can process, and learners continually test hypotheses and filter input through knowledge of their first language. Instruction that focuses the learner's attention is needed to isolate and highlight the crucial parts of the input, especially with complex structures of syntax (Gass, Svetics, and Lemelin, 2003). For example, second language cues that are absent or marked differently in the first language may have low salience for a learner. Cues that are redundant or accompanied and resolved by other contextual resources may not be explicitly noticed and learned either (such as *the two cats*, in which both the inflection and the number term indicate plurality).

In a meta-analysis to evaluate the effectiveness of different instructional techniques, Norris and Ortega (2000) found that focused second language instruction was more effective than the control conditions. Explicit teaching that included rule explanation as part of the instruction produced stronger effects than implicit teaching that included neither rule presentation nor directions to attend to particular linguistic forms (see also Long, 1983; Nassaji, 2009). A third finding was that instruction that begins with learners doing meaningful tasks but also presents opportunities to provide information about linguistic structures (e.g., an error) produced comparable results as instruction in which an ordered sequence of linguistic forms is taught outside a communicative context (e.g., teaching a sequence of grammatical structures), especially with explicit instruction in both (Norris and Ortega, 2000). In addition, Ellis (2005) reports that teaching formulaic expressions (e.g., I don't understand) and basic rules of chunked materials (e.g., I don't + verb) may help learners develop familiarity with the English language and master structures used frequently for communicating. Less is known about how instruction interacts with contextual variables, such as the proficiency of the learner (Gass, Svetics, and Lemelin, 2003), type of language outcome measured (Norris and Ortega, 2000), complexity and type of linguistic structure (DeKeyser and Sokalski, 1996; Gass, Svetics, and Lemelin, 2003), and characteristics of learners' first language (Williams, 2005).

As described in Chapter 2, research with young language learners also shows the benefit of direct instruction on phonological awareness, decoding, vocabulary, comprehension, and writing (Goldenberg, 2008). Sometimes derided as "drill and kill," direct and explicit instruction simply means making the components and requirements of complex literacy tasks obvious and salient, and it generally can be done in motivating ways. The most effective language instruction for young children combines interactive instruction involving discussions among teachers and learners and direct approaches that involve explicit teaching, modeling of correct language usage, and feedback (Genesee et al., 2006; Goldenberg, 2008).

Focus on Both Form and Meaning and Providing Feedback

There is much debate about how to draw the learner's attention to an error in a linguistic structure without disrupting the communicative inter-actions that are also needed for learning. Similar issues arise in any situation in which the long-term flow of an activity is part of the instruction. A standard approach in other areas is to use video or other capture techniques and then replay the moment at which a small correction is needed, after the overall event occurs, during postproblem reflection opportunities (Katz, Connelly, and Allbritton, 2003; Lesgold and Nahemow, 2001).

A principle of learning is that students benefit from feedback on their performance in a learning task. Feedback is especially important in language development because, despite some linguistic errors, the meaning of a communication may still be clear. Because communication is not disrupted, incorrect forms may not be challenged and continue to be used. Therefore, second language educators emphasize the importance of giving feedback on what is not an acceptable form, even when the form is comprehensible, as well as explicitly teaching the structures to prevent and correct such errors (Ellis, 2005; Lyster, 1998). These findings are consistent with research on "negative suggestion effects" showing that learning wrong information can be reduced when feedback is immediate.

A common tool used in classrooms is to provide language feedback: "recasting" or responding to a learner's error by restating what the learner has said while modeling the correct form (e.g., *Learner*: *She go to school.* *Teacher*: *She goes to school?* with stress on "goes."). Recasts are useful because they can occur as part of the conversation and do not disrupt the flow of communication. They temporarily focus the learner's attention on language itself. Because recasts are usually subtle, they may not be noticed or used, and so they tend to be more effective when made more explicit (e.g., signaling the error with stress).

In a study of eight Somali-speaking young adults, those with higher literacy in their first language were better able than those with lower literacy to learn to form questions in English using recasts that teachers provided (Bigelow and Tarone, 2004; Tarone, Bigelow, and Hansen, 2007). At this point, it is not clear whether the development of complex syntactic structures, such as relative clauses, requires more explicit or additional or more varied supports (e.g., presenting information visually, in writing) for those with low literacy. Learning from recasts can be limited unless classroom instruction focuses explicitly on language itself (through explicit prior instruction on the form, for example) or unless, consistent with the Somali study, the learners are at a more advanced stage (Ellis, Loewen, and Erlam, 2006; Lyster, 1998; Nassaji, 2009; Nicholas, Lightbown, and Spada, 2001).

Encouraging a learner to generate the correct form can be effective for learning (Loewen and Philip, 2006). This finding is consistent with the generation effect, which states that learning is enhanced when learners produce answers in comparison to having them recognize answers. Such "desirable difficulties" also can present challenges that require cognitive effort (e.g., to retrieve the correct form) and thereby lead to longer retention and learning. In sum, although recasts have been studied extensively and systematically in second language classrooms, research is needed to determine how best to use recasts to facilitate learning for adults.

Rich and Elaborated Input

Rich and elaborated input provides the learners with opportunities to experience and learn certain structural patterns in the language related to phonology, morphology, syntax, or pragmatics, although they may not be aware of learning the grammatical rules that govern the structures. Through intensive exposure to language, learners develop an implicit understanding of the patterns in a language—for example, how often certain structures or words are used. Nevertheless, these incidental opportunities for learning about the structure of a language are not sufficient, especially for learning the more complex structures presented in text, and require explicit attention to form (Ellis, 2005; see Chapter 3 for a similar description of language and literacy development in a first language).

As described in Chapter 3, adult literacy instruction often includes authentic reading materials. The term authentic often carries the incorrect connotation that explicit teaching is not necessary for learning to read and that exposure to "real-world" language and text is enough (see Condelli and Wrigley, 2004, for a similar argument). For language learners, and even for adults developing literacy in a first language, the spoken and especially more formal written input in authentic communications can be overwhelming. Although one option could be to simplify the input, such simplified materials do not allow learners to experience the complex structures of the second language that they need to learn. A more promising approach is to use "elaborated" input (Long, 2009) that includes linguistic supports, such as redundancy, paraphrasing, synonyms, clear signaling, and marking to increase topic salience, making the information flow chronologically, using shorter sentences, and so on. Likewise in written and especially spoken language elaborations, instruction includes frequent clarification requests and comprehension checks (Long, 2009; Yano, Long, and Ross, 1994). However, making the language more comprehensible does not mean using child-like content. Adult learners need materials that are interesting and relevant to their knowledge development needs.

Development of Language and Knowledge for Learning and Reading Comprehension

Francis and colleagues (2006) have compiled research-based recommendations for helping adolescent newcomers in schools who have limited English proficiencies and have difficulty especially with reading and writing academic texts. The literacy difficulties of these students may stem from limited oral proficiency in English, limited exposure to English texts, and possible gaps in background knowledge for the topic. Taking all of these factors into consideration, it is suggested that effective instruction for adolescent newcomers includes content-based literacy instruction, with an emphasis on developing academic language. In this approach, there are dual, integrated objectives: teachers address content through language and teach language through content. In addition, explicit instruction is used to teach reading comprehension and writing for academic purposes.

Effective vocabulary instruction for adolescent newcomers is explicit, systematic, extensive, and intensive (Francis et al., 2006). Explicit instruction involves not only direct instruction of the meanings of specific key words but also direct instruction in effective word learning strategies, such as breaking words down into parts, using contextual clues, and using dictionaries as references. Systematic instruction requires teachers to thoughtfully choose the key words that they teach and create multiple opportunities for meaningful exposure to the words and their meanings. Extensive vocabulary instruction is incorporated into every lesson, integrated across the curriculum. Finally, intensive vocabulary instruction provides depth of knowledge, such as an understanding of multiple meanings of words, their different forms, and different contexts of use and situated in larger conceptual frameworks. These instructional strategies are accompanied by high-quality ongoing classroom assessments to monitor students' progress and, if needed, appropriate intervention for newcomers with word reading difficulties (Francis et al., 2006).

Initiatives to improve the academic vocabulary of language learners in upper elementary and middle schools (August et al., 2009; Lesaux, Kieffer, and Kelley, 2009; Vaughn et al., 2009) have integrated the teaching of academic vocabulary with learning in content areas, such as social studies and science. Instead of teaching vocabulary as an itemized list of new words, the instruction integrates the words into discussion of what Vaughn et al. (2009) calls "big ideas," such as human rights. The target words are taught using a combination of strategies, including reading, writing, oral discussions, and multimedia (e.g., videos to build background knowledge). The words are used and practiced in different contexts. In addition to teaching specific words, these programs also explicitly model and teach word analysis and comprehension strategies. Some also use students' first language, Spanish, as a resource. There is also peer support, dyad and group work of the learners.

ALIAS (Academic Language Instruction for All Students) is a good example of such a program developed for middle school students (Lesaux et al., 2009). As the name implies, this program targets all students, both native speakers and English language learners. The curriculum provides rich and systematic instruction of high-utility academic words. There are multiple, planned exposures to each word through reading, writing, class discussions, and group activities. The students are encouraged to talk about these concepts, engage through personal connections and class discussions, and finally use the words in writing. The evaluation of the program indicates that for native speakers as well as language learners, there was significant growth in the targeted vocabulary, in word analysis, and, most importantly, in reading comprehension—although it should be noted that the size of the gain was relatively small compared with the amount of gain needed, and the practical meaning of the gains was not clear.

As discussed in Chapter 3, contextualized literacy instruction is an approach that is consistent with principles of learning and has sufficient preliminary support to warrant further research on its effectiveness with adults. Few data exist for adult language learners. The Integrated Basic Education and Skills Training program, or I-BEST, in Washington state is a program in which basic skills instructors and college-level career-technical faculty jointly design and teach college-level occupational courses for adult basic skills students. The program aims to increase successful completion of postsecondary occupational education and training (Jenkins, Zeidenberg, and Kienzl, 2009). The instruction of basic skills is integrated with instruction in college-level career-technical skills courses. The tracking of these students for 2 years showed that I-BEST students (both adult basic education and ESL students) had better basic skills (assessed by Comprehensive

Adult Student Assessment Systems) and the persistence to continue their education (e.g., earning college or vocational credits, certification). These students were not randomly assigned, however, but rather self-selected into I-BEST programs, so the results need to be interpreted cautiously. The effectiveness of embedded programs has not been evaluated systematically. Observations and interviews indicate that teacher specialization or boundaries and coordination within programs can present challenges to effective implementation (Cara et al., 2006; Guenther, 2002).

Access to Language and Literacy Practice Outside Classrooms

Learning continues outside the classroom where adult language learners can experience continued interactions in both spoken and written English (Reder, 2008). Successful language learning requires extensive second language input and opportunities to interact with others and to use language to express their own ideas, thoughts, and views (Ellis, 2009). Exposure to rich language patterns is also helpful, because learners are quite sensitive and readily notice the common patterns in a language (Vouloumanos, 2008). Thus, it is important not to isolate language learners from native speakers and to maximize exposure to the second language using many different venues.

Technology is a promising tool to provide practice outside the classroom through opportunities to use Internet sites, distance learning, and email. Although some new research has accumulated with adult language learners, most research on technology's effectiveness with this population is old and ambiguous (Abraham, 2008; Torgerson, Porthouse, and Brooks, 2003). A new generation of research is needed because the feasibility, usefulness, and effectiveness of self-access models via technologies for adult language learners have not been fully explored (Wrigley, 2009).

Leveraging Knowledge in the First Language, When Available

Given the possibilities of transfer discussed earlier, more needs to be known about how best to use the first language to support development of English literacy. It is also reasonable to expect that acknowledging and valuing a learner's first language are motivating, since they acknowledge and build on the knowledge and capabilities of the learner. When the first language is used as an aid to clarify instructions and tasks, learners show more growth in second language reading comprehension and oral proficiency (Condelli, Wrigley, and Yoon, 2009). Systematic use of the first language may not be feasible in many languages other than Spanish because of lack of qualified teachers and materials.

Integrated Multimodal Instruction

Research with monolinguals indicates that higher order comprehension skills necessary for reading can also be developed through discussions of material presented in different modalities, such as visual or auditory (Kendeou et al., 2008). Using technology to present information in a variety of modalities shows particular promise for language instruction, since language and content presented in a variety of modalities (visual, auditory, text-based) reinforce each other. In addition, visual and auditory presentations can provide varied input that is not available in print, such as regional accents, speed of discourse, pronunciation, and pragmatic uses of language. Research with monolinguals indicates that higher order comprehension skills necessary for reading can also be developed through discussions of material presented in different modalities, such as visual or auditory (Kendeou et al., 2008). As Hanley, Herron, and Cole (1995) report, visual support in the form of descriptive pictures significantly improved comprehension scores for English-speaking students learning French.

Anecdotal evidence from the adult literacy field consistently stresses that adults in literacy programs enjoy using technology (Benbunan-Fich and Hiltz, 1999; Parke and Tracy-Mumford, 2000). Cromley (2000) suggests that access to technology results in greater learner engagement and retention. Technologies for acquiring English have shown positive impacts on the frequency of revision and the complexity of content in the writing of adults learning a second language (Li and Cumming, 2001).

As explained earlier, speaking, listening, reading, and writing are all interrelated modes of communication (Hornberger, 1989). Even with very young language learners, providing exposure to oral and written language together is more effective in developing vocabulary and phonological awareness (Farver, Lonigan, and Eppe, 2009). Likewise, for adults, it is not a good strategy to provide only oral language instruction while waiting until reading and writing reach a certain level of proficiency. It is also useful to include and integrate both decoding and comprehension instruction (see Chapter 6 for further discussion of instructional approaches).

Writing

As for native speakers, writing is an essential part of instruction for adult language learners. It offers an opportunity to practice second language skills related to both reading and writing, and it can be another way to track second language proficiencies. Writing can also help to meet the learner's practical needs for communication because those with limited literacy in their first language tend to take notes (and use other cognitive strategies) to overcome this limitation (Klassen and Burnaby, 1993).

Cross-sectional studies suggest that uses of vocabulary, syntax, morphology, signaling, and rhetorical devices in writing improve with second language proficiency, as does the coherence and fluency of writing (Chenoweth and Hayes, 2001; Cumming, 2001; Sasaki, 2000; Sasaki and Hirose, 1996). First and second language writing processes are fundamentally similar, and knowledge of the first language is used in second language writing. But those with weak second language skills tend to devote more attention to form (e.g., finding the right word or syntactic structure in the second language by translating from the first language) and thus devote less attention to the macro processes of generating ideas, planning, revising, and editing (Sasaki, 2000). A promising avenue for research is to understand more about how to develop these macro processes in second language instruction (Sasaki, 2000). Other promising instructional strategies provide additional scaffolds and support, such as prediscussions of the writing topic, peers evaluating and responding to each other's work (Berg, 1999), and teacher-student dialogue journals (Peyton and Seyoum, 1989). As Cumming (in press) summarizes, educators can facilitate second language writing development by providing extensive opportunities to write and by responding to that writing, modeling relevant text types and discourse interactions, by enhancing students' self-control over their composing and learning processes, and by organizing curricula and assessments appropriate to learners' abilities, purposes, and interests. Finally, extensive reading and vocabulary development in the second language are also helpful for writing.

Writing is a complex cognitive skill that is influenced by social and cultural aspects of the learner's environment. Although the basic components of writing discussed in Chapter 4 apply to all adults, several other factors affect writing for second language learners. These include significant variability in first language background, educational level, second language proficiency, length of time in the new country, acculturation and familiarity with second language writing contexts, and the purposes and needs for writing. This complex web of factors has yet to be considered in a comprehensive model of second language writing development (Cumming, in press). Research is needed, especially with adult language learners in adult education settings, to track learners' progress in the use of text features, their use of composition processes for different tasks and writing environments, and how progress changes as a function of different types of instruction (Cumming and Riazi, 2000).

As for reading, more needs to be understood about how to develop second language writing in content domains and how to support writing outside the classroom. A rare study of second language writing in the workplace illustrates how the specific style of writing and vocabulary required in a particular workplace evolves. In this observational research, newly graduated Francophone nurses who received mentoring, were encouraged to interact informally with peers, and had opportunities to observe others who modeled forms of communication in the workplace developed both their expressive communication skills in the second language and the specific workplace genre for completing patient charts and discharge papers (Parks, 2001; Parks and Maguire, 1999). Such studies show the potential for developing language, reading, and writing in a second language outside the classroom.

Affective Aspects of Learning and Instruction

Field research indicates the importance of attending to the affective aspects of instruction (Wrigley, 2009), although more systematic research on English language learners' affective responses to literacy instruction is needed to develop motivating and supportive approaches. Field observations show that beginning learners are reluctant to use English inside and outside the classroom because they may feel insecure about their linguistic skills. English learners can become demotivated, frustrated with the slow pace of literacy instruction; repetitive instruction (e.g., as teachers try to catch up students who have missed a class); a focus on topics that are not well matched to the learner's education level, interests, or familiarity with U.S. culture (e.g., a focus on holidays when content related to science and technology and topical discussions is preferred). Those whose goal it is to transition to training or postsecondary education mention the lack of focus on academic vocabulary in high beginning or intermediate classes.

As mentioned earlier, the general principles for supporting motivation and persistence in Chapter 5 are likely to apply to language learners. Given the unique contexts that surround language learners, it is important to make the learning environment safe, supportive, and comfortable (Hardman, 1999); to make instruction useful and valuable to the learner (Burt, Peyton, and Adams, 2003); to encourage support through collaborations and peers (Baynham et al., 2007; Cener for Applied Lingistics, 2010; Slavin, 1996; Taylor et al., 2007; Watanabe and Swain, 2007; see Torgerson, Porthouse, and Brooks, 2003, for a review); and to use relevant topics, activities, and texts for instruction. Although not yet systematically evaluated, cooperative learning and other forms of peer support may matter even more for adult language learners. Even when adults in certain ESL classes reported feeling frustrated at times, they reported enjoying meeting people and getting to know other speakers of Spanish (Klassen and Burnaby, 1993), so the social aspects of the instructional environment may be especially powerful in motivating persistence.

Assessment

Adequate assessments are lacking for English language learners. The need to develop more valid and comprehensive approaches to the assessment of adults' reading and writing skills also applies to this population.

Four additional issues specific to the English language learner population have emerged in research and practice: (1) assessment of learners' linguistic and cultural backgrounds and existing language proficiencies, (2) the need to avoid the use of tests developed for native speakers of English, (3) assessment of incremental progress in subcomponents of spoken and written language proficiency, and (4) assessment of affective and psychological outcomes.

Learner Background and Existing Proficiencies

The heterogeneity of adult English language learners requires having systematic ways to assess the backgrounds and such factors as first and second language and literacy proficiencies that influence English literacy development. Currently, teachers report that it is a challenge to provide instruction that is sufficiently common to all in a classroom while differentiating instruction to meet the needs of all learners (Wrigley, 2009). As more is understood about the factors that affect English language and literacy development for different English language learner populations, more reliable and valid assessments can be developed to help make placement decisions and inform instructional planning.

Use of Tests Developed for Native English Speakers

Assessments in English that are developed for native speakers may not provide valid information about language learners for two reasons. If linguistic complexity rather than the content of a test item causes low performance, the assessment does not reliably assess that content knowledge (Abedi, 2006). This type of measurement error occurs on tests other than reading, such as mathematics tests, which are sometimes incorrectly assumed to be relatively independent of linguistic proficiency (Abedi, 2002, 2006; Abedi and Lord, 2001).

Second, because reading comprehension, whether in a first or second language, is tied to background knowledge (Garcia, 1991; Lesser, 2007), a language learner may show poor comprehension not because of poor language or comprehension ability but because the topic is unfamiliar. In fact, for Spanish college students learning English, discipline-related background knowledge and language proficiency compensated for each other. Those with low English proficiency could read texts successfully if they had prior knowledge about the topic, and those with high English proficiency comprehended texts even if they had low background knowledge about the topic (Uso-Juan, 2007).

Such interrelationships between language proficiency and background knowledge have not been systematically explored with adult language learners. The possibility of existing background knowledge (in the first language) compensating for low linguistic proficiency is intriguing, and further research can identify if and how background knowledge in the first language can be used as an instructional tool while building English proficiency.

Assessment of Incremental Progress in All of the Subcomponents of Spoken and Written Language

Another challenge in assessing language learners is the complexity of language acquisition. Understanding spoken or written language requires integrating multiple sources of information, such as word meanings, syntactic rules, and background knowledge. Because assessments usually tap into only a subset of language skills (e.g., vocabulary) or include measures that are too broad (e.g., oral proficiency), they may not assess the full range of language skill. Moreover, different components of language develop at different rates and in an incremental fashion. For example, vocabulary knowledge is not a simple dichotomy of knowing or not knowing a word's meaning. Rather, knowledge is a continuum that ranges from not knowing a word, to recognizing it, to knowing it roughly, to describing it very accurately and knowing its uses in different contexts (Schoonen and Verhallen, 2008; Vermeer, 2001). Such incremental growth in linguistic knowledge is not reflected in vocabulary tests. An analysis of the 19 most common assessments for language learners (many of which are not widely used or standardized) identified the need for assessments that measure a greater range of language skills and more detailed proficiency levels (Center for Applied Linguistics, 2010). Assessments are needed for different purposes. Although global measures at the program level may be sufficient for accountability purposes, more fine-grained assessments are needed at the individual level to assess language and literacy growth for planning instruction and providing feedback to learners (see Center for Applied Linguistics, 2010, for a review).

Given the integrated development of spoken and written language, proficiencies in both written and spoken English should be assessed. Language and literacy in the first language and level of education are also important to assess to guide instruction because, as reviewed earlier, these are closely linked to second language development.

Assessments that involve selected or constrained responses (e.g., multiple choice or completion) show the largest effects of instruction because they match instruction closely. Free response tasks that require spoken or written answers are better measures of learners' second language proficiency, however, because they relate most closely to language use outside the classroom (Ellis, 2009; Norris and Ortega, 2000). Developing tests of the second type, especially for language learners, is a challenge, but, as for all adults in literacy instruction, it is important to develop reliable and valid measures to assess performance on relevant real-world tasks (Purcell-Gates et al., 2002).

Assessment of Affective and Psychological Outcomes

A range of affective and psychological influences on learning and desired outcomes are important to evaluate in addition to language and literacy skill. These include self-efficacy in the use of spoken and written English, effortless and confident navigation of new contexts in the culture, and the ability to interact comfortably with native speakers, all of which remain difficult to quantify.

SUMMARY AND DIRECTIONS FOR RESEARCH

The number of adults who need to develop their English literacy skills in the United States is substantial and growing, and the population is extremely diverse. These adults differ in languages spoken, education levels, literacy skill in the first language, knowledge of English, familiarity with U.S. culture, and other characteristics. The adults differ in the component skills they need to develop and bring to the challenging task of learning to use and comprehend a second language. Some English learners need to understand how the English writing system represents the spoken language and how to decode and read words in English. They often need to develop vocabulary and knowledge of linguistic features, such as syntax and morphology. Background knowledge related to the culture, the texts to be comprehended, and purpose of a literacy task all may need attention to help adults use their skills to make inferences and create a rich mental representation of the meaning of text. Communicative expression may need to be developed in both spoken and written modalities.

Various cognitive, linguistic, social, affective, and cultural factors influence the development of literacy in a second language. These include education and proficiency in the first language, age, type and degree of existing English proficiency, aptitude for language, possible learning disabilities, cultural and background knowledge, and interest. All of these factors must be considered in the development of instruction for adults learning English as a second language.

Research on effective practices for developing English language and literacy in adults is severely limited, especially those with low levels of education and literacy in the first language. Thus, this chapter reviews three additional sources of information to identify promising practices to study further with adult English language learners: (1) studies of second language teaching in high school and college settings, (2) studies of children who have limited literacy in their first language and who are developing both oral and written language skills in English and thus may provide insights

---

BOX 8-2
Practices to Apply and Study with English Language Learners

Engaging and differentiated instruction for adults who vary in

- English language and literacy skills,
- first language proficiency,
- educational background, and
- familiarity with U.S. culture.

Instruction that integrates explicit instruction with opportunities for the implicit learning of language and literacy, with a focus on

- both linguistic form and meaning with feedback,
- development of vocabulary and content knowledge for learning and reading comprehension,
- extensive practice outside the classroom,
- leveraging knowledge of the first language,
- multimodal instruction,
- attention to writing,
- attention to the affective aspects of learning and instruction, and
- sound assessment of literacy skill and affective and psychological outcomes of instruction.

---

into effective practices for adults with limited education or literacy facility in a first language, and (3) practitioner descriptions of practices used in adult education ESL classes and that warrant more systematic research attention. Box 8-2 shows practices to apply and study in future research. A particular challenge is the need to differentiate instruction for adults in a classroom who vary in first language proficiency, educational background, and familiarity with U.S. culture.

Box 8-3 summarizes directions for research. The overarching priorities for this research agenda are to (a) develop and evaluate effective instructional methods for diverse populations of English language learners; (b) develop adequate assessment methods; (c) identify or develop the technologies that can facilitate the learning of language and literacy skills for adult English language learners who differ in their knowledge of English language and literacy, first language literacy, and educational and linguistic backgrounds; and (d) specify the training and supports instructors need to implement the instructional approaches effectively. Standard terms and definitions for describing the subgroups of this diverse population of adults will need to be used in this research to produce more reliable, valid, and interpretable information about the approaches that generalize across subgroups and the specific approaches that meet a particular group's literacy development needs.

BOX 8-3
Directions for Research on English as a
Second Language Instruction

- Experiments to identify effective instructional practices for different groups of language learners (with varying first languages, knowledge of English, first language literacy skills, educational backgrounds, and reasons for attending instruction) to help instructors differentiate instruction.
- Studies to specify the length, type, and intensity of instruction that is the most effective for different language learner groups.
- Systematic and longitudinal analyses of language teaching practices (integrating language structures with language use and meaningful content) and documentation of outcomes for adult language learners.
- Comprehensive description and analysis of the components of effective programs at multiple levels (instructional content, teaching practices, student interactions, and so on) using quantitative and qualitative methods that link components to outcomes.
- Background variables that have an impact on outcomes and that are important to assess at program entry and for differentiated instruction.
- Characteristics of learners and aspects of language exposure (both inside and outside the classroom) that predict learning and a range of other desired outcomes that include persistence, continuation with further education, finding employment, and lifelong learning.
- The relation between first language skills and the development of spoken and written English skills and identification of opportunities for transferring skills and strategies.
- Ways to provide effective multimodal language instruction (speaking, reading, writing, visual presentations) and technology.
- Ways to integrate classroom instruction with informal learning opportunities provided by interactions in communities and through the use of technology.
- The most effective ways to integrate language and literacy development with content instruction.
- Development and evaluation of "integrated instruction" models that combine language and literacy education with academic and career education.
- Assessments that (a) provide enough information about language and literacy skills and progress to be useful for planning instruction and providing feedback to learners, (b) are valid measures of practically important language and literacy competencies, and (c) measure affective, cultural, and psychological factors that affect learning.
- Teacher knowledge and professional development to effectively administer and use assessments and flexibly adapt the curriculum to meet learners' needs.

9

Conclusions and Recommendations

It is clear that a significant proportion of U.S. adults do not have the high level of literacy in both print and digital media required for negotiating many aspects of life in the 21st century. As noted in Chapter 1, more than 90 million U.S. adults are estimated to lack adequate literacy (Kutner et al., 2007); only 38 percent of U.S. twelfth graders are at or above proficient in reading (National Assessment of Educational Progress, 2008); and more than 50 percent of recent 250,000 community college student enrollees were referred to at least one developmental (remedial) education course to remediate weak skills during their college tenure (Bailey, Jeong, and Cho, 2010), with about one-third of them referred specifically for reading. Furthermore, the estimated 2.6 million adults enrolled in federally funded programs in 2005 showed variable progress in their literacy skills, and their skill gains were insufficient to achieve functional literacy (Tamassia et al., 2007).

This committee was asked to (1) synthesize research findings on literacy and learning from cognitive science, neuroscience, behavioral and social science, and education; (2) identify from the research the main factors that affect literacy development in adolescence and adulthood, both in general and with respect to the specific populations served in education programs for adults; (3) analyze the implications of the research for informing curricula and instruction used to develop adults' literacy; and (4) recommend a more systemic approach to subsequent research, practice, and policy. To focus our work, we defined the target population (to whom we refer generally as "adults") to be adolescents and adults ages 16 and older who need to develop their literacy skills outside the K-12 system. This definition is consistent with eligibility for participation in federally funded adult literacy education programs. We considered research on learning and literacy that would be most relevant to those eligible or likely to attend formal literacy instruction in programs of four general types: adult basic education, adult secondary education, English as a second language programs offered in a wide range of settings (e.g., community-based programs, local education agencies, community colleges, workplace, prisons, etc.), and developmental education courses for academically underprepared students in college.

Ideally, conclusions and recommendations for adult literacy instruction would be grounded in clear research findings demonstrating the efficacy of the recommended approaches. When rigorous demonstrations of efficacy do not exist, the next best approach would be to recommend both instructional practices consistent with available evidence on adult literacy and rigorous efficacy studies to confirm these recommendations. Findings from research on cognition and learning with the target population would also be most useful.

The present situation is more complex. There is a surprising lack of research on the effectiveness of the various instructional practices for adults seeking to improve their literacy skills. The lack of relevant research is especially striking given the long history of both federal funding for adult education programs, albeit stretched thin, and reliance on developmental education courses to remediate college students' skills. Few studies of adult literacy focus on the development of reading and writing skills. There is also inadequate knowledge about assessment and ongoing monitoring of adult students' proficiencies, weaknesses, instructional environments, and progress, which might guide instructional planning.

Similarly, basic research on adult cognition and learning is constrained for our purposes. It relies on study samples of convenience (college students in introductory psychology courses) or elderly populations, and it does not usually include adults with relatively low education or literacy skills. In addition, it is well known that literacy research has focused mainly on young children first learning to read and decode text. Major research efforts launched by the U.S. Department of Education, the National Institute of Child Health and Human Development, and others on the development of literacy in adolescence and adulthood are too new to have produced numerous peer-reviewed publications. As discussed in Chapter 2, research is emerging with adolescents on topics that we think are important to pursue with the target population given their literacy development needs (e.g., academic or disciplinary literacy and discussion-based approaches). More research is needed with adolescent and adult populations to evaluate the effectiveness of instructional practices and specify learning trajectories and the interaction of factors—cognitive, social, linguistic, economic, neurobiological—that may affect literacy development in subpopulations of adolescents and adults who vary greatly in literacy development needs, education levels, socioeconomic status, linguistic background, and other characteristics.

Given the dearth of relevant research with the target adult population, this report draws on what is available: extensive research on reading and writing processes and difficulties of younger students, emerging research on literacy and learning in adolescents and adults with normal reading capability, and extremely limited research on adult literacy learners. Until the necessary research is conducted with adults who receive literacy instruction outside the K-12 system, the committee concluded that it is reasonable to apply the wealth of available research on learning and literacy with other populations. Findings from this research provide guidance about the reading and writing skills to target with instruction and principles for designing instructional practices, technologies, assessments, and preparation for teachers. With our conclusions, we recommend a program of research and innovation to validate, identify the boundaries of, and extend current knowledge to improve instruction for adults and adolescents outside school and create the supports needed for learning and achievement.

The request to the committee stressed the need for guidance from research to inform the design of instructional curricula and practices for use in programs, and not broader improvements to adult education delivery systems or access to programs—important as such improvements might be. In drawing conclusions from the research and recommending a more systemic approach to research, practice, and policy, however, we recognize four main issues related to the adult literacy system: (1) the variability in the profiles of adult learners, (2) the variability of instructor preparation, (3) the existence of many different types of programs that have varied literacy development aims and practices, and (4) the instructional and other supports that enable adults to persist in programs and practice skills outside the classroom. We urge attention to these issues in research and policy because they impinge directly on the quality of instruction, the feasibility of completing the recommended research, and the potential for broad dissemination and implementation of the practices that emerge as effective from research findings.

CONCLUSIONS

Adult Learners and Learning Environments

Conclusion 1: The population of adult learners is heterogeneous. Optimal reading and writing instruction will therefore vary according to goals for literacy development and learning, knowledge and skill, interests, neurocognitive profiles, and cultural and linguistic backgrounds. The contexts in which adults receive literacy instruc-

tion also are highly variable with respect to (1) place and purpose of instruction, (2) literacy development aims and practices, and (3) instructor preparation.

Learners have diverse instructional needs, varying motivations for acquiring greater literacy, and diverse educational, economic, linguistic, and cultural backgrounds. Some adults have specific neurocognitive challenges associated with disability that have not been addressed with the appropriate interventions, and others simply have not had the social and educational environment as children that would support learning to read and write well and with proficiency in multiple contexts and domains. Moreover, adult learners vary, sometimes substantially, in the level of facility they have already attained.

The contexts in which adults receive literacy instruction are highly varied. People who need to develop their literacy skills receive instruction in many different types of programs, including adult basic education, community colleges, general educational development (GED) programs, workplace literacy programs, university remedial education programs, citizenship programs, English language learning programs, basic skills and job training centers, among others. While some of the adults receiving literacy instruction may have attained certain levels and forms of literacy, they lack the range and level of reading and writing skills required for education, work, parental and family responsibilities, and other purposes. The literature on adult literacy indicates that a wide range of largely untested theoretical frameworks, practices, texts, and tools are used in literacy instruction with adults. At present, there are neither clear objectives for the development of literacy skills nor standards for curricula and practice that take into consideration research on component reading and writing skills, valued literacy tasks linked to learning goals, and the social and cultural backgrounds and motivations of learners. Programs also differ in whether they provide or facilitate access to services for transportation, child care, and psychological counseling, which might affect the ability of certain segments of the population to engage in and persist with learning.

Instructors vary in their knowledge of reading and writing development, assessment, curriculum development, and pedagogy. The training instructors receive is generally limited, and professional development is constrained by lack of funding, inflexible locations, work, and other life demands. To be effective, however, the instructors must reliably assess learners' skills, plan and differentiate instruction, and select and adapt materials and learning activities to meet the skill development needs of learners who differ greatly in their neurobiological, psychosocial, cultural, and linguistic characteristics, as well as in their level of literacy attainment. Thus, teachers need to have the requisite tools for instruction and the technical knowledge and expertise, professional development, and ongoing supports as needed for effective implementation. This training and support must include knowledge and skills for teaching adults with disabilities. Teachers of English learners need access to specific help in understanding their students' capabilities and challenges, communicating with them effectively, and using available support techniques to help them engage with English texts. They also need to understand how adults develop proficiency in a second language and have knowledge of the characteristics of English language.

Principles of Effective Literacy Instruction

Conclusion 2: Effective literacy instruction

- targets (as needed) word recognition, fluency, vocabulary, reading comprehension, background knowledge, strategies for deeper analysis and understanding of texts, and the component skills of writing;
- combines explicit teaching and extensive practice with motivating and varied texts, tools, and tasks matched to the learner's skills, educational and cultural backgrounds, and literacy needs and goals;
- explicitly targets the automation and integration of component skills and the transfer of skills to tasks valued by society and the learner; and
- includes formative assessments to monitor progress, provide feedback, and adjust instruction.

Students who have not mastered the foundational component skills of reading and writing require instruction targeted to their skill level and practice with reading and writing in amounts substantial enough to produce high levels of competence in the component skills. As discussed in Chapter 2, a large body of research with K-12 students has identified the major components of reading and writing and principles of instructional practice that are important to typically developing and struggling learners. A sizeable literature on efficacious interventions for struggling learners in K-12 education points to additional principles for developing literacy and overcoming specific areas of difficulty among adults:

1. Interventions that directly target specific learning difficulties in the context of broader reading and writing instruction result in better literacy outcomes for struggling readers and writers.
2. Intervention must include explicit instruction to support generalization and transfer of learning, with abundant and varied opportunities for practice.

3. Struggling learners require more intense instruction, more explicit instruction, and even more opportunities to practice inside and outside the classroom.

4. Attributions, beliefs, and motivational profiles of struggling learners must be understood and targeted during instruction.

5. Intervention should be differentiated to meet the particular needs of adults, including those with disabilities. Research is needed to test whether and when subgroups of adult learners might benefit from different types of instruction.

Decades of research points to principles of learning (see Box 4-1 in Chapter 4) and motivation (see Box 5-1 in Chapter 5) that warrant inclusion in the design of adult literacy instruction. The principles are derived from research with both adults and younger populations and converge with findings from research on effective literacy instruction for K-12 students. The research has not included samples of low-literate adults, however; further efforts are needed to design and evaluate the effectiveness of instructional approaches consistent with these principles for adults who need to develop their literacy.

Conclusion 3: Although knowledge of effective literacy instruction for adults is lacking, research with younger populations can be used to guide the development of instructional approaches for adults if the instruction is modified to account for two major differences between adults and younger populations: (1) adults may experience age-related neurocognitive declines that affect reading and writing processes and speed of learning and (2) adults have varied and more substantial life experiences and knowledge and different motivations for learning that need attention in instructional design. Research with adult literacy learners is required to validate, identify the boundaries of, and extend current knowledge to identify how best to meet the particular literacy development needs of well-defined subgroups of adults.

Except for a few intervention studies, the study of instruction in the component literacy skills and processes has not been a priority in research with adults, nor has the research incorporated knowledge of the practices that develop reading and writing skills in K-12 students. Research even for younger populations is not complete with respect to understanding the components of literacy, interrelations among the components, how to most effectively develop each component, or why literacy may not be sufficiently developed in every adult. Significant research remains to be undertaken with individuals of all ages to develop more comprehensive models of adult reading comprehension and of adult writing to guide assessment and instruction. Similarly, questions remain about fluency and its relation to other components of literacy, and the best ways to teach vocabulary remain to be fully tested. Significant work remains to be done to identify the social and contextual factors that affect the literacy development of adolescents and adults, neurobiological mechanisms of reading and writing development, and age-related changes in reading and writing processes, all of which have implications for the design of instruction and development of assessments to measure progress.

Yet the practices already validated to develop reading and writing skills in younger students should work for older students, provided that the instruction is modified in two ways. First, findings from cognitive science and aging show that the increased knowledge and decreased speed and information processing capacity of cognitive processes that occurs with age may, at the margin, require some tuning of instruction for older learners. Second, although general principles of motivation should apply to learners of all ages, the particular motivations to read or write are often different at different ages. Instruction for adolescents and adults may need to be designed differently to motivate these populations to persist.

Compared with children progressing through a more typical trajectory of literacy development, adolescents and adults may have more knowledge and possess forms of literacy while still needing to fill gaps in component skills, acquire content knowledge, and develop types and levels of literacy proficiency needed for education, work, and practical life. Engagement of learners in higher levels of literacy and learning need not wait until all the gaps in lower level skills have been filled, however. Scaffolds, such as prompts and visual displays, can provide the supports learners need to engage with texts and develop complex thinking usually prohibited by the lack of fully fluent foundational skills. To become facile in executing component skills for particular purposes, adults require both explicit teaching and plentiful opportunities to practice skills typical of those needed to achieve functional goals. For this reason and for increased motivation, it is important to facilitate the development and integration of component skills as much as possible using texts, activities, and tools that relate to the adult learners' interests, learning goals, and everyday functional literacy needs.

> **Conclusion 4: Literacy development is a complex skill that requires thousands of hours of practice to reach the levels needed for full opportunity in modern life, yet many adults do not persist long enough in adult education programs or developmental education courses. Many factors—instructional, cognitive, economic, and social—affect persistence. At present, research does not indicate which methods are most effective in supporting adults' persistence and engagement with instruction. Enough is known, however, from**

research on motivation, literacy, and learning with other populations to suggest how to design motivating instructional environments, create more time for practice, and ensure that the time is
efficiently used. The efficacy of these approaches will need to be
tested rigorously.

A most significant challenge to the design of literacy development
opportunities for adults is getting the adults to participate and persevere.
Findings show low completion rates for developmental education courses in
college, lack of persistence in adult education programs, and high rates of
attrition from research studies on instructional effectiveness for adults with
low- to intermediate-level skills. Moreover, even if completed, the available
programs cannot, by themselves, provide enough practice to build needed
facility levels. Future interventions must be designed on the assumption that
a main reason for the lack of substantial progress is that significant portions
of the needed practice have not occurred for adults with inadequate literacy.

Motivation involves multiple factors that are related but not identical.
First, the adult needs to be present for and persist with instruction. Con-
venient instructional opportunities may be critical to supporting repeated
access. Many adult literacy programs are offered at specific sites, often sites
that low-income adults cannot easily reach. Accordingly, the total time
spent going to a class, attending the class, and going home may be much
longer than the time spent in the literacy-enhancing activity. This challenge
to access and participation suggests that if some literacy instruction or
practice could be provided to adults in forms they could access at home,
the yield from whatever time they choose to invest would be much higher.
Certainly, as discussed later, information technologies can be exploited for
this purpose.

Time for learning competes with time for work. Transportation from
home to a study site and child care responsibilities can be major barriers.
Increased access to child care and transportation and other social services,
such as counseling, may help with retention of learners in programs and
with their persistence in literacy practice. Financial support and incentives
may be necessary even for highly motivated learners. Although research on
the factors that motivate adults to persist in literacy programs is limited, we
encourage the development and testing of approaches that have been used
with some success to motivate adherence to health promotion programs
(e.g., weight loss, smoking cessation). Reminder systems used in health
care may also prove of benefit in encouraging repeated presence for classes.

Having some level of choice in the source, location, and form of instruction is likely to increase motivation. For this reason and because effective literacy is built up over thousands of hours, it is extremely worthwhile
to include out-of-class practice opportunities in any program. Technology

has the potential to expand time for practice beyond what institutions can afford to provide via human instructors. Substantial innovation may be required, however, to provide adults with access to technologies. In some cases, community-based centers with computers that afford some level of privacy or computer loan programs so that students can work at home may be helpful for increasing access and retention. Just as schools sometimes team with other institutions to provide after-school learning opportunities, adult literacy programs may need to team with a range of other entities to provide easily accessible learning time in addition to formal classes "on campus."

Second, when present in the instructional setting, adults need to be motivated and engaged with learning through the instructional interactions, texts, tasks, and tools available in their learning environment. Learners are more engaged and more likely to persist when literacy instruction and practice includes valued learning activities designed to scaffold progress. As described in Chapter 5, research shows the importance of setting clear goals and a path toward longer term goals. To engage in and persist with learning, learners need help to set realistic goals and expectations about the amount of effort and practice required. Learners can underestimate the amount of practice and effort required to achieve fluency and often need help with monitoring their progress and regulating their behavior toward goal attainment. Instruction also needs to help learners develop self-efficacy and feelings of control and autonomy. Thus, learners are likely to benefit from realistic expectations about the amount of practice needed to achieve literacy development goals and feedback that allows for recognizing both progress and the amount of work needed to achieve the next goal.

Even when learners are eager to improve their literacy, they can possess deeply rooted and maladaptive attributions and beliefs about their literacy skills as a result of past experiences with learning in school, past failed attempts at remedial literacy instruction, and labels assigned to them based on skill and background. Because adult literacy learners have a history of failure and embarrassment at reading and academic learning, it is important to explore through research whether persistence might be increased through learning communities. Collaborative learning arrangements, both group learning and learner interactions via online environments, are promising ways to increase engagement.

English Language Learners

Conclusion 5: The component skills of reading and writing in English and the principles of effective literacy instruction derived from research with native English speakers are likely to apply to English language learners. Consistent with principles of learning, effective

> instruction meets the particular skill development needs of English learners, which differ in several respects from the needs of native speakers, and uses existing knowledge of content, language, and literacy whether in the native or the English language.

English language learners are the largest subgroup of adults enrolled in adult education programs. Although treated as a monolithic category, in reality they vary dramatically in what they need to become more literate in English. Some are literate in a first language and hence may need little practice in recognizing or spelling words or even basic comprehension skills. Many are U.S. citizens who speak English well but have low- to intermediate-level English literacy skills. Others are recent immigrants who lack basic literacy skills in any language. Some English learners may be challenged by the lack of opportunities to use and be exposed to English.

The principles of effective literacy instruction discussed in Chapter 2 for typically developing learners should apply to English learners as well. Instruction will need to target, however, the particular skill development needs of the specific English learner, which can differ depending on the degree of literacy in a first language. For example, English learners show weaker vocabulary and comprehension relative to native English speakers but often show relative strength in decoding, especially if they are literate in their first language. Some of those learning English may benefit from some cultural background knowledge to support their learning and performance, for example, in reading comprehension.

Adult English language learners who can read fluently in their native language often can use some of their first language and literacy skills to facilitate learning to read and write in their second language. This means that adult literacy instruction would be most effective if tailored to the level of literacy they have developed in their native language.

A particular challenge to address in adult literacy instruction for English learners is developing their language and literacy skills at the same time. Second language learning past childhood can be difficult and differs from language learning at younger ages in two important ways: it usually is learned via explicit instruction more than through implicit learning, and it also usually is more closely tied to reading.

Experiences in second language instruction with young language learners, high schools, and colleges suggests several principles that may be effective with adult language learners, although these principles await systematic evaluations in adult education contexts. These include a balanced and integrated focus on oral language, reading, and writing; providing meaningful, genuine, and relevant materials and tasks; utilizing learners' first language strengths; a focus on both form and meaning; providing frequent and explicit feedback; providing opportunities to experience and apply linguistic structures in varied contexts, including outside the classroom; and being sensitive to learner's existing levels and readiness as new linguistic concepts are introduced.

Assessment

Conclusion 6: Improved adolescent and adult literacy programs require the development of measures and comprehensive systems of assessment that (1) include measures of language and literacy skills related to a range of literacy forms and tasks, domain knowledge, cognitive abilities, and valued functional as well as psychological outcomes; (2) include measures for differentiated placement and instruction, diagnosis, formative assessment, and accountability that are all aligned to work toward common learning goals; and (3) produce information at learner, classroom, and program levels that is useful to learners, instructors, program administrators, and policy makers.

Three types of assessment are needed: diagnostic, formative, and accountability assessment. The different forms of measurement serve different purposes. *Diagnostic assessment* gives detailed information to instructors about which skill components the learner possesses and which need to be developed. *Formative assessment* provides the information needed to improve instruction by focusing attention on skills that need to be improved as instruction progresses. *Accountability assessment* provides funders and the public with a sense of how well the program and systems that serve adult literacy learners are working. There is a focus on the development of effective diagnostic and formative assessment of learners' progress during the course of instruction, so that it can be focused efficiently and improved continually. Instructors also need training in how to use diagnostic assessments to guide instructional choices and formative assessments to improve instruction.

To be feasible to implement, classroom instruction must share common elements whenever possible while being differentiated enough to meet each learner's needs for skill development and practical goals for learning, and thus assessments are needed to help differentiate instruction. Although some attempts have been made to assess adults' profiles for instructional purposes, the reliability and validity of any particular approach to assessing profiles of skills and other characteristics for the purpose of planning instruction remains to be established (see Chapter 3).

The validity of measures for both practice and research needs attention with respect to (1) the suitability of the measures for adults, (2) comprehensive coverage of the multiple dimensions of component skills (especially those most likely to be weak in adult learners), and (3) the measurement of reading, writing, and language skills that society demands and values. To elaborate: there are no satisfactory ways to comprehensively assess the range of literacy skills that adults bring to instruction and their growth over time. The use of grade level equivalents to measure skill levels and gains needs to be rethought because adults begin instruction with widely varied skills that do not fit neatly into grade level categories. Longitudinal research would help to inform the development of valid measures for adults by elucidating patterns and variations in the growth of adults' literacy skills across the lifespan and in response to instruction.

In both research and practice, better measurement tools are especially needed to more adequately assess all aspects of reading comprehension. The measures that are available and that have been used in the few intervention studies focus on a narrow range of skill (e.g., very low or intermediate). To evaluate effective instructional practices, measures used in research must have sufficient breadth and complexity to measure the important dimensions of literacy and language. Sufficient breadth and depth of measurement is important for testing hypotheses about how particular practices affect learners' growth and address specific areas of reading and language difficulty. Use of only a single composite score on a standardized assessment, by contrast, or measurement of a narrow skill set should be avoided to maximize understanding and return on investment, especially in large-scale effectiveness research. There is a need to conceptualize and develop multidimensional measures in tandem with the development and testing of integrated reading comprehension models and comprehensive approaches to instruction. In doing this work, attention is needed to construct validity. Across studies, the same measures have been used to assess different constructs, and different measures have been used to assess the same constructs, indicating a need to systematically clarify both the constructs that are important to assess and valid ways to define and measure them.

The same comprehensive and multidimensional approaches are needed for research and assessment of writing and writing development. Moreover, because writing assessment is often costly and time-consuming, considerable attention needs to be devoted to developing valid automatic computerized scoring systems that will prove useful to teachers and learners alike.

Studies must measure outcomes of literacy instruction that have external validity, meaning that they measure component skills needed to perform valued literacy tasks for education, work, and other life goals. Measurements of growth in the ability to use and compose texts for these purposes are needed for both print and digital text forms.

There are many reasons why people think that universal literacy is important, so studies need to measure the extent to which all the goals of interest are realized. These might include such outcomes as GED attainment and job improvement, self-confidence, continuing one's education, civic engagement or participation in other aspects of social life, avocational engagement in literate activity, and so on. Although more needs to be known about how to reliably assess them, such noncognitive outcomes contribute to a complete view of the effectiveness of adult literacy instruction. Despite a long history of psychological and sociocultural research on the constructs of motivation, engagement, and persistence, the best ways to measure the related constructs still need to be determined or developed for use in studies with the target population.

Technology

Conclusion 7: Technologies for learning can help to resolve problems facing adult learners caused by time and space constraints. Technology can assist with multiple aspects of learning and assessment that include diagnosis, feedback, scaffolding, embedded practice with skills in meaningful tasks, tracking of learner progress, and accommodations to create more effective and efficient instruction. Given the costs of human labor, technology also may offer a more cost-effective means of achieving the extended levels of practice needed to gain reading and writing facility.

Technologies for learning, including social networking tools, have advanced to the point that literacy instruction and practice no longer need to be offered only in the traditional classroom. Technology has the potential to scaffold literate activity to make learning more efficient. Technology also can assist with assessment, especially by leveraging recent model tracing, Bayesian network, and natural language processing advances. Technology can be used for placement, feedback, and tracking of learner progress for more effective and efficient instruction. Writing is improved by intelligent tutoring systems and automated scoring systems that diagnose and give feedback on language and discourse deficits at multiple levels. Technology also can assist with accommodation, and in particular text-to-speech and speech-to-text technologies can help to support both reading and writing development.

Many adult learners can benefit from technology that can guide, coach, or scaffold engagement with literacy tasks. For example, electronic texts might include software routines that monitor how long various pieces of a text are engaged and use that information to provide prompts that encourage persistence in deep processing. Pop-up questions can allow students to self-assess the depth of their engagement.

Technology tools exist or could be developed to link the instruction and practice of specific literacy skills to particular tasks and purposes designed to meet goals of the adult learner. Technology can be leveraged to create motivating environments for acquiring reading and writing skills that include virtual worlds, animated agents, and multiparty simulations or games that simulate or have a close correspondence to the learners' everyday lives.

Developing the literacy skills for using collaborative communication technologies can be motivating as well as valuable, because they help learners maintain connections with important people in their social world and develop the pragmatic understandings needed to comprehend and compose texts for effective communication. Although some adults may be somewhat familiar with these tools, the rich use of collaborative technologies will require training, not only for students but also for their instructors, and they may enhance persistence in literacy programs that use them.

The human resource cost of education, as well as other cultural opportunities, tends to rise faster than the general cost of living. This means that deeper levels of instructional support by human teachers may be less feasible to support publicly as time passes. Technology can leverage human teaching, especially to provide more and deeper opportunities to engage texts. In addition, given the temporal barriers many adult learners face to increase literacy opportunity, technology can make added literacy engagement opportunities more accessible and more portable.

> **Conclusion 8: Society increasingly requires broader, more intensive and more complex forms of literacy given new communication technologies. Adults need to be able to use contemporary tools of literacy and become facile with forms of reading and writing that are valued and expected for education, work, health maintenance, social and civic participation, and other life tasks.**

Literate practice always involves tools and technologies. Society has moved from pen and paper to digital forms of expression through information media and multimodal communications. To be functionally literate today, an adult will need to also have made this move. Adults need opportunities to learn valued literacy skills, which include the tools and forms of communication and information seeking that have resulted from the information revolution and which society now expects adults to possess as part of being literate and skilled.

Research is just beginning to examine practices and proficiencies related to the use of new information and communication technologies that are now part of being literate in 21st-century society (see Appendix B). Various theories regarding digital media and learning offer ideas about how to develop proficiencies related to these technologies to meet adults' learning goals. An important direction for research in the next decade will be to investigate online reading, writing, and learning to identify the underlying cognitive, social, and cultural mechanisms involved in learning, engagement, and performance with technologies. The features of instructional practices and learning environments must also be identified that promote technology-related literacy proficiencies for adult populations with different levels of literacy.

Specific questions for research include the following: What are the competencies involved in reading and writing online and comprehending and creating multimodal texts? What instructional materials and programs are effective in developing digital literacy skills? How should the development of digital literacy skills be incorporated into adult literacy programs: for example, what is the most effective ordering and configuration of media and modalities in the teaching of reading and writing certain digital multimodal texts? Should literacy development always begin with print-based texts or should it start with texts in multimodal and digital media? How should learning environments be structured to help adults with diverse educational, economic, cultural, and linguistic backgrounds and familiarity with information and communication technologies develop their digital literacy?

Formative and intervention research is needed to determine how adult learners use digital literacy practices in informal and work contexts. For example: How do adults with a need to further develop their literacy take up and use Web 2.0 technologies (wiki-writing, social networking, blogging) in their everyday lives? How might these new technologies be used for collaboration in literacy instruction to develop desired skills?

New forms of assessment are needed to measure adults' proficiency with digital and multimodal forms of literacy. A coherent approach is required to specify instructional goals for digital and multimodal forms and design the necessary measures and assessment tools for assessing these skills.

Adult Literacy Instruction: State of the Evidence

Conclusion 9: There is a lack of research and data of the kind required to better define, prevent, and remediate problems that adolescents and adults enrolled in instruction outside compulsory schooling are experiencing with developing their literacy skills in the United States.

This report provides priorities for literacy research with adults in light of the gaps in current knowledge of adult learners, effective instruction, and adults' learning environments (see Box 3-2 in Chapter 3). It also points to additional priorities for research with English language learners (see Box 8-1 in Chapter 8). As discussed in Chapter 3, the lack of relevant research on adult learners is due to several factors that have affected both the quantity and the quality of the information available. Key among these is that the level of funding has been insufficient and too sporadic to systematically accumulate knowledge and stimulate sophisticated uses of new technologies. To provide an adequate research base for better adult literacy improvement efforts, several things are needed:

- First, exploratory studies are needed to identify approaches that show promise of effecting substantial improvement.
- Then, support is needed both to develop scalable instructional programs reflecting that promise and to test these new approaches rigorously.
- Finally, further research may be needed to ensure that general findings are applicable to the entire range of adult literacy learners or to specify for whom they work.

Methodological improvements and development of standard protocols for collecting information about adult learners, instructional interventions, and instructional environments are required to yield an interpretable body of information about adults' literacy skills and the practices and other conditions that support adults' learning.

RECOMMENDATIONS

In Chapter 1, we present the conceptual framework that guided our synthesis of research and gathering of other information on adult literacy (see Figure 1-2). The framework also specifies the major categories of variables that require attention in a comprehensive and systematic program of research to develop adults' literacy skills. Although many important specific hypotheses remain to be tested about how best to support adults' learning, this figure conveys that the overall research effort must be multifaceted in order to provide an adequate answer to the primary question: What instructional practices (interactions, texts, tools, etc.) and other supports for learning are effective for developing component and valued functional literacy skills, for which learners, and under which conditions? Implementing the recommendations will require productive collaborations among researchers from multiple disciplines, along with partnerships including these researchers, instructors, program administrators, and the learners themselves. It will also require attending to systemic constraints and political realities that are largely beyond the committee's purview, as well as strong leadership of the U.S. Department of Education, especially the Office of Vocational and Adult Education and the Institute of Education Sciences, the U.S. Department of Labor, and other sponsoring research agencies.

A sustained and systematic research effort is needed that begins with well-designed pilot studies of instructional practices and other interventions. Funds will be needed first to adopt and evaluate promising approaches at initial test sites. In the same time frame, advances in measurement and assessment must be made, which will require the collaboration of programs.

> **Recommendation 1: Federal and state policy makers should move quickly to build on and expand the existing infrastructure of adult literacy education to support the use of instructional approaches, curricula, materials, tools, and assessments of learners consistent with (a) research on reading, writing, learning, language, and adult development; (b) research on the effectiveness of instructional approaches; and (c) knowledge of sound assessment practices.**

Although the evidence is mostly on groups not quite identical to the target group (children still in school, students in college who participate in psychological studies, and the elderly), a substantial body of research exists to guide the selection and implementation of instructional practices in reading, writing, and oral language for adolescents and adults with literacy development needs that range from minimal to substantial. Thus, some practices warrant application immediately, based on evidence from other populations, while research is undertaken to assess the extent to which they produce improvements for various segments of the adult population.

> **Recommendation 2: Federal and state policy makers should ensure that professional development and technical assistance for instructors are widely accessible and consistent with the best research on reading, writing, learning, language, and adult development.**

The variability in instructor preparation is a clear impediment to both ensuring instructional effectiveness on a broad scale and conducting the needed research. There is a critical need to ensure that instructors possess knowledge and skills that are consistent with the most reliable research on literacy development and learning.

Although recommendations about specific mechanisms for delivering instructor preparation are beyond the charge to the committee, it is worth noting that instructors experience many of the same constraints on their professional development (lack of funding, inflexible locations, work and other life demands) as those who participate in literacy programs. Given these constraints, options to consider include online courses supported by the U.S. Department of Education to deliver instruction in the science of teaching reading and writing and a process that involves researchers and practitioners in the development and evaluation of professional development content, to ensure that it is consistent with the most recent research and validated best practice. Education and technical assistance efforts for instructors themselves need evaluation to determine whether they result in more effective implementation of taught practices and continuous improvement of offerings. It may be possible to offer a collection of professional development modules that serve both high school and adult literacy instructors, even if subsets of the modules need to be specialized for one group or the other. Along with such programming, attention must be given to providing appropriate incentive structures to ensure that instructors needing the support take advantage of it. There is also a need for data to identify the characteristics of teachers associated with effective implementation of literacy instruction across the four general types of literacy education programs (basic education, secondary education, English as a second language, and developmental education in colleges).

> **Recommendation 3: Policy makers, providers of literacy programs, and researchers should collaborate to systematically implement and evaluate options (instructional components, technology components, social service components, incentives) aimed at maximizing persistence with literacy learning.**

Achieving literacy requires thousands of hours of practice. The problem of high attrition from instructional programs (as well as the relatively brief length of those programs altogether) must be resolved if adults are to receive sufficient amounts of practice and instruction and if reliable evidence is to accumulate on the instructional methods that are effective when adults engage with learning. Although research documents the challenges that adults experience with persistence and engagement, it does not provide clear evidence about specific practices and policies that address these challenges for particular groups of adults. Systematic implementation and evaluation of various approaches is required to identify the mix of strategies that will engage learners of different backgrounds for the large amounts of time required for instruction and practice to be effective. The interventions should be developed with consideration of the factors that are likely to cause attrition and lack of perseverance. Programs can then select strategies that are most appropriate with an understanding of the specific situations of their students.

> **Recommendation 4: To inform local, state, and federal decisions aimed at optimizing the progress of adult learners, the committee strongly recommends strategic and sustained investments in a coordinated and systemic approach to program improvement, evaluation, and research about adult literacy learners.**

A variety of federal units currently play a role in the education of adult learners and in research to understand and intervene with this population. Key among them are the Office of Vocational and Adult Education, the Institute of Education Sciences and the Office of English Language Acquisition of the U.S. Department of Education, the U.S. Department of Labor, the National Institute of Child Health and Human Development of the National Institutes of Health, and the U.S. Department of Defense. Other agencies that might play a role in shaping and monitoring adult literacy education efforts include the National Institute on Aging of the National Institutes of Health and the National Science Foundation. However the proposed research and programmatic changes are implemented, they will benefit from a coordination infrastructure that ensures continued focus on the primary goal of producing a better educated workforce and citizenry.

The five-goal structure used in the Institute of Education Sciences' approach to research and development is very close to the research strategy needed, although more attention will be required to defining subgroups of learners that require specific variations in instructional approaches to meet their needs. The sequence includes exploration, innovation, efficacy testing, scaling up, and assessment development. Some of the practices of the National Institutes of Health and the National Science Foundation that represent focused, long-term strategies might also be helpful, including registries for related research findings and possibly the designation of multidisciplinary centers to pursue synergistic programs of work that are guided by an overarching research plan and regularly reviewed by an advisory group of scientists for adherence to the plan.

Research Design

The research called for in this report should meet the following requirements:

- Research should address the diversity of populations for whom literacy improvement is a concern, including high school dropouts, low-literate English language learners with varying levels of first language literacy, students with documented disabilities, students in career and technical education, academically underprepared college students, and other adults who fared poorly in the K-12 system.
- Research should use rigorous designs and integrated multidisciplinary perspectives that can clarify the effective components of instructional practice and why they work, with adequate experimental power to clarify both what does and what does not work for specific subgroups of the population. Planned variation experiments would be one approach that is valuable for this purpose. The research should include detailed qualitative and quantitative information on learner and instructional contexts, because the diversity of learners and instructional contexts may affect whether the results generalize.

- Research should include longitudinal designs to determine which approaches produce substantial and durable literacy improvement and to track the developmental trajectories of students in an instructional program to provide some insight into what types of individual differences might be instructionally relevant.
- Research should use the best methods for reducing attrition known to be effective in conducting research with difficult-to-study populations.
- Research should determine that the approaches and effects are achievable and sustainable in the instructional context and thoroughly analyze the instructional practices, the instructors, the instructional environment, and provided supports.

Priorities for Basic and Applied Research

As the committee notes throughout this report, a substantial program of research is required to better articulate the specific literacy needs and challenges of adult learners, the literacy demands they face, and the cognitive, neurological, linguistic, social, cultural, and systemic factors that affect their learning. This research should address the following aspects:

- **Characteristics of literacy learners:** The range of specific literacy needs of the population needs to be better understood, including competencies in a native language that can support the development of English literacy and the challenges to learning faced by specific subgroups of English learners. Done well, such research would provide a stronger basis for the differentiation of adult literacy instruction and for grouping of learners who need substantially different learning opportunities.
- **Specification of the literacy skills required in today's society:** The specific literacy skills required for meeting certain educational or career milestones need to be documented, including the literacy skills associated with knowledge building, collaborative problem solving, and effective use of new communications media. This information would permit a move from indexing the success of adult literacy instruction using traditional measures, which are based mostly on the learning that typically occurs in elementary school, to the assessment of literacy skills and levels required for adults' educational and economic success and full social and civic participation.
- **Knowledge of the cognitive, linguistic, and neural underpinnings of instruction:** The underlying cognitive, linguistic, and neural functions need to be further developed as part of instruction for both

typical adult literacy learners and those with learning disabilities. Such research would allow better adaptation of instructional approaches to cognitive differences among children, adolescents, and working-age adults, and the specific challenges faced by some adults trying to become more literate.

- **Contextual influences on literacy development throughout the life span:** This would include research on the multiple paths of literacy development and, more specifically, the ways in which various forces (cognitive, linguistic, social, cultural, instructional, and systemic) interact to affect typical and atypical literacy development from childhood through adulthood. This research would provide knowledge about the population needed to better address the challenges that adult learners experience in developing their literacy skills outside K-12 education.

Priorities for Translational Science

Translational science bridges the gap between the type of knowledge derived from small-scale, controlled research and that required for implementation in large systems that serve diverse individuals in diverse contexts. To improve adult literacy instruction, translational research is needed in four areas to inform the selection and use of practices and products that effectively develop valued literacy skills: (1) instructional approaches and materials grounded in principles of learning and instruction derived mainly from other populations, (2) supports for persistence, (3) technologies to assist with and expand opportunities for learning, and (4) assessments of learners and their instructional environments.

The research will need to include a strong instructor training component and thorough description and analysis of the practices used and instructor characteristics to inform improved instructor recruitment, training, professional development, and ongoing supports required to deliver instruction effectively. It should include large-scale data collection and information gathering. Strong leadership will be required from the U.S. Departments of Education and Labor and other sponsoring research agencies. Partnerships will need to be developed among interdisciplinary teams of researchers, practitioners, curriculum developers, and administrators to systematically build this knowledge and to identify and address barriers to implementation.

Instructional Approaches and Materials

New and modified approaches to remedial literacy instruction are needed that both develop the skills that society demands for education, work, social and civic participation, and health maintenance and apply the principles of learning, cognitive and neural function, and motivation derived from research with other populations to diverse subgroups of adult learners. An interdisciplinary effort involving researchers, practitioners, and curriculum developers is needed to create a coherent system of literacy activities, practices, texts, and tools that are linked to the particular literacy development needs of the learner.

The effort should address the need for appropriate texts for practicing reading skills to develop fluency and accumulate useful knowledge. Adolescents and adults lack a sufficient range of high-interest texts matched to assessed proficiencies and designed to develop literacy skills while developing knowledge needed to achieve broader goals. "Authentic" (real-world) materials often contain too many literacy elements that learners have not yet mastered and so can be overwhelming and frustrating if presented without substantial scaffolding; there is a need to develop materials and evaluation strategies that instructors can use to select materials that present appropriate challenges to learners according to their skill levels. One promising possibility is to add to existing online work environment tools that can scaffold developing literacy. Tools already exist that scaffold the comprehension of free-standing texts, and it should be possible to build similar tools into basic work systems that allow adults to stretch their literacy levels and thus gain added literacy practice.

Persistence

It is vital to study the mix of practices, program components, and policies that support persistence with literacy instruction and that would also serve to reduce the high rates of attrition reported in research studies with the population. Research should be conducted to identify how to maximize persistence and progress by designing programs that attend comprehensively to the cognitive, social, cultural, psychological, and motivational needs of the learner. Literacy is a skill requiring thousands of hours of practice. Adults with inadequate literacy skills have not had sufficient practice and often have not found learning in school to be pleasant. Research should be conducted to encourage attendance, sustained practice, and engagement with instruction. This research should apply and extend current knowledge, focusing in particular on aspects of the learner, the learning environment, learning activities, texts, and materials that affect persistence. In addition to understanding persistence in programs, work is needed to determine how to facilitate persistence with specific literacy tasks.

Technology

Developing and identifying effective uses of technology are important for several reasons. First, technologies can free literacy practice from being dependent on a specific learning location. This is important because learning is usually limited for adults as a result of limited program funds and locations available (a few hours of instruction are offered a few days per week), participants' work schedules, and other life demands.

Second, technologies can help to standardize instructional offerings across the many places of instruction that have shared populations with common literacy development needs and learning goals. Third, technologies have the potential to provide some of the scaffolding needed for progress with literacy skills and engagement with complex texts and tasks while filling gaps in lower level reading skills. Intelligent interactive media should be developed to motivate and scaffold practice by adults with literacy needs and incorporate specific work and life goals and interests.

Fourth, technology has the potential to help overcome the high cost of intelligent human labor, in this case literacy instructors. For example, web-based and automated evaluation, diagnosis, and prescription of further learning opportunities could be developed both to support instructors and to support adults in reading practice. Technology for use in classrooms must also be engineered to be accessible to the instructors with appropriate instructor training.

Assessment of Learners and Instructional Environments

A valid, coherent, and comprehensive system of assessment should be developed for diagnosis, planning instruction, and accountability. The system should comprehensively assess knowledge, skills, and valued psychological and functional outcomes. It should be aligned to produce different but linked forms of measurement for assessing learning at the learner, classroom, and program levels. The system should generate information that is appropriate and useful for the particular purposes and audiences: learners, instructors, program administrators, or policy makers in local, state, and federal governments. Effective assessment tools would address all of the components of literacy and map onto the primary valued learning outcomes for adult remedial and basic education. The needed assessments would, among other things, measure the ability to comprehend and use text meaning for purposes (e.g., for academic learning, health maintenance, civic participation, work). Valid measures must be developed that are (1) appropriate for use with adults and for learners' cultural and linguistic backgrounds, (2) provide comprehensive coverage of the multiple dimensions of component skills, and (3) measure the reading, writing, and language skills that society demands and values.

Few studies examine the characteristics of programs in adult education associated with improved learner outcomes. One reason for this lack of research is that few measures are available to assess learning environments in adult education. Such work is just beginning even for K-12 schooling. Thus, in addition to better measures of adult outcomes, standard ways of measuring the quality of the educational environment are needed that are derived from research on language, learning, and literacy. These measures would assess instructional interactions, texts, and implementation of instruction and contextual factors (e.g., content of teacher preparation, uses of technology outside school) that support or constrain the implementation of effective practices and adults' opportunities to learn and practice new skills.

Large-Scale Data Collection and Information Gathering

Information about the literacy skills of adults in the United States and in the diverse systems that offer adult literacy instruction should be gathered and analyzed on a continual and long-term basis to know whether the population is becoming more literate and whether efforts to improve literacy are effective at a macro level as well as in specific individual efficacy studies.

Allocations of funding for adult literacy programs signal an understanding of the magnitude and importance of the literacy problem in the United States. Yet the only assessment tools used at the federal level to evaluate the effectiveness of adult literacy education programs are global accountability measures that relate only superficially to the specific literacy proficiencies that need to be developed. In addition, these measures do not convey how much more a literate U.S. society is as a result of investments in adult literacy instruction or how to focus efforts to improve instructional practices and adult learning. While current efforts to survey literacy in the U.S. population and collect information on adult literacy programs and learners are important, there is a need to modify them to track progress in the components of reading and writing that have been identified in research and proficiency in performing important literacy tasks. There is also a need to gather data on the instructional interactions, materials, and tools used in literacy instruction to better understand current practices, plan the appropriate professional development of instructors, create effective out-of-classroom learning opportunities, and better match literacy instruction to emerging literacy demands for work, education, health, and functioning in society. Finally, it is important to have data on the personal writing and reading goals of the adult learner population, so that the gap between broad social goals and personal goals can be negotiated. It may be productive to embed questions relating to literacy in broader longitudinal surveys.

CONCLUDING THOUGHTS: LEADERSHIP AND PARTNERSHIP

The current approaches to adult literacy instruction represent well-intentioned and partly productive efforts of adult literacy program providers, community colleges, state agencies, and the U.S. Departments of

Education and Labor, operating under several constraints. Although it is wise not to change practice without rigorous experimental confirmation that a new approach is more effective, the available research on literacy and learning with other populations strongly indicates that better approaches to instruction are possible. The request to this committee—to synthesize the knowledge base on learning and literacy to inform instructional practice and develop a more systemic approach to research, practice, and policy—is a necessary step to improve adult learning in the United States. The relevant agencies should encourage research that is sufficiently focused and sustained to accumulate knowledge about how to improve adult literacy instruction and make substantial progress in adults' literacy.

Meaningful change will be difficult, however, given the current level of investment, the need for substantial instructor training as part of any change in current practice, the needed research and innovation, and the extent of additional learning that many adults will require. Success will depend on a strong partnership of school districts, states, and the federal government. It will also require strong and sustained partnerships between researchers and practitioners at various levels.

Although many federal programs and agencies contribute to adult education services, it is the Office of Vocational and Adult Education in the U.S. Department of Education that administers the Adult Education and Family Literacy Act, enacted as Title II of the Workforce Investment Act, which is the principal source of federal support for adult basic and literacy education programs for those who are at least 16 years old, not enrolled in high school, and lack basic skills, a high school diploma, or proficiency in English. The law specifies that agencies eligible to provide adult literacy instruction consider whether the programs they choose to fund use practices that research has "proven to be effective in teaching individuals to read" (Workforce Investment Act [WIA], Title II, Section 231 (e4)(B)). It also gives the secretary of education the authority to establish and carry out a program of national leadership activities to enhance the quality of adult education and literacy programs nationwide (WIA, Title II, Section 223). Thus, current legislation provides the authority and one possible source of existing funds for collaborating with other appropriate funders.[1]

---

[1]The Adult Education and Family Literacy Act (which is Title II of WIA) aims broadly to help adults become literate and build the knowledge and skills for employment and self-sufficiency, completion of secondary education, and full participation in the educational development of their children. The legislation directs how federal funds are distributed by formula to states, defines goals for adult programs, and defines core indicators of performance. The Office of Vocational and Adult Education contributes an estimated 25 percent of the total funds used for adult literacy programs. States must provide matching funds to qualify for the allocations made on the basis of census data. States competitively award most of the funds to local institutions to provide adult literacy programs and retain 12.5 percent for overall

The nature of the work to be done will require partnerships among researchers, practitioners, curriculum developers, and administrators to systematically build the needed knowledge and tools and to identify and address barriers to implementation. Major employers, existing training and education organizations, faith-based groups, and other community groups will need to be enlisted to help in the effort. A number of organizations have been started by business and civic groups to promote literacy, especially "21st-century literacy," but these organizations have, for the most part, been advocates for change rather than participants in effecting change. Just as government must play a role in sponsoring the needed research, providing program incentives, and monitoring progress, it also will be important for the business community to move from a role of advocacy alone to also providing input into literacy requirements, providing onsite learning opportunities, being accommodating of needed research on effectiveness, and helping to provide incentives to boost motivation to complete literacy programs. Substantial national leadership will be needed to sustain investment and strategic direction through periods of uncertainty and economic variability. Having an educated, literate workforce is essential to the preservation of the U.S. economy in the information age.

As with any field, the dissemination of knowledge and effective practice from research to policy makers, administrators, and instructors in the field of adult literacy is a subject of inquiry in its own right. The committee hopes that those with a mission to improve adult literacy will, as part of acting on the recommendations in this report, participate in the steps needed to identify and address the factors that will affect the conduct of the recommended research and the implementation of the findings into widespread practice.

---

program improvement. Federal funding for programs has remained relatively level since 2001, with an annual appropriation of about $560 million. An additional sum is provided annually for research, technical assistance, and other national leadership activities, which in 2010 were funded at 13.3 million, or .021 percent of the total $628.2 million adult education and family literacy budget (U.S. Department of Education, 2010).

References and Bibliography

Abadzi, H. (2003). Improving reading performance in adult literacy classes of Burkina Faso. In H. Abadzi (Ed.), *Improving adult literacy outcomes: Lessons from cognitive research for developing countries*. Washington, DC: Directions in Development, World Bank.

Abar, B., and Loken, E. (2010). Self-regulated learning and self-directed study in a pre-college sample. *Learning and Individual Differences, 20*, 25-29.

Abedi, J. (2002). Standardized achievement tests and English language learners: Psychometrics issues. *Educational Assessment, 8*(3), 231-257.

Abedi, J. (2006). Psychometric issues in the ELL assessment and special education eligibility. *Teachers College Record, 108*(11), 2,282-2,303.

Abedi, J., and Lord, C. (2001). The language factor in mathematics tests. *Applied Measurement in Education, 14*, 219-234.

Abraham, L. (2008). Computer-mediated glosses in second language reading comprehension and vocabulary learning: A meta-analysis. *Computer Assisted Language Learning, 21*(3), 199-226.

Abrahamsson, N., and Hyltenstam, K. (2008). The robustness of aptitude effects in near-native second language acquisition. *Studies in Second Language Acquisition, 30*(4), 481-509.

Abutalebi, J. (2008). Neural aspects of second language representation and language control. *Acta Psychologica, 128*(3), 466-478.

Abutalebi, J., and Green, D. (2007). Bilingual language production: The neurocognition of language representation and control. *Journal of Neurolinguistics, 20*, 242-275.

Abutalebi, J., Cappa, S.F., and Perani, D. (2001). The bilingual brain as revealed by functional neuroimaging. *Bilingualism: Language and Cognition, 4*, 179-190.

Achugar, M., and Schleppegrell, M.J. (2005). Beyond connectors: The construction of cause in history textbooks. *Linguistics and Education, 16*(3), 298-318.

Ackerman, P.L. (1988). Determinants of individual differences during skill acquisition: Cognitive abilities and information processing. *Journal of Experimental Psychology: General, 117*, 288-318.

Ackerman, P.L. (2008). Knowledge and cognitive aging. In F.I.M. Craik and T.A. Salthouse (Eds.), *Handbook of aging and cognition* (3rd ed.). New York: Psychology Press.

Ackerman, P.L., and Beier, M.E. (2006). Determinants of domain knowledge and independent study learning in an adult sample. *Journal of Educational Psychology, 98*, 366-381.

Ackerman, P.L., and Rolfhus, E.L. (1999). The locus of adult intelligence: Knowledge, abilities, and nonability traits. *Psychology and Aging, 14*, 314-330.

Ackerman, P.L., Bowen, K.R., Beier, M.E., and Kanfer, R. (2001). Determinants of individual differences and gender differences in knowledge. *Journal of Educational Psychology, 93*, 797-825.

ACT. (undated). *College readiness standards.* Iowa City, IA: American College Testing. Available: http://www.act.org/standard/ [Feb. 2010].

Adams, M. (1990). *Beginning to read: Thinking and learning about print.* Cambridge, MA: MIT Press.

Adams, R., and Burt, M. (2002). *Research on the reading development of adult English language learners: An annotated bibliography.* Washington, DC: National Center for ESL Literacy Education. Available: http://www.eric.ed.gov/PDFS/ED467498.pdf [Sept. 2011].

Ainley, M., Hidi, S., and Berndorff, D. (2002). Interest, learning, and the psychological processes that mediate their relationship. *Journal of Educational Psychology, 94*, 545-561.

Ainsworth, S. (2008). How do animations influence learning? In D.H. Robinson and G. Schraw (Eds.), *Recent innovations on educational technologies that facilitate student learning* (pp. 37-67). Charlotte, NC: Information Age.

Ainsworth, S., and Loizou, A.T. (2003). The effects of self-explaining when learning with texts or diagrams. *Cognitive Science, 27*, 669-681.

Airasian, P.W. (1994). *Classroom assessment* (2nd ed.). New York: McGraw-Hill.

Akamatsu, N. (2003). The effects of first language orthographic features on second language reading in text. *Language Learning, 53*, 207-231.

Akkus, R., Gunel, M., and Hand, B. (2007). Comparing an inquiry-based approach known as the science writing heuristic to traditional science teaching practices: Are there differences? *International Journal of Science Education, 29*(14), 1,745-1,765.

Al Otaiba, S., and Fuchs, D. (2002). Characteristics of children who are unresponsive to early literacy intervention: A review of the literature. *Remedial and Special Education, 23*, 300-316.

Alamprese, J. (2009). Developing learners' reading skills in adult basic education programs. In S. Reder and J. Brynner (Eds), *Tracking adult literacy and numeracy skills* (pp. 107-131). New York: Routledge.

Alamprese, J., MacArthur, C., Price, C., and Knight, D. (2011). Effects of a structured decoding curriculum on adult literacy learners' reading development. *Journal of Research on Education Effectiveness, 4*(2), 154-172.

Albert, M., Jones, K., Savage, C., Berkman, L., Seeman, T., Blazer, D., et al. (1995). Predictors of cognitive change in older persons: MacArthur studies of successful aging. *Psychology and Aging, 10*, 578-589.

Albin, M., Benton, S., and Khramtsova, I. (1996). Individual differences in interest and narrative writing. *Contemporary Educational Psychology, 21*, 305-324.

Aleven, V., Stahl, E., Schworm, S., Fischer, F., and Wallace, R. (2003). Help seeking and help design in interactive learning environments. *Review of Educational Research, 73*, 277-320.

Alexander, P.A. (1997). Mapping the multidimensional nature of domain learning: The interplay of cognitive, motivational, and strategic forces. In M.L. Maehr and P.R. Pintrich (Eds.), *Advances in motivation and achievement* (vol. 10, pp. 213-250). Greenwich, CT: JAI Press.

Alexander, P.A. (2003). Profiling the adolescent reader: The interplay of knowledge, interest, and strategic processing. . In C. Fairbanks, J. Worthy, B. Maloch, J.V. Hoffman, and D. Schallert (Eds.), *53rd yearbook of the National Reading Conference* (pp. 47-65). Milwaukee, WI: National Reading Conference.

Alexander, P.A., and Jetton, T.L. (2000). Learning from text: A multidimensional and developmental perspective. In M. Kamil, P.D. Pearson, R. Barr, and P. Mosenthal (Eds.), *Handbook of reading research* (pp. 285-310). Mahwah, NJ: Lawrence Erlbaum Associates.

Alexander, P.A., and Jetton, T.L. (2003). Learning from traditional and alternative texts: New conceptualizations for the Information Age. In A.C. Graesser, M.A. Gernsbacher, and S.R. Goldman (Eds.), *Handbook of discourse processes* (pp. 199-232). Mahwah, NJ: Lawrence Erlbaum Associates.

Alexander, P.A., and Judy, J.E. (1988). The interaction of domain-specific and strategic knowledge in academic performance. *Review of Educational Research, 58*, 375-404.

Alexander, P.A., Kulikowich, J.M., and Jetton, T.L. (1994). The role of subject-matter knowledge and interest in the processing of linear and nonlinear and nonlinear texts. *Review of Educational Research, 64*, 201-252.

Alexander, P.A., Kulikowich, J.M., and Schulze, S.K. (1994a). How subject-matter knowledge affects recall and interest on the comprehension of scientific exposition. *American Educational Research Journal, 31*, 313-337.

Alexander, P.A., Kulikowich, J.M., and Schulze, S.K. (1994b). The influence of topic knowledge, domain knowledge, and interest on the comprehension of scientific exposition. *Learning and Individual Differences, 6*, 379-397.

Alexander, P.A., Graham, S., and Harris, K. (1998). A perspective on strategy research: Progress and prospects. *Educational Psychology Review, 10*, 129-154.

Allen-DeBoer, R.A., Malmgren, K.W., and Glass, M.-E. (2006). Reading instruction for youth with emotional and behavioral disorders in a juvenile correctional facility. *Behavioral Disorders, 32*(1), 18-28.

Allyn, F.A., and Burt, J.S. (1998). Pinch my wig or winch my pig: Spelling, spoonerisms and other language skills. *Reading and Writing: An Interdisciplinary Journal, 10*, 51-74.

Alozie, N.M., Moje, E.B., and Krajcik, J.S. (2010). An analysis of the supports and constraints for scientific discussion in high school project-based science. *Science Education, 94*(3), 395-427.

Alvermann, D.E., and Xu, S.H. (2003). Children's everyday literacies: Intersections of popular culture and language arts instruction. *Language Arts, 81*(2), 145-155.

American Educational Research Association, American Psychological Association, and National Council on Measurement in Education. (1985). *Standards for educational and psychological testing.* Washington, DC: American Psychological Association.

American Psychiatric Association. (2000). *Diagnostic and statistical manual of mental disorders* (4th ed.) Washington, DC: American Psychiatric Association.

Ames, C. (1992). Classrooms: Goals, structures, and student motivation. *Journal of Educational Psychology, 84*(3), 261-271.

Ames, C., and Ames, R.E. (1984). Goal structures and motivation. *Elementary School Journal, 85*(1), 39-52.

Ames, C., and Archer, J. (1988). Achievement goals in the classroom: Students' learning strategies and motivation processes. *Journal of Educational Psychology, 80*(3), 260-267.

Ander, P.L., Hoffman, J.V., and Duffy, G.G. (2000). Teaching teachers to teach reading: Paradigm shifts, persistent problems, and challenges. In M.L. Kamil, P.B. Mosenthal, P.D. Pearson, and R. Barr (Eds.), *Handbook of reading research* (vol. III, pp. 719-742). Mahwah, NJ: Lawrence Erlbaum Associates.

Anderman, E.M. (1997). Motivation and school reform. In M.L. Maehr and P.R. Pintrich (Eds.), *Advances in motivation and achievement* (vol. 10, pp. 303-337). Greenwich, CT: JAI Press.

Anderman, E.M., and Anderman, L.H. (2010). *Classroom motivation.* Upper Saddle River: Pearson.

Anderman, E.M., and Maehr, M.L. (1994). Motivation and schooling in the middle grades. *Review of Educational Research, 64*(2), 287-309.

Anderman, E.M., and Wolters, C. (2006). Goals, values, and affect: Influences on student motivation. In P. Alexander and P. Winne (Eds.), *Handbook of educational psychology* (2nd ed., pp. 369-389). Mahwah, NJ: Lawrence Erlbaum Associates.

Anderman, E.M., and Young, A.J. (1994). Motivation and strategy use in science: Individual differences and classroom effects. *Journal of Research in Science Teaching, 31*(8), 811-831.

Anderman, E.M., Maehr, M.L., and Midgley, C. (1999). Declining motivation after the transition to middle school: Schools can make a difference. *Journal of Research and Development in Education, 32,* 131-147.

Anderman, E., Jensen, J., Haleman, D., and Goldstein, B. (2002). Motivation to improve adult education in under-educated adults in rural communities. In D. McInerney (Ed.), *Research on sociocultural influences on motivation and learning* (vol. 2, pp. 183-206). Greenwich, CT: Information Age.

Andersen, S.M., and Kooij, C.S. (2007) Adult literacy education and human rights: A view from Afghanistan. *Globalisation, Societies and Education, 5*(3), 315-331.

Anderson, J.R., Corbett, A.T., Koedinger, K.R., and Pelletier, R. (1995). Cognitive tutors: Lessons learned. *The Journal of Learning Sciences, 4*(2), 167-207.

Anderson, R.C. (2001). Influence of oral discussion on written argument. *Discourse Processes, 32,* 155-175.

Anderson, R.C., and Pearson, P.D. (1984a). A schema-theoretic view of basic processes in reading comprehension. In P.D. Pearson, R. Barr, M.L. Kamil, and P. Mosenthal (Eds.), *Handbook of reading research* (vol. 1, pp. 255-291). New York: Longman.

Anderson, R.C., and Pearson, P.D. (1984b). A schema-theoretic view of basic processes in reading comprehension. In P.D. Pearson, R. Barr, M.L. Kamil, and P. Mosenthal (Eds.), *Handbook of reading research* (vol. II, pp. 225-253). New York: Longman.

Anderson, R.C., and Pichert, J.W. (1978). Recall of previously unrecallable information following a shift in perspective. *Journal of Verbal Learning and Verbal Behavior, 17,* 1-12.

Anderson, R.C., Nguyen-Jahiel, K., McNurlen, B., Archodidou, A., Kim, S., Reznitskaya, A., Tillmanns, M., and Gilbert, L. (2001). The snowball phenomenon: Spread ways of talking and ways of thinking across groups of children. *Cognition and Instruction, 19*(1), 1-46.

Anderson, T.H., and Armbruster, B.B. (1984). Content area textbooks. In R.C. Anderson, J. Osborne, and R.J. Tierney (Eds.), *Learning to read in American schools: Basal readers and content texts* (pp. 193-226). Hillsdale, NJ: Lawrence Erlbaum Associates.

Anderson-Inman, L. (2004). Reading on the web: Making the most of digital text. *Wisconsin State Reading Association Journal, 4,* 8-14.

Anderson-Inman, L., and Horney, M.A. (2007). Supported eText: Assistive technology through text transformations. *Reading Research and Practice, 14,* 153-160.

Anderson-Inman, L., Horney, M.A., Chen, D., and Lewin, L. (1994, April). Hypertext literacy: Observations from the electro text project. *Language Arts, 71,* 37-45.

Andrews, R., Torgerson, C., Beverton, S., Freeman, A., Locke, T., Low, G., Robinson, A., and Zhu, D. (2006). The effect of grammar teaching on writing development. *British Educational Research Journal, 32*(1), 39-55.

Anson, C.M.B.R. (1995). *Journals in the classroom: Writing to learn*. Norwood, MA: Christopher-Gordon.

Anyon, J. (1981). Social class and school knowledge. *Curriculum Inquiry, 11*, 1-42.

Aoki, A. (2005). Assessing learning achievements and development impact: Ghana's National Functional Literacy Program. *Australian Journal of Adult Learning, 45*(1), 63-81.

Applebee, A. (1984). Writing and reasoning. *Review of Educational Research, 54*, 577-596.

Applebee, A., and Langer, J. (2006). *The state of writing instruction: What existing data tell us*. Albany, NY: Center on English Learning and Achievement.

Applebee, A., Langer, J., Nystrand, M., and Gamoran, A. (2003). Discussion-based approaches to developing understanding: Classroom instruction and student performance in middle and high school English. *American Educational Research Journal, 40*, 685-730.

Ariely, D., Gneezy, U., and Lowenstein, G. (2009). Large stakes and big mistakes. *Review of Economic Studies, 76*, 451-469.

Armbruster, B.B., and Anderson, T.H. (1985). Producing "considerate" expository text: Or easy reading is damned hard writing. *Journal of Curriculum Studies, 17*(3), 247-263.

Arnold, E.M., Goldston, D.B., Walsh, A.K., Reboussin, B.A., Daniel, S.S., Hickman, E., and Wood, F.B. (2005). Severity of emotional and behavioral problems among poor and typical readers. *Journal of Abnormal Psychology, 33*, 205-217.

Aronson, J., Lustina, M.J., Good, C., Keough, K., Steele, C. M., and Brown, J. (1999). When white men can't do math: Necessary and sufficient factors in stereotype threat. *Journal of Experimental Social Psychology, 35*(1), 29-46.

Arrington, C. M., and Logan, G. D. (2004). The cost of a voluntary task switch. *Psychological Science, 15*(9), 610-615.

Atkinson, R. (2002). Optimizing learning from examples using animated pedagogical agents. *Journal of Educational Psychology, 94*, 416-427.

Atkinson, R.C., and Hansen, D.N. (1966). Computer-assisted instruction in initial reading: The Stanford project. *Reading Research Quarterly, 2*, 5-26.

Attali, Y., and Burstein, J. (2006). Automated essay scoring with e-rater R V.2. *Journal of Technology, Learning and Assessment, 4*(3).

Attar, D. (2005). Dismay and disappointment: Perspectives of inexperienced adult learners on becoming webpage readers. *International Journal of Educational Research, 43*, 495-508.

Atwell, N. (1987). *In the middle*. Portsmouth, NH: Heinemann.

Au, K.H. (1998). Social constructivism and the school literacy learning of students of diverse backgrounds. *Journal of Literacy Research, 30*(2), 297-319.

Au, K.H., and Kawakami, A.J. (1994). Cultural congruence in instruction. In E.R. Hollins, J.E. King, and W. Hayman (Eds.), *Teaching diverse populations: Formulating a knowledge base* (pp. 5-23). Albany, NY: State University of New York Press.

Au, K.H., and Mason, J.M. (1983). Cultural congruence in classroom participation structures: Achieving a balance of rights. *Discourse Processes, 6*, 145-167.

August, D., and Shanahan, T. (Eds.) (2006). *Developing literacy in second-language learners: Report of the National Literacy Panel on Language-Minority Children and Youth*. Mahwah, NJ: Lawrence Erlbaum Associates.

August, D., Branum-Martin, L., Cardenas-Haan, E., and Francis, D.J. (2009). The impact of an instructional intervention on the science and language learning of middle grade English language learners. *Journal of Research on Educational Effectiveness, 2*, 345-376.

Austin, J.T., and Vancouver, J.B. (1996). Goal constructs in psychology: Structure, process, and content. *Psychological Bulletin, 120*(3), 338-375.

Ausubel, D.P. (1968). *Educational psychology: A cognitive view*. New York: Holt, Rinehart, and Winston.

Azevedo, R. (2005). Computer environments as metacognitive tools for enhancing learning. *Educational Psychologist, 40*, 193-198.

Azevedo, R., and Bernard, R.M. (1995). A meta-analysis of the effect of feedback in computer-based instruction. *Journal of Educational Computing Research*, *13*, 109-125.

Azevedo, R., and Cromley, J.G. (2004). Does training on self-regulated learning faciliate students' learning with hypermedia. *Journal of Educational Psychology*, *96*, 523-535.

Azevedo, R., and Witherspoon, A.M. (2009). Self-regulated learning with hypermedia. In D. J. Hacker, J. Dunlosky and A. C. Graesser (Eds.), *Handbook of metacognition in education* (pp. 319-339). Mahwah, NJ: Routledge.

Azevedo, R., Witherspoon, A.M., Graesser, A.C., McNamara, D., Chauncey, A., Siler, E., Cai, Z., Rus, V., and Lintean, M. (2009). MetaTutor: Analyzing self-regulated learning in a tutoring system for biology. In V. Dimitrova, R. Mizoguchi, B. du Boulay, and A. Graesser (Eds.), *Artificial intelligence in education* (pp. 635-637). Amsterdam, the Netherlands: IOS Press.

Baard, P.P., Deci, E.L., Ryan, R.M. (2004). Intrinsic need satisfaction: A motivational basis of performance and well-being in two work settings. *Journal of Applied Social Psychology*, *34*, 2,045-2,068.

Bäckman, L., and Nilsson, L.-G. (1985). Prerequisites for lack of age differences in memory performance. *Experimental Aging Research*, *11*, 67-73.

Badway, N., and Grubb, W.N. (1997). *A sourcebook for reshaping the community college: Curriculum integration and the multiple domians of career preparation* (vols. 1-2). Berkeley, CA: National Center for Research in Vocational Education.

Baer, J., Kutner, M., and Sabatini, J. (2009). *Basic reading skills and the literacy of America's least literate adults: Results from the 2003 National Assessment of Adult Literacy (NAAL) supplemental studies* (NCES 2009-481). Washington, DC: National Center for Education Statistics, Institute of Education Sciences, U.S. Department of Education.

Bahktin, M.M. (1981). *The dialogic imagination*. [C. Emerson and M. Holquist, Trans., M. Holquist (Ed.)]. Austin: University of Texas Press.

Bahrick, H.P., Bahrick, L.E., Bahrick, A.S., and Bahrick, P.E. (1993). Maintenance of foreign language vocabulary and the spacing effect. *Psychological Science*, *4*, 316-321.

Bailey, T. (2009). Challenge and opportunity: Rethinking the role and function of developmental education in community college. *New Directions for Community Colleges*, *145*, 11-30.

Bailey, T., Jeong, D.W., and Cho, S.W. (2010). Referral, enrollment, and completion in developmental education sequences in community colleges. *Economics of Education Review*, *29*, 255-270.

Bain, R.B. (2000). Into the breach: Using research and theory to shape history instruction. In P. Seixas, P. Stearns, and S. Wineberg (Eds.), *Teaching, learning and knowing history: National and international perspectives* (pp. 331-353). New York: New York University Press.

Bain, R.B. (2005). They thought the world was flat? HPL principles in teaching high school history. In National Research Council, *How students learn: History, mathematics, and science in the classroom* (pp. 179-214). Committee on *How People Learn*, A Targeted Report for Teachers. M.S. Donovan and J.D. Bransford, Eds. Division of Behavioral and Social Sciences and Education. Washington, DC: The National Academies Press.

Bain, R.B. (2006). Rounding up unusual suspects: Facing the authority hidden in the history classroom. *Teachers College Record*, *108*(10), 2,080-2,114.

Bain, R.B. (2007). *Knowledge for teaching history: The whens and whats of teacher learning*. Paper presented at the U.S. Department of Education Teaching American History Conference.

Baker, E.D., Hope, L., and Karandjeff, K. (2009). *Contextualized teaching and learning: A faculty primer.* Sacramento: The Research and Planning Group for California Community Colleges, Center for Student Success. Available: http://www.careerladdersproject.org/docs/CTL.pdf [Sept. 2011].

Baker, E.L., and Mayer, R.E. (1999) Computer-based assessment of problem solving. *Computers in Human Behavior, 15,* 269-282.

Baker, L. (1985). Differences in standards used by college students to evaluate their comprehension of expository prose. *Reading Research Quarterly, 20,* 298-313.

Baker, L. (1999). Opportunities at home and in the community that foster reading engagement. In J.T. Guthrie and D.E. Alvermann (Eds.), *Engaging in reading: Processes, practices, and policy implications* (pp. 105-133). New York: Teachers College Press.

Baker, R.S., D'Mello, S.K., Rodrigo, M.T., and Graesser, A.C. (2010). Better to be frustrated than bored: The incidence, persistence, and impact of learners' cognitive-affective states during interactions with three different computer-based learning environments. *International Journal of Human-Computer Studies, 68,* 223-241.

Bakhtin, M.M. (1986). *Speech genres and other late essays.* [V.W. McGee, Trans., C. Emerson, and M. Holquist (Eds.)]. Austin: University of Texas Press.

Balatti, J., Black, S., and Falk, I. (2007). Teaching for social capital outcomes: The case of adult literacy and numeracy courses. *Australian Journal of Adult Learning, 47*(2), 245-263.

Baldwin, T.T., Magjuka, R.J., and Loher, B.T. (1991). The perils of participation: Effects of choice on trainee motivation and learning. *Personnel Psychology, 44,* 51-65.

Ball, A.F. (1997). Expanding the dialogue on culture as a critical component when assessing writing. *Assessing Writing, 4,* 169-202.

Baltes, P.B., and Baltes, M.M. (1990). Psychological perspectives on successful aging: The model of selective optimization with compensation. In P.B. Baltes and M.M. Baltes (Eds.), *Successful aging: Perspectives from the behavioral sciences* (pp. 1-34). New York: Cambridge University Press.

Bandura, A. (1977). Self-efficacy: Toward a unifying theory of behavioral change. *Psychological Review, 84,* 191-215.

Bandura, A. (1986). *Social foundations of thought and action: A social cognitive theory.* Englewood Cliffs, NJ: Prentice-Hall.

Bandura, A. (1989a). Human agency in social cognitive theory. *American Psychologist, 44,* 1,175-1,184.

Bandura, A. (1989b). Regulation of cognitive processes through perceived self-efficacy. *Developmental Psychology, 25,* 729-735.

Bandura, A. (1997). *Self-efficacy: The exercise of control.* New York: W.H. Freeman.

Banerjee, M., and Gregg, N. (2009). Redefining accessibility in an era of alternative media for postsecondary students with learning disabilities. *Learning Disabilities: A Multidisciplinary Journal, 45,* 233-245.

Bangert-Drowns, R.L. (1993). The word processor as an instructional tool: A meta-analysis of word processing in writing instruction. *Review of Educational Research, 63*(1), 69-93.

Bangert-Drowns, R.L., Kulik, C.C., Kulik, J.A., and Morgan, M.T. (1991). The instructional effect of feedback in test-like events. *Review of Educational Research, 61,* 213-238.

Bangert-Drowns, R.L., Hurley, M.M., and Wilkinson, B. (2004). The effects of school-based writing-to-learn interventions on academic achievement: A meta-analysis. *Review of Educational Research, 74,* 29-58.

Banich, M.T., and Caccamise, D. (2010). (Eds.). *Generalization of knowledge: Multidisciplinary perspectives.* New York: Psychology Press.

Barab, S.A., and Roth, W.-M. (2006). Curriculum-based ecosystems: Supporting knowing from an ecological perspective. *Educational Researcher, 35*(5), 3-13.

Barab, S.A., Thomas, M., Dodge, T., Cartreaux, R., and Tuzun, H. (2005). Making learning fun: Quest Atlantis, a game without guns. *Education Technology Research and Development, 53*(1), 86-107.

Barkley, R.A. (2006). *Attention deficit hyperactivitydisorder: A handbook for diagnosis and treatment* (2nd ed.). New York: Guilford Press.

Barnett, S. M., and Ceci, S. J. (2002). When and where do we apply what we learn? A taxonomy for far transfer. *Psychological Bulletin, 128*, 612-637.

Bartholomae, D. (1980). The study of error. *College Composition and Communication, 31*(3), 253-269.

Barton, D., and Hamilton, M. (1998). *Local literacies: Reading and writing in one community.* London, England: Routledge.

Batalova, J., and Fix, M. (2010). A profile of limited English proficient adult immigrants. *Peabody Journal of Education, 85*, 511-534.

Batchedler, J.S., and Koski, D.D. (2003). Technology in the adult education classroom: Evaluating achievement on the test of adult basic education. *MPAEA Journal of Adult Education, 32*(2), 59-70.

Baumann, J.F., Kame'enui, E.J., and Ash, G.E. (2003). Research on vocabulary instruction: Voltaire redux. In J. Flood, J.M. Jensen, D. Lapp, and J.R. Squire (Eds.), *Handbook of research in teaching the English language arts* (2nd ed., pp. 752-785). New York: MacMillan.

Baumeister, R.F., Smart, L., and Boden, J.M. (1996). Relation of threatened egotism to violence and aggression: The dark side of high self-esteem. *Psychological Bulletin, 103*, 5-33.

Baumeister, R.F., Campbell, J.D., Krueger, J.L., and Vohs, K.D. (2003). Does high self-esteem cause better performance, interpersonal success, happiness, or healthier lifestyles? *Psychological Science in the Public Interest, 4*, 1-44.

Baumeister, R.F., Vohs, K.D., and Tice, D.M. (2007). The strength model of self-control. *Current Directions in Psychological Science, 16*, 351-355.

Baylor, A.L., and Kim, Y. (2005). Simulating instructional roles through pedagogical agents. *International Journal of Artificial Intelligence in Education, 15*, 95-115.

Baynham, M., Roberts, C., Cooke, M., Simpson, J., Ananiadou, K., Callaghan, J., McGoldrick, J., and Wallace, C. (2007). *Effective teaching and learning ESOL.* London, England: National Research and Development Centre for Adult Literacy and Numeracy. Available: http://www.nrdc.org.uk/uploads/documents/doc_3341.pdf [Sept. 2011].

Beach, K. (1995). Activity as a mediator of sociocultural change and individual development: The case of school-work transition in Nepal. *Mind, Culture, and Activity, 2*, 285-302.

Beach, R., Hull, G., and O'Brien, D. (in press). Transforming English language arts in a web 2.0 world. In D. Lapp and D. Fisher (Eds.), *Handbook of research on teaching the English language arts* (3rd ed., sec. IV, pp. 161-167). Cosponsored by the International Reading Association and the National Council of Teachers of English. New York: Routledge.

Beaulieu, C., Plewes, C., Paulson, L.A., Roy, D., Snook, L., Concha, L., and Philips, L. (2005). Imaging brain connectivity in children with diverse reading ability. *NeuroImage, 25*, 1,266-1,271.

Beaverstock, C., and McIntyre, S. (2008). Dividing and conquering: Successful writing processes for adult learners. *Adult Basic and Literacy Education Journal, 2*(2), 104-108.

Beaverstock, C., Bhaskaran, S., and Brinkley, J. (2009). Transforming adult students into authors: The writer to writer challenge. *Adult Basic and Literacy Education Journal, 3*(1), 50-59.

Beck, A. (2005). A place for critical literacy. *Journal of Adolescent and Adult Literacy, 48*(5), 392-400.

Beck, I.L., and McKeown, M.G. (1986). Application of theories of reading to instruction. In N. L. Stein (Ed.), *Literacy in American schools: Learning to read and write* (pp. 63-83). Chicago, IL: University of Chicago Press.

Beck, I.L., and McKeown, M.G. (2002). Questioning the author: Making sense of the social studies. *Educational Leadership, 60*(3), 44-47.

Beck, I.L., and McKeown, M.G. (2006). *Improving comprehension with questioning the author: A fresh and enhanced view of a proven approach.* New York: Scholastic.

Beck, I.L., and McKeown, M.G. (2007). Different ways for different goals, but keep your eye on the higher verbal goals. In R.K. Wagner, A.E. Muse, and K.R. Tannenbaum (Eds.), *Vocabulary acquisition: Implications for reading comprehension* (pp. 182-204). New York: Guilford Press.

Beck, I.L., McKeown, M.G., and Gromoll, E.W. (1989). Learning from social studies texts. *Cognition and Instruction, 6*(2), 99-158.

Beck, I.L., McKeown, M.G., Sandora, C., Kucan, L., and Worthy, J. (1996). Questioning the author: A year-long classroom implementation to engage students with text. *The Elementary School Journal, 96*(4).

Beck, I.L., McKeown, M.G., Hamilton, R.L., and Kucan, L. (1997). *Questioning the author: An approach for enhancing student engagement with text.* Newark, DE: International Reading Association.

Beck, I.L., McKeown, M.G., and Kucan, L. (2002). *Bringing words to life: Robust vocabulary instruction.* New York: Guilford Press.

Beder, H. (1999). *The outcomes and impacts of adult literacy education in the United States.* (Information Analyses No. NCSALL-R-6R309B60002.) Boston, MA: National Center for the Study of Adult Learning and Literacy.

Beidler, A. (1969). *The effects of the Peabody language development kit on the intelligence, reading, listening, and writing of disadvantaged children in the primary grades.* Unpublished doctoral dissertation, Lehigh University.

Beier, M.E., and Ackerman, P.L. (2001). Current-events knowledge in adults: An investigation of age, intelligence, and nonability determinants. *Psychology and Aging, 16,* 615-628.

Beier, M.E., and Ackerman, P.L. (2003). Determinants of health knowledge: An investigation of age, gender, personality, and interests. *Journal of Personality and Social Psychology, 84,* 439-448.

Beier, M.E., and Ackerman, P.L. (2005). Age, ability, and the role of prior knowledge on the acquisition of new domain knowledge: Promising results in a real-world learning environment. *Psychology and Aging, 20,* 341-355.

Beilock, S.L. (2008). Math performance in stressful situations. *Current Directions in Psychological Science, 17,* 339-343.

Beilock, S.L., Rydell, R.J., and McConnell, A. R. (2007). Stereotype threat and working memory: Mechanisms, alleviation, and spill over. *Journal of Experimental Psychology: General, 136,* 256-276.

Beilock, S.L., Gunderson, E.A., Ramirez, G., and Levine, S.C. (2010). Female teachers' math anxiety affects girls' math achievement. *Proceedings of the National Academy of Sciences, 107*(5), 1,060-1,063.

Belzer, A. (Ed.). (2007). *Toward defining and improving quality in adult basic education.* Mahway, NJ: Lawrence Erlbaum Associates.

Belzer, A., and St. Clair, R. (2003). *Opportunities and limits: An update on adult literacy education.* (Information series No. 391.) Columbus, OH: ERIC Clearinghouse on Adult, Career, and Vocational Education.

Benbunan-Fich, R. and Starr, R. Hiltz, (1999). Impacts of asynchronous learning networks on individual and group problem solving: A field experiment, *Group Decision and Negotiation, 8,* 409-426.

Benseman, J., Sutton, A., and Lander, J. (2005). *Working in the light of evidence, as well as aspiration. A literature review of the best available evidence about effective adult literacy, numeracy and language teaching.* Prepared for the Tertiary Education Learning Outcomes Policy Group, Ministry of Education, New Zealand.

Benson, N.J. (2000). Analysis of specific deficits: Evidence of transfer in disabled and normal readers following oral-motor awareness training. *Journal of Educational Psychology, 92*(4), 646-658.

Benson, N.J., Lovett, M.W., and Kroeber, C.L. (1997). Training and transfer-of-learning effects in disabled and normal readers: Evidence of specific deficits. *Journal of Experimental Child Psychology, 64*(3), 343-366.

Bereiter, C., and Scardamalia, M. (1985). Cognitive coping strategies and the problem of "inert knowledge." In S.F. Chipman, J.W. Segal, and R. Glaser (Eds.), *Thinking and learning skills: Vol. 2. Current research and open questions* (pp. 65-80). Hillsdale, NJ: Lawrence Erlbaum Associates.

Bereiter, C., and Scardamalia, M. (2003). Learning to work creatively with knowledge. In E. De Corte, L. Verschaffel, N. Entwistle, and J. van Merriënboer (Eds.), *Powerful learning environments: Unraveling basic components and dimensions* (pp. 55-68, Advances in Learning and Instruction Series). Oxford, England: Elsevier Science.

Berg, E.C. (1999). The effects of trained peer response on ESL students' revision types and writing quality. *Journal of Second Language Writing, 8*(3), 215-241.

Bergin, C. (2001). The parent-child relationship during beginning reading. *Journal of Literacy Research, 33*(4), 681-706.

Berkeley, S., Mastropieri, M.A., and Scruggs, T.W. (2011). Reading comprehension strategy instruction and attribution retraining for secondary students with learning and other mild disabilities. *Journal of Learning Disabilities, 44*, 18-32.

Berkman, N., DeWalt, D., Pignone, M., Sheridan, S., Lohr, K., Lux, L., Sutton, S., Swinson, T., and Bonito, A. (2004). *Literacy and health outcomes: Evidence report/technology assessment no. 87.* (AHRQ Publication No. 04-E007-2.) Rockville, MD: Agency for Healthcare Research and Quality. Available: http://www.ahrq.gov/downloads/pub/evidence/pdf/literacy/literacy.pdf [Dec. 2010].

Berman, I. (2009). Supporting adolescent literacy achievement. *Issue Brief*, Feb. 25, 1-15.

Berman, J. (2001). Industry output and employment projections to 2010. *Monthly Labor Review*, Nov., 40.

Berne, J. (2004). Think-aloud protocol and adult learners. *Adult Basic Education, 14*(3), 153-173.

Berninger, V.W. (1994). *The varieties of orthographic knowledge.* Dordrecht, the Netherlands: Kluwer Academic Press.

Berninger, V.W., and Amtmann, D. (2003). Preventing written expression disabilities through early and continuing assessment and intervention for handwriting and/or spelling problems: Research into practice. In H.L. Swanson, K.R. Harris, and S. Graham (Eds.), *Handbook of learning disabilities* (pp. 345-363). New York: Guilford Press.

Berninger, V.W., and Fuller, F. (1992). Gender differences in orthographic, verbal, and compositional fluency: Implications for assessing writing disabilities in primary grade children. *Journal of School Psychology, 30*, 363-382.

Berninger, V.W., and Richards, T.L. (2002). *Brain literacy for educators and psychologists.* New York: Academic Press.

Berninger, V.W., and Winn, W.D. (2006). Implications of the advancements in brain research and technology for writing development, writing instruction, and educational evolution. In C. MacArthur, S. Graham, and J. Fitzgerald (Eds), *Handbook of writing research* (pp. 96-114). New York: Guilford Press.

Berninger, V.W., Vaughan, K.B., Abbott, R.D., Abbott, S.P., Rogan, L.W., Brooks, A., Reed, E., and Graham, S. (1997). Treatment of handwriting problems in beginning writers: Transfer from handwriting to composition. *Journal of Educational Psychology, 89*(4), 652-666.

Berninger, V.W., Vaughan, K., Abbott, R.D., Brooks, A., Abbott, S.P., Rogan, L., Reed, E., and Graham S. (1998). Early intervention for spelling problems: Teaching functional spelling units of varying size with a multiple-connections framework. *Journal of Educational Psychology, 90*(4), 587-605.

Berninger, V.W., Vaughan, K., Abbott, R.D., Begay, K., Coleman, K.B., Curtain, G., Hawkins, J.M., and Graham, S. (2002). Teaching spelling and composition alone and together: Implications for the simple view of writing. *Journal of Educational Psychology, 94*(2), 291-304.

Berninger, V.W., Abbott, R.D., Thomson, J., Wagner, R., Swanson, H.L., Wijsman, E.M., and Raskind, W. (2006). Modeling developmental phonological core deficits within a working-memory architecture in children and adults with developmental dyslexia. *Scientific Studies of Reading, 10*(2), 165-198.

Berninger, V.W., Nagy, W., and Beers, S. (2011). Child writers' construction and reconstruction of single sentences and construction of multi-sentence texts: contributions of syntax and transcription to translation. *Reading and Writing, 24*(2).

Berns, R.G., and Erickson, P.M. (2001). *Contextual teaching and learning: Preparing students for the new economy* (The Highlight Zone: Research @Work No. 5). Louisville, KY: University of Louisville, National Research Center for Career and Technical Education.

Berry, A.B., and Mason, L.H. (in press). The effects of self-regulated strategy development on the writing of expository essays for adults with written expression difficulties: Preparing for the GED. Submitted to *Remedial and Special Education*.

Berry, J.M., West, R.L., and Dennehey, D.M. (1989). Reliability and validity of the memory self-efficacy questionnaire. *Developmental Psychology, 25*, 701-713.

Berry, J.M., Hastings, E., West, R.L., Lee, C., and Cavanaugh, J.C. (2010). Memory aging: Deficits, beliefs, and interventions. In J.C. Cavanaugh and C.K. Cavanaugh (Eds.), *Aging in America* (vol. 1, pp. 255-299). Denver, CO: Praeger.

Bever, T.G. (1981). Normal acquisition processes explain the critical period for language learning. In K.C. Diller, (Ed.), *Individual differences and universals in language learning aptitude*. Rowley, MA: Newbury House.

Bialystok, E., and Hakuta, K. (1995). *In other words: The science and psychology of second-language acquisition*. New York: Basic Books.

Bialystok, E., Craik, F.I.M., Grady, C., Chau, W., Ishii, R., Gunji, A., and Pantev, C. (2005). Effect of bilingualism on cognitive control in the Simon task: Evidence from MEG. *NeuroImage, 24*, 40-49.

Biber, D. (1988). *Variation across speech and writing*. Cambridge, England: Cambridge University Press.

Biber, D. (1986). Spoken and written textual dimensions in English: Resolving the contradictory findings. *Language, 62*, 384-414.

Biber, D., and Conrad, S. (2006). *Register, genre, and style*. Cambridge, England: Cambridge University Press.

Biber, D., Conrad, S., and Reppen, R. (1998). *Corpus linguistics: Investigating language structure and uses*. Cambridge, England: Cambridge University Press.

Bigelow, M., and Schwarz, R.L. (2010). *Adult English language learners with limited literacy*. Washington, DC: National Institute for Literacy.

Bigelow, M., and Tarone, E. (2004). The role of literacy level in second language acquisition: Doesn't who we study determine what we know? *TESOL Quarterly, 38*(4), 689-700.

Bilal, D., and Kirby, J. (2002). Differences and similarities in information seeking: Children and adults as web users. *Information Processing and Management, 38,* 649-670.

Bilalic, M., McLeod, P., and Gobet, F. (2008). Inflexibility of experts—Reality or myth? Quantifying the Einstellung effect in chess masters. *Cognitive Psychology, 56,* 73-102.

Binder, K.S., Chace, K.H., and Manning, M.C. (2007). Sentential and discourse context effects: Adults who are learning to read compared with skilled readers. *Journal of Research in Reading, 30*(4), 360-378.

Birdsong, D. (2006). Age and second language acquisition and processing: A selective overview. *Language Learning, 56*(Suppl 1), 9-49.

Birren, J.E., and Morrison, D.F. (1961). Analysis of the WAIS subtests in relation to age and education. *Journal of Gerontology, 16,* 363-369.

Bishara, A.J., and Jacoby, L.L. (2008). Aging, spaced retrieval, and inflexible memory performance. *Psychonomic Bulletin and Review, 15,* 52-57.

Bitan, T., Booth, J.R., Choy, J., Burman, D.D., Gitelman, D.R., and Mesulam, M.M. (2005). Shifts of effective connectivity within a language network during rhyming and spelling. *Journal of Neuroscience, 25*(22), 5,397-5,403.

Bjork, R.A. (1988). Retrieval practice and maintenance of knowledge. In M.M. Gruneberg, P.E. Morris, and R.N. Sykes (Eds.) *Practical aspects of memory: Current research and issues* (vol. 1, pp. 396-401). Hoboken, NJ: John Wiley & Sons.

Bjork, R.A. (1994). Memory and metamemory considerations in the training of human beings. In J. Metcalfe and A. Simamura (Eds.) *Metacognition: Knowing about knowing* (pp. 185-205). Cambridge, MA: MIT Press.

Bjork, R.A. (1999). Assessing our own competence: Heuristics and illusions. In D. Gopher and A. Koriat (Eds.), *Attention and performance XVII: Cognitive regulation of performance, interaction of theory and application* (pp. 435-459). Cambridge, MA: MIT Press.

Bjork, R.A., and Linn, M.C. (2006). The science of learning and the learning of science: Introducing desirable difficulties. *American Psychological Society Observer, 19,* 29-39.

Blachman, B.A., Schatschneider, C., Fletcher, J.M., Francis, D.J., Clonan, S.M., and Shaywitz, B.A. (2004). Effects of intensive reading remediation for second and third graders and a 1-year follow-up. *Journal of Educational Psychology, 96,* 444-461.

Black, A., and Deci, E. (2000). The effects of instructors' autonomy support and students' autonomous motivation on learning organic chemistry: A self-determination theory perspective. *Science Education, 84,* 740-756.

Black, R.W. (2009). Online fan fiction, global identities, and imagination. *Research in the Teaching of English, 43*(4), 397-425.

Blackburn, M.V. (2005). Agency in borderland discourses: Examining language use in a community center with black queer youth. *Teachers College Record, 107*(1), 89-113.

Block, C.C., and Pressley, M. (Eds.). (2002). *Comprehension instruction: Research-based best practices.* New York: Guilford Press.

Block, C.C., Parris, S.R., Reed, K.L., Whiteley, C.S., and Cleveland, M.D. (2009). Instructional approaches that significantly increase reading comprehension. *Journal of Educational Psychology, 101*(2), 262-281.

Blok, H., Oostdam, R., Otter, M.E., and Overmaat, M. (2002). Computer-assisted instruction in support of beginning reading instruction: A review. *Review of Educational Research, 72*(1), 101-130.

Blommaert, J., Street, B.V., and Turner, J. (2007). Academic literacies—What have we achieved and where to from here? [Edited transcript of a recorded discussion.] *Journal of Applied Linguistics, 4*(1), 137-148.

Bloom, B.S. (1956). *Taxonomy of educational objectives, handbook I: The cognitive domain.* New York: David McKay.

Bloom, K.C., and Shuell, T.J. (1981). Effects of massed and distributed practice on the learning and retention of second-language vocabulary. *Journal of Educational Research, 74*, 245-248.

Blumenfeld, P., Mergendoller, J., and Swarthout, D. (1987). Task as a heuristic for understanding student learning and motivation. *Journal of Curriculum Studies, 19*, 135-148.

Blumenfeld, P., Soloway, E., Marx, R., Krajcik, J.S., Guzdial, M., and Palincsar, A.S. (1991). Motivating project-based learning: Sustaining the doing, supporting the learning. *Educational Psychologist, 25*, 369-398.

Blumenfeld, P., Marx, R.W., Krajcik, J., Fishman, B., and Soloway, E. (2000). Creating useable innovations in systemic reform: Scaling up technology-embedded project-based science in urban schools. *Educational Psychologist, 35*, 149-164.

Blumenfeld, P., Marx, R.W., and Harris, C. (2006). Learning environments. In I. Siegel and A. Renninger (Eds.), *Handbook of child psychology* (vol. 4, pp. 297-342). Hoboken, NJ: John Wiley & Sons.

Blumenthal, A. J. (2002). English as a second language at the community college: An exploration of contexts and concerns. *New Directions for Community Colleges, 117*(Spring), 45-53.

Boiché, J.C., Sarrazin, P.G., Grouzet, F.M., and Pelletier, L.G. (2008). Students' motivational profiles in physical education and achievement outcomes: A self-determination theory perspective. *Journal of Educational Psychology, 100*, 688-701.

Bonk, C.J., and Reynolds, T. H. (1992). Early adolescent composing within a generative-evaluative computerized prompting framework. *Computers in Human Behavior, 8*, 39-62.

Bonk, C.J., Middleton, J., Reynolds, T., and Stead, L. (1990). *The index of writing awareness: One tool for measuring early adolescent metacognition in writing.* Paper presented at the Annual Meeting of the American Educational Research Association, Washington, DC.

Booth, J.R., Burman, D.D., Van Santen, F.W., Harasaki, Y., Gitelman, D.R., Parrish, T.B., and Marsel Mesulam, M.M. (2001). The development of specialized brain systems in reading and oral-language. *Neuropsychology, Development, and Cognition: Section C, Child Neuropsychology, 7*(3), 119-141.

Borkowski, J.G., Weyhing, R.S., and Carr, M. (1988). Effects of attributional retraining on strategy-based reading comprehension in learning disabled students. *Journal of Educational Psychology, 80*(1), 46-53.

Boroch, D., Fillpot, J., Hope, L., Johnstone, R., Mery, P., Serban, A., and Gabriner, R.S. (2007). *Basic skills as a foundation for student success in California community colleges.* Sacramento: The Research and Planning Group for California Community Colleges, Center for Student Success. Available: http://www.cccbsi.org/Websites/basicskills/Images/Lit_Review_Student_Success.pdf [Sept. 2011].

Bottge, B.A. (1999). Effects of contextualized math instruction on problem solving of average and below-average achieving students. *Journal of Special Education, 33*, 81-92.

Bottge, B.A. (2009-2012). (PI). *Developing mathematics understanding of students with disabilities using enhanced anchored instruction.* U.S. Department of Education Institute of Education Sciences four-year grant under Mathematics and Science Special Education Research, University of Kentucky College of Education.

Bottge, B.A., and Hasselbring, T.S. (1993). A comparison of two approaches for teaching complex, authentic mathematics problems to adolescents in remedial math classes. *Exceptional Children, 59*, 556-566.

Bottge, B.A., and Rueda, E. (2006, April). *Capturing math understanding: A comparison of two assessment methods.* Paper presented at the annual meeting of the American Educational Research Association, San Francisco.

Bottge, B.A., Heinrichs, M., Chan, S., and Serlin, R. (2001). Anchoring adolescents' understanding of math concepts in rich problem-solving environments. *Remedial and Special Education, 22*, 299-314.

Bottge, B.A., Heinrichs, M., Mehta, Z., and Hung, Y. (2002). Weighing the benefits of anchored math instruction for students with disabilities in general education classes. *Journal of Special Education, 35*, 186-200.

Bottge, B.A., Heinrichs, M., Chan, S.Y., Mehta, Z.D., and Watson, E. (2003). Effects of video-based and applied problems on the procedural math skills of average- and low-achieving adolescents. *Journal of Special Education Technology, 18*(2), 5-22.

Bottge, B.A., Heinrichs, M., Mehta, Z.D., Rueda, E., Hung, Y., and Danneker, J. (2004). Teaching mathematical problem solving to middle school students in math, technology education, and special education classrooms. *RMLE Online, 27*(1). Available: http://www.nmsa.org/portals/0/pdf/publications/RMLE/rmle_vol27_no1_article1.pdf [Sept. 2011].

Bottge, B.A., Rueda, E., Serlin, R., Hung, Y.-H., and Kwon, J. (2007). Shrinking achievement differences with anchored math problems: Challenges and possibilities. *Journal of Special Education, 41*, 31-49.

Bouchard, T.J., and Hare, M. (1970). Size, performance, and potential in brainstorming groups. *Journal of Applied Psychology, 54*, 51-55.

Boudett, K.P., and Friedlander, D. (1997). Does mandatory basic education improve achievement test scores of AFDC recipients? *Evaluation Review, 21*(5), 568-588.

Bourdieu, P. (1982). *Language and symbolic power.* Cambridge, MA: Harvard University Press.

Bourdieu, P., and Passeron, J. (1977/1990). *Reproduction in education, society and culture.* London, England: Sage.

Bourdieu, P., and Wacquant, L.J.D. (1992). *An invitation to reflexive sociology.* Chicago: University of Chicago Press.

Bourdin, B., and Fayol, M. (1993). *Comparing speaking span and writing span: A working memory approach.* Paper presented at the Meeting of the European Association for Research in Learning and Instruction, Aix-en-Provence, France.

Bourdin, B., and Fayol, M. (1994). Is written language production more difficult than oral language production? A working memory approach. *International Journal of Psychology, 29*, 591-620.

Boutwell, M.A. (1989). Partnership for change. In A. Fingeret and P. Jurmo (Eds.), *Participatory literacy education* (pp. 43-52). San Francisco: Jossey-Bass.

Bowe, C.M., Lahey, L., Armstrong, E., and Kegan, E. (2003). Questioning the "big assumptions": Addressing personal contradictions that impede professional development. *Medical Education, 37*, 715-722.

Bower, G.H., and Clark, M.C. (1969). Narrative stories as mediators for serial learning. *Psychonomic Science, 14*, 181-182.

Bower, G.H., Black, J.B., and Turner, T.J. (1979). Scripts in memory for text. *Cognitive Psychology, 11*, 177-220.

Bowles, S., and Gintis, H. (1976). *Schooling in capitalist America: Educational reform and the contradictions of economic life.* New York: Basic Books.

Boyd, D. (2008). Why youth ♥ social network sites: The role of networked publics in teenage social life. In D. Buckingham (Ed.), *Youth, identity, and digital media.* Cambridge, MA: MIT Press.

Bradley, L., and Bryant, P. (1985). *Rhyme and reason in reading and spelling.* Ann Arbor: University of Michigan Press.

Bradley, R., Danielson, L., and Hallahan, D. (2002). *Identification of learning disabilities: Research to practice.* Mahwah, NJ: Lawrence Erlbaum Associates.

Brambati, S.M., Termine, C., Ruffino, M., Stella, G., Fazio, F., Cappa, S.F., and Perani, D. (2004). Regional reductions of gray matter volume in familial dyslexia. *Neurology*, 63(4), 742-745.

Brantmeier, C. (2005). Effects of reader's knowledge, text type, and test type on L1 and L2 reading comprehension in Spanish. *Modern Language Journal*, 89(1), 37-53.

Branum-Martin, L., Mehta, P.D., Fletcher, J.M., Carlson, C.D., Ortiz, A., Carlo, M., and Francis, D.J. (2006). Bilingual phonological awareness: Multilevel construct validation among Spanish-speaking kindergarteners in transitional bilingual education classrooms. *Journal of Educational Psychology*, 98, 170-181.

Brass, J.J. (2008). Local knowledge and digital movie composing in an after-school literacy program. *Journal of Adolescent and Adult Literacy*, 51(8), 464-473.

Braze, D., Tabor, W., Shankweiler, D.P., and Mencl, W.E. (2007). Speaking up for vocabulary: Reading skill differences in young adults. *Journal of Learning Disabilities*, 40(3), 226-243.

Breetvelt, I., Van den Bergh, H. and Rijlaarsdam, G. (1994). Relations between writing processes and text quality: When and how. *Cognition and Instruction*, 12, 103-123.

Breetvelt, I., Van den Bergh, H. and Rijlaarsdam, G. (1996). Rereading and generating and their relation to text quality: An application of mutilevel analysis on writing process data. In G. Rijlaarsdam, H. Van den Bergh, and M. Couzjin (Eds.), *Theories, models and methodologies on writing research* (pp. 10-21). Amsterdam, the Netherlands: Amsterdam University Press.

Brehmer, Y., Li, S.-C., Müller, V., von Oertzen, T., and Lindenberger, U. (2007). Memory plasticity across the life span: Uncovering children's latent potential. *Developmental Psychology*, 43, 465-478.

Brehmer, Y., Li, S.-C., Straube, B., Stoll, G., von Oertzen, T., Müller, V., and Lindenberger, U. (2008). Comparing memory skill maintenance across the life span: Preservation in adults, increase in children. *Psychology and Aging*, 23(2), 227-238.

Breznitz, Z. (2006). *Fluency in reading: Synchronization of processes*. Mahwah, NJ: Lawrence Erlbaum Associates.

Brittenham, R., Cook, R., Hall, J.B., Moore-Whitesell, P., Ruhl-Smith, C., Shafii-Mousavi, M., Showalter, J., Smith, K., and White, K. (2003). Connections: An integrated community of learners. *Journal of Developmental Education*, 27(1), 18-25.

Britton, B.K., and Gulgoz, S. (1991). Using Kintsch's computational model to improve instructional text: Effects of repairing inference calls on recall and cognitive structures. *Journal of Educational Psychology*, 83, 329-345.

Brockett, R.G., and Hiemstra, R. (1991). *Self-direction in adult learning: Perspectives in theory, research, and practice*. New York: Routledge.

Brooks, G., Davies, R. Puckett, L., Hutchison, D., Kendall, S., and Wilkin, A. (2001). *Progress in adult literacy: Do learners learn?* London, England: Basic Skills Agency.

Brooks, G., Burton, M., Cole, P., and Szczerbinski, M. (2007). *Effective teaching and learning: Reading*. London, England: National Research and Development Centre for Adult Literacy and Numeracy.

Brown, A.L., and Palincsar, A. (1982). Inducing strategic learning from texts by means of informed, self-control training. *Topics in Learning and Learning Disabilities*, 2(1), 1-17.

Brown, A.L., Collins, A., and Duguid, P. (1989). Situated cognition and the culture of learning. *Educational Researcher*, 18(1), 32-42.

Brown, W.E., Eliez, S., Menon, V., Rumsey, J.M., White, C.D., and Reiss, A.L. (2001). Preliminary evidence of widespread morphological variations of the brain in dyslexia. *Neurology*, 56, 781-783.

Brozo, W.G. (1990). Hiding out in secondary content classrooms: Coping strategies of unsuccessful readers. *Journal of Reading*, 33(5), 324-328.

Bruck, M. (1990). Word-recognition skills of adults with childhood diagnoses of dyslexia. *Developmental Psychology, 26*(3), 439-454.

Bruck, M. (1992). Persistence of dyslexics' phonological awareness deficits. *Developmental Psychology, 28*, 874-886.

Bruck, M. (1993). Component spelling skills of college students with childhood diagnoses of dyslexia. *Learning Disability Quarterly, 16*, 171-184.

Bruck, M. and Waters, G. (1990). Effects of reading skill on component spelling skills. *Applied Psycholinguistics, 9*, 77-92.

Bruner, J.S. (1960). *The process of education.* New York: Vintage Books.

Brunning, R., and Horn, C. (2000). Developing motivation to write. *Educational Psychologist, 35*, 25-38.

Brunswick, N., McCrory, E., Price, C., Frith, C.D., and Frith, U. (1999). Explicit and implicit processing of words and pseudowords by adult developmental dyslexics: A search for Wernicke's Wortschatz. *Brain, 122*, 1,901-1,917.

Bryan, L. (1996). Cooperative writing groups in community college. *Journal of Adolescent and Adult Literacy, 40*(3), 188.

Buckingham, D. (2003). *Media education: Literacy, learning, and culture.* Cambridge, England: Polity.

Bull, S., and Kay, J. (2007). Student models that invite the learner in: The SMILI open learner modeling framework. *International Journal of Artificial Intelligence in Education, 17*, 89-120.

Buonomano, D.V., and Merzenich, M.M. (1998). Cortical plasticity: From synapses to maps. *Annual Review of Neuroscience, 21*, 149-186.

Burgess, M. (2009). Using WebCT as a supplemental tool to enhance critical thinking and engagement among developmental reading students. *Journal of College Reading and Learning, 39*(2), 9-33.

Burke, D.M., and Peters, L. (1986). Word associations in old age: Evidence for consistency in semantic encoding during adulthood. *Psychology and Aging, 1*(4), 283-292.

Burke, D.M., and Shafto, M.A. (2004). Aging and language production. *Current Directions in Psychological Science, 13*(1), 21-24.

Burke, D.M., White, H., and Diaz, D.L. (1987). Semantic priming in young and older adults: Evidence for age constancy in automatic and attentional processes. *Journal of Experimental Psychology-Human Perception and Performance, 13*(1), 79-88.

Burke, D.M., Mackay, D.G., Worthley, J.S., and Wade, E. (1991). On the tip of the tongue— What causes word-finding failures in young and older adults. *Journal of Memory and Language, 30*(5), 542-579.

Burns, M., Appleton, J., and Stehouwer, J. (2005). Meta-analytic review of responsiveness-to-intervention research: Examining field-based and research-implemented models. *Journal of Psychoeducational Assessment, 23*, 381-394.

Burstein, J. (2003). The e-rater® scoring engine: Automated essay scoring with natural language processing. In M.D. Shermis and J. Burstein (Eds.), *Automated essay scoring: A cross-disciplinary perspective.* Hillsdale, NJ: Lawrence Erlbaum Associates.

Burt, J.S., and Fury, M.B. (2000). Spelling in adults: The role of reading skills and experience. *Reading and Writing, 13*, 1-30.

Burt, J.S., and Shrubsole, C.S. (2000). Processing of phonological representations and adult spelling proficiency. *Australian Journal of Psychology, 52*(2), 100-109.

Burt, M., Peyton, J.K., and Adams, R. (2003). *Reading and adult English language learners: A review of the research.* Washington, DC: Center for Applied Linguistics.

Burt, M., Peyton, J.K., and Van Duzer, C. (2005). *How should adult ESL reading instruction differ from ABE reading instruction?* Washington, DC: Center for Adult English Language Acquisition. Available: http://www.marshalladulteducation.org/pdf/briefs2/How_Should_Adult_ESL_Reading_Instruction_Differ_from%20_ABE_Reading_Instruction.pdf [Sept. 2011].

Burton, K.D., Lydon, J.E., D'Alessandro, D.U., and Koestner, R. (2006). The differential effects of intrinsic and identified motivation on well-being and performance: Prospective, experimental and implicit approaches to self-determination theory. *Journal of Personality and Social Psychology, 91,* 750-762.

Burton, M., Davey, J., Lewis, M., Ritchie, L., and Brooks, G. (2010). *Progress for adult literacy learners.* London, England: National Research and Development Centre for Adult Literacy and Numeracy.

Bus, A.G., van Ijzendoorn, M.H., and Pellegrini, A.D. (1995). Joint book reading makes for success in learning to read: A meta-analysis on intergenerational transmission of literacy. *Review of Educational Research, 65,* 1-21.

Butler, A.C., and Roediger, H.L., III. (2007). Testing improves long-term retention in a simulated classroom setting. *European Journal of Cognitive Psychology, 19,* 514-527.

Butler, A.C., Karpicke, J.D., and Roediger, H.L. (2008) Correcting a metacognitive error: Feedback increases retention of low-confidence correct responses. *Journal of Experimental Psychology: Learning, Memory, and Cognition, 34,* 918-928.

Butler, D.L., and Winne, P.H. (1995). Feedback and self-regulated learning: A theoretical synthesis. *Review of Educational Research, 65*(3), 245-281.

Butler, D.L., Lauscher, H., Jarvis-Selinger, S., and Beckingham, B. (2004). Collaboration and self-regulation in teachers' professional development. *Teaching and Teacher Education, 20*(5), 435-455.

Byrne, M.E., Crowe, T.A., and Hale, S.T. (1996). Metalinguistic and pragmatic abilities of participants in adult literacy programs. *Journal of Communication Disorders, 29*(1), 37-49.

Cahalan-Laitusis, C. (2003). *Accommodations on high-stakes writing tests for students with disabilities.* Research report no. RR-04-13. Princeton, NJ: Educational Testing Service. Available: http://www.ets.org/Media/Research/pdf/RR-04-13.pdf [Sept. 2011].

Cain, K., and Oakhill, J. (Eds.). (2007). *Children's comprehension problems in oral and written language: A cognitive perspective.* New York: Guilford Press.

Cain, K., Oakhill, J., and Elbro, C. (2002). The ability to learn new word meanings from context by school-age children with and without language comprehension difficulties. *Journal of Child Language, 30,* 681-694.

Cain, K., Oakhill, J.V., and Lemmon, K. (2004). Individual differences in the inference of word meanings from context: The influence of reading comprehension. *Journal of Educational Psychology, 96*(4), 671-681.

Calkins, L.M. (1994). *The art of teaching writing.* Portsmouth, NH: Heinemann.

Callahan, M., and Chumney, D. (2009). "Write like college": How remedial writing courses at a community college and a research university position "at-risk" students in the field of higher education. *Teachers College Record, 111*(7), 1,619-1,664.

Cameron, J., and Pierce, W.D. (1994). Reinforcement, reward, and intrinsic motivation: A meta-analysis. *Review of Educational Research, 64*(3), 363-423.

Cameron, J., and Pierce, W.D. (1996). The debate about rewards and intrinsic motivation: Protests and accusations do not alter the results. *Review of Educational Research, 66*(1), 39-51.

Cameron, J., Banko, K.M., and Pierce, W.D. (2001). Pervasive negative effects of rewards on intrinsic motivation: The myth continues. *Behavior Analyst, 24*(1), 1-44.

Caplan, D. (2004). Functional neuroimaging studies of written sentence comprehension. *Scientific Studies of Reading, 8*(3), 225-240.

Caplan, D., and Waters, G.S. (1999). Verbal working memory and sentence comprehension. *Behavioral and Brain Sciences*, 22(1), 77-94.

Cara, O., and Litster, J.H. (2009). Teacher attitudes toward the "skills for life" national strategy for imporving adult litercy and numeracy skills. In S. Reder and J. Bynner (Eds.), *Tracking adult literacy and numeracy skills: Findings from longitudinal research* (pp. 177-199). New York: Routledge.

Cara, O., Casey, H., Eldred, J., Grief, S., Hodge, R., Ivanic, R., Jupp, T., Lopex, D., and McNeil, B. (2006). *You wouldn't expect a math teacher to teach plastering: Embedding literacy, language and numeracy in post-16 vocational programmes, the impact on learning and achievement.* London, England: National Research and Development Centre for Adult Literacy and Numeracy.

Carlisle, J.F. (1995). Morphological awareness and early reading achievement. In L.B. Feldman (Ed.), *Morphological aspects of language processing* (pp. 189-209). Hillsdale, NJ: Lawrence Erlbaum Associates.

Carlisle, J.F. (2000). Awareness of the structure and meaning of morphologically complex words: Impact on reading. *Reading and Writing: An Interdisciplinary Journal*, 12, 169-190.

Carlisle, J.F. (2004). Morphological processes that influence learning to read. In C.A. Stone, E.R. Silliman, B.J. Ehren, and E. Apel (Eds.), *Handbook of language and literacy: Development and Disorders* (pp. 318-390). New York: Guilford Press.

Carlisle, J.F., and Rice, M.S. (2002). *Improving reading comprehension: Research-based principles and practices.* Baltimore, MD: York Press.

Carlisle, J.F., and Stone, A. (2003). The effects of morphological structure on children's reading of derived words. In E. Assink and D. Santa (Eds), *Reading complex words: Cross-language studies* (pp. 27-52). New York: Kluwer Academic Press.

Carlo, M.S., August, D., McLaughlin, B., Snow, C.E., Dressler, C. and Lippman, D. (2004). Closing the gap: Addressing the vocabulary needs of English language learners in bilingual and mainstream classrooms. *Reading Research Quarterly*, 39(2), 188-215.

Carlson, C.D., and Francis, D. (2002). Increasing the reading achievement of at-risk children through direct instruction: Evaluation of the Rodeo Institute for Teacher Excellence (RITE). *Journal of Education for Students Placed at Risk. Special Issue: Research on Direct Instruction in Reading*, 7(2), 141-166.

Carnevale, A., and Derochers, D. (2003). *Standards for what? The economic roots of K-16 reform.* Princeton, NJ: Educational Testing Service.

Carr, T.H., and Posner, M.I. (1994). The impact of learning to read on the functional anatomy of language processing. In B. de Gelder and J. Morais (Eds.), *Language and literacy: Comparative Approaches* (p. 32). Cambridge, MA: MIT Press.

Carrell, P.L. (1984). Schema theory and ESL reading: Classroom implications and applications. *Modern Language Journal*, 68(4), 332-343.

Carrigan, V.L. (n.d.). *Contextualizing basic skills and career technical education (CTE) curricula.* Sacramento, CA: Workplace Learning Resource Center, Los Rios Community College District. Available: http://www.wplrc.org/app/doc/Contextualizing%20Basic%20Skills%20into%20CTE%20curricula.pdf [Sept. 2011].

Carroll, J.B. (1993). *Human cognitive abilities: A survey of factor analytic studies.* New York: Cambridge University Press.

Carter, S. (2006). Redefining literacy as a social practice. *Journal of Basic Writing*, 25(2), 94-125.

Carver, C.S., and Scheier, M.F. (Eds.). (2000). *Handbook of self-regulation.* New York: Academic Press.

Casey, B., Erkut, S., Ceder, I., and Young, J.M. (2008). Use of a storytelling context to improve girls' and boys' geometry skills in kindergarten. *Journal of Applied Developmental Psychology, 29,* 29-48.

Castleton, G. (2002). Workplace literacy as a contested site of educational activity. *Journal of Adolescent and Adult Literacy, 45*(7), 556-566.

Castro-Caldas, A., Petersson, K.M., Reis, A., Stone-Elander, S., and Ingvar, M. (1998). The illiterate brain—Learning to read and write during childhood influences the functional organization of the adult brain. *Brain, 121,* 1,053-1,063.

Catrambone, R. (1996). Generalizing solution procedures learned from examples. *Journal of Experimental Psychology: Learning, Memory, and Cognition, 22,* 1,020-1,031.

Catts, H.W., and Hogan, T. (2003). Language basis of reading disabilities and implications for early identification and remediation. *Reading Psychology, 24,* 223-246.

Catts, H.W., Adlof, S.M., and Ellis, W.S. (2006). Language deficits in poor comprehenders: A case for the simple view of reading. *Journal of Speech, Language, and Hearing Research, 49,* 278-293.

Caverly, D.C., Nicholson, S.A., and Radcliffe, R. (2004). The effectiveness of strategic instruction for college developmental readers. *Journal of College Reading and Learning, 35,* 25-49.

Cazden, C.B. (1985). Social context of learning to read. In H. Singer and R.B. Ruddell (Eds.), *Theoretical models and processes of reading* (pp. 595-629). Newark, DE: International Reading Association.

Cazden, C.B. (1988). *Classroom discourse: The language of teaching and learning.* Portsmouth, NH: Heinemann.

Cazden, C.B., Hymes, D., and John, W.J. (Eds.). (1972). *Functions of language in the classroom.* New York: Teachers College Press.

Ceci, S.J. (1991). How much does schooling influence general intelligence and its cognitive components? A reassessment of the evidence. *Developmental Psychology, 27*(5), 703-722.

Center for Applied Linguistics. (2010). *Education for adult English language learners in the United States: Trends, research, and promising practices.* Washington, DC: Author.

Cepeda, N.J., Pashler, H., Vul, E., Wixted, J.T., and Rohrer, D. (2006). Distributed practice in verbal recall tasks: A review and quantitative synthesis. *Psychological Bulletin, 132,* 354-380.

Chafe, W., and Tannen, D. (1987). The relation between written and spoken language. *Annual Review of Anthropology, 16,* 383-407.

Chaiklin, S., and Lave, J. (Eds.) (1996). *Understanding practice: Perspectives on activity and context.* New York: Cambridge University Press.

Chambliss, M.J. (1995). Text cues and strategies successful readers use to construct the gist of lengthy written arguments. *Reading Research Quarterly, 30,* 778-807.

Chambliss, M.J., and Calfee, R. (1998). *Textbooks for learning: Nurturing children's minds.* Boston, MA: Blackwell.

Chambliss, M.J., and Murphy, P.K. (2002). Fourth and fifth graders representing the argument structure in written texts. *Discourse Processes, 34*(1), 91-115.

Chamot, A.U. (2000). Literacy characteristics of Hispanic adolescent immigrants with limited prior education. In *Proceedings of a research symposium on high standards in reading for students from diverse language groups: Research, practice and policy* (pp. 188-202). Washington, DC: U.S. Department of Education, Office of Bilingual Education and Minority Languages Affairs.

Chandler-Olcott, K., and Mahar, D. (2003). "Tech-Savviness" meets multiliteracies: Exploring adolescent girls' technology mediated literacy practices. *Reading Research Quarterly, 38*(3), 356-385.

Chard, D.J., Vaughn, S., and Tyler, B. (2002). A synthesis of research on effective interventions for building reading fluency with elementary students with learning disabilities. *Journal of Learning Disabilities, 35*(5), 386-406.

Chard, D.J., Ketterlin-Geller, L.R., Baker, B.K., Doabler, C., and Apichatabutra, C. (2009). Repeated reading intervention for students with learning disabilities: Status of the evidence. *Exceptional Children, 75,* 263-281.

Charness, N. (2006). The influence of work and occupation on brain development. In P.B. Baltes, P.A. Reuter-Lorenz, and F. Rösler (Eds.), *Lifespan development and the brain: The perspective of biocultural co-constructivism* (pp. 255-276). New York: Cambridge University Press.

Charness, N., Krampe, R. Th., and Mayr, U. (1996). The role of practice and coaching in entrepreneurial skill domains: An international comparison of life-span chess skill acquisition. In K.A. Ericsson (Ed.), *The road to excellence: The acquisition of expert performance in the arts and sciences, sports, and games* (pp. 51-80). Mahwah, NJ: Lawrence Erlbaum Associates.

Chase, W.G., and Simon, H.A. (1973). The mind's eye in chess. In W.G. Chase (Ed.), *Visual information processing* (pp. 215-281). New York: Academic Press.

Chatzisarantis, N.L.D., and Hagger, M.S. (2007). Mindfulness and the intention-behavior relationship within the theory of planned behavior. *Personality and Social Psychology Bulletin, 33*(5), 663-676.

Chee, M., Tan, E., and Thiel, T. (1999). Mandarin and English single word processing studied with functional magnetic resonance imaging. *Journal of Neuroscience, 19,* 3,050-3,056.

Cheeseman Day, J., and Newburger, E.C. (2002). *The big payoff: Educational attainment and synthetic estimates of work-life earnings.* Washington, DC: U.S. Census Bureau.

Chenoweth, N.A., and Hayes, J.R. (2001). Fluency in writing. *Written Communication, 18*(1), 80-98.

Chi, M.T.H., Glaser, R., and Rees, E. (1982). Expertise in problem solving. In R.S. Sternberg (Ed.), *Advances in the psychology of human intelligence* (vol. 1, pp. 1-75). Hillsdale, NJ: Lawrence Erlbaum Associates.

Chi, M.T.H., Glaser, R., and Farr, M.J. (Eds.). (1988). *The nature of expertise.* Hillsdale, NJ: Lawrence Erlbaum Associates.

Chi, M.T.H., de Leeuw, N., Chiu, M., and LaVancher, C. (1994). Eliciting self-explanations improves understanding. *Cognitive Science, 18,* 439-477.

Chi, M.T.H., Siler, S.A., and Jeong, H. (2004). Can tutors monitor students' understanding accurately? *Cognition and Instruction, 22*(3), 363-387.

Chi, M.T.H., Roy, M., and Hausmann, R.G.M. (2008) Observing tutorial dialogues collaboratively: Insights about human tutoring effectiveness from vicarious learning. *Cognitive Science, 32*(2), 301-341.

Chinn, C., and Brewer, W. (1993). The role of anomalous data in knowledge acquisition: A theoretical framework and implications for science instruction. *Review of Educational Research, 63,* 1-49.

Chisman, F., and Crandall, J. (2007). Passing the torch: Strategies for innovation in community college ESL. New York: Council for Advancement of Adult Literacy. Available: http://caalusa.org/eslexecsummary.pdf [Sept. 2011].

Chiu, C.W., and Pearson, P.D. (1999). *Synthesizing the effects of tests accommodations for special education and limited English proficient students.* Paper presented at the National Conference on Large-Scale Assessment, June, Snowbird, UT.

Cho, K., and Schunn, C.D. (2007). Scaffolded writing and rewriting in the discipline: A web-based reciprocal peer review system. *Computers and Education, 48*(3), 409-426.

Cho, K., and Schunn, C.D. (2010). Developing writing skills through students giving instructional explanations. In M.K. Stein and L. Kucan (Eds.), *Instructional explanations in the disciplines: Talk, texts and technology*. New York: Springer.

Cho, K., Schunn, C., and Wilson, R. (2006). Validity and reliability of scaffolded peer assessment of writing from instructor and student perspectives. *Journal of Educational Psychology, 98*(4), 891-901.

Cho, K., Schunn, C.D., and Kwon, K. (2007). Learning writing by reviewing in science. In *CSCL '07 Proceedings of the 8th International Conference on Computer-Supported Collaborative Learning*. Available: http://dl.acm.org/citation.cfm?id=1599600&picked= prox&cfid=41750636&cftoken=53704519 [Sept. 2011].

Choi, I., Nisbett, R.E., and Norenzayan, A. (1999). Causal attribution across cultures: Variation and universality. *Psychological Bulletin, 125*(1), 47-63.

Choi, I., Koo, M., and Choi, J.A. (2007). Individual differences in analytic versus holistic thinking. *Personality and Social Psychology Bulletin, 33*, 691-705.

Christensen, C.A. (2005). The role of orthographic-motor integration in the production of creative and well structured written text for students in secondary school. *Educational Psychology, 25*, 441-453.

Christenson, S.L. Thurlow, M.L., Ysseldyke, J.E., and McVicar, R. (1989). Written language instruction for students with mild handicaps: Is there enough quantity to ensure quality. *Learning Disability Quarterly, 12*, 219-222.

Chu, R.J.-C., and Tsai, C.-C. (2009). Self-directed learning readiness, Internet self-efficacy and preferences toward constructivist Internet-based learning environments among higher-aged adults. *Journal of Computer Assisted Learning, 25*, 489-501.

Church, J.A., Coalson, R.S., Lugar, H.M., Petersen, S.E., and Schlaggar, B.L. (2008). A developmental fMRI study of reading reveals changes in phonological and visual mechanisms over age. *Cerebral Cortex, 18*, 2,054-2,065.

Cirino, P.K., Israelian, M.K., Morris, M.K., and Morris, R.D. (2005). Evaluation of the double-deficit hypothesis in college students referred for learning difficulties. *Journal of Learning Disabilities, 38*(1), 29-44.

Clark, H.H. (1996). *Using language*. Cambridge, England: Cambridge University Press.

Clark, R.C., and Mayer, R.E. (2003). *e-learning and the science of instruction: Proven guidelines for consumers and designers of multimedia learning*. San Francisco, CA: Jossey-Bass.

Clough, G., Jones, A.C., McAndrew, P., and Scanlon, E. (2008). Informal learning with PDAs and smartphones. *Journal of Computer Assisted Learning, 24*, 359-371.

Clover, D.E. (2007). From sea to cyberspace: Women's leadership and learning around information and communication technologies in coastal Newfoundland. *International Journal of Lifelong Education, 26*(1), 75-88.

Cobb, P., and Bowers, J. (1999). Cognitive and situated learning perspectives in theory and practice. *Educational Researcher, 28*(2), 4-15.

Cobb, P., Confrey, J., diSessa, A., Lehrer, R., and Schauble, L. (2003). Design experiments in educational research. *Educational Researcher, 32*(1), 9-13.

Cobo-Lewis, A., Eilers, R.E., Pearson, B.Z., and Umbel, V.C. (2002). Interdependence of Spanish and English knowledge in language and literacy among bilingual children. In D.K. Oller and R.E. Eilers (Eds.), *Language and literacy in bilingual children* (pp. 118-132). Clevedon, England: Multilingual Matters.

Coffin, C. (2001). Theoretical approaches to written language. In A. Burns and C. Coffin (Eds.), *Analysing English in a global context* (pp. 93-122). London, England: Routledge.

Coffin, C. (2006). Mapping subject-specific literacies. *NALDIC Quarterly, 3*(3), 13-26.

Coffin, C., and Hewings, A.O.H.K. (2004). Applying English grammar: Functional and corpus approaches. In C. Coffin, A. Hewings, and K. O'Halloran (Eds.), *Applying English grammar: Functional and corpus approaches*. London, England: Arnold.

Cognition and Technology Group at Vanderbilt. (1990). Anchored instruction and its relationship to situated cognition. *Educational Researcher, 19*(3), 2-10.

Cognition and Technology Group at Vanderbilt. (1997). *The Jasper project: Lessons in curriculum, instruction, assessment, and professional development.* Mahwah, NJ: Lawrence Erlbaum Associates.

Cohen, A.M., and Brawer, F.B. (2003). *The American community college* (4th ed.). San Francisco, CA: Jossey-Bass.

Cohen, A.S., Gregg, N., and Deng, M. (2005). The role of extended time and item content on a high-stakes mathematics test. *Learning Disabilities Research and Practice, 20*(4), 225-233.

Cohen, E.G. (1994). *Designing groupwork: Strategies for heterogeneous classrooms.* New York: Teachers College Press.

Cohen, E.G., and Lotan, R.A. (Eds.). (1997). *Working for equity in heterogeneous classrooms: Sociological theory in practice.* New York: Teachers College Press.

Cohen, G. (1981). Inferential reasoning in old age. *Cognition, 9,* 59-72.

Cohen, L., Dehaene, S., Naccache, L., Lehéricy, S., Dehaene-Lambertz, G., Hénaff, M-A, and Michel, F. (2000). The visual word form area: Spatial and temporal characterization of an initial stage of reading in normal subjects and posterior split-brain patients. *Brain, 123*(2), 291-307.

Cohen, L., Lehericy, S., Chochon, F., Lemer, C., Rivaud, S., and Dehaene, S. (2002). Language-specific tuning of visual cortex? Functional properties of the visual word form area. *Brain, 125,* 1,054-1,069.

Coiro, J. (2003). Reading comprehension on the internet: Expanding our understanding of reading comprehension to encompass new literacies. *The Reading Teacher, 56,* 458-464.

Coiro, J., and Dobler, E. (2007). Exploring the online comprehension strategies used by sixth-grade skilled readers to search for and locate information on the internet. *Reading Research Quarterly, 42*(2), 214-257.

Coiro, J., Knobel, M., Lankshear, C., and Leu, D.J. (2009a). Central issues in new literacies and new literacies research. In J. Coiro, M. Knobel, C. Lankshear, and D.J. Leu (Eds.), *Handbook of research on new literacies* (pp. 1-22). New York: Routledge.

Coiro, J., Knobel, M., Lanksear, C., and Leu, D.J. (Eds.). (2009b). *Handbook of research on new literacies.* New York: Routledge.

Cole, M. (1996). *Cultural psychology: A once and future discipline.* Cambridge, MA: Harvard University Press.

Cole, R., van Vuuren, S., Pellom, B., Hacioglu, K., Ma, J., and Movellan, J. (2003). Perceptive animated interfaces: First steps toward a new paradigm for human computer interaction. *Proceedings of the Institute of Electrical and Electronics Engineers, 91,* 1,391-1,405.

Coleman, C., and Gregg, N. (2005). *Assessing adult writing disorders: Beyond standardized test scores.* Paper presented at the 9th European Congress of Psychology, July, Granada, Spain.

Coleman, C., Gregg, N., McLain, L., and Belair, L. (2009). Spelling and writing fluency: A comparison of performance errors and verbosity across young adults with and without dyslexia. *Assessment for Effective Intervention, 34*(2), 94-105.

Coleman, J.S. (1990). *Foundations of social theory.* Cambridge, MA: Harvard University Press.

Collatos, A., Morrell, E., Nuno, A., and Lara, R. (2004). Critical sociology in K-16 early intervention: Remaking Latino pathways to higher education. *Journal of Hispanic Higher Education, 3*(2), 164-180.

Collier, V.P. (1987). Age and rate of acquisition of second language for academic purposes. *TESOL Quarterly, 21,* 617-641.

Collins, A., Brown, J.S., and Newman, S.E. (1989). Cognitive apprenticeship: Teaching the crafts of reading, writing, and mathematics. In L.B. Resnick (Ed.), *Knowing, learning, and instruction: Essays in honor of Robert Glaser* (pp. 453-494). Hillsdale, NJ: Lawrence Erlbaum Associates.

Collins, W.M., and Levy, B.A. (2008). Developing fluent text processing with practice: Memorial influences on fluency and comprehension. *Canadian Psychology, 49*(2), 133-139.

Collopy, R.M.B., and Bowman, P. (2005). *The impact of a six traits analytic writing model on student achievement.* Paper presented at the Annual Meeting of the American Educational Research Association.

Comings, J. (2009). Student persistence in adult literacy and numeracy programs. In S. Reder and J. Bynner (Eds.), *Tracking adult literacy and numeracy skills: Findings from longitudinal research* (pp. 160-176). New York: Routledge.

Comings, J., and Scoricone, L. (2007). *Adult literacy research: Opportunities and challenges.* Occasional Paper of the National Center for the Study of Adult Learning and Literacy, Harvard Graduate School of Education.

Conati, C. (2002). Probabilistic assessment of user's emotions in educational games. *Journal of Applied Artificial Intelligence, 16*, 555-575.

Conati, C., and VanLehn, K. (2000). Toward computer-based support of meta-cognitive skills: A computational framework to coach self-explanation. *International Journal of AI in Education, 11*, 398-415.

Conati, C., Gertner, A., and VanLehn, K. (2002). Using Bayesian networks to manage uncertainty in student modeling. *User Modeling and User-Adapted Interaction, 12*, 371-417.

Condelli, L. (2006). *A review of the literature in adult numeracy: Research and conceptual issues.* Washington, DC: U.S. Department of Education.

Condelli, L., and Wrigley, H.S. (2004). *Real world research: Combining qualitative and quantitative research for adult ESL.* Paper presented at the National Research and Development Centre Second International Conference for Adult Literacy and Numeracy, March 25-27, Loughborough, England. Available: http://www.leslla.org/publications. htm [Sept. 2011].

Condelli, L., Wrigley, H.S. and Yoon, K.W. (2009). "What works" for adult literacy students of English as a second language. Developing learners' reading skills in adult basic education programs. In S. Reder and J. Brynner (Eds.), *Tracking adult literacy and numeracy skills* (pp. 132-159). New York: Routledge.

Conley, M., Kerner, M., and Reynolds, J. (2005). Not a question of should, but a question of how: Literacy knowledge and practice into secondary teacher preparation through tutoring in urban middle schools. *Action in Teacher Education, 27*(2), 22-32.

Connell, J.P., and Wellborn, J.G. (1991). Competence, autonomy, and relatedness: A motivational analysis of self-system processes. In R. Gunnar and L.A. Sroufe (Eds.), *Minnesota symposia on child psychology* (vol. 23, pp. 43-77). Hillsdale, NJ: Lawrence Erlbaum Associates.

Connell, J.P., Spencer, M.B., and Aber, J.L. (1994). Educational risk and resilience in African American youth: Context, self, and action outcomes in school. *Child Development, 65*, 493-506.

Connelly, V., Dockrell, J., and Barnett, J. (2005). The slow hand writing of undergraduate students constrains performance in essay exams. *Educational Psychology, 25*, 99-107.

Connor, C.M., Morrison, F.J., and Katch, E.L. (2004). Beyond the reading wars: Exploring the effect of child-instruction interactions on growth in early reading. *Scientific Studies of Reading, 8*, 305-336.

Connor, C.M., Morrison, F.J., Fishman, B.J., Schatschneider, C., and Underwood, P. (2007). The early years: Algorithm-guided individualized reading instruction. *Science, 315*, 464-465.

Connor, C.M., Piasta, S.B., Fishman, B., Glasney, S., Schatschneider, C., Crowe, E., Underwood, P., and Morrison, F.J. (2009). Individualizing student instruction precisely: Effects of child by instruction interactions on first graders' literacy development. *Child Development, 80,* 77-100.

Constable, R.T., Pugh, K.R., Berroya E., Mencl, W.E.,Westerveld. M., Ni, W., and Shankweiler, D. (2004). Sentence complexity and input modality effects in sentence comprehension: An fMRI Study. *NeuroImage, 22,* 11-21.

Cook-Gumperz, J. (1986). Literacy and schooling: An unchanging equation? In J. Cook-Gumperz (Ed.), *The social construction of literacy* (pp. 16-44). Cambridge, England: Cambridge University Press.

Cooke, A., Grossman, M., DeVita, C., Gonzalez-Atavales, J., Moore, P., Chen, W., Gee, J., and Detre, J. (2006). *Brain and Language, 96,* 14-36.

Cooper, G., and Sweller, J. (1987). The effects of schema acquisition and rule automation on mathematical problem-solving transfer. *Journal of Educational Psychology, 79,* 347-362.

Corcoran, J. (2009). *The bridge to literacy: No child—or adult—left behind.* New York: Kaplan.

Coryell, J.E., and Chlup, D.T. (2007). Implementing e-learning components with adult English language learners: Vital factors and lessons learned. *Computer Assisted Language Learning, 20*(3), 263-278.

Coté, N., Goldman, S., and Saul, E.U. (1998). Students making sense of informational text: Relations between processing and representation. *Discourse Processes, 25,* 1-53.

Cottingham, S., Metcalf, K., and Phnuyal, B. (1998). The REFLECT approach to literacy and social change: A gender perspective. *Gender and Development, 6*(2), 27-34.

Cotugno, M. (2009). Encouraging GED students write now!: The studio as a bridge. *Adult Basic and Literacy Education Journal, 3*(3), 171-174.

Cowan, P. (1999). "Drawn" into the community: Re-considering the artwork of Latino adolescents. *Visual Studies, 14*(1), 91-107.

Cowan, P. (2004). Devils or angels: Literacy and discourse in lowrider culture. In J. Mahiri (Ed.), *What they don't learn in school: Literacy in the lives of urban youth* (pp. 47-74). New York: Peter Lang.

Craig, H.K., Zhang, L., Hensel, S.L., and Quinn, E.J. (2009). African American English-speaking students: An examination of the relationship between dialect shifting and reading outcomes. *Journal of Speech, Language, and Hearing Research, 52*(4), 839-855.

Craig, S.D., Sullins, J., Witherspoon, A., and Gholson, B. (2006). The deep-level reasoning effect: The role of dialogue and deep-level-reasoning questions during vicarious learning. *Cognition and Instruction, 24,* 565-591.

Craik, F.I.M., and Jennings, J.M. (1992). Human memory. In F.I.M. Craik and T.A. Salthouse (Eds.), *The handbook of aging and cognition* (pp. 51-110). Hillsdale, NJ: Lawrence Erlbaum Associates.

Craik, F.I.M., and Lockhart, R.S. (1972). Levels of processing: A framework for memory research. *Journal of Verbal Learning and Verbal Behavior, 11,* 671-684.

Craik, F.I.M., and Salthouse, T.A. (Eds.) (2000). *The handbook of aging and cognition* (2nd ed.). Mahwah, NJ: Lawrence Erlbaum Associates.

Crain, S., and Shankweiler, D. (1988). Syntactic complexity and reading acquisition. In A. Davison and G.M. Green (Eds.), *Linguistic complexity and text comprehension. Readability issues reconsidered* (pp. 167-192). Hillsdale, NJ: Lawrence Erlbaum Associates.

Cranton, P. (2000). *Planning instruction for adult learners.* Toronto: Wall and Emerson.

Crinion, J., Turner, R., Grogan, A., Hanakawa, T., Noppeney, U., Devlin, J.T., Aso, T., Urayama, S., Fukuyama, H., Stockton, K., Usui, K., Green, D.W., and Price, C.J. (2006). Language control in the bilingual brain. *Science, 312*(5,779), 1,537-1,540.

Crocker, J., Lee, S.J., and Park, L.E. (2004). The pursuit of self-esteem: Implications for good and evil. In A.G. Miller (Ed.), *The social psychology of good and evil* (pp. 271-302). New York: Guilford Press.

Cromley, J.G. (2000). Learning with computers: The theory behind the practice. *Focus on Basics, 4.* Boston: The National Center for the Study of Adult Learning and Literacy/ World Education.

Cromley, J.G., and Azevedo, R. (2007). Testing and refining the direct and inferential mediation model of reading comprehension. *Journal of Educational Psychology, 99*(2), 311-325.

Cromley, J.G., and Azevedo, R. (2009). Locating information with extended hypermedia. *Education Technology Research and Development, 57*(3), 287-313.

Cronbach, L.J., and Snow, R.E. (1977). *Aptitude and instructional methods: A handbook for research on interaction.* New York: Irvington.

Csikszentmihalyi, M. (1975). *Beyond boredom and anxiety.* San Francisco, CA: Jossey-Bass.

Csikszentmihalyi, M. (1990). *Flow: The psychology of optimal experience.* New York: Harper-Row.

Csikszentmihalyi, M., Abuhamdeh, S., and Nakamura, J. (2005). Flow. In A.J. Elliot and C.S. Dweck (Eds.), *Handbook of competence and motivation* (pp. 598-608). New York: Guilford Press.

Cull, W. L. (2000). Untangling the benefits of multiple study opportunities and repeated testing for cured recall. *Applied Cognitive Psychology, 14,* 215-235.

Cumming, A. (2001). Learning to write in a second language. *IJES, 1*(2), 1-23. Available: http://www.um.es/ijes/vol1n2/02-CUMMING.pdf [Sept. 2011].

Cumming, A. (in press). Writing development in second language acquisition. To appear in A. Ohta (Vol. Ed.) and C. Chapelle (Series Ed.), *Social, dynamic and complexity theory approaches to second language acquisition, encyclopedia of applied linguistics.* Malden, MA: Wiley-Blackwell.

Cumming, A., and Riazi, A. (2000). Building models of adult second-language writing instruction. *Learning and Instruction. Special Issue: Second Language Acquisition and Writing: A Multidisciplinary Perspective, 10*(1), 55-71.

Cunningham, A.E. and Stanovich, K.D. (1990). Assessing print exposure and orthographic processing skill in children: A quick measure of reading experience. *Journal of Educational Psychology, 82*(4), 733-740.

Cunningham, A.E., and Stanovich, K.E. (1998). What reading does for the mind. *American Educator, 22,* 8-15.

Cunningham, A.E., Perry, K.E., and Stanovich, K.E. (2001). Converging evidence for the concept of orthographic processing. *Reading and Writing, 14,* 549-568.

Curtis, M.E., and Longo, A.M. (2001). Teaching vocabulary to adolescents to improve comprehension. *Reading Online, 5*(4).

Cutler, L., and Graham, S. (2008). Primary grade writing instruction: A national survey. *Journal of Educational Psychology, 100,* 907-919.

Cutting, L.E., and Scarborough, H.S. (2006). Prediction of reading comprehension: Relative contributions of word recognition, language proficiency, and other cognitive skills can depend on how comprehension is measured. *Scientific Studies of Reading, 10*(3), 277-299.

Dahlin, E., Neely, A.S., Larsson, A., Bäckman, L., and Nyberg, L. (2008). Transfer of learning after updating training mediated by the striatum. *Science, 320,* 1,510-1,512.

Damasio, A.R. and Damasio, H. (1983). The anatomic basis of pure alexia. *American Academy of Neurology, 33,* 1,573.

D'Amico, D., and Schnee, E. (1997). "It changed something inside of me": English language learning, structural barriers to employment and workers' goals in a workplace literacy program. In G. Hull (Ed.), *Changing work, changing workers: Critical perspectives on language, literacy, and skills* (pp. 117-140). Albany, NY: State University of New York Press.

Daneman, M., and Merikle, P. M. (1996). Working memory and language comprehension: A meta-analysis. *Psychonomic Bulletin and Review, 3*(4), 422-433.

Daneman, M., Hannon, B., and Burton, C. (2006). Are there age-related differences in shallow semantic processing of text? Evidence from eye movements. *Discourse Processes, 42,* 177-203.

Daneman, M., Lennertz, T. and Hannon, B. (2007). Shallow semantic processing of text: Evidence from eye movements. *Language and Cognitive Processes, 22,* 83-105.

Daniel, S.S., Walsh, A.K., Goldston, D.B., Arnold, E.M., Reboussin, B.A., and Wood, F.B. (2006). Suicidality, school dropout, and reading problems among adolescents. *Journal of Learning Disaiblities, 39,* 507-514.

Dardour, M. (2000). The literacy campaign in rural Morocco: Drawing some lessons. Prospects. *Quarterly Review of Comparative Education, 30*(1), 125-142.

Darkenwald, G.G., and Valentine, T. (1985). Outcomes of participation in adult basic skills education. *Lifelong Learning, 8*(5), 17-22.

Davenport, J., and Davenport, J.A. (1985). A chronology and analysis of the andragogy debate. *Adult Education Quarterly, 35,* 152-159.

Davidson, R.K., and Strucker, J. (2002). Patterns of word-recognition errors among adult basic education native and nonnative speakers of English. *Scientific Studies of Reading, 6,* 299-316.

Davies, J., and Merchant, G. (2009). *Web 2.0 for schools: Learning and social participation.* New York: Peter Lang.

Daw, N.W. (1994). Mechanisms of plasticity in the visual cortex. *Investigative Ophthalmology, 35,* 4,168-4,179.

de Certeau, M. (1984). *The practice of everyday life.* Berkeley: University of California Press.

de Jong, E.J. (2004). After exit: Academic achievement patterns of former English language learners. *Educational Policy Analysis Archives, 12.* Available: http://epaa.asu.edu/epaa/v12n50/v12n50.pdf [Sept. 2011].

De La Paz, S., and Graham, S. (1995). Dictation: Applications to writing for students with learning disabilities. In T. Scruggs and M. Mastropieri (Eds.), *Advances in Learning and Behavioral Disabilities, 9,* 227-247. Greenwich, CT: JAI Press.

De La Paz, S., Swanson, P., and Graham, S. (1998). Contribution of executive control to the revising problems of students with writing and learning difficulties. *Journal of Educational Psychology, 90,* 448-460.

de Vega, M., Glenberg, A.M., and Graesser, A.C. (Eds.). (2008). *Symbols and embodiment: Debates on meaning and cognition.* Oxford, England: Oxford University Press.

Deacon, S.H., Parrila, R., and Kirby, J. (2006). Processing of derived forms in high-functioning dyslexics. *Annals of Dyslexia, 56*(1), 103-128.

Deacon, S.H., Wade-Woolley, L., and Kirby, J. (2007). Crossover: The role of morphological awareness in French immersion children's reading. *Developmental Psychology, 43*(3), 732-746.

DeCaro, M S., Rotar, K.E., Kendra, M.S., and Beilock, S.L. (2010). Diagnosing and alleviating the impact of performance pressure on mathematical problem solving. *The Quarterly Journal of Experimental Psychology: Human Experimental Psychology, 63*(8), 1,619-1,630.

DeCharms, R. (1968). *Personal causation.* New York: Academic Press.

Deci, E.L. (1972). Intrinsic motivation, extrinsic reinforcement, and inequity. *Journal of Personality and Social Psychology, 22*, 113-120.

Deci, E.L. (1975). *Intrinsic motivation.* New York: Plenum.

Deci, E.L., and Ryan, R.M. (1985). Intrinsic motivation and self-determination in human behavior. New York: Plenum.

Deci, E.L., and Ryan, R.M. (1987). The support of autonomy and the control of behavior. *Journal of Personality and Social Psychology, 53*, 1,024-1,037.

Deci, E., and Ryan, R.M. (2002a). *Handbook of self-determination research.* Rochester, NY: University of Rochester Press.

Deci, E.L., and Ryan, R.M. (2002b). The paradox of achievement: The harder you push, the worse it gets. In J. Aronson (Ed.), *Improving academic achievement: Impact of psychological factors on education* (pp. 61-87). Orlando, FL: Academic Press.

Deci, E., and Ryan, R.M. (2008). Facilitating optimal motivation and psychological well-being across life's domains. *Canadian Psychology, 49*, 14-23.

Deci, E.L., Schwartz, A.J., Sheinman, L., and Ryan, R.M. (1981). An instrument to assess adults' orientations toward control versus autonomy with children: Reflections on intrinsic motivation andf perceived competence. *Journal of Educational Psychology, 73*, 642-650.

Deci, E.L., Connell, J.P., and Ryan, R.M. (1989). Self-determination in a work organization. *Journal of Applied Psychology, 74*, 580-590.

Deci, E.L., Eghrari, H., Patrick, B.C., and Leone, D. (1994). Facilitating internalization: The self-determination theory perspective. *Journal of Personality, 62*, 119-142.

Deci, E.L., Koestner, R., and Ryan, R.M. (1999). The undermining effect is a reality after all—Extrinsic rewards, task interest, and self-determination: Reply to Eisenberger, Pierce, and Cameron (1999) and Lepper, Henderlong, and Gingras (1999). *Psychological Bulletin, 125*(6), 692-700.

Deci, E.L., Koestner, R., and Ryan, R.M. (2001). Extrinsic rewards and intrinsic motivation in education: Reconsidered once again. *Review of Educational Research, 71*(1), 1-27.

Deci, E.L., La Guardia, J.G., Moller, A.C., Scheiner, M.J., and Ryan, R.M. (2006). On the benefits of giving as well as receiving autonomy support: Mutuality in close friendships. *Personality and Social Psychology Bulletin, 32*, 313-327.

Dede, C., and Grotzer, T. (2009). *Black's Nook EcoMUVE: Learning about ecosystems complexity: Teacher guide.* Technical Report on Institute for Education Sciences Grant R305A080514, Harvard University, Cambridge, MA.

DeFries, J.C., and Baker, L.A. (1983). Parental contributions to longitudinal stability of cognitive measures in the Colorado family reading study. *Child Development, 54*(2), 388-395.

Dehaene, S. (2009). *Reading in the brain.* New York: Penguin.

Dehaene, S., Naccache, L., Cohen, L., Bihan, D.L., and Mangin J. (2001). Cerebral mechanisms of word masking and unconscious repetition priming, *Nature Neuroscience, 4*(7), 752-758.

Dejerine, J. (1891). Sur un cas de cécité verbale avec agraphie, suivi d'autopsie. *Comptes Rendus des Séances et Mémoires de la Société de Biologie, 4*, 61-90.

DeKeyser, R.M., and Sokalski, K.J. (1996). The differential role of comprehension and production practice. *Language Learning, 46*, 613-642.

Delgado-Gaitan, C. (1994). Socializing young children in Mexican-American families: An intergenerational perspective. In P.M. Greenfield and R. Cocking (Eds.), *Cross-cultural roots of minority child development* (pp. 55-87). Hillsdale, NJ: Lawrence Erlbaum Associates.

Delgado-Gaitan, C. (1996). *Protean literacy: Extending the discourse on empowerment.* London, England: The Falmer Press.

Delis, D.C., Kaplan, E., and Kramer, J.H. (2001). *Delis-Kaplan executive function system.* San Antonio, TX: Psychological Corporation.

Dellatolas, G., Braga, L.W., Souza, L.D. N., Filho, G.N., Queiroz, E., and DeLoache, G. (2003). Cognitive consequences of early phase of literacy. *Journal of the International Neuropsychological Society, 9*(5), 771-782.

Delpit, L. (1995). *Other people's children: Cultural conflict in the classroom.* New York: New Press.

Dempster, F.N. (1997). Distributing and managing the conditions of encoding and practice. In E.L. Bjork and R.A. Bjork (Eds), *Human memory* (pp. 197-236). San Diego, CA: Academic Press.

Denissen, J.J.A., Zarrett, N.R., and Eccles, J.S. (2007). I like to do it, I'm able, and I know I am: Longitudinal couplings between domain-specific ability/achievement, self-concept, and interests. *Child Development, 78,* 430-447.

Deno, S., Marston, D., and Mirkin, P. (1982). Valid measurement procedures for continuous evaluation of written expression. *Exceptional Children, 48,* 368-371.

Denzin, N.K., and Lincoln, Y.S. (Eds.). (2005). *The Sage handbook of qualitative research* (3rd ed.). Thousand Oaks, CA: Sage.

Derby, D.C. (2007). Predicting degree completion: Examining the interaction between orientation course participation and ethnic background. *Community College Journal of Research and Practice, 31*(11), 883-894.

Deshler, D.D., Ellis, E.S., and Lenz, B.K. (1996). *Teaching adolescents with learning disabilities: Strategies and methods, second edition.* Denver, CO: Love.

Detterman, D.K.S.R.J. (1993). *Transfer on trial: Intelligence, cognition, and instruction.* Norwood, NJ: Ablex.

Deul, R.K. (1992). Motor skill disorder. In S.R. Hooper, G.W. Hynd, and R.E. Mattison (Eds.), *Developmental disorders: Diagnostic criteria and clinical assessment* (pp. 239-282). Mahwah, NJ: Lawrence Erlbaum Associates.

Deutsch, G.K., Dougherty, R.F., Bammer, R., Siok, W.T., Gabrieli, J.D., and Wandell, B.A. (2005). Children's reading performance is correlated with white matter structure measured by diffusion tensor imaging. *Cortex,* 354-363.

Dickinson, C.M., and Rabbitt, P.M.A. (1991). Simulated visual impairment: Effects on text comprehension and reading speed. *Clinical Vision Science, 6,* 301-308.

Diehl, M., and Stroebe, W. (1987). Productivity loss in brainstorming groups: Toward the solution of a riddle. *Journal of Personality and Social Psychology, 53,* 497-509.

Dietrich, J.A., and Brady, S.A. (2001). Phonological representations of adult poor readers: An investigation of specificity and stability. *Applied Psycholinguistics, 22*(3), 383-418.

DiGennaro, K. (2008). Assessment of Generation 1.5 learners for placement into college writing courses. *Journal of Basic Writing, 27*(1), 61-79.

Dijkstra, K. Yaxley, R.H., Madden, C.J., and Zwaan, R.A. (2004). The role of age and perceptual symbols in language comprehension. *Psychology and Aging, 19,* 352-356.

Dillon, A., and Gabbard, R. (1998). Hypermedia as an educational technology: A review of the quantitative research literature on learner comprehension, control, and style. *Review of Educational Research, 68,* 322-349.

Dillon, J.T. (1988). The remedial status of student questioning. *Journal of Curriculum Studies, 20*(3), 197-210.

Dillon-Black, L. (1998). A rose abused: Literacy as transformation. *Journal of Adolescent and Adult Literacy, 42*(1), 20-24.

Dinsmore, D.L., Fox, E., Parkinson, M.M., and Rahman, T. (2010, April). *A deeper look at why readers succeed or fail.* Paper presented at the American Educational Research Association, Denver, CO.

Dirkx, J.M., and Jha, L.R. (1994). Completion and attrition in adult basic education: A test of two pragmatic prediction models. *Adult Education Quarterly, 45*(1), 269-285.

Dirkx, J.M., and Prenger, S.M. (1997). *A guide for planning and implementing instruction for adults: A theme-based approach.* San Francisco, CA: Jossey-Bass.

Dixon, R.A., and Gould, O.N. (1998). Younger and older adults collaborating on retelling everyday stories. *Applied Development Science, 2,* 160-171.

Dixon, R.A., and Hultsch, D.F. (1983). Structure and development of metamemory in adulthood. *Journals of Gerontology, 38*(6), 682-688.

D'Mello, S.K., and Graesser, A.C. (2010). Multimodal semi-automated affect detection from conversational cues, gross body language, and facial features. *User Modeling and User-Adapted Interaction, 20,* 187.

D'Mello, S.K., Craig, S.D., Witherspoon, A., McDaniel, B., and Graesser, A.C. (2008). Automatic detection of learner's affect from conversational cues. *User Modeling and User-Adapted Interaction, 18,* 45-80.

D'Mello, S.K., King, B., Chipman, P., and Graesser, A.C. (2010). Towards spoken human-computer tutorial dialogues. *Human Computer Interaction, 25*(4), 289-323.

Dockrell, J., Lindsay, G., and Connelly, V. (2009). The impact of specific language impairment on adolescents' written text. *Exceptional Children, 75,* 427-446.

Dodds, P.V.W., and Fletcher, J. D. (2004) Opportunities for new "smart" learning environments enabled by next generation web capabilities. *Journal of Education Multimedia and Hypermedia, 13*(4), 391-404.

Doignon, J.P., and Falmagne, J.C. (1999). *Knowledge spaces.* Berlin, Germany: Springer.

Donovan, C., and Smolkin, L. (2006). Children's understanding of genre and writing development. In C. MacArthur, S. Graham, and J. Fitzgerald (Eds.), *Handbook of writing research.* New York: Guilford Press.

Dougherty, R.F., Ben-Shachar, M., Deutsch, G.K., Hernandez, A., Fox, G.R., and Wandell, B.A. (2007). Temporal-callosal pathway diffusivity predicts phonological skills in children. *Proceedings of the National Academy of Sciences, 104,* 8,556-8,561.

Doupe, A.J., and Kuhl, P.K. (1999). Birdsong and human speech: Common themes and mechanisms. *Annual Review of Neuroscience, 22,* 567-631.

Dowden, T. (2007). Relevant, challenging, integrative and exploratory curriculum design: Perspectives from theory and practice for middle-level schooling in Australia. *Australian Educational Researcher, 34*(2), 51-71.

Draganski, B., Gaser, C., Busch, V., Schuierer, G., Bogdahn, U., and May, A. (2004). Changes in grey matter induced by training. *Nature, 427,* 311-312.

Draganski, B., Gaser, C., Kempermann, G., Kuhn, H.G., Winkler, J., Büchel, C., and May, A. (2006). Temporal and spatial dynamics of brain structure changes during extensive learning. *Journal of Neuroscience, 26*(23), 6,314-6,317.

Dressler, C., and Kamil, M.L. (2006). First- and second-language literacy. In D. August and T. Shanahan (Eds.), *Developing literacy in second-language learners: Report of the national literacy panel on language-minority children and youth* (pp. 197-238). Mahwah, NJ: Lawrence Erlbaum Associates.

Droop, M., and Verhoeven, L. (1998). Background knowledge, linguistic complexity, and second-language reading comprehension. *Journal of Literacy Research, 30*(2), 253-271.

Droop, M., and Verhoeven, L. (2003). Language proficiency and reading ability in first- and second-language learners. *Reading Research Quarterly, 38*(1), 78-103.

Duffy, G.G. (2005). Developing metacognitive teachers: Visioning and the expert's changing role in teacher education and professional development. In S.E. Israel, C.C. Block, K.L. Bauserman, and K. Kinnucan-Welsch (Eds.), *Metacognition in literacy learning: Theory, assessment, instruction, and professional development* (pp. 299-314). Mahwah, NJ: Lawrence Erlbaum Associates.

Duggan, G.B., and Payne, S.J. (2009). Text skimming: The process and effectiveness of foraging through text under time pressure. *Journal of Experimental Psychology: Applied, 15*, 228-242.

Duijnhouwer, H., Prins, F.J., and Stokking, K.M. (2010). Progress feedback effects on students' writing mastery goal, self-efficacy beliefs, and performance. *Educational Research and Evaluation, 16*(1), 53-74.

Duin, A., and Graves, M. (1987). Intensive vocabulary instruction as a prewriting technique. *Reading Research Quarterly, 22*, 311-330.

Duke, N.K., and Carlisle, J.F. (2011). The development of comprehension. In M.L. Kamil, P.D. Pearson, E.B. Moje, and P. Afflerbach (Eds.), *Handbook of reading research* (vol. IV, pp. 199-228). London, England: Routledge.

Duke, N.K., and Pearson, D. (2002). Effective practices for developing reading comprehension. In A.E. Farstrup and S.J. Samuels (Eds.). *What research has to say about reading instruction* (3rd ed., pp. 205-242). Newark, DE: International Reading Association.

Dunlosky, J., and Hertzog, C. (1998). Training programs to improve learning in later adulthood: Helping older adults educate themselves. In D.J. Hacker, J. Dunlosky, and A.C. Graesser (Eds.), *Metacognition in educational theory and practice* (pp. 249-275). Mahwah, NJ: Lawrence Erlbaum Associates.

Dunlosky, J., and Lipko, A. (2007). Metacomprehension: A brief history and how to improve its accuracy. *Current Directions in Psychological Science, 16*, 228-232.

Dunlosky, J., and Metcalfe, J. (2008). *Metacognition: A textbook for cognitive, educational, life span and applied psychology*. Thousand Oaks, CA: Sage.

Dunlosky, J., Kubat-Silman, A.K., and Hertzog, C. (2003). Training monitoring skills improves older adults' self-paced associative learning. *Psychology and Aging, 18*, 340-345.

Dunlosky, J., Hertzog, C., and Powell-Moman, A. (2005). The contribution of mediator-based deficiencies to age differences in associative learning. *Developmental Psychology, 41*, 389-400.

Durgunoğlu, A.Y. (2000). *Adult literacy: Issues of personal and community development*. Final report submitted to the Spencer Foundation, Chicago, IL.

Durgunoğlu, A.Y. (2002). Cross-linguistic transfer in literacy development and implications for language learners. *Annals of Dyslexia, 52*, 189-204.

Durgunoğlu, A.Y. (2009). *Effects of first language oral proficiency on second language (reading) comprehension*. Paper prepared for the National Research Council Workshop on the Role of Language in School Learning: Implications for Closing the Gap, October 15-16, Hewlett Foundation, Menlo Park, CA. Available: http://www7.nationalacademies.org/cfe/Paper_Aydin_Durgunoglu.pdf [Sept. 2011].

Durgunoğlu, A.Y., and Hughes, T. (in press). Preservice teachers' perceived preparedness, self-efficacy and English language learners. *International Journal of Teaching and Learning in Higher Education*.

Durgunoğlu, A.Y., and Oney, B. (1999). A cross-linguistic comparison of phonological awareness and word recognition. *Reading and Writing, 11*, 281-299.

Durgunoğlu, A.Y., and Oney, B. (2002). Phonological awareness in literacy development: It's not only for children. *Scientific Studies of Reading, 6*, 245-266.

Durgunoğlu, A.Y., Mir, M., and Arino-Marti, S. (2002). The relationship between bilingual children's reading and writing in their two languages. In S. Ransdell and M.L. Barbier (Eds), *Psycholinguistic approaches to understanding second-language writing* (pp. 81-100). Dordrecht, the Netherlands: Kluwer Academic Press.

Durgunoğlu, A.Y., Peynircioğlu, Z., and Mir, M. (2002). The role of formal definitions in reading comprehension of bilingual students. In R. Heredia and J. Altarriba (Eds), *Sentence processing in bilinguals* (pp. 299-316). Amsterdam, the Netherlands: Elsevier.

Durunoğlu, A.Y., Oney, B., and Kuscul, H. (2003). Development and evaluation of an adult literacy program in Turkey. *International Journal of Educational Development, 23*(1), 17-36.

Durik, A.M., Vida, M., and Eccles, J.S. (2006). Task values and ability beliefs as predictors of high school literacy choices: A developmental analysis. *Journal of Educational Psychology, 98*, 382-393.

Durkin, D. (1966). *Children who read early.* New York: Teachers College Press.

Dweck, C.S. (2002). Messages that motivate: How praise molds students' beliefs, motivation, and performance (in surprising ways). In J. Aronson (Ed.), *Improving academic achievement: Impact of psychological factors on education* (pp. 61-87). Orlando, FL: Academic Press.

Dweck, C.S. (2008). Can personality be changed? The role of beliefs in personality and change. *Current Directions in Psychological Science, 17*, 391-394.

Dweck, C.S., and Leggett, E.L. (1988). A social-cognitive approach to motivation and personality. *Psychological Review, 95*(2), 256-273.

Dymock, D. (2007). *Community adult language, literacy and numeracy provision in Australia: Diverse approaches and outcomes.* Research report. Adelaide, South Australia: National Centre for Vocational Education Research.

Dymock, D., and Billett, S. (2008). *Assessing and acknowledging learning through non-accredited community adult language, literacy and numeracy programs.* Research report. Adelaide, South Australia: National Centre for Vocational Education Research.

Dynarski, M., Agodini, R., Heaviside, S., Novak, T., Carey, N., Campuzano, L., Means, B., Murphy, R., Penuel, W., Javitz, H., Emery, D., and Sussex, W. (2007). *Effectiveness of reading and mathematics software products: Findings from the first student cohort.* Washington, DC: National Center for Educational Evaluation.

Dyson, A. (1995). Writing children: Reinventing the development of childhood literacy. *Written Communication, 12*, 4-46.

Eason, S.H., and Cutting, L.E. (2009). Examining sources of poor comprehension in older poor readers: Preliminary findings, issues, and challenges. In R.K. Wagner, C.S. Schatschneider, and C. Phythian-Sence (Eds.), *Beyond decoding: The behavioral and biological foundations of reading comprehension* (pp. 263-283). New York: Guilford Press.

Eccles, J.S., and Midgley, C. (1989). Stage/environment fit: Developmentally appropriate classrooms for early adolescents. In R.E. Ames and C. Ames (Eds.), *Research on motivation in education* (vol. 3, pp. 139-185). New York: Academic Press.

Eccles, J.S., and Wigfield, A. (2002). Motivational beliefs, values, and goals. *Annual Review of Psychology, 53*(1), 109-132.

Eccles, J.S., Adler, T.F., Futterman, R., Goff, S.B., Kaczala, C.M., Meece, J.L., and Midgley, C. (1983). Expectancies, values, and academic behaviors. In J.T. Spence (Ed.), *Achievement and achievement motivation* (pp. 75-146). San Francisco, CA: W.H. Freeman.

Eccles, J.S., Lord, S., and Midgley, C. (1991). What are we doing to early adolescents? The impact of educational contexts on early adolescents. *American Journal of Education, 99*, 521-542.

Eccles, J.S., Midgley, C., Wigfield, A., Miller-Buchannan, C., Reuman, D., Flanagan, C., and MacIver, D. (1993a). Development during adolescence: The impact of stage-environment fit on young adolescents' experiences in schools and families. *American Psychologist, 48*, 90-101.

Eccles, J.S., Wigfield, A., Midgley, C., Reuman, D., MacIver, D., and Feldlaufer, H. (1993b). Negative effects of traditional middle schools on students' motivation. *Elementary School Journal, 93*, 553-574.

Eckert, M.A., Leonard, C.M., Richards, T.L., Aylward, E.H., Thomson, J., and Berninger, V.W. (2003). Anatomical correlates of dyslexia: Frontal and cerebellar findings. *Brain, 126*, 482-494.

Eden, G.F., Jones, K.M., Cappell, K., Gareau, L., Wood., F.B., Zeffrio, T.A., Dietz, N.A.E., Agnew, J.A., and Flowers, D.L. (2004). Neural changes following remediation of adult developmental dyslexia. *Neuron, 44*, 411-422.

Edmonds, M.S., Vaughn, S., Wexler, J., Reutebuch, C.K., Cable, A., Tackett, K.K., and Schnackenberg, J.W. (2009). A synthesis of reading interventions and effects on reading comprehension outcomes for older struggling readers. *Review of Educational Research, 79*(1), 262-300.

Education Commission of the States (2000). *State funding for community colleges: A 50-state survey.* Denver, CO: Center for Community College Policy, Education Commission of the States.

Ehri, L.C. (1987). Learning to read and spell words. *Journal of Reading Behavior, 19*, 5-31.

Ehri, L.C. (1998). Grapheme-phoneme knowledge is essential for learning to read words in English. In J.L. Metsala and L.C. Ehri (Eds.), *Word recognition in beginning literacy* (pp. 3-40). Mahwah, NJ: Lawrence Erlbaum Associates.

Ehri, L.C., Nunes, S.R., Stahl, S.A., and Willows, D.M. (2001). Systematic phonics instruction helps students learn to read: Evidence from the National Reading Panel's meta-analysis. *Review of Educational Research, 71*(3), 393-447.

Eisenberger, R., Pierce, W.D., and Cameron, J. (1999). Effects of reward on intrinsic motivation—Negative, neutral, and positive: Comment on Deci, Koestner, and Ryan (1999). *Psychological Bulletin, 125*(6), 677-691.

Eisner, E.W. (1994). *Cognition and curriculum reconsidered* (2nd ed.). New York: Teachers College Press.

Ekkens, K., and Winke, P. (2009). Evaluating workplace English language programs. *Language Assessment Quarterly, 6*(4), 265-287.

Elbow, P. (1976). *Writing without teachers.* New York: Oxford University Press.

Elder, L., and Richard, P. (2002). Critical thinking: Teaching students how to study and learn. *Journal of Developmental Education, 26*, 34-35.

Elliot, A.J., and Dweck, C.S. (Eds.). (2005). *Handbook of competence and motivation.* New York: Guilford Press.

Elliot, A.J., and Harackiewicz, J.M. (1996). Approach and avoidance achievement goals and intrinsic motivation: A mediational analysis. *Journal of Personality and Social Psychology, 70*(3), 461-475.

Elliot, A.J., McGregor, H.A., and Gable, S. (1999). Achievement goals, study strategies, and exam performance: A mediational analysis. *Journal of Educational Psychology, 91*(3), 549-563.

Elliott, S. (2003). IntelliMetric: From here to validity. In M.D. Shermis and J. Burstein (Eds.), *Automated essay scoring: A cross-disciplinary perspective.* Hillsdale, NJ: Lawrence Erlbaum Associates.

Ellis, N. (2005). At the interface: Dynamic interactions of explicit and implicit language knowledge. *Studies in Second Language Acquisition, 27*(2), 305-352.

Ellis, R., Loewen, S., and Erlam, R. (2006). Implicit and explicit corrective feedback and the acquisition of L2 grammar. *Studies in Second Language Acquisition, 28*, 339-368.

Engeström, Y. (1987). *Learning by expanding: An activity-theoretical approach to developmental research.* Helsinki, Finland: Orienta-Konsultit Oy.

Englert, C.S. (1990). Unraveling the mysteries of writing through strategy instruction. In T.E. Scruggs and B.Y.L. Wond (Eds), *Intervention research in learning disabilities* (pp. 186-223). New York: Springer-Verlag.

Englert, C.S., and Thomas, C. (1987). Sensitivity to text structure in reading and writing: A comparison between learning disabled and non-learning disabled students. *Learning Disability Quarterly*, *10*, 93-105.

Englert, C.S., Mariage, T., Garmon, A., and Tarrant, K. (1988a). Accelerating reading progress in Early Literacy Project classrooms. *Learning Disability Quarterly*, *19*, 142-159, 180.

Englert, C.S., Raphael, T., Fear, K., and Anderson, L. (1988b). Students' metacognitive knowledge about how to write informational texts. *Learning Disability Quarterly*, *11*, 18-46.

Englert, C.S., Raphael, T., Anderson, L., Anthony, H., Stevens, D., and Fear, K. (1991). Making writing and self-talk visible: Cognitive strategy instruction in regular and special education classrooms. *American Educational Research Journal*, *28*, 337-373.

Englert, C.S., Garmon, A., Mariage, T., Rozendal, M., Tarrant, K., and Urba, J. (1995). The early literacy project: Connecting across the literacy curriculum. *Learning Disability Quarterly*, *18*, 253-275.

Englert, C.S., Mariage, T.V., Garmon, M.A., and Tarrant, K.L. (1998). Accelerating reading progress in early literacy project classrooms: Three exploratory studies. *Remedial and Special Education*, *19*(3), 142-159.

Englert, C.S., Mariage, T.V., and Dunsmore, K. (2006). Tenets of sociocultural theory in writing instruction research. In C.A. MacArthur, S. Graham, and J. Fitzgerald (Eds.), *Handbook of writing research* (pp. 208-221). New York: Guilford Press.

Engstrom, E.U. (2005). Reading, writing, and assistive technology: An integrated developmental curriculum for college students. *Journal of Adolescent and Adult Literacy*, *48*(1), 30-39.

Ercetin, G. (2003). Exploring ESL learners' use of hypermedia reading glosses. *CALICO Journal*, *20*(2), 261-283.

Erickson, F. (2004). Teaching, learning and research in "real reading": Some observations from a laboratory school. In J. Worthy, B. Maloch, J.V. Hoffman, D.L. Schallert, and C.M. Fairbanks (Eds.), *53rd yearbook of the national reading conference* (pp. 45-59). Oak Creek, WI: National Reading Conference.

Erickson, F., and Mohatt, G. (1982). Cultural organization of participation structures in two classrooms of Indian students. In G. Spindler (Ed.), *Doing the ethnography of schooling*. New York: Holt, Rinehart and Winston.

Erickson, K.I., Colcombe, S.J., Wadhwa, R., Bherer, L., Peterson, M.S., Scalf, P.E., Kim, J.S., Alvarado, M., and Kramer, A.F. (2007). Training induced functional activation changes in dual-task processing: An fMRI study. *Cerebral Cortex*, *17*(1), 192-204.

Ericsson, K.A. (2006). The influence in experience and deliberate practice on the development of superior expert performance. In K.A. Ericsson, N. Charness, P. J. Feltovich, and R.R. Hoffman (Eds.), *The Cambridge handbook of expertise and expert performance* (pp. 683-703). Cambridge, England: Cambridge University Press.

Ericsson, K.A., and Kintsch, W. (1994). *Long-term working memory*. Available: http://comminfo.rutgers.edu/~kantor/t/MLIS/551/public_dump/morris_a_11.html [Sept. 2011].

Ericsson, K.A., Krampe, R.Th., and Tesch-Römer, C. (1993). The role of deliberate practice in the acquisition of expert performance. *Psychological Review*, *100*, 363-406.

Evans, G.W., and Schamberg, M.A. (2009). Childhood poverty, chronic stress, and adult working memory. *Proceedings of the National Academy of Sciences*, *106*(16), 6,545-6,549.

Evans, K.S. (1996). A closer look at literature discussion groups: The influence of gender on student response and discourse. *The New Advocate*, *9*, 183-196.

Eves-Bowden, A. (2001). What basic writers think about writing. *Journal of Basic Writing*, *20*(2), 71-87.

Eviatar, Z., Ganayim, D., and Ibrahim, R. (2004). Orthography and the hemispheres: Visual and lilnguistic aspects of letter processing. *Neuropsychology*, *18*, 174-184.

Fallon, D. (1995). Making dialogue dialogic: A dialogic approach to adult literacy instruction. *Journal of Adolescent and Adult Literacy, 39*(2), 138-147.

Farrell, L., and Fenwick, T. (Eds.). (2007). *Educating the global workforce: Knowledge, knowledge work and knowledge workers.* World Yearbook of Education Series. London, England: Routledge.

Farver, J., Lonigan, C., and Eppe, S. (2009). Effective early literacy skill development for young Spanish-speaking English language learners: An experimental study of two methods. *Child Development, 80,* 703-719.

Federmeier, K.D., Van Petten, C., Schwartz, T.J., and Kutas, M. (2003). Sounds, words, sentences: Age-related changes across levels of language processing. *Psychology & Aging, 18,* 858-872.

Ferstl, E.C. (2006). The functional neuroanatomy of text comprehension: What's the story so far? In F. Schmalhofer and C. Perfetti (Eds.), *Higher level language processes in the brain: Inference and comprehension processes* (pp. 53-102). Mahwah, NJ: Lawrence Erlbaum Associates.

Ferstl, E.C., Neumann, J., Bogler, C., and Von Cramon, D.Y. (2008). The extended language network: A meta-analysis of neuroimaging studies on text comprehension. *Human Brain Mapping, 29*(5), 581-593.

Feyereisen, P. (2009). Enactment effects and integration processes in younger and older adults memory for actions. *Memory, 17,* 374-385.

Fiebach, C.J., Friederici, A.D., Müller, K., von Cramon, D.Y., and Hernandez, A.E. (2003). Distinct brain representations for early and late learned words. *NeuroImage, 19,* 627-637.

Fielding, L., and Pearson, P.D. (1994). Reading comprehension: What works. *Educational Leadership, 51*(5), 62-68.

Findley, M.J., and Cooper, H.M. (1983). Locus of control and academic achievement: A literature review. *Journal of Personality and Social Psychology, 44,* 419-247.

Fingeret, A. (1989). The social and historical context of participatory literacy education. In A. Fingeret and P. Jurmo (Eds.), *Participatory literacy education* (pp. 5-15). San Francisco, CA: Jossey-Bass.

Fingeret, A., and Drennon, C. (1997). *Literacy for life: Adult learners, new practices.* New York: Teachers College Press.

Fingeret, H.A., Tom, A., Dyer, P., Morley, A., Dawson, J., Harper, L., Lee, D., McCue, M., and Niks, M. (1994). *Lives of change: An ethnographic evaluation of two learner centered literacy programs.* Raleigh, NC: Literacy South.

Fiore, K., and Elsasser, N. (1987). "Strangers no more": A liberatory literacy curriculum. In I. Shore (Ed.), *Freire for the classroom: A sourcebook for liberatory teaching* (pp. 87-103). Portsmouth, NJ: Boynton/Cook.

Fisher, M.T. (2007). *Writing in rhythm: Spoken word poetry in urban classrooms.* New York: Teachers College Press.

Fitzgerald, J. (1995). English-as-a-second-language learners' cognitive reading processes: A review of research in the United States. *Review of Educational Research, 65,* 145-190.

Fitzgerald, J., and Markham, L. (1987). Teaching children about revision in writing. *Cognition and Instruction, 4,* 3-24.

Fitzgerald, J., and Shanahan, T. (2000). Reading and writing relations and their development. *Educational Psychologist, 35,* 39-50.

Fitzgerald, J., and Teasley, A. (1986). Effects of instruction in narrative structure on children's writing. *Journal of Educational Psychology, 78,* 424-432.

Fitzgerald, N.B., and Young, M.B. (1997). The influence of persistence on literacy learning in adult education. *Adult Education Quarterly, 47*(2), 78-91.

Flege, J.E., Yeni-Komshian, G.H., and Liu, S. (1999). Age constraints on second-language acquisition. *Journal of Memory and Language, 41*(1), 78-104.

Fleisher, L.S., Jenkins, J. R., and Pany, D. (1979). Effects on poor readers' comprehension of training in rapid decoding. *Reading Research Quarterly, 15*, 30-48.

Fletcher, J.D. (2002). Is it worth it? Some comments on research and technology in assessment and instruction. In National Research Council, *Technology and assessment: Thinking ahead, proceedings from a workshop* (Ch. 3, pp. 26-39). Board on Testing and Assessment, Center for Education. Division of Behavioral and Social Sciences and Education. Washington, DC: National Academy Press.

Fletcher, J.D. (2003). Evidence for learning from technology-assisted instruction. In H.F. O'Neil, Jr. and R. Perez (Eds.), *Technology applications in education: A learning view* (pp. 79-99). Hillsdale, NJ: Lawrence Erlbaum Associates.

Fletcher, J.D., and Tobias, S. (2007). *What research has to say (thus far) about designing computer games for learning.* Unpublished manuscript, Institute for Defense Analysis, Alexandria, VA.

Fletcher, J.D., Hawley, D.E., and Piele, P.K. (1990). Costs, effects, and utility of microcomputer assisted instruction in the classroom. *American Educational Research Journal, 27*(4), 783-806.

Fletcher, J.M., Denton, C., and Francis, D.J. (2005). Validity of alternative approaches for the identification of learning disabilities: Operationalizing unexpected achievement. *Journal of Learning Disabilities, 38*, 545-552.

Fletcher, J.M., Lyon, G.R., Fuchs, L.S., and Barnes, M.A. (2007). *Learning disabilities: From identification to intervention.* New York: Guilford Press.

Flower, L. (1979). Writer-based prose: A cognitive basis for problems in writing. *College English, 41*(1), 19-37.

Flowerday, T., Schraw, G., and Stevens, J. (2004). The role of choice and interest in reader engagement. *Journal of Experimental Education, 72*, 93-114.

Floyd, R.G., Gregg, N., Keith, T.Z., and Meisinger, E.C. (in review). *Explanation of reading comprehensionfrom early childhood using models from CHC theory: Support for integrative models of reading comprehension.* Unpublished manuscript, University of Memphis.

Flugman, B., Perin, D., and Spiegal, S. (2003). *An exploratory case study of 16-20-year old students in adult education programs.* New York: Center for Advanced Study of Education. Available: http://web.gc.cuny.edu/dept/case/adult_ed/Adult_Ed_TimesRoman_Final_Rpt.pdf [Sept. 2011].

Foley, D. (1990). *Learning capitalist culture: Deep in the heart of Tejas.* Philadelphia: University of Pennsylvania Press.

Foley, D. (1991). Reconsidering anthropological explanations of ethnic school failure. *Anthropology and Education Quarterly, 22*, 60-86.

Foley, W.A. (1999). Information structure. In K. Brown and J. Miller (Eds.), *Concise encyclopedia of grammatical categories* (pp. 204-213). Amsterdam, the Netherlands: Elsevier.

Foltz, P.W., Kintsch, W., and Landauer T.K. (1998). The measurement of textual coherence with latent semantic analysis. *Discourse Processes, 25*, 285-307.

Foorman, B.R. (1994). Phonological and orthographic processing: Separate but equal? In V.W. Berninger (Ed.), *The varieties of orthographic knowledge* (pp. 321-357). Dordrecht, the Netherlands: Kluwer Academic Press.

Foorman, B.R., Francis, D.J., Fletcher, J.M., Schatschneider, C., and Mehta, P. (1998). The role of instruction in learning to read: Preventing reading failure in at-risk children. *Journal of Educational Psychology, 90*(1), 37-55.

Foorman, B.R., Chen, D.-T., Carlson, C., Moats, L., Francis, D.J., and Fletcher, J.M. (2003). The necessity of the alphabetic principle to phonemic awareness instruction. *Reading and Writing, 16*(4), 289-324.

Foorman, B.R., Goldenberg, C., Carlson, C., Saunders, W., and Pollard-Durodola, S.D. (2004). How teachers allocate time during literacy instruction in primary-grade English language learner classrooms. In P. McCardle and V. Chhabra (Eds.), *The voice of evidence in reading research* (pp. 289-328). Baltimore, MD: Paul H. Brookes.

Forbus, K., Gentner, D., and Law, K. (1995). MAC/FAC: A model of similarity-based retrieval. *Cognitive Science, 19*, 141-205.

Ford, M.J., and Forman, E. (2006). Redefining disciplinary learning in classroom contexts. *Review of Research in Education, 30*(1), 1-32.

Fordham, S. (1996). *Blacked out.* New York: Routledge.

Forell, K. (2006). Ideas in practice: Bringin' hip-hop to the basics. *Journal of Developmental Education, 30*(2), 28-33.

Forman, E.A., Minick, N., and Stone, C.A. (Eds.). (1993). *Contexts for learning: Sociocultural dynamics in children's development.* New York: Oxford University Press.

Forness, S.R., Kavale, K.A., Blum, I.M., and Lloyd, J.W. (1997). What works in special education and related services: Using meta-analysis to guide practice. *Teaching Exceptional Children, 29*(6), 4-9.

Foucault, M. (1980). The order of discourse. In R. Young (Ed.), *Untying the text: A poststructuralist reader* (pp. 51-78). London, England: Routledge.

Fradd, S.H., Lee, O., Sutman, F.X., and Saxton, M.K. (2001). Promoting science literacy with English language learners through instructional materials development: A case study. *Bilingual Research Journal, 25*(4), 479-501.

Francis, D.J., Fletcher, J.M., Catts, H.W., and Tomblin, J.B. (2005). Dimensions affecting the assessment of reading comprehension. In S.A. Stahl and S.G. Paris (Eds.), *Children's reading comprehension and assessment* (pp. 369-394). Mahwah, NJ: Lawrence Erlbaum Associates.

Francis, D.J., Rivera, M., Lesaux, N., Kieffer, M., and Rivera, H. (2006). *Practical guidelines for the education of English language learners: Research-based recommendations for serving adolescent newcomers.* Portsmouth, NH: RMC Research Corporation, Center on Instruction. Available: http://www.centeroninstruction.org/files/ELL2-Newcomers.pdf [Sept. 2011].

Fredricks, J.A., Blumenfeld, P.C., and Paris, A.H. (2004). School engagement: Potential of the concept, state of the evidence. *Review of Educational Research, 74*(1), 49-109.

Freedman, S. (1994). *Exchanging writing, exchanging culture: Lessons in school reform from the United States and Great Britain.* Cambridge, MA: Harvard University Press.

Freire, P. (1970). *Pedagogy of the oppressed.* New York: Continuum.

Freund, A.M., and Baltes, P.B. (1998). Selection, optimization, and compensation as strategies of life management: Correlations with subjective indicators of successful aging. *Psychology and Aging, 13*, 531-543.

Freund, A.M., and Baltes, P.B. (2002). Life-management strategies of selection, optimization, and compensation: Measurement by self-report and construct validity. *Journal of Personality and Social Psychology, 82*, 642-662.

Friedlander, D., and Martinson, K. (1996). Effects of mandatory basic education for adult AFDC recipients. *Educational Evaluation and Policy Analysis, 18*(4), 327-337.

Friend, R. (2001). Teaching summarization as a content area reading strategy. *Journal of Adolescent and Adult Literacy, 44*(4), 320-329.

Frijters, J.C., Lovett, M.W., Steinbach, K.A., Wolf, M., Sevcik, R.A., and Morris, R. (2011). Cognitive and neuropsychological predictors of response to reading intervention. *Journal of Learning Disabilities, 44*(2), 150-166.

Frijters, J.C., Lovett, M.W., Sevcik, R.S., Donohue, D.K., and Morris, R.W. (in preparation). *Change in attributions for reading success and failure across associated with intensive reading intervention.* Brock University, Ontario, Canada.

Frith, U. (1980). Unexpected spelling problems. In U. Frith (Ed.), *Cognitive processes in spelling* (pp. 495-515). London, England: Academic Press.

Frost, R. (1998). Towards a strong phonological theory of visual word recognition: True issues and false trails. *Psychological Bulletin, 123*, 71-99.

Fuchs, D., and Fuchs, L.S. (2005). Peer-assisted learning strategies: Promoting word recognition, fluency, and reading comprehension in young children. *Journal of Special Education, 39*(1), 34-44.

Fuchs, L.S., and Fuchs, D. (2001). Principles for the prevention and intervention of mathematics difficulties. *Learning Disabilities: Research and Practice, 16*(2), 85-95.

Fuchs, L.S., Fuchs, D., Bentz, J., Phillips, N., and Hamlett, C. (1994). The nature of students' interactions during peer tutoring with and without prior training and experience. *American Educational Research Journal, 31*, 75-103.

Fuchs, L.S., Fuchs, D., and Kazdan, S. (1999). Effects of peer-assisted learning strategies on high school students with serious reading problems. *Remedial and Special Education, 20*, 309-318.

Fuchs, L.S., Fuchs, D., Kazdan, S., and Allen, S. (1999). Effects of peer-assisted learning strategies in reading with and without training in elaborated help giving. *Elementary School Journal, 99*, 201-219.

Fuller, C. (2009). "No disrespect": Literature discussion as social action in the adult education classroom. In R. Rogers, M. Mosley, and M.A. Kramer (Eds.), *Designing socially just learning communities* (pp. 76-87). New York: Routledge.

Furnham, A. (2009). The validity of a new self-report measure of multiple intelligence. *Current Psychology: Research and Reviews*, 225-239.

Gaber-Katz, E., and Watson, G.M. (1991). *The land that we dream of...: A participatory study of community-based literacy.* Toronto, Canada: OISE Press.

Gagne, R.M. (1985). *The conditions of learning and theory of instruction* (4th ed.). New York: Holt, Rinehart, and Winston.

Gagne, R.M., Wager, W.W., Golas, K.C., and Keller, J.M. (2005). *Principles of instructional design* (5th ed.). Belmont, CA: Wadsworth/Thompson Learning.

Galaburda, A.M. (2005). Dyslexia—A molecular disorder or neuronal migration: The 2004 Norman Geschwind memorial lecture. *Annals of Dyslexia, 55*(2), 151-165.

Galaburda, A.M., Sherman, G.F., Rosen, G.D., Aboitiz, and Geschwind, N. (1985). Developmental dyslexia: Four consecutive patients with cortical anomalies. *Annals of Enurology, 18*(2), 222-233.

Galaburda, A.M., LoTurco, J.J., Ramus, F, Fitch, R.H., and Rosen G.D. (2006). From genes to behavior in developmental dyslexia. *Nature Neuroscience, 9*(10), 1,213-1,217.

Galletta, A., and Cross, W.E., Jr. (2007). Past as present, present as past. Historicizing black eduation and interrogating "integration." In A. Fuligni (Ed.), *Contesting stereotypes and creating identities: Social categories, social identities, and educational participation* (pp. 15-41). New York: Russell Sage Foundation Press.

Gallo, M.L. (2004). *Reading the world of work: A learner-centered approach to workplace literacy and ESL.* Malabar, FL: Krieger.

Gao, X., Noh, S. R., Eskew, R.T., and Stine-Morrow, E.A.L. (2011). Visual noise disrupts conceptual integration in reading. *Psychonomic Bulletin and Review, 18*, 83-88.

Garcia, G.E. (1991). Factors influencing the English reading test performance of Spanish-speaking Hispanic children. *Reading Research Quarterly, 26*(4), 371-392.

García, J-N., and de Caso, A.M. (2004). Effects of a motivational intervention for improving the writing of children with learning disabilities. *Learning Disability Quarterly, 27*(3), 141-159.

Garcia-Sánchez, J.-N., and Fidalgo-Redondo, R. (2006). Effects of two types of self-regulatory instruction programs on students with learning disabilities in writing products, processes, and self-efficacy. *Learning Disability Quarterly, 29*(3), 181-211.

Gardner, H. (1983). *Frames of mind: The theory of multiple intelligences.* New York: Basic Books.

Gardner, H. (1999). *Intelligence reframed.* New York: Basic Books.Gardner, H. (2004). Audiences for the theory of multiple intelligences. *Teachers College Record, 106,* 212-220.

Garner, R., and Gillingham, M. (1996). *Conversations across time, space, and culture.* Mahwah, NJ: Lawrence Erlbaum Associates.

Garrod, S., and Pickering, M. (2004). Why is conversation so easy? *Trends in Cognitive Science, 8*(1), 8-11.

Garrison, D.R. (1997). Self-directed learning: Toward a comprehensive model. *Adult Education Quarterly, 48,* 18-33.

Gass, S.M., Svetics, I., and Lemelin, S. (2003). Differential effects of attention. *Language Learning, 5*(3), 497-545.

Gee, J.P. (1996). Discourses and literacies. In *Social linguistics and literacies: Ideology in discourses* (2nd ed., pp. 122-148). London, England: Taylor and Francis.

Gee, J.P. (2004a). New times and new literacies: Themes for a changing world. In A. Ball and S.W. Freedman (Eds.), *Bakhtinian perspectives on language, literacy, and learning* (pp. 279-306). Cambridge, England: Cambridge University Press.

Gee, J.P. (2004b). *What video games have to teach us about language and literacy.* New York: Palgrave Macmillan.

Gee, J.P. (2007). *What video games have to teach us about learning and literacy* (2nd ed., revised and updated). New York: Palgrave Macmillan.

Gee, J.P. (2009). Digital media and learning as an emerging field, part 1: How we got here. *International Journal of Learning and Media, 1*(2), 13-23.

Gee, J.P., Michaels, S., and O'Connor, M.C. (1992). Discourse analysis. In M.D. LeCompte, W.L. Millroy, and J. Preissle (Eds.), *The handbook of qualitative research in education* (pp. 227-291). San Diego: Academic Press.

Geier, R., Blumenfeld, P.C., Marx, R.W., Krajcik, J.S., Fishman, B., and Soloway, E. (2008). Standardized test outcomes for students engaged in inquiry-based science curriculum in the context of urban reform. *Journal of Research in Science Teaching, 45*(8), 922-939.

Genesee, F. (2001). Bilingual first language acquisition: Exploring the limits of the language faculty. *Annual Review of Applied Linguistics, 21,* 153-168.

Genesee, F., and Geva, E. (2006). Cross-linguistic relationships in working memory, phonological processes, and oral language. In D. August and T. Shanahan (Eds.), *Developing literacy in second-language learners: Report of the national literacy panel on language-minority children and youth* (pp. 175-183). Mahwah, NJ: Lawrence Erlbaum Associates.

Genesee, F., Lindholm-Leary, K., Saunders, W., and Christian, D. (2006). *Educating English language learners.* New York: Cambridge University Press.

Georgakopoulou, A. (2006a). The other side of the story: Towards a narrative analysis of narratives-in-interaction. *Discourse Studies, 8*(2), 235-257.

Georgakopoulou, A. (2006b). Thinking big with small stories in narrative and identity analysis. *Narrative Inquiry, 16*(1), 122-130.

Georgakopoulou, A. (2007). *Small stories, interaction and identities.* Amsterdam, the Netherlands: John Benjamins.

Gernsbacher, M.A., Varner, K.R., and Faust, M.E. (1990). Investigating differences in general comprehension skill. *Journal of Experimental Psychology: Learning, Memory, and Cognition, 16*(3), 430-445.

Gersten, R., Fuchs, L.S., Williams, J.P., and Baker, S. (2001). Teaching reading comprehension strategies to students with learning disabilities: A review of the research. *Review of Educational Research*, 71, 279-320.

Geschwind, N. (1965). Disconnection syndromes in animals and man. *Brain*, 88, 237-294.

Gholson, B., and Craig, S.D. (2006). Promoting constructive activities that support learning during computer-based instruction. *Educational Psychology Review*, 18, 119-139.

Gholson, B., Witherspoon, A., Morgan, B., Brittingham, J.K., Coles, R., Graesser, A. C., Sullins, J., and Craig, S.D. (2009). Exploring the deep-level reasoning questions effect during vicarious learning among eighth to eleventh graders in the domains of computer literacy and Newtonian physics. *Instructional Science*, 37, 487-493.

Gick, M.L., and Holyoak, K.J. (1980). Analogical problem solving. *Cognitive Psychology*, 12, 306-355.

Giedd, J.N., Castellanos, F.X., Rajapakse, J.C., Vaituzis, A.C., and Rapoport, J.L. (1997). Sexual dimorphism of the developing human brain. *Progress in Neuro-Psychopharmacology and Biological Psychiatry*, 21(8), 1,185-1,201.

Gilbert, J., and Graham, S. (2010). Teaching writing to elementary students in grades 4 to 6: A national survey. *Elementary School Journal*, 110, 494-518.

Gillespie, M. (2001). Research in writing: Implications for adult literacy. *Review of Adult Learning and Literacy*, 2(3). Available: http://www.ncsall.net?id=561 [Sept. 2011].

Glenberg, A.M. (1997). What memory is for? *Behavior and Brain Sciences*, 20, 1-55.

Glenberg, A.M., and Kaschak, M.P. (2002). Grounding language in action. *Psychonomic Bulletin and Review*, 9, 558-565.

Glenberg, A.M., and Robertson, D.A. (1999). Indexical understanding of instructions. *Discourse Processes*, 28, 1-26.

Glenberg, A.M., Gutierrez, T., Levin, J.R., Japuntich, S., and Kaschak, M.P. (2004). Activity and imagined activity can enhance young children's reading comprehension. *Journal of Educational Psychology*, 96, 424-436.

Glucksberg, S. (1962). The influence of strength of drive on functional fixedness and perceptual recognition. *Journal of Experimental Psychology*, 63, 36-41.

Gold, P.C., and Horn, P.L. (1982). Achievement in reading, verbal language, listening comprehension, and locus of control of adult illiterates in a volunteer tutorial project. *Perceptual and Motor Skills*, 54(3), 1,243-1,250.

Gold, P.C., and Johnson, J. A. (1982). Prediction of achievement in reading, self-esteem, auding and verbal language by adult illiterates in a psychoeducational tutorial program. *Journal of Clinical Psychology*, 38(3), 513-522.

Goldberg, A., Russell, M., and Cook, A. (2003). The effect of computers on student writing: A meta-analysis of studies from 1992 to 2002. *Journal of Technology, Learning, and Assessment*, 2(1), 1-51. Available: http://escholarship.bc.edu/jtla/vol2/1/ [Sept. 2011].

Goldblatt, E. (1995). *Round my way: Authority and double-consciousness in three urban high school writers*. Pittsburgh, PA: Pittsburgh University Press.

Golden, J.M. (1988). Text and the mediation of text. *Linguistics and Education*, 1(1), 19-43.

Goldenberg, C. (2008) Teaching English language learners. *American Educator*, summer, 8-44.

Goldman, S.R. (1997). Learning from text: Reflections on the past and suggestions for the future. *Discourse Processes*, 23, 357-398.

Goldman, S.R., and Hasselbring, T.S. (1997). Achieving meaningful mathematics literacy for students with learning disabilities. *Journal of Learning Disabilities*, 30(March/April), 198-208.

Goldman, S.R., Graesser, A.C., and van den Broek, P. (Eds.). (1999). *Narrative comprehension, causality, and coherence: Essays in honor of Tom Trabasso*. Mahwah, NJ: Lawrence Erlbaum Associates.

Goldman, S.R., Duschl, R.A., Ellenbogen, K., Williams, S., and Tzou, C.T. (2003). Science inquiry in a digital age: Possibilities for making thinking visible. In H. van Oostendorp (Ed.), *Cognition in a digital world* (pp. 253-284). Mahwah, NJ: Lawrence Erlbaum Associates.

Goldman, S. R., Lawless, K. A., Pellegrino, J. P., Braasch, J. L., Manning, F., and Gomez, K. (2011). A technology for assessing multiple source comprehension: An essential skill of the 21st century. In J. Clarke-Midura, M. Mayrath, and D. Robinson (Eds.), *Technology-based assessments for 21st century skills: Theoretical and practical implications from modern research*. Charlotte, NC: Information Age.

Goldrick-Rab, S. (2007). *Promoting academic momentum at community colleges: Challenges and opportunities*. CCRC Working Paper No. 5. New York: Community College Research Center, Teachers College, Columbia University.

Goldschmidt, M.M., Notzold, N., and Miller, C.Z. (2003). ESL student transition to college: The 30-hour program. *Journal of Developmental Education, 27*(2), 12-17.

Goldstone, R.L., and Sakamoto, Y. (2003). The transfer of abstract principles governing complex adaptive systems. *Cognitive Psychology, 46*, 414-466.

Goldstone, R.L, and Son, J.Y. (2005). The transfer of scientific principles using concrete and idealized simulations. *Journal of the Learning Sciences, 14*, 69-110.

Gomez, K., Gomez, L., Kwon, S., and Sherrer, J. (2007). Supporting reading-to-learn in science: The application of summarization technology in multicultural urban high school classrooms. In R. Bloymeyer, T. Ganesh, and H. Waxman (Eds.), *Research in technology use in multicultural settings*. Charlotte, NC: Information Age.

Goodyear, P., Jones, C., Asensio, M., Hodgson, V., and Steeples, C. (2005). Networked learning in higher education: Students' expectations and experiences. *Higher Education, 50*(3), 473-508.

Gopher, D., Weil, M., and Bareket, T. (1994). Transfer of skill from a computer game trainer to flight. *Human Factors, 36*, 387-405.

Gorard, S., Selwyn, N., and Williams, S. (2000). Must try harder! Problems facing technological solutions to non-participation in adult learning. *British Educational Research Journal, 26*(4), 507-521.

Gorard, S., Selwyn, N., and Madden, L. (2003). Logged on to learning: Assessing the impact of technology on participation in lifelong learning. *International Journal of Lifelong Education, 22*(3), 281-296.

Gordon, B.L. (2008). Requiring first-year writing classes to visit the writing center: Bad attitudes or positive results? *Teaching English in the Two-Year College, 36*(2), 154-163.

Gott, S.P., and Lesgold, A.M. (2000). Competence in the workplace: How cognitive performance models and situated instruction can accelerate skill acquisition. In R. Glaser (Ed.), *Advances in instructional psychology*. Hillsdale, NJ: Lawrence Erlbaum Associates.

Gottardo, A., and Mueller, J. (2009). Are first- and second-language factors related in predicting second-language reading comprehension? A study of Spanish-speaking children acquiring English as a second language from first to second grade. *Journal of Educational Psychology, 101*(2), 330-344.

Gottesman, R.L., Bennett, R.E., Nathan, R.G., and Kelly, M.S. (1996). Inner-city adults with severe reading difficulties: A closer look. *Journal of Learning Disabilities, 29*(6), 589-597.

Gough, P.B. (1996). How children learn to read and why they fail. *Annals of Dyslexia, 46*, 3-20.

Gough, P.B., and Tunmer, W.E. (1986). Decoding, reading, and reading disability. *RASE: Remedial and Special Education, 7*(1), 6-10.

Grabe, W., and Stoller, F.L. (2002). *Teaching and researching reading*. New York: Longman.

Graesser, A.C. (2007). An introduction to strategic reading comprehension. In D.S. McNamara (Ed.), *Reading comprehension strategies: Theories, interventions, and technologies* (pp. 3-26). New York: Lawrence Erlbaum Associates.

Graesser, A.C., and Bertus, E.L. (1998). The construction of causal inferences while reading expository texts on science and technology. *Scientific Studies of Reading, 2*, 247-269.

Graesser, A.C., and Forsyth, C. (in press). Discourse comprehension. In D. Reisberg (Ed.), *Oxford handbook of cognitive psychology.* Oxford, England: Oxford University Press.

Graesser, A.C., and King, B. (2008). Technology-based training. In National Research Council, *Human behavior in military contexts* (pp. 127-149). Committee on Opportunities in Basic Research in the Behavioral and Social Sciences for the U.S. Military. J.J. Blascovich and C.H. Hartel (Eds.). Board on Behavioral, Cognitive, and Sensory Sciences. Division of Behavioral and Social Sciences and Education. Washington, DC: The National Academies Press.

Graesser, A.C., and McMahen, C.L. (1993). Anomalous information triggers questions when adults solve problems and comprehend stories. *Journal of Educational Psychology, 85*, 136-151.

Graesser, A.C., and McNamara, D.S. (2010). Self-regulated learning in learning environments with pedagogical agents that interact in natural language. *Educational Psychologist, 45*(4), 234-244.

Graesser, A.C., and McNamara, D.S. (2011). Computational analyses of multilevel discourse comprehension. *Topics in Cognitive Science, 3*(2), 371-398.

Graesser, A.C., and Olde, B.A. (2003). How does one know whether a person understands a device? The quality of the questions the person asks when the device breaks down. *Journal of Educational Psychology, 95*, 524-536.

Graesser, A.C., and Ottati, V. (1996). Why stories? Some evidence, questions, and challenges. In R.S. Wyer (Ed.), *Knowledge and memory: The real story* (pp. 121-132). Hillsdale, NJ: Lawrence Erlbaum Associates.

Graesser, A.C., and Person, N.K. (1994). Question asking during tutoring. *American Educational Research Journal, 31*, 104-137.

Graesser, A.C., Haberlandt, K.F., and Koizumi, D. (1987). How is reading time influenced by knowledge-based inferences and world knowledge? In B. Britton and S.M. Glynn (Eds.), *Executive control processes in reading.* Hillsdale, NJ: Lawrence Erlbaum Associates.

Graesser, A.C., Singer, M., and Trabasso, T. (1994). Constructing inferences during narrative text comprehension. *Psychological Review, 101*, 371-395.

Graesser, A.C., Person, N.K., and Magliano, J.P. (1995). Collaborative dialogue patterns in naturalistic one-to-one tutoring. *Applied Cognitive Psychology, 9*, 1-28.

Graesser, A.C., Millis, K.K., and Zwaan, R.A. (1997). Discourse comprehension. *Annual Review of Psychology, 48*, 163-189.

Graesser, A.C., Olde, B., and Klettke, B. (2002). How does the mind construct and represent stories? In M.C. Green, J.J. Strange, and T.C. Brock (Eds.), *Narrative impact: Social and cognitive foundations* (pp. 231-263). Mahwah, NJ: Lawrence Erlbaum Associates.

Graesser, A.C., Gernsbacher, M.A., and Goldman, S.R. (Eds.). (2003). *Introduction to the handbook of discourse processes.* Mahwah, NJ: Lawrence Erlbaum Associates.

Graesser, A.C., McNamara, D.S., Louwerse, M.M., and Cai, Z. (2004). Coh-Metrix: Analysis of text on cohesion and language. *Behavior Research Methods, Instruments, and Computers, 36*(2), 193-202.

Graesser, A.C., McNamara, D.S., and VanLehn, K. (2005). Scaffolding deep comprehension strategies through PointandQuery, AutoTutor, and iSTART. *Educational Psychologist, 40*, 225-234.

Graesser, A.C., Lu, S., Olde, B.A., Cooper-Pye, E., and Whitten, S. (2005). Question asking and eye tracking during cognitive disequilibrium: Comprehending illustrated texts on devices when the devices break down. *Memory and Cognition, 33,* 1,235-1,247.

Graesser, A.C., Cai, Z., Louwerse, M., and Daniel, F. (2006). Question understanding aid (QUAID): A web facility that helps survey methodologists to improve the comprehensibility of questions. *Public Opinion Quarterly, 70,* 3-22.

Graesser, A.C., Halpern, D.F., and Hakel, M. (2007). *25 principles of learning.* Washington, DC: Taskforce on Lifelong Learning at Work and at Home. Available: http://www.psyc. memphis.edu/learning/whatweknow/index.shtml [Sept. 2011].

Graesser, A.C., Wiley, J., Goldman, S.R., O'Reilly, T., Jeon, M., and McDaniel, B. (2007). SEEK Web tutor: Fostering a critical stance while exploring the causes of volcanic eruption. *Metacognition and Learning, 2,* 89-105.

Graesser, A.C., Jeon, M., and Dufty, D. (2008). Agent technologies designed to facilitate interactive knowledge construction. *Discourse Processes, 45,* 298-322.

Graesser, A.C., D'Mello, S.K., and Person, N., (2009). Meta-knowledge in tutoring. In D.J. Hacker, J. Dunlosky, and A.C. Graesser (Eds.), *Metacognition in educational theory and practice.* Mahwah, NJ: Lawrence Erlbaum Associates.

Graff, H. (1987). *The legacies of literacy: Continuities and contradictions in western culture and society.* Bloomington: University of Indiana Press.

Graham, S. (1982). Written composition research and practice: A unified approach. *Focus on Exceptional Children, 14,* 1-16.

Graham, S. (1990a). On communicating low ability in the classroom. In S. Graham and V. Folkes (Eds.), *Attribution theory: Applications to achievement, mental health, and interpersonal conflict* (pp. 17-36). Hillsdale, NJ: Lawrence Erlbaum Associates.

Graham, S. (1990b). The role of production factors in learning disabled students'compositions. *Journal of Educational Psychology, 82,* 781-791.

Graham, S. (1997). Executive control in the revising of students with learning and writing difficulties. *Journal of Educational Psychology, 89,* 223-234.

Graham, S. (1999). Handwriting and spelling instruction for students with learning disabilities: A review. *Learning Disability Quarterly, 22,* 78-98.

Graham, S. (2000). Should the natural learning approach replace traditional spelling instruction. *Journal of Educational Psychology, 92,* 235-247.

Graham, S. (2006a). Strategy instruction and the teaching of writing. In C.A. MacArthur, S. Graham, and J. Fitzgerald (Eds.), *Handbook of writing research* (pp. 187-207). New York: Guilford Press.

Graham, S. (2006b). Writing. In P. Alexander and P. Winne (Eds.), *Handbook of educational psychology* (pp. 457-478). Mahwah, NJ: Lawrence Erlbaum Associates.

Graham, S., and Gilbert, J. (2010). Teaching writing to elementary students in grades 4 to 6: A national survey. *Elementary School Journal, 110*(4), 494-518.

Graham, S. and Harris, K. (1999). Assessment and intervention in overcoming writing difficulties: An illustration from the self-regulated strategy development model. *Language, Speech and Hearing Services in Schools, 30,* 255-264.

Graham, S., and Harris, K.R. (2000a). The role of self-regulation and transcription skills in writing and writing development. *Educational Psychologist, 35,* 3-12.

Graham, S., and Harris, K.R. (2000b). Writing development: Introduction to the special issue. *Educational Psychologist, 35*(1), 1.

Graham, S., and Harris, K.R. (2003). Students with learning disabilities and the process of writing: A meta-analysis of SRSD studies. In H.L. Swanson, K.R. Harris, and S. Graham (Eds.), *Handbook of learning disabilities* (pp. 323-344). New York: Guilford Press.

Graham, S., and Harris, K. (2005). *Writing better: Effective strategies for teaching students with learning disabilities.* Baltimore, MD: Paul H. Brookes.

Graham, S., and Hebert, M. (2010). *Writing to reading.* Washington, DC: Alliance for Excellence in Education.

Graham, S., and Perin, D. (2007a). A meta-analysis of writing instruction for adolescent students. *Journal of Educational Psychology, 99*(3), 445-476.

Graham, S., and Perin, D. (2007b). What we know, what we still need to know: Teaching adolescents to write. *Scientific Studies of Reading, 11*(4), 313-335.

Graham, S., and Perin, D. (2007c). *Writing next: Effective strategies to improve writing of adolescents in middle and high schools.* New York: Carnegie Corporation of New York.

Graham, S., and Weintraub, N. (1996). A review of handwriting research: Progress and prospects from 1980-1994. *Educational Psychology Review, 8*, 7-86.

Graham, S., Schwartz, S., and MacArthur, C. (1993). Knowledge of writing and the composing process, attitude toward writing, and the self-efficacy for students with and without learning disabilities. *Journal of Learning Disabilities, 26*, 237-249.

Graham, S., Berninger, V., Abbott, R., Abbott, S., and Whitaker, D. (1997). The role of mechanics in composing of elementary school students: A new methodological approach. *Journal of Educational Psychology, 89*, 170-182.

Graham, S., Berninger, V.W., Weintraub, N., and Schafer, W. (1998). The development of handwriting fluency and legibility in grades l through 9. *Journal of Educational Research, 92*, 42-52.

Graham, S., Harris, K.R., and Fink, B. (2000). Is handwriting causally related to learning to write? Treatment of handwriting problems in beginning writers. *Journal of Educational Psychology, 92*, 620-633.

Graham, S., Harris, K.R., and Fink-Chorzempa, B. (2002). Contribution of spelling instruction to the spelling, writing, and reading of poor spellers. *Journal of Educational Psychology, 94*, 669-686.

Graham, S., Harris, K.R., MacArthur, C., and Fink-Chorzempa, B. (2003). Primary grade teachers' instructional adaptations for weaker writers: A national survey. *Journal of Educational Psychology, 95*, 279-293.

Graham, S., Berninger, V., and Fan, W. (2007). The structural relationship between writing attitude and writing achievement in young children. *Contemporary Educational Psychology, 32*, 516-536.

Graham, S., Harris, K.R., and Olinghouse, N. (2007). Addressing executive function problems in writing: An example from the self-regulated strategy development model. In L. Meltzer (Ed.), *Executive function in education* (pp. 216-236). New York: Guilford Press.

Graham, S., Capizzi, A., Hebert, M., and Morphy, P. (2010). *Teaching writing to middle school students: A national survey.* Paper submitted for publication.

Grant, E., and Standing, L. (1989 Oct). Effects of rapid decoding training on reading speed and comprehension. *Perceptual and Motor Skills, 69*(2), 515-521.

Graves, D. (1983). *Writing: Teachers and children at work.* Exeter, NH: Heinemann.

Green, C.S., and Bavelier, D. (2003). Action video game modifies visual selective attention. *Nature, 423*, 534-537.

Green, J.L. (1983). Exploring classroom discourse: Linguistic perspectives on teaching-learning processes. *Educational Psychologist, 18*(3), 180-199.

Greenberg, D., Ehri, L.C., and Perin, D. (1997). Are word-reading processes the same or different in adult literacy students and third-fifth graders matched for reading level? *Journal of Educational Psychology, 89*, 262-275.

Greenberg, D., Ehri, L. C., and Perin, D. (2002). Do adult literacy students make the same word-reading and spelling errors as children matched for word-reading age? *Scientific Studies of Reading, 6*(3), 221-244.

Greenberg, D., Pae, H., Morris, R., Calhoon, M., and Nanda, A. (2009). Measuring adult literacy students' reading skills using the Gray Oral Reading Test. *Annals of Dyslexia, 59*(2), 133-149.

Greenberg, D., Morris, R., Wise, J., Nanda, A., and Pae, H. (2011). A randomized-control study of instructional approaches for struggling adult readers. *Journal of Research on Education Effectiveness, 4,* 101-117.

Greenhow, C., Robelia, B., and Hughes, J.E. (2009). Learning, teaching, and scholarship in a digital Age: Web 2.0 and classroom research: What path should we take now? *Educational Researcher, 38*(4), 246-259.

Greenleaf, C., Schoenbach, R., Cziko, C., and Mueller, F. (2001). Apprenticing adolescent readers to academic literacy. *Harvard Educational Review, 71*(1), 79-129.

Greeno, J.G., Smith, D.R., and Moore, J.L. (1993). Transfer of situated learning. In D.K. Detterman and R.J. Sternberg (Eds.), *Transfer on trial: Intelligence, cognition, and instruction* (pp. 99-167). Norwood, NJ: Ablex.

Gregg, L., and Steinberg, E. (Eds.). (1980). *Cognitive processes in writing.* Hillsdale, NJ: Lawrence Erlbaum Associates.

Gregg, N. (2007).Underserved and underprepared: Postsecondary learning disabilities. *Learning Disabilities Research and Practice, 22*(4), 219-228.

Gregg, N. (2009). *Adolescents and adults with learning disabilities and ADHD: Assessment and accommodations.* New York: Guilford Press.

Gregg, N. (in press). Increasing access to learning for the adult basic education learner with learning disabilities: Evidence-based accommodation research. *Journal of Learning Disabilities.*

Gregg, N., and Banerjee, M. (2005). Reading comprehension solutions for college students with dyslexia in an era of technology: An integrated approach. In G. Reid (Ed.), *The Routledge companion to dyslexia* (pp. 265-285). New York: Routledge.

Gregg, N., and Hartwig, J. (2005). Written expression assessment: An integrated approach. In S.W. Lee (Ed.), *Encyclopedia of school psychology* (pp. 590-600). New York: Sage.

Gregg, N., and McAlexander, P. (1989). The relation between sense of audience and specific learning disabilities: An exploration. *Annals of Dyslexia, 39,* 206-226.

Gregg, N., and Nelson, J. (in press). A meta-analysis of the test accommodation research specific to adolescents and adults with LD. *Journal of Learning Disabilities.*

Gregg, N., Hoy, C., McAlexander, P., and Hayes, C. (1991). Written sentence production error patterns of college writers with learning disabilities. *Reading and Writing: An Interdisciplinary Journal, 3,* 169-185.

Gregg, N., Sigalas, S., Hoy, C., Weisenbaker, J., and McKinley, C. (1996). Sense of audience and the adult writer: A study across competence levels. *Reading and Writing: An Interdisciplinary Journal, 8,* 121-137.

Gregg, N., Coleman, C., Stennett, R., Davis, M., Nielsen, K., Knight, D., and Hoy, C. (2002). Sublexical and lexical processing of young adults with learning disabilities and attention deficit/hyperactivity disorder. In E. Witruk, A.D. Friedrici, and T. Lachmann (Eds.), *Basic functions of language, reading, and reading disability* (pp. 329-358). Dordrecht, the Netherlands: Kluwer Academic Press.

Gregg, N., Coleman, C., and Knight, D. (2003). Learning disabilities assessment and the use of the WJ III. In F. Schrank and D. Flannigan (Eds.), *WJ III.* Hillside, NJ: Lawrence Erlbaum Associates.

Gregg, N., Hoy, C., Flaherty, D.A., Norris, P., Coleman, C., Davis, M., and Jordan, M. (2005). Documenting decoding and spelling accommodations for postsecondary students demonstrating dyslexia: It's more than processing speed. *Learning Disabilities: A Contemporary Journal, 3,* 1-17.

Gregg, N., Coleman, C., Davis, M., and Chalk, J.C. (2007). Timed essay writing: Implications for high-stakes tests. *Journal of Learning Disabilities, 40,* 306-318.

Gregg, N., Bandalos, D., Coleman, C., Davis, M., Robinson, K., and Blake, K. (2008).The validity of a battery of phonemic and orthographic awareness tasks for adults with and without dyslexia and attention deficit/hyperactivity disorder. *Remedial and Special Education, 29,* 175-190.

Grief, S., Meyer, B., and Burgess, A. (2007) *Effective teaching and learning: Writing.* NRDC Research Report. New York: National Resources Defense Council.

Griffin, P., and Cole, M. (1984). Current activity for the future: The zo-ped. In B. Rogoff and J. Wertsch (Eds.), *Children's learning in the "zone of proximal development"* (pp. 45-63). San Francisco, CA: Jossey-Bass.

Griffin, T.D., Wiley, J., and Thiede, K.W. (2008). Individual differences, rereading, and self-explanation: Concurrent processing and cue validity as constraints on metacognitive accuracy. *Memory and Cognition, 36,* 93-103.

Griffin, T.D., Jee, B.D., and Wiley, J. (2009). The effects of domain knowledge on metacomprehension accuracy. *Memory and Cognition, 37,* 1,001-1,013.

Grigg, W., Donahue, P., and Dion, G. (2007). *The nation's report card: 12th grade reading and mathematics.* NCES 2007-468. Washington, DC: U.S. Department of Education.

Grigorenko, E.L. (2004). Genetic bases of developmental dyslexia: A capsule review of heritability estimates. *Enfance, 3,* 273-287.

Grigorenko, E.L. (2009). Dynamic assessment and response to intervention: Two sides of the same coin. *Journal of Learning Disabilities, 42,* 111-132.

Grigorenko, E.L., and Naples, A.J. (2009). The devil is in the details: Decoding the genetics of reading. In P. McCardle and K. Pugh (Eds.), *Helping children learn to read: Current issues and new directions in the integration of cognition, neurobiology and genetics of reading and dyslexia* (pp. 133-148). New York: Psychological Press.

Grisso, T., Steinberg, L., Woolard, J., Cauffman, E., Scott, E., and Graham, S. (2003). Juveniles' competence to stand trial: A comparison of adolescents' and adults'capacities as trial defendants. *Law and Human Behavior, 27*(4), 333-363.

Groff, P. (1978). Children's oral language and their written composition. *Elementary School Journal, 78,* 180-191.

Grolnick, W.S., and Ryan, R.M. (1987). Autonomy in children's learning: An experimental and individual difference investigation. *Journal of Personality and Social Psychology, 52,* 890-898.

Grolnick, W.S., and Ryan, R.M. (1989). Parent styles associated with children's self-regulation and competence in school. *Journal of Educational Psychology, 81,* 143-154.

Grotzer, T.A. (2003). Learning to understand the forms of causality implicit in scientific explanations. *Studies in Science Education, 39,* 1-74.

Grubb, W.N. (1996). *Working in the middle: Strengthening education and training for the mid-skilled labor force.* San Francisco, CA: Jossey-Bass.

Grubb, W.N. (1999). *Honored but invisible: An inside look at teaching in community colleges.* New York: Routledge.

Grubb, W.N. (2008). *Narrowing the multiple achievement gaps in California: Ten goals for the long haul.* Paper prepared for the Superintendent of Public Instruction's P-16 Council. Available: http://www.closingtheachievementgap.org/cs/ctag/download/resources/88/Grubb_Paper.pdf?x-r=pcfile_d [Sept. 2011].

Grubb, W.N. (2010). *Outside the instructional triangle: Historical and institutional perspectives on remediation.* Paper commissioned by the Committee on Learning Sciences: Foundations and Applications to Adolescent and Adult Literacy, Division of Behavior and Social Sciences, and Education, National Research Council, Washington, DC.

Grubb, W.N., and Cox, R.D. (2005). Pedagogical alignment and curricular consistency: The challenges for developmental education. *New Directions for Community Colleges, 129,* 93-103.

Grubb, W.N., and Kalman, J. (1994). Relearning to earn: The role of remediation in vocational education and job training. *American Journal of Education, 103*(1), 54-93.

Grubb, W.N., and Kraskouskas, E. (1992). *A time to every purpose: Integrating occupational and academic instruction in community colleges and technical institutes.* Berkeley: National Center for Research in Vocational Education, University of California at Berkeley.

Guastello, E.F. (2001). Parents as partners: Improving children's writing. In W.M. Linek, E. G. Sturtevant, J.A.R. Dugan, and P.E. Linder (Eds.), *Celebrating the voices of literacy: Yearbook of the College Reading Association* (pp. 279-295). Readyville, TN: College Reading Association.

Guenther, J. (2002). *What makes "good" literacy and numeracy provision?: Case study research of regional Australia.* Melbourne: Adult Literacy and Numeracy Australian Research Consortium, Nathan Queensland Centre.

Guerrero, S., and Sire, B. (2001). Motivation to train from the workers' perspective: Example of French companies. *The International Journal of Human Resource Management, 12,* 988-1,004.

Guglielmi, R.S. (2008). Native language proficiency, English literacy, academic achievement, and occupational attainment in limited-English-proficient students: A latent growth modeling perspective. *Journal of Educational Psychology, 100*(2), 322-342.

Guglielmino, P.J., and Roberts, D.G. (1992). A comparison of self-directed learning readiness in U.S. and Hong Kong samples and the implications for job performance. *Human Resource Development Quarterly, 2,* 261-271.

Gumperz, J.J. (1972). Verbal strategies in multilingual communication. *Georgetown University round table on languages and linguistics, 1970.* Washington, DC: Georgetown University Press.

Gumperz, J.J. (1981). Conversational inferences and classroom learning. In J. Green and C. Wallat (Eds.), *Ethnographic approaches to face-to-face interaction* (pp. 3-23). Norwood, NJ: Ablex.

Gumperz, J.J. (1982). *Language and social identity.* Cambridge, England: Cambridge University Press.

Gustavson, L. (2007). *Youth learning on their own terms.* New York: Routledge.

Guthrie, J.T. (2004). Classroom contexts for engaged reading: An overview. In J.T. Guthrie, A. Wigfield, and K.C. Perencevich (Eds.), *Motivating reading comprehension: Concept-oriented reading instruction* (pp. 1-24). Mahwah, NJ: Lawrence Erlbaum Associates.

Guthrie, J.T., and Davis, M.H. (2003). Motivating struggling readers in middle school through an engagement model of classroom practice. *Reading and Writing Quarterly, 19,* 59-85.

Guthrie, J.T., and Humenick, N.M. (2004). Motivating students to read: Evidence for classroom practices that increase reading motivation and achievement. In P. McCardle and V. Chhabra (Eds.), *The voice of evidence in reading research* (pp. 329-354). Baltimore, MD: Paul H. Brookes.

Guthrie, J.T., and McCann, A.D. (1997). Characteristics of classrooms that promote motivations and strategies for learning. In J.T. Guthrie and A. Wigfield (Eds.), *Reading engagement: Motivating readers through integrated instruction* (pp. 128-134). Newark, DE: International Reading Association.

Guthrie, J.T., and Wigfield, A. (2000). Engagement and motivation in reading. In M.L. Kamil, P.B. Mosenthal, P.D. Pearson, and R. Barr (Eds.), *Handbook of reading research* (vol. III, pp. 403-422). New York: Lawrence Erlbaum Associates.

Guthrie, J.T., and Wigfield, A. (2005). Roles of motivation and engagement in reading com-prehension assessment. In S. Paris and S. Stahl (Eds.), *Children's reading comprehension and assessment* (pp. 187-213). Mahwah, NJ: Lawrence Erlbaum Associates.

Guthrie, J.T., Van Meter, P., McCann, A.D., Wigfield, A., Bennett, L., Poundstone, C.C., Rice, M.E., Faibisch, F.M., Hunt, B., and Mitchell, A.M. (1996). Growth in literacy engage-ment: Changes in motivations and strategies during concept-oriented reading instruction. *Reading Research Quarterly, 31*(3), 306-332.

Guthrie, J.T., Anderson, E., Alao, S., and Rinehart, J. (1999). Influences of concept-oriented reading instruction on strategy use and conceptual learning from text. *The Elementary School Journal, 99*(4), 343-366.

Guthrie, J.T., Wigfield, A., and Perencevich, K.C. (2004). *Motivating reading comprehension: Concept-oriented reading instruction.* Mahwah, NJ: Lawrence Erlbaum Associates.

Guthrie, J.T., Wigfield, A., Barbosa, P., Perencevich, K.C., Taboada, A., Davis, M.H., Scafiddi, N.T., and Tonks, S. (2004). Increasing reading comprehension and engagement through concept-oriented reading instruction. *Journal of Educational Psychology, 96*, 403-423.

Guthrie, J.T., Hoa, L.W., Wigfield, A., Tonks, S.M., and Perencevich, K.C. (2006a). From spark to fire: Can situational reading interest lead to long-term reading motivation? *Reading Research and Instruction, 45*, 91-113.

Guthrie, J.T., Wigfield, A., Humenick, N.M., Perencevich, K.C., Taboada, A., and Barbosa, P. (2006b). Influences of stimulating tasks on reading motivation and comprehension. *Journal of Educational Research, 99*(4), 232-245.

Guthrie, J.T., Taboada, A., and Coddington, C.S. (2007). Engagement practices for strategy learning in concept-oriented reading instruction. In D.S. McNamara (Ed.), *Reading com-prehension strategies: Theory, interventions, and technologies* (pp. 241-266). Mahwah, NJ: Lawrence Erlbaum Associates.

Guthrie, J.T., McRae, A., Coddington, C.S., Klauda, S.L., Wigfield, A., and Barbosa, P. (2009). Impacts of comprehensive reading instruction on diverse outcomes of low-achieving and high-achieving readers. *Journal of Learning Disabilities, 42*, 195-214.

Guthrie, J.T., Wigfield, A., and You, W. (in press). Instructional contexts for engagement and achievement in reading. In S. Christensen, A. Reschly, and C. Wylie (Eds.), *Handbook of research on student engagement.* New York: Springer Science.

Gutiérrez, K.D. (2008). Developing a sociocritical literacy in the third space. *Reading Research Quarterly, 43*(2), 148-164.

Gutiérrez, K.D., Rymes, B., and Larson, J. (1995). Script, counterscript, and underlife in the classroom: James Brown versus Brown v. Board of Education. *Harvard Educational Review, 65*, 445-471.

Gutiérrez, K.D., Baquedano-López, P., Alvarez, H., and Chiu, M. M. (1999). Building a culture of collaboration through hybrid language practices. *Theory into Practice, 38*(2), 87-93.

Haas, C., and Witte, S. (2001). Writing as embodied practice: The case of engineering stan-dards. *Journal of Business and Technical Communication, 15*(4), 413-457.

Haberlandt, K., and Graesser, A.C. (1985). Component processes in text comprehension and some of their interactions. *Journal of Experimental Psychology: General, 114*, 357-374.

Hacker, D.J., Dunlosky, J., and Graesser, A.C. (2009). *Handbook of metacognition in educa-tion.* New York: Routledge.

Hackman, D.A., and Farah, M.J. (2009). Socioeconomic status and the developing brain. *Trends in Cognitive Sciences, 13*(2), 65-73.

Hairston, W., Burdette, J., Flowers, D., and Wood, F. (2005). Altered temporal profile of visual-auditory multisensory interactions in dyslexia. *Experimental Brain Research, 166*(3-4), 474-480.

Hakel, M., and Halpern, D.F. (2005). How far can transfer go? Making transfer happen across physical, temporal, and conceptual space. In J. Mestre (Ed.), *Transfer of learning: From a modern multidisciplinary perspective* (pp. 357-370). Greenwich, CT: Information Age.

Hakuta, K. (1993). *Second-language acquisition, bilingual education, and prospects for a language-rich nation. Restructuring learning: 1990 summer institute papers and recommendations by the Council of Chief State School Officers.* Washington, DC: Council of Chief State School Officers.

Hakuta, K., Bialystok, E., and Wiley, E. (2003). Critical evidence: A test of the critical-period hypothesis for second-language acquisition. *Psychological Science, 14*, 31-38.

Hall, L.A. (2007). Understanding the silence: Struggling readers discuss decisions about reading expository text. *Journal of Educational Research, 100*(3), 132-141.

Hallenbeck, M.J. (1996). The cognitive strategy in writing: Welcome relief for adolescents with learning disabilities. *Learning Disabilities Research and Practice, 11*, 107-119.

Halliday, M.A.K. (1973). *Explorations in the functions of language.* New York: Elsevier.

Halliday, M.A.K., and Hasan, R. (1976). *Cohesion in English.* London, England: Longman.

Halvari, A.M., and Halvari, H. (2006). Motivational predictors of change in oral health: An experimental test of self-determination theory. *Motivation and Emotion, 30*, 295-306.

Hamada, M., and Koda, K. (2008). Influence of first language orthographic experience on second language decoding and word learning. *Language Learning, 58*(1), 1-31.

Hampson, M., Tokoglu, F., Sun, Z., Schafer, R.J., Skudlarski, P., Gore, J.C., and Constable, R.T. (2006). Connectivity-behavior analysis reveals that functional connectivity between left BA39 and Broca's area varies with reading ability. *NeuroImage, 31*, 513-519.

Hampton, K.N., Sessions, L.F., Her, E.J., and Rainie, L. (2009). *How the Internet and mobile phones impact Americans' social networks.* Available: http://pewresearch.org/pubs/1398/internet-mobile-phones-impact-american-social-networks [Sept. 2011].

Hamre, B.K., and Pianta, R.C. (2005). Can instructional and emotional support in the first-grade classroom make a difference for children at risk of school failure? *Child Development, 76*(5), 949-967.

Hand, B., Wallace, C., and Yang, E. (2004). Using the science writing heuristic to enhance learning outcomes from laboratory activities in seventh grade science: Quantitative and qualitative aspects. *International Journal of Science Education, 26*, 131-149.

Handley-More, D., Deitz, J., Billingsley, F.F., and Coggins, T.E. (2003). Facilitating written work using computer word processing and word prediction. *American Journal of Occupational Therapy, 57*, 139-151.

Hanley, J.E.B., Herron, C.A., and Cole, S.P. (1995). Using video as an advance organizer to a written passage in the FLES classroom. *The Modern Language Journal, 79*, 57-66.

Hannon, B., and Daneman, M. (2004). Shallow semantic processing of text: An individual-differences approach. *Discourse Processes, 37*, 187-204.

Hannon, P., Pahl, K., Bird, V., Taylor, C., and Birch, C. (2006). *Community-focused provision in adult literacy, numeracy and language: An exploratory study.* NRDC Research Report. London, England: National Research and Development Centre for Adult Literacy and Numeracy. Available: http://www.nrdc.org.uk/content.asp?CategoryID=440&ArticleID=359 [Sept. 2011].

Harackiewicz, J.M., Barron, K.E., Tauer, J.M., Carter, S.M., and Elliot, A.J. (2000). Short-term and long-term consequences of achievement goals: Predicting interest and performance over time. *Journal of Educational Psychology, 92*, 316-330.

Hardman, J.C. (1999). A community of learners: Cambodians in an adult ESL classroom. *Language Teaching Research, 3*, 145-66.

Hardre, P.L., and Reeve, J. (2003). A motivational model of rural students' intentions to persist in, versus drop out of, high school. *Journal of Educational Psychology, 95*, 347-356.

Hargittai, E., and Hinnant, A. (2008). Digital inequality: Differences in young adults' use of the Internet. *Communication Research, 35*(5), 602-621.

Harris, K.R., Graham, S., and Pressley, M. (1992). Cognitive-behavioral approaches in reading and written language: Developing self-regulated learners. In N.N. Singh and I.L. Beale (Eds.), *Learning disabilities: Nature, theory, and treatment* (pp. 415-451). New York: Springer-Verlag.

Harris, K.R., Graham, S., Reid, R., McElroy, K., and Hamby, R.S. (1994). Self-monitoring of attention versus self-monitoring of performance: Replication and cross-task comparison studies. *Learning Disability Quarterly, 17,* 121-138.

Harris, K.R., Graham, S., and Mason, L.H. (2006). Self-regulated strategy development for 2nd-grade students who struggle with writing. *American Educational Research Journal, 43,* 295-340.

Harrison, A.G., Larochette, A.-C., and Nichols, E. (2007). Students with learning disabilities in postsecondary education: Selected initial characteristics. *Exceptionality Education Canada, 17*(2), 135-154.

Hart, B., and Risley, T.R. (1992). American parenting of language-learning children: Persisting differences in family-child interactions observed in natural home environments. *Developmental Psychology, 28*(6), 1,096-1,105.

Hart, B., and Risley, T.R. (1995). *Meaningful differences in the everyday experiences of young American children.* Baltimore, MD: Paul H. Brookes.

Hart, E.R., and Speece, D.L. (1998). Reciprocal teaching goes to college: Effects for postsecondary students at risk for academic failure. *Journal of Educational Psychology 90,* 670-681.

Harter, S. (1999). *The construction of the self: A developmental perspective.* New York: Guilford Press.

Harter, S., Whitesell, N.R., and Kowalski, P. (1992). Individual differences in the effects of educational transitions on young adolescents' perceptions of competence and motivational orientation. *American Educational Research Journal, 29,* 777-808.

Hartley, J.T. (1988). Geriatric psycholinguistics: Syntactic limitations of oral and written language. In L.L. Light (Ed.), *Language, memory, and aging.* New York: Cambridge University Press.

Hartley, J.T., and Harris, J.L. (2001). Reading the typography of text. In J.L. Harris, A.G. Kamhi, and K.E. Pollack (Eds.), *Literacy in African American communities* (pp. 109-125). Mahwah, NJ: Lawrence Erlbaum Associates.

Hartley, J.T., Stojack, C.C., Mushaney, T.J., Annon, T.A.K., and Lee, D.W. (1994). Reading speed and prose memory in older and younger adults. *Psychology and Aging, 9*(2), 216-223.

Hassel, H., and Giordano, J.B. (2009). Transfer institutions, transfer of knowledge: The development of rhetorical adaptability and underprepared writers. *Teaching English in the Two-Year College, 37*(1), 24-40.

Hatcher, J., Snowling, M.J., and Griffiths, Y.M. (2002). Cognitive assessment of dyslexic students in higher education. *British Journal of Educational Psychology, 72,* 119-133.

Hayati, A.M., and Shariatifar, S. (2009). Mapping strategies. *Journal of College Reading and Learning, 39*(3), 53-67.

Hayes, E. (2000). Youth in adult literacy education programs. In J. Comings, B. Garner, and C. Smith (Eds.), *Annual review of adult learning and literacy* (vol. 1, pp. 74-10). San Francisco, CA: Jossey-Bass.

Hayes, J. (1996). A new framework for understanding cognition and affect in writing. In M. Levy and S. Ransdell (Eds.), *The science of writing: Theories, methods, individual differences, and applications* (pp. 1-27). Mahwah, NJ: Lawrence Erlbaum Associates.

Hayes, J.R., and Flower, L. (1980). Identifying the organization of writing processes. In L. Gregg and E. Steinberg (Eds.), *Cognitive processes in writing* (pp. 3-30). Hillsdale, NJ: Lawrence Erlbaum Associates.

Hayes, J.R., and Simon, H.A. (1977). Psychological differences among problem isomorphs. In J. Castellan, D.B. Pisoni, and G. Potts (Eds.), *Cognitive theory* (vol. 2). Hillsdale, NJ: Lawrence Erlbaum Associates.

Heath, S.B. (1982). What no bedtime story means: Narrative skills at home and school. *Language in Society, 11*(1), 49-76.

Heath, S.B. (1983). *Ways with words: Language, life, and work in communities and classrooms.* Cambridge, England: Cambridge University Press.

Heath, S.B. (1994). The children of Trackton's children: Spoken and written language in social change. In R.B. Ruddell, M.R. Ruddell, and H. Singer (Eds.), *Theoretical models and processes of reading* (4th ed., pp. 208-230). Newark, DE: International Reading Association.

Heath, S.B. (1998). *Living the arts through language and learning: A report on community-based youth organizations.* Americans for the Arts Monographs, vol. 2. Washington, DC: Americans for the Arts. Available: http://www.americansforthearts.org/NAPD/files/9603/Living%20the%20Arts%20Through%20Language%20and%20Learning%20(November%20'98).pdf [Sept. 2011].

Heath, S.B., and McLaughlin, M.W. (Eds.) (1993). *Identity and inner-city youth: Beyond ethnicity and gender.* New York: Teachers College Press.

Heckhausen, J. (1999). *Developmental regulation in adulthood.* New York: Cambridge University Press.

Heckhausen, J., Wrosch, C., and Schulz, R. (2010). A motivational theory of life-span development. *Psychological Review, 117*, 32-60.

Hegarty, M., and Just, A. (1993). Constructing mental models of machines from text and diagrams. *Journal of Memory and Language, 32*, 717-742.

Heider, R. (1958). *The psychology of interpersonal relations.* New York: Wiley.

Heinrich, A., Schneider, B.A., and Craik, F.I.M. (2008). Investigating the influence of continuous babble on auditory short-term memory performance. *Quarterly Journal of Experimental Psychology, 61*, 735-751.

Heller, C.E. (1997). *Until we are strong together: Women writers in the Tenderloin.* New York: Teachers College Press.

Henderlong, J., and Lepper, M.R. (2002). The effect of praise on children's intrinsic motivation: A review and synthesis. *Psychological Bulletin, 128*(5), 774-795.

Hensch, T.K. (2003). Controlling the critical period. *Neuroscience Research, 47*, 17-22.

Hernandez, A., Li, P., and MacWhinney, B. (2005). The emergence of competing modules in bilingualism. *TRENDS in Cognitive Science, 9*, 220-225.

Hertzog, C., and Dunlosky, J. (2004). Aging, metacognition, and cognitive control. In B. Ross (Ed.), *The psychology of learning and motivation* (vol. 45, pp. 215-251). New York: Elsevier.

Hertzog, C., and Hultsch, D.F. (2000). Metacognition in adulthood and old age. In F.I.M. Craik and T.A. Salthouse (Eds.), *The handbook of cognition and aging* (2nd ed., pp. 417-466). Mahwah, NJ: Lawrence Erlbaum Associates.

Hertzog, C., Touron, D.R., and Hines, J.C. (2007). Does a time-monitoring deficit influence older adults' delayed retrieval shift during skill acquisition? *Psychology and Aging, 22*, 607-624.

Hertzog, C., Kramer, A.F., Wilson, R.S., and Lindenberger, U. (2008). Enrichment effects on adult cognitive development: Can the functional capacity of older adults be preserved and enhanced? *Psychological Science in the Public Interest, 9*, 1-65.

Hess, T.M. (1994). Social cognition in adulthood: Aging-related changes in knowledge and processing mechanisms. *Developmental Review*, 14(4), 373-412.

Hess, T.M., and Slaughter, S.J. (1990). Schematic knowledge influences on memory for scene information in young and older adults. *Developmental Psychology*, 26, 855-865.

Hess, T.M., Auman, C., Colcombe, S.J., and Rahhal, T.A. (2003). The impact of stereotype threat on age differences in memory performance. *Journal of Gerontology: Psychological Sciences*, 58B, P3-P11.

Hetzroni, O.E., and Shrieber, B. (2004). Word processing as an assistive technology tool for enhancing academic outcomes of students with writing disabilities in the general classroom. *Journal of Learning Disabilities*, 37, 143-154.

Hicks, D. (2004). Growing up girl in working-poor America: Textures of language, poverty, and place. *ETHOS*, 32(2), 214-232.

Hidi, S. (1990). Interest and its contribution as a mental resource for learning. *Review of Educational Research*, 60, 549-571.

Hidi, S., and Boscolo, P. (2006). Motivation and writing. In C. MacArthur, S. Graham, and J. Fitzgerald (Eds.), *Handbook of Writing Research* (pp. 144-156). New York: Guilford Press.

Hidi, S., and Harackiewicz, J. M. (2000). Motivating the academically unmotivated: A critical issue for the 21st century. *Review of Educational Research*, 70, 151-179.

Hidi, S., Berndorff, D., and Ainley, M. (2002). Children's argument writing, interest and self-efficacy: An intervention study. *Learning and Instruction*, 12(4), 429-446.

Higgins, E.L., and Raskind, M.H. (1995). Compensatory effectiveness of speech recognition on the written composition performance of postsecondary students with learning disabilities. *Learning Disability Quarterly*, 18, 159-174.

Hillocks, G. (1986). *Research on written composition: New directions for teaching*. Urbana, IL: National Council of Teachers of English.

Hillocks, G. (2002). *The testing trap: How state writing assessments control learning*. New York: Teachers College Press.

Hinshelwood, J. (1917). *Congenital word blindness*. London, England: H.K. Lewis.

Hoadley, C.M. (2005). Design-based research methods and theory building: A case study of research with SpeakEasy. *Educational Technology*, 45(10), 42-47.

Hock, M.F., and Mellard, D.F. (2005). Reading comprehension strategies for adult literacy outcomes. *Journal of Adolescent and Adult Literacy*, 49(3), 192-200.

Hock, M.F., and Mellard, D.F. (2011). Efficacy of learning strategies instruction in adult education. *Journal of Research on Educational Effectiveness*, 4(2), 134-153.

Hock, M.F., Deshler, D.D., and Schumaker, J.B. (1999). Tutoring programs for academically underprepared college students: A review of the literature. *Journal of College Reading and Learning*, 29(2), 101-122.

Hodges, R., and White, W.G., Jr. (2001). Encouraging high-risk student participation in tutoring and supplemental instruction. *Journal of Developmental Education*, 24(3), 2-4, 6, 8, 10, 43.

Hofer, J., and Larson, P. (1997). Building community and skills through multilevel classes. *Focus on Basics*, 1(C). Available: http://ncsall.net/?id=445 [Sept. 2011].

Hohenshell, L.M., and Hand, B. (2006). Writing-to-learn-strategies in secondary school cell biology: A mixed method study. *International Journal of Science Education*, 28, 261-289.

Holland, D., and Leander, K. (2004). Ethnographic stduies of positioning and subjectivity: An introduction. *ETHOS*, 32(2), 127-139.

Holland, D., Lachicotte, W., Skinner, D., and Cain, C. (1998). *Identity and agency in cultural worlds*. Cambridge, MA: Harvard University Press.

Holliway, D., and McCutchen, D. (2004). Audience perspective in young writers' composing and revising. In L.Allal, L. Chanquoy, and P. Largy (Eds.), *Revision: Cognitive and
instructional processes* (pp. 87-101). Boston, MA: Kluwer.

Holmes,V.M., and Castles, A.E. (2001). Unexpectedly poor spelling in university students.
Scientific Studies of Reading, 5, 319-350.

Holmes, V.M., and Malone, N. (2004). Adult spelling strategies. *Reading and Writing, 17*(6),
537-566.

Holton, E.F., Wilson, L.S., and Bates, R.A. (2009). Toward the development of a generalized instrument to measure andragogy. *Human Resource Development Quarterly, 20*,
169-193.

Hooper, S., Swartz, C., Wakely, M., de Kruif, R., and Montgomery, J. (2002). Executive functioning in elementary school children with and without problems in written expression.
Journal of Learning Disabilities, 35, 57-68.

Hoover, W.A., and Gough, P.B. (1990). The simple view of reading. *Reading and Writing: An
Interdisciplinary Journal, 2*, 127-160.

Hornberger, N. (1989). Continua of biliteracy. *Review of Educational Research, 59*(3),
271-296.

Horney, M.A., and Anderson-Inman, L. (1994). The electro text project: Hypertext reading
patterns of middle school students. *Journal of Educational Multimedia and Hypermedia,
3*, 71-91.

Horney, M.A., and Anderson-Inman, L. (1999). Supported text in electronic reading environments. *Reading and Writing Quarterly, 15*, 127-168.

Horwitz, B., Rumsey, J.M., and Donohume, B.C. (1998). Functional connectivity of the
angular gyrus in normal reading and dyslexia. *Proceedings of the National Academy of
Sciences, 95*, 8,939-8,944.

Houchins, D.E., Jolivette, K., Krezmien, M.P., and Baltodano, H.M. (2008). A multi-state
study examining the impact of explicit reading instruction with incarcerated students.
Journal of Correctional Education, 59(1), 65-85.

Houck, C., and Billingsley, B. (1989). Written expression of students with and without learning disabilities: Differences across grades. *Journal of Learning Disabilities, 22*, 561-565.

Hsueh-chao, M.H., and Nation, P. (2000). Unknown vocabulary density and reading comprehension. *Reading in a Foreign Language, 13*(1), 403-430.

Hu, X., and Graesser, A. C. (2004). Human use regulatory affairs advisor (HURAA): Learning about research ethics with intelligent learning modules. *Behavior Research Methods,
Instruments, and Computers, 36*, 241-249.

Hua, H., and Burchfield, S. (2003). *The effect of integrated basic education programs on
women's social and economic well-being in Bolivia.* Paper presented at the Annual Meeting of the Comparative and International Education Society, March, New Orleans, LA.
Available: http://www.eric.ed.gov/PDFS/ED479954.pdf [Sept. 2011].

Hua, J., Tembe, W.D., and Dougherty, E.R. (2009). Performance of feature-selection methods
in the classification of highdimension data. *Pattern Recognition, 42*, 409-424.

Hughes, K.L., and Scott-Clayton, J. (2011). *Assessing developmental assessment in commu-
nity colleges.* CCRC Working Paper No. 19. New York: Community College Research
Center, Teachers College, Columbia University. Available: http://ccrc.tc.columbia.edu/
[Feb. 2011].

Hull, G. (1999). What's in a label? Complicating notions of the skills-poor worker. *Written
Communication, 16*(4), 379-411.

Hull, G., and Bartholomae, D. (1984). Basic writing: A survey. In M.G. Moran and R.F.
Lunsford (Eds.), *Research in composition and rhetoric* (pp. 265-302). Westport, CN:
Greenwood Press.

Hull, G., and Nelson, M. (2005). Locating the semiotic power of multimodality. *Written Communication*, 22(2), 224-262.

Hull, G., and Rose, M. (1989). Rethinking remediation: Towards a social/cognitive understanding of problematic reading and writing. *Written Communication*, 8, 139-154.

Hull, G., and Rose, M. (1990). This wooden shack place: The logic of an unconventional reading. *College Composition and Communication*, 41(3), 287-298.

Hull, G., and Schultz, K. (2001). Literacy and learning out of school: A review of theory and research. *Review of Educational Research*, 71(4), 575-611.

Hull, G., and Zacher, J. (2007). Enacting identities: An ethnography of a job training program. *Identity: An International Journal of Theory and Research*, 7(1), 71-102.

Hull, G., Kenney, N., Marple, S, and Forsman-Schneider, A. (2006). *Many versions of masculine: Explorations of boys' identity formation through multimodal composing in an after-school program*. Occasional Papers Series. New York: Robert F. Bowne Foundation.

Hull, G., Stornaiuolo, A., and Sahni, U. (2010). Cultural citizenship and cosmopolitan practice: Global youth communicate online. *English Education*, 42(4), 331-367.

Hulstijn, J., and Laufer, B. (2001). Some empirical evidence for the involvement load hypothesis in vocabulary acquisition. *Language Learning*, 51, 539-558.

Hultsch, D.F., and Dixon, R.A. (1983). The role of pre-experimental knowledge in text processing in adulthood. *Experimental Aging Research*, 9, 17-22.

Hunt, E., and Pellegrino, J.W. (2002). Issues, examples, and challenges in formative assessment. *New Directions for Teaching & Learning, 89*, 73.

Hunt, K. (1965). *Grammatical structures written at three grade levels*. Champaign, IL: National Council of Teachers of English.

Hurry, J., Brazier, L., Wilson, A., Emslie-Henry, R., and Snapes, K. (2010). *Improving the literacy and numeracy of young people in custody and in the community*. London, England: National Research and Development Centre for Adult Literacy and Numeracy.

Hymes, D.H. (1971). *On communicative competence*. Philadelphia: University of Pennsylvania Press.

Hymes, D.H. (1980). *Language in education: Ethnolinguistic essays*. Washington, DC: Center for Applied Linguistics.

Hymes, D.H. (1994). Toward ethnographies of communication. In J. Maybin (Ed.), *Language and literacy in social practice* (pp. 11-22). Clevedon, England: Open University.

Hynd-Shanahan, C., Holschuh, J.P., and Hubbard, B.P. (2004). Thinking like a historian: College students' reading of multiple historical documents. *Journal of Literacy Research*, 36(2), 141-176.

Indefrey, P., and Levelt, W.J. (2004). The spatial and temporal signatures of word production components. *Cognition*, 92, 101-144.

Institute of Medicine. (2004). *Health literacy: A prescription to end confusion*. Committee on Health Literacy. Board on Neuroscience and Behavioral Health. L. Nielsen-Bohlman, A.M. Panzer, and D.A. Kindig (Eds.). Washington, DC: The National Academies Press.

Israel, S.E., Block, C.C., Bauserman, K.L., and Kinnucan-Welsch, K. (2005). *Metacognition in literacy learning: Theory, assessment, instruction, and professional development*. Mahwah, NJ: Lawrence Erlbaum Associates.

Ito, M., Horst, H.A., Bittanti, M., Boyd, D., Herr-Stephenson, B., Lange, P.G., Pascoe, C.J., and Robinson, L., with Baumer, S., Cody, R., Mahendran, D., Martinez, K., Perkel, D., Sims, C., and Tripp, L. (2008). *Living and learning with new media: Summary of findings from the digital youth project*. Available: http://digitalyouth.ischool.berkeley.edu/report [Sept. 2011].

Ito, M., Baumer, S., Bittanti, M., Boyd, D., Cody, R., Herr-Stephenson, B., Horst, H.A., Lange, P.G., Mahendran, D., Martinez, K.Z., Pascoe, C.J., Perkel, D., Robinson, L., Sims, C., and Tripp, L., with Antin, J., Finn, M., Law, A., Manion, A., Mitnick. S., Scholssberg, D., and Yardi, S. (2009). *Hanging out, messing around, geeking out: Living and learning with new media.* Cambridge, MA: MIT Press.

Iyengar, S.S., and Lepper, M.R. (2000). When choice is demotivating: Can one desire too much of a good thing? *Journal of Personality and Social Psychology, 70,* 996-1,006.

Jacobs, J.E., Lanza, S., Osgood, D.W., Eccles, J.S., and Wigfield, A. (2002). Changes in children's self-competence and values: Gender and domain differences across grades one through twelve. *Child Development, 73*(2), 509-527.

Jacobson, E. (2008). Learning and collaborating in the adult literacy education wiki. *E-Learning, 5*(4), 370-383.

Jaeggi, S.M., Buschkuehl, M., Jonides, J., and Perrig, W. (2008). *Improving fluid intelligence with training on working memory.* Available: http://www.pnas.org/content/early/2008/04/25/0801268105.full.pdf+html [Sept. 2011].

James, K.H., and Gauthier, I. (2006). Letter processing automatically recruits a sensory-motor brain network. *Neuropsychologia, 44,* 2,937-2,949.

Janzen, J. (2007) Preparing teachers of second language reading. *TESOL Quarterly, 41*(4), 707-729.

Jenkins, D., Zeidenberg, M., and Kienzl, G.S. (2009). *Educational outcomes of the I-BEST, Washington State community and technical college system's integrated basic education and skills training program: Findings from a multivariate analysis.* CCRC Working Paper No. 16. New York: Community College Research Center, Teachers College, Columbia University. Available: http://www.eric.ed.gov/PDFS/ED505331.pdf [Sept. 2011].

Jenkins, H., Clinton, K., Purushotma, R., Robison, A.J., and Weigel, M. (2009). *Confronting the challenge of participatory culture: Media education for the 21st Century.* An occasional paper on digital media and learning. Available: http://digitallearning.macfound.org/atf/cf/%7B7E45C7E0-A3E0-4B89-AC9C-E807E1B0AE4E%7D/JENKINS_WHITE_PAPER.PDF [Sept. 2011].

Jensen, A.P. (1998). *The g factor: The science of mental ability.* Westport, CT: Praeger.

Jewitt, C., and Kress, G. (Eds.). (2003). *Multimodal literacy.* New York: Peter Lang.

Jiang, N. (2007). Selective integration of linguistic knowledge in adult second language learning. *Language Learning, 57,* 1-33.

Jiménez, R.T. (1997). The strategic reading abilities and potential of five low-literacy Latina/o readers in middle school. *Reading Research Quarterly, 32*(3), 224-243.

Jocson, K.M. (2008). *Youth poets: Empowering literacies in and out of schools.* New York: Peter Lang.

Johnson, E.B. (2002). *Contextual teaching and learning: What it is and why it's here to stay.* Thousand Oaks, CA: Corwin Press.

Johnson, F., Garza, S., and Ballmer, N. (2009). Theory to practice: Building the 21st century writing community. *Journal of College Reading and Learning, 39*(2), 83-92.

Johnson, J.S., and Newport, E.L. (1989). Critical period effects in second language learning: The influence of maturational state on the acquisition of English as a second language. *Cognitive Psychology, 21,* 60-99.

Johnson, L.W., and Valente, A. (2008). Tactical language and culture training systems: Using artificial intelligence to teach foreign languages and cultures. In *Proceedings of the Twentieth Conference on Innovative Applications of Artificial Intelligence.* Menlo Park, CA: AAAI Press.

Johnson, M.M.S., Schmidt, F.A., and Pietrukowicz, M. (1989). The memory advantages of the generation effect: Age and process differences. *Journal of Gerontology: Psychological Sciences, 44,* P91-P94.

Johnson, R.E. (2003). Aging and the remembering of text. *Developmental Review*, *23*(3), 261-346.

Johnson, W.L., and Beal, C. (2005). Iterative evaluation of a large-scale intelligent game for language learning. In C. Looi, G. McCalla, B. Bredeweg, and J. Breuker (Eds.), *Artificial intelligence in education: Supporting learning through intelligent and socially informed technology* (pp. 290-297). Amsterdam, the Netherlands: IOS Press.

Johnston, A.M., Barnes, M.A., and Desrochers, A. (2008). Reading comprehension: Developmental processes, individual differences, and interventions. *Canadian Psychology*, *49*(2), 125-132.

Johnstone, C.J., Altman, J., Thurlow, M.L., and Thompson, S.J. (2006). *A summary of research on the effects of test accommodations: 2002 through 2004*. Technical Report No. 45. Minneapolis: University of Minnesota, National Center on Educational Outcomes. Available: http://education.umn.edu/NCEO/OnlinePubs/Tech45/ [Sept. 2011].

Johnstone, C.J., Thompson, S.J., Bottsford-Miller, N.S., and Thurlow, M.L. (2008). Universal design and multimethod approaches to item review. *Educational Measurement: Issues and Practice*, *27*, 25-36.

Jopp, D., and Hertzog, C. (2007). Activities, self-referent memory beliefs and cognitive performance: Evidence for direct and mediated relations. *Psychology and Aging*, *22*, 811-825.

Juchniewicz, M.M. (2007). Beginning with literacy needs: Community college program development that considers individual students' contexts. *Community College Journal of Research and Practice*, *31*, 199-215.

Juel, C. (1988). Learning to read and write: A longitudinal study of 54 children from first through fourth grade. *Journal of Educational Psychology*, *80*, 437-447.

Juel, C., and Minden-Cupp, C. (2000). Learning to read words: Linguistic units and instructional strategies. *Reading Research Quarterly*, *35*, 458-492.

Jurafsky, D., and Martin, J.H. (2008). *Speech and language processing* (2nd ed.). Upper Saddle River, NJ: Prentice Hall.

Jurmo, P. (2004). Workplace literacy education: Definitions, purposes, and approaches. *Focus on Basics*, *7*(B), 22-26. Available: http://www.ncsall.net/?id=629 [Sept. 2011].

Just, M.A., and Carpenter, P.A. (1992). A capacity theory of comprehension: Individual differences in working memory. *Psychological Review*, *99*, 122-149.

Just, M.A., and Varma, S. (2007). The organization of thinking: What functional brain imaging reveals about the neuroarchitecture of complex cognition. *Cognitive, Affective, and Behavioral Neuroscience*, *7*, 153-191.

Just, M.A., Carpenter, P.A., and Varma, S. (1999). Computational modeling of high-level cognition and brain function. *Human Brain Mapping*, *8*(2-3), 128-136.

Justice, L.M., Mashburn, A., Pence, K., and Wiggins, A. (2008). Experimental evaluation of a comprehensive language-rich curriculum in at-risk preschools. *Journal of Speech, Language, and Hearing Research*, *51*, 1-19.

Kaakinen, J.K., and Hyönä, J. (2007). Perspective effects in repeated reading: An eye movement study. *Memory and Cognition*, *35*, 1,323-1,326.

Kaakinen, J.K., and Hyönä, J. (2008). Perspective-driven text comprehension. *Applied Cognitive Psychology*, *22*, 319-334.

Kaakinen, J.K., and Hyönä, J. (2010). Task effects on eye movements during reading. *Journal of Experimental Psychology: Learning, Memory, and Cognition*, *36*, 1,561-1,566.

Kaakinen, J.K., Hyönä, J., and Keenan, J.M. (2003). How prior knowledge, WMC, and relevance of information affect eye fixations in expository text. *Journal of Experimental Psychology: Learning, Memory, and Cognition*, *29*, 447-457.

Kafai, Y.B., Peppler, K., and Chiu, G. (2007). High tech programmers in low-income communities: Seeding reform in a community technology center. In C. Steinfield, B. Pentland, M. Ackerman, and N. Contractor (Eds.), *Communities and technologies* (pp. 545-564). New York: Springer.

Kafai, Y.B., Peppler, K.A., and Chapman, R.N. (2009). *The computer clubhouse: Constructionism and creativity in youth communities.* New York: Teachers College Press.

Kagitcibasi, C., Goksen, F., and Gulgoz, S. (2005). Functional adult literacy and empowerment of women: Impact of a functional literacy program in Turkey. *Journal of Adolescent and Adult Literacy, 48*(6), 472-489.

Kalchman, M., and Koedinger, K.R. (2005). Teaching and learning functions. In National Research Council, *How students learn: History, mathematics and science in the classroom* (pp. 351-396). Committee on *How People Learn*, A Targeted Report for Teachers. M.S. Donovan and J.D. Bransford (Eds.). Division of Behavioral and Social Sciences and Education. Washington, DC: The National Academies Press.

Kallenbach, S., and Viens, J. (2002). *Open to interpretation: Multiple intelligences theory in adult literacy education.* London, England: National Centre for the Study of Adult Learning and Literacy.

Kalyuga, S., Chandler, P., and Sweller, J. (1999). Managing split-attention and redundancy in multimedia instruction. *Applied Cognitive Psychology, 13,* 351-371.

Kalyuga, S., Chandler, P., Tuovinen, J., and Sweller, J. (2001). When problem solving is superior to studying worked examples. *Journal of Educational Psychology, 93,* 579-588.

Kambouri, M., Thomas, S., and Mellar, H. (2006). Playing the literacy game: A case study in adult education. *Learning, Media and Technology, 31*(4), 395-410.

Kamil, M.L. (2004). The current state of quantitative research. *Reading Research Quarterly, 39*(1), 100-108.

Kamil, M.L., Borman, G.D., Dole, J., Kral, C.C., Salinger, T., and Torgesen, J. (2008). *Improving adolescent literacy: Effective classroom and intervention practices: A practice guide.* NCEE No. 2008-4027. Washington, DC: Institute of Education Sciences, U.S. Department of Education. Available: http://ies.ed.gov/ncee/wwc/pdf/practiceguides/adlit_pg_082608.pdf [Sept. 2011].

Kang, S.H.K., McDermott, K.B., and Roediger, H.L. III. (2007). Test format and corrective feedback modify the effect of testing on long-term retention. *European Journal of Cognitive Psychology, 19,* 528-558.

Kanner, B.G., and Wertsch, J.V.(1991). Beyond a transmission model of communication. *Educational Psychology Review, 3*(2), 103-109.

Kaplan, A., Middleton, M.J., Urdan, T., and Midgley, C. (2002). Achievement goals and goal structures. In C. Midgley (Ed.), *Goals, goal structures, and patterns of adaptive learning* (pp. 21-53). Mahwah, NJ: Lawrence Erlbaum Associates.

Kaplan, D., and Walpole, S. (2005). A stage-sequential model of reading transitions: Evidence from the Early Childhood Longitudinal Study. *Journal of Educational Psychology, 97,* 551-563.

Kaplan, S., and Berman, M.G. (2010). Directed attention as a common resource for executive functioning and self-regulation. *Perspectives on Psychological Science, 5,* 43-57.

Karpicke, J.D., and Roediger, H.L. III. (2007). Repeated retrieval during learning is the key to long-term retention. *Journal of Memory and Language, 57,* 151-162.

Karweit, N. (1998). Contextual learning: A review and synthesis. In A.M. Milne (Ed.), *Educational reform and vocational education* (pp. 53-84). Washington, DC: U.S. Department of Education, Office of Educational Research and Improvement, and National Institute on Postsecondary Education, Libraries, and Lifelong Learning.

Kaspar, L.F. (1996). Writing to read: Enhancing ESL students' reading proficiency through written response to text. *Teaching English in the Two-Year College, 23,* 25-33.

Katanoda, K., Yoshikawa, K., and Sugishita, M. (2001). A functional MRI study on the neural substrates for writing. *Human Brain Mapping, 13*, 34-42.

Katz, S., Connelly, J., and Allbritton, D. (2003). Going beyond the problem given: How human tutors use post-solution discussions to support transfer. *International Journal of Artificial Intelligence in Education, 13*, 79-116.

Kauffman, J.M., and Hallahan, D.P. (Eds.). (2011). *Handbook of special education.* London, England: Routledge.

Kausler, D.H., Wiley, J.G., and Philips, P.L. (1990). Adult age differences in memory for massed and distributed repeated actions. *Psychology and Aging, 5*, 530-534.

Kavale, K.A., and Reese, J.H. (1992). The character of learning disabilities: An Iowa profile. *Learning Disability Quarterly, 15*, 74-94.

Kavanagh, J.F., and Mattingly, I.G. (Eds.). (1972). *Language by ear and eye.* Cambridge, MA: MIT Press.

Kebritchi, M., Hirumi, A., and Bai, H. (2010). The effect of modern mathematics computer games on mathematics achievement and class motivation. *Computers and Education, 55*, 427-443.

Keenan, J.M., Betjemann, R.S., and Olson, R.K. (2008). Reading comprehension tests vary in the skills they assess: Differential dependence on decoding and oral comprehension. *Scientific Studies of Reading, 12*(3), 281-300.

Keith, N., and Frese, M. (2008). Effectiveness of error management training: A meta-analysis. *Journal of Applied Psychology, 93*, 59-69.

Keller, T.A., and Just, M.A. (2009). Altering cortical connectivity: Remediation-induced changes in the white matter of poor readers. *Neuron, 64*(5), 624-631.

Keller, T.A., Carpenter, P.A., and Just, M.A. (2001). The neural basis of sentence comprehension: An fMRI examination of syntactic and lexical processing. *Cerebral Cortex, 11*, 223-237.

Kellogg, R. (1986). Designing idea processors for document composition. *Behavior Research, Methods, Instruments, and Computers, 18*, 118-128.

Kellogg, R. (1987). Effects of topic knowledge on the allocation of processing time and cognitive effort to writing processes. *Memory and Cognition, 15*, 256-266.

Kellogg, R. (1993a). Observations on the psychology of thinking and writing. *Composition Studies, 21*, 3-41.

Kellogg, R. (1993b). *The psychology of writing.* New York: Oxford University Press.

Kemmelmeier, M., and Oyserman, D. (2001). Gendered influence of downward social comparisons on current and possible selves. *Journal of Social Issues, 57*(1), 129-148.

Kemper, S. (1987). Syntactic complexity and elderly adults prose recall. *Experimental Aging Research, 13*(1-2), 47-52.

Kemper, S., Rash, S., Kynette, D., and Norman, S. (1990). Telling stories: The structure of adults' narratives. *European Journal of Cognitive Psychology, 2*(3), 205-228.

Kemper, S., Jackson, J.D., Cheung, H., and Anagnopoulos, C.A. (1993). Enhancing older adults' reading comprehension. *Discourse Processes, 15*, 405-428.

Kemper, S., Greiner, L.H., Marquis, J.G., Prenovost, K., and Mitzner, T.L. (2001). Language decline across the life span: Findings from the nun study. *Psychology and Aging, 16*(2), 227-239.

Kemple, J., Corrin, W., Nelson, E., Salinger, T., Herrmann, S., and Drummond, K. (2008). *The enhanced reading opportunities study: Early impacts and implementation findings.* Washington, DC: U.S. Department of Education, Institute of Education Sciences.

Kendeou, P., and van den Broek, P. (2005). The effects of readers' misconceptions on comprehension of science texts. *Journal of Educational Psychology, 97*, 235-245.

Kendeou, P., and van den Broek, P. (2007). The effects of prior knowledge in text structure on comprehension processes during reading scientific texts. *Memory and Cognition, 35,* 1,567-1,577.

Kendeou, P., Bohn-Gettler, C., White, M.J., and van den Broek, P. (2008). Children's inference generation across different media. *Journal of Research in Reading, 31*(3), 259-272.

Kerr, N.L., and Tindale, R.S. (2004). Group performance and decision making. *Annual Review of Psychology, 55,* 623-655.

Khatiwada, I., McLaughlin, J., Sum, A., and Palma, S. (2007, December). *The fiscal consequences of adult educational attainment.* Prepared for the National Commission on Adult Literacy. Boston, MA: Northeast University, Center for Labor Market Studies.

Kieffer, M.J. (2008). Catching up or falling behind? Initial English proficiency, concentrated poverty, and the reading growth of language minority learners in the United States. *Journal of Educational Psychology, 100*(4), 851-868.

Kim, I.-H., Anderson, R.C., Nguyen-Jahiel, K., and Archodidou, A. (2007). Discourse patterns during children's collaborative online discussions. *Journal of the Learning Sciences, 16,* 333-370.

Kim, J., Taft, M., and Davis, C. (2004). Orthographic-phonological links in the lexicon: When lexical and sublixical information conflict. *Reading and Writing: An International Journal, 17,* 187-218.

Kim, K.H.S., Relkin, N.R., Lee, K.-M., and Hirsch, J. (1997). Distinct cortical areas associated with native and second languages. *Nature, 388*(6,638), 171-174.

Kindler, A.L. (2002). *Survey of the states' limited English proficient students and available educational programs and services: 2000-2001summary report.* Washington, DC: National Clearinghouse for English Language Acquisition.

King, A. (1994). Guiding knowledge construction in the classroom: Effects of teaching children how to question and how to explain. *American Educational Research Journal, 31,* 338-368.

King, K.P. (2000). The adult ESL experience: Facilitating perspective transformation in the classroom. *Adult Basic Education, 10,* 69-89.

Kintsch, E., Coccamise, D., Franzke, M., Johnson, N., and Dooley, S. (2007). Summary street: Computer-guided summary writing. In T. Landauer, D.S. McNamara, S. Dennis, and W. Kintsch (Eds.), *Handbook of latent semantic analysis* (pp. 263-278). Mahwah, NJ: Lawrence Erlbaum Associates.

Kintsch, W. (1994). Text comprehension, memory, and learning. *American Psychologist, 49,* 294-303.

Kintsch, W. (1998). *Comprehension: A paradigm for cognition.* Cambridge, England: Cambridge University Press.

Kintsch, W., and van Dijk, T.A. (1978). Toward a model of text comprehension and production. *Psychological Review, 85,* 363-394.

Kintsch, W., and Vipond, D. (1979). Reading comprehension and readability in educational practice and psychological theory. In L.G. Nilsson (Ed.), *Perspectives on memory research* (pp. 329-366). Hillsdale, NJ: Lawrence Erlbaum Associates.

Kintsch, W., Welsch, D., Schmalhofer, F., and Zimny, S. (1990). Sentence memory: A theoretical analysis. *Journal of Memory and Language, 29*(2), 133-159.

Kirkpatrick, D.L. (1994). *Evaluation training programs. The four levels.* San Francisco, CA: Berrett-Koehler.

Kirsch, I., Jungeblut, A., Jenkins, L., and Kolstad, A. (2002). *Adult literacy in America: A first look at the findings of the National Adult Literacy Survey* (3rd ed.). NCES Report No. NCES 1993-275. Washington, DC: National Center for Education Statistics.

Kirsch, I., Braun, H., Yamamoto, K., and Sum, A. (2007). *America's perfect storm: Three forces changing our nation's future.* Princeton, NJ: Educational Testing Service.

Kirschner, P.A., Sweller, J., and Clark, R.E. (2006). Why minimal guidance during instruction does not work: An analysis of the failure of constructivist, discovery, problem-based, experiential, and inquiry-based teaching. *Educational Psychologist, 41,* 75-86.

Kiuhara, S.A., Graham, S., and Hawken, L.S. (2009). Teaching writing to high school students: A national survey. *Journal of Educational Psychology, 101*(1), 136-160.

Klahr, D. (2002). *Exploring science: The cognition and development of discovery processes.* Cambridge, MA: MIT Press.

Klassen, C. and Burnaby, B. (1993). "Those who know": Views on literacy among adult immigrants in Canada. *TESOL Quarterly, 27,* 377-397.

Klauda, S.L., and Guthrie, J.T. (2008). Relationships of three components of reading fluency to reading comprehension. *Journal of Educational Psychology, 100*(2), 310-321.

Klein, D., Milner, B., Zatorre, R., Zhoa, V., and Nikelski, J. (1999). Cerebral organization in bilinguals: A PET study of Chinese-English verb generation. *Neuroreport, 10,* 2,841-2,846.

Klein, D., Zatorre, R.J., Chen, J.-K., Milner, B., Crane, J., Belin, P., and Bouffard, M. (2006). Bilingual brain organization: A functional magnetic resonance adaptation study. *NeuroImage, 31,* 366-375.

Klein, P.D. (1999). Reopening inquiry into cognitive processes in writing-to-learn. *Educational Psychology Review, 11*(3), 203-270.

Kliegl, R., Smith, J., and Baltes, P.B. (1989). Testing-the-limits and the study of adult age differences in cognitive plasticity of a mnemonic skill. *Developmental Psychology, 25,* 247-256.

Klingberg, T., Hedehus, M., Temple, E., Salz, T., Gabrieli, J.D., Moseley, M.E., and Poldrack, R.A. (2000). Microstructure of temporo-parietal white matter as a basis for reading ability: Evidence from diffusion tensor magnetic resonance imaging. *Neuron, 25*(2), 493-500.

Klinger, J.K., and Vaughn, S. (1999). Students' perceptions of instruction in inclusion classrooms: Implications for students with learning disabilities. *Exceptional Children, 66,* 23-37.

Klingner, J.K., Artiles, A.J., and Méndez Barletta, L. (2006). English language learners who struggle with reading: Language acquisition or LD? *Journal of Learning Disabilities, 39*(2), 108-128.

Kluger, A.N., and DiNisi, A. (1996) Feedback interventions: Toward the understanding of a two-edged sword. *Current Directions in Psychological Science, 7*(3), 67-72.

Knobel, M. (1999). *Everyday literacies.* New York: Lang.

Knobel, M., and Lankshear, C. (2008). Digital literacy and participation in online social networking spaces. In C. Lankshear and M. Knobel (Eds.), *Digital literacies: Concepts, policies and practices* (pp. 247-278). New York: Peter Lang.

Knowles, M.S. (1970). *The modern practice of adult education: Andragogy versus pedagogy.* New York: Association Press.

Knowles, M.S., Holton, E.F., and Swanson, R.A. (2005). *The adult learner* (6th ed.). New York: Elsevier.

Knudson, R. (1991). Development and use of a writing attitude survey in grades 4 to 8. *Psychological Reports, 68,* 807-816.

Knudson, R. (1992). Development and application of a writing attitude survey for grades 1 to 3. *Psychological Reports, 70,* 711-720.

Knudson, R. (1995). Writing experiences, attitudes, and achievement of first to sixth graders. *Journal of Educational Research, 89,* 90-97.

Koda, K. (1999). Development of L2 intraword orthographic sensitivity and decoding skills. *Modern Language Journal, 83,* 51-64.

Koedinger, K.R., and Nathan, M.J. (2004). The real story behind story problems: Effects of representations on quantitative reasoning. *Journal of the Learning Sciences, 13*(2), 129-164.

Koedinger, K.R., Anderson, J.R., Hadley, W.H., and Mark, M. (1997). Intelligent tutoring goes to school in the big city. *International Journal of Artificial Intelligence in Education, 8,* 30-43.

Koestner, R., Losier, G. F., Vallerand, R. J., and Carducci, D. (1996). Identified and introjected forms of political internalization: Extending self-determination theory. *Journal of Personality and Social Psychology, 70,* 1,025-1,036.

Kohn, A. (1994). The truth about self-esteem. *Phi Delta Kappan,* 272-283. Available: http://www.alfiekohn.org/teaching/tase.htm [Sept. 2011].

Kohn, A. (1996). By all available means: Cameron and Pierce's defense of extrinsic motivators. *Review of Educational Research, 66*(1), 1-4.

Koriat, A., Ma'ayan, H., and Nussinson, R. (2006). The intricate relationship between monitoring and control in metacognition: Lessons for the cause-and-effect relationship between subjective experience and behavior. *Journal of Experimental Psychology: General, 135,* 36-69.

Kornell, N., and Bjork, R. (2007). The promise and perils of self-regulated study. *Psychonomic Bulletin and Review, 14,* 219-224.

Kornell, N., and Metcalfe, J. (2006). Study efficacy and the region of proximal learning framework. *Journal of Experimental Psychology: Learning, Memory, and Cognition, 32,* 609-622.

Kornell, N., Castel, A.D., Eich, T.S., and Bjork, R.A. (2010). Spacing as a friend of both memory and induction in young and old adults. *Psychology and Aging, 25,* 498-503.

Kotrlik, J.W., and Redmann, D.H. (2005). Extent of technology integration in instruction by adult basic education teachers. *Adult Education Quarterly, 55*(3), 200-219.

Kovacs, A., and Mehler, J. (2009). Flexible learning of multiple speech structures in bilingual infants. *Science, 325,* 611-612.

Kozeracki, C. (2005). Preparing faculty to meet the needs of developmental students. *New Directions for Community Colleges, 129,* 39-49.

Kozeracki, C.A., and Brooks, J.B. (2006). Emerging institutional support for developmental education. *New Directions for Community Colleges, 136,* 63-73.

Kozma, R. (2000). Reflections on the state of educational technology research and development. *Educational Technology Research and Development, 48*(1), 5-15.

Kozulin, A., and Gindis, B. (2007). Sociocultural theory and education of children with special needs. In H. Daniels, M, Cole, and J. Wertsch (Eds.), *The Cambridge companion to Vygotsky* (pp. 332-362). New York: Cambridge University Press.

Krajcik, J., Blumenfeld, P.C., Marx, R.W., Bass, K.M., and Fredricks, J. (1998). Inquiry in project-based science classrooms: Initial attempts by middle school students. *Journal of the Learning Sciences, 7,* 313-350.

Kramer, A.F., Larish, J.F., and Strayer, D.L. (1995). Training for attentional control in dual task settings: A comparison of young and old adults. *Journal of Experimental Psychology: Applied, 1,* 50-76.

Kramer, A.F., Larish, J.L., Weber, T.A., and Bardell, L. (1999). Training for executive control: Task coordination strategies and aging. In D. Gopher and A. Koriat (Eds.), *Attention and performance xvii: Cognitive regulation of performance: Interaction of theory and application* (pp. 617-652). Cambridge, MA: MIT Press.

Kramer, M.A., and Jones, R. (2009). Designing a critical literacy lab in an adult education center. In R. Rogers, M. Mosley, and M.A. Kramer (Eds.), *Designing socially just learning communities: Critical literacy education across the lifespan* (pp. 113-124). New York: Routledge.

Krampe, R.T., and Charness, N. (2006). Aging and expertise. In K.A. Ericsson, N. Charness, P.J. Feltovich, and R.R. Hoffman (Eds.), *The Cambridge handbook of expertise and expert performance* (pp. 723-742). New York: Cambridge University Press.

Krapp, A., Hidi, S., and Renninger, K.A. (1992). Interest, learning, and development. In K.A. Renninger, S. Hidi, and A. Krapp (Eds.), *The role of interest in learning and development* (pp. 3-25). Hillsdale, NJ: Lawrence Erlbaum Associates.

Kress, G. (2003). *Literacy in the new media age.* London, England: Routledge.

Kroll, J.F., and Linck, J.A. (2007). Representation and skill in second language learners and proficient bilinguals. In I. Kecskes and L. Albertazzi (Eds.), *Cognitive aspects of bilingualism* (pp. 237-269). New York: Springer.

Kronbichler, M., Wimmer, H., Staffen, W., Hutzler, F., Mair, A., and Gunther, L. (2008). Developmental dyslexia: Gray matter abnormalities in occipitotemporal cortex. *Human Brain Mapping, 29,* 613-625.

Kruidenier, J.J. (2002). *Research-based principles for adult basic education: Reading instruction.* Available http://www.nifl.gov/publications/pdf/adult_ed_02.pdf [Sept. 2011].

Kruidenier, J.J., MacArthur, C.A., and Wrigley, H.S. (2010). *Adult education literacy instruction: A review of the research.* Washington, DC: National Institute for Literacy.

Kucer, S.B. (2001). *Dimensions of literacy: A conceptual base for teaching reading and writing in school settings.* Mahwah, NJ: Lawrence Erlbaum Associates.

Kuhn, M.R., and Stahl, S.A. (2003). Fluency: A review of developmental and remedial practices. *Journal of Educational Psychology, 95*(1), 22-40.

Kuhn, M.R., Schwanenflugel, P.J., Morris, R.D., Morrow, L.M., Woo, D.G., Meisinger, E.B., Sevcik, R.A., Bradley, B.A., and Stahl, S.A. (2006). Teaching children to become fluent and automatic readers. *Journal of Literacy Research, 38*(4), 357-387.

Kulik, C.-L. C., and Kulik, J.A. (1991). Effectiveness of computer-based instruction: An updated analysis. *Computers in Human Behaviour, 7,* 75-94.

Kuperberg, G.R., Sitnikova, T., and Lakshmanan, B.M. (2008). Neuroanatomical distinctions within the semantic system during sentence comprehension: Evidence from functional magnetic resonance imaging. *NeuroImage, 40,* 367-388.

Kutner, M., Greenberg, E., and Bauer, J. (2005). *National Assessment of Adult Literacy (NAAL): A first look at the literacy of America's adults in the 21st century.* NCES 2006-470. Washington, DC: National Center for Education Statistics. Available: http://nces.ed.gov/NAAL/PDF/2006470.PDF [Sept. 2011].

Kutner, M. Greenberg, E., Jin, Y., and Paulsen, C. (2006). *The health literacy of American adults: Results from the 2003 National Assessment of Adult Literacy.* NCES 2006-483. Washington, DC: National Center for Education Statistics. Available: http://nces.ed.gov/pubs2006/2006483_1.pdf [Sept. 2011].

Kutner, M., Greenberg, E., Jin,Y., Boyle, B., Hsu, Y., and Dunleavy, E. (2007). *Literacy in everyday life: Results from the 2003 national assessment of adult literacy.* NCES 2007-480. Washington, DC: National Center for Education Statistics. Available: http://nces.ed.gov/pubs2007/2007480.pdf [Sept. 2011].

Kvasny, L. (2005). The role of the habitus in shaping discourses about the digital divide. *Journal of Computer-Mediated Communication, 10*(2). Available: http://onlinelibrary.wiley.com/doi/10.1111/j.1083-6101.2005.tb00242.x/full [Sept. 2011].

Labov, W. (1970). *The study of non-standard English.* Champaign, IL: National Council of Teachers of English.

Labov, W., and Robins, C. (1969). A note on the relation of reading failure to peer-group status in urban ghettos. *Teachers College Record, 70,* 395-405.

Lachman, M.E. (1983). Perceptions of intellectual aging: Antecedent or consequences of intellectual functioning? *Developmental Psychology, 19,* 482-498.

Lachman, M.E. (2006). Perceived control over aging-related declines: Adaptive beliefs and behaviors. *Current Directions in Psychological Science, 15,* 282-286.

Lachman, M.E., Weaver, S.L., Bandura, M., Elliott, E., and Lewkowicz, C.J. (1992). Improving memory and control beliefs through cognitive restructuring and self-generated strategies. *Journal of Gerontology: Psychological Sciences, 47,* 293-299.

Laing, S.P., and Kamhi, A. (2003). Alternative assessment of language and literacy in culturally and linguistically diverse populations. *Language, Speech, and Hearing Services in the Schools, 34,* 44-55.

Lakes, R.D. (1996). *Youth development and critical education: The promise of democratic action.* Albany, NY: State University of New York Press.

Lam, W.S.E. (2000). L2 literacy and the design of self: A case study of a teenager writing on the Internet. *TESOL Quarterly, 34*(3), 457-482.

Lam, W.S.E. (2006). Re-envisioning language, literacy, and the immigrant subject in new mediascapes. *Pedagogies: An International Journal, 1*(3), 171-195.

Landauer, T.K., Laham, D., and Foltz, P.W. (2000). The intelligent essay assessor. *IEEE Intelligent Systems, 15,* 27-31.

Landauer, T.K., Laham, D., and Foltz, P.W. (2003). Automatic essay assessment. *Assessment in Education: Principles, Policy and Practice, 10*(3), 295-308.

Langer, J.A., Bartolome, L., Vasquez, O., and Lucas, T. (1990). Meaning construction in school literacy tasks: A study of bilingual students. *American Educational Research Journal, 27*(3), 427-471.

Langston, M.C., and Graesser, A.C. (1993). The "Point and Query" Interface: Exploring knowledge by asking questions. *Journal of Educational Multimedia and Hypermedia, 2,* 355-368.

Lankshear, C., and Knobel, M. (2003). *New literacies.* Philadelphia: Open University Press.

Larsen, S.C., and Hammill, D.P. (1989). *Test of legible handwriting.* Austin, TX: PROED.

Laufer, B. (1997). The lexical plight in second language reading: Words you don't know, words you think you know, and words you can't guess. In J. Coady and T. Huckin (Eds.), *Secondary language vocabulary acquisition: A rationale for pedagogy* (pp. 20-34). Cambridge, England: Cambridge University Press.

Lave, J. (1988). *Cognition in practice: Mind, mathematics and culture in everyday life.* Cambridge, England: Cambridge University Press.

Lave, J., and Wenger, E. (1991). *Situated learning: Legitimate peripheral participation.* Cambridge, England: Cambridge University Press.

Lave, J., and Wenger, E. (1998). *Communities of practice: Learning, meaning, and identity.* Cambridge, England: Cambridge University Press.

Lazar, M., Bean, R., and Van Horn, B. (1998). Linking the success of a basic skills program to workplace practices and productivity. *Journal of Adolescent and Adult Literacy, 41*(5), 352.

Leander, K.M. (2004). "They took out the wrong context": Uses of time-space in the practice of positioning. *ETHOS, 32*(2), 188-213.

Leander, K.M., and Lovvorn, J.F. (2006). Literacy networks: Following the circulation of texts, bodies, and objects in the schooling and online gaming of one youth. *Cognition and Instruction, 24*(3), 291-340.

Leander, K.M., and McKim, K.K. (2003). Tracing the everyday "sittings" of adolescents on the Internet: A strategic adaptation of ethnography across online and offline spaces. *Education, communication, and information, 3*(2), 211-240.

Lee, C.D. (1993). *Signifying as a scaffold for literary interpretation: The pedagogical implications of an African American discourse genre.* NCTE Research Report No 26. Urbana, IL: National Council of Teachers of English.

Lee, C.D. (1995). A culturally based cognitive apprenticeship: Teaching African American high school students skills in literary interpretation. *Reading Research Quarterly, 30*(4), 608-630.

Lee, C.D. (2001). Is October Brown Chinese? A cultural modeling activity system for underachieving students. *American Educational Research Journal, 38*(1), 97-141.

Lee, C.D. (2007). *Culture, literacy, and learning: Taking bloom in the midst of the whirlwind.* New York: Teachers College Press.

Lee, C.D., and Spratley, A. (2006). *Reading in the disciplines and the challenges of adolescent literacy.* Report to the Carnegie Corporation of New York. New York: Carnegie Corporation of New York.

Lee, C.D., and Spratley, A. (2010). *Reading in the disciplines: The challenges of adolescent literacy.* Final report from Carnegie Corporation of New York's Council on Advancing Adolescent Literacy. New York: Carnegie Corporation of New York.

Lee, O. (1999). Science knowledge, world views, and information sources in social and cultural contexts: Making sense after a natural disaster. *American Educational Research Journal, 36*(2), 187-219.

Lee, O., and Fradd, S.H. (1998). Science for all, including students from non-English language backgrounds. *Educational Researcher, 27*(3), 12-21.

Lee, O., Buxton, C., Lewis, S., and LeRoy, K. (2006). Science inquiry and student diversity: Enhanced abilities and continuing difficulties after an intervention. *Journal of Research in Science Teaching, 43*, 607-636.

Leeser, M. (2007). Learner-based factors in L2 reading comprehension and processing grammatical form: Topic familiarity and working memory. *Language Learning, 57*(2), 229-270.

Lemke, J. (1998). Analyzing verbal data: Principles, methods, and problems. In K. Tobin and B. Fraser, (Eds), *International handbook of science education* (pp. 1,175-1,189). London, England: Kluwer Academic.

Lenhart, A. (2010). *Cell phones and American adults.* A project of the Pew Research Center. Available: http://pewinternet.org/Reports/2010/Cell-Phones-and-American-Adults.aspx [Sept. 2011].

Lenhart, A., Purcell, K., Smith, A., and Zickuhr, K. (2010a). *Social media and young adults.* A project of the Pew Research Center. Available: http://pewinternet.org/Reports/2010/Social-Media-and-Young-Adults.aspx [Sept. 2011].

Lenhart, A., Ling, R., Campbell, S., and Purcell, K. (2010b). *Teens and mobile phones.* A project of the Pew Research Center. Available: http://pewinternet.org/Reports/2010/Teens-and-Mobile-Phones.aspx [Sept. 2011].

Leikin, M., and Hagit, E.Z. (2006). Morphological processing in adult dyslexia. *Journal of Psycholinguistic Research, 35*, 471-490.

Lenneberg, E.H. (1967). *Biological foundations of language.* New York: Wiley.

Lensmire, T. (1994). *When children write: Critical re-visions of the writing workshop.* New York: Teachers College Press.

Leong, C.K. (1999). Phonological and morphological processing in adult students with learning/reading disabilities. *Journal of Learning Disabilities, 32*, 224-238.

Lepper, M.R., and Henderlong, J. (2000). Turning "play" into "work" and "work" into "play": 25 years of research on intrinsic versus extrinsic motivation. In C. Sansone and J. M. Harackiewicz (Eds.), *Intrinsic and extrinsic motivation: The search for optimal motivation and performance* (pp. 257-307). San Diego, CA: Academic Press.

Lepper, M.R., and Woolverton, M. (2002). The wisdom of practice: Lessons learned from the study of highly effective tutors. In J. Aronson (Ed.), *Improving academic achievement: Impact of psychological factors on education* (pp. 135-158). Orlando, FL: Academic Press.

Lepper, M.R., Greene, D., and Nisbett, R.E. (1973). Undermining children's intrinsic interest with extrinsic reward: A test of the "overjustification" hypothesis. *Journal of Personality and Social Psychology, 28,* 129-137.

Lepper, M.R., Keavney, M., and Drake, M. (1996). Intrinsic motivation and extrinsic rewards: A commentary on Cameron and Pierce's meta analysis. *Review of Educational Research, 66,* 5-32.

Lerner, J.W. (1989). Educational intervention in learning disabilities. *Journal of the American Academy of Child and Adolescent Psychiatry, 28,* 326-331.

Lesaux, N.K., and Geva, E. (2006). Synthesis: Development of literacy in language-minority students. In D. August and T. Shanahan (Eds.), *Developing literacy in second-language learners: Report of the national literacy panel on language-minority children and youth* (pp. 53-74). Mahwah, NJ: Lawrence Erlbaum Associates.

Lesaux, N.K., and Kieffer, M.J. (2010) Exploring sources of reading comprehension difficulties among language minority learners and their classmates in early adolescence. *American Educational Research Journal, 47*(3), 596-632.

Lesaux, N.K., Koda, K., Siegel, L., and Shanahan, T. (2006). Development of literacy. In D. August and T. Shanahan (Eds.), *Developing literacy in second-language learners: Report of the National Literacy Panel on Language-Minority Children and Youth* (pp. 75-122). Mahwah, NJ: Lawrence Erlbaum Associates.

Lesaux, N.K., Rupp, A., and Siegel, L.S. (2007). Growth in reading skills of children from diverse linguistic backgrounds: Findings from a 5-year longitudinal study. *Journal of Educational Psychology, 99*(4), 821-834.

Lesaux, N.K., Kieffer, M., and Kelley, J. (2009). *Academic language instruction for all students: Effects of a large-scale vocabulary intervention.* Available: http://www.cal.org/create/events/CREATE2009/postconference/handouts/Kieffer_handout.pdf [Sept. 2011].

Lesaux, N.K., Kieffer, M.J., Faller, E., and Kelley, J. (2010). The effectiveness and ease of implementation of an academic vocabulary intervention for linguistically diverse students in urban middle schools. *Reading Research Quarterly, 45*(2), 198-230.

Lesgold, A.M. (in press). Practical issues in the deployment of new training technology. In P.J. Durlach and A.M. Lesgold, (Eds.), *Adaptive technologies for training and education.* Cambridge, England: Cambridge University Press.

Lesgold, A.M., and Nahemow, M. (2001). Tools to assist learning by doing: Achieving and assessing efficient technology for learning. In D. Klahr and S. Carver (Eds.), *Cognition and instruction: Twenty-five years of progress* (Part III, Ch. 3). Mahwah, NJ: Lawrence Erlbaum Associates.

Lesgold, A.M., Lajoie, S.P., Bunzo, M., and Eggan, G. (1992). SHERLOCK: A coached practice environment for an electronics trouble-shooting job. In J.H. Larkin and R.W. Chabay (Eds.), *Computer-assisted instruction and intelligent tutoring systems: Shared goals and complementary approaches* (pp. 201-238). Hillsdale, NJ: Lawrence Erlbaum Associates.

Lesser, J. (2007). Learner-based factors in L2 reading comprehension and processing grammatical form: Topic familiarity and working memory. *Language Learning, 57,* 229-270.

Leu, D.J., and Reinking, D. (2005). *Teaching Internet comprehension to adolescents: Developing Internet comprehension strategies among poor, adolescent students at risk to become dropouts.* U.S. Department of Education Institute of Education Sciences Research Grant. Available: http://www.newliteracies.uconn.edu/ies.html [Sept. 2011].

Leu, D.J., Coiro, J., Castek, J., Harman, D.K., Henry, L.A., and Reinking, D. (in press). Research on instruction and assessment in the new literacies of online reading comprehension. In C. Collins Block, S. Parris, and P. Afflerback (Eds.), *Comprehension instruction: Research-based best practices.* New York: Guilford Press.

Leu, D.J., Zawilinski, L., Castek, J., Banerjee, M., Housand, B.C., Liu, Y., and O'Neill, M. (in press). What is new about the new literacies of online reading comprehension? In L. Rush, A.J. Eakle, and A. Berger (Eds.), *Secondary school literacy: What research reveals for classroom practice.* Urbana, IL: National Council of Teachers of English.

Levesque, C.S., Zuehlke, N., Stanek, L., and Ryan, R.M. (2004). Autonomy and competence in German and U.S. university students: A comparative study based on self-determination theory. *Journal of Educational Psychology, 96,* 68-84.

Levin, B.E. (1990). Organizational deficits in dyslexia: Possible frontal lobe dysfunction. *Developmental Neuropsychology, 6,* 95-110.

Levy, M., and Ransdell, S. (1996) (Eds). *The science of writing: Theories, methods, individual differences, and applications.* Mahwah, NJ: Lawrence Erbaum Associates.

Levy, S., Rasher, S., Carter, S., Harris, L., Berbaum, M., Mandernach, J., Bercovitz, L., and Martin, L. (2008). Health literacy curriculum works for adult basic education students. *Focus on Basics, 9*(B), 33-39.

Lewis, C., and Fabos, B. (2005). Instant messaging, literacies, and social identities. *Reading Research Quarterly, 40*(4), 470-501.

Li, J. (2006). The mediation of technology in ESL writing and its implications for writing assessment. *Assessing Writing, 11,* 5-21.

Li, J., and Cumming, A. (2001). Word processing and second language writing: A longitudinal case study. *International Journal of English Studies, 1*(2), 127-152.

Li, K.Z., Lindenberger, U., Freund, A.M., and Baltes, P.B. (2001). Walking while memorizing: Age-related differences in compensatory behavior. *Psychological Science, 12,* 230-237.

Liberman, I.Y. (1971). Basic research in speech and lateralization of language: Some implications for reading disability. *Bulletin of the Orton Society, 21,* 71-87.

Liberman, I.Y., and Shankweiler, D. (1991). Phonology and the beginning reader: A tutorial. In L. Rieben and C.A. Perfetti (Eds.), *Learning to read: Basic research and its implications.* Hillsdale, NJ: Lawrence Erlbaum Associates.

Lidz, C.S., and Peña, E.D. (1996). Dynamic assessment: The model, its relevance as a non-biased approach, and its application to Latino American preschool children. *Language, Speech, and Hearing Services in the Schools, 27,* 367-372.

Lieberman, I.Y., Shankweiler, D., Fischer, F.W., and Carter, B. (1974). Reading and the awareness of linguistic segments. *Journal of Experimental Child Psychology, 18,* 201-212.

Lien, M.C., Allen, P.A., Ruthruff, E., Grabbe, J., McCann, R.S., and Remington, R.W. (2006). Visual word recognition without central attention: Evidence for greater automaticity with advancing age. *Psychology and Aging, 21*(3), 431-447.

Liepmann, H. (1900). Das krankheitsbild der apraxie [The clinical profile of apraxia]. *Monatsschrift Fur Psychiatrie und Neurologie, 8,* 15-44, 102-132, 182-192.

Light, L.L., and Capps, J.L. (1986). Comprehension of pronouns in young and older adults. *Developmental Psychology, 22*(4), 580-585.

Light, L.L., Valencialaver, D., and Zavis, D. (1991). Instantiation of general terms in young and older adults. *Psychology and Aging, 6*(3), 337-351.

Light, L.L., Capps, J.L., Singh, A., and Owens, S.A.A. (1994). Comprehension and use of anaphoric devices in young and older adults. *Discourse Processes, 18*(1), 77-103.

Liimatainen, L., Poskiparta, M., Karhila, P., and Sjögren, A. (2001). The development of reflective learning in the context of health counseling and health promotion during nurse education. *Journal of Advanced Nursing, 34,* 648-658.

Liming, D., and Wolf, M. (2008). Job outlook by education, 2006-16. *Occupational Outlook Quarterly,* Fall, 2-29. U.S. Bureau of Labor Statistics. Available: http://www.bls.gov/opub/ooq/2008/fall/art01.pdf [Sept. 2011].

Linan-Thompson, S. (2009). *Building language and promoting concept knowledge in social studies classes*. Available: http://www.cal.org/create/events/CREATE2009/postconference/handouts/Linan-Thompson_handout.pdf [Sept. 2011].

Linderholm, T., and van den Broek, P. (2002). The effects of reading purpose and working memory capacity on the proocessing of expository text. *Journal of Educational Psychology*, *94*, 778-784.

Linnenbrink, E.A., and Pintrich, P. (2002). The role of motivational beliefs in conceptual change. In M. Limon and L. Mason (Eds.), *Reconsidering conceptual change: Issues in theory and practice*. Dordretch, the Netherlands: Kluwer Academic Press.

Lipson, M.Y., and Wixson, K.K. (1997). *Assessment and instruction of reading and writing disability: An interactive approach* (2nd ed.). Boston, MA: Addison Wesley Longman.

Lipstein, R., and Renninger, K.A. (2007). Interest for writing: How teachers can make a difference. *English Journal*, *96*(4), 79-85.

Litman, D.J., and Forbes-Riley, K. (2006). Recognizing student emotions and attitudes on the basis of utterances in spoken tutoring dialogues with both human and computer tutors. *Speech Communication*, *48*(5), 559-590.

Litman, D.J., Rosé, C.P., Forbes-Riley, K., VanLehn, K., Bhembe, D., and Silliman, S. (2006). Spoken versus typed human and computer dialogue tutoring. *International Journal of Artificial Intelligence in Education*, *16*(2), 145-170.

Liu, Y., Dunlap, S., Fiez, J., and Perfetti, C.A. (2007). Evidence for neural accommodation to a writing system following learning. *Human Brain Mapping*, *28*, 1,223-1,234.

Locke, E., Shaw, K., Saari, L., and Latham, G. (1981). Goal setting and task performance: 1969-1980. *Psychological Bulletin*, *90*, 125-152.

Loewen, S., and Philip, J. (2006). Recasts in the adult L2 classroom: Characteristics, explicitness and effectiveness. *Modern Language Journal*, *90*, 536-556.

Loftus, G.R., and Loftus, E.F. (1983). *Mind at play: The psychology of video games*. New York: Basic Books.

Logan, K.J. (2004, November). *Some effects of conversational context on utterance form, function, and fluency*. Paper presented at the annual convention of the American Speech-Language-Hearing Association, Philadelphia, PA.

Logan, J.M., and Balota, D.A. (2009). Expanded vs. equal interval spaced retrieval practice: Exploring different schedules of spacing and retention interval in younger and older adults. *Aging, Neuropsychology, and Cognition*, *15*, 257-280.

Long, M. (1983). Does second language instruction make a difference? A review of research. *TESOL Quarterly*, *17*, 359-382.

Long, M.H. (2009). Methodological principles for language teaching. In M.H. Long and C.J. Doughty (Eds), *The handbook of language teaching* (pp. 373-394). Oxford, England: Blackwell.

Long, M.H., and Crookes, G. (1992). Three approaches to task-based language teaching. *TESOL Quarterly*, *26*, 1, 27-56.

Loomer, B., Fitzsimmons, R., and Sterge, M. (1990). *Spelling research and practice*. Iowa City, IA: Useful Learning.

Losh, E. (2005). In country with tactical Iraqi: Trust, identity, and language learning in a military video game. In *Digital Experience: Proceedings of the Digital Arts and Culture Conference 2005* (pp. 69-78). Dec. 1-3, IT University, Copenhagen, Denmark.

Lovegrove, W., Martin, F., and Slaghuis, W. (1986). A theoretical and experimental case for a visual deficit in specific reading disability. *Cognitive Neuropsychology*, *3*, 225-267.

Lovett, M.W., Ransby, M.J., Hardwick, N., Johns, M.S., and Donaldson, S.A. (1989). Can dyslexia be treated? Treatment-specific and generalized treatment effects in dyslexic children's response to remediation. *Brain and Language*, *37*, 90-121.

Lovett, M.W., Warren-Chaplin, P.M., Ransby, M.J., and Borden, S.L. (1990). Training the word recognition skills of reading disabled children: Treatment and transfer effects. *Journal of Educational Psychology, 82,* 769-780.

Lovett, M.W., Borden, S.L., DeLuca, T., Lacerenza, L., Benson, N.J., and Brackstone, D. (1994). Treating the core deficits of developmental dyslexia: Evidence of transfer-of-learning following phonologically- and strategy-based reading training programs. *Developmental Psychology, 30*(6), 805-822.

Lovett, M.W., Lacerenza, L., and Borden, S.L. (2000). Putting struggling readers on the PHAST track: A program to integrate phonological and strategy-based remedial reading instruction and maximize outcomes. *Journal of Learning Disabilities, 33*(5), 458-476.

Lovett, M.W., Lacerenza, L., Borden, S.L., Frijters, J.C., Steinbach, K.A., and De Palma, M. (2000). Components of effective remediation for developmental reading disabilities: Combining phonological and strategy-based instruction to improve outcomes. *Journal of Educational Psychology, 92*(2), 263-283.

Lovett, M.W., Barron, R.W., and Benson, N.J. (2003). Effective remediation of word identification and decoding difficulties in school-age children with reading disabilities. In H.L. Swanson, K. Harris, and S. Graham (Eds.), *Handbook of learning disabilities* (pp. 273-292). New York: Guilford Press.

Lovett, M.W., Lacerenza, L., Murphy, D., Steinbach, K.A., De Palma, M., and Frijters, J.C. (2005). The importance of multiple-component interventions for children and adolescents who are struggling readers. In J. Gilger and S. Richardson (Eds.), *Research-based education and intervention: What we need to know* (pp. 67-102). Baltimore, MD: International Dyslexia Association.

Lovett, M.W., De Palma, M., Frijters, J., Steuinbach, K., Temple, M., Benson, N., and Lacerenza, L. (2008a). Interventions for reading difficulties: A comparison of response to intervention by ELL and EFL struggling readers. *Journal of Learning Disabilities, 41*(4), 333-352.

Lovett, M.W., Lacerenza, L., De Palma, M., Benson, N.J., Steinbach, K.A., and Frijters, J.C. (2008b). Preparing teachers to remediate reading disabilities in high school: What is needed for effective professional development? *Teaching and Teacher Education, 24*(4), 1,083-1,097.

Lowe, R.S.W., and Schnotz, W. (2007). *Learning with animation: Research and implications for design.* New York: Cambridge University Press.

Luke, A. (1993). Stories of social regulation: The micropolitics of classroom narrative. In B. Green (Ed.), *The insistence of the letter: Literacy studies and curriculum theorizing* (pp. 137-153). London, England: Falmer Press.

Luke, A. (1995). Genres of power? Literacy education and the production of capital. In R. Hasan and G. Williams (Eds.), *Literacy in society* (pp. 308-338). London, England: Longman.

Luo, L., Hendricks, T., and Craik, F.I.M. (2007). Age differences in recollection: Three patterns of enhanced encoding. *Psychology and Aging, 22,* 269-280.

Luria, G.E. (1987). *The development of self-monitoring as a study strategy training and generalization to prose recall* (Dissertation: Thesis Ph.D. in Education—University of California, Berkeley, May).

Lyon, G.R., Fletcher, J.M., Shaywitz, S.E., Shaywitz, B.A., Torgesen, J.K., Wood, F.B., Schulte, A., and Olson, R. (2001). Rethinking learning disabilities. In C.E. Finn, Jr., R.A.J. Roherrham, and C.R. Hokanson, Jr. (Eds.), *Rethinking special education for a new century* (pp. 259-287). Washington, DC: Thomas B. Fordham Foundation and Progressive Policy Institute.

Lyon, G.R., Fletcher, J.M., and Barnes, M.A. (2003). Learning disabilities. In E.J. Mash and R.A. Barkley (Eds.), *Child psychopathology* (2nd ed., pp. 520-586). New York: Guilford Press.

Lyster, R. (1998). Recasts, repetition, and ambiguity in L2 classroom discourse. *Studies in Second Language Acquisition, 20,* 51-81.

Lyytinen, H., Ronimus, M., Alanko, A., Poikkeus, A., and Taanila, M. (2007). Early identification of dyslexia and the use of computer game-based practice to support reading acquisition. *Nordic Psychology, 59*(2), 109-126.

Maas, A., D'Etole, C., and Cadinu, M. (2008). Checkmate? The role of gender stereotypes in the ultimate intellectual sport. *European Journal of Social Psychology, 38,* 231-245.

MacArthur, C.A. (2006). The effects of new technologies on writing and writing processes. In C.A. MacArthur, S. Graham, and J. Fitzgerald (Eds.), *Handbook of writing research* (pp. 248-262). New York: Guilford Press.

MacArthur, C.A. (2008). *Research relevant to the connection between reading and writing in adult basic education: A working paper.* Presented at a meeting of the Adult Literacy Research Working Group, Washington, DC.

MacArthur, C.A., and Cavalier, A. (2004). Dictation and speech recognition technology as accommodations in large-scale assessments for students with learning disabilities. *Exceptional Children, 71,* 43-58.

MacArthur, C.A., and Lembo, L. (2009). Strategy instruction in writing for adult literacy learners. *Reading and Writing, 22*(9), 1,021-1,039.

MacArthur, C.A., Graham, S., and Fitzgerald, J. (2006). (Eds.). *Handbook of writing research.* New York: Guilford Press.

MacArthur, C.A., Konold, T., Glutting, J., and Alamprese, J. (2010a). Reading component skills of learners in adult basic education. *Journal of Learning Disabilities, 43*(2), 108-121.

MacArthur, C., Konold, T., Glutting, J., and Alamprese, J. (2010b). *Subgroups of adult basic education learners with different profiles of reading skills.* Available: http://www.springer link.com/content/q02801u756523t58/fulltext.pdf [Sept. 2011].

MacIver, D.J., and Epstein, J.L. (1993). Middle grades research: Not yet mature, but no longer a child. *Elementary School Journal, 93,* 519-531.

MacKay, D.G., and Abrams, L. (1998). Age-linked declines in retrieving orthographic knowledge: Empirical, practical, and theoretical implications. *Psychology and Aging, 13,* 647-662.

Mackey, M. (2007). Slippery texts and evolving literacies. *E-Learning, 4*(3), 319-328.

Maclay, C.M., and Askov, E.N. (1988). Computers and adult beginning readers: An intergenerational approach. *Lifelong Learning, 11*(8), 23-28.

MacLeod, J. (1987). *Ain't no makin' it: Leveled aspirations in a low-income neighborhood.* Boulder, CO: Westview Press.

MacLeod, J. (1995). *Ain't no makin' it: Aspirations and attainment in a low-income neighborhood.* Boulder, CO: Westview Press.

Macrine, S.L., and Sabbatino, E.D. (2008). Dynamic assessment and remediation approach: Using the DARA approach to assist struggling readers. *Reading and Writing Quarterly, 24,* 52-76.

MacWhinney, B. (2005) A unified model of language acquisition. In J.F. Kroll and A.M.B. de Groot (Eds.), *Handbook of bilingualism: Psycholinguistic approaches.* New York: Oxford University Press.

Madden, D.J. (1988). Adult age-differences in the effects of sentence context and stimulus degradation during visual word recognition. *Psychology and Aging, 3*(2), 167-172.

Madden, M. (2010). *Older adults and social media.* Washington, DC: Pew Internet & American Life Project. Available: http://pewinternet.org/Reports/2010/Older-Adults-and-Social-Media.aspx [Sept. 2011].

Madden, M., and Smith, A. (2010). *Reputation management and social media.* Washington, DC: Pew Internet & American Life Project. Available: http://pewinternet.org/Reports/2010/Reputation-Management.aspx [Sept. 2011].

Madigan, R., Linton, P., and Johnston, S. (1996). The paradox of writing apprehension. In M. Levy and S. Ransdell (Eds.), *The science of writing: Theories, methods, individual differences, and applications* (pp. 295-307). Mahwah, NJ: Lawrence Erlbaum Associates.

Maehr, M.L. (1976). Continuing motivation: An analysis of a seldom considered educational outcome. *Review of Educational Research, 46,* 443-462.

Maehr, M.L., and Anderman, E.M. (1993). Reinventing schools for early adolescents: Emphasizing task goals. *Elementary School Journal, 93,* 593-610.

Maehr, M.L., and Midgley, C. (1996). *Transforming school cultures.* Boulder, CO: Westview Press.

Magliano, J., Trabasso, T., and Graesser, A.C. (1999). Strategic processing during comprehension. *Journal of Educational Psychology, 91,* 615-629.

Magnusson, S.J., and Sullivan Palincsar, A. (2005). *Teaching to promote the development of scientific knowledge and reasoning about light at the elementary school level. In National Research Council, How students learn: History, mathematics, and science in the classroom* (pp. 421-474). Committee on *How People Learn, A Targeted Report for Teachers,* M.S. Donovan and J.D. Bransford (Eds.). Division of Behavioral and Social Sciences and Education. Washington, DC: The National Academies Press.

Maguire, E.A., Gadian, D.G., Johnsrude, I.S., Good, C.D., Ashburner, J., Frackowiak, R.S.J., and Frith, C.D. (2000). Navigation-related structural change in the hippocampi of taxi drivers. *Proceedings of the National Academy of Sciences, 97,* 4,398-4,403.

Maguire, E.A., Spiers, H.J., Good, C.D., Hartley, T., Frakowiak, R.S.J., and Burgess, N. (2003). Navigation expertise and the human hippocampus: A structural brain imaging analysis. *Hippocampus, 13,* 208-217.

Mahiri, J., and Sablo, S. (1996). Writing for their lives: The non-school literacy of California. *Journal of Negro Education, 65*(2), 164-180.

Maki, R.H. (1998). Test predictions over text material. In D.J. Hacker, J. Dunlosky, and A.C. Graesser (Eds.), *Metacognition in educational theory and practice* (pp. 117-144). Mahwah, NJ: Lawrence Erlbaum Associates.

Malone, L.D., and Mastropieri, M.A. (1992). Reading comprehension instruction: Summarization and self-monitoring training for students with learning disabilities. *Exceptional Children, 58*(3), 270-279.

Malone, T.W., and Lepper, M.R. (1987). Making learning fun: A taxonomy of intrinsic motivations for learning. In R.E. Snow and M.J. Farr (Eds.), *Aptitude, learning and instruction: Conative and affective process analyses* (vol. 3, pp. 223-253). Hillsdale, NJ: Lawrence Erlbaum Associates.

Manderlink, G., and Haraciewicz, J.M. (1984). Proximal vs. distal goal setting and intrinsic motivation. *Journal of Personality and Social Psychology, 47,* 918-928.

Mandl, H., Stein, N.L., and Trabasso, T. (1984). *Learning and comprehension of text.* Hillsdale, NJ: Lawrence Erlbaum Associates.

Manis, F., and Lindsey, K. (2010). Cognitive and oral language contributors to reading disabilities in Spanish-English bilinguals. In A.Y. Durgunoğlu and C. Goldenberg (Eds.), *Language and literacy development in bilingual settings.* New York: Guilford Press.

Manis, F., Lindsey, K.A., and Bailey, C.E. (2004). Development of reading in grades K-2 in Spanish-speaking English-language learners. *Learning Disabilities Research and Practice, 19,* 214-224.

Marian, V., Spivey, M., and Hirsch, J. (2003). Shared and separate systems in bilingual language processing: Converging evidence from eyetracking and brain imaging. *Brain and Language, 86,* 70-82.

Markus, H., and Nurius, P. (1986). Possible selves. *American Psychologist, 41*(9), 954-969.

Markus, H.R., and Kitiyama, S. (2010). Cultures and selves: A cycle of mutual constitution. *Perspectives on Psychological Science, 5*(4), 420-430.

Martin, J.H., and Friedberg, A. (1986). *Writing to read: A parents' guide to the new early learning program for young children.* New York: Warner Books.

Martino, N.L., Norris, J., and Hoffman, P.R. (2001). Reading comprehension instruction: Effects of two types. *Journal of Developmental Education, 25*(1), 2-12.

Marx, R.W., Blumenfeld, P.C., Krajcik, J.S., and Soloway, E. (1997). Enacting project-based science. *The Elementary School Journal, 97,* 341-358.

Marx, R.W., Blumenfeld, P.C., Krajcik, J.S., Fishman, B., Soloway, E., Geier, R., and Tal, R.T. (2004). Inquiry-based science in the middle grades: Assessment of learning in urban systemic reform. *Journal of Research in Science Teaching, 41*(10), 1,063-1,080.

Marzano, R.J., and Kendall, J. S. (2007). *The new taxonomy of educational objectives* (2nd ed.).Thousand Oaks, CA: Corwin Press.

Masgoret, A-M., and Gardner, R.C. (2003). Attitudes, motivation, and second language learning: A meta-analysis of studies conducted by Gardner and Associates. *Language Learning, 53*(1),123-163.

Mason, L.H. (2004). Explicit self-regulated strategy development versus reciprocal questioning: Effects on expository reading comprehension among struggling readers. *Journal of Educational Psychology, 96*(2), 283-296.

Masunaga, H., and Horn, J. (2001). Expertise and age-related changes in components of intelligence. *Psychology and Aging, 16,* 293-311.

Mathes, P.G., and Fuchs, L.S. (1994). Peer tutoring in reading for students with mild disabilities: A best evidence synthesis. *School Psychology Review, 23,* 59-80.

Mathews-Aydinli, J. (2008). Overlooked and understudied? A survey of current trends in research on adult English language learners. *Adult Education Quarterly, 58*(3), 198-213.

Mathieu, J.E., and Martineau, J.W. (1997). Individual and situational influences on training motivation. In J.K. Ford, S.W.J. Kozlowski, K. Kraiger, E. Salas, and M.S. Teachout (Eds.), *Improving training effectiveness in work organizations* (pp. 193-221). Mahwah, NJ: Lawrence Erlbaum Associates.

Matsuda, P.K. (2003). Basic writing and second language writers: Toward an inclusive definition. *Journal of Basic Writing, 22*(2), 67-89.

Matute-Bianchi, M.E. (1991). Situational ethnicity and patterns of school performance among immigrants and non-immigrant Mexican-descent students. In M. Gibson and J.U. Ogbu (Eds.), *Minority status and schooling: A comparative study of immigrant and involuntary minorities* (pp. 205-247). New York: Garland.

Mautone, P.D., and Mayer, R.E. (2007). Cognitive aids for guiding graph comprehension. *Journal of Educational Psychology, 99*(3), 640-652.

Mavrogenes, N., and Bezruczko, N. (1993). Influences on writing development. *Journal of Educational Research, 86,* 237-245.

Mayberry, R. (2009). Early language acquisition and adult language ability: What sign language reveals about the critical period for language. In M. Marschark and P. Spencer (Eds.), *Oxford handbook of deaf studies, language, and education* (vol. 2, part 4, pp. 281-291). New York: Oxford University Press.

Mayer, R.E. (2005). *The Cambridge handbook of multimedia learning.* New York: Cambridge University Press.

Mayer, R.E. (2009). *Multimedia learning* (2nd ed). New York: Cambridge University Press.

Mayer, R.E., and Moreno, R. (2003). Nine ways to reduce cognitive load in multimedia learning. *Educational Psychologist, 38*, 43-52.

McAlexander, P.J. (2000). Developmental classroom personality and response to peer review. *Research and Teaching in Developmental Education, 17*(1), 5-12.

McCardle, P., Mele-McCarthy, J., Cutting, L., Leos, K., and D'Emilio, T. (2005). Learning disabilities in English language learners: Identifying the issues. *Learning Disabilities Research and Practice, 20*(1), 1-5.

McCardle, P., Chhabra, V., and Kapinus, B. (2008). *Reading research in action: A teacher's guide for student success.* Baltimore, MD: Paul H. Brookes.

McCarthy, P. M., Myers, J.C., Briner, S.W., Graesser, A.C., and McNamara, D.S. (2009). Are three words all we need? A psychological and computational study of genre recognition. *Journal for Language Technology and Computational Linguistics, 1*, 23-57.

McCaslin, M., and Good, T.L. (1996). The informal curriculum. In D.C. Berliner and R.C. Calfee (Eds.), *Handbook of educational psychology* (pp. 622-670). New York: Macmillan.

McCloskey, M., Caramazza, A., and Green, B. (1980). Curvilinear motion in the absence of external forces: Native beliefs about the motion of objects. *Science, 210*, 1,139-1,141.

McConachie, S., and Petrosky, T. (2010). *Content matters: A disciplinary literacy approach to improving student learning.* San Francisco, CA: Jossey-Bass.

McConachie, S., Hall, M., Resnick, L., Ravi, A.K., Bill, V.L., Bintz, J., and Taylor, J.A. (2006). Task, text, and talk: Literacy for all subjects. *Educational Leadership, 64*(2), 8-14.

McCrudden, M.T., and Schraw, G. (2007). Relevance and goal-focusing in text processing. *Educational Psychology Review, 19*, 113-139.

McCutchen, D. (1994). The magical number three, plus or minus two: Working memory in writing. In E. Butterfield (Ed.), *Children's writing: Towards a process theory of the development of skilled writing* (pp. 1-30). Greenwich, CT: JAI Press.

McCutchen, D. (2000). Knowledge acquisition, processing, efficiency, and working memory: Implications for a theory of writing. *Educational Psychologist, 35*, 13-23.

McCutchen, D. (2006). Cognitive factors in the development of children's writing. In C.A. MacArthur, S. Graham, and J. Fitzgerald (Eds.), *Handbook of writing research* (pp. 115-130). New York: Guilford Press.

McCutchen, D. Hull, G., and Smith, W. (1987). Editing strategies and error correction in basic writing. *Written Communication, 4*(2), 139-154.

McDaniel, M.A., Roediger, H.L., and McDermott, K.B. (2007). Generalizing test enhanced learning from the laboratory to the classroom. *Psychonomic Bulletin and Review, 14*, 200-206.

McDaniel, M.A., Anderson, J.L., Derbish, M.H., and Morrisette, N. (2007). Testing the testing effect in the classroom. *European Journal of Cognitive Psychology, 19*, 494-513.

McDermott, R.P. (1978). Pirandello in the classroom: On the possibility of equal educational opportunity in American culture. In M.C. Reynolds (Ed.), *Futures of exceptional children: Emerging structures.* Reston, VA: Council for Exceptional Children.

McDermott, R.P., and Varenne, H. (1995). Culture as disability. *Education and Anthropology Quarterly, 26*, 323-348.

McDonald, J.L. (2006). Beyond the critical period: Processing-based explanation for poor grammaticality judgment performance by late second language learners. *Journal of Memory and Language, 55*, 381-401.

McDonald, J.L. (2008). Differences in the cognitive demands of word order, plural, and subject-verb agreement constructions. *Psychonomic Bulletin and Review, 15*(5), 980-984.

McEneaney, J.E., Li, L., Allen, K., and Guzniczak, L. (2009). Stance, navigation, and reader response in expository hypertext. *Journal of Literacy Research, 41*(1), 1-45.

McGinnis, D. (2009). Text comprehension products and processes in young, young-old, and old-old adults. *Journals of Gerontology Series B-Psychological Sciences and Social Sciences, 64*(2), 202-211.

McGinnis, D., and Zelinski, E.M. (2000). Understanding unfamiliar words: The influence of processing resources, vocabulary knowledge, and age. *Psychology and Aging, 15*(2), 335-350.

McGinnis, D., and Zelinski, E.M. (2003). Inference generation during discourse processing: Evidence for the superordinate processing hypothesis in old-old adults. *Psychology and Aging, 18*, 497-509.

McGinnis, D., Goss, R.J., Tessmer, C., and Zelinski, E.M. (2008). Inference generation in young, young-old and old-old adults: Evidence for semantic architecture stability. *Applied Cognitive Psychology, 22*(2), 171-192.

McGraw, K.O., and McCullers, J.C. (1979). Evidence of a detrimental effect of extrinsic incentives on breaking a mental set. *Journal of Experimental Social Psychology, 15*, 285-294.

McKenna, M.C., and Robinson, R.D. (2009). *Teaching through text: Reading and writing in the content areas* (5th ed.). Boston, MA: Pearson Education.

McKeown, M.G., and Beck, I.L. (1988). Learning vocabulary: Different ways for different goals. *Remedial and Special Education, 9*(1), 42-46.

McKeown, M.G., and Beck, I.L. (1994). Making sense of accounts of history: Why young students don't and how they might. In G. Leinhardt, I.L. Beck, and C. Stainton (Eds.), *Teaching and learning in history*. Hillsdale, NJ: Lawrence Erlbaum Associates.

McKeown, M.G., Beck, I.L., Omanson, R.C., and Pople, M.T. (1985). Some effects of the nature and frequency of vocabulary instruction on the knowledge and use of words. *Reading Research Quarterly, 20*, 522-535.

McKeown, M.G., Beck, I.L., and Blake, R.G.K. (2009). Rethinking reading comprehension instruction: A comparison of instruction for strategies and content approaches. *Reading Research Quarterly, 44*(3), 218-253.

McNamara, D.S. (2004). SERT: Self-explanation reading training. *Discourse Processes, 38*, 1-30.

McNamara, D.S. (Ed.). (2007a). *Reading comprehension strategies: Theories, interventions, and technologies*. Mahwah, NJ: Lawrence Erlbaum Associates.

McNamara, D.S. (Ed.). (2007b). *Theories of text comprehension: The importance of reading strategies to theoretical foundations of reading comprehension*. Mahwah, NJ: Lawrence Erlbaum Associates.

McNamara, D.S., and Kintsch, W. (1996). Learning from text: Effects of prior knowledge and text coherence. *Discourse Processes, 22*, 247-287.

McNamara, D.S., and Magliano, J. (2008). Towards a comprehensive model of comprehension. In B. Ross (Ed.), *The Psychology of Learning and Motivation, 51*(9), 297-384.

McNamara, D.S., and Magliano, J. (2009). Self-explanation and metacognition. In D.J. Hacker, J. Dunlosky, and A.C. Graesser (Eds.), *Handbook of metacognition in education* (pp. 60-81). New York: Routledge.

McNamara, D.S., Kintsch, E., Songer, N.B., and Kintsch, W. (1996). Are good texts always better? Interactions of text coherence, background knowledge, and levels of understanding in learning from text. *Cognition and Instruction, 14*(1), 1-43.

McNamara, D.S., Levinstein, I.B., and Boonthum, C. (2004). iSTART: Interactive strategy trainer for active reading and thinking. *Behavioral Research Methods, Instruments, and Computers, 36*, 222-233.

McNamara, D.S., de Vega, M., and O'Reilly, T. (2007). Comprehension skill, inference making, and the role of knowledge. In F. Schmalhofer, and C.A. Perfetti (Eds.), *Higher level language processes in the brain: Inference and comprehension processes* (pp. 233-251). Mahwah, NJ: Lawrence Erlbaum Associates.

McNamara, D.S., O'Reilly, T., Rowe, M., Boonthum, C., and Levinstein, I.B. (2007a). iSTART: A web-based tutor that teaches self-explanation and metacognitive reading strategies. In D.S. McNamara (Ed.), *Reading comprehension strategies: Theories, interventions, and technologies*. Mahwah, NJ: Lawrence Erlbaum Associates.

McNamara, D.S., Ozuru, Y., Best, R., and O'Reilly, T. (2007b). The 4-pronged comprehension strategy framework. In D.S. McNamara (Ed.), *Reading comprehension strategies: Theories, interventions, and technology* (pp. 465-496). New York: Lawrence Erlbaum Associates.

McNamara, D.S., Jackson, G.T., and Graesser, A.C. (2010). Intelligent tutoring and games (ITaG). In Y.K. Baek (Ed.), *Gaming for classroom-based learning: Digital role-playing as a motivator of study* (pp. 44-65). Hershey, PA: IGI Global.

McNeil, B., and Smith, L. (2004). *Success factors in informal learning: Young adults' experiences of literacy, language and numeracy.* Interim report summary. London, England: National Research and Development Centre for Adult literacy. Available: http://www.nrdc.org.uk/publications_details.asp?ID=40# [Sept. 2011].

Meade, M.L., and Roediger, H.L. (2009). Age differences in collaborative memory: The role of retrieval manipulations. *Memory and Cognition, 37,* 962-975.

Medina, P. (1999). *The outcomes and impacts of adult literacy education in the United States. Appendix A: Abstracts of studies reviewed.* No. NCSALL-R-6AR309B960002. Boston, MA: National Center for the Study of Adult Learning and Literacy.

Meece, J.L., and Miller, S.D. (1999). Changes in elementary school children's achievement goals for reading and writing: Results of a longitudinal and an intervention study. *Scientific Studies of Reading, 3*(3), 207-229.

Meece, J.L., Wigfield, A., and Eccles, J. S. (1990). Predictors of math anxiety and its consequences for young adolescents' course enrollment intentions and performances in mathematics. *Journal of Educational Psychology, 82,* 60-70.

Meece, J. L., Herman, P., and McCombs, B. L. (2003). Relations of learner-centered teaching practices to adolescents' achievement goals. *International Journal of Educational Research, 39,* 457-475.

Meece, J.L., Anderman E.M., and Anderman, L.H. (2006). Structures and goals of educational settings: Classroom goal structure, student motivation, and academic achievement. In S.T. Fiske, A.E. Kazdin, and D.L. Schacter (Eds.), *Annual review of psychology* (vol. 57, pp. 487-504). Stanford, CA: Annual Reviews.

Mehan, H., Hertweck, A., and Meihls, J.L. (1986). *Handicapping the handicapped: Decision making in students' educational careers.* Stanford, CA: Stanford University Press.

Mehta, P.D., Foorman, B.R., Branum-Martin, L., and Taylor, W.P. (2005). Literacy as an unidimensional multilevel construct: Validation, sources of influence, and implications in a longitudinal study in grades 1 to 4. *Scientific Studies of Reading, 9*(2), 85-116.

Mellard, D., and Fall, E. (in press). Component model of reading comprehension for adult education participants. *Learning Disabilities Quarterly.*

Mellard, D., and Patterson, M. (2008). Contrasting adult literacy learners with and without specific learning disabilities. *Remedial and Special Education, 29*(3), 133-144.

Mellard, D., Fall, E., and Mark, C. (2008). Reading profiles for adults with low literacy: Cluster analysis with power and speeded measures. *Reading and Writing, 22,* 975-992.

Mellard, D., Fall, E., and Woods, K. (2010). A path analysis of reading comprehension for adults with low literacy. *Journal of Learning Disabilities, 43*(2), 154-165.

Mellard, D., Woods, K., and Fall, E. (2011). Assessment and instruction of oral reading fluency among adults with low literacy. *Adult Basic Education and Literacy Journal, 5,* 3-14.

Meltzer, L.J. (1994). Assessment of learning disabilities: The challenge of evaluating the cognitive strategies and processes underlying learning. In G.R. Lyon (Ed.), *Frames of reference for the assessment of learning disabilities: New views on measurement issues* (pp. 571-606). Baltimore, MD: Paul H. Brookes.

Menard-Warwick, J., and Dabach, D.B. (2004). "In a little while I could be in front": Social mobility, class, and gender in the computer practices of two Mexicano families. *Journal of Adolescent and Adult Literacy, 47*(5), 380-389.

Menon, V., and Desmond, J.E. (2001). Left superior parietal cortex involvement in writing: Integrating fMRI with lesion evidence. *Cognitive Brain Research, 12,* 337-340.

Mercado, C. (1992). Researching research: A classroom-based student-teacher-researchers collaborative project. In A. Ambert and M. Alvarez (Eds.), *Puerto Rican children on the mainland: Interdisciplinary perspectives* (pp. 167-192). New York: Garland.

Merino, B.J., and Hammond, L. (1998). Family gardens and solar ovens: Making science education accessible to culturally and linguistically diverse students. *Multicultural Education, 5*(3), 34-37.

Merriam, S.B., Caffarella, R.S., and Baumgartner, L.M. (2007). *Learning in adulthood: A comprehensive guide* (3rd ed.). New York: Wiley.

Merrifield, J. (1997). If job training is the answer, what is the question? Research with displaced women textile workers. In G. Hull (Ed.), *Changing work, changing workers: Critical perspectives on language, literacy, and skills* (pp. 273-294). Albany, NY: State University of New York Press.

Meschyan, G., and Hernandez, A.E. (2006). Impact of language proficiency and orthographic transparency on bilingual word reading: An fMRI investigation. *NeuroImage, 29,* 1,135-1,140.

Messemer, J.E., and Valentine, T. (2004). The learning gains of male inmates participating in a basic skills program. *Adult Basic Education, 14*(2), 67-89.

Metcalfe, J. (2002). Is study time allocated selectively to a region of proximal learning? *Journal of Experimental Psychology: General, 131,* 349-363.

Metcalfe, J., and Kornell, N. (2003). The dynamics of learning and allocation of study time to a region of proximal learning. *Journal of Experimental Psychology: General, 132,* 530-542.

Metcalfe, J., and Kornell, N. (2005). A region of proximal learning model of study time allocation. *Journal of Memory and Language, 52,* 463-477.

Metcalfe, J., and Kornell, N. (2007). Principles of cognitive science in education: The effects of generation, errors and feedback. *Psychonomic Bulletin and Review, 14,* 225-229.

Meyer, B.J.F., and Poon, L.W. (2001). Effects of structure strategy training and signaling on recall of text. *Journal of Educational Psychology, 93,* 141-159.

Meyer, B.J.F., and Rice, G.E. (1989). Prose processing in adulthood: The text, the reader, and the task. In L.W. Poon, D.C. Rubin, and B.A. Wilson (Eds.), *Everyday cognition in adulthood and late life* (pp.157-174). Cambridge, England: Cambridge University Press.

Meyer, B.J.F., and Wijekumar, K. (2007). Web-based tutoring of the structure strategy: Theoretical background, design, and findings. In D.S. McNamara (Ed.), *Reading comprehension strategies: Theories, interventions, and technologies* (pp. 347-375). Mahwah, NJ: Lawrence Erlbaum Associates.

Meyer, B.J.F., Brandt, D.M., and Bluth, G.J. (1980). Use of top-level structure in text: Key for reading comprehension of ninth-grade students. *Reading Research Quarterly, 16*(1), 72-103.

Meyer, B.J.F., Young, C.J., and Bartlett, B.J. (1989). *Memory improved: Reading and memory enhancement across lifespan through strategic text structures.* Hillsdale, NJ: Lawrence Erlbaum Associates.

Meyer, B.J.F., Marsiske, M., and Willis, S.L. (1993). Text processing variables predict the readability of everyday documents read by older adults. *Reading Research Quarterly, 28*, 235-248.

Meyer, B.J F., Talbot, A.P., and Ranalli, C K. (2007). Why older adults make more immediate treatment decisions about cancer than younger adults. *Psychology and Aging, 22*, 505-524.

Meyer, D.K., and Turner, J.C. (2006). Re-conceptualizing emotion and motivation to learn in classroom contexts. *Educational Psychology Review, 18*, 377-390.

Meyer, M.S., and Felton, R.H. (1999). Repeated reading to enhance fluency: Old approaches and new direction. *Annals of Dyslexia, 49*, 283-306.

Meyler, A., Keller, T.A., Cherkassy, V.L., Gabrieli, J.E.D., and Just, M.A. (2008). Modifying the brain activation of poor readers during sentence comprehension with extended remedial instruction: A longitudinal study of neuroplasticity. *Neuropsychologia, 46*, 2,580-2,592.

Mezirow, J. (1981). A critical theory of adult learning and education. *Adult Education Quarterly, 32*, 3-24.

Mezirow, J. (1996). Contemporary paradigms of learning. *Adult Education Quarterly, 46*, 158-173.

Mezirow, J. (1998). On critical reflection. *Adult Education Quarterly, 48*, 185-198.

Michael, E.B., Keller, T.A., Carpenter, P.A., and Just, M.A. (2001). An fMRI investigation of sentence comprehension by eye and by ear: Modality fingerprints on cognitive processes. *Human Brain Mapping, 13*, 239-252.

Michaels, S., and O'Connor, M.C. (1990). *Literacy as reasoning within multiple discourse: Implications for policy and educational reform.* Paper presented at the Council of Chief State School Officers Summer Institute on Restructuring Learning, Educational Development Center, Literacies Institute, Newton, MA.

Middleton, M.J., and Midgley, C. (1997). Avoiding the demonstration of lack of ability: An underexplored aspect of goal theory. *Journal of Educational Psychology, 89*(4), 710-718.

Midgley, C. (2002). *Goals, goal structures, and patterns of adaptive learning.* Mahwah, NJ: Lawrence Erlbaum Associates.

Midgley, C., and Urdan, T. (2001). Academic self-handicapping and achievement goals: A further examination. *Contemporary Educational Psychology, 26*, 61-75.

Mikulecky, L. (1998). Adjusting school writing curricula to reflect expanded workplace writing. In M. Garay and S. Bernhardt (Eds.), *Expanding literacies: English teaching and the new workplace* (pp. 201-224). Albany, NY: State University of New York Press.

Mikulecky, L., and Lloyd, P. (1997). Evaluation of workplace literacy programs: A profile of effective instructional practices. *Journal of Literacy Research, 29*(4), 555-585.

Miles, J.R., and Stine-Morrow, E.A.L. (2004). Age differences in self-regulated learning from reading sentences. *Psychology and Aging, 19*, 626-636.

Miller, B., Esposito, L., and McCardle, P. (2011). A public health approach to improving the lives of adult learners: An introduction to a special issue on adult literacy interventions. *Journal of Research on Educational Effectiveness, 4*, 87-100.

Miller, J., and Schwanenflugel, P.J. (2006). Prosody of syntactically complex sentences in the oral reading of young children. *Journal of Educational Psychology, 98*(4), 839-853.

Miller, L.M.S. (2003). The effects of age and domain knowledge on text processing. *Journals of Gerontology Series B-Psychological Sciences and Social Sciences, 58*(4), P217-P223.

Miller, L.M.S. (2009). Age differences in the effects of domain knowledge on reading efficiency. *Psychology and Aging, 24*, 63-74.

Miller, L.M.S., and Gagne, D.D. (2005). The effects of age and control beliefs on reading strategies. *Aging, Neuropsychology, and Cognition, 12*, 129-148.

Miller, L.M.S., and Lachman, M.E. (1999). The sense of control and cognitive aging: Toward a model of mediational processes. In T. Hess and F. Blanchard-Fields (Eds.), *Social cognition* (pp.17-41). New York: Academic Press.

Miller, L.M.S., and Stine-Morrow, E.A.L. (1998). Aging and the effects of knowledge on on-line reading strategies. *Journal of Gerontology: Psychological Sciences, 53B*, P223-P233.

Miller, L.M.S., and West, R.L. (2010). The effects of age, control beliefs, and feedback on self-regulation of reading and problem solving. *Experimental Aging Research, 36*, 40-63.

Miller, L.M.S., Lachman, M.E., Hess, T.M., and Blanchard-Fields, F. (1999). The sense of control and cognitive aging: Toward a model of mediational processes. In T.M. Hess and F. Blanchard-Fields (Eds.), *Social cognition and aging* (pp. 17-41). New York: Academic Press.

Miller, L.M.S., Stine-Morrow, E.A.L., Kirkorian, H.L., and Conroy, M.L. (2004). Adult age differences in knowledge-driven reading. *Journal of Educational Psychology, 96*(4), 811-821.

Miller, L.M.S., Cohen, J.A., and Wingfield, A. (2006). Contextual knowledge reduces demands on working memory during reading. *Memory and Cognition, 34*, 1,355-1,367.

Miller, M., Linn, R., and Gronlund, N. (2009). *Measurement and assessment in teaching* (10th ed.). Upper Saddle River, NJ: Pearson Education.

Miller, S., and Meece, J. (1997). Enhancing elementary students' motivation to read and write: A classroom intervention study. *Journal of Educational Research, 90*, 286-299.

Minot, W.S., and Gamble, K.R. (1991). Self-esteem and writing apprehension of basic writers: Conflicting evidence. *Journal of Basic Writing, 2*, 116-125.

Mishler, E.G. (2004). Historians of the self: Restoring lives, revising identities. *Research in Human Development, 1*(1), 101-121.

Mislevy, R.J., Steinberg, L.S., and Almond, R.G. (2003). On the structure of educational assessments. *Measurement: Interdisciplinary Research and Perspectives, 1*, 3-67.

Mitchell, D.C., Hunt, R.R., and Schmitt, F.A. (1986). The generation effect and reality monitoring: Evidence from dementia and normal aging. *Journal of Gerontology, 41*, 79-84.

Mitrovic, A., Martin, B., and Suraweera, P. (2007). Intelligent tutors for all: The constraint-based approach. *IEEE Intelligent Systems, 22*(4), 38-45.

Moats, L.C. (1994). The missing foundation in teacher education: Knowledge of the structure of spoken and written language. *Annals of Dyslexia, 44*, 81-102.

Moats, L.C. (2004). *Language essentials for teachers of reading and spelling (LETRS), Module 2, the speech sounds of English, and Module 3, spellography for teachers.* Longmont, CO: Sopris West Educational Services.

Moats, L.C. (2005). *Language essentials for teachers of reading and spelling (LETRS).* Longmont, CO: Sopris West Educational Services.

Moats, L.C., and Dakin, K.E. (2007). *Basic facts about dyslexia and other reading problems.* Baltimore, MD: The International Dyslexia Association.

Moats, L.C., Foorman, B.R., and Taylor, W.P. (2006). How quality of writing instruction impacts high-risk fourth graders' writing. *Reading and Writing: An Interdisciplinary Journal, 19*, 363-391.

Moje, E. B. (1995). Talking about science: An interpretation of the effects of teacher talk in a high school classroom. *Journal of Research in Science Teaching, 32*, 349-371.

Moje, E. B. (1996). "I teach students, not subjects": Teacher-student relationships as contexts for secondary literacy. *Reading Research Quarterly, 31*, 172-195.

Moje, E.B. (1997). Exploring discourse, subjectivity, and knowledge in chemistry class. *Journal of Classroom Interaction, 32*(2), 35-44.

Moje, E.B. (2000a). *All the stories that we have: Adolescents' insights on literacy and learning in secondary school.* Newark, DE: International Reading Association.

Moje, E.B. (2000b). To be part of the story: The literacy practices of gangsta adolescents. *Teachers College Record, 102*, 652-690.

Moje, E.B. (2002). Re-framing adolescent literacy research for new times: Studying youth as a resource. *Reading Research and Instruction, 41*(3), 211-228.

Moje, E.B. (2006a). Achieving identities: Why youth identities matter in their school achievement. In V.O. Pang and R. Jiménez (Eds.), *Race and language* (vol. 2, pp. 133-156). Westport, CT: Greenwood Press/Praeger.

Moje, E.B. (2006b). Motivating texts, motivating contexts, motivating adolescents: An examination of the role of motivation in adolescent literacy practices and development. *Perspectives, 32*(3), 10-14.

Moje, E.B. (2007). Developing socially just subject-matter instruction: A review of the literature on disciplinary literacy. In L. Parker (Ed.), *Review of research in education* (pp. 1-44). Washington, DC: American Educational Research Association.

Moje, E.B. (2008a). Foregrounding the disciplines in secondary literacy teaching and learning: A call for change. *Journal of Adolescent and Adult Literacy, 52*(2), 96-107.

Moje, E.B. (2008b).Youth cultures, literacies, and identities in and out of school. In J. Flood, S.B. Heath, and D. Lapp (Eds.), *Handbook of research in teaching the communicative and visual arts* (pp. 207-219). Mahwah, NJ: Lawrence Erlbaum Associates.

Moje, E.B. (2009). A call for new research of new and multi-literacies. *Reseach in the Teaching of English, 43*(4), 348-362.

Moje, E.B., and Luke, A. (2009). Review of research: Literacy and identity—Examining the metaphors in history and contemporary research. *Reading Research Quarterly, 44*(4), 415-437.

Moje, E.B., and Martinez, M. (2007). The role of peers, families, and ethnic identity in the educational persistence of Latino youth. In A. Fuligni (Ed.), *Contesting stereotypes and creating identities* (pp. 209-238). New York: Russell Sage.

Moje, E.B., and Speyer, J. (2008). The reality of challenging texts in high school science and social studies: How teachers can mediate comprehension. In K.A. Hinchman and H.K. Sheridan-Thomas (Eds.), *Best practices in adolescent literacy instruction* (pp. 185-211). New York: Guilford Press.

Moje, E.B., and Wade, S.E. (1997). What case discussions reveal about teacher thinking. *Teaching and Teacher Education, 13*, 691-712.

Moje, E.B., Dillon, D.R., and O'Brien, D.G. (2000). Re-examining the roles of the learner, the text, and the context in secondary literacy. *Journal of Educational Research, 93*, 165-180.

Moje, E.B., Young, J., Readence, J.E., and Moore, D.W. (2000). Reinventing adolescent literacy for new times: A commentary on perennial and millennial issues in adolescent literacy. *Journal of Adolescent and Adult Literacy, 43*, 400-411.

Moje, E.B., Willes, D.J., and Fassio, K. (2001a). Constructing and negotiating literacy in a writer's workshop: Literacy teaching and learning in the seventh grade. In E.B. Moje and D.G. O'Brien (Eds.), *Constructions of literacy: Studies of literacy teaching and learning in secondary classrooms and schools* (pp. 193-212). Mahwah, NJ: Lawrence Erlbaum Associates.

Moje, E.B., Collazo, T., Carrillo, R., and Marx, R.W. (2001b). "Maestro, what is 'quality'?": Language, literacy, and discourse in project-based science. *Journal of Research in Science Teaching, 38*(4), 469-496.

Moje, E.B., Peek-Brown, D., Sutherland, L.M., Marx, R.W., Blumenfeld, P., and Krajcik, J. (2004a). Explaining explanations: Developing scientific literacy in middle school project-based science reforms. In D. Strickland and D.E. Alvermann (Eds.), *Bridging the gap: Improving literacy learning for preadolescent and adolescent learners in grades 4-12* (pp. 227-251). New York: Carnegie Corporation.

Moje, E.B., Ciechanowski, K.M., Kramer, K.E., Ellis, L.M., Carrillo, R., and Collazo, T. (2004b). Working toward third space in content area literacy: An examination of everyday funds of knowledge and discourse. *Reading Research Quarterly, 39*(1), 38-71.

Moje, E.B., Overby, M., Tysvaer, N., and Morris, K. (2008). The complex world of adolescent literacy: Myths, motivations, and mysteries. *Harvard Educational Review, 78,* 107-154.

Moje, E.B., Sutherland, L.M., Solomon, T.E., and Vanderkerkof, M. (2010). *Integrating literacy instruction into secondary school science inquiry: The challenges of disciplinary literacy teaching and professional development.* Available: http://www-personal.umich.edu/~moje/pdf/MojeEtAlScienceLiteracyTeachingStrategies2010.pdf [Feb. 2012].

Molden, D.C., and Dweck, C.S. (2006). Finding "meaning" in psychology: A lay thoeries approach to self-regulation, social perception, and social development. *American Psychologist, 61,* 192-203.

Moll, K., and Landerl, K. (2009). Double disassociation between reading and spelling deficits. *Scientific Studies of Reading, 13,* 359-382.

Moll, L.C. (1992). Literacy research in community and classrooms: A sociocultural approach. In R. Beach, J.L. Green, M.L. Kamil, and T. Shanahan (Eds.), *Multidisciplinary perspectives in literacy research* (pp. 211-244). Urbana, IL: National Conference on Research in English and National Council of Teachers of English.

Moll, L.C. (1994). Literacy research in community and classrooms: A sociocultural approach. In R.B. Ruddell and M.R. Ruddell (Authors) and H. Singer (Ed.), *Theoretical models and processes of reading* (4th ed., pp. 179-207). Newark, DE: International Reading Association.

Moll, L.C., and Diaz, S. (1993). Change as the goal of educational research. In E. Jacob and C. Jordan (Eds.), *Minority education: Anthropological perspectives* (pp. 67-79). Norwood, NJ: Ablex.

Moll, L.C., and Gonzales, N. (1994). Lessons from research with language minority children. *Journal of Reading Behavior, 26,* 439-456.

Moll, L.C., and Greenberg, J. (1990). Creating zones of possibilities: Combining social contexts for instruction. In L.C. Moll (Ed.), *Vygotsky and education* (pp. 319-348). New York: Cambridge University Press.

Moll, L.C., and Whitmore, K.F. (1993). Vygotsky in classroom practice: Moving from individual transmission to social transaction. In E.A. Forman, N. Minick, and C.A. Stone (Eds.), *Contexts for learning: Sociocultural dynamics in children's development* (pp. 19-42). New York: Oxford University Press.

Moll, L.C., Veléz-Ibañéz, C., and Greenberg, J. (1989). *Year-one progress report: Community knowledge and classroom practice: Combining resources for literacy instruction.* Tucson: University of Arizona.

Moller, A.C., Deci, E.L., and Ryan, R.M. (2006). Choice and ego-depletion: The moderating role of autonomy. *Personality and Social Psychology Bulletin, 32,* 1,024-1,036.

Moni, K.B., Jobling, A., and van Kraayenoord, C.C. (2007). "They're a lot cleverer than I thought": Challenging perceptions of disability support staff as they tutor in an adult literacy program. *International Journal of Lifelong Education, 26*(4), 439-459.

Moreno, R. (2007). Optimising learning from animations by minimizing cognitive load: Cognitive and affective consequences of signaling and segmentation methods. *Applied Cognitive Psychology, 21,* 765-781.

Moreno, R., and Mayer, R.E. (2004). Personalized messages that promote science learning in virtual environments. *Journal of Educational Psychology, 96,* 165-173.

Moreno, R., and Mayer, R.E. (2007). Interactive multimodal learning environments. *Educational Psychology Review, 19,* 309-326.

Morgan, A.M. (2004). Educating low-literacy adults: To teach or not to teach? *International Journal of Educational Reform, 13*(2), 151-158.

Morgan, P.L., Fuchs, D., Compton, D.L., Cordray, D.S., and Fuchs, L.S. (2008). Does early reading failure decrease children's reading motivation? *Journal of Learning Disabilities*, *41*, 387-404.

Morphy, P., and Graham, S. (2010). Word processing programs and weaker writers/readers: A meta-analysis of research findings. *Reading and Writing*, March, 1-38.

Morra, A.M., and Asis, M.I. (2009). The effect of audio and written teacher responses on EFL student revision. *Journal of College Reading and Learning*, *39*(2), 68-82.

Morrell, E. (2002). Toward a critical pedagogy of popular culture: Literacy development among urban youth. *Journal of Adolescent and Adult Literacy*, *46*, 72-77.

Morrell, E. (2004). *Linking literacy and popular culture*. New York: Christopher-Gordon.

Morrell, E., and Collatos, A. (2003). *Critical pedagogy in a college access program for students of color*. Paper presented at the American Educational Research Association, April, Chicago, IL.

Morrell, E., and Duncan-Andrade, J. (2003). What they do learn in school: Hip-hop as a bridge to canonical poetry. In J. Mahiri (Ed.), *What they don't learn in school: Literacy in the lives of urban youth* (pp. 247-268). New York: Peter Lang.

Morris, R.D., Lovett, M.W., Wolf, M., Sevcik, R.A., Steinbach, K.A., Frijters, J.C., and Shapiro, M.B. (2010). Multiple-component remediation for developmental reading disabilities: IQ, socioeconomic status, and race as factors on remedial outcome. *Journal of Learning Disabilities* [first published on May 5, 2010 before print]. Abstract available: http://www.ncbi.nlm.nih.gov/pubmed/20445204 [Sept. 2011].

Morrow, D.G., Leirer, V.O., Andrassy, J. M., Tanke, E.D., and Stine-Morrow, E.A.L. (1996). Medication instruction design: Younger and older adult schemas for taking medication. *Human Factors*, *38*, 556-573.

Morrow, D.G., Miller, L.M.S., Ridolfo, H.E., Magnor, C., Fischer, U.M., Kokayeff, N.K., and Stine-Morrow, E. (2009). Expertise and age differences in pilot decision making. *Aging, Neuropsychology, and Cognition*, *16*(1), 33-55.

Mortensen, L., Smith-Lock, K., and Nickels, L. (2008). Text structure and patterns of cohesion in narrative texts written by adults with a history of language impairment. *Reading and Writing*, *22*, 735-752.

Mosenthal, P.B. (1996). Understanding the strategies of document literacy and their conditions of use. *Journal of Educational Psychology*, *88*, 314-332.

Mosenthal, P.B, Conley, M., Colella, A., and Davidson-Mosenthal, R. (1985). The influence of prior knowledge and teacher lesson structure on children's production of narratives. *Elementary School Journal*, *85*, 621-634.

Mostow, J. (2008). Experience from a reading tutor that listens: Evaluation purposes, excuses, and methods. In C.K. Kinzer and L. Verhoeven (Eds.), *Interactive literacy education: Facilitating literacy environments through technology* (pp. 117-148). Mahwah, NJ: Lawrence Erlbaum Associates.

Mull, C., Sitlington, P.L., and Alper, S. (2001). Postsecondary education for students with learning disabilities: A synthesis of the literature. *Exceptional Children*, *68*(1), 97-118.

Mulligan, N.W., and Hornstein, S.L. (2003). Memory for actions: Self-performed tasks and reenactment effect. *Memory and Cognition*, *31*, 412-421.

Muraven, M., and Baumeister, R.F. (2000). Self-regulation and depletion of limited resources: Does self-control resemble a muscle? *Psychological Bulletin*, *126*, 247-259.

Murphy, P.K., Wilkinson, I.A.G., Soter, A.O., Hennessey, M.N., and Alexander, J.F. (2009). Examining the effects of classroom discussion on students' comprehension of text: A meta-analysis. *Journal of Educational Psychology*, *101*(3), 740-764.

Murray, D. (1978). Internal revision: A process of discovery. In C. Cooper and L. Odell (Eds.), *Research on composing: Points of departure* (pp. 85-103). Urbana, IL: National Council of Teachers of English.

Myerson, J., Emery, L., White, D.A., and Hale, S. (2003). Efects of age, domain, and processing demands on memory span: Evidence for differential decline. *Aging, Neuropsychology, and Cognition, 10,* 20-27.

Nagy, W.E. (1984). *Limitations of vocabulary instruction: Technical report no. 326.* Expanded version of a paper presented at the 68th Annual Meeting of the American Educational Research Association, April 23-27, New Orleans, LA. Available: http://www.eric.ed.gov/PDFS/ED248498.pdf [Sept. 2011].

Nagy, W.E. (2007). Metalinguistic awareness and the vocabulary-comprehension connection. In R.K. Wagner, A.E. Muse, and K.R. Tannenbaum (Eds.), *Vocabulary acquisition implications for reading comprehension.* New York: Guilford Press.

Nagy, W.E., and Anderson, R.C. (1984). How many words are there in printed school English? *Reading Research Quarterly, 19,* 304-330.

Nagy, W.E., and Scott, J.A. (2000). Vocabulary processes. In M.L. Kamil, P. Mosenthal, P.D. Pearson, and R. Barr (Eds.), *Handbook of reading research* (vol. III, pp. 269-284). Mahwah, NJ: Lawrence Erlbaum Associates.

Nagy, W.E., Herman, P.A. and Anderson, R.C. (1985). Learning words from context. *Reading Research Quarterly, 20,* 233-253.

Nagy, W.E. Anderson, R., Schommer, M., Scott, J., and Stallman, A.C. (1989). Morphological families and word recognition. *Reading Research Quarterly, 24,* 262-282.

Nagy, W.E., García, G.E., Durgunoğlu, A.Y., and Hancin-Bhatt, B.J. (1993). Spanish-English bilingual students' use of cognates in English reading. *Journal of Reading Behavior, 25,* 241-259.

Nakamoto, J., Lindsey, K.A., and Manis, F.R. (2008). A cross-linguistic investigation of English language learners' reading comprehension in English and Spanish. *Scientific Studies of Reading, 12*(4), 351-371.

Nanda, A., Greenberg, D., and Morris, R. (2010). Modeling child-based theoretical reading constructs with struggling adult readers. *Journal of Learning Disabilities, 43*(2), 139-153.

Nash, A., and Kallenbach, S. (2009). *Making it worth the stay: Findings from the New England adult learner persistence project.* Boston, MA: New England Literacy Resource Center. Available: http://www.nelrc.org/persist/report09.pdf [Sept. 2011].

Nassaji, H. (2009). Effects of recasts and elicitations in dyadic interaction and the role of feedback explicitness *Language Learning, 59*(2), 411-452.

National Assessment of Educational Progress. (2008). *The nation's report card: Writing 2007* (NCES). Washington, DC: U.S. Department of Education.

National Assessment of Educational Progress. (2010). *The nation's report card: Grade 12 reading and mathematics 2009 national and pilot state results* (NCES). Washington, DC: U.S. Department of Education.

National Center for Education Statistics. (2009). *Digest of education statistics, 2008.* NCES 2009-020, Chapter 3. Washington, DC: U.S. Department of Education.

National Center for Education Statistics. (2010a). *The condition of education, 2010.* NCES 2010-028, Indicator 5. Washington, DC: U.S. Department of Education.

National Center for Education Statistics. (2010b). *Public school graduates and dropouts from the common core of data: School year 2007-08 first look.* Available: http://nces.ed.gov/pubs2010/2010341.pdf [Sept. 2011].

National Center on Education and the Economy (1997). *New standards performance standards* (vols. 1-3). [Reprinted in 1998.] Available: http://www.ncee.org/publications/new-standards-2/ [Sept. 2011].

National Commission on Writing. (2004). *Writing: A ticket to work . . . or a ticket out: A survey of business leaders.* The College Board Advocacy and Policy Center. Available: http://www.writingcommission.org/prod_downloads/writingcom/writing-ticket-to-work.pdf [Sept. 2011].

National Commission on Writing. (2005). *Writing: A powerful message from state government*. The College Board Advocacy and Policy Center. Available: http://www.writing commission.org/prod_downloads/writingcom/powerful-message-from-state.pdf [Sept. 2011].

National Council of Teachers of English. (2008). *21st century curriculum and assessment framework*. Adopted by the NCTE Executive Committee, Nov. 19. Available: http:// www.ncte.org/positions/statements/21stcentframework [Sept. 2011].

National Council of Teachers of English. (2009). *Writing between the lines—and everywhere else*. Available: http://www.ncte.org/topics/betweenlines [Sept. 2011].

National Council on Disability. (2003). *Addressing the needs of youth with disabilities in the juvenile justice system: The current status of evidence-based research*. Washington, DC: Urban Institute Justice Policy Center. Available: http://www.ncd.gov/newroom/ publications/2003/juvenile.htm [Sept. 2011].

National Governors Association and Council of Chief State School Officers. (2009). *Common core state standards* (draft). Available: http://www.corestandards.org/ [Sept. 2011].

National Institute of Child Health and Human Development. (2000a). *Report of the National Reading Panel. Teaching children to read: An evidence-based assessment of the scientific research literature on reading and its implications for reading instruction*. Available: http://www.nationalreadingpanel.org/Publications/summary.htm [Sept. 2011].

National Institute of Child Health and Human Development. (2000b). *Report of the National Reading Panel. Teaching children to read: An evidence-based assessment of the scientific research literature on reading and its implications for reading instruction: Reports of the subgroups*. Available: http://www.nationalreadingpanel.org/Publications/subgroups. htm [Sept. 2011].

National Reporting System for Adult Education. (2001). *Measures and methods for the national reporting system for adult education—Implementation guidelines*. Washington, DC: Division of Adult Education and Literacy, Office of Vocational and Adult Education, U.S. Department of Education.

National Research Council. (1998). *Preventing reading difficulties in young children*. C.E. Snow, P. Griffin, and M.S. Burns (Eds.). Committee on the Prevention of Reading Difficulties in Young Children. Commission on Behavioral and Social Sciences and Education. Washington, DC: National Academy Press.

National Research Council. (1999). *How people learn: Bridging research and practice*. M.S. Donovan and J.W. Pellegrino (Eds.). Committee on Learning Research and Educational Practice, Commission on Behavioral and Social Sciences and Education. Washington, DC: National Academy Press.

National Research Council. (2000). *How people learn: Brain, mind, experience, and school. Expanded edition*. Committee on Development in the Science of Learning. J.D. Bransford, A.L. Brown, and R.R. Cocking (Eds.) with additional material from the Committee on Learning Research and Educational Practice. M.S. Donovan, J.D. Bransford, and J.W. Pellegrino (Eds.). Commission on Behavioral and Social Sciences and Education. Washington, DC: National Academy Press.

National Research Council. (2005). *How students learn: History, mathematics, and science in the classroom*. Committee on *How People Learn*, A Targeted Report for Teachers, M.S. Donovan and J.D. Bransford (Eds.). Division of Behavioral and Social Sciences and Education. Washington, DC: The National Academies Press.

National Research Council. (2008). *Learning science in informal environments: People, places, and pursuits*. Committee on Learning Science in Informal Environments. P. Bell, B. Lowenstein, A.W. Shouse, and M. Feder (Eds.). Board on Science Education, Center for Education. Division of Behavioral and Social Sciences and Education. Washington, DC: The National Academies Press.

National Research Council. (2011). *Learning science through computer games and simulations*. Committee on Science Learning: Computer Games, Simulations, and Education. M.A. Honey and M. Hilton (Eds.). Board on Science Education, Division of Behavioral and Social Sciences and Education. Washington, DC: The National Academies Press.

National Research Council and Institute of Medicine. (2002). *Community programs to promote youth development*. Committee on Community-Level Programs for Youth. J. Eccles and J.A. Gootman (Eds.). Board on Children, Youth, and Families. Division of Behavioral and Social Sciences and Education. Washington, DC: National Academy Press.

National Writing Project. (2007). *The 2007 survey on teaching writing: American public opinion on the importance of writing in schools*. Conducted for the National Writing Project. Available: http://www.nwp.org/cs/public/download/nwp_file/8856/NWP_2007_Survey_Report.pdf?x-r=pcfile_d\ [Sept. 2011].

Nelson, N., and Calfee, R. (1998). The reading-writing connection. In N. Nelson and R. Calfee (Eds.), *Ninety-seventh yearbook of the National Society for the Study of Education, part II* (pp. 1-52). Chicago, IL: National Society for the Study of Education.

Nelson, T.O. (1996). Consciousness and metacognition. *American Psychologist, 51*, 102-116.

Nelson, T.O., Dunlosky, J., Graf, A., and Narens, L. (1994). Utilization of metacognitive judgments in the allocation of study during multitrial learning. *Psychological Science, 5*, 207-213.

Neufeld, P. (2005). Comprehension instruction in content area classes. *The Reading Teacher, 59*(4), 302-312.

Neuman, S.B. (1999). Books make a difference: A study of access to literacy. *Reading Research Quarterly, 34*, 286-301.

Neuman, S.B., and Celano, D. (2001). Access to print in low- and middle-income communities: An ecological study of 4 neighborhoods. *Reading Research Quarterly, 36*, 8-26.

New London Group. (1996). A pedagogy of multiliteracies: Designing social futures. *Harvard Educational Review, 66*(1), 60-92.

Newman, L., Wagner, M., Cameto, R., and Knokey, A.M. (2009). *The post-high school outcomes of youth with disabilities up to 4 years after high school*. A report of findings from the National Longitudinal Transition Study-2 (NLTS2). Menlo Park, CA: SRI International. Available: http://www.nlts2.org/reports/2009_04/index.html [Sept. 2011].

Newport, E.L. (1990). Maturational constraints on language learning. *Cognitive Science, 14*, 11-28.

Nicholas, H., Lightbown, P., and Spada, N. (2001). Recasts as feedback to language learners. *Language Learning, 51*, 719-758.

Nicholls, J.G. (1984). Achievement motivation: Conceptions of ability, subjective experience, task choice, and performance. *Psychological Review, 91*, 328-346.

Nicolson, R.I., Fawcett, A.J., and Dean, P. (2001). Developmental dyslexia: The cerebellar deficit hypothesis. *Trends in Neurosciences, 24*(9), 508-511.

Niemiec, C.P., Lynch, M.F., Vansteenkiste, M., Bernstein, J., Deci, E.L., and Ryan, R.M. (2006). The antecedents and consequences of autonomous self-regulation for college: A self-determination theory perspective on socialization. *Journal of Adolescence, 29*, 761-775.

Niogi, S.N., and McCandliss, B.D. (2006). Left lateralized white matter microstructure accounts for individual differences in reading ability and disability. *Neuropsychologia, 44*, 2,178-2,188.

Nisbett, R. (2003). *The geography of thought: How Asians and Westerners think differently... and why*. New York: The Free Press.

Nisbett, R.E., Peng, K., Choi, I., and Norenzayan, A. (2001). Culture and systems of thought: Holistic versus analytic cognition. *Psychological Review, 108*(2), 291-310.

Nissen, H.J., Damerow, P., and Englund, R.K. (1993). *Archaic bookkeeping.* Chicago: University of Chicago Press.

Nobal, K.G., McCandliss, B.D., and Farah, M.J. (2007). Socioeconomic gradients predict individual differences in neurocognitive abilities. *Developmental Science, 10*(4), 464-480.

Noble, K.G., Wolmetz, M.E., Ochs, L.G., Farah, M.J., and McCandliss, B.D. (2006). Brain-behavior relationships in reading acquisition are modulated by socioeconomic factors. *Developmental Science, 9*(6), 642-654.

Noh, S.R., Shake, M.C., Parisi, J.M., Joncich, A.D., Morrow, D.G., and Stine-Morrow, E.A.L. (2007). Age differences in learning from text: The effects of content preexposure on reading. *International Journal of Behavioral Development, 31*(2), 133-148.

Noice, H., and Noice, T. (2006). What studies of actors and acting can tell us about memory and cognitive functioning. *Current Directions in Psychological Science, 15*, 14-18.

Noice, H., and Noice, T. (2008). An arts intervention for older adults living in subsidized retirement homes. *Aging, Neuropsychology, and Cognition, 16*, 56-79.

Noice, H., Noice, T., Perrig-Chiello, P., and Perrig, W. (1999). Improving memory in older adults by instructing them in professional actors' learning strategies. *Applied Cognitive Psychology, 13*, 315-328.

Noice, H., Noice, T., and Kennedy, C. (2000). Effects of enactment by professional actors at encoding and retrieval. *Memory, 8*, 353-363.

Nolen, S.B. (1988). Reasons for studying: Motivational orientations and study strategies. *Cognition and Instruction, 5*, 269-287.

Nolen, S.B. (2003). *The development of interest and motivation to read and write.* Paper presented at the 10th bi-annual meeting of the European Association for Research on Learning and Instruction, August, Padova, Italy.

Nolen, S.B., and Haladyna, T.M. (1990). Motivation and studying in high school science. *The Journal of Research in Science Teaching, 27*, 115-126.

Noll, E. (1998). Experiencing literacy in and out of school: Case studies of two American Indian youths [Sioux Indians]. *Journal of Literacy Research, 30*(2), 205-232.

Noordman, L.G.M., and Vonk, W. (1992). Readers' knowledge and control of inferences in reading. *Language and Cognitive Processes, 7*, 373-391.

Norenzayan, A., and Nisbett, R.E. (2000). Culture and causal cognition. *Current Directions in Psychological Science, 9*(4), 132-135.

Norman, S., Kemper, S., and Kynette, D. (1992). Adult reading comprehension: Effects of syntactic complexity and working memory. *Journals of Gerontology, 47*(4), 258-265.

Norris, J.M., and Ortega, L. (2000). Effectiveness of L2 instruction: A research synthesis and quantitative meta-analysis. *Language Learning, 50*, 417-528.

North Central Regional Educational Laboratory. (2003). *enGauge 21st century skills for 21st century learners: Literacy in the digital age.* Available: http://www.ncrel.org/engauge [Sept. 2011].

Nosarti, C., Mechelli, A., Green, D.W., and Price, C.J. (2009). The impact of second language learning on semantic and nonsemantic first language reading. *Cerebral Cortex, 20*(2), 315-327.

Nuckles, M., Hubner, S., and Renkl, A. 2009. Enhancing self-regulated learning by writing learning protocols. *Learning and Instruction, 19*, 259-271.

Nystrand, M. (2006). Research on the role of classroom discourse as it affects reading comprehension. *Research in the Teaching of English, 40*, 392-412.

Nystrand, M., Wu, L., Gamoran, A., Zeiser, S., and Long, D. (2003). Questions in time: Investigating the structure and dynamics of unfolding classroom discourse. *Discourse Processes, 35*, 135-196.

Oakhill, J., Cain, K., and Bryant, P.E. (2003). The dissociation of word reading and text comprehension: Evidence from component skills. *Language and Cognitive Processes, 18*, 443-468.

O'Brien, E.J., Raney, G.E., Albrecht, J.E., and Rayner, K. (1997). Processes involved in the resolution of explicit anaphors. *Discourse Processes, 23*, 1-24.

O'Brien, E.J., Rizzella, M.L., Albrecht, J.E., and Halleran, J.G. (1998). Updating a situation model: A memory-based text processing view. *Journal of Experimental Psychology: Learning, Memory, and Cognition, 24*, 1,200-1,210.

O'Connor, C. (1997). Dispositions toward (collective) struggle and educational resilience in the inner city: A case analysis of six African-American high school students. *American Educational Research Journal, 34*, 593-629.

O'Connor, R. Notari-Syverson, A., and Vadasky, P. (1996). Ladders to literacy: The effects of teacher-led phonological activities for kindergarten children with and without disabilities. *Exceptional Children, 63*, 117-130.

Oddi, L.F. (1986). Development and validation of an instrument to identify self-directed continuing learners. *Adult Education Quarterly, 38*, 21-31.

Ogbu, J.U. (1978). *Minority education and caste: The American system in cross-cultural perspective.* New York: Academic Press.

Ogbu, J.U. (1987). Variability in minority school performance: A problem in search of an explanation. *Anthropology and Educational Quarterly, 18*, 312-334.

Ogbu, J.U. (1991). Immigrant and involuntary minorities in comparative perspective. In J.U. Ogbu and M.A. Gibson (Eds.), *Minority status and schooling: A comparative study of immigrant and involuntary minorities* (pp. 3-33). New York: Garland.

Ogbu, J.U. (1993). Frameworks—Variability in minority school performance: A problem in search of an explanation. In E. Jacob and C. Jordan (Eds.), *Minority education: Anthropological perspectives* (pp. 83-112). Norwood, NJ: Ablex.

Olinghouse, N., and Graham, S. (2009). The relationship between the writing knowledge and the writing performance of elementary-grade students. *Journal of Educational Psychology, 101*, 37-50.

O'Neil, H. (Ed.). (2005). *What works in distance learning: Guidelines.* Greenwich, CT: Information Age.

O'Neil, H.F., Wainess, R., and Baker, E.L. (2005). Classification of learning outcomes: Evidence from the computer games literature. *The Curriculum Journal, 16*, 455-474.

Ordóñez, C.L., Carlo, M.S., Snow, C.E., and McLaughlin, B. (2002). Depth and breadth of vocabulary in two languages: Which vocabulary skills transfer? *Journal of Educational Psychology, 94*(4), 719-728.

O'Reilly, T., and McNamara, D.S. (2007). The impact of science knowledge, reading skill, and reading strategy knowledge on more traditional "high-stakes" measures of high school students' science achievement. *American Educational Research Journal, 44*, 161-197.

Organisation for Economic Co-operation and Development. (2010). *Are the new millenium learners making the grade? Technology use and educational performance in PISA.* Paris, France: Author. Available: http://www.oecdbookshop.org/oecd/display.asp?k=5KSCG4 J39DHB&lang=en [Sept. 2011].

Organisation for Economic Co-operation and Development and Statistics Canada. (2005). *Learning a living: First results of the adult literacy and life skills survey.* Paris, France: Author. Available: http://www.statcan.gc.ca/pub/89-603-x/2005001/4071714-eng.htm [Sept. 2011].

Orpwood, G., Schollen, L., Marinelli-Henriques, P., and Assiri, H. (2010). *College mathematics project 2009* (Final report). Seneca, Ontario: Seneca College of Applied Arts and Technology, York-Seneca Institute for Mathematics, Science and Technology Education.

Osborn Popp, S.E., Ryan, J.M., Thompson, M.S., and Behrens, J.T. (2003). *Operationalizing the rubric: The effect of benchmark selection on the assessed quality of writing*. Presented at the annual meeting of the American Educational Research Association, April, Chicago, IL.

Osborne, J. (2010). Arguing to learn in science: The role of collaborative, critical discourse. *Science, 328*, 463-466.

O'Sullivan, P.J., Ysseldyke, J.E., Christenson, S.L., and Thurlow, M.L. (1990). Mildly handicapped elementary students' opportunity to learn during reading instruction in mainstream and special education settings. *Reading Research Quarterly, 25*, 131-146.

Ouyang, R. (1993). A meta-analysis: Effectiveness of computer-assisted instruction at the level of elementary education (K-6). Doctoral dissertation, Indiana University of Pennsylvania. *Dissertation Abstracts International, 54*, 02A.

Oyserman, D. (1987). *Possible selves and behavior: The case of juvenile delinquency*. Thesis dissertation, University of Michigan.

Oyserman, D., Bybee, D., and Terry, K. (2006). Possible selves and academic outcomes: How and when possible selves impel action. *Journal of Personality and Social Psychology, 91*, 188-204.

Oyserman, D., Brickman, D., and Rhodes M. (2007). Racial ethnic identity: Content and consequences for African American, Latino and Latina youth. In A. Fuligni (Ed.), *Contesting stereotypes and creating identities: Social categories, social identities and educational participation* (pp. 91-114). New York: Russell Sage.

Paas, F., and van Merriënboer, J. (1994). Variability of worked examples and transfer of geometrical problem-solving skills: A cognitive-load approach. *Journal of Educational Psychology, 86*, 122-133.

Padak, N., and Baradine, B. (2004). Engaging readers and writers in adult education contexts. *Journal of Adolescent and Adult Literacy, 48*(2), 126-137.

Paivio, A. (1986). *Mental representations: A dual coding approach*. Oxford, England: Oxford University Press.

Pajares, F. (2003). Self-efficacy beliefs, motivation, and achievement in writing: A review of the literature. *Reading and Writing Quarterly, 19*, 139-158.

Pajares, F., and Valiante, G. (2006). Self-efficacy beliefs and motivation in writing. In C.A. MacArthur, S. Graham, and J. Fitzgerald (Eds.), *Handbook of writing research* (pp. 158-170). New York: Guilford Press.

Palincsar, A.S., and Brown, A.L. (1984). Reciprocal teaching of comprehension-fostering and monitoring activities. *Cognition and Instruction, 1*, 117-175.

Palincsar, A.S., and Magnusson, S.J. (2001). The interplay of first-hand and text-based investigations to model and support the development of scientific knowledge and reasoning. In S.M. Carver and D. Klahr (Eds.), *Cognition and Instruction: 25 years of progress* (pp. 152-193). Mahwah, NJ: Lawrence Erlbaum Associates.

Palincsar, A., and Magnusson, S. (2005). The interplay of first-hand and second-hand investigations to model and support the development of scientific knowledge and reasoning. In S. Carver and D. Klahr (Eds.), *Cognition and instruction: Twenty-five years of progress* (pp. 151-193). Mahwah, NJ: Lawrence Erlbaum Associates.

Pan, W., Guo, S., Alikonis, C., and Bai, H. (2008). Do intervention programs assist students to succeed in college?: A multilevel longitudinal study. *College Student Journal, 42*(1), 90-98.

Papadopoulou, E. (2008). *Vocabulary instruction and the writing performance of 3rd grade struggling writers*. Ann Arbor, MI: ProQuest Information and Learning. Available: http://books.google.com/books?id=EvTVuT1jgdgC&dq=Vocabulary+instruction+and+the+writing+performance+of+3rd+grade+struggling+writers&source=gbs_navlinks_s [Sept. 2011].

Papert, S. (1981). Computers and computer cultures. *Creative Computing, 7*(3), 82-92.

Paquette, K., and Kaufman, C.C. (2008). Merging civic and literacy skills. *The Social Studies, 99*(4), 187-190.

Paradis, M. (2004). *A neurolinguistic theory of bilingualism.* Philadelphia, PA: John Benjamins.

Park, D.C., and Huang, C.M. (2010). Culture wires the brain: A cognitive neuroscience perspective. *Perspectives on Psychological Science, 5*, 391-400.

Park, D.C., and Reuter-Lorenz, P. (2009). The adaptive brain: Aging neurocognitive scaffolding. *Annual Review of Psychology, 60*, 173-196.

Park, D.C., Lautenschlager, G., Hedden, T., Davidson, N.S., Smith, A.D., and Smith, P.K. (2002). Models of visuospatial and verbal memory across the adult life span. *Psychology and Aging, 17*, 299-320.

Parke, M., and Tracy-Mumford, F. (2000). *How states are implementing distance education for adult learners.* Washington, DC: National Institute for Literacy.

Parks, S. (2001). Moving from school to the workplace: Disciplinary innovation, border crossings, and the reshaping of a written genre. *Applied Linguistics, 22*(4), 405-438.

Parks, S., and Maguire, M.H. (1999). Coping with on-the-job writing in ESL: A constructivist-semiotic perspective. *Language Learning, 49*(1), 143-175.

Parr, B.A., Edwards, M.C., and Leising, J.G. (2008). Does a curriculum integration intervention to improve the mathematics achievement of students diminish their acquisition of technical competence? An experimental study in agricultural mechanics. *Journal of Agricultural Education, 49*(1), 61-71.

Partnership for 21st Century Skills. (2002). *Learning for the 21st century: A report and MILE guide for 21st century skills.* Available: http://www.p21.org/images/stories/otherdocs/p21up_Report.pdf [Sept. 2011].

Partnership for 21st Century Skills. (2003). *The road to 21st century learning: A policymaker's guide to 21st century skills.* Available: http://www.p21.org/index.php?option=com_content&task=view&id=30&Itemid=185 [Sept. 2011].

Partnership for 21st Century Skills. (2006). *Results that matter: 21st century skills and high school reform.* Available: http://www.p21.org/index.php?option=com_content&task=view&id=204&Itemid=185 [Sept. 2011].

Partnership for 21st Century Skills. (2007). *The intellectual and policy foundations of the 21st century skills framework.* Available: http://www.p21.org/index.php?option=com_content&task=view&id=925&Itemid=185 [Oct. 2011].

Partnership for 21st Century Skills. (2009). *P21 framework definitions.* Available: http://www.p21.org/index.php?option=com_content&task=view&id=925&Itemid=185 [Oct. 2011].

Pashler, H., Cepeda, J.T., Wixted, J.T., and Rohrer, D. (2005).When does feedback facilitate learning of words? *Journal of Experimental Psychology: Learning, Memory, and Cognition, 31*, 3-8.

Pashler, H., Bain, P.M., Bottge, B.A., Graesser, A., Koedinger, K., and McDaniel, M., (2007). *Organizing instruction and study to improve student learning: IES practice guide.* NCER 2007-2004. Washington, DC: National Center for Education Research.

Pashler, H., McDaniel, M., Roher, D., and Bjork, R. (2009). Learning styles: Concepts and evidence. *Psychological Science in the Public Interest, 9*, 105-119.

Patrick, H., Anderman, L.H., and Ryan, A.M. (2002). Social motivation and the classroom social environment. In C. Midgley (Ed.), *Goals, goal structures, and patterns of adaptive learning* (pp. 85-108). Mahwah, NJ: Lawrence Erlbaum Associates.

Pattamadilok, C., Perre, L., Dufau, S., and Ziegler, J.C. (2009). On-line orthographic influences on spoken language in a semantic task. *Journal of Cognitive Neuroscience, 21*, 169-179.

Pattamadilok, C., Knierim, I.N., Duncan, K.J.K., and Devlin, J.T. (2010). How does learning to read affect speech perception? *Journal of Neuroscience, 30*, 8,435-8,444.

Patterson, M. (2008). Learning disability prevalence and adult education program characteristics. *Learning Disabilities Research and Practice, 23*(1), 50-59.

Paulesu, E., Démonet, J.-F., Fazio, F., McCrory, E., Chanoine, V., Brunswick, N., Cappa, S.F., Cossu, G., Habib, M., Frith, C.D., and Frith, U. (2001). Dyslexia: Cultural diversity and biological unity. *Science, 291*, 2,165-2,167.

Paxton, R. J. (1997). "Someone with like a life wrote it": The effects of a visible author on high school history students. *Journal of Educational Psychology, 89*(2), 235-250.

Pearl, J., and Russell, S. (2002). Bayesian networks. In M.A. Arbib (Ed.), *Handbook of brain theory and neural networks* (pp. 157-160). Cambridge, MA: Bradford Books (MIT Press).

Pearson, P.D., and Duke, N.K. (2002). Comprehension instruction in the primary grades. In C.C. Block and M. Pressley (Eds.), *Comprehension instruction: Research-based best practices* (pp. 247-258). New York: Guilford Press.

Pearson, P.D., Roehler, L.R., Dole, J.A., and Duffy, G.G. (1992). Developing expertise in reading comprehension. In S.J. Samuels (Ed.), *What research has to say about reading instruction* (pp. 145-199). Newark, DE: International Reading Association.

Pease-Alvarez, L., and Hakuta, K. (1992). Enriching our views of bilingualism and bilingual education. *Educational Researcher, 21*(2), 4-6.

Pekrun, R. (2006). The control-value theory of achievement emotions: Assumptions, corollaries, and implications for educational research and practice. *Educational Psychology Review, 18*, 315-341.

Pellegrini, A.D., Galda, L., Flor, D., Bartini, M., and Charak, D. (1997). Close relationships, individual differences, and early literacy learning. *Journal of Experimental Child Psychology, 67*, 409-422.

Pelletier, L.G., Dion, S., Tuson, K.M., and Green-Demers, I. (1999). Why do people fail to adopt environmental behaviors? Towards a taxonomy of environmental amotivation. *Journal of Applied Social Psychology, 29*, 2,481-2,504.

Pennington, B.F., and Bishop, D.V.M. (2009). Relations among speech, language, and reading disorders. *Annual Review of Psychology, 60*, 283-306.

Pennington, B.F., and Olson, R.K. (2005). Genetics of dyslexia. In M.J. Snowling and C. Hulme (Eds.), *The science of reading: A handbook* (pp. 453-472). Oxford, England: Blackwell.

Peppler, K., and Kafai, Y. (2007). From SuperGoo to Scratch: Exploring creative digital media production in informal learning. *Learning, Media, and Technology, 32*(2), 149-166.

Perfetti, C.A. (1985). *Reading ability.* New York: Oxford University Press.

Perfetti, C.A. (1992). The representation problem in reading acquisition. In P.B. Gough, L.C. Ehri, and R. Treiman (Eds.), *Reading acquisition* (pp. 145-174). Hillsdale, NJ: Lawrence Erlbaum Associates.

Perfetti, C.A. (1999). Constructing meaning: The role of decoding. In J. Oakhill (Ed.), *Reading development and the teaching of reading: A psychological perspective.* Oxford, England: Blackwell.

Perfetti, C.A. (2007). Reading ability: Lexical quality to comprehension. *Scientific Studies of Reading, 11*, 357-383.

Perfetti, C.A., and Hart, L. (2002). The lexical quality hypothesis. In L. Verhoeven (Ed.), *Precursors of functional literacy* (pp. 189-213). Philadelphia, PA: John Benjamins.

Perfetti, C.A., Marron, M.A., and Foltz, P.W. (1996). Sources of comprehension failure: Theoretical perspectives and case studies. In C. Coroldi and J. Oakhill (Eds.), *Reading comprehension difficulties: Processes and intervention* (pp. 137-165). Mahwah, NJ: Lawrence Erlbaum Associates.

Perfetti, C.A., Liu, Y., Fiez, J., Nelson, J., Bolger, D.J., and Tan, L-H. (2007). Reading in two writing systems: Accommodation and assimilation of the brain's reading network. *Bilingualism: Language and Cognition, 10*(2), 131-146.

Perin, D. (2001). Academic-occupational integration as a reform strategy for the community college: Classroom perspectives. *Teachers College Record, 103*(2), 303-335.

Perin, D. (2004). Remediation beyond developmental education community colleges: The use of learning assistance centers to increase academic preparedness in community colleges. *Community College Journal of Research and Practice, 28*, 559-582.

Perin, D. (2006). Can community colleges protect both access and standards? The problem of remediation. *Teachers College Record, 108*(3), 339-373.

Perin, D. (2011). *Facilitating student learning through contextualization*. Working Paper No. 29, Community College Research Center Asessment of Evidence Series. New York: Teachers College, Columbia University.

Perin, D., and Charron, K. (2006). Lights just click on every day. In T. Bailey and V.S. Morest (Eds.), *Defending the community college equity agenda* (pp. 155-194). Baltimore, MD: Johns Hopkins University Press.

Perin, D., and Greenberg, D. (1994). Understanding dropouts in an urban worker education program: Retention patterns, demographics, student perceptions, and reasons given for early departure. *Urban Education, 29*(2), 169-287.

Perin, D., and Greenberg, D. (2007). Research-based reading instruction in an adult basic education program. *Adult Basic Education and Literacy Journal, 1*(3), 123-132.

Perin, D., Keselman, A., and Monopoli, M. (2003). The academic writing of community college remedial students: Text and learner variables. *Higher Education, 45*(1), 19-42.

Perin, D., Flugman, B., and Spiegel, S. (2006). Last chance gulch: Youth participation in urban adult basic education programs. *Adult Basic Education, 16*(3), 171-188.

Perin, D., Hare, R.J., Peverly, S.T., and Mason, L.H. (2010). Contextualized written summarization by academically underprepared community college students. Unpublished manuscript.

Perre, L., and Ziegler, J.C. (2008). On-line activation of orthography in spoken word recognition. *Brain Research, 1,188*, 132-138.

Petrill, S.A., Deater-Deckard, K., Thompson, L.A., DeThorne, L.S., and Schatschneider, C. (2006a). Genetic and environmental effects of serial naming and phonological awareness on early reading outcomes. *Journal of Educational Psychology, 98*(1), 112-121.

Petrill, S.A., Deater-Deckard, K., Thompson, L.A., DeThorne, L.S., and Schatschneider, C. (2006b). Reading skills in early readers: Genetic and shared environmental influences. *Journal of Learning Disabilities, 39*, 48-55.

Peyton, J.K., and Seyoum, M. (1989). The effect of teacher strategies on students' interactive writing: The case of dialogue journals. *Research in the Teaching of English, 23*(3), 310-334.

Pharness, G. (2001). From where we live, how far can we see? In P. Campbell and B. Burnaby (Eds.), *Participatory practices in adult education* (pp. 197-218). Mahwah, NJ: Lawrence Erlbaum Associates.

Philipose, L.E., Gottesman, R.F., Newhart, M., Kleinman, J.T., Herskovits, E.H., Pawlak, M.A., Marsh. E.B., Davis, C., Heidler-Gary, J., and Hillis, A.E. (2007). Neural regions essential for reading and spelling of words and pseudowords. *Annals of Neurology, 62*(5), 481-492.

Philips, S.U. (1972). Participant structure and communicative competence: Warm Springs children in community and classroom. In C. Cazden, D. Hymes, and W.J. John (Eds.), *Functions of language in the classroom* (pp. 370-394). New York: Teachers College Press.

Philips, S.U. (1983). *The invisible culture: Communication in classroom and community on the Warm Springs Indian Reservation*. Long Grove, IL: Waveland Press.

Piaget, J. (1952). *The origins of intelligence*. New York: International University Press.

Pianta, R.C., La Paro, K.M., and Hamre, B.K. (2008). *Classroom assessment scoring system: Manual K-3*. Baltimore, MD: Paul H. Brookes.

Pianta, R.C., Belsky, J., Vandergrift, N., Houts, R., and Morrison, F.J. (2008). Classroom effects on children's achievement trajectories in elementary school. *American Educational Research Journal, 45*(2), 365-397.

Pickering, M.J., and Garrod, S. (2004). Toward a mechanistic psychology of dialogue. *Behavioral and Brain Sciences, 27*(2).

Piestrup, A.M. (1973). *Black dialect interference and accommmodation of reading instruction in first grade*. Monographs of the Language Behavior Research Laboratory No. 4. Berkeley: University of California.

Pinker, S. (1994). *The language instinct*. New York: William Morrow.

Pinsent-Johnson, C. (2007). Developing practice-based performance assessment. In P. Campbell (Ed.), *Measures of success: Assessment and accountability in adult basic education* (pp. 15-46). Edmonton, Alberta: Grass Roots Press.

Pintrich, P. R. (1999). The role of motivation in promoting and sustaining self-regulated learning. *International Journal of Educational Research, 31*(6), 459-470.

Pintrich, P. R. (2000a). Multiple goals, multiple pathways: The role of goal orientation in learning and achievement. *Journal of Educational Psychology, 92*, 544-555.

Pintrich, P.R. (2000b). The role of goal orientation in self-regulated learning. In M. Boekaerts, P. Pintrich, and M. Zeidner (Eds.), *Handbook of self-regulation* (pp. 452-502). New York: Academic Press.

Pintrich, P.R. (2003). A motivational science perspective on the role of student motivation in learning and teaching contexts. *Journal of Educational Psychology, 95*, 667-686.

Pintrich, P.R., and De Groot, E.V. (1990). Motivational and self-regulated learning components of classroom academic performance. *Journal of Educational Psychology, 82*(1), 33-40.

Pintrich, P.R., and Garcia, T. (1991). Student goal orientation and self-regulation in the college classroom. In M.L. Maehr and P.R. Pintrich (Eds.), *Advances in motivation and achievement* (vol. 7). Bingley, England: Emerald Group.

Pintrich, P.R., and Schrauben, B. (1992). Students' motivational beliefs and their cognitive engagement in clasroom academic tasks. In D.H. Schunk and J. Meece (Eds.), *Student perceptions in the classroom* (pp. 149-179). Hillsdale, NJ: Lawrence Erlbaum Associates.

Pintrich, P. R., and Schunk, D. H. (1996). *Motivation in education: Theory, research, and applications*. Englewood Cliffs, NJ: Prentice-Hall.

Pintrich, P.R., and Zusho, A. (2002). The development of academic self-regulation: The role of cognitive and motivational factors. In A. Wigfield and J.S. Eccles (Eds.), *Development of achievement motivation* (pp. 249-284). San Diego: Academic Press.

Pintrich, P.R., Marx, R.W., and Boyle, R.A. (1993). Beyond cold conceptual change: The role of motivational beliefs and classroom contextual factors in the process of conceptual change. *Review of Educational Research, 63*, 167-199.

Pintrich, P.R., Smith, D.A., Garcia, T., and McKeachie, W.J. (1993). Reliability and predictive validity of the Motivation Strategies for Learning Questionnaire (MSLQ). *Educational and Psychological Measurement, 53*, 801-813.

Pirolli, P. (2005). Rational analysis of information foraging on the web. *Cognitive Science, 29*, 343-373.

Pirolli, P. (2007). *Information foraging theory: Adaptive interaction with information*. New York: Oxford University Press.

Pirolli, P., and Card, S. (1999). Information foraging. *Psychological Review, 106*, 643-675.

Pittman, T.S., Davey, M.E., Alafat, K.A., Wetherill, K.V., and Kramer, N.A. (1980). Informational versus controlling verbal rewards. *Personality and Social Psychology Bulletin, 6*, 228-233.

Planty, M., Hussar, W., Snyder, T., Kena, G., Kewal-Ramani, A., Kemp, J., Bianco, K., and Dinkes, R. (2009). *The condition of education 2009.* NCES 2009-081. Washington, DC: National Center for Education Statistics, Institute of Education Sciences, U.S. Department of Education.

Plomin, R., and Kovas, Y. (2005). Generalist genes and learning disabilities. *Psychological Bulletin, 131*(4), 592-617.

Poldrack, R.A., Wagner, A.D., Prull, M.W., Desmond, J.E., Glover, G.H., and Gabrieli, J.D. (1999). Functional specialization for semantic and phonological processing in the left inferior prefrontal cortex. *NeuroImage, 10*, 15-35.

Popadopoulou, E. (2007). *The impact of vocabulary instruction on the vocabulary knowledge and writing performance of third grade students.* Unpublished doctoral dissertation, University of Maryland.

Popken, R. (1991). A study of topic sentence use in technical writing. *The Technical Writing Teacher, 18*, 49-58.

Pratt, A., and Brady, S. (1988). Relation of phonological awareness to reading disability in children and adults. *Journal of Educational Psychology, 80*(3), 319-323.

Prensky, M. (2000). *Digital game-based learning.* New York: McGraw-Hill.

Pressley, M. (1991). Can learning-disabled children become good information processors? How can we find out? In L.V. Feagans, E.J. Short, and L.J. Meltzer (Eds.), *Subtypes of learning disabilities: Theoretical perspectives and research* (pp. 137-162). Hillsdale, NJ: Lawrence Erlbaum Associates.

Pressley, M. (2000). What should comprehension instruction be the instruction of? In M.L. Kamil, P.B. Mosenthal, P.D. Pearson, and R. Barr (Eds.), *Handbook of reading research* (vol. III, pp. 545-561). Mahwah, NJ: Lawrence Erlbaum Associates.

Pressley, M. (2002) Effective beginning reading instruction. *Journal of Literacy Research, 34*, 165-188.

Pressley, M., and Afflerbach, P. (1995). *Verbal protocols of reading: The nature of constructively responsive reading.* Hillsdale, NJ: Lawrence Erlbaum Associates.

Pressley, M., and Wharton-McDonald, R. (1997). Skilled comprehension and its development through instruction. *School Psychology Review, 26*, 448-466.

Pressley, M., Simmons, S., Snyder, B.L., and Cariglia-Bull, T. (1989a). Strategy instruction research comes of age. *Learning Disability Quarterly, 12*, 16-30.

Pressley, M., Goodchild, F., Fleet, J., Zajchowski, R., and Evans, E.D. (1989b). The challenges of classroom strategy instruction. *Elementary School Journal, 89*(3), 301-342.

Pressley, M., Wood, E., Woloshyn, V.E., Martin, V., King, A., and Menke, D. (1992). Encouraging mindful use of prior knowledge: Attempting to construct explanatory answers facilitates learning. *Educational Psychologist, 27*, 91-109.

Pressley, M., Wharton-McDonald, R., Hampson, J.M., and Echevarria, M. (1998). The nature of literacy instruction in ten grade-4/5 classrooms in upstate New York. *Scientific Studies of Reading, 2*, 159-191.

Pressley, M., Disney, L., and Anderson, K. (2007). Landmark vocabulary instructional research and the vocabulary instructional research that makes sense now. In R.K. Wagner, A.E. Muse, and K.R. Tannenbaum (Eds.), *Vocabulary acquisition: Implications for reading comprehension* (pp. 205-232). New York: Guilford Press.

Prins, E. (2010). Salvadoran campesinos/as' literacy practices and perceptions of the benefits of literacy: A longitudinal study with former literacy participants. *International Journal of Educational Development, 30*(4), 418-427.

Prins, E., Toso, B., and Schafft, K. (2009). "It feels like a little family to me": Social interaction and support among women in adult education and family literacy. *Adult Education Quarterly, 59*(4), 335-352.

Prior, P. (2006). A sociocultural theory of writing. In C. MacArthur, S. Graham, and J. Fitzgerald (Eds.), *Handbook of writing research* (pp. 54-65). New York: Guilford Press.

Puchner, L. (2003). Women and literacy in rural Mali: A study of the socio-economic impact of participating in literacy programs in four villages. *International Journal of Educational Development, 23*(4), 439-458.

Pugh, K., Mencl, W.E., Shaywitz, B.A., Shaywitz, S.E., Fulbright, R.K., Constable R.T., Skudlarski, P., Marchione, K.E., Jenner, A.R., Fletcher, J.M., Liberman, A.M., Shankweiler, D.P., Katz, L., Lacadie, C., and Gore, J.C. (2000). The angular gyrus in developmental dyslexia: Task-specific differences in functional connectivity in posterior cortex. *Psychological Science, 11*, 51-56.

Pugh, K.R., Sandak, R., Frost, S.J., Moore, D., and Mencl, W.E. (2006a). Examining reading development and reading disability in diverse languages and cultures: Potential contributions from functional neuroimaging. *Journal of American Indian Education, 45*(3), 60-76.

Pugh, K.R., Frost, S.J., Sandak, R., Gillis, M., Moore, D., Jenner, A.R., and Mencl, W.E. (2006b). What does reading have to tell us about writing? Preliminary questions and methodological challenges in examining the neurobilological foundations of writing and writing disabilities. In C.A. MacArthur, S. Graham, and J. Fitzgerald (Eds.), *Handbook of writing research* (pp. 433-448). New York: Guilford Press.

Pugh, K.R., Frost, S.J., Sandak, R., Landi, N., Rueckl, J.G., Constable, R.T., Fulbright, R., Katz, L., and Mencl, W.E. (2008). Effects of stimulus difficulty and repetition on printed word identification: An fMRI comparison of non-impaired and reading disabled adolescent cohorts. *Journal of Cognitive Neuroscience, 207*, 1,146-1,160.

Pugh, K.R., Frost, S.J., Sandak, R., Landi, N., Moore, D., Della Porta, G., Reuckl, J.G., and Mencl, W.E. (2010). Mapping the word reading circuitry in skilled and disabled readers. In P.L. Cornelissen, P.C. Hansen, M.L. Kringelback, and K. Pugh (Eds.), *The neural basis of reading*. New York: Oxford University Press.

Pulido, D. (2004). The relationship between text comprehension and second language incidental vocabulary acquisition: A matter of topic familiarity? *Language Learning, 54*, 469-523.

Purcell, K. (2010). *The state of online video*. Washington, DC: Pew Internet & American Life Project. Available: http://www.pewinternet.org/Reports/2010/State-of-Online-Video.aspx [Oct. 2011].

Purcell, K., Rainie, L., Mitchell, A., Rosenstiel, T., and Olmstead, K. (2010). *Understanding the participatory news consumer*. Washington, DC: Pew Internet & American Life Project. Available: http://www.pewinternet.org/Reports/2010/Online-News.aspx [Oct. 2011].

Purcell-Gates, V. (1995). *Other people's words: The cycle of low literacy*. Cambridge, MA: Harvard University Press.

Purcell-Gates, V., Degener, S. Jacobson, E. and Soler, M. (2002). Impact of authentic adult literacy instruction on adult literacy practices. *Reading Research Quarterly, 37*(1), 70-92.

Purves, A.C. (1992). Reflections on research and assessment in written composition. *Research in the Teaching of English, 26*(1), 108-122.

Putnam, R.D. (2000). *Bowling alone: The collapse and revival of American community*. New York: Simon and Schuster.

Qian, D.D. (1999). Assessing the roles of depth and breadth of vocabulary knowledge in reading comprehension. *The Canadian Modern Language Journal, 56*, 262-305.

Rachal, J.R. (1984). The computer in the ABE and GED classroom: A review of the literature. *Adult Education Quarterly, 35*(2), 86-95.

Rachal, J.R. (1995). Adult reading achievement comparing computer-assisted and traditional approaches: A comprehensive review of the experimental literature. *Reading Research and Instruction*, *34*(3), 239-258.

Rachal, J.R. (2002). Andragogy's detectives: A critique of the present and a proposal for the future. *Adult Education Quarterly*, *52*(3), 210-227.

Radvansky, G.A., and Dijkstra, K. (2007). Aging and situation model processing. *Psychonomic Bulletin and Review*, *14*, 1,027-1,042.

Radvansky, G.A., Zwaan, R.A., Curiel, J.M., and Copeland, D.E. (2001). Situation models and aging. *Psychology and Aging*, *16*, 145-160.

Rahhal, T.A., Hasher, L., and Colcombe, S.J. (2001). Instructional manipulations and age differences in memory: Now you see them, now you don't. *Psychology and Aging*, *16*, 697-706.

Raiser, V. (1981). Syntactic maturity, vocabulary diversity, mode of discourse and theme selection in the free writing of learning disabled adolescents. *Dissertation Abstracts International*, *42*, 2,544-A.

Rak, C.F., and Patterson, L.E. (1996). Promoting resilience in at-risk children. *Journal of Counseling and Development*, *74*, 368-373.

Randel, J.M., Morris B.A., Wetzle, C.D., and Whitehead, B.V. (1992). The effectiveness of games for educational purposes: A review of recent research. *Simulation and Gaming*, *23*, 261-276.

Ranker, J. (2008). Composing across multiple media. *Written Communication*, *25*(2), 196-234.

Rapp, D.N. (2008). How do readers handle incorrect information during reading? *Memory and Cognition*, *36*, 688-701.

Rapp, D.N., van den Broek, P., McMaster, K.L., Kendeou, P., and Espin, C.A. (2007). Higher-order comprehension processes in struggling readers: A perspective for research and intervention. *Scientific Studies of Reading*, *11*(4), 289-312.

Rawson, K.A., and Kintsch, W. (2005). Rereading effects depend on time of test. *Journal of Educational Psychology*, *97*, 70-80.

Rawson, K.A., and Van Overschelde, J.P. (2008). How does knowledge promote memory? The distinctiveness theory of skilled memory. *Journal of Memory and Language*, *58*, 646-668.

Rawson, K.A., Dunlosky, J., and Thiede, K.W. (2000). The rereading effect: Metacomprehension accuracy improves across reading trials. *Memory and Cognition*, *28*(6), 1,004-1,010.

Rayner, K., Foorman, B.R., Perfetti, C.A., Pesetsky, D., and Seidenberg, M.S. (2001). How psychological science informs the teaching of reading. *Psychological Science in the Public Interest*, *2*(2), 31-74.

Re, A., Pedron, M., and Cornoldi, C. (2007). Expressive writing difficulties in children described as exhibiting ADHD symptoms. *Journal of Learning Disabilities*, *40*, 244-255.

Read, C., and Ruyter, L. (1985). Reading and spelling skills in adults of low literacy. *Remedial and Special Education*, *6*(6), 43-51.

Reader, W.R., and Payne, S.J. (2007). Allocating time across multiple texts: Sampling and satisficing. *Human-Computer Interaction*, *22*(3), 263-298.

Reder, S. (2008). The development of literacy and numeracy in adult life. In S. Reder and J. Brynner (Eds.), *Tracking adult literacy and numeracy skills: Findings from longitudinal research* (pp. 59-84). New York: Routledge.

Reece, J.E., and Cumings, G. (1996). Evaluating speech-based composition methods: Planning, dictation, and the listening word processor. In C.M. Levy and S. Ransdell (Eds.), *The science of writing: Theories, methods, individual differences, and applications* (pp. 361-380). Mahwah, NJ: Lawrence Erlbaum Associates.

Reichle, E.D., and Perfetti, C.A. (2003). Morphology in word identification: A word experience model that accounts for morpheme frequency effects. *Scientific Studies of Reading*, *7*, 219-237.

Reis, A., Guerreiro, M., and Petersson, K.M. (2003). A sociodemographic and neuropsychological characterization of an illiterate population. *Applied Neuropsychology, 10*(4), 191-204.

Renkl, A., Atkinson, R.K., and Grosse, C.S. (2004) How fading worked solution steps works: A cognitive load perspective. *Instructional Science, 32,* 59-82.

Renkl, A., Atkinson, R., Maier, U., and Staley, R. (2002). From example study to problem solving: Smooth transitions help learning. *Journal of Experimental Education, 70,* 293-315.

Renninger, K.A. (2000). Individual interest and its implications for understanding intrinsic motivation. In C. Sansone and J.M. Harackiewicz (Eds.), *Intrinsic motivation: Controversies and new directions* (pp. 373-404). San Diego, CA: Academic Press.

Renninger, K.A., Hidi, S., and Krapp, A. (1992). *The role of interest in learning and development.* Hillsdale, NJ: Lawrence Erlbaum Associates.

Reynolds, T.H., and Bonk, C. (1996). Facilitating college writers' revisions within a generative-evaluative computerized prompting framework. *Computers and Composition, 13,* 93-108.

Reznitskaya, A., Anderson, R.C., Dong, T., Li, Y., Kim, I.-H., and Kim, S.-Y. (2008). Learning to think well: Application of argument schema theory to literacy instruction. In C.C. Block and S.R. Parris (Eds.), *Comprehension instruction: Research-based best practices* (2nd ed., pp. 196-214). New York: Guilford Press.

Reznitskaya, A., Kuo, L.-J., Glina, M., and Anderson, R.C. (2009). Measuring argumentative reasoning: What's behind the numbers. *Learning and Individual Differences, 19,* 219-224.

Rhoder, C.A., and French, J.N. (1994). Workplace literacy: From survival to empowerment and human development. *Journal of Reading, 38*(2), 110-120.

Rhoder, C.A., and French, J.N. (1995). Participant-generated text: A vehicle for workplace literacy. *Journal of Adolescent and Adult Literacy, 39*(2), 110-118.

Rice, G.E., Meyer, B.J.F., and Miller, D.C. (1989). Using text structure to improve older adults recall of important medical information. *Educational Gerontology, 15*(5), 527-542.

Rich, R. and Shepherd, M.J. (1993). Teaching text comprehension strategies to adult poor readers. *Reading and Writing, 5,* 387-402.

Richards, T., Berninger, V., and Fayol, M. (2009). fMRI activation differences between 11-year old good and poor spellers' access in working memory to temporary and long-term orthographic representations. *Journal of Neurolinguistics, 22*(4), 327-353.

Rideout, V.J., Foehr, U.G., and Roberts, D.F. (2010). *Generation M2: Media in the lives of 8-to 18-year-olds.* Menlo Park, CA: Henry J. Kaiser Family Foundation. Available: http://www.kff.org/entmedia/mh012010pkg.cfm [Oct. 2011].

Ridgeway, C.L., Boyle, E.H., Kuipers, K.J., and Robinson, D.T. (1998). How do status beliefs develop? The role of resources and interaction. *American Sociological Review, 63,* 331-350.

Rieber, L.P. (1996). Animation as feedback in a computer-based simulation: Representation matters. *Educational Technology Research and Development, 44*(1), 5-22.

Riediger, M., Li, S.-C., and Linderberger, U. (2006). Selection, optimization, and compensation as developmental mechanisms of adaptivere resource allocation: Review and preview. *Handbook of the psychology of aging* (6th ed., pp. 289-313). New York: Elsevier.

Rigby, C.S., Deci, E., Patrick, B.C., and Ryan, R.M. (1992). Beyond the intrinsic-extrinsic dichotomy: Self-determination in motivation and learning. *Motivation and Emotion, 16*(3), 165-185.

Ridgeway, C.L. (2001). Gender, status, and leadership. *Journal of Social Issues, 57,* 637-655.

Riley, M.W., and Riley, J.W. Jr. (1994). Structural lag. In M.W. Riley, R.L. Kahn, and A. Foner (Eds.), *Age and structural lag* (pp. 15-36). New York: Wiley.

Riley, M.W., and Riley, J.W. Jr. (2000) Age integration: Conceptual and historical background. *The Gerontologist, 40(3),* 266-270.

Rimrodt, S.L., Peterson, D.J., Denckla, M.B., Kaufmann, W.E., and Cutting, L.E. (2010). White matter microstructural differences linked to left perisylvian language network in children with dyslexia. *Cortex, 46,* 739-749.

Rindermann, H., and Ceci, S.J. (2009). Educational Policy and Country Outcomes in International Cognitive Competence Studies. *Perspectives on Psychological Science, 4,* 551-577.

Ritter, S., Anderson, J.R., Koedinger, K.R., and Corbett, A. (2007) Cognitive Tutor: Applied research in mathematics education. *Psychonomic Bulletin and Review, 14(2),* 249-255.

Ritterfeld, U., Cody, M., and Vorderer, P. (2008). (Eds.), *Serious games: Mechanisms and effects.* Mahwah, NJ: Routledge/Taylor and Francis.

Rivera, L. (2008). *Laboring to learn: Women's literacy and poverty in the post-welfare era.* Urbana: University of Illinois Press.

Roberts, D., and Mather, N. (1997). Orthographic dyslexia: The neglected subtype. *Learning Disabilities Research and Practice, 12(4),* 236-250.

Roberts, T.A., and Meiring, A. (2006). Teaching phonics in the context of children's literature or spelling: Influences on first-grade reading, spelling, and writing and fifth-grade comprehension. *Journal of Educational Psychology, 98(4),* 690-713.

Roberts, T.A., and Neal, H. (2004). Relationships among preschool English language learner's oral proficiency in English, instructional experience and literacy development. *Contemporary Educational Psychology, 29,* 283-311.

Robertson, L. (2007). An adult education teacher's journey with evidence-based reading instruction. *Adult Basic and Literacy Education Journal, 1(3),* 157-160.

Robinson, P. (2001). Task complexity, task difficulty and task production: Exploring interactions in a componential framework. *Applied Linguistics, 22(1),* 27-57.

Robinson, P., and Ellis, N.C. (2008). Conclusion: Cognitive linguistics, second language acquisition and L2 instruction—Issues for research. In P. Robinson and N.C. Ellis (Eds.), *Handbook of cognitive linguistics and second language acquisition* (pp. 489-545). New York: Routledge/Taylor and Francis.

Rochford, R.A. (2003). Assessing learning styles to improve the quality of performance of community college students in developmental writing programs: A pilot study. *Community College Journal of Research and Practice, 27,* 665-677.

Rodríguez, A.J. (2010). *Science education as a pathway to teaching language literacy.* Boston, MA: Sense.

Roediger, H.L. III., and Karpicke, J. D. (2006). The power of testing memory: Basic research and implications for educational practice. *Psychological Science, 1,* 181-210.

Roediger, H.L. III, and Marsh, E. J. (2005). The positive and negative consequences of multiple-choice testing. *Journal of Experimental Psychology: Learning, Memory, and Cognition, 31,* 1,155-1,159.

Roeser, R.W., Midgley, C., and Urdan, T. C. (1996). Perceptions of the school psychological environment and early adolescents psychological and behavioral functioning in school: The mediating role of goals and belonging. *Journal of Educational Psychology, 88,* 408-422.

Roeser, R.W., Peck, S.C. and Nasir, N.S. (2006). Self and identity processes in school motivation, learning, and achievement. In P.A. Alexander and P.H. Winne (Eds.), *Handbook of educational psychology* (2nd ed., pp. 391-424). Mahwah, NJ: Lawrence Erlbaum Associates.

Rogers, L.A., and Graham, S. (2008). A meta-analysis of single subject design writing intervention research. *Journal of Educational Psychology Review, 100(4),* 879-906.

Rogers, R., and Kramer, M.A. (2008). *Adult education teachers: Designing critical literacy practices.* Mahwah, NJ: Lawrence Erlbaum Associates.

Rogoff, B. (1990). *Apprenticeship in thinking: Cognitive development in social context.* New York: Oxford University Press.

Rogoff, B. (1993). *Guided participation in cultural activity by toddlers and caregivers.* Chicago, IL: University of Chicago.

Rogoff, B. (1995). Observing sociocultural activity on three planes: participatory appropriation, guided participation, and apprenticeship. In J.V. Wertsch, P.D. Rio, and A. Alvarez (Eds.), *Sociocultural studies of mind* (pp. 139-164). Cambridge, England: Cambridge University Press.

Rogoff, B., and Gardner, W., (1984). Adult guidance of cognitive development. In B. Rogoff and J. Lave (Eds.), *Everyday cognition: Its development in social context* (pp. 95-116). Cambridge, MA: Harvard University Press.

Rogoff, B., and Lave, J. (1984). *Everyday cognition: Its development in social context.* Cambridge, MA: Harvard University Press.

Rogoff, B., and Wertsch, J.V. (1984). *Children's learning in the "zone of proximal development."* San Francisco, CA: Jossey-Bass.

Rohrer, D., and Taylor, K. (2006). The effects of overlearning and distributed practice on the retention of mathematics knowledge. *Applied Cognitive Psychology, 20,* 1209-1224.

Rojewski, J.W., and Gregg, N. (2011). Career choice patterns and behaviors of work-bound youth with high incidence disabilities. In J.M. Kaufman and D.P. Hallahan (Eds.), *Handbook of special education* (pp. 584-593). New York: Routledge.

Rojewski, J.W., and Kim, H. (2003). Career choice patterns and behavior of work-bound youth during early adolescence. *Journal of Career Development, 30,* 89-108.

Rolla San Francisco, A., Mo, M., Carlo, M., August, D., and Snow, C, (2006). The influences of language of literacy instruction and vocabulary on the spelling of Spanish-English bilinguals. *Reading and Writing, 19,* 627-642.

Romance, N.R., and Vitale, M.R. (1992). A curriculum strategy that expands time for in-depth elementary science instruction by using science-based reading strategies: Effects of a year-long study in grade four. *Journal of Research in Science Teaching, 29(6),* 545-554.

Romance, N.R., and Vitale, M.R. (2001). Implementing an in-depth expanded science model in elementary schools: Multi-year findings, research issues, and policy implications. *International Journal of Science Education, 23(4),* 373-404.

Roscoe, R.D., and Chi, M.T.H. (2007). Understanding tutor learning: Knowledge-building and knowledge-telling in peer tutors' explanations and questions. *Review of Educational Research, 77,* 534-574.

Rose, M. (1984). *Writer's block: The cognitive dimension.* Carbondale, IL: Southern Illinois University Press.

Rosebery, A.S., and Warren, B. (Eds.). (1998). *Boats, balloons, and classroom video: Science teaching as inquiry.* Portsmouth, NH: Heinemann.

Rosebery, A.S., Warren, B., and Conant, F.R. (1992). Appropriating scientific discourse: Findings from language minority classrooms. *Journal of the Learning Sciences, 2(1),* 61-94.

Rosenblum, S., Weiss, P.L., and Parush, S. (2004). Handwriting evaluation for developmental dysgraphia: Process versus product. *Reading and Writing: An Interdisciplinary Journal, 17,* 433-458.

Rosenshine, B., and Meister, C. (1994). Reciprocal teaching: A review of the research. *Review of Educational Research, 64(4),* 479-530.

Rosenshine, B., Meister, C., and Chapman, S. (1996). Teaching students to generate questions: A review of the intervention studies. *Review of Educational Research, 66,* 181-221.

Ross, M. (1975). Salience of reward and intrinsic motivation. *Journal of Personality and Social Psychology, 32,* 245-254.

Ross, M., and Wang, Q. (2010). Why we remember and what we remember: Culture and autobiographical memory perspectives. *Psychological Science, 5(4),* 401-409.

Ross, S. (2000). Individual differences and learning outcomes in the certificates in spoken and written English. In G. Bridley (Ed.), *Studies in immigrant English language assessment* (vol. 1, pp. 191-214). Sydney, Australia: National Centre for English Language Teaching and Research.

Rouet, J. (2006). *The skills of document use: From text comprehension to web-based learning.* Mahwah, NJ: Lawrence Erlbaum Associates.

Rounds, J., and Armstrong, P.I. (2005). Assessment of needs and values. In S.D. Brown and R.W. Lent (Eds.), *Career development and counseling: Putting theory and research to work* (pp. 305-329). Hoboken, NJ: John Wiley & Sons.

Rowley, K., and Meyer, N. (2003). The effect of a computer tutor for writers on student writing achievement. *Journal of Educational Computing Research, 29,* 169-187.

Rowley, K., Carsons, P., and Miller, T. (1998). A cognitive technology to teach composition skills: Four studies with the R-WISE writing tutor. *Journal of Educational Computing Research, 18,* 259-296.

Rubin, D.C. (1984). Social cognition and written communication. *Written Communication, 1*(2), 211-245.

Rubin, D.C. (1995). *Memory in oral traditions: The cognitive psychology of epic, ballads, and counting-out rhymes.* New York: Oxford University Press.

Rubin, D.C., and Looney, J. (1990). Facilitation of audience awareness: Revision processes of basic writers. In G. Kirsch and D. Roen (Eds.), *A sense of audience in written communication* (pp. 280-292). Newbury Park, CA: Sage.

Rudner, L.M., Garcia, V., and Welch, C. (2006). An evaluation of the IntelliMetric essay scoring system. *Journal of Technology, Learning and Assessment, 4,* 1-22.

Rumelhart, D. (1994). Toward an interactive model of reading. In R.B. Ruddel, M.R. Ruddell, and H. Singer (Eds.), *Theoretical models and processes of reading* (4th ed., pp. 864-894). Newark, DE: International Reading Association.

Rumsey, I., and Ballard, K.D. (1985). Teaching self-management strategies for independent story writing to children with classroom behavior difficulties. *Educational Psychology, 5,* 147-157.

Rumsey, J.M., Nace, K., Donohue, B., Wise, D., Maisog, J.M., and Andreason, P.A. (1997a). A positron emission tomographic study of impaired word recognition and phonological processing in dyslexic men. *Archives of Neurology, 54,* 562-573.

Rumsey, M.H., Donohue, C., Nace, K., Maisong, M., and Andreason, P. (1997b). Phonological and orthographic components of word recognition: A PET-rCBF scan study. *Brain, 120,* 739-759.

Russell, D. (1997). Rethinking genre in school and society: An activity theory analysis. *Written Communication, 14,* 504-554.

Ryan, R.M., and Deci, E.L. (1996). When paradigms clash: Comments on Cameron and Pierce's claim that rewards do not undermine intrinsic motivation. *Review of Educational Research, 66,* 33-38.

Ryan, R.M., and Deci, E.L. (2000). Self-determination theory and the facilitation of intrinsic motivation, social development, and well-being. *American Psychologist, 55*(1), 68-78.

Ryan, R.M. and Deci, E.L. (2008). A self-determination theory approach to psychotherapy: The motivational basis for effective change. *Canadian Psychology, 49,* 186-193.

Ryan, R.M., and Grolnick, W.S. (1986). Origins and pawns in the classroom: Self-report and projective assessments of children's perceptions. *Journal of Personality and Social Psychology, 50,* 550-558.

Ryan, R.M., Connell, J.P., and Plant, R.W. (1990). Emotions in non-directed text learning. *Learning and Individual Differences, 2,* 1-17.

Ryan, R.M., Rigby, S., and King, K. (1993). Two types of religious internalization and their relations to religious orientations and mental health. *Journal of Personality and Social Psychology, 65*, 586-596.

Ryan, R.M., Stiller, J., and Lynch, J.H. (1994). Representations of relationships to teachers, parents, and friends as predictors of academic motivation and self-esteem. *Journal of Early Adolescence, 14*, 226-249.

Ryan, R.M., Rigby, S., and Przybylski, A. (2006). The motivational pull of video games: A self-determination theory approach. *Motivation and Emotion, 30*, 344-360.

Rydell, R.J., Rydell, M.T., and Boucher, K.L. (2010). The effect of negative performance stereotypes on learning. *Journal of Personality and Social Psychology, 99*, 883-896.

Ryes Warner, J., and Vorhause, J. (2008). *The learner study: The impact of the skills for life strategy on literacy, language and numeracy learners.* London, England: Institute of Education, University of London.

Sabatini, J.P. (2002). Efficiency in word reading of adults: Ability group comparisons. *Scientific Studies of Reading, 6*(3), 267-298.

Sabatini, J.P., Sawaki, Y., Shore, J., and Scarborough, H. (2010). Relationships among reading skills of adults with low literacy. *Journal of Learning Disabilities, 43*(2), 122-138.

Sabatini, J.P., Shore, J., Holtzman, S., and Scarborough, H.S. (2011). Relative effectiveness of reading intervention programs for adults with low literacy. *Journal of Research on Education Effectiveness, 4*, 118-133.

Saddler, B., and Graham, S. (2005). The effects of peer-assisted sentence-combining instruction on the writing performance of more and less skilled young writers. *Journal of Educational Psychology, 97*(1), 43-54.

Saddler, B., and Graham, S. (2007). The relationship between writing knowledge and writing performance among more and less skilled writers. *Reading and Writing Quarterly, 23*, 231-247.

Salahu-Din, D., Persky, H., and Miller, J. (2008). *The nation's report card: Writing 2007.* NCES 2008-468. Washington, DC: National Center for Education Statistics, U.S. Department of Education.

Salmelin, R., Service, E., Kiesila, P., Uutela, K., and Salonen, O. (1996). Impaired visual word processing in dyslexia revealed with magnetoencephalography. *Annals of Neurology, 40*, 157-162.

Salthouse, T.A. (1996). The processing-speed theory of adult age differences in cognition. *Psychological Review, 103*, 403-428.

Sandler, A., Watson, T., Footo, M., Levine, M., Coleman, W., and Hooper, S. (1992). Neurodevelopmental study of writing disorders in middle childhood. *Developmental and Behavioral Pediatrics, 13*, 17-23.

Sandlin, J A., and Clark, M.C. (2009). From opportunity to responsibility: Political master narratives, social policy, and success stories in adult literacy education. *Teachers College Record, 111*(4), 999-1,029.

Sandmel, K., and Graham, S. (in press). The process writing approach: A meta-analysis. *Journal of Educational Research.*

Sarkari, S., Simos, P.G., Fletcher, J.M., Castillo, E.M., Breier, J.I., and Papanicolaou, A.C. (2002). Functional brain imaging. *Seminars in Pediatric Neurology, 9*, 227-236.

Sarroub, L.K. (2001). The sojourner experience of Yemeni American high school students: An ethnographic portrait. *Harvard Educational Review, 71*(3), 390-415.

Sarroub, L.K. (2002). In-betweenness: Religion and conflicting visions of literacy. *Reading Research Quarterly, 37*(2), 130-148.

Sarroub, L.K. (2004). *All American Yemeni girls: Being Muslim in a public school.* Philadelphia: University of Pennsylvania Press.

Sarroub, L.K. (2008). Glocalism in literacy and marriage in transnational lives. *Critical Inquiry in Language Studies [Special Issue: Immigration, Language, and Education]*, 6(1-2), 63-80.

Sasaki, M. (2000). Toward an empirical model of EFL writing processes: An exploratory study. *Journal of Second Language Writing*, 9(3), 259-291.

Sasaki, M., and Hirose, K. (1996). Explanatory variables for EFL students' expository writing. *Language Learning*, 46(1), 137-174.

Saunders, W., Foorman, B.R., and Carlson, C. (2006). Is a separate block of time for oral English language development in programs for English learners needed? *Elementary School Journal*, 107(2), 181-199.

Savage, R.S., Abrami, P., Hipps, G., and Deault, L. (2009). A randomized controlled trial study of the ABRACADABRA reading intervention program in grade 1. *Journal of Educational Psychology*, 101(3), 590-604.

Sawyer, R., Graham, S., and Harris, K.R. (1992). Direct teaching, strategy instruction, and strategy instruction with explicit self-regulation: Effects on learning disabled students'composition skills and self-efficacy. *Journal of Educational Psychology*, 84, 340-352.

Scammacca, N., Roberts, G., Vaughn, S., Edmonds, M., Wexler, J., Reutebuch, C.K., and Torgesen, J.K. (2007). *Interventions for adolescent struggling readers: A meta-analysis with implications for practice*. Portsmouth, NH: RMC Research Corporation, Center on Instruction.

Scarborough, H.S. (2002). Connecting early language and literacy to later reading (dis)abilities: Evidence, theory, and practice. In S.B. Neuman and D.K. Dickinson (Eds.), *Handbook of early literacy research* (pp. 97-125). New York: Guilford Press.

Scardamalia, M., and Bereiter, C. (1985). Fostering the development of self-regulation in children's knowledge processing. In S. Chipman, J. Segal, and R. Glaser (Eds.), *Thinking and learning skills: Current research and open questions* (vol. 2, pp. 563-577). Hillsdale, NJ: Lawrence Erlbaum Associates.

Schaefer, S., Krampe, R., Lindenberger, U., and Baltes, P.B. (2008). Age differences between children and young adults in the dynamics of dual-task prioritization: Body (balance) vs. mind (memory). *Developmental Psychology*, 44, 747-757.

Schaie, K.W. (2005). *Developmental influences on adult intelligence: The Seattle longitudinal study*. New York: Oxford University Press.

Schatschneider, C., Fletcher, J.M., Francis, D.J., Carlson, C.D., and Foorman, B.R. (2004). Kindergarten prediction of reading skills: A longitudinal comparative analysis. *Journal of Educational Psychology*, 96(2), 265-282.

Schiefele, U. (1996a). *Motivation and learning with text*. Gottingen, Germany: Hogrefe.

Schiefele, U. (1996b). Topic interest, text representation, and quality of experience. *Contemporary Educational Psychology*, 21(1), 3-18.

Schiefele, U., Krapp, A., and Winteler, A. (1992). Interest as a predictor of academic achievement: A meta-analysis of research. In K.A. Renninger, S. Hidi, and A. Krapp (Eds.), *The role of interest in learning and development* (pp. 183-212). Hillsdale, NJ: Lawrence Erlbaum Associates.

Schiff, R., and Raveh, M. (2006). Deficient morphological processing in adults with developmental dyslexia: Another barrier to efficient word recognition. *Dyslexia*, 13, 110-129.

Schlagel, B. (2007). Best practices in spelling and handwriting. In S. Graham, C.A. MacArthur, and J. Fitzgerald (Eds.), *Best practices in writing instruction* (pp. 179-201). New York: Guilford Press.

Schlaggar, B.L., and McCandliss, B.D. (2007). Development of neural systems for reading. *Annual Reviews of Neuroscience*, 30, 475-503.

Schleppegrell, M.J. (2004). *The language of schooling: A functional linguistics perspective.* Mahwah, NJ: Lawrence Erlbaum Associates.

Schleppegrell, M.J. (2007). The linguistic challenges of mathematics teaching and learning: A research review. *Reading and Writing Quarterly, 23*(2), 139-159.

Schleppegrell, M.J., and Achugar, M. (2003). Learning language and learning history: A functional linguistics approach. *TESOL Journal, 12*(2), 21-27.

Schleppegrell, M.J., Achugar, M., and Oteíza, T. (2004). The grammar of history: Enhancing content-based instruction through a functional focus on language. *TESOL Quarterly, 38*(1), 67-93.

Schmidt, J.L., Deshler, D.D., Schumaker, J.B., and Alley, G.R. (1988). Effects of generalization instruction on the written language performance of adolescents with learning disabilities in the mainstream classroom. *Reading, Writing, and Learning Disabilities, 4,* 291-309.

Schmidt, R.A., and Bjork, R.A. (1992). New conceptualizations of practice: Common principles in three paradigms suggest new concepts for training. *Psychological Science, 3,* 207-217.

Schmidt, R.A., Young, D.E., Swinnen, S., and Shapiro, D.C. (1989). Summary knowledge of results for skill acquisition: Support for the guidance hypothesis. *Journal of Experimental Psychology: Learning, Memory, and Cognition, 15,* 352-359.

Schmitz, B., and Skinner, E. (1993). Perceived control, effort, and academic performance: Interindividual, intraindividual, and time series analyses. *Journal of Personality and Social Psychology, 64,* 1,010-1,028.

Schoonen, R., and Verhallen, M. (2008). The assessment of deep word knowledge in young first and second language learners. *Language Testing, 25*(2), 211-236.

Schoonen, R., Gelderen, A. van, Glopper, K. de, Hulstijn, J., Simis, A., Snellings, P., and Stevenson, M. (2003). First language and second language writing: The role of linguistic knowledge, speed of processing and metacognitive knowledge. *Language Learning, 53*(1), 165-202.

Schraw, G., and Lehman, S. (2001). Situational interest: A review of the literature and directions for future research. *Educational Psychology Review, 13,* 23-52.

Schultz, K. (1997). "Do you want to be in my story?": Collaborative writing in an urban elementary school classroom. *Journal of Literacy Research, 29,* 253-287.

Schultz, K., and Fecho, B. (2000). Society's child: Social context and writing development. *Educational Psychologist, 35,* 51-62.

Schumacher, J.B., Hoffmann, P., Schmal, C., Schulte-Korne, G., and Nothen, M.M. (2007). Genetics of dyslexia: The evolving landscape. *Journal of Medical Genetics, 44,* 289-297.

Schumaker, J.B., Deshler, D.D., Alley, G.R., Warner, M.M., Clark, F.L., and Nolan, S. (1982). Error monitoring: A learning strategy for improving adolescent academic performance. In W.M. Cruickshank and J.W. Lerner (Eds.), *Coming of age: The best of ACLD* (vol. 3, pp. 170-183). Syracuse, NY: Syracuse University Press.

Schunk, D.H. (1991). Self-efficacy and academic motivation. *Educational Psychologist, 26,* 207-232.

Schunk, D.H. (1996). *Learning theories: An educational perspective* (2nd ed.). Englewood Cliffs, NJ: Merrill.

Schunk, D.H. (2003). Self-efficacy for reading and writing: Influence of modeling, goal setting, and self-evaluation. *Reading and Writing Quarterly, 19,* 159-172.

Schunk, D.H., and Pajares, F. (2002). The development of academic self-efficacy. In A. Wigfield and J. Eccles (Eds.), *Development of achievement motivation* (pp. 16-31). San Diego: Academic Press.

Schunk, D.H., and Pajares, F. (2005). Competence beliefs and academic functioning. In A.J. Elliot and C.S. Dweck (Eds.), *Handbook of Competence and Motivation* (pp. 85-104). New York: Guilford Press.

Schunk, D.H., and Rice, J.M. (1992). Influence of reading-comprehension strategy information on children's achievement outcomes. *Learning Disability Quarterly, 15*(1), 51-64.

Schunk, D., and Swartz, C.W. (1993a). Goals and progress feedback: Effects on self-efficacy and writing achievement. *Contemporary Educational Psychology, 18,* 337-354.

Schunk, D.H., and Swartz, C.W. (1993b). Writing strategy instruction with gifted students: Effects of goals and feedback on self-efficacy and skills. *Roeper Review, 15,* 225-230.

Schunk, D.H., and Zimmerman, B.J. (Eds.). (1994). *Self-regulation of learning and performance.* Hillsdale, NJ: Lawrence Erlbaum Associates.

Schunk, D.H., and Zimmerman, B.J. (2006). Competence and control beliefs: Distinguishing the means and ends. In P.A. Alexander and P.H. Winne (Eds.), *Handbook of educational psychology* (pp. 349-367). Mahwah, NJ: Lawrence Erlbaum Associates.

Schunk, D.H., and Zimmerman, B.J. (Eds.). (2008). *Motivation and self-regulated learning: Theory, research, and applications.* Mahwah, NJ: Lawrence Erlbaum Associates.

Schutte, N.S., and Malouff, J.M. (2007). Dimensions of reading motivation: Development of an adult reading motivation scale. *Reading Psychology: An International Quarterly, 28,* 469-489.

Schwanenflugel, P.J., Hamilton, A.M., Kuhn, M.R., Wisenbaker, J., and Stahl, S.A. (2004). Becoming a fluent reader: Reading skill and prosodic features in the oral reading of young readers. *Journal of Educational Psychology, 96,* 119-129.

Schwartz, D., and Bransford, D. (1998). A time for telling. *Cognition and Instruction, 16*(4), 475-522.

Scientific Learning Corporation. (2010). *Scientific Learning reading assistant™ expanded edition.* Available: http://www.scilearn.com/products/reading-assistant/ [Oct. 2011].

Scordaras, M. (2009). Just not enough time: Accelerated composition courses and struggling ESL writers. *Teaching English in the Two-Year College, 36*(3), 270-279.

Scott, C. (1999). Learning to write. In H. Catts and A. Kamhi (Eds.), *Language and reading disorders* (pp. 224-258). Boston, MA: Allyn and Bacon.

Scott, C., and Windsor, J. (2000). General language performance measures in spoken and written narrative and expository discourse of school-age children with language learning disabilities. *Journal of Speech, Language, and Hearing Research, 43,* 324-339.

Scribner, S., and Cole, M. (1981). *The psychology of literacy.* Cambridge, MA: Harvard University Press.

Scrivener, S., Bloom, D., LeBlanc, A., Paxson, C., Rouse, C., and Sommo, C. (2008). *Opening doors: A good start. Two-year effects of a freshmen learning community program at Kingsborough Community College.* New York: MDRC.

Seeman, T., McAvay, G., Merrill, S., Albert, M., and Rodin, J. (1996). Self-efficacy beliefs and change in cognitive performance: McArthur studies of successful aging. *Psychology and Aging, 11,* 538-551.

Seghier, M.L., and Price, C.J. (2010). Reading aloud boosts connectivity through the putamen. *Cerebral Cortex, 20*(3), 570-582.

Seidenberg, M.S., and McClelland, J.L. (1989). A distributed, developmental model of word recognition and naming. *Psychological Review, 96,* 523-568.

Seidenberg, M.S., and Zevin, J.D. (2006). Connectionist models in developmental cognitive neuroscience: Critical periods and the paradox of success. In Y. Munakata and M. Johnson (Eds.), *Processes of change in brain and cognitive development: Attention and performance XXI* (pp. 585-612). New York: Oxford University Press.

Sekaquaptewa, D., and Thompson, M. (2003). Solo status, stereotype threat, and performance expectancies: Their effects on women's performance. *Journal of Experimental Social Psychology, 39,* 68-74.

Selwyn, N. (2004). The information aged: A qualitative study of older adults' use of information and communications technology. *Journal of Aging Studies, 18,* 369-384.

Selwyn, N., and Gorard, S. (2004). Exploring the role of ICT in facilitating adult informal learning. *Education, Communication and Information, 4*(2), 293-310.

Sénéchal, M., and Cornell, E.H. (1993). Vocabulary acquisition through shared reading experiences. *Reading Research Quarterly, 28*, 361-374.

Sexton, M., Harris, K.R., and Graham, S. (1998). Self-regulated strategy development and the writing process: Effects on essay writing and attributions. *Exceptional Children, 64*(3), 295-311.

Shaffer, D.W. (2007). *How computer games help children learn.* New York: Palgrave.

Shanahan, T. (2006). Relations among oral language, reading, and writing development. In C. MacArthur, S. Graham, and J. Fitzgerald (Eds.), *Handbook of writing research* (pp. 171-183). New York: Guilford Press.

Shanahan, T., and Shanahan, C. (2008). Teaching disciplinary literacy to adolescents: Rethinking content-area literacy. *Harvard Educational Review, 78*(1), 40-61.

Shankweiler, D., and Crain, S. (1986). Language mechanisms and reading disorder: A modular approach. *Cognition, 24*, 139-168. [Reprinted in *The onset of literacy: Cognitive processes in reading acquisition.* Cambridge, MA: Bradford Books, MIT Press.]

Shankweiler, D., Mencl, W.E., Braze, D., Tabor, W., Pugh, K.R., and Fulbright, R. (2008). Reading differences and brain: Cortical integration of speech and print in sentence processing varies with reader skill. *Developmental Neuropsychology, 33*(6), 745-775.

Share, D.L., and Stanovich, K.E. (1995). Cognitive processes in early reading development: Accommodating individual differences into a model of acquisition. *Issues in Education: Contributions from Educational Psychology, 1*, 1-57.

Shaughnessy, M. (1979). *Errors and expectations.* Oxford, England: Oxford University Press.

Shaywitz, B.A., Shaywitz, S.E., Pugh, K.R., Mencl, W.E., Fulbright, R.K., Skudlarski, P., Constable, R.T., Marchione, K.E. Fletcher, J.M., Lyon, G.R., and Gore, J.C. (2002). Disruption of posterior brain systems for reading in children with developmental dyslexia. *Biological Psychiatry, 52*, 101-110.

Shaywitz, B.A., Shaywitz, S.E., Blachman, B.A., Pugh, K.R., Fulbright, R.K., Skudlarski, P., Mencl, W.E., Constable, R.T., Holahan, J.M., Marchione, K.E., Fletcher, J.M., Lyon, G.R., and Gore, J.C. (2004). Development of left occipitotemporal systems for skilled reading in children after a phonologically-based intervention. *Biological Psychiatry, 55*, 926-933.

Shaywitz, S.E. (2003). *Overcoming dyslexia: A new and complete science-based program for reading problems at any level.* New York: Knopf.

Shaywitz, S.E., Shaywitz, B.A., Pugh, K.R., Fulbright, R.K., Constable, R.T., Mencl, W.E., Shankweiler, D.P., Liberman, A.M., Skudlarski, P., Fletcher, J.M., Katz, L., Marchione, K.E., Lacadie, C., Gatenby, C., and Gore, J.C. (1998). Functional disruption in the organization of the brain for reading in dyslexia. *Proceedings of the National Academy of Sciences, 95*, 2,636-2,641.

Shaywitz, S.E., Shaywitz, B.A., Fulbright, R.K., Skudlarski, P., Mencl,W.E., Constable, R.T., Pugh, K.R., Holahan, J.M., Marchione, K.E., Fletcher, J.M., Lyon, G.R., and Gore, J.C. (2003). Neural systems for compensation and persistence: Young adult outcome of childhood reading disability. *Society of Biological Psychiatry, 54*, 25-33.

Shaywitz, S.E., Mody, M., and Shaywitz, B.A. (2006). Neural mechanisms in dyslexia. *Current Directions in Psychological Science, 15*, 278-281.

Shearer, B. (2004). Multiple intelligences theory after 20 years. *Teachers College Record, 106*, 2-16.

Sheen, Y., Wright, D., and Moldawa, A. (2009). Differential effects of focused and unfocused written correction on the accurate use of grammatical forms by adult ESL learners. *System: An International Journal of Educational Technology and Applied Linguistics, 37*(4), 556-569.

Sheldon, K.M., and Krieger, L.K. (2007). Understanding the negative effects of legal education on law students: A longitudinal test of self-determination theory. *Personality and Social Psychology Bulletin, 33*, 883-897.

Shell, D., Colvin, C., and Brunning, R. (1995). Self-efficacy, attribution, and outcome expectancy mechanisms in reading and writing achievement: Grade-level and achievement-level differences. *Journal of Educational Psychology, 87*, 386-398.

Shermis, M.D., and Burstein, J. (Eds.) (2003). *Automated essay scoring: A cross-disciplinary perspective.* Hillsdale, NJ: Lawrence Erlbaum Associates.

Shermis, M.D., Burstein, J., Higgins, D., and Zechner, K. (2010). *Automated essay scoring: Writing assessment and instruction.* Available: http://www.mkzechner.net/AES_IEE09.pdf [Oct. 2011].

Shippen, M.E. (2008). A pilot study of the efficacy of two adult basic literacy programs for incarcerated males. *Journal of Correctional Education, 59*(4), 339-347.

Shor, I. (1987). Monday morning fever: Critical literacy and the generative theme of "work." In I. Shor (Ed.), *Freire for the classroom* (pp. 104-121). Portsmouth, NH: Boynton/Cook.

Shute, V.J. (2006). *Focus on formative feedback.* ETS Research Report. Princeton, NJ: Educational Testing Service.

Shute, V.J. (2008). Focus on formative feedback. *Review of Educational Research, 78*, 153-189.

Shute, V.J., Ventura, M., Bauer, M.I., and Zapata-Rivera, D. (2009). Melding the power of serious games and embedded assessment to monitor and foster learning: Flow and grow. In U. Ritterfeld, M. Cody, and P. Vorderer (Eds.), *Serious games: Mechanisms and effects* (pp. 295-321). Mahwah, NJ: Routledge/Taylor and Francis.

Siegel, J. (2007). Keeping it real: Authentic materials in a GED class. *Adult Basic Education and Literacy Journal, 1*(2), 100-102.

Siegel, M. (1995). More than words: The generative power of transmediation for learning. *Canadian Journal of Education, 20*, 455-475.

Silani, G., Frith, U., Demonet, J.F., Fazio, F., Perani, D., Price, C., Frith, C.D., and Paulesu, E. (2005). Brain abnormalities underlying altered activation in dyslexia: A voxel-based morphometry study. *Brain, 128*, 2,453-2,461.

Silva, E. (2008). *Measuring skills for the 21st century.* Washington, DC: Education Sector. Available: http://www.educationsector.org/publications/measuring-skills-21st-century [Oct. 2011].

Silver-Pacuilla, H. (2006). Access and benefits: Assistive technology in adult literacy. *Journal of Adolescent and Adult Literacy, 50*(2), 114-125.

Simmons, D.C., Fuchs, L.S., Fuchs, D., Mathes, P.I., and Hodge, J.P. (1995). Effects of explicit teaching and peer tutoring on the reading achievement of learner-disabled and low-performing students in regular classrooms. *The Elementary School Journal, 95*, 387-408.

Simos, P.G., Breier, J.I., Fletcher, J.M., Foorman, B.R., Mouzaki, A., and Papanicoloau, A.C. (2001). Age-related changes in regional brain activation during phonological decoding and printed word recognition. *Developmental Neuropsychology, 29*(2), 191-210.

Simos, P.G., Breier, J.I., Fletcher, J.M., Foorman, B.R., Castillo, E.M., and Papanicolaou, A.C. (2002a). Brain mechanisms for reading words and pseudowords: An integrated approach. *Cerebral Cortex, 12*, 297-305.

Simos, P.G., Fletcher, J.M., Bergman, E., Breier, J.I., Foorman, B.R., Castillo, E.M., Davis, R.N., Fitzgerald, M., and Papanicolaou, A.C. (2002b). Dyslexia-specific brain activation profile becomes normal following successful remedial training. *Neurology, 58*, 1,203-1,213.

Simpson, M.L., Hynd, C.R., Nist, S.L., and Burrell, K.I. (1997). College academic assistance programs and practices. *Educational Psychology Review, 9*(1), 39-87.

Sinatra, G.M., Brown, K.J., and Reynolds, R.E. (2002). Implications of cognitive resources allocation for comprehension strategies instruction. In C.C. Block and M. Pressley (Eds.), *Comprehension instruction: Research-based best practices* (pp. 62-76). New York: Guilford Press.

Singer, M., Halldorson, M., Lear, J.C., and Andrusiak, P. (1992). Validation of causal bridging inferences in discourse understanding. *Journal of Memory and Language, 31*, 507-524.

Sireci, S.G., and Pitoniak, M. (2006). *Assessment accommodations: What have we learned from research?* Paper presented at the 2006 Educational Testing Service symposium on Accommodating Students with Disabilities on State Assessments.

Sireci, S.G., Scarpati, S.E., and Li, S. (2005). Test accommodations for students with disabilities: An analysis of the interaction hypothesis. *Review of Educational Research, 75*, 457-490.

Sissel, P.A. (1996). Reflection as vision: Prospects for future literacy programming. *New Directions for Adult and Continuing Education, 70*, 97-103.

Skaalvik, E.M. (1997). Issues in research on self-concept. In M.L. Maehr and P.R. Pintrich (Eds.), *Advances in motivation and achievement* (vol. 10, pp. 51-98). Greenwich, CN: JAI Press.

Skinner, E.A. (1995). *Perceived control, motivation, and coping.* Newbury Park, CA: Sage.

Skinner, E.A., Zimmer-Gembeck, and Connell, J.P. (1998). *Individual differences and the development of perceived control.* Monographs of the Society for Research in Child Development, No. 254. Indianapolis, IN: Wiley-Blackwell.

Slavin, R.E. (1991). Reading effects of IBM's "writing to read" program: A review of evaluations. *Educational Evaluation and Policy Analysis, 13*, 1-11.

Slavin, R.E. (1995). *Cooperative learning* (2nd ed.). Boston, MA: Allyn and Bacon.

Slavin, R.E. (1996). Research on cooperative learning and achievement: What we know, what we need to know. *Contemporary Educational Psychology, 21*, 43-69.

Slavin, R.E. (1999). Comprehensive approaches to cooperative learning. *Theory into Practice, 38*, 74-79.

Slavin, R.E., and Cheung, A. (2003). *Effective reading programs for English language learners: A best-evidence synthesis.* Baltimore, MD: Johns Hopkins University, Center for Research on the Education of Students Placed at Risk. Available: http://www.csos.jhu.edu/crespar/techReports/Report66.pdf [Oct. 2011].

Slavin, R.E. and Cheung, A. (2005). A synthesis of research on language of reading instruction. *Review of Educational Research, 75*, 247-284.

Sloutsky, V.M., Kaminski, J.A., and Heckler, A.F. (2005). The advantage of simple symbols for learning and transfer. *Psychonomic Bulletin and Review, 12*, 508-513.

Smith, A. (2010a). *Home broadband 2010.* Washington, DC: Pew Internet & American Life Project. Available: http://pewinternet.org/Reports/2010/Home-Broadband-2010.aspx [Oct. 2011].

Smith, A. (2010b). *Mobile access 2010.* Washington, DC: Pew Internet & American Life Project. Available: http://pewinternet.org/Reports/2010/Mobile-Access-2010.aspx [Oct. 2011].

Smith, B.P. (2006). The (computer) games people play. In P. Vorderer and J. Bryant (Eds.), *Playing video games: Motives, responses, and consequences* (pp. 43-56). Mahwah, NJ: Lawrence Erlbaum Associates.

Smith, B.Q. (2004). Genre, medium, and learning to write: Negotiating identities, enacting school-based literacies in adulthood. *Journal of College Reading and Learning, 34*(2), 75-96.

Smith, C., and Gillespie, M. (2007). *Research on professional development and teacher change: Implications for adult basic education.* Available: http://www.ncsall.net/fileadmin/resources/ann_rev/smith-gillespie-07.pdf [Oct. 2011].

Smith, D., Gilmore, P., Goldman, S., and McDermott, R. (1993). Failure's failure. In E. Jacob and C. Jordan (Eds.), *Minority education: Anthropological perspectives* (pp. 209-231). Norwood, NJ: Ablex.

Smith, R. (2010). Feeling supported: Curricular learning communities for basic skills courses and students who speak English as a second language. *Community College Review*, *37*(3), 261-284.

Smith, S., Rebok, G.W., Smith, W., Hall, S.E., and Alvin, M. (1983). Adult age differences in the use of story structure in delayed free recall. *Experimental Aging Research*, *9*, 191-195.

Smitherman, G. (1986). *Talkin and testifyin: The language of black America.* Detroit, MI: Wayne State University Press.

Smith-Lock, K., Nickels, L., and Mortensen, L. (2008). Story writing skills of adults with a history of language-impairments. *Reading and Writing*, *22*, 713-734.

Snow, C.E. (2002). *Reading for understanding: Toward a research and development program in reading comprehension.* Santa Monica, CA: RAND.

Snow, C.E. (2010). Academic language and the challenge of reading for learning about science. *Science*, *328*, 450-452.

Snow, C.E., and Uccelli, P. (2008). The challenge of academic language. In D. Olson and N. Torrance (Eds.), *The Cambridge handbook of literacy* (Ch. 7, pp. 112-133). Cambridge, England: Cambridge University Press.

Snow, C.E., Griffin, P., and Burns, M.S. (2005). *Knowledge to support the teaching of reading: Preparing teachers for a changing world.* San Francisco, CA: Jossey-Bass.

Snow, C.E., Lawrence, J., and White, C. (2009). Generating knowledge of academic language among urban middle school students. *Journal of Research on Educational Effectiveness*, *2*, 325-344.

Snyder, V. (2002). The effect of course-based reading strategy training on the reading comprehension skills of developmental college students. *Research and Teaching in Developmental Education*, *18*(2), 37-41.

Soenens, B., and Vansteenkiste, M. (2005). Antecedents and outcomes of self-determination in three life domains: The role of parents' and teachers' autonomy support. *Journal of Youth and Adolescence*, *34*, 589-604.

Soep, E., and Chavez, V. (2005). Youth radio and the pedagogy of collegiality. *Harvard Educational Review*, *75*(4), 409-434.

Soifer, R., Young, D.L., and Irwin, M. (1989). The academy: A learner-centered workplace literacy program. In A. Fingeret and P. Jurmo (Eds.), *Participatory literacy education* (pp. 65-72). San Francisco, CA: Jossey-Bass.

Solomon, T.C., Van der Kerkhof, M.H., and Moje, E.B. (2010). When is a detail seductive? On the challenges of constructing and teaching from engaging science texts. In A.J. Rodriguez (Ed.), *Science education as a pathway to teaching language literacy.* Rotterdam, the Netherlands: Sense.

Son, L.K. (2004). Spacing one's study: Evidence for a metacognitive control strategy. *Journal of Experimental Psychology: Learning, Memory, and Cognition*, *30*, 601-604.

Son, L.K., and Metcalfe, J. (2000). Metacognitive and control strategies in study-time allocation. *Journal of Experimental Psychology: Learning, Memory, and Cognition*, *26*, 204-221.

Son, L.K., and Sethi, R. (2006). Metacognitive control and optimal learning. *Cognitive Science*, *30*, 759-774.

Song, B. (2006). Failure in a college ESL course: Perspectives of instructors and students. *Community College Journal of Research and Practice*, *30*(5/6), 417-431.

Sonnenschein, S., Stapleton, L.M., and Benson, A. (2010). The relation between the type and amount of instruction and growth in children's reading competencies *American Educational Research Journal*, 47(2), 358-389.

Sonntag, C.M., and McLaughlin, T.F. (1984). The effects of training students in paragraph writing. *Education and Treatment of Children*, 7, 49-59.

Sowell, E.R., Thompson, P.M., Leonard, C.M., Welcome, S.E., Kan, E., and Toga, A.W. (2004). Longitudinal mapping of cortical thickness and brain growth in normal children. *Journal of Neuroscience*, 24, 8,223-8,231.

Spada, N., and Lightbown, P. (2008). Form-focused instruction: Isolated or integrated? *TESOL Quarterly*, 42(2), 181-207.

Sparks, R.L., Philips, L., and Javorsky, J. (2003). Students classified as LD who petitioned for or fulfilled the college foreign language requirement: Are they different? A replication study. *Journal of Learning Disabilities*, 36(4), 348-362.

Sparks, R.L., Patton, J., Ganschow, L., and Humbach, N. (2009a). Long-term crosslinguistic transfer of skills from L1 to L2. *Language Learning*, 59, 203-243.

Sparks, R.L., Patton, J., Ganschow, L., and Humbach, N. (2009b). Long-term relationships among early first language skills, second language aptitude, second language affect and later second language proficiency. *Applied Psycholinguistics*, 30, 725-755.

Spear-Swerling, L. (2004). Fourth-graders' performance on a state-mandated assessment involving two different measures of reading comprehension. *Reading Psychology*, 25, 121-148.

Sperling, C. (2009). *The Massachusetts community colleges developmental education best policy and practice audit: Final report.* Boston: Massachusetts Community Colleges Executive Office. Available: http://www.masscc.org/pdfs/09AnnualReport1.pdf [Oct. 2011].

Spieler, D.H., and Balota, D.A. (2000). Factors influencing word naming in younger and older adults. *Psychology and Aging*, 15(2), 225-231.

Spiro, R.J., Feltovich, P.J., Jacobson, M.J., and Coulson, R.C. (1991). Cognitive flexibility, constructivism, and hypertext: Random access instruction for advanced knowledge acquisition in ill-structured domains. *Educational Technology*, 31, 24-33.

Spurling, S., Seymour, S., and Chisman, F. (2008). *Pathways and outcomes: Tracking ESL student performance.* A longitudinal study of ESL service at City College of San Francisco. New York: Council for Advancement of Adult Literacy. Available: http://www.caalusa.org/pathways-outcomes/pathways-outcomesfull.pdf [Oct. 2011].

Stahl, S.A. (2004). What do we know about fluency? Findings of the National Reading Panel. In P. McCardle and V. Chhabra (Eds.), *The voice of evidence in reading research* (pp. 187-211). Baltimore, MD: Paul H. Brookes.

Stahl, S.A., and Fairbanks, M.M. (1986). The effects of vocabulary instruction: A model-based meta-analysis. *Review of Educational Research*, 56, 72-110.

Stahl, S.A., McKenna, M.C. and Pagnucco, J.R. (1994). The effects of whole language instruction: An update and a reappraisal. *Educational Psychologist*, 29, 175-185.

Stanley, L.D. (2003). Beyond access: Psychosocial barriers to computer literacy. *The Information Society*, 19(5), 407-416.

Stanovich, K.E. (1980). Toward an interactive compensatory model of individual differences in the development of reading fluency. *Reading Research Quarterly*, 16, 32-71.

Stanovich, K.E. (1986). Matthew effects in reading: Some consequences of individual differences in the acquisition of literacy. *Reading Research Quarterly*, 21, 360-407.

Stanovich, K.E., and Stanovich, P.J. (1995). How research might inform the debate about early reading acquisition. *Journal of Research in Reading [Special Issue: The Contribution of Psychological Research]*, 18(2), 87-105.

Stanovich, K.E., and West, R.R. (1989). Exposure to print and orthographic processing. *Reading Research Quarterly*, 24, 402-484.

Stanovich, K.E., West, R.F., and Cunningham, A.E. (1991). Beyond phonological processes: Print exposure and orthographic processing. In S. Brady and D. Shankweiler (Eds.), *Phonological processes in literacy* (pp. 219-235). Hillsdale, NJ: Lawrence Erlbaum Associates.

Stanovich, K.E., West, R.F., and Harrison, M.R. (1995). Knowledge growth and maintenance across the life span: The role of print exposure. *Developmental Psychology, 31*, 811-826.

Staudinger, U.M., and Baltes, P.B. (1996). Interactive minds: A facilitative setting for wisdom-related performance? *Journal of Personality and Social Psychology, 71*, 746-762.

Steele, C.M. (1997). A threat in the air: How stereotypes shape intellectual identity and performance. *American Psychologist, 52*, 613-629.

Steele, C.M., and Aronson, J. (1995). Stereotype threat and the intellectual test performance of African-Americans. *Journal of Personality and Social Psychology, 69*, 797-811.

Steffe, L.P., and Thompson, P.W. (2000). Teaching experiment methodology: Underlying principles and essential elements. In R. Lesh and A.E. Kelly (Eds.), *Research design in mathematics and science education* (pp. 267-307). Hillsdale, NJ: Lawrence Erlbaum Associates.

Stefl-Mabry, J. (1998). Designing a web-based reading course. *Journal of Adolescent and Adult Literacy, 41*(7), 556.

Stein, J. (2001). The sensory basis of reading problems. *Developmental Neuropsychology, 20*(2), 509-534.

Steinberg, L. Brown, B., and Dornbusch, S.M. (1996). *Beyond the classroom: Why school reform has failed and what parents need to do.* New York: Simon and Schuster.

Sticht, T.G. (1988). Adult literacy education. *Review of Research in Education, 15*(1), 59-96.

Sticht, T.G. (2005). *Functional context education: Making learning relevant in the 21st century: Workshop participant's notebook.* Available: http://www.nald.ca/library/research/fce/FCE.pdf [Oct. 2011].

Stiggins, R. (1997). *Student-centered classroom assessment* (2nd ed.). Upper Saddle River, NJ: Prentice-Hall.

Stine, E.A.L., and Hindman, J. (1994). Age differences in reading time allocation for propositionally dense sentences. *Aging, Neuropsychology, and Cognition, 1*(1), 2-16.

Stine, E.A.L., and Wingfield, A. (1990). How much do working memory deficits contribute to age differences in discourse memory? *European Journal of Cognitive Psychology, 2*(3), 289-304.

Stine, E.A.L., Wingfield, A., and Myers, S.D. (1990). Age differences in processing information from television news: The effects of bisensory augmentation. *Journal of Gerontology: Psychological Sciences, 45*, P1-P8.

Stine-Morrow, E.A.L., and Miller, L.M.S. (2009). Aging, self-regulation, and learning from text. In B.H. Ross (Ed.), *Psychology of learning and motivation: Advances in research and theory* (vol. 51, pp. 255-296). San Diego, CA: Elsevier Academic Press.

Stine-Morrow, E.A.L., and Shake, M.C. (2009). Language in aged persons. In L. Squire (Ed.), *New encyclopedia of neuroscience* (pp. 337-342) New York: Elsevier.

Stine-Morrow, E.A.L., Loveless, M.K., and Soederberg, L.K. (1996). Resource allocation in on-line reading by younger and older adults. *Psychology and Aging, 11*, 475-486.

Stine-Morrow, E.A.L., Miller, L.M.S., and Nevin, J.A. (1999). The effects of context and feedback on age differences in spoken word recognition. *Journal of Gerontology: Psychological Sciences, 54B*, P125-P134.

Stine-Morrow, E.A.L., Gagne, D.D., Morrow, D.G., and DeWall, B.H. (2004). Age differences in rereading. *Memory and Cognition, 32*, 696-710.

Stine-Morrow, E.A.L., Shake, M.C., Miles, J.R., and Noh, S.R. (2006a). Adult age differences in the effects of goals on self-regulated sentence processing. *Psychology and Aging, 21*, 790-803.

Stine-Morrow, E.A.L., Miller, L.M.S., and Hertzog, C. (2006b). Aging and self-regulated language processing. *Psychological Bulletin, 132,* 582-606.

Stine-Morrow, E.A.L., Gagne, D.D., Miller, L.M.S., and Hertzog, C. (2008). Self-regulated reading in adulthood. *Psychology and Aging, 23*(1), 131-153.

Stoddard, B., and MacArthur, C. A. (1993). A peer editing strategy: Guiding learning disabled students in response and revision. *Research in the Teaching of English, 27,* 76-103.

Stodden, R., Jones, M.A., and Chang, K.B.T. (2002). *Services, supports, and accommodations for individuals with disabilities: An analysis across secondary education, postsecondary education, and employment.* Paper presented at the Capacity Building Institute, March, Honolulu, HI.

Stoehr, T. (2005). Is it a crime to be illiterate? Changing lives through literature: Offenders program report. *Change, 41*(7), 28-35.

Stone, J.R., III, Alfeld, C., Pearson, D., Lewis, M.V., and Jensen, S. (2006). *Building academic skills in context: Testing the value of enhanced math learning in CTE (Final study).* St. Paul, MN: National Research Center for Career and Technical Education. Available: http://136.165.122.102/UserFiles/File/Math-in-CTE/MathLearningFinalStudy.pdf [Oct. 2011].

Stothard, S.E., and Hulme, C. (1996). A comparison of reading comprehension and decoding difficulties in children. In C. Cornoldi and J. Oakhill (Eds.), *Reading comprehension difficulties: Processes and intervention* (pp. 93-112). Mahwah, NJ: Lawrence Erlbaum Associates.

Street, B.V. (1984). *Literacy in theory and practice.* New York: Cambridge University Press.

Street, B.V. (1994). Literacy, culture, and history. In J. Maybin (Ed.), *Language and literacy in social practice* (pp. 139-150). Clevedon, England: Multilingual Matters.

Street, B.V. (2003). What's "new" in New Literacy Studies? Critical approaches to literacy in theory and practice. *Current Issues in Comparative Education, 5*(2), 77-91.

Street, B.V. (2009). *"Hidden" features of academic paper writing* (Draft version). Final to be published in Working Papers in Educational Linguistics, University of Pennsylvania.

Street, C.A. (2005). A reluctant writer's entry into a community of writers. *Journal of Adolescent and Adult Literacy, 48*(8), 636-641.

Streeter, L., Psotka, J., Laham, D., and MacCuish, D. (2002). *The credible grading machine: Automated essay scoring in the DoD.* Paper presented at Interservice/Industry, Simulation and Education Conference (I/ITSEC), Dec. 2-5, Orlando, FL.

Stromswold, K. (1995). The cognitive and neural bases of language acquisition. In M. Gazzaniga (Ed.), *The cognitive neurosciences* (pp. 855-870). Cambridge, MA: MIT Press.

Strong American Schools. (2008). *Diploma to nowhere.* Available: http://www.deltacostproject.org/resources/pdf/DiplomaToNowhere.pdf [Oct. 2011].

Strucker, J., and Davidson, R. (2003). *Adult reading components study (ARCS).* NCSALL Research Brief. Available: http://www.ncsall.net/fileadmin/resources/research/brief_strucker2.pdf [Oct. 2011].

Strucker, J., Yamamoto, K., and Kirsch, I. (2007). *The relationship of the component skills of reading to IALS performance: Tipping points and five classes of adult literacy learners.* Cambridge, MA: National Center for the Study of Adult Learning and Literacy.

Sturm, J.M., and Rankin-Erickson, J.L. (2002). Effects of hand-drawn and computer-generated concept mapping on the expository writing of students with learning disabilities. *Learning Disabilities Research and Practice, 17,* 124-139.

Swanson, H.L. (1999). Reading research for students with learning disabilities: A meta-analysis of intervention outcomes. *Journal of Learning Disabilities, 32*(6), 504-532.

Swanson, H.L., and Alexander, J.E. (1997). Cognitive processes as predictors of word recognition and reading comprehension in learning-disabled and skilled readers: Revisiting the specificity hypothesis. *Journal of Educational Psychology, 89*(1), 128-158.

Swanson, H.L. and Ashbaker, H. (2000). Working memory, short-term memory, speech rate, word recognition, and reading comprehension in learning disabled readers: Does the executive system have a role? *Intelligence, 28*, 1-30.

Swanson, H.L., and Hsieh, C.-J. (2009). Reading disabilities in adults: A selective meta-analysis of the literature. *Review of Educational Research, 79*(4), 1,362-1,390.

Swanson, H.L., and Saez, L.S. (2003). Memory difficulties in children and adults with learning disabilities. In H.L. Swanson, K.R. Harris, and S. Graham (Eds.), *Handbook of learning disabilities* (pp. 182-198). New York: Guilford Press.

Swanson, H.L., and Siegel, L.S. (2001). Learning disabilities as a working memory deficit. *Issues in Education: Contributions from Educational Psychology, 7*(1), 1-48.

Swanson, H.L., Hoskyn, M., and Lee, C. (1999). *Interventions for students with learning disabilities: A meta-analysis of treatment outcomes.* New York: Guilford Press.

Swanson, H.L., Harris, K.R., and Graham, S. (Eds.). (2003). *Handbook of learning disabilities.* New York: Guilford Press.

Swanson, H.L., Howard, C.B., and Saez, L. (2007). Reading comprehension and working memory in children with learning disabilities in reading. In K. Cain and J. Oakhill (Eds.), *Children's comprehension problems in oral and written language: A cognitive perspective* (pp.157-190). New York: Guilford Press.

Swanson, H.L., Rosston, K., Gerber, M., and Solari, E. (2008). Influence of oral language and phonological awareness on children's bilingual reading. *Journal of School Psychology, 46*(4), 413-429.

Swanson, L., and Berninger, V. (1996). Individual differences in children's working memory and writing skills. *Journal of Experimental Child Psychology, 63*, 358-385.

Sweller, J., and Chandler, P. (1991). Evidence for cognitive load theory. *Cognition and Instruction, 8*, 351-362.

Swezy, R.W., and Llaneras, R.E. (1997). Models in training and instruction. In G. Salvendy (Ed.), *Handbook of human factor and ergonomics* (pp. 512-577). New York: John Wiley & Sons.

Szupnar, K.K., McDermott, K.B., and Roediger, H.L., III. (2007). Expectation of a final cumulative test enhances long-term retention. *Memory and Cognition, 35*, 1,007-1,013.

Taboada, A., Tonks, S.M., Wigfield, A., and Guthrie, J.T. (2009). Effects of motivational and cognitive variables on reading comprehension. *Reading and Writing, 22*, 85-106.

Taconnat, L., Froger, C., Sacher, M., and Isingrini, M. (2008). Generation and associative encoding in young and old adults. *Experimental Psychology, 55*, 23-30.

Tallal, P. (1980). Auditory temporal perception, phonics, and reading disabilities in children. *Brain and Language, 9*, 182-198.

Tallal, P. (2004). Improving language and literacy is a matter of time. *Nature Reviews Neuroscience, 5*, 721-728.

Tamassia, C., Lennon, M., Yamamoto, K., and Kirsch, I. (2007). *Adult education in America: A first look at results from the Adult Education Program and Learner Surveys.* Princeton, NJ: Educational Testing Service. Available: http://www.ets.org/research/policy_research_reports/aeps-report [Oct. 2011].

Tan, L.H., Spinks, J.A., Feng, C.M., Siok, W.T., Perfetti, C.A., Xiong, J., Fox, P.T., and Gao, J.H. (2003). Neural systems of second language reading are shaped by native language. *Human Brain Mapping, 18*, 155-166.

Tarone, E., Bigelow, M., and Hansen, K. (2007). The impact of alphabetic print literacy level on oral second language acquisition. In N.R. Faux (Ed.), *Low-educated adult second language and literacy acquisition proceedings of symposium* (pp. 99-122). Richmond, VA: Literacy Institute at Virginia Commonwealth University.

Taylor, E.W. (2007). An update of transformative learning theory: A critical review of the empirical literature (1999-2005). *International Journal of Lifelong Education, 26*, 173-191.

Taylor, K. (2006). Autonomy and self-directed learning: A developmental journey. In C. Hoare (Ed.), *Handbook of adult development and learning* (Ch. 9, pp. 196-218). New York: Oxford University Press.

Taylor, M., Abasi, A., Pinsent-Johnson, C., and Evans, K. (2007). Collaborative learning in communities of literacy practice. *Adult Basic Education and Literacy Journal, 1,* 4-11.

Taylor, R.T., and McAtee, R. (2003). Turning a new page to life and literacy. *Journal of Adolescent and Adult Literacy, 46*(6), 476-480.

Teale, W.H. (1986). Home background and young children's literary development. In W.H. Teale and E. Sulzby (Eds.), *Emergent literacy: Writing and reading* (pp. 173-206). Norwood, NJ: Ablex.

Temple, E., Deutsch, G.K., Poldrack, R.A., Miller, S.L., Tallal, P., Merzenich, M.M., and Gabrieli, J.D.E. (2003). Neural deficits in children with dyslexia ameliorated by behavioral remediation: Evidence from functional MRI. *Proceedings of the National Academy of Sciences, 100,* 2,860-2,865.

Tett, L., and Maclachlan, K. (2008). Learners, tutors and power in adult literacies research in Scotland. *International Journal of Lifelong Education, 27*(6), 659-672.

Tharp, R.G., and Gallimore, R. (1991). *Rousing minds to life: Teaching, learning, and schooling in social context.* Cambridge, England: Cambridge University Press.

Therriault, D.J., Rinck, M., and Zwaan, R.A. (2006). Assessing the influence of dimensional focus during situation model construction. *Memory and Cognition, 34,* 78-89.

Therrien, W.J. (2004). Fluency and comprehension gains as a result of repeated reading: A meta-analysis. *Remedial and Special Education, 25*(4), 252-261.

Therrien, W.J., and Hughes, C.A. (2008). Comparison of repeated reading and question generation on students' reading fluency and comprehension. *Learning Disabilities: A Contemporary Journal, 6*(1), 1-17.

Thibodeau, A. (1964). *A study of the effects of elaborative thinking and vocabulary enrichment exercises on written composition.* Unpublished doctoral dissertation, Boston University.

Thiede, K.W., and Dunlosky, J. (1999). Toward a general model of self-regulated study: An analysis of selection of items for study and self-paced study time. *Journal of Experimental Psychology: Learning, Memory, and Cognition, 25,* 1,024-1,137.

Thiede, K.W., Anderson, M.C.M., and Therriault, D.J. (2003). Accuracy of metacognitive monitoring affects learning of texts. *Journal of Educational Psychology, 95,* 66-73.

Thomas, C., Englert, C., and Gregg, S. (1987). An analysis of errors and strategies in the expository writing of learning disabled students. *Remedial and Special Education, 8,* 21-30.

Thomas, R.L. (2009). Using distance learning to increase literacy among TANF participants. *Journal of Technology in Human Services, 27*(3), 216-226.

Thompson, E.J.D. (2002). *Putting bread on the table: Literacy and livelihood in Kenya.* Nairobi, Kenya: Knowledge and Information Management, Adult Education for Development.

Thonus, T. (2003). Serving generation 1.5 learners in the university writing center. *TESL Journal, 12*(1), 17-24.

Tierney, R., and Shanahan, T. (1991). Research on the reading-writing relationship: Interactions, transactions, and outcomes. In R. Barr, M. Kamil, P. Mosenthal, and D. Pearson (Eds.), *The handbook of reading research* (vol. 2, pp. 246-280). New York: Longman.

Tierney, R., Readence, J., and Dishner, E. (1995). *Reading strategies and practices: A compendium.* Boston, MA: Allyn and Bacon.

Tindal, G., and Fuchs, L. (1999). *A summary of research on test changes: An empirical basis for defining accommodations.* Lexington: University of Kentucky, Mid-South Regional Resource Center.

Tindal, G., and Ketterlin-Geller, L.R. (2004). *Research on mathematics test accommodations relevant to NAEP testing.* NAGB Conference on Increasing the Participation of SD and LEP Students in NAEP. Available: http://www.eric.ed.gov/PDFS/ED500433.pdf [Oct. 2011].

Tindal, G., Heath, B., Hollenbeck, K., Almond, P., and Harniss, M. (1998). Accommodating students with disabilities on large-scale tests: An empirical study of student response and test administration demands. *Exceptional Children, 64,* 439-450.

Tokowicz, N., and MacWhinney, B. (2005). Implicit and explicit measures of sensitivity to violations in second language grammar. An event-related potential investigation. *Studies in Second Language Acquisition, 27,* 173-204.

Topping, K. (1996). The effectiveness of peer tutoring in further and higher education: A typology and review of the literature. *Higher Education, 32,* 321-345.

Toppino, T.C., and Brochin, H.A. (1989). Learning from tests: The case of true-false examinations. *Journal of Educational Research, 83,* 119-124.

Toppino, T.C., and Luipersbeck, S.M. (1993). Generality of the negative suggestion effect in objective tests. *Journal of Educational Research, 86,* 357-362.

Torgerson, C.J., and Zhu, D. (2003). A systematic review and meta-analysis of the effectiveness of ICT on literacy learning in English. In *Research Evidence in Education Library* (pp. 5-16). London, England: EPPI-Centre, Social Science Research Unit, Institute of Education. Available: http://eppi.ioe.ac.uk/EPPIWebContent/reel/review_groups/english/eng_rv2/eng_rv2.pdf [Oct. 2011].

Torgerson, C.J., Porthouse, J., and Brooks, G. (2003). A systematic review and meta-analysis of randomised controlled trials evaluating interventions in adult literacy and numeracy. *Journal of Research in Reading, 26,* 234-255.

Torgerson, C.J., Brooks, G., Porthouse, J., Burton, M., Robinson, A., Wright, K., and Watt, I. (2004). *Adult literacy and numeracy and literacy instructions and outcomes: A review of controlled trials.* Available: http://www.nrdc.org.uk/uploads/documents/doc_2850.pdf [Oct. 2011].

Torgerson, C.J., Porthouse, J., and Brooks, G. (2005). A systematic review of controlled trials evaluating interventions in adult literacy and numeracy. *Journal of Research in Reading, 28*(2), 87-107.

Torgesen, J.K. (2004). Lessons learned from the last 20 years of research on interventions for students who experience difficulty learning to read. In P. McCardle and V. Chhabra (Eds.), *The voice of evidence in reading research* (Ch. 15, Part IV, Reading Research Evidence in the Classroom). Baltimore: MD: Paul H. Brookes.

Torgesen, J.K., Wagner, R.K., Rashotte, C.A., Rose, E., Lindamood, P., Conway, T., and Garvan, C. (1999). Preventing reading failure in young children with phonological processing disabilities: Group and individual responses to instruction. *Journal of Educational Psychology, 91*(4), 579-593.

Torgesen, J.K., Alexander, A.W., Wagner, R.K., Rashotte, C.A., Voeller, K.K.S., and Conway, T. (2001). Intensive remedial instruction for children with severe reading disabilities: Immediate and long-term outcomes from two instructional approaches. *Journal of Learning Disabilities, 34*(1), 33-58.

Torrance, M., and Galbraith, D. (2006). The processing demands of writing. In C.A. MacArthur, S. Graham, and J. Fitzgerald (Eds.), *Handbook of writing research* (pp. 67-82). New York: Guilford Press.

Toso, B.W., Prins, E., Drayton, B., Tnanadass, E., and Gungor, R. (2009). Finding voice: Shared decision making and student leadership in a family literacy program. *Adult Basic Education and Literacy Journal, 3*(3), 151-160.

Tough, A. (1978). *The adult's learning projects: A fresh approach to theory and practice in adult learning* (2nd ed.). Toronto: Ontario Institute for Studies in Education.

Trabasso, T., and van den Broek, P. (1985). Causal thinking and the representation of narrative events. *Journal of Memory and Language, 24*(5), 612-630.

Trabasso, T., Secco, T., and Van den Broek, P. (1984). Causal cohesion and story coherence. In H. Mandl, N.L. Stein, and T. Trabasso (Eds.), *Learning and comprehension of text* (pp. 83-111). Hillsdale, NJ: Lawrence Erlbaum Associates.

Traxler, M., and Gernsbacher, M. (1993). Improving written communication through perspective-taking. *Language and Cognitive Processes, 8*, 311-344.

Treiman, R. (1993). *Beginning to spell.* New York: Oxford University Press.

Tulving E. (1967). The effects of presentation and recall of material in free-recall learning. *Journal of Verbal Learning and Verbal Behavior, 6*, 175-184.

Turkeltaub, P.E., Gareau, L., Flowers, D.L., Zeffiro, T.A., and Eden, G.F. (2003). Development of neural mechanisms for reading. *Nature Neuroscience, 6*, 767-773.

Tversky, B., Morrison, J.B., and Betrancourt, M. (2002). Animation: Can it facilitate? *International Journal of Human-Computer Studies, 57*, 247-262.

United Nations Education, Social, and Cultural Organization. (2004). *The plurality of literacy and its implications for policies and programmes.* UNESCO Education Sector Position Paper. Available: http://unesdoc.unesco.org/images/0013/001362/136246e.pdf [Oct. 2011].

University of the State of New York. (2005). *English language arts core curriculum (prekindergarten-grade 12).* Albany, NY: University of the State of New York, the State Education Department. Available: http://www.emsc.nysed.gov/ciai/ela/elacore.pdf [Oct. 2011].

Urdan, T.C. (2004). Predictors of academic self-handicapping and achievement: Examining achievement goals, classroom goal structures, and culture. *Journal of Educational Psychology, 96*, 251-264.

Urdan, T.C., and Maehr, M.L. (1995). Beyond a two-goal theory of motivation and achievement: A case for social goals. *Review of Educational Research, 65*, 213-243.

Urdan, T., and Midgley, C. (2001). Academic self-handicapping: What we know, what more there is to learn. *Educational Psychology Review, 13*, 115-138.

Urdan, T., Midgley, C., and Anderman, E.M. (1998). The role of classroom goal structure in students' use of self-handicapping strategies. *American Educational Research Journal, 35*, 101-122.

U.S. Census Bureau (2007). *Educational attainment: People 18 years old and over, by total money earnings in 2006, age, race, Hispanic origin, and sex.* Available: http://pubdb3.census.gov/macro/032007/perinc/new04_001.htm [Oct. 2011].

U.S. Department of Education. (2010). *Fiscal year 2010 budget summary.* Available: http://www2.ed.gov/about/overview/budget/budget10/summary/edlite-section3c.html [Feb. 2012].

U.S. Department of Health and Human Services (2008). *Quick guide to health literacy.* Washington, DC: Office of Disease Prevention and Health Promotion. Available: http://www.health.gov/communication/literacy/quickguide/ [Oct.2011].

Uso-Juan, E. (2007). The compensatory nature of discipline-related knowledge and English-language proficiency in reading English for academic purposes. *The Modern Language Journal, 90*, 210-227.

Vadasy, P.F., and Sanders, E.A. (2008). Repeated reading intervention: Outcomes and interactions with readers' skills and classroom instruction. *Journal of Educational Psychology, 100*(2), 272-290.

Valdés, G. (1998). The world outside and inside schools: Language and immigrant children. *Educational Researcher, 27*(6), 4-18.

Vallerand, R.J. (1997). Toward a hierarchical model of intrinsic and extrinsic motivation. In M.P. Zanna (Ed.), *Advances in experimental social psychology* (vol. 29, pp. 271-360). San Diego, CA: Academic Press.

Vallerand, R.J., and Bissonnette, R. (1992). Intrinsic, extrinsic, and amotivational styles as predictors of behavior: A prospective study. *Journal of Personality, 60,* 599-620.

Vallerand, R.J., Pelletier, L.G., Biais, M.R., Briere, N.M., Senecal, C., and Vallieres, E.F. (1992). The academic motivation scale: A measure of intrinsic, extrinsic, and amotivation in education. *Educational and Psychological Measurement, 52,* 1,003-1,017.

Vallerand, R.J., Pelletier, L.G., Blais, M.R., Briere, N.M., Senecal, C., and Vallieres, E.F. (1993). On the assessment of intrinsic, extrinsic and amotivation in education: Evidence on the concurrent and construct validity of the academic motivation scale. *Educational and Psychological Measurement, 53,* 159-172.

Vallerand, R.J., Fortier, M.S., and Guay, F. (1997). Self-determination and persistence in a real-life setting: Toward a motivational model of high school dropout. *Journal of Personality and Social Psychology, 72,* 1,161-1,176.

van Ark, B., Inklaar, R., and McGuckin, R.H. (2003). ICT productivity in Europe and the United States: Where do the differences come from? *CESifo Economic Studies, 49,* 295-318.

Van den Bergh, H. and Rijlaarsdam, G. (1996). The dynamics of composing: Modeling writing process data. In C. Levy and S. Ransdell (Eds.), *The science of writing* (pp. 207-232). Mahwah, NJ: Lawrence Erbaum Associates.

van den Broek, P., Risden, K., and Husebye-Hartmann, E. (1995). The role of reader's standards of coherence in the generation of inference during reading. In E.P. Lorch and E.J. O'Brien (Eds.), *Sources of coherence in reading* (pp. 353-374). Hillsdale, NJ: Lawrence Erlbaum Associates.

van den Broek, P., Lorch, R., Linderholm, T., and Gustafson, M. (2001). The effects of readers' goals on inference generation and memory for texts. *Memory and Cognition, 29*(8), 1,081-1,087.

van den Broek, P., Virtue, S., Everson, M.G., and Tzeng, Y., and Sung, Y. (2002). Comprehension and memory of science texts: Inferential processes and the construction of a mental representation. In J. Otero, J. Leon, and A.C. Graesser (Eds.), *The psychology of science text comprehension* (pp. 131-154). Mahwah, NJ: Lawrence Erlbaum Associates.

van den Broek, P., Rapp, D.N., and Kendeou, P. (2005). Integrating memory-based and constructionist processes in accounts of reading comprehension. *Discourse Processes, 39,* 299-316.

van den Broek, M., Verschelden, G., and Boonaert, T. (2008). E-learning in a low-status female profession: The role of motivation, anxiety and social support in the learning divide. *Journal of Computer Assisted Learning, 24,* 181-190.

van den Broek, P., White, M.J., Kendeou, P., and Carlson, S. (2009). Reading between the lines: Developmental and individual differences in cognitive processes in reading comprehension. In R. K. Wagner, C. Schatschneider, and C. Phythian-Sence (Eds.), *Beyond decoding: The behavioral and biological foundations of reading comprehension* (pp. 107-123). New York: Guilford Press.

Vanderberg, R., and Swanson, H.L. (2007). Which components of working memory are imporant in the writing process? *Reading and Writing, 20,* 721-752.

Van der Linden, M., Collette, F., Salmon, E., Delfiore, G., Degueldre, C., Luxen, A., and Franck, G. (1999). The neural correlates of updating information in verbal working memory. *Memory, 7*(5-6), 549-560.

Van der Linden, D., Sonnentag, S., Frese, M., and Van Dyck, C. (2001). Exploration strategies, performance, and error consequences when learning a complex computer task. *Behavior and Information Technology, 20,* 189-198.

Van Dijk, T.A., and Kintsch, W. (1983). *Strategies of discourse comprehension.* New York: Academic Press.

Van Eck, R. (2007). Building artificially intelligent learning games. In D. Gibson, C. Aldrich, and M. Prensky (Eds.), *Games and simulations in online learning research and development frameworks* (pp. 271-307). Hershey, PA: Idea Group.

van Gelderen, A., Schoonen, R., Stoel, R.D., de Glopper, K., and Hulstijn, J. (2007). Development of adolescent reading comprehension in language 1 and language 2: A longitudinal analysis of constituent components. *Journal of Educational Psychology, 99,* 477-491.

VanLehn, K. (2006). The behavior of tutoring systems. *International Journal of Artificial Intelligence in Education, 16*(3), 227-265.

VanLehn, K., Lynch, C., Taylor, L., Weinstein, A., Shelby, R.H., Schulze, K.G., Treacy, D., and Wintersgill, M. (2002). Minimally invasive tutoring of complex physics problem solving. In S.A. Cerri, G. Gouarderes, and F. Paraguacu (Eds.), *Intelligent tutoring systems, 6th international conference* (pp. 367-376). Berlin, Germany: Springer.

VanLehn, K., Graesser, A.C., Jackson, G.T., Jordan, P., Olney, A., and Rose, C.P. (2007). When are tutorial dialogues more effective than reading? *Cognitive Science, 31,* 3-62.

VanLehn, K., Graesser, A.C., Jackson, G.T., Jordan, P., Olney, A., and Rose, C.P. (in press). When are tutorial dialogues more effective than reading? *Cognitive Science.*

Van Merrienboer, J., Jeroen, J.G., Kester, L., and Pass, F. (2006). Teaching complex rather than simple tasks: Balancing intrinsic and germane load to enhance transfer of learning. *Applied Cognitive Psychology, 20,* 343-352.

Van Orden, G.C., Pennington, B.F., and Stone, G.O. (1990). Word identification in reading and the promise of subsymbolic psycholinguistics. *Psychological Review, 97,* 488-522.

Vansteenkiste, M., Simons, J., Lens, W., Sheldon, K.M., and Deci, E.L. (2004). Motivating learning, performance, and persistence: The synergistic role of intrinsic goals and autonomy-support. *Journal of Personality and Social Psychology, 87,* 246-260.

Vaughn, S., Klinger, J., and Hughes, M. (2000). Sustainability of research-based practices. *Exceptional Children, 66*(2), 163-171.

Vaughn, S., Martinez, L.R., Linan-Thompson, S., Reutebuch, C.K., Carlson, C.D., and Francis, D.J. (2009). Enhancing social studies vocabulary and comprehension for seventh-grade English language learners: Findings from two experimental studies. *Journal of Research on Educational Effectiveness, 2,* 297-324.

Vellutino, F.R., Fletcher, J.M., Snowling, M.J., and Scanlon, D.M. (2004). Specific reading disability (dyslexia): What have we learned in the past four decades? *Journal of Child Psychology and Psychiatry and Allied Disciplines, 45*(1), 2-40.

Vellutino, F.R., Scanlon, D.M., and Chen, R.S. (1994). The increasingly inextricable relationship between orthographic and phonological coding in learning to read: Some reservations about current methods of operationalizing orthographic coding. In V.W. Berninger (Ed.), *The varieties of orthographic knowledge, I1:Theoretical and developmental issues* (pp. 47-112). Dordrecht, the Netherlands: Kluwer Academic Press.

Verhaeghen, P. (2003). Aging and vocabulary scores: A meta-analysis. *Psychology and Aging, 18,* 232-239.

Verhaeghen, P., and Salthouse, T.A. (1997). Meta-analysis of age-cognition relations in adulthood: Estimates of linear and non-linear effects and structural models. *Psychological Bulletin, 122,* 231-249.

Verhoeven, L., and Van Leeuwe, J. (2008). Prediction of the development of reading comprehension: A longitudinal study. *Applied Cognitive Psychology [Special Issue: Advances in Text Comprehension: Model, Process and Development], 22*(3), 407-423.

Vermeer, A. (2001). Breadth and depth of vocabulary in relation to l1/l2 acquisition and frequency of input. *Applied Psycholinguistics, 22*(2), 217-234.

Vernon, D.T., and Blake, R.L. (1993). Does problem based learning work? A meta analysis of evaluation research. *Academic Medicine, 68,* 550-563.

Vitale, M.R., and Romance, N.R. (2007). A knowledge-based framework for unifying content-area reading comprehension strategies. In D. McNamara (Ed.), *Reading comprehension strategies: Theories, interventions, and technologies* (pp. 73-104). Mahwah, NJ: Lawrence Erlbaum Associates.

Vitale, M.R., Romance, N.R., and Dolan, F. (2006). A knowledge-based framework for the classroom assessment of student science understanding. In M. McMahon, P. Simmons, R. Sommers, D. DeBaets, and F. Crawley (Eds.), *Assessment in science: Practical experiences and education research* (pp. 1-14). Arlington, VA: NSTA Press.

Vohs, K.D., Baumeister, R.F., Schmeichel, B.J., Twenge, J.M., Nelson, N.M., and Tice, D.M. (2008). Making choices impairs subsequent self-control: A limited-resource account of decision making, self-regulation, and active initiative. *Journal of Personality and Social Psychology, 94,* 883-898.

Vorderer, P., and Bryant, J. (Eds.). (2006). *Playing video games: Motives, responses, and consequences.* Mahwah, NJ: Lawrence Erlbaum Associates.

Vosniadou, S., and Brewer, W.F. (1992). Mental models of the earth: A study of conceptual change in childhood. *Cognitive Psychology, 24,* 535-585.

Voss, J., Vesonder, G., and Spilich, G. (1980). Text generation and recall by high-knowledge and low-knowledge individuals. *Journal of Verbal Learning and Verbal Behavior, 19,* 651-667

Vouloumanos, A. (2008). Fine-grained sensitivity to statistical information in adult word learning. *Cognition, 107*(2), 729-742.

Vrugt, A., Oort, F., and Zeeberg, C. (2002). Goal orientations, perceived self-efficacy and study results among beginner and advanced students. *British Journal of Educational Psychology, 72,* 385-397.

Vygotsky, L.S. *Mind in society.* (1978). Cambridge, MA: Harvard University Press.

Vygotsky, L.S. (1986). *Thought and language.* Trans. Alex Kozulin. Cambridge, MA: MIT Press.

Vygotsky, L.S. (1993). *The collected works of L.S. Vygotsky, volume 2: The fundamentals of defectology (abnormal psychology and learning disabilities).* Trans. by J.E. Know and C.B. Stevens, R.W. Rieber, and A.S. Carton (Eds.). New York: Plenum Press.

Vygotsky, L.S. (1998). *The collected works of L.S. Vygotsky, volume 5: Child psychology.* Trans. by J.E. Know and C.B. Stevens and R.W. Rieber (Eds.). New York: Plenum Press.

Wade, S.E. (1992). How interest affects learning from text. In K.A. Renninger, S. Hidi, and A. Krapp (Eds.), *The role of interest in learning and development* (pp. 255-277). Hillsdale, NJ: Lawrence Erlbaum Associates.

Wade, S.E., Schraw, G., Buxton, W.M., and Hayes, M.T. (1993). Seduction of the strategic reader: Effects of interest on strategy and recall. *Reading Research Quarterly, 28,* 93-114.

Wade, S.E., Buxton, W.M., and Kelly, M. (1999). Using think-alouds to examine reader-text interest. *Reading Research Quarterly, 34*(2), 194-216.

Wagner, D.A., Venezky, R.L., and Street, B.V. (Eds.). (1999). *Literacy: An international handbook.* Boulder, CO: Westview Press.

Wagner, M., Newman, L., Cameto, R., Garza, N., and Levine, P. (2005). *After high school: A first look at the postschool experiences of youth with disabilities.* Menlo Park, CA: SRI International.

Wagner, M., Newman, L., Cameto, R., Levine, P., and Marder, C. (2007). *Perceptions and expectations of youth with disabilities. A special topic report from the National Longitudinal Transition Study-2 (NLTS2).* NCSER 2007-3006. Menlo Park, CA: SRI International

Wagner, R.K., Torgesen, J.K., and Rashotte, C.A. (1994). Development of reading-related phonological processing abilities: New evidence of bidirectional causality from a latent variable longitudinal study. *Developmental Psychology, 30*(1), 73-87.

Wagner, R.K., Torgesen, J.K., Rashotte, C.A., Hecht, S.A., Barker, T.A., Burgess, S.R., Donahue, J., and Garon, T. (1997). Changing relations between phonological processing abilities and word-level reading as children develop from beginning to skilled readers: A five-year longitudinal study. *Developmental Psychology, 33*(3), 468-479.

Wagner, R.K., Torgesen, J.K., and Rashotte, C.A. (1999). *Comprehensive test of phonological processing.* Austin, TX: Prod-Ed.

Wagner, R.K., Puranik, C.S., Foorman, B., Foster, E., Gehron, L., Tschinkel, E., and Kantor, P.T. (2011). Modeling the development of written language. *Reading and Writing: An Interdisciplinary Journal, 24*(2), 203-220.

Wakely, M., Hooper, S., de Kruif, R., and Swartz, C. (2006). Subtypes of written expression in elementary school children: A linguistic-based model. *Developmental Neuropsychology, 29,* 125-159.

Walberg, H., and Ethington, C. (1991). Correlates of writing performance and interest: A U.S. national assessment study. *Journal of Educational Research, 84,* 198-203.

Wallace, D., Hayes, J., Hatch, J., Miller, W., Moser, G., and Silk, C. (1996). Better revision in eight minutes? Prompting first-year college writers to revise globally. *Journal of Educational Psychology, 88,* 682-688.

Wallace, G.W., and Bott, D.A. (1989). Statement-pie: A strategy to improve the paragraph-writing skills of adolescents with learning disabilities. *Journal of Learning Disabilities, 22,* 541-553.

Wang, D. (2009) Factors affecting the comprehension of global and local main idea. *Journal of College Reading and Learning, 39,* 34-52.

Ward, J., and Edwards, J. (2002). *Learning journeys: Learners' voices. Learners' views on progress and achievement in literacy and numeracy.* London, England: Learning and Skills Development Agency.

Ward, J.V. (1990). Racial identify formation and transformation. In C. Gilligan, N.D. Lyons, and T.J. Hammer (Eds.), *Making connections: The relational worlds and adolescent girls at Emma Willard School* (pp. 215-238). Cambridge, MA: Harvard University Press.

Warren, B., Rosebery, A., and Conant, F. (1989). *Cheche Konnen: Science and literacy in language minority classrooms.* Report No. 7305. Cambridge, MA: Bolt, Beranek, and Newman.

Warren, B., Rosebery, A., and Conant, F. (1994). Discourse and social practice: Learning science in a language minority classroom. In D. Spener (Ed.), *Adult biliteracy in the United States* (pp. 191-210). Washington, DC: Center for Applied Linguistics.

Warren, B., Ballenger, C., Ogonowski, M., Rosebery, A., and Hudicourt-Barnes, J. (2001). Rethinking diversity in learning science: The logic of everyday languages. *Journal of Research in Science Teaching, 38,* 1-24.

Warren-Peace, P., Parrish, E., Peace, C.B., and Xu, J. (2008). Senior surfing: Computer use, aging, and formal training. *AACE Journal, 16*(3), 253-274.

Warrington, E.T., and Shallice, T. (1980). Word from dyslexia. *Brain, 103,* 99-112.

Waszak, F., Li, S.-C., and Hommel, B. (2010). The development of attentional networks: Cross-sectional findings from a a life span sample. *Developmental Psychology, 46,* 337-349.

Watanabe,Y., and Swain, M. (2007). Effects of proficiency differences and patterns of pair interaction on second language learning: Collaborative dialogue between adult ESL learners. *Language Teaching Research, 11*(2), 121-142.

Waterhouse, L. (2006a). Inadequate evidence for muliple intelligences, the Mozart effect, and emotional intelligence theories. *Educational Psychologist, 41,* 247-255.

Waterhouse, L. (2006b). Muliple intelligences, the Mozart effect, and emotional intelligence: A critical review. *Educational Psychologist, 41*, 207-225.

Waterhouse, P.J., and Deakin, R. (1995). Changing approaches to workplace literacy. *Journal of Reading, 38*(6), 498-500.

Weaver, C. (1990). *Understanding whole language.* Portsmouth, NH: Heinemann.

Webb, S. (2006). Can ICT reduce social exclusion? The case of an adult's English language. *British Educational Research Journal, 32*(3), 481-507.

Weibel, M.C. (1994). Literature, whole language, and adult literacy instruction. *Adult Learning, 6*(2), 9-12.

Weinbaum, A., and Rogers, A.M. (1995). *Contextual learning: A critical aspect of school-to-work transition programs* (ED381666). Washington, DC: Office of Educational Research and Improvement.

Weiner, B. (1985). An attribution theory of achievement motivation and emotion. *Psychological Review, 92*, 548-573.

Weiner, B. (1986). *An attributional theory of motivation and emotion.* New York: Springer-Verlag.

Weiner, B. (1992). *Human motivation: Metaphors, theories, and research.* Newbury Park, CA: Sage.

Weiner, B. (2005). Motivation from an attribution perspective and the social psychology of perceived competence. In A.J. Elliot and C.S. Dweck (Eds.), *Handbook of competence and motivation* (pp. 73-84). New York: Guilford Press.

Weiss G., and Hechtman, L. (1993). *Hyperactive children grown up* (2nd ed.). New York: Guilford Press.

Weiss, M.J., Visher, M.G., and Wathington, H. (with Teres, J., and Schneider, E.). (2010). *Learning communities for students in developmental reading: An impact study at Hillsborough Community College.* New York: Columbia University, Teachers College, National Center for Postsecondary Research.

Welch, D.C., and West, R.L. (1995). Self-efficacy and mastery: Its application to issues of environmental control, cognition, and aging. *Developmental Review, 15*, 150-171.

Wells, G. (1999). *Dialogic inquiry: Toward a sociocultural practice and theory of education.* New York: Cambrige University Press.

Wenger, E. (1998). *Communities of practice: Learning meaning, and identity.* New York: Cambridge University Press.

Werner, E.E. (1984). Resilient children. *Young Children, 40*, 68-72.

Wertsch J.V. (1991). *Voices of the mind: A sociocultural approach to mediated action.* Cambridge, MA: Harvard University Press.

Wertsch, J.V., Del Rio, P., and Alvarez, A. (2005). Sociocultural studies: History, action, and mediation. In J.V. Wertsch, P. Del Rio, and A. Alvarez (Eds.), *Sociocultural studies of mind* (pp. 187-214). New York: Cambridge University Press.

West, R.L., and Craik, F.I.M. (1999). Age-related decline in prospective memory: The role of cue accessibility and cue sensitivity. *Psychology and Aging, 14*, 264-272.

West, R.L., Thorn, R.M., and Bagwell, D.K. (2003). Memory performance and beliefs as a function of goal setting and aging. *Psychology and Aging, 18*, 111-125.

West, R.L., Bagwell, D.K., and Dark-Freudeman, A. (2005). Memory and goal setting: The response of older and younger adults to positive and objective feedback. *Psychology and Aging, 20*, 195-201.

Wexler, J., Vaughn, S., Roberts, G., and Denton, C.A. (2010). The efficacy of repeated reading and wide reading practice for high school students with severe reading disabilities. *Learning Disabilities Research and Practice, 25*(1), 2-10.

Wheeler, M.A., and Roediger, H.L. III. (1992).Disparate effects of repeated testing: Reconciling Ballard's (1913) and Bartlett's (1932) results. *Psychological Science, 3*, 240-245.

White, B., and Frederiksen, J. (1998). Inquiry, modeling, and metacognition: Making science accessible to all students. *Cognition and Instruction, 16*, 3-117.

White, B., and Frederiksen, J. (2005). A theoretical framework and approach for fostering metacognitive development. *Educational Psychologist, 40*, 211-233.

White, S., and Dillow, S. (2005). *Key concepts and features of the 2003 National Assessment of Adult Literacy.* Available: http://nces.ed.gov/pubsearch/pubsinfo.asp?pubid=2006471 [Oct. 2011].

Wigfield, A., and Eccles, J. (1992). The development of achievement task values: A theoretical analysis. *Developmental Review, 12*, 265-310.

Wigfield, A., and Eccles, J.S. (2000). Expectancy: Value theory of motivation. *Contemporary Educational Psychology, 25*, 68-81.

Wigfield, A., and Eccles, J.S. (2002). The development of competence beliefs and values from childhood through adolescence. In A. Wigfield and J.S. Eccles (Eds.), *Development of achievement motivation* (pp. 92–120). San Diego, CA: Academic Press.

Wigfield, A., and Guthrie, J.T. (1997). Relations of children's motivation for reading to the amount and breadth of their reading. *Journal of Educational Psychology, 89*, 420-432.

Wigfield, A., and Karpathian, M. (1991). Who am I and what can I do? Children's self concepts and motivation in achievement situations. *Educational Psychologist, 26*, 233-261.

Wigfield, A., Eccles, J.S., and Rodriguez, D. (1998). The development of children's motivation in school contexts. *Review of Research in Education, 23*, 73-118.

Wigfield, A., Guthrie, J.T., Perencevich, K.C., Taboada, A., Klauda, S.L., McRae, A., and Barbosa, P. (2008). The role of reading engagement in mediating effects of reading comprehension instruction on reading outcomes. *Psychology in the Schools, 45*(5), 432-445.

Wiggins, R. (1968). *A study of the influence of oral instruction on students' ability in written sentence structure.* Unpublished doctoral dissertation, University of South Carolina.

Wiley, J., Goldman, S.R., Graesser, A.C., Sanchez, C.A., Ash, I.K., and Hemmerich, J.A. (2009). Source evaluation, comprehension, and learning in Internet science inquiry tasks. *American Educational Research Journal, 46*, 1,060-1,106.

Wilkinson, I.A.G., and Fung, I.Y.Y. (2002). Small-group composition and peer effects. *International Journal of Educational Research, 37*, 425-447.

Willans, J., and Seary, K. (2007). "I'm not stupid after all"—Changing perceptions of self as a tool for transformation. *Australian Journal of Adult Learning, 47*(3), 433-452.

Williams, G.C., and Deci, E.L. (1996). Internalization of biopsychosocial values by medical students: A test of self-determination theory. *Journal of Personality and Social Psychology, 70*, 767-779.

Williams, G.C., Saizow, R., Ross, L., and Deci, E.L. (1997). Motivation underlying career choice for internal medicine and surgery. *Social Science and Medicine, 45*, 1,705-1,713.

Williams, J.N. (2005). Learning without awareness. *Studies in Second Language Acquisition, 27*(2), 269-304.

Williams, J.P. (2006). Stories, studies, and suggestions about reading. *Scientific Studies of Reading, 10*, 121-142.

Williams, J.P., Hall, K.M., and Lauer, K.D. (2004). Teaching expository text structure to young at-risk learners: Building the basics of comprehension instruction. *Exceptionality, 12*, 129-144.

Williams, J.P., Hall, K.M., Lauer, K.D., Stafford, K.B., De Sisto, L.A., and deCani, J.S. (2005). Expository text comprehension in the primary grade classroom. *Journal of Educational Psychology, 97*, 538-550.

Williams, J.P., Nubla-Kung, A.M., Pollini, S., Stafford, K.B., Garcia, A., and Snyder, A.E. (2007). Teaching cause-effect structure through social studies content to at-risk second graders. *Journal of Learning Disabilities, 40*, 111-120.

Williams, J.P., Stafford, K.B., Lauer, K.D., Hall, K.M., and Pollini, S. (2009). Embedding reading comprehension training in content-area instruction. *Journal of Educational Psychology, 101*, 1-20.

Willingham, D. (1998). A neuropsychological theory of motor skill learning. *Psychological Review, 105*, 558-584.

Willis, P. (1977). *Learning to labour: How working class kids get working class jobs.* Surrey, England: Gower.

Wineburg, S.S. (1991). Historical problem solving: A study of the cognitive process used in the evaluation of documentary and pictorial evidence. *Journal of Educational Psychology, 83* (1), 73-87.

Wineburg, S.S. (1998). Reading Abraham Lincoln: An expert-expert study in the interpretation of historical texts. *Cognitive Science, 22*, 319-346.

Wingfield, A., and Grossman, M. (2006). Language and the aging brain: Patterns of neural compensation revealed by functional brain imaging. *Journal of Neurophysiology, 96*(6), 2,830-2,839.

Wingfield, A., Poon, L.W., Lombardi, L., and Lowe, D. (1985). Speed of processing in normal aging: Effects of speech rate, linguistic structure and processing time. *Journals of Gerontology, 40*(5), 579-585.

Wingfield, A., Tun, P.A., and McCoy, S.L. (2005). Hearing loss in older adults: What it is and how it interacts with cognitive performance. *Current Directions in Psychological Science, 14*, 144-148.

Winn, B.D., Skinner, C.H., Oliver, R., Hale, A.D., and Ziegler, M. (2006). The effects of listening while reading and repeated reading on the reading fluency of adult learners. *Journal of Adolescent and Adult Literacy, 50*(3), 196-205.

Winne, P.H. (2001). Self-regulated learning viewed from models of information processing. In B. Zimmerman and D. Schunk (Eds.), *Self-regulated learning and academic achievement: Theoretical perspectives* (pp. 153-189). Mahwah, NJ: Lawrence Erlbaum Associates.

Wise, B.W., and VanVuuren, S. (2007) Choosing software gems to improve children's reading. *Perspectives, 33*(3), 34-42.

Wise, B.W., Ring, J., and Olson, R.K. (2000). Individual differences in gains from computer-assisted remedial reading with more emphasis on phonological analysis or accurate reading in context. *Journal of Experimental Child Psychology, 77*, 197-235.

Wisely, W.C. (2009). *Effectiveness of contextual approaches to developmental math in California community colleges.* Unpublished doctoral dissertation, University of the Pacific, Stockton, CA.

Wittrock, M. (1990). Generative processes of comprehension. *Educational Psychologist, 24*, 345-376.

Wolf, M. (2007). *Proust and the squid: The story and science of the reading brain.* New York: Harper.

Wolf, M., and Bowers, P.G. (1999). The double-deficit hypothesis for the developmental dyslexias. *Journal of Educational Psychology, 91*(3), 415-438.

Wolf, M., and Katzir-Cohen, T. (2001). Reading fluency and its intervention. *Scientific Studies of Reading, 5*(3), 211-239.

Wolf, M., Miller, L., and Donnelly, K. (2000). Retrieval, automaticity, vocabulary elaboration, orthography (RAVE-O): A comprehensive, fluency-based reading intervention program. *Journal of Learning Disabilities, 33*(4), 375-386.

Wolfe, M.B.W., Schreiner, M.E., Rehder, B., Laham, D., Foltz, P., Kintsch, W., and Landauer, T. (1998). Learning from text: Matching readers and texts by latent semantic analysis. *Discourse Processes, 25*, 309-336.

Wolters, C. (2004). Advancing goal theory: Using goal structures and goal orientations to predict students' motivation, cognition, and achievement. *Journal of Educational Psychology, 96,* 236-250.

Wong, B., Wong, R., and Blenkinsop, J. (1989). Cognitive and metacognitive aspects of learning disabled adolescents' composing problems. *Learning Disability Quarterly, 12,* 300-322.

Wong, B.Y.L. (1991). Assessment of metacognitive research in learning disabilities: Theory, research, and practice. In H.L. Swanson (Ed.), *Handbook on the assessment of learning disabilities* (pp. 265-284). Austin, TX: Pro-Ed.

Wong, B.Y.L. (1994). Instructional parameters promoting transfer of learned strategies in students with learning disabilities. *Learning Disability Quarterly, 17,* 110-119.

Wong, B.Y.L., Harris, K.R., Graham, S., and Butler, D.L. (2003). Cognitive strategies instruction research in learning disabilities. In H.L. Swanson, K.R. Harris, and S. Graham (Eds.), *Handbook of learning disabilities* (pp. 383-402). New York: Guilford Press.

Wong-Fillmore, L. (1991). When learning a second language means losing the first. *Early Childhood Research Quarterly, 6,* 323-346.

Woodcock, D. McGrew, K. and Mather, N. (2001). *Woodcock-Johnson III (cognitive and achievement batteries).* Itasca, IL: Riverside.

Woodin, T. (2008). "A beginner reader is not a beginner thinker": Student publishing in Britain since the 1970s. *Paedagogica Historica, 44*(1/2), 219-232.

Woolf, B.P. (2009). *Building intelligent interactive tutors.* Burlington, MA: Morgan Kaufmann.

Wortham, S. (2004). From good student to outcast: The emergence of a classroom identity. *Ethos, 32*(2), 164-187.

Worthy, J., and Viise, N.M. (1996). Morphological, phonological, and orthographic differences between the spelling of normally achieving children and basic literacy adults. *Reading and Writing, 8,* 139-154.

Wright, D.C., and Klumpp, A. (2004). Collaborative inhibition is due to the product, not the process, of recalling in groups. *Psychonomic Bulletin and Review, 11,* 1,080-1,083.

Wrigley, H.S. (2007). Beyond the life boat: Improving language, citizenship, and training services for immigrants and refugees. In A. Belzer (Ed.), *Toward defining and improving quality in adult basic education: Issues and challenges* (pp. 221-239). Mahwah, NJ: Lawrence Erlbaum Associates.

Wrigley, H.S. (2009). *Literacy education for adult English language learners: A perspective on the state of research and practice.* Paper commissioned by the Committee on Learning Sciences: Foundations and Applications to Adolescent and Adult Literacy, Division of Behavioral, Social Sciences, and Education, National Research Council, Washington, DC.

Wrigley, H.S., Chen, J., White, S., and Soroui, J. (2009). Assessing the literacy skills of adult immigrants and adult English language learners. *New Directions for Adult and Continuing Education, 121,* 5-24.

Wrosch, C., Heckhausen, J., and Lachman, M.E. (2000). Primary and secondary control strategies for managing healtlh and financial stress across adulthood. *Psychology and Aging, 15,* 387-399.

Wylie, R.C. (1979). *The self-concept: Theory and research on selected topics* (revised ed.). Lincoln: University of Nebraska Press.

Xue, G., Dong, Q., Jin, Z., Zhang, L., and Wang, Y. (2004). An fMRI study with semantic access in low proficiency second language learners. *NeuroReport, 15,* 791-796.

Yancey, K.B. (2009). *Writing in the 21st century.* Urbana, IL: National Council of Teachers of English. Available: http://www.ncte.org/press/21stcentwriting [Oct. 2011].

Yano, Y., Long, M.H., and Ross, S. (1994). The effects of simplified and elaborated texts on foreign language reading comprehension. *Language Learning, 44*(2), 189-219.

Yeh, K-C., Gregory, J.P., and Ritter, F.E. (2010). One laptop per child: Polishing up the XO laptop user experience. *Ergonomics in Design: The Quarterly of Human Factors Applications, 18*(3), 8-13.

Yoon, B. (2008). Uninvited guests: The influence of teachers' roles and pedagogies on the positioning of English language learners in the regular classroom. *American Educational Research Journal, 45,* 495-522.

Young, A.R., and Bowers, P.G. (1995). Individual difference and text difficulty determinants of reading fluency and expressiveness. *Journal of Experimental Child Psychology, 60*(3), 428-454.

Young, G., and Browning, J. (2005). Learning disabilities/dyslexia and employment: A mythical view. In G. Reid and A. Fawcett (Eds.), *Dyslexia in context: Research, policy and practice* (pp. 25-59). London, England: Whurr.

Yule, V. (1996). Take-home video for adult literacy. *International Review of Education, 42*(1), 187-203.

Zachry, E.M., and Schneider, E. (2009). *Promising instructional reforms in developmental education. A case study of three Achieving the Dream colleges.* New York: MDRC. Available: http://www.mdrc.org/publications/504/full.pdf [Oct. 2011].

Zareva, A., Schwanenflugel, P., and Nikolova, Y. (2005). Relationship between lexical competence and language proficiency. *Studies in Second Language Acquisition, 27*(4), 567-595.

Zeidenberg, M., Jenkins, D., and Calcagno, J.C. (2007). *Do student success courses actually help community college students succeed?* CCRC Brief, No. 36. New York: Community College Research Center, Teachers College, Columbia University.

Zelinski, E., and Gilewski, M. (1988). Assessment of memory complaints by rating scales and questionnaires. *Psychopharmacology Bulletin, 24*(4), 523.

Zellermayer, M., Salomon, G., Globerson, T., and Givon, H. (1991). Enhancing writing-related metacognitions through a computerized writing partner. *American Educational Research Journal, 28,* 373-391.

Zhang, S., and Duke, N.K. (2008). Strategies for Internet reading with different reading purposes: A descriptive study of 12 good Internet readers. *Journal of Literacy Research, 40*(1), 128-162.

Ziegler, J.C., and Goswami, U. (2006). Becoming literate in different languages: similar problems, different solutions. *Developmental Science, 9,* 429-453.

Ziegler, M., Ebert, O., and Cope, O. (2004). Using cash incentives to encourage progress of welfare recipients in adult basic education. *Adult Basic Education, 14,* 18-31.

Zimmerman, B.J. (1989). A social cognitive view of self-regulated academic learning. *Journal of Educational Psychology, 81*(3), 329-339.

Zimmerman, B.J. (1990). Self-regulating academic learning and achievement: The emergence of a social cognitive perspective. *Educational Psychology Review, 2,* 173-201.

Zimmerman, B.J. (1994). Dimensions of academic self-regulation: A conceptual framework for education. In D.H. Schunk and B.J. Zimmerman (Eds.), *Self-regulation of learning and performance: Issues and educational applications* (pp. 3-21). Hillsdale, NJ: Lawrence Erlbaum Associates.

Zimmerman, B.J. (2000a). Attaining self-regulation: A social cognitive perspective. In M. Boekaerts, P.R. Pintrick, and M. Zeidner (Eds.), *Handbook of self-regulation* (pp. 13-39). San Diego, CA: Academic Press.

Zimmerman, B.J. (2000b). Self-efficacy: An essential motive to learn. *Contemporary Educational Psychology, 25*(1), 82-91.

Zimmerman, B.J. (2001). Theories of self-regulated learning and academic achievement: An overview and analysis. In B.J. Zimmerman and D. Schunk (Eds.), *Self-regulated learning and academic achievement: Theoretical perspectives* (pp. 1-37). Mahwah, NJ: Lawrence Erlbaum Associates.

Zimmerman, B.J., and Bandura, A. (1994). Impact of self-regulatory influences on writing course attainment. *American Educational Research Journal, 31*, 845-862.

Zimmerman, B.J., and Reisemberg, R. (1997). Becoming a self-regulated writer: A social cognitive perspective. *Contemporary Educational Psychology, 22*, 73-101.

Zuckerman, M., Porac, J., Lathin, D., Smith, R., and Deci, E.L. (1978). On the importance of self-determination for intrinsically motivated behaviour. *Personality and Social Psychology Bulletin, 4*, 443-446.

Zukin, C., Keeter, S., Andolina, M., Jenkins, K., and Delli Carpini, M.X. (2006). *A new engagement? Political participation, civic life, and the changing American citizen.* New York: Oxford University Press.

Zwaan, R.A. (1994). Effect of genre expectations on text comprehension. *Journal of Experimental Psychology: Learning, Memory, Cognition, 20*, 920-933.

Zwaan, R.A. (2003). The immersed experiencer: Toward an embodied theory of language comprehension. In H.R. Brian (Ed.), *Psychology of learning and motivation* (vol. 44, pp. 35-62). Available: http://www.sciencedirect.com/science/bookseries/00797421/44 [Oct. 2011].

Zwaan, R.A., and Radvansky, G.A. (1998). Situation models in language comprehension and memory. *Psychological Bulletin, 123*, 162-185.

Zwaan, R.A., and Singer, M. (2003). Text comprehension. In A.C. Graesser and M.A. Gernsbacher (Eds.), *Handbook of discourse processes* (pp. 83-121). Mahwah, NJ: Lawrence Erlbaum Associates.

Zwaan, R.A., Magliano, J.P., and Graesser, A.C. (1995). Dimensions of situation model construction in narrative comprehension. *Journal of Experimental Psychology: Learning, Memory, and Cognition, 21*, 386-397.

Appendix A

Biographical Sketches of Committee Members and Staff

Alan M. Lesgold (*Chair*) is dean of the School of Education at the University of Pittsburgh. Prior to this position, he served as the executive associate director of the Learning Research and Development Center at the University of Pittsburgh from 1997 to 2000. Other previous positions at the University of Pittsburgh include professor of psychology and intelligent systems, codirector of the Graduate Program in Intelligent Systems Studies and the Faculty of Arts and Sciences, and Director of the Learning Skills Research Unit at the Research and Development Center. He is a fellow of the American Psychological Association (APA) Divisions of Experimental Psychology, Applied Experimental and Engineering Psychology, and Educational Psychology. He was secretary/treasurer of the Cognitive Science Society from 1988 to 1997 and continues to serve on its board of governors. In 1995, he was awarded the Educom Medal by Educom and the APA for contributions to educational technology. With colleagues, he developed a technology of intelligently coached learning-by-doing over the period from 1986 to 1999. More recently, he and colleagues developed a technology for supporting rich collaborative engagement of students and professionals with complex issues and complex bodies of knowledge, including professional development for teachers. He is a national associate of the National Research Council of the National Academies and was a member of the Board on Testing and Assessment from 1993 through 1998. He has a Ph.D. in psychology from Stanford University (1971).

Karen S. Cook is the Ray Lyman Wilbur professor of sociology, director of the Institute for Social Science Research (IRiSS), and vice provost for faculty development and diversity at Stanford University. Her current research focuses on social exchange theory and issues of trust in social relations and networks. She has studied power-dependence relations and physician-patient trust, including how interactions between physicians and patients with different racial, ethnic, and cultural backgrounds affect health outcomes. She is the coeditor of the Russell Sage Foundation Trust Series and has published on trust in the series (*Cooperation Without Trust?*, *eTrust: Forming Relationships in the Online World*, and *Whom Do You Trust?*). She is the coeditor of the *Annual Review of Sociology*, and in 2004, she received the American Sociological Association's Cooley-Mead Award for Career Contributions to Social Psychology. She was a fellow at the Center for Advanced Study in the Behavioral Sciences (1998-1999) and was elected to the American Academy of Arts and Sciences in 1996 and the National Academy of Sciences in 2007. She has a Ph.D. in sociology from Stanford University.

Aydin Yücesan Durgunoğlu is professor of psychology at the University of Minnesota, Duluth. She conducts research on the literacy development of adults and children in both monolingual and multilingual contexts, including among Spanish- and Hmong-speaking adults. Her work has focused on cross-linguistic transfer and the cognitive underpinnings of spoken and written language development. She has coedited two books on literacy development in multilingual contexts. She was one of the developers of the Mother Child Education Foundation's adult literacy program in Turkey. This program has been implemented in 18 provinces and has reached over 100,000 people in the last 15 years. She and her colleagues have been continuously evaluating and revising the program and are currently developing its web-based version. The program won a UNESCO King Sejong Literacy Prize in 2006. She serves as an associate editor of *Applied Psycholinguistics*. She has a Ph.D. in cognitive psychology from Purdue University.

Arthur C. Graesser is professor of experimental and cognitive psychology, adjunct professor in computer science, and codirector of the Institute of Intelligent Systems at the University of Memphis. His primary research interests are in cognitive science, discourse processing, and the learning sciences. More specific interests include knowledge representation, question asking and answering, tutoring, text comprehension, inference generation, conversation, reading, education, memory, emotions, computational linguistics, artificial intelligence, and human-computer interaction. He served as editor of the journal *Discourse Processes* (1996-2005) and is the current editor of *Journal of Educational Psychology* (2009-2014). In addition to publishing many articles in journals, books, and conference proceedings, he has written two books and edited nine books (including *Handbook of Dis-*

course Processes and *Handbook of Metacognition in Education*). He and his colleagues have designed, developed, and tested software in learning, language, and discourse technologies, including AutoTutor, Auto-Tutor-Lite, MetaTutor, GuruTutor, HURA Advisor, SEEK Web Tutor, Operation ARIES!, Coh-Metrix, Question Understanding Aid (QUAID), QUEST, and Point & Query. He has a Ph.D. in psychology from the University of California, San Diego.

Steve Graham is the Currey-Ingram professor of special education and literacy at Vanderbilt Peabody College. His research interests include learning disabilities, writing instruction and writing development, and the development of self-regulation. He is the past editor of *Exceptional Children* and *Contemporary Educational Psychology*. He is the coauthor of the *Handbook of Writing Research*, *Handbook of Learning Disabilities*, *Writing Better*, and *Making the Writing Process Work*. He is also the lead author of an Institute of Education Sciences's practice guide (under development) on effective writing for students in the elementary grades. In 2001, he was elected a fellow of the International Academy for Research in Learning Disabilities. He is the recipient of career research awards from the Council for Exceptional Children and Special Education Research Interest Group in the American Educational Research Association. He has an an Ed.D. in special education from the University of Kansas.

Noel Gregg is distinguished research professor at the University of Georgia. She is a faculty member in the Department of Psychology and the Department of Communication Sciences and Special Education, as well as the director of the Regents' Center for Learning Disorders. Her areas of specialization include adolescents and adults with learning disabilities and attention deficit/hyperactivity disorder (AD/HD), accommodations, alternative media, assessment, written language disorders, and test validity. She has been a national expert witness for several key legal cases pertaining to accommodating adults with learning disabilities and AD/HD on high-stakes tests. She has published four books, including *Assessing and Accommodating the Adolescent and Adult Populations with Learning Disabilities and AD/HD*, as well as numerous scientific articles and book chapters. She has a Ph.D. in communication disorders from Northwestern University.

Joyce L. Harris is associate professor in the Communication Sciences and Disorders Department at the University of Texas at Austin and director of the Language and Cognitive Aging Laboratory. Her current research involves the study of text comprehension in aging, particularly the comprehension of text-based health information. Harris teaches courses in acquired neurogenic language disorders in adults and the sociocultural bases of communication. She is coeditor of, and chapter contributor to, *Literacy in African American Communities*. Other print scholarship focuses on normal and disordered communicative process across the human life span. Harris has served as an associate editor for language for the *Journal of Speech, Language, and Hearing Research*, chair of the National Black Association for Speech-Language and Hearing's board of directors, and as a member of the publication board of the American Speech-Language-Hearing Association, of which she is a fellow and life member. Harris holds a Certificate of Clinical Competence in Speech-Language Pathology (CC-SLP) from the American Speech-Language-Hearing Association, and a Ph.D. from the University of Texas at Austin.

Glynda A. Hull is professor of education in language, literacy, and culture at the University of California, Berkeley. She has also been professor of English education in the Department of Teaching and Learning of the Steinhardt School of Culture, Education, and Human Development at New York University. Her expertise is in adult cognition, learning, education, and adult identity formation. Her work focuses on workplace literacy, adult writing in and out of schools, use of multimedia technologies with at-risk students, and understanding the roles that literacy and new information technologies play in the workplace, particularly for low-income and at-risk populations. She has expertise in the use of qualitative and ethnographic methods. Her books include *School's Out! Bridging Out-of-School Literacies with Classroom Practice* and *Changing Work, Changing Workers: Critical Perspectives on Language, Literacy, and Skills*. She has a Ph.D. from the University of Pittsburgh.

Maureen W. Lovett is professor of paediatrics and medical sciences at the University of Toronto, and a senior scientist in the Neurosciences and Mental Health Program at the Hospital for Sick Children in Toronto. She is founder and director of the hospital's Learning Disabilities Research Program, a clinical research unit dedicated to developing and evaluating different forms of remediation for children and youth with developmental reading disabilities. Her research program is devoted to the study of reading disorders in children and adolescents and methods of intervention for their effective remediation. She is recognized internationally for contributions to reading disabilities research and for the development of interventions that address basic learning problems that interfere with the ability to read. She studies individual differences in response to intervention among children with language-based learning disabilities and developmental neurocognitive disorders, as well as methodological and training issues in the rehabilitation of neurocognitive disorders. She completed postdoctoral training in neuropsychology at the Hospital for Sick Children. She has a Ph.D. in psychology from McGill University.

Daryl F. Mellard is associate research professor in the School of Education and director of the Division of Adult Studies, Center for Research on Learning, at the University of Kansas. His research focuses on education and employment issues for adults and interventions to improve adult literacy in adult education and other programs, such as Job Corps. As coprincipal investigator of the National Research Center on Learning Disabilities, he directed its review of Responsiveness to Intervention and conducted studies of education, social, and employment issues for adults with disabilities. He just completed a 5-year study to develop, implement, and study the effectiveness of adult literacy interventions for low-literate adults, including the role of decoding, vocabulary, fluency and comprehension instruction and explicitness of instruction. A current development study focuses on developing literacy skills of Job Corps participants in vocational trades. He has served as a cochair to the Kansas Coalition on Adult Literacy and Learning Disabilities and on the board of directors for a local independent living center. He has a Ph.D. in education from the University of Kansas.

Elizabeth B. Moje is associate dean for research and the Arthur F. Thurnau professor of literacy, language, and culture in educational studies at the University of Michigan. She also serves as a faculty associate in the university's Institute for Social Research and a faculty affiliate in Latino/a studies. Her work focuses on adolescents and their development of literacy skills in such areas as social studies and science. She is an expert on adolescent identities related to literacy and how these develop through participating in literacy practices of homes and communities and in ethnic, popular, and school cultures. She was a member of the Carnegie Corporation of New York's Adolescent Literacy Council and research chair of the National Conference on Research on Language and Literacy. She also served as a reading expert on the Steering Committee for the Program for International Student Assessment and is a member of the William T. Grant Foundation's Scholar Award Selection Committee. Her books include *Reframing Sociocultural Research on Literacy: Identity, Agency, and Power*; *Constructions of Literacy: Studies of Literacy Teaching and Learning In and Out of Secondary Schools*; and *All The Stories We Have: Adolescents' Insights on Literacy and Learning in Secondary School*. She is coeditor of the *Handbook of Reading Research*, Volume IV. She has a Ph.D. in literacy and language from Purdue University.

Kenneth Pugh is president and director of research at Haskins Laboratories, a Yale University–affiliated interdisciplinary institute dedicated to the investigation of the biological basis of language and human communication. He also holds the appointment of professor in the Department of Psychology at the University of Connecticut, and is associate professor in the Department of Linguistics at Yale University and the director of the Yale

Reading Center. His primary research interests are in the areas of cognitive neuroscience and psycholinguistics. He was among the first scientists to use functional magnetic resonance imaging (fMRI) to reveal brain activity associated with reading and reading disabilities. His current research employs combined behavioral and neurobiological measures in the study of typical and atypical reading and language development, with a particular focus on learning and plasticity in people with reading disabilities. He has a Ph.D. in experimental psychology from the Ohio State University.

Chris Schatschneider is professor in the Department of Psychology at Florida State University. His expertise is in early reading development in children and learning disabilities. His research focuses on individual differences in the development of reading and the discovery and measurement of skills needed to acquire reading, which can be used to identify children who are at risk for reading problems. He completed a postdoctoral fellowship in statistics and research methodology at the University of Houston and is an expert in quantitative methods, statistics, and research design. His interests include multilevel modeling, growth-curve analyses, theory building and testing, intervention design in field settings, and item-response theory. He serves as an associate director at the Florida Center for Reading Research at Florida State University; and he was a member of the National Early Literacy Panel, which synthesized scientific research on the development of literacy in children. He has a Ph.D. in psychology from Case Western Reserve University.

Mark S. Seidenberg is the Hilldale professor and the Donald O. Hebb professor in the Department of Psychology at the University of Wisconsin. He is a cognitive neuroscientist who studies language and reading. His work on language acquisition focuses on the role of statistical learning and the bases of age-related changes in the capacity to learn language (the critical period phenomenon). His reading research addresses the nature of skilled reading, how children learn to read, dyslexia, and the brain bases of reading, using the tools of modern cognitive neuroscience: behavioral experiments, computational models, and neuroimaging. His current work focuses on how language background affects early school achievement, reading achievement of low-income and minority children, and the role of home-school dialect differences in the "achievement gap." He has published research articles in psychology, linguistics, neuroscience, and education and was recently honored as one of the 250 most-cited researchers in the areas of psychology and psychiatry. Seidenberg is a fellow of the American Association for the Advancement of Science, the Cognitive Science Society, and the Association for Psychological Science. He has a Ph.D. in psychology from Columbia University and was a postdoctoral fellow at the Center for the Study of Reading.

Elizabeth A.L. Stine-Morrow is professor in the Department of Educational Psychology and Beckman Institute for Advanced Science and Technology at the University of Illinois, Urbana-Champaign. She is a researcher in cognitive aging—examining how language comprehension and memory change through adulthood and how strategic and contextual factors contribute to the capacity for lifelong learning. She has served as associate editor for *Memory and Cognition* (2007-2009) and the *Journal of Gerontology: Psychological Sciences* (2009-2010) and is currently associate editor for *Psychology and Aging*. She is a fellow of the American Psychological Association and of the Gerontological Society of America. She was a postdoctoral fellow at the Center for the Study of Aging and Human Development at the Duke Medical Center, a research scientist at Brandeis University, and on the faculty for many years at the University of New Hampshire. She has a Ph.D. in general-experimental psychology from the Georgia Institute of Technology.

Melissa Welch-Ross (*Study Director*) is senior program officer in the National Research Council's Division of Behavioral and Social Sciences and Education. Previously, she served as a special expert in research and policy analysis in the Office of the Assistant Secretary for Planning and Evaluation, Division of Children and Youth Policy, of the U.S. Department of Health and Human Services. She earlier launched and directed the Early Learning and School Readiness Research Program for the National Institute of Child Health and Human Development at the National Institutes of Health. She has held faculty appointments at George Mason University and Georgia State University, where she conducted longitudinal research on early memory development and published other experiments on social cognition and memory. She has served terms as consulting editor for the journals *Child Development* (2002-2007) and *Developmental Psychology* (1999-2004) and was lead editor of the 2007 *Handbook on Communicating and Disseminating Behavioral Science*. She has a Ph.D. in developmental psychology from the University of Florida.

Appendix B

Literacy in a Digital Age

Digital and online media are rapidly evolving new tools that are changing the ways that people communicate, read, and write. Adolescents and adults are taking up these communication technologies at an unprecedented pace and on a previously unattainable scale. Adults' use of social networking, for example, increased 33 percent between 2009 and 2010 (Madden, 2010), and 72 percent of all adults were texting in 2010 (Lenhart, 2010).[1]

In today's world, expectations for literacy include use of digital and online media to communicate with a wide range of other people and to produce, find, evaluate, and synthesize knowledge in innovative and creative ways to meet the varied demands of education and work. Indeed, in the last decade, government, business, and education organizations have asserted in commissioned reports, position statements, and syntheses of research that certain skills are needed in the 21st century for full civic and economic participation in this increasingly networked, mobile, and globally interconnected world (see North Central Regional Educational Laboratory, 2003; National Council of Teachers of English, 2008, 2009; Organisation for Economic Co-operation and Development, 2010; Organisation for Economic Co-operation and Development and Statistics Canada, 2005; Partnership for 21st Century Skills, 2002, 2003, 2007, 2009).

---

[1] The committee did not evaluate the methodology of polls used to get the usage numbers reported in this appendix. Although the methodologies generally appear to be sound, there are questions about whether the subset of the population who need literacy enhancement might be underrepresented, simply due to lesser likelihood of pollsters reaching them and lesser likelihood of their responding to these kinds of surveys.

Researchers have begun to study the particular social practices, skills, strategies, and dispositions associated with full participation in this technological and media-saturated society (Jenkins et al., 2009). An assumption of this research is that literacy is connected to a range of skills used in conjunction with information and communication technologies (ICT) to select, analyze, evaluate, synthesize, and share information (Organisation for Economic Co-operation and Development, 2010); to think critically and creatively (Silva, 2008); to make and apply knowledge flexibly and adaptively (Partnership for 21st Century Skills, 2009); to develop proficiency with tools of technology (including the design and creation of a variety of texts for multiple, global audiences, and various purposes) (National Council of Teachers of English, 2008); and to communicate and collaborate effectively (e.g., North Central Regional Educational Laboratory, 2003). Many of these critical thinking and learning competencies are not new or unique, but there is a need to understand the digital and online literacy skills that are required to live in a globalized and technologically mediated society transformed by new economic, social, and political realities.

Although most research on new media and literacy has focused on adolescents in out-of-school contexts, researchers have begun to document how adults use information and communication technologies in their everyday lives and in their pursuit of continuing education (Lenhart, 2010; Madden, 2010; Mellar and Kambouri, 2004; Smith, 2010a, 2010b; Tamassia et al., 2007).

In this appendix, we report findings from 32 empirical studies conducted between 1995 and 2009 on the relation between new information and communication technologies and adults' literacy practices and beliefs involving new media.[2] The first section of this appendix draws from these studies and other widely cited studies to describe practices and proficiencies related to the use of new technologies that now contribute to what it means to be literate. The second section examines what the research says about

---

[2]Our review included peer-reviewed journals from 1995 to 2010. It excluded studies that did not focus explicitly on literacy and technology. The primary search term used was "adult"; secondary search terms were "literacy," "reading," and "writing"; tertiary search terms (combined with each secondary term) were "computer," "digital," "ICT," "information and communication technology," "information technology," "internet," "multimedia," "multimodal," "online," "technology," and "web." Databases used were ERIC, JSTOR, and Google Scholar. Four categories of journals were also searched individually: (1) general education journals (*American Education Research Journal, Harvard Educational Review, International Journal of Educational Research*), (2) literacy journals (*Written Communication, Journal of Literacy Research, Reading and Writing, Reading Research Quarterly*), (3) technology journals (*Journal of Computer Assisted Learning; Journal of Computer Mediated Communication; International Journal of Learning and Media; Learning, Media, and Technology*), and (4) adult education journals (*Adult Education Quarterly, International Journal of Lifelong Education, Adult Basic Education and Literacy Journal*).

how and why people engage in these literacy practices. The third section examines various instructional practices and learning environments that promote these proficiencies, especially for adult populations with different levels of literacy. The final section notes that empirical research on the role of new media in adult literacy development is scant, particularly for those adults who struggle with foundational reading and writing skills. The frameworks available in the field of digital media and learning to explain why adults need to develop proficiencies relating to these technologies to meet their learning goals can inform future studies. This issue and recommendations for research are discussed in Chapter 9.

ADULT LITERACY PRACTICES AND PROFICIENCIES

As digital reading—whether on computers or, increasingly, mobile devices—becomes more commonplace, a central question for literacy researchers is how these contexts affect reading patterns and comprehension processes (Alexander and Jetton, 2003). Research on the online reading practices of youth in educational settings has emerged as a focus (Coiro et al., 2009), as has research on the online reading practices of adults, particularly ones who struggle with reading and writing in print (Attar, 2005; Ercetin, 2003; Mackey, 2007; McEneaney et al., 2009; Zhang and Duke, 2008). Early research on online reading processes with proficient readers (both youth and adults) suggests that reading online is not isomorphic with reading print texts (Coiro and Dobler, 2007; Zhang and Duke, 2008). Reading both online and printed texts requires the integration of prior knowledge, the use of inferential reasoning strategies, and frequent self-regulation, but online reading also demands that readers use these skills and strategies in ways that are different and may involve more complex and adaptive combinations (Coiro and Dobler, 2007; Zhang and Duke, 2008).

Readers in online contexts must draw on prior knowledge not only of the topic and text structures but also of online structures such as hyperlinks, websites, and search engines (Coiro and Dobler, 2007; Miller et al., 2004; Zhang and Duke, 2008). While studies have primarily been conducted with proficient youth (Coiro and Dobler, 2007) or proficient adults (Zhang and Duke, 2008), the importance of prior knowledge to reading success suggests that struggling adult readers, particularly those with less prior knowledge about ICT structures, are likely to struggle with online reading, especially since traditional reading competencies are needed in more complex combinations for online comprehension (Cromley and Azevedo, 2009). In addition to drawing on more sources of prior knowledge, readers of online texts must use extended and multilayered inferential reasoning strategies. In particular, they must make more forward inferences, that is, predictions (Coiro and Dobler, 2007), as well as more flexible and adaptive self-regulation of reading processes, particularly across short time cycles, different reading purposes, and physical spaces (Coiro and Dobler, 2007; Zhang and Duke, 2008).

Interactive media, such as the Internet, place special demands on the reader for strategic search, coordination of multiple sources, and discernment of relevance and credibility. Readers in such environments make implicit and explicit decisions about the level of resources to invest in particular texts and supporting multimedia materials, and about when to shift attention among them (Duggan and Payne, 2009; Pirolli, 2007; Pirolli and Card, 1999; Reader and Payne, 2007). Thus, searching for information (e.g., perusing web pages) and consuming information (e.g., reading the text on a particular web page) are separable processes, with particular cognitive underpinnings (Hills et al., in press). Individual differences in both working memory and knowledge can impact the effectiveness with which information is obtained and integrated in such interactive environments (Sharit et al., 2009).

A number of studies examining the Internet search strategies of adults, including inexperienced adult computer users, have found that (1) prior knowledge about the topic, computers, and online text structures facilitates search capabilities (both in speed and in success) and (2) navigation of online structures plays a crucial role in finding and reading information (Attar, 2005; Cromley and Azevedo, 2009; McEneaney et al., 2009; Rouet, 2006). Prior knowledge and navigation skills mattered more than age in determining whether users were successful in their tasks (Cromley and Azevedo, 2009), suggesting that as inexperienced adults become more familiar with online structures of websites and hypertext, they can develop more proficient reading practices. This conclusion is further supported by findings from the latest Program for International Student Assessment study, which found that increased familiarity with computers and the Internet was associated with higher test scores (Organisation for Economic Co-operation and Development, 2010), although socioeconomic status might have contributed to this correlation.

One of the central difficulties facing inexperienced users, either adult or youth, in navigating online reading contexts is the ability to recover from breakdowns in meaning. Proficient Internet readers have self-regulation strategies to fix up and repair breakdowns that are part of their overall reading strategies (Bilal and Kirby, 2002; Coiro and Dobler, 2007; Zhang and Duke, 2008). But inexperienced users struggle to monitor and repair breakdowns in meaning (Attar, 2005; Bilal and Kirby, 2002), having problems similar to those that struggling readers encounter in reading print texts (Pearson et al., 1992). Furthermore, inexperienced adults encountered more difficulties in mapping what they know onto the new Internet context and struggled in navigating the spaces of the web pages (Attar, 2005). However, knowing what strategies to employ in which circumstances while planning, predicting, monitoring, and evaluating is particularly important in online reading contexts, which demand more flexible and often simultaneous deployment of strategies across even faster cycles of self-regulation (Coiro and Dobler, 2007; Zhang and Duke, 2008).

Research with adult users of information and communication technologies shows that such a central capacity for online reading is flexible deployment of appropriate strategies depending on one's purpose and stance (Clover, 2007; Cromley and Azevedo, 2009; Mackey, 2007; McEneaney et al., 2009; Zhang and Duke, 2008). This adaptive capacity is important not only in comprehending text but also in reading multimodal texts that combine images, audio, graphics, and video in complex combinations, a kind of multiliterate meaning-making capacity enabling users to do many things at once (Clover, 2007) and to make meaning across and with multiple representations. Research that looks at search strategies across different age groups suggests that there is no single ideal hypermedia search strategy (Cromley and Azevedo, 2009) but that a variety of strategies must be deployed, sometimes simultaneously, according to people's varied stances toward and purposes for reading and searching (McEneaney et al., 2009). Whether seeking to be entertained, to gain general knowledge, or to find specific information, readers monitor their reading processes, apply their prior knowledge, and evaluate online texts using a range of strategies flexibly and adaptively (Zhang and Duke, 2008). As texts increasingly point to other texts through hyperlinks and incorporate multiple and hybrid text structures and multimedia content, readers must read not only strategically but also intertextually—across modes, media, genres, and content (Mackey, 2007; Perfetti, Britt, and Georgi, 1995; Rouet, 2006).

Just as adults need to develop a sophisticated strategic repertoire to navigate online contexts, so too do they need to develop a strategic and flexible composing repertoire for writing in multimodal contexts. Research on multimodal composing processes facilitated by information and communication technologies suggests that this involves sophisticated textual work (Brass, 2008). Writers can now reappropriate symbolic materials across a range of modes—audio, video, graphics, etc.—and take advantage of intertextual possibilities in new contexts (Ranker, 2008), drawing on prior knowledge, locally meaningful texts, and popular culture in multiple combinations. This kind of multimodal braiding of meaning from different sources, now seen as a commonplace strategy by many (Mackey, 2007), allows writers to compose new meanings by layering and synthesizing across a number of available modes, with the created meaning transcending the collection of its constitutive parts (Hull and Nelson, 2005; Ranker, 2008).

With an expanding number of ways to create meaningful communications through the orchestration of these multiple modes, the explicitly performative and multivoiced nature of many digital texts, and the circulation of these texts, readers and writers are faced with increasing textual complexity (Lewis and Fabos, 2005; Mackey, 2007; National Council of Teachers of English, 2008). Writers in complex digital contexts must be strategic in how they compose, to whom, and for what purposes (Mackey, 2007; Ranker, 2008), not least because of the potential to connect to people in new ways, across national and generational borders (Chandler-Olcott and Mahar, 2003; Lam, 2006). Multimodal composing also offers rich implications for writers' identities, especially in inviting experimentation and playfulness (Boyd, 2008; Chandler-Olcott and Mahar, 2003; Lam, 2006). Research suggests that using computers to compose might facilitate adults' negotiation of this textual complexity by encouraging revision and self-monitoring (Li, 2006), although the impact of composing in digital contexts has not been sufficiently explored with adults who are less familiar with ICT or traditional print literacy practices.

ADULTS' ENGAGEMENT WITH INFORMATION AND COMMUNICATION TECHNOLOGIES

Recent surveys of U.S. households point to a more connected, more participatory, and more engaged public than ever before. More people report getting online and using new technologies to connect to one another, with 74 percent of all adults over 18 now online[3] (including 93 percent of young adults ages 18-29) (Lenhart et al., 2010a). Most of these users are taking advantage of digital connectivity by getting online via cell phones (Smith, 2010a); texting (Lenhart, 2010); watching videos online (Purcell, 2010); blogging (Lenhart et al., 2010a); reading, commenting on, or creating the news (Purcell et al., 2010); and connecting on social networking sites (Madden, 2010), although it remains unclear whether the target adolescent and adult literacy population uses the more literacy-demanding of ICT affordances. In particular, older Americans are connecting with others online in increasing numbers, and although most still prefer email to communicate, more older adults are connecting via social networking sites (the number grew from 22 to 42 percent of all online adults over age 50 in the last year) (Madden, 2010), with 46 percent of all online adults now having at least one social networking profile (Madden and Smith, 2010). Some reports indicate that this digital connectedness is beneficial (or at least not harmful) in creating core social networks to fight social isolation, with most people who connect online reporting a broader and more diverse core social support network (Hampton et al., 2009). However, many of the same social stratification issues that affect young adults offline are

---

[3]See footnote 1.

replicated online, with users from a resource-rich background also reaping more benefits from their online practices (Hargittai and Hinnant, 2008). While issues of access remain a concern, more people of all income and education levels are getting online, many of whom are using mobile devices to close the participation gap (Smith, 2010a).

A number of studies have explored why some adults engage with information and communication technologies and others remain nonusers or limited users. It appears that motivation and disposition are more important indicators than access in determining who gets online or uses computers (Attar, 2005; Selwyn, 2004; Selwyn and Gorard, 2004; Smith, 2004, 2010a, 2010b; Stanley, 2003; Vandenbroeck et al., 2008; Warren-Peace, 2008). In particular, anxiety plays an important role (Vandenbroeck et al., 2008), as some unconnected older adults report being fearful, lacking self-efficacy around computer use, or not imagining themselves as the kind of people who engage with such technologies (Stanley, 2003). A recent Pew Research Center report found that 21 percent of the American adults surveyed do not get online, with more than half of them saying that they do not feel comfortable or knowledgeable about it (Smith, 2010a). Charness and Boot (2009) also found both attitudinal and cognitive barriers to Internet use and recommend a combination of training and better design to enhance accessibility. Other adults report not being interested in going online (Smith, 2010a) or do not see its usefulness to their daily lives (Smith, 2010a; Selwyn, 2004). Selwyn and Kvasny (2006) both argue that use of information and communication technologies among adults is multifaceted and historical, tied less to issues of access and more to historic inequalities and relationships around technology use that people develop over time in their local, everyday communities.

This issue of people's perceptions of new technologies—which are of course mediated by people's social, historical, and cultural backgrounds—plays a central role in whether and how adults use them (Chu and Tsai, 2009; Gorard, Selwyn, and Williams, 2000). Although most adult education programs in the United States (80 percent) offer some use of computers for instructional activities, it is unclear how these programs are addressing participants' motivation and disposition toward using information and communication technologies, including going online (Tamassi et al., 2007). Since studies have indicated that self-efficacy and self-determination around ICT use are important to how those adults use new technologies (Chu and Tsai, 2009; Vandenbroeck et al., 2008), it seems central to know how adult basic education programs support historically underserved populations who may be disenfranchised from their use (Coryell and Chlup, 2007; Clover, 2007; Jacobson, 2008; Webb, 2006). Just as there is less research on other aspects of the adult literacy population, so also there is less clarity about their inclusion in samples from which inferences about the ubiquity of technology use are made. Better understanding of the technology access and use patterns of the target population of this report is particularly important, given research that indicates that increased ICT use improves participants' attitudes and motivation, including more positive attitudes about their own self-efficacy in reading and writing and a wider strategic repertoire (Chu and Tsai, 2009; Clough et al., 2007; Ercetin, 2003; Kambouri et al., 2006).

INSTRUCTIONAL PRACTICES AND LEARNING ENVIRONMENTS

Although the research on particular instructional practices with information and communication technologies that have implications for adults' literacy practices is not extensive (see Tamassi et al., 2007), some studies do indicate that more experience and familiarity with online reading and writing have positive implications for users' attitudes toward online literacy practices, particularly for ones that integrate technology throughout the course (Goodyear et al., 2005). For example, Attar's (2005) longitudinal study of adult education participants in the United Kingdom indicates that explicit instruction about the structure of online interfaces helped make the logic of web pages, hypertext, and search engines more transparent. This explicit and guided instruction helped participants become more familiar with language about the Internet and increased their knowledge about (and thus comfort with) online texts and interfaces. Similarly, Warren-Peace's small-scale study (2008) reported that structured guidance helped the two older adults in the study become more familiar with technologies over time and increased their enjoyment in engaging in them. Furthermore, in Ercetin's (2003) study of adult participants enrolled in a program of English as a second language, practice and experience in guided reading in new media environments helped participants find reading more enjoyable, suggesting that offering adults opportunities to engage with information and communication technologies might increase self-efficacy.

Some studies, while not specifically on the target U.S. adolescent and adult literacy learner population and often on small samples, also suggest that increased engagement and familiarity with online literacy practices have implications for literacy learning more broadly. For example, Kambouri and colleagues (2006) examined the literacy practices of 13 young adults in three UK literacy centers who played a high-quality educational game designed to engage learners who were disaffected by traditional literacy practices (but who were experienced with the video game genre). Findings indicate that users were more actively engaged in creating intertextual connections (especially incorporating their lived experiences into the formal educational context), innovating new literacy practices around the game, and developing their critical literacy practices (including taking control over their learning). Other work (Dede and Grotzner, 2009; Shaffer, 2006) has emphasized the need to access technical information (such as reading text) as it is needed in serious game environments and that mentorship is needed in order to coordinate games and academic material to achieve science learning. This underscores the challenges of integrating subject-matter content in motivating games. In a different context, a longitudinal study of adult women involved in community technologies in rural villages, Clover (2007) found that engagement with them, including resistance, increased women's critical literacy capacities, empowering them to decide how best to adapt literacy practices involving technology to their everyday purposes.

A number of studies suggest that programs that create supportive learning environments that take into account adults' prior life experiences and offer opportunities for self-directed learning seem to set the stage for successful learning experiences. Controlling one's learning environment is important for learners' self-efficacy and motivation (Chu and Tsai), which may be why many youth turn to online communication contexts outside formal educational contexts for the opportunity to shape their environments (Chandler-Olcott and Mahar, 2003; Lam, 2006; Lewis and Fabos, 2005) and why many adults seek out informal learning opportunities via mobile and online practices (Clough et al., 2007). In adult learning settings, successful programs are ones in which students are supported individually, are given enough time to work on computers (including for personal purposes), and allow collaboration between students and between teachers and students (Coryell and Chlup, 2007). Furthermore, programs that offer structure and guidance can have an impact on how relevant adult participants find information and communication technologies as well as their attitudes toward learning with them (Warren-Peace et al., 2008).

However, learning environments that include top down administration, particularly involving staff members who believe that technology is neutral and who are not adequately trained, can lead to resistance, dropping out, or other problems with participant attitudes toward learning (Clover, 2007). Furthermore, the presence of technologies alone in these programs cannot overcome the social and cultural inequities that affect adults' beliefs and attitudes toward lifelong learning and technology (Gorard, Selwyn, and Madden, 2003; Kvasny, 2006), which can also affect teachers' integration of them into adult basic education programs (Kotrlik and Redmann, 2005). After years of absence from formal learning situations or having negative earlier schooling experiences, adult students can be intimidated by overly structured, test-centered programs (Stanley, 2003). Many times these programs, full of young people, presume basic computer literacy or English proficiency, and they do not take into account how adults who have not been involved with ICT use can be intimidated and anxious about adopting these new roles in unfamiliar educational settings (Attar, 2005; Stanley, 2003). Furthermore, many of these programs have a narrow view of technology and literacy, prescribing constrained uses of computers and not taking into account the wide range of purposes people might have in using technology (Kvasny, 2006). This may account for why some studies examining computer-aided instruction do not necessarily find that achievement scores improve, particularly when computers are used in ways with which students do not identify and without teacher support (Batchedler and Koski, 2003). When considering technology-enhanced instruction, programs that allow students to work at their own pace, offer individualized instruction, have strong community ties, and support learners with myriad work and familial responsibilities have been shown to promote literacy learning through ICT use with their adult students (Clover, 2007; Coryell and Chlup, 2007; Menard-Warwick and Dabach, 2004; Silver-Pacuilla, 2006; Stanley, 2003).

FUTURE RESEARCH

Research, especially experiments, on how to develop literacy with new media is scant, but the available theoretical literature on new technologies for literacy can inform future studies. Specific priority areas for research are discussed in Chapter 9.

REFERENCES

Alexander, P.A., and Jetton, T.L. (2003). Learning from traditional and alternative texts: New conceptualizations for the information age. In A.C. Graesser, M.A. Gernsbacher, and S.R. Goldman (Eds.), *Handbook of discourse processes* (pp. 199-232). Mahwah, NJ: Lawrence Erlbaum Associates.

Attar, D. (2005). Dismay and disappointment: Perspectives of inexperienced adult learners on becoming web page readers. *International Journal of Educational Research, 43*, 495-508.

Barab, S.A., and Roth, W.-M. (2006). Curriculum-based ecosystems: Supporting knowing from an ecological perspective. *Educational Researcher, 35*(5), 3-13.

Barab, S.A., Thomas, M., Dodge, T., Cartreaux, R., and Tuzun, H. (2005). Making learning fun: Quest Atlantis, a game without guns. *Education Technology Research and Development, 53*(1), 86-107.

Barton, D., and Hamilton, M. (1998). *Local literacies: Reading and writing in one community.* London, England: Routledge.

Batchedler, J.S., and Koski, D.D. (2003). Technology in the adult education classroom: Evaluating achievement on the test of adult basic education. *MPAEA Journal of Adult Education, 32*(2), 59-70.

Bilal, D., and Kirby, J. (2002). Differences and similarities in information seeking: Children and adults as web users. *Information Processing and Management, 38*, 649-670.

Black, R.W. (2009). Online fan fiction, global identities, and imagination. *Research in the Teaching of English, 43*(4), 397-425.

Boyd, D. (2008). Why youth ♥ social network sites: The role of networked publics in teenage social life. In D. Buckingham (Ed.), *Youth, identity, and digital media.* Cambridge, MA: MIT Press.

Brass, J.J. (2008). Local knowledge and digital movie composing in an after-school literacy program. *Journal of Adolescent and Adult Literacy*, *51*(8), 464-473.

Brown, A.L., Collins, A., and Duguid, P. (1989). Situated cognition and the culture of learning. *Educational Researcher*, *18*(1), 32-42.

Chandler-Olcott, K., and Mahar, D. (2003). "Tech-savviness" meets multiliteracies: Exploring adolescent girls' technology mediated literacy practices. *Reading Research Quarterly*, *38*(3), 356-385.

Chu, R. J.-C., and Tsai, C.-C. (2009). Self-directed learning readiness, Internet self-efficacy and preferences towards constructivist Internet-based learning environments among higher-aged adults. *Journal of Computer Assisted Learning*, *25*, 489-501.

Clough, G., Jones, A.C., McAndrew, P., and Scanlon, E. (2008). Informal learning with PDAs and smartphones. *Journal of Computer Assisted Learning*, (24), 359-371.

Clover, D.E. (2007). From sea to cyberspace: Women's leadership and learning around information and communication technologies in coastal Newfoundland. *International Journal of Lifelong Education*, *26*(1), 75-88.

Coiro, J., and Dobler, E. (2007). Exploring the online reading comprehension strategies used by sixth-grade skilled readers to search for and locate information on the Internet. *Reading Research Quarterly*, *42*(2), 214-257.

Coiro, J., Knobel, M., Lankshear, C., and Leu, D.J. (2009). Central issues in new literacies and new literacies research. In J. Coiro, M. Knobel, C. Lankshear, and D.J. Leu (Eds.), *Handbook of research on new literacies* (pp. 1-22). New York: Routledge.

Cole, M. (1996). *Cultural psychology.* Cambridge, MA: Harvard University Press.

Coryell, J.E., and Chlup, D.T. (2007). Implementing E-Learning components with adult English language learners: Vital factors and lessons learned. *Computer Assisted Language Learning*, *20*(3), 263-278.

Cromley, J.C., and Azevedo, R. (2009). Locating information with extended hypermedia. *Education Technology Research and Development*, *57*, 287-313.

Duggan, G.B., and Payne, S.J. (2009). Text skimming: The process and effectiveness of foraging through text under time pressure. *Journal of Experimental Psychology: Applied, 15*, 228-242.

Ercetin, G. (2003). Exploring ESL learners' use of hypermedia reading glosses. *CALICO Journal*, *20*(2), 261-283.

Gee, J. P. (2009). Digital media and learning as an emerging field, part 1: How we got here. *International Journal of Learning and Media*, *1*(2), 13-23.

Goodyear, P., Jones, C., Asensio, M., Hodgson, V., and Steeples, C. (2005). Networked learning in higher education: Students' expectations and experiences. *Higher Education*, *50*(3), 473-508.

Gorard, S., Selwyn, N., and Williams, S. (2000). Must try harder! Problems facing technological solutions to non-participation in adult learning. *British Educational Research Journal*, *26*(4), 507-521.

Gorard, S., Selwyn, N., and Madden, L. (2003). Logged on to learning: Assessing the impact of technology on participation in lifelong learning. *International Journal of Lifelong Education*, *22*(3), 281-296.

Hampton, K.N., Sessions, L.F., Her, E.J., and Rainie, L. (2009). *How the Internet and mobile phones impact Americans' social networks.* Retrieved from Pew Internet and American Life Project: http://pewresearch.org/pubs/1398/internet-mobile-phones-impact-american-social-networks.

Hargittai, E., and Hinnant, A. (2008). Digital inequality: Differences in young adults' use of the Internet. *Communication Research*, *35*(5), 602-621.

Hills, T., Todd, P.M., and Jones, M. (2009). Optimal foraging in semantic memory. In N.A. Taatgen and H. van Rijn (Eds.), *Proceedings of the 31st annual conference of the Cognitive Science Society*. Amsterdam, the Netherlands, July 29-August 1.

Hull, G., and Nelson, M.E. (2005). Locating the semiotic power of multimodality. *Written Communication, 22*(2), 224-261.

Ito, M., Horst, H., Bittanti, M., Boyd, dD., Herr-Stephenson, B., Lange, P.G., et al. (2008). *Living and learning with new media: Summary of findings from the Digital Youth Project*. Available: http://digitalyouth.ischool.berkeley.edu/report [Nov. 2011].

Jacobson, E. (2008). Learning and collaborating in the adult literacy education wiki. *E-Learning, 5*(4), 370-383.

Jenkins, H., Clinton, K., Purushotma, R., Robison, A.J., and Weigel, M. (2009). *Confronting the challenge of participatory culture: Media education for the 21st century*. Available: http://digitallearning.macfound.org/atf/cf/%7B7E45C7E0-A3E0-4B89-AC9C-E807 E1B0AE4E%7D/JENKINS_WHITE_PAPER.PDF [Nov. 2011].

Kambouri, M., Thomas, S., and Mellar, H. (2006). Playing the literacy game: A case study in adult education. *Learning, Media and Technology, 31*(4), 395-410.

Kotrlik, J.W., and Redmann, D.H. (2005). Extent of technology integration in instruction by adult basic education teachers. *Adult Education Quarterly, 55*(3), 200-219.

Kress, G. (2003). *Literacy in the new media age*. London: Routledge.

Kvasny, L. (2005). The role of habitus in shaping discourses about the digital divide. *Journal of Computer-Mediated Communication, 10*(2). Available: http://onlinelibrary.wiley.com/doi/10.1111/j.1083-6101.2005.tb00242.x/full [Nov. 2011].

Lam, W.S.E. (2006). Re-envisioning language, literacy, and the immigrant subject in new mediascapes. *Pedagogies: An International Journal, 1*(3), 171-195.

Lankshear, C., and Knobel, M. (2003). *New literacies*. Philadelphia: Open University Press.

Lave, J., and Wenger, E. (1991). *Situated learning: Legitimate peripheral participation*. Cambridge: Cambridge University Press.

Lenhart, A. (2010). *Cell phones and American adults*. Available: http://pewinternet.org/Reports/2010/Cell-Phones-and-American-Adults.aspx [Nov. 2011].

Lenhart, A., Ling, R., Campbell, S., and Purcell, K. (2010a). *Teens and mobile phones*. Available: http://pewinternet.org/Reports/2010/Teens-and-Mobile-Phones.aspx [Nov. 2011].

Lenhart, A., Purcell, K., Smith, A., and Zickuhr, K. (2010b). *Social media and mobile Internet use among teens and young adults*. Available: http://pewinternet.org/Reports/2010/Social-Media-and-Young-Adults.aspx [Nov. 2011].

Lewis, C., and Fabos, B. (2005). Instant messaging, literacies, and social identities. *Reading Research Quarterly, 40*(4), 470-501.

Li, J. (2006). The mediation of technology in ESL writing and its implications for writing assessment. *Assessing Writing, 11*, 5-21.

Mackey, M. (2007). Slippery texts and evolving literacies. *E-Learning, 4*(3), 319-328.

Madden, M. (2010). *Older adults and social media*. Available: http://pewinternet.org/Reports/2010/Older-Adults-and-Social-Media.aspx [Nov. 2011].

Madden, M., and Smith, A. (2010). *Reputation management and social media*. Available: http://pewinternet.org/Reports/2010/Reputation-Management.aspx [Nov. 2011].

McEneaney, J.E., Li, L., Allen, K., and Guzniczak, L. (2009). Stance, navigation, and reader response in expository hypertext. *Journal of Literacy Research, 41*(1), 1-45.

Mellar, H., and Kambouri, M. (2005). Observing ICT use in adult literacy, numeracy, and language classrooms. *Literacy and Numeracy Studies, 14*(2), 61-74.

Menard-Warwick, J., and Dabach, D.B. (2004). "In a little while I could be in front": Social mobility, class, and gender in the computer practices of two Mexicano families. *Journal of Adolescent and Adult Literacy, 47*(5), 380-389.

Miller, L.M.S., Stine-Morrow, E.A.L., Kirkorian, H. L., and Conroy, M.L. (2004). Adult age differences in knowledge-driven reading. *Journal of Educational Psychology*, 96(4), 811-821.

Moje, E.B. (2009). A call for new research of new and multi-literacies. *Research in the Teaching of English*, 43(4), 348-362.

National Council of Teachers of English. (2008). *21st century curriculum and assessment framework*. Available: http://www.ncte.org/positions/statements/21stcentframework [Nov. 2011].

National Council of Teachers of English. (2009). *Writing between the lines and everywhere else*. Available: http://www.ncte.org/topics/betweenlines [Nov. 2011].

New London Group. (1996). A pedagogy of multiliteracies: Designing social futures. *Harvard Educational Review*, 66(1), 60-92.

North Central Regional Educational Laboratory. (2003). *engauge 21st century skills: Literacy in the digital age*. Available: http://www.ncrel.org/engauge [Nov. 2011].

Organisation for Economic Co-operation and Development. (2010). *Are the new millenium learners making the grade? Technology use and educational performance in PISA*. Available: http://www.oecdbookshop.org/oecd/display.asp?k=5KSCG4J39DHBandlang=en [Nov. 2011].

Organisation for Economic Co-operation and Development and Statistics Canada. (2005). *Learning a living: First results of the Adult Literacy and Life Skills Survey*. Available: http://www.statcan.gc.ca/pub/89-603-x/2005001/4071714-eng.htm [Nov. 2011].

Partnership for 21st Century Skills. (2002). *Learning for the 21st century: A report and mile guide for 21st century skills*. Available: http://www.p21.org/index.php?option=com_contentandtask=viewandid=925andItemid=185 [Nov. 2011].

Partnership for 21st Century Skills. (2003). *The road to 21st century learning: A policymaker's guide to 21st century skills*. Available: http://www.p21.org/index.php?option=com_contentandtask=viewandid=925andItemid=185 [Nov. 2011].

Partnership for 21st Century Skills. (2006). *Results that matter: 21st century skills and high school reform*. Available: http://www.p21.org/index.php?option=com_contentandtask=viewandid=204andItemid=185 [Nov. 2011].

Partnership for 21st Century Skills. (2007). *The intellectual and policy foundations of the 21st century skills framework*. Available: http://www.p21.org/index.php?option=com_contentandtask=viewandid=925andItemid=185 [Nov. 2011].

Partnership for 21st Century Skills. (2009). *P21 framework definitions*. Available: http://www.p21.org/index.php?option=com_contentandtask=viewandid=925andItemid=185 [Nov. 2011].

Pearson, P.D., Roehler, L.R., Dole, J.A., and Duffy, G.G. (1992). Developing expertise in reading comprehension. In S.J. Samuels (Ed.), *What research has to say about reading instruction* (pp. 145-199). Newark, DE: International Reading Association.

Pirolli, P. (2007). Information foraging theory: Adaptive interaction with information. New York: Oxford University Press.

Pirolli, P., and Card, S.K. (1999). Information foraging. *Psychological Review*, 106, 643-675.

Purcell, K. (2010). *The state of online video*. Available: http://www.pewinternet.org/Reports/2010/State-of-Online-Video.aspx [Nov. 2011].

Purcell, K., Rainie, L., Mitchell, A., Rosenstiel, T., and Olmstead, K. (2010). *Understanding the participatory news consumer*. Available: http://www.pewinternet.org/Reports/2010/Online-News.aspx [Nov. 2011].

Ranker, J. (2008). Composing across multiple media. *Written Communication*, 25(2), 196-234.

Reader, W.R.,and Payne, S.J. (2007). Allocating time across multiple texts: Sampling and satisficing. *Human Computer Interaction*, 22(3), 263-298.

Rideout, V.J., Foehr, U.G., and Roberts, D.F. (2010). *Generation M2: Media in the lives of 8-18 year olds*. Available: http://www.kff.org/entmedia/mh012010pkg.cfm [Nov. 2011].

Rouet, J-F. (2006). *The skills of document use*. Mahwah, NJ: Lawrence Erlbaum Associates.

Selwyn, N. (2004). The information aged: A qualitative study of older adults' use of information and communications technology. *Journal of Aging Studies, 18*, 369-384.

Selwyn, N., and Gorard, S. (2004). Exploring the role of ICT in facilitating adult informal learning. *Education, Communication and Information, 4*(2), 293-310.

Sharit, J., Hernandez, M., Czaja, S.J., and Pirolli, P. (2009). Investigating the roles of knowledge and cognitive abilities in older adult information seeking on the Web. *ACM Transactions of Computer-Human Interaction, 15*(1), 3-1-3-25.

Silva, E. (2008). *Measuring skills for the 21st century*. Available: http://www.educationsector.org [Nov. 2011].

Silver-Pacuilla, H. (2006). Access and benefits: Assistive technology in adult literacy. *Journal of Adolescent and Adult Literacy, 50*(2), 114-125.

Smith, A. (2010a). *Home broadband 2010*. Available: http://pewinternet.org/Reports/2010/Home-Broadband-2010.aspx [Nov. 2011].

Smith, A. (2010b). *Mobile access 2010*. Available: http://pewinternet.org/Reports/2010/Mobile-Access-2010.aspx [Nov. 2011].

Smith, B.Q. (2004). Genre, medium, and learning to write: Negotiating identities, enacting school-based literacies in adulthood. *Journal of College Reading and Learning, 34*(2), 75-96.

Stanley, L.D. (2003). Beyond access: Psychosocial barriers to computer literacy. *The Information Society, 19*(5), 407-416.

Street, B. (1984). *Literacy in theory and practice*. Cambridge: Cambridge University Press.

Street, B. (2003). What's "new" in new literacy studies? Critical approaches to literacy in theory and practice. *Current Issues in Comparative Education, 5*(2), 77-91.

Tamassia, C., Lennon, M., Yamamoto, K., and Kirsch, I. (2007). *Adult education in America: A first look at results from the adult education program and learner surveys*. Available: http://www.ets.org/research/policy_research_reports/aeps-report [Nov. 2011].

Vandenbroeck, M., Verschelden, G., and Boonaert, T. (2008). E-learning in a low-status female profession: The role of motivation, anxiety and social support in the learning divide. *Journal of Computer Assisted Learning, 24*, 181-190.

Warren-Peace, P., Parrish, E., Peace, C.B., and Xu, J. (2008). Senior surfing: Computer use, aging, and formal training. *AACE Journal, 16*(3), 253-252.

Webb, S. (2006). Can ICT reduce social exclusion? The case of an adults' English language. *British Educational Research Journal, 32*(3), 481-507.

White, S., and Dillow, S. (2005). *Key concepts and features of the 2003 National Assessment of Adult Literacy*. Available: http://nces.ed.gov/pubsearch/pubsinfo.asp?pubid=2006471 [Nov. 2011].

Yancey, K.B. (2009). *Writing in the 21st century*. Available: http://www.ncte.org/press/21stcentwriting [Nov. 2011].

Yule, V. (1996). Take-home video for adult literacy. *International Review of Education, 42*(1), 187-203.

Zhang, S., and Duke, N.K. (2008). Strategies for Internet reading with different reading purposes: A descriptive study of 12 good Internet readers. *Journal of Literacy Research, 40*(1), 128-162.

Appendix C

Interventions to Develop the Component Literacy Skills of Low-Literate Adults

A. Study Populations and Sample Characteristics

Investigator:	Greenberg	Levy	MacArthur
Project Title	*Research on Reading Instruction for Low-Literate Adults*	*Testing Impact of Health Literacy in Adult Literacy and Integrated Family Approach Programs*	*Building a Knowledge Base for Teaching Adult Decoding*
Study Population	Adult literacy program with 3rd-to-5th-grade reading ability	ABE ASE Adult English literacy	ABE
Sample Characteristics			
Size	Descriptive n = 425 Intervention n = 198	Intervention n = 1,907 Assessment n = 98	Descriptive n = 486 Intervention n = 349
Age	Intervention M = 37 (range 16-78 yrs)		Descriptive M = 35 (SD = 14) Intervention M = 37 (SD = 14) (range 16-76 years)
Gender	Intervention = 67% female	Intervention = 75% female	Descriptive = 67% female Intervention = 66% female
Reading Level	Intervention screened to be 3rd-to-5th-grade level	By NRS reading levels • ABE beginner n = 63 • ABE intermediate n = 284 • ABE advanced n = 75 • ASE n = 80 • ELL beginner n = 494 • ELL intermediate n = 431 • ELL advanced n = 141	NRS low-intermediate level Nelson Reading Comprehension (standard score for 6th grade spring) M = 36.2 (SD = 16.4), 4.6 GLE
Native English speakers	Intervention = 56%		Descriptive = 69% Intervention = 65%

Mellard	Sabatini	Wood
Improving Literacy Instruction for Adults	*Relative Effectiveness of Reading Programs for Adults*	*Young Adult Literacy Problems: Prevalence and Treatment*
ABE ASE	ABE with below 7th grade reading ability and sufficient English language ability	Descriptive 10th grade public high school with English as first language Intervention: Adults with developmental dyslexia
Descriptive n = 319 Intervention n = 205	Descriptive n = 579 Intervention n = 148	Descriptive n = 188 Intervention n = 19
Descriptive M = 32 yrs (SD = 15.2); Mdn = 24 yrs Intervention M = 28 years (SD = 13.7); Mdn = 22 yrs	Descriptive M = 36 (range 17-76 yrs)	Descriptive M =15 yrs Intervention M = 44 yrs
Descriptive = 60% female Intervention = 63% female	Descriptive = 67% female	Descriptive = 44% female Intervention = 26% female
Descriptive: WRMT-R Passage comprehension standard score M = 72.3 (SD 22.8) Intervention: WRMT-R Passage comprehension (standard scores) Bridging M = 60.3 (SD = 22.3), n = 15 Fluency M = 89.0 (SD = 14.3), n = 12 Prediction M = 79.4 (SD = 16.2), n = 31 Summarization M = 77.1 (SD = 18.7), n = 42 Descriptive = 82%	Screened for below 7th grade level	Descriptive: = 50% "poor readers"; 50% "typical readers" Intervention Standard scores WRAT read words M = 85.6 WAIS full IQ M = 101.9

B. Intervention Practices, Intensity, Duration, and Attrition Rates

Intervention Descriptors	Greenberg	Levy	MacArthur
Practices	4 instructional interventions 1. Decoding and fluency 2. Decoding, comprehension, and fluency 3. Extensive reading 4. Decoding, comprehension, extensive reading, and fluency	Directed health literacy curriculum	Enriched decoding and spelling curriculum
Intensity and Duration	Planned: 2 hrs/day × 4 days/wk for up to 100 hrs over Minimum for analyses: 60 hrs, with at least 20 hrs after course midpoint	42 hrs of classroom instruction over 12-16 wks	Duration approximately 8 mos Hrs of reading instruction $M = 57$
Attrition	50%		38%

Mellard	Sabatini	Wood
4 learning strategies interventions	3 instructional interventions adapted for adults	Structured multisensory phonological instruction from Lindamood-Bell Learning Corporation
1. Bridging (word reading)	1. Corrective reading	
2. Fluency (repeated readings)	2. RAVE O	
3. Prediction (comprehension)	3. Guided repeated readings	
4. Summarization (comprehension)		
Whole-group classroom instruction	Supplemental one-to-one tutoring	Tutored 112 hrs over 8 wks
• Bridging–19 hrs	1-hr session × 3 days per wk for 15 wks	
• Fluency–13 hrs		
• Prediction–30 hrs	45 contact hrs	
• Summarization–18 hrs	Completers' 12-15 hrs of instruction over 3-5 wks	
• Bridging–48%	50%	0%
• Fluency–3%		
• Prediction–60%		
• Summarization–42%		

C. Study Instruments by Measurement Construct by Study (Measures marked with * showed significant pre-post gain compared with a control group. Measures marked with ** showed differences from "business as usual control.")

Measurement Construct	Greenberg	Levy	MacArthur
Phonological Processing	CTOPP Elision CTOPP blending CTOPP rapid letter naming	—	—
Decoding and Word Recognition	TOWRE phonemic decoding efficiency TOWRE sight word efficiency WJ-III letter-word identification WJ-III word attack**	TOWRE phonemic decoding efficiency TOWRE sight word efficiency Adams & Huggins irregular word reading task	TOWRE phonemic decoding efficiency* WJ-R word attack WJ-R letter-word identification WJ-R letter-sound survey WRAT3 word reading
Vocabulary	Boston Naming Test* PPVT	Boston Naming Test	Nelson word meaning
Fluency	WJ-III reading fluency* GORT-4 fluency	WJ-III fluency	Researcher-designed oral passage reading TOWRE sight word efficiency
Comprehension	WJ-III passage comprehension GORT-4 comprehension	TABE-R** BEST literacy** CELSA**	Nelson reading comprehension

Mellard	Sabatini	Wood
CTOPP Elision	CTOPP Elision	Lindamood Auditory Conceptualization Test
CTOPP blending	CTOPP blending	Test of Auditory Analysis Skill**
CTOPP rapid color naming	CTOPP rapid letter naming	
CTOPP rapid letter naming	CTOPP rapid digit naming	
CTOPP rapid digit naming	CTOPP memory for digits	
	CTOPP nonword repetition	
	WJ-III spelling of sounds	
TOWRE phonemic decoding efficiency	TOWRE phonemic decoding efficiency*	DST nonwords
TOWRE sight word efficiency	TOWRE sight word efficiency*	DST real words
WRMT-R word attack	WJ-III letter-word identification*	DST Phonemic Transfer Index**
WRMT-R word identification	WJ-III word attack*	WJ-R word attack**
	NAAL BRS oral word reading, pseudo-word reading	WJ-R letter-word identification
		Visual Symbol Imagery**
WAIS-III vocabulary	Boston Naming Test	Boston Naming Test
PPVT	WJ-III picture vocabulary	
TOSWRF	WJ-III reading fluency*	RAN digits, letters
Reading fluency passages from QRI	NAAL BRS oral passage reading	
GORT-4 fluency		
CASAS reading	WJ-III passage comprehension*	WJ-R passage comprehension
WRMT-R passage comprehension	WJ-III oral comprehension	Gates-MacGinite reading comprehension
GORT-4 comprehension		WRAT3 reading achievement
		GORT-3

continued

Measurement Construct	Greenberg	Levy	MacArthur
Other Cognitive Ability or Skills	PIAT-R spelling subtest TOLD I Word ordering subtest	Orally administered, research-designed/ validated evaluation instrument—health literacy knowledge, self-efficacy, and intention*	WRAT3 spelling test Researcher-designed spelling test Self-efficacy scales

NOTES:

ABE/ASE = Adult basic education and adult secondary education

BEST Literacy = Basic English Skills Test (Center for Applied Linguistics, 1987 for Levy)

BEST Plus = Basic English Skills Test (Center for Applied Linguistics)

BNT = Boston Naming Test (Kaplan, Goodglass, and Weintraub, 1983, 2001)

CASAS = Comprehensive Adult Student Assessment System (CASAS, 2001)

CELF = Clinical Evaluation of Language Fundamentals (Semel, Wiig, and Secord, 1987)

CELSA = Combined English Language Skills Assessment (Thompson, 1994)

CTOPP = Comprehensive Test of Phonemic Processing (Wagner, Torgesen, and Rashotte, 1999)

DST = Decoding Skills Test (Richardson and DiBenedetto, 1985)

fMRI = Functional MRI (magnetic resonance imaging)

GORT = Gray Oral Reading Tests-3 and 4 (Wiederholt and Bryant, 1994, 2001)

K-SADS-E = Schedule for Affective Disorders and Schizoprenia for School-age Children—Epidemiologic Version, 5th ed. (Orvaschel and Puig-Antich, 1994)

LAC = Lindamood Auditory Conceptualization Test (Lindamood and Lindamood, 1971)

LSS = Letter Sound Survey (Venezky, 2003)

NAAL = National Assessment of Adult Literacy (Basic Reading Skills and Passage Reading) (Baer, Kutner, and Sabatini, 2009)

Nelson Reading Test (Hanna, Schell, and Schreiner, 1977)

NRS = National Reporting System for Adult Education

PIAT-R = Peabody Individual Achievement Test-Revised, spelling subtest (Frederick and Markwardt, 1997)

Mellard	Sabatini	Wood
WAIS-III block design	WJ-III story recall	K-SADS-E (psychiatric disorders and suicidal behaviors)
WAIS-III information	WJ-III understanding directions	
CELF		Dropout–first time left school for any reason
WJ-III story recall	BEST Plus	
WJ-III auditory working memory		WASI**
		fMRI

PPVT = Peabody Picture Vocabulary Test–III (Dunn and Dunn, 1997, 1998)

QRI = Qualitative Reading Inventory-3 (Leslie and Caldwell, 2000)

RAN = Rapid Automatized Naming (Denckla and Rudel, 1976)

RAVE O = Retrieval Rate, Automaticity, Vocabulary Elaboration, Engagement with Language, and Orthography (Wolf, Miller, and Donnelly, 2000)

TAAS = Test of Auditory Analysis Skill (Rosner and Simon, 1971; Rosner, 1979)

TABE-R = Test of Adult Basic Education-Revised (CTB/McGraw-Hill, 1996)

TOLD I:3 = Test of Language Development, Intermediate, 3rd Edition (Hammil and Newcomer, 1997)

TOSWRF = Test of Silent Word Reading Fluency (Mather et al., 2004)

TOWRE = Test of Word Reading Efficiency (Torgesen, Wagner, and Rashotte, 1999)

VSI = Visual Symbol Imagery (Bell, 1997)

WAIS-III = Wechsler Adult Intelligences Scale III (Wechsler, 1997)

WASI = Wechsler Abbreviated Scales of Intelligence (Wechsler, 1999)

WJ-III = Woodcock-Johnson III, Tests of Achievement (Woodcock, McGrew, and Mather, 2001)

WJ-R = Woodcock-Johnson Psycho-educational Battery, Tests of Achievement, Revised (Woodcock and Johnson, 1989, 1990)

WRAT3 = Wide Range Achievement Test-Revision 3 (Wilkinson, 1993)

WRMT-R = Woodcock Reading Mastery Tests-Revised (Woodcock, 1998)

REFERENCES

Alamprese, J., MacArthur, C., Price, C., and Knight, D. (2011). Effects of a structured decoding curriculum on adult literacy learners' reading development. *Journal of Research on Education Effectiveness, 4*(2), 154-172.

Eden, G.F., Jones, K.M., Cappell, K., Gareau, L., Wood, F.B., Zeffrio, T.A., Dietz, N.A.E., Agnew, J.A., and Flowers, D.L. (2004). Neural changes following remediation of adult developmental dyslexia. *Neuron, 44*, 411-422.

Greenberg, D., Wise, J., Morris, R., Fredrick, L., Rodrigo, V., Nanda, A., and Pae, H. (2011). A randomized-control study of instructional approaches for struggling adult readers. *Journal of Research on Education Effectiveness, 42*(2), 101-117.

Hock, M., and Mellard, D. (2011). Efficacy of learning strategies instruction in adult education. *Journal of Research on Education Effectiveness, 4*(2), 134-153.

Levy, S., Rasher, S., Carter, S., Harris, L., Berbaum, M., Mandernach, J., Bercovitz, L., and Martin, L. (2008). Health literacy curriculum works for adult basic education students. *Focus on Basics, 9*(B), 33-39.

Sabatini, J., Shore, J., Holtzman, and Scarborough, H. (2011). Relative effectiveness of reading intervention programs for adults with low literacy. *Journal of Research on Education Effectiveness, 4*(2), 118-133.

Appendix D

Search Procedures and Reviewed Studies of Adult Literacy Instruction

Appendix D is not printed in this volume but is available online. Go to http://www.nap.edu/catalog.php?record_id=13242.